British History for AS Level

1867 - 1918

Derek Peaple & Tony Lancaster

Edited by Steve Lancaster

CPL

Causeway Press

Dedication

To Jackie, Jane, Sarah, Ruth, Lisa, Maisie and Esme

Acknowledgements

Cover design	Caroline Waring-Collins (Waring Collins Ltd)
Page design	Rebecca Leatherbarrow (Waring Collins Ltd)
Graphic origination	Rebecca Leatherbarrow (Waring Collins Ltd)
Graphics	Chris Collins (Waring Collins Ltd)
Readers	Mary Walton and Heather Doyle

Thanks to Leigh Wilson for her work on Unit 3.

Picture Credits

Brick 177; Fotomas Index 109tl, 212t; Hulton Getty 28, 77, 83, 86, 221b; ILP 159; Liberal Democrats 206; Mansell Collection 62; Mary Evans Picture Library 6, 12, 13, 21 (both), 29, 34, 43, 44, 52, 61, 71b, 72, 102, 127, 146l, 163t, 188, 199, 207, 212b, 228 (both), 234, 244, 251 (both), 267, 279, 286; Museum of London 93, 94, 101 (both), 109tr; Robert Opie collection 250; Public Record Office 109b; National Museum of Labour History 119, 132, 137, 143; Punch Magazine 178; Topham Picturepoint 155, 193, 221t, 229, 259 (both), 268, 294, 295.

Cover pictures

Museum of London (Emmeline Pankhurst)
Mary Evans Picture Library (David Lloyd George)
Topham Picturepoint (union banner, tariff reform poster)

Every effort has been made to locate the copyright owners of material used in this book. Any omissions brought to the attention of the publisher are regretted and will be credited in subsequent printings.

British Library Cataloguing in Publication Data
A catalogue record for this book is available from the British Library.

ISBN 1 902796 17 9

Causeway Press Limited
PO Box 13, Ormskirk, Lancs, L39 5HP

© Derek Peaple, Tony Lancaster & Steve Lancaster
First impression, 2000

Printed and bound by Omnia Books Ltd, Westerhill Road, Bishopbriggs, Glasgow, G64 2QR.

Contents

Party and policy under Gladstone and Disraeli

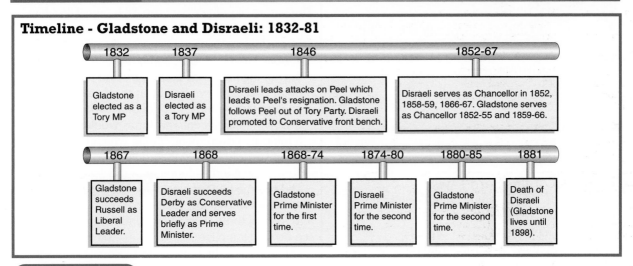

Timeline - Gladstone and Disraeli: 1832-81

1832	1837	1846	1852-67
Gladstone elected as a Tory MP	Disraeli elected as a Tory MP	Disraeli leads attacks on Peel which leads to Peel's resignation. Gladstone follows Peel out of Tory Party. Disraeli promoted to Conservative front bench.	Disraeli serves as Chancellor in 1852, 1858-59, 1866-67. Gladstone serves as Chancellor 1852-55 and 1859-66.

1867	1868	1868-74	1874-80	1880-85	1881
Gladstone succeeds Russell as Liberal Leader.	Disraeli succeeds Derby as Conservative Leader and serves briefly as Prime Minister.	Gladstone Prime Minister for the first time.	Disraeli Prime Minister for the second time.	Gladstone Prime Minister for the second time.	Death of Disraeli (Gladstone lives until 1898).

Introduction

Mid-Victorian politics were dominated by two men - William Ewart Gladstone and Benjamin Disraeli. To use Disraeli's phrase, both men 'climbed to the top of the greasy pole' in the late 1860s, both serving twice as Prime Minister in the period 1868-85 (Gladstone in 1868-74 and 1880-85 and Disraeli in 1868 and 1874-80). Although the two men both set out on their careers in the 1830s as Conservatives, they travelled along different political paths. Gladstone followed Robert Peel out of the Conservative Party in 1846 and, over the next two decades, evolved into a Liberal Prime Minister. Disraeli, on the other hand, remained in the Conservative Party throughout his career. In 1846, it was Disraeli who launched the attacks on Peel that led to Peel's ejection from the Conservative Party. This propelled Disraeli onto the Conservative front bench and, in 1868, to the Conservative leadership and into 10 Downing Street.

Both Gladstone and Disraeli built up formidable reputations in their lifetimes, reputations that reached almost legendary proportions after their deaths. But, for historians today, this is a major problem. The temptation is to assume that both were great men who achieved great deeds. But, was this the case? Is it right, for example, to describe Gladstone's first administration as 'brilliantly successful' and 'perhaps the most impressive in achievement of any in Victoria's long reign'. Similarly, is it right to claim that Disraeli's second administration was distinctive because he began to put into practice his 'One Nation' Conservatism, a new philosophical approach that he had been working on years before he became Prime Minister? It is questions like these that the first three parts of this unit address.

Because the careers of Gladstone and Disraeli ran, to some extent, in parallel and because the two men were Party Leaders at the same time, much attention has been paid to the rivalry between the two men. But, to what extent was this rivalry a matter of genuine personal dislike and how deep did it go? The final part of this unit tackles these questions.

UNIT SUMMARY

Part 1 examines Gladstone's early career and his rise to power. It then goes on to make an assessment of his first administration.

Part 2 begins by looking at Disraeli's background and personality. It explores his rise to power and then considers the extent to which his second administration was an attempt to put his political ideas into practice.

Part 3 focuses on Gladstone's second administration. Why did he become Prime Minister for a second time? What were the main domestic social and political issues in Gladstone's second administration? Why were fewer reforms introduced than had been introduced in the first administration?

Part 4 is concerned with the rivalry between Gladstone and Disraeli. What were the origins of the rivalry? How big were the differences between the two men?

1 Gladstone's first administration

Key questions

1. What were the main features of domestic politics 1846-68?

2. What was Gladstone's position in 1868?

3. What were the key political and social issues in Gladstone's government of 1868-74?

1.1 What were the main features of domestic politics 1846-68?

The repeal of the Corn Laws

The year 1846 was a turning point because it was the year in which the Conservative Prime Minister, Robert Peel, repealed the Corn Laws. For some Conservatives (those who supported protectionism), this was the ultimate betrayal. The Corn Laws had protected their interests by keeping the price of corn artificially high (the 1815 Corn Law laid down that no corn could be imported until the price reached 80 shillings a quarter). This ensured that landowners made a good profit (many Conservative MPs were landowners). For other Conservatives, however, repeal was an important step on the road towards genuine free trade which, they believed, would lead to greater economic growth and prosperity.

The result was a major split in the Conservative Party in 1846. In effect, the party split into two parts (the pro-free trade Peelites and the Protectionists) and, by doing so, shook up the political system:

'Between 1806 and 1846, the Tories in one guise or another had ruled the country for 29 out of 40 years and the period during which the Whigs held office had been too chaotic and faction-ridden to make them an acceptable substitute...The situation was very different after 1846. The Whigs might not have gained greatly in public esteem, but with the Peelites out of office and the Protectionists regarded as unfit to rule, they were the only possibility. The period that followed was one of party weakness, great confusion, much cross-voting and...weakness in government too.' (Blake 1985, pp.77-78)

It was during the period after 1846 that a loose coalition gradually developed into what became labelled as the 'Liberal Party'. This coalition, made up of Whigs, radicals and Peelites (see Box 1.1, note 2), formed all the majority governments of the period 1846-65. The dominant figure in these governments was Lord Palmerston who was Foreign Secretary (1846-52), Home Secretary (1852-5) and Prime Minister (1855-58 and 1859-65).

It was also during this period of confused party lines that Gladstone and Disraeli emerged as key players in the House of Commons.

The nature of politics, 1846-68

The nature of politics between 1846 and 1868 has been summarised as follows:

'A coalition government was made up of the various Liberal groups, compromising and bargaining until they could agree no more and a point of breakdown had been reached. The government would go out of office without dissolving Parliament. The Tories would then form a minority government, during which the non-Tory groups would resolve their differences, defeat the Tories, force a dissolution, win the general election and resume power.' (Matthew 1984, p.466)

The Conservatives lost six general elections in a row and formed three short-lived minority governments - see Box 1.1 on page 3.

The parties of the period were loosely organised and did not enter office with a distinctive programme. There was no mass membership or national party structure and, as a result, there was no organised upward pressure on governments to implement a well-defined programme. The Peelites and the Whigs were officially united in June 1859 (the official birth of the Liberal Party), but Liberals throughout the period were disunited:

'The key to the apparently chaotic situation lay in the inability of the various politicians known by the collective label "Liberal" to cooperate harmoniously. There were no less than six occasions in the 1850s when governments resigned after suffering defeats in the House of Commons.' (Jenkins 1998, p.2)

During this period, much political power remained in the hands of the landowning aristocracy. Box 1.1, for example, illustrates the continued power of the aristocracy in the senior ranks of government.

Attitudes towards domestic reform 1846-68

By the mid-19th century, rapid industrialisation and urbanisation had produced a range of social problems that affected large numbers of people. Governments in the period 1846-68, however, were reluctant to pass legislation to provide remedies for these problems. In particular, governments were reluctant to support legislation which regulated living or working conditions. Palmerston's reply to a query about whether any Bills along these lines would be included in the Queen's Speech of 1864 was typical:

'Oh. There is really nothing to be done. We cannot go on adding to the Statute Book ad infinitum [for ever]. Perhaps we may have a little law reform or bankruptcy reform; but we cannot go on legislating for ever.' (quoted in Woodward 1938, p.163)

BOX 1.1	General elections and Prime Ministers 1847-1868	
General Elections	**Prime Ministers**	**Government**
1847	Lord John Russell	Whig
	Lord Derby (1852)	Conservative
1852	Lord Aberdeen	Coalition
	Lord Palmerston (1855)	Whig
1857	Lord Palmerston	Whig
	Lord Derby (1858-59)	Conservative
1859	Lord Palmerston	Liberal
1865	Lord Russell	Liberal
	Lord Derby (1866-68)	Conservative
	Benjamin Disraeli (1868)	Conservative
1868	William Gladstone	Liberal

Note 1 - Lord John Russell was the third son of the Duke of Bedford and was, therefore, born into one of the wealthiest families in Britain. Since he was a younger son of a duke, he did not inherit a title (younger sons were given the title 'Lord' as a courtesy title) and was able to join the House of Commons as an MP in 1813. He remained in the Commons until 1861 when he was given an earldom and went to the Lords. Lord Palmerston was an Irish peer and was, therefore, allowed to sit in the House of Commons (he did so for 58 years). Like Lord John Russell and the other Prime Ministers in the period 1847-68, Palmerston had an aristocratic background. Indeed, the only Commoners to become Prime Minister in the 19th century, apart from Robert Peel, were Gladstone and Disraeli.

Note 2 - Whigs were landowning aristocrats. They supported freedom from arbitrary government but were not, generally, enthusiastic reformers. They formed the conservative wing of the Liberal Party, attached to the defence of property and privilege. Radicals tended to come from the middle class. They were keen to extend opportunities by removing aristocratic privileges. Most believed there should be minimal government interference in economic affairs. The Peelites were those who left the Conservative Party when it split over the repeal of the Corn Laws in 1846.

Adapted from Gardiner & Wenborn 1995.

There were a number of reasons for this reluctance to intervene.

1. The laissez-faire approach

One reason was the move from protection to free trade. Free trade was the economic approach favoured by middle-class manufacturers who were becoming an increasingly influential group. Matthew suggests that the series of Budgets introduced by Gladstone as Chancellor of the Exchequer in 1853-55 and 1859-65 was designed to meet the expectations of this group:

'The manufacturing classes wanted free trade; Gladstone saw that they got it.' (Matthew 1984, p.466)

Gladstone's Budgets swept away most of the remaining tariffs and reduced income tax in 1865. By taking this approach, Gladstone revealed his support for laissez-faire economics. 'Laissez-faire' is French for 'leave alone'. Supporters of a laissez-faire economics oppose government intervention. They want a free market in which the government leaves them alone. This allows little scope for social reform:

'Laissez-faire was manifested in three ways. First the cost of government remained tiny. Secondly, the British government dismantled the complex controls it had previously exercised over the economy. Only women and children were afforded any legal protection from exploitation. Thirdly...responsibility for social welfare was laid squarely at the door of individuals.' (Winstanley 1990, p.7)

2. Economic prosperity

The economic prosperity of the mid-Victorian period may also have been a reason why there was a reluctance to undertake reforms. It is possible to exaggerate this new-found prosperity, but there was a gradual improvement in terms of wages and employment opportunities by the end of the 1840s. The 1850s and 1860s have been described by one historian as the 'Age of Equipoise' (Burn 1968). Burn suggested a balance had been achieved between the landowning classes (the aristocracy) and the rising industrial (working) and commercial (middle) classes, again resulting in a feeling that major reforms were not necessary. It should be noted, however, that Burn's view has been challenged:

'The historian Trygve Tholfsen has questioned Professor Burn's description of the period as "The Age of Equipoise". Instead, he sees mid-Victorian Britain as "a stable culture in a state of inner tension".' (Behagg 1995, p.232)

Behagg argues that the apparent lack of class conflict in the period after 1846 (or more accurately, after 1848 when Chartism ended as a mass movement - see Unit 2, pages 39-40) was short-lived.

3. Other reasons

Other reasons why there was a reluctance to introduce domestic reforms in the period 1846-68 include:

- a lack of ideological differences between the political parties - both main parties were reluctant to alter the status quo
- Palmerston's opposition to electoral reform (see Unit 2, page 40)
- Palmerston's ability to keep the public's attention on foreign policy matters after 1855 -

he was particularly successful in arousing patriotic sentiment and had a keen eye for a popular cause, like the unification of Italy. Although there was a reluctance to undertake major reform in the period 1846-66, the years 1866-67 were dominated by the debates over electoral reform which led, eventually, to the second Reform Act (see Unit 2, Section 1.3). This made a big impact on the two main parties (see Unit 2, Part 2) and helped to shape the direction taken by the Liberal government elected in 1868.

1.2 What was Gladstone's position in 1868?

Gladstone's early career

Gladstone entered Parliament at the age of 23 and began his career as a staunch Tory. His early years are outlined in Box 1.2.

Gladstone 1846-68

Most historians agree that the period 1846-59 was a difficult phase in Gladstone's career. Winstanley's summary is typical:

'The 1850s were not happy years for Gladstone. Despite holding office as Chancellor of the Exchequer between 1852 and 1855 and gaining a reputation for financial management, he was, like most Peelites, uncertain of his future. He would be happier, he explained to Sir James Graham in 1852, "on the liberal side of the Conservative Party rather than on the conservative side of the Liberal Party". (Winstanley 1990, p.38)

During this period, Gladstone was offered posts in both Whig and Conservative governments and it was only in 1859 that he finally decided to make a commitment - by joining Palmerston's Liberal government.

The transformation from staunch Conservative to Liberal was remarkable and is difficult to explain.

BOX 1.2 William Gladstone (1809-98)

(i) The early years

William Gladstone was born in 1809. His father was a wealthy Liverpool merchant and he sent his son through the conventional upper-class educational route of Eton College and Christ Church College, Oxford. At Oxford, Gladstone gained a reputation as one of the most talented men of his generation. Politics was not the only career Gladstone considered. He was a deeply religious man and thought about a career in the Church of England. Eventually, however, he came to the conclusion that the best way to serve the Church was through politics. When he became an MP in 1832, his stance was that of a reactionary - he opposed factory reform, the abolition of slavery and anything else which smacked of reform. Throughout the 1830s, he was convinced that there was a conspiracy to destroy the Anglican Church and he became, in the words of the Whig Macaulay, 'the rising hope of those stern and unbending Tories' who believed the privileges of the Church had to be defended at all costs. He served as a junior minister in Peel's short government of 1835. Then, in 1839, he married Catherine Glynne, the daughter of a wealthy landowner. By marrying into a landed family, he combined the older landed interests with the newer commercial interests represented by the Tory Party of the 1830s and 1840s. Between 1841-43, he served under Peel as Vice President of the Board of Trade and, in 1843, was promoted to the Cabinet as President of the Board of Trade. But, in January 1845 he felt obliged to resign over the government's decision to increase its grant to the Irish Catholic college at Maynooth (Gladstone had publicly argued that the state should only support the Church of England - though he changed his mind on this after the Maynooth Affair). He was brought back into the Cabinet in December 1845 as Secretary for War and the Colonies and was a keen supporter of Peel's decision to repeal the Corn Laws in 1846.
Adapted from Cooper 1995 and Gardiner & Wenborn 1995.

(ii) The career as a whole

1832	MP for Newark	1859-65	Chancellor of the Exchequer under Palmerston and Russell
1834-35	Under-secretary of War		
1841-43	Vice-President of the Board of Trade	1866	Leader of House of Commons
1843-45	President of the Board of Trade	1868-74	Prime Minister for the first time
1845-46	Secretary for War and the Colonies	1880-85	Prime Minister for the second time
1846-59	Part of Peelite group in Parliament	1886	Prime Minister for the third time - defeat over Home Rule for Ireland
1852-55	Chancellor of the Exchequer under Aberdeen and Palmerston	1892-94	Prime Minister for the fourth time

Biography Box

Gladstone is often described as 'an enigma'. Historians have offered different interpretations - for example:

- Gladstone was naive and high minded - his deep religious views produced a moral stance which fitted better with that of Liberals
- Gladstone was a political opportunist - he thought his career would best be served as a Liberal
- Gladstone was genuinely open to new ideas - he would change his mind, if convinced by new arguments
- Gladstone's fixed belief in free trade and a laissez-faire approach brought him closer to the Liberals
- Gladstone's dislike of Disraeli made it difficult for him to contemplate rejoining the Conservatives.

Gladstone - Liberal Leader

Historians have suggested that there are four main reasons why Gladstone was the obvious choice as Leader of the Liberal Party after the downfall of Lord John Russell's government in 1866.

First, the Liberal Party had been dominated by Lord Palmerston, but he died in 1865. Then, Lord John Russell, who had taken over the leadership from Palmerston, announced his retirement (in December 1867). In addition:

'Twelve senior members of the Cabinet died in the five years after 1859, among them able and popular men...who would have posed a major challenge to Gladstone's succession.' (Winstanley 1990, p.40)

Second, Gladstone's achievements as Chancellor - both in 1852-55 and 1859-65 - had established his reputation as a political heavyweight and gained him popularity:

'He had made Liberalism synonymous with free trade and low-taxing, low-spending government, as well as supremely competent administration. His own reputation rose higher and spread wider. Gladstone's technical expertise was admired by the political élite, while his tax cuts left more

money in people's pockets. He was becoming a popular hero.' (Cooper 1995, p.247)

Third, he was able to gain support from both wings of the Liberal Party - from the Whigs as well as the radicals:

'Between 1859 and 1865, he was building up goodwill among the radicals and an increasing number of the public...At the same time, given his immense talent, he was able to retain the grudging support of the Whigs.' (Watts 1995, p.75)

And fourth, Gladstone was a great self-publicist who knew how to exploit the press to enhance his profile. As Chancellor, he had fought to repeal paper duties (tax on the use of paper). When his proposal was blocked by the Lords, he reintroduced it as part of the Budget in a general finance Bill - ensuring that the Lords would not block it again. Not only did this constitutional battle endear him to the radicals, it also ensured that he gained an excellent press:

'As a result of his repeal of the paper duties, Gladstone could generally rely on a favourable press - the most powerful and rapidly expanding public medium of the day. Largely Liberal by inclination, but particularly grateful to Gladstone for his part in reducing the costs of production, the new press lavished fulsome praise on him... Realising the potential of the press, Gladstone had long deliberately courted it. Even in the 1850s, he regularly supplied journalists with details of his activities. From about 1860, he went further...He "leaked" official information anonymously to his contact at the *Telegraph*...The press was particularly useful in broadening the impact of another of Gladstone's initiatives - public speaking...When, in October 1862, Gladstone embarked on his first orchestrated public-speaking tour of the North, the spectacle of him sailing down the Tyne at the head of a convoy of steamers...was shared by readers all over the country.' (Winstanley 1990, p.43)

MAIN POINTS - Sections 1.1-1.2

- The year 1846 was a turning point because the repeal of the Corn Laws split the Conservative Party and, by so doing, shook up the political system.
- The pattern between 1846-68 was for a coalition of Whigs, radicals and Peelites (from 1859, the 'Liberal Party') to form a government, split, allow a minority Conservative government to be set up and then reunite, forcing a general election.
- There was little domestic reform in the period 1846-68 because of (1) laissez-faire attitudes (2) economic prosperity (3) lack of ideological diversity (4) Palmerston's opposition and (5) Palmerston's ability to keep the public's attention on foreign policy matters.
- Gladstone began his career as a staunch Tory. He served in the Cabinet in Peel's second administration and supported the repeal of the Corn Laws in 1846.

- The period 1846-59 was a difficult phase. He was offered posts in Whig and Conservative governments, only making a commitment in 1859 when he joined Palmerston's Liberal government.
- Gladstone's transformation from staunch Conservative to Liberal has been explained by reference to (1) his deep religious views (2) political opportunism (3) flexibility (4) his fixed belief in free trade and a laissez-faire approach and (5) dislike of Disraeli.
- There are four main reasons why Gladstone was chosen as Liberal Leader in 1867 - (1) key competitors had retired or died (2) he had secured his reputation as Chancellor in the 1850s (3) he had support from both Whigs and radicals and (4) he was a great self-publicist.

Activity 1.1 Gladstone as Chancellor

ITEM 1 Delivering the Budget

This picture shows Gladstone delivering the Budget in 1860. Gladstone enjoyed working with detailed figures and had the capacity to communicate his enthusiasm. His Budget speeches raised what, under his predecessors, had been rather humdrum occasions to one of the chief moments of the political year. His Budget speeches were huge - four hours were not uncommon. They were delivered from notes only. Gladstone unfolded the record of national financial progress and the details of his financial proposals as if he was the detective at the end of a novel, unravelling a complete plot and bringing all the details into clear and dramatic relationship.

Adapted from Matthew 1987.

ITEM 2 A historian's view (1)

Gladstone first became Chancellor in December 1852. His colleagues' expectations of him were amply fulfilled when, in April 1853, he produced one of the century's most celebrated Budgets. The Budget was vital for the survival of Lord Aberdeen's government since its position in the Commons was weak - any accident which drew the Tories, the Irish and radicals into one lobby would force the government into a minority. Gladstone's Budget speech lasted four and three-quarters hours, but his audience seemed anything but bored. The principles behind the Budget were Peelite (the sort of principles that had been supported by Robert Peel). Laissez-faire and retrenchment were its keywords. The state should interfere with the natural progress of the nation's economic life as little as possible and cut its own spending to a minimum. In practice, this meant the reduction or abolition of tariffs, the elimination of bureaucratic waste and keeping a tight rein on defence expenditure. Government spending should be reduced to a minimum. In 1853, income tax was retained at seven pence in the pound, but Gladstone projected its abolition in 1860. When the Crimean War of 1853-56 intervened (Gladstone believed it could have been avoided), this wrecked his plans for retrenchment, leading to Gladstone's resignation in 1855. When he became Chancellor again in 1859, his Budgets continued along the same lines as that of 1853.

Adapted from Cooper 1995.

ITEM 3 A historian's view (2)

Gladstone's policies as Chancellor were in line with the trend towards free trade and his desire to free manufacturers from restraints helped Britain to compete abroad. Such policies contributed to an enormous increase in industry and trade which was good for manufacturers and also for members of the working class who might expect to profit from the increased prosperity of the nation - particularly by gaining higher wages. But, his policies offered them little direct help with social problems since retrenchment in public spending meant that money was not spent on projects that would have done this. But, this was a time when laissez-faire doctrines held sway and Gladstone was a man of his times. He pursued his goals with passion and conviction and his desire for economy and good administration was basic to his outlook. He even insisted that the address on the labels on his government dispatch bag should be erased so that the bags could be reused. Aware as he was of social evils, however, he did not see it as the role of government to correct them, even if it could do so. He was keen that the state should enable individuals to improve themselves. Beyond his financial achievements, Gladstone used his Chancellorship to demonstrate his considerable talents and expertise to fellow parliamentarians. Even more important, perhaps, he won admiration from potential voters. Lower prices, reduced taxation and an attack on the Lords (over paper duty) helped to increase his popularity.

Adapted from Watts 1995.

1.3 What were the key political and social issues in Gladstone's government of 1868-74?

The Irish Question

Britain's links with Ireland went back to the 12th century, but it was only in the 17th century that British forces began to conquer large parts of Ireland and to settle them with British colonists. By seizing land from the local (mainly Catholic) inhabitants, these (mainly Protestant) colonists sowed the seeds for later conflict. During the 18th century, Britain controlled the Irish government via a Protestant-dominated Irish Parliament. Irish Catholics remained very much second-class citizens. In 1798, an uprising organised by a mainly Catholic group, the Society of United Irishmen, failed, but the British government decided to incorporate Ireland into the UK and rule it directly. The result was the Act of Union of 1801. Direct rule of Ireland proved difficult from the start. The bulk of the population was opposed to British rule and protest took both a constitutional and a revolutionary form. By the time Gladstone came to power, the 'Irish question' had come to be dominated by three main concerns - land, religion and education, and Ireland's political status:

- the land question - what should the relationship between landlord and tenants be?
- the question of religion and education - what should the status of the various religious groups be and who should control the education of the young?
- the political question - what should the relationship between Ireland and Great Britain be?

The 1868 general election campaign

The 1868 general election campaign was dominated by a religious question - the disestablishment of the Church of Ireland. This meant breaking links between the Protestant Church of Ireland and the British state, placing the Church of Ireland on the same legal basis as the Catholic Church and other 'non-conformist' churches (non-conformists or 'dissenters' are Protestants who do not belong to the Church of England - examples are Methodists and Unitarians). The existence of an established Protestant Church in Ireland had been the source of grievance to the majority of Irish people for many years (the majority of Irish people were Catholics and did not recognise the Church of Ireland). But, events in 1867 focused public attention on Ireland. It was in 1867 that Fenian activity was at its height - see Box 1.3.

By focusing on the issue of the disestablishment of the Church of Ireland, Gladstone gained a number of advantages. First, it was an issue which he believed in - he had first publicly voiced his support for it in 1865 (by then, he had come a long way from his view in the 1830s that the Anglican Church must be defended at all costs). Second, focusing on this issue gave the Liberals a big advantage over the Conservatives:

'Gladstone was responsible for a brilliant party stroke which exploited one of the Prime Minister's [ie Disraeli's] major weaknesses. Conservatives were defenders of the Protestant Church and Disraeli felt he had to rally to the cause.' (Watts 1995, p.78)

BOX 1.3 Fenian activity in 1867

The Fenians were Irish republicans who were prepared to use force to remove British rule from Ireland. In March 1867, Fenians organised an armed uprising in the hope of overthrowing British rule. Like previous republican uprisings, this was a flop, easily put down by the authorities. Then, in September 1867, two Fenian leaders were arrested in Manchester. A week later, as they were being transferred from court to prison, their prison van was ambushed. The prisoners were freed, but one police officer was shot dead. Subsequently, three men were arrested, tried and hanged. All three had taken part in the attack, but none had fired the fatal shot. Then, in December 1867, Richard O'Sullivan Burke, the Fenians' armaments organiser, was arrested in London and taken to Clerkenwell prison to await trial. On 13 December, Fenians placed a huge bomb outside the prison wall, hoping that Burke would be exercising and able to escape when it exploded. In fact, Burke was locked in his cell. The bomb caused enormous damage, killing 12 Londoners and wounding 30 more. The incidents in Manchester and London created a wave of panic throughout mainland Britain because Irish republican violence had previously been confined to Ireland.

Adapted from Kee 1972.

And third, Gladstone was able to unite Whigs, Peelites and radicals in Parliament and to mobilise the support of both non-conformist and Catholic voters:

'In Irish Church disestablishment Gladstone had thus found a cause which reunited not only the Parliamentary Liberal Party, but made the most his support in the country for the forthcoming election. A remarkable combination of dissenters with Irish and even English Catholics formed behind him.' (Feuchtwanger 1985, p.57)

In the 1868 general election the Liberals won about the same number of seats in England as they had in 1865, while they made gains in the 'Celtic fringe' (where Catholicism and non-conformism was much more common than in England):

- Ireland - from five seats in 1865 to 25 in 1868
- Wales - from 18 seats in 1865 to 22 in 1868
- Scotland - from 41 seats in 1865 to 52 in 1868.

Overall, the Liberals won 387 seats while the Conservatives won 271 seats. As a result, Gladstone was invited to form the government.

The historical debate

There is a debate among historians about the success and significance of Gladstone's first administration. Some historians are enthusiastic and claim that it was a 'great reforming ministry':

'It has widely been viewed as a brilliantly successful, perhaps the most impressive in achievement of any in Victoria's long reign. Not for nothing is it often called a "great reforming ministry"; certainly, it was one of the greatest, and Gladstone's most successful.' (Watts 1995, pp.82-83)

Others, however, are less impressed:

'Gladstone's first ministry muddled through a series of measures...ad hoc [unplanned] legislation which antagonised [angered] the Whigs while disappointing the radicals.' (Belchem 1990, p.37)

Gladstone's 'programme'

There is a consensus amongst historians that, when he was appointed Prime Minister, Gladstone had no grand programme of reform in mind. Rather, the programme of reform which developed was the product of a number of factors:

'Gladstone himself was the driving force behind the Irish legislation; in some areas such as education or army reform, there was a wide consensus that action was needed; trade union legislation was brought in as a consequence of a Royal Commission reporting; licensing legislation and the [secret] ballot were expected to come from a Liberal government.' (Feuchtwanger 1985, p.60)

Nevertheless, some historians have argued that the reforms which were introduced were all consistent with the principles of 'Gladstonian Liberalism'. In other words, they all fitted with the laissez-faire approach:

'There was little by way of social improvement to help the lowly-paid, the badly-housed, the sick or the unemployed, or to improve working conditions. Nor was there likely to be, for the Liberal Party believed that it was not the role of government to regulate social and economic life, and laissez-faire philosophy combined with a deep aversion to increasing government expenditure and a preference for low taxation made social provision unlikely.' (Watts 1995, p.93)

While some historians discuss the successes (and failures) of Gladstone's first administration as if he personally was responsible for all the measures that were taken, others point out that, apart from the legislation on Ireland, Gladstone left initiatives to his Cabinet colleagues:

'Gladstone had a very delicate sense of the independence of individual ministers, but once a policy or Bill had been adopted by the Cabinet, he considered it his duty as Prime Minister to throw his formidable parliamentary abilities behind the policy or Bill if this support was needed.' (Feuchtwanger 1985, p.60)

Gladstone and Ireland

When the telegram arrived telling William Gladstone that he was to become Prime Minister for the first time, he was engaged in one of his favourite occupations - felling trees. He was accompanied by Evelyn Ashley who recalled 30 years later:

'After a few minutes, the blows ceased and Mr Gladstone, resting on the handle of his axe, looked up, and with deep earnestness in his face exclaimed: "My mission is to pacify Ireland". He then resumed his task and never said another word until the tree was down.' (quoted in Shannon 1999, p.57)

Whatever Gladstone's motives, Gladstone's decision to tackle the Irish Question had important consequences. While it would be simplistic to argue that the measures taken during Gladstone's first term as Prime Minister were alone responsible for sparking the struggle over Home Rule which developed in the 1880s (see Section 3.2 below), there is good reason to suggest that they raised rather than lowered the political temperature in Ireland. The steps that were taken are outlined in Box 1.4 on page 9.

The impact of Gladstone's Irish reforms

Each of the four steps described in Box 1.4 alienated sections of the population in Ireland. First, disestablishing the Church of Ireland alienated Irish Anglicans because it raised concerns that the privileged position of Protestants was under threat. Second, the land reform did not go far enough to satisfy tenants and it outraged many landlords:

'The Irish Land Act was not very successful even in its own terms. The problem of defining legally

BOX 1.4 | Gladstone and Ireland 1868-74

Gladstone's first administration took four steps in the hope of solving the Irish Question.

1. The Irish Church Act, 1869

This Act aimed to disestablish the Church of Ireland (ie to break the link between the Church and the state) and to disendow it (ie to strip it of its endowments - its property and assets). From 1 January 1871, the Church became a voluntary body governed by a General Synod. To compensate the Church for its losses, it was agreed that £10 million would be granted to the clergy for pensions and as compensation. Most clerics chose to pay their money to the Representative Church Body which was set up look after Church property and finances. A further £13 million was set aside for education and relief of the poor. An important clause in the Bill allowed tenant farmers on Church land to buy their land - an opportunity taken up by c.6,000 tenants. Also, there was a clause cutting state grants to the Presbyterian Church and to the Catholic Maynooth College - to ensure that all churches were on the same footing.

2. The Irish Land Act, 1870

The Act was divided into three parts. The first part dealt with the 'Ulster custom'. The custom in Ulster (and in some areas outside Ulster) was only to evict tenants if they did not pay their rent and to allow tenants to have 'free sale' (when moving from a farm, they could claim compensation for the improvements they had made during their time there). Until 1870, these rights were customary, but after the Land Act was passed, they had the force of law. The second part of the Act dealt with eviction, making it compulsory for landlords to compensate evicted tenants for any improvements the tenants had made and to pay damages if a tenant was evicted for anything other than non-payment. The third part of the Act allowed tenants who wanted to buy land from their landlord to borrow from the state two-thirds of the purchase price. This part of the Act is often referred to as the "Bright Clauses" because it was the MP John Bright who proposed the clauses in the Act which made these provisions.

3. The Irish Universities Bill, 1873

The Irish Universities Bill proposed that a non-denominational University of Dublin should be set up which incorporated Trinity College (an Anglican college) and new and already established Catholic colleges. The measure was controversial because it would have meant Protestants and Catholics studying at the same institution (Gladstone hoped that education under one roof would ease the sectarian divide). The Bill was defeated in the House of Commons by three votes (in March 1873). The defeat led to Gladstone's resignation, though Disraeli's refusal to take office (for tactical reasons) meant that the administration limped on until February 1874.

4. Coercion and the release of Fenian prisoners

Due to rural unrest in Ireland, the Peace Preservation Act was passed in April 1870 and the Westmeath Act in 1871. These Acts gave the police increased powers to arrest and detain suspects without trial. In December 1870, by way of contrast, the decision was made to release Fenian prisoners as a gesture of goodwill.

Adapted from Kee 1972 and Shannon 1999.

---

where the "Ulster Custom" existed was extraordinarily complicated. The "Bright Clauses" too were a failure since they offered no incentive for the landlord to sell, and few tenants could afford the one-third of the purchase price needed to buy their holding. Above all, the eviction clauses had little impact since the question of controlling rents was ignored; and tenants on long leases were, in any case, outside the provisions of the Act.' (Adelman 1996, p.78)

Furthermore, as Foster (1988, p.397) notes, the Act was threatening to landlords since it interfered with property rights and implied that tenants had a moral right to own the land which they farmed. The Bill was opposed by many Whigs for this reason. Third, the University Bill failed to take into account the sectarianism (division over religious beliefs - in this case between Catholics and Protestants) which existed in Ireland and pleased

neither Protestants (who wanted Trinity College to remain independent) nor Catholics (who were strongly opposed to mixed education because they believed the Protestant authorities would use it to promote Protestantism). And fourth, any good will arising from the release of Fenian prisoners was cancelled out by the coercive Peace Preservation Act and the Westmeath Act. Besides, the Protestant élite (the so-called 'Protestant Ascendancy') did not appreciate the release of Fenians. Again, it seemed to be a sign that their privileged position was under threat:

'Gladstone's Irish legislation, though a long way short of revolutionary, had a symbolic significance far beyond its immediate effects. It signalled a fresh way of looking at Irish problems...Above all, it gave notice that the Protestant Ascendancy was no longer immutable [unchangeable] and invulnerable.' (Lyons 1971, p.146)

A great reforming ministry?

The reputation that Gladstone's first administration gained as a 'great reforming ministry' arose in part from the sheer number of reforms which were implemented during the period 1868-74. The problem that the government soon faced, however, was that, while some groups were disappointed because the reforms did not go far enough, other groups disliked the reforms because they went too far. As a result, important sections of the electorate were alienated and the government's re-election prospects severely damaged.

Reforms which alienated religious groups

It was noted above that one reason for Gladstone's success in the 1868 general election was support from non-conformists for disestablishment of the Church of Ireland. Two reforms in his first administration, however, succeeded in alienating this support - namely, the 1870 Education Act and 1872 Licensing Act. The provisions of these acts are outlined in Box 1.5.

BOX 1.5 | Reforms which alienated religious groups

1. The 1870 Education Act

The 1870 Education Act made the following provisions:

- School Boards were to be set up to build elementary schools in areas where schools were not provided by religious organisations (in Britain as a whole, about 2 million children did not receive elementary education)
- School Boards were to be elected by local ratepayers
- School Boards were to have the power to raise local rates
- religious teaching in Board Schools was to be undenominational and based on simple Bible teaching
- parents had the right to withdraw child from religious teaching
- schooling was not free and not compulsory, though School Boards could make it compulsory in their areas
- schools run by religious bodies continued where they already existed, with increased grant aid.

This Act created the first national network of schools, significantly extending the responsibility of the state in this area.

2. The Licensing Act, 1872

This Act gave powers to magistrates to grant licences and check for the adulteration of alcoholic drinks. It also fixed closing times for pubs.

Adapted from Cooper 1995 and Lee 1994.

Summary Box

The 1870 Education Act

Historians agree that there were two main reasons why the 1870 Education Act was passed:

- a series of inquiries had revealed that many children did not receive even an elementary education and it was recognised that Britain needed an educated workforce if it was to compete with the rest of the world
- the 1867 Reform Act had given large numbers of working-class men the vote (see Unit 2, Sections 1.3 and 2.1) and it was generally agreed (in Parliament at least) that voters would only be able to use their vote responsibly if they had at least a basic education.

The problem with setting up a national system of elementary education was that education was closely tied up with religious affiliation:

'Education was a religious battlefield in which Anglicans and non-conformists vied for the upper hand. Church of England schools outnumbered their rivals by roughly 3:1. Anglicans, organising themselves into the National Education Union (1869), were determined that this lead be maintained, and with it the distinctive religious identity of their schools. The radical/non-conformist-influenced National Education League (1869), by contrast, pressed for the absorption of the Anglican schools within a new nationwide system.' (Cooper 1995, p.264)

In the battle over the Bill in Parliament, Anglican MPs gained a number of concessions, leaving non-conformists both in Parliament and outside feeling resentful:

'Hardline non-conformists felt badly let down. The government's education legislation had failed to advance the cause of non-conformity. Instead, in vote after vote, non-conformists had been left in the minority, outnumbered by a broad front of Anglican Liberals and Anglican Conservatives. They felt this humiliation deeply. Temporarily at least, there was a rupture between the Party Leader and his non-conformist foot soldiers.' (Cooper 1995, p.264)

It should be pointed out that it was not just non-conformists who were alienated by the Education Act. Radicals were also disappointed that attendance in the new Board Schools would be neither compulsory nor free.

The Licensing Act, 1872

The temperance (anti-alcohol) movement was dominated by non-conformists. For many members of this movement, the 1872 Act did not go far enough because it did not reduce the number of pubs:

'There was a strong temperance movement which sought to persuade people to renounce [give up] alcohol and it urged measures to remove temptation by curbing the number of public houses and restricting their opening times.' (Watts 1995, p.89)

Lee argues that Gladstone was concerned about excessive drunkenness, but:

Summary Box

BOX 1.6 Reforms which alienated the aristocracy

1. Civil Service Examinations, 1870
An Order in Council set up, for the first time, open competitive examinations for entry into the Civil Service in all Departments of State except the Foreign and Home Offices (the Home Office was added in 1873). As a result, appointments in the Civil Service were gained by merit rather than influence or patronage.

2. The University Tests Act, 1871
This removed the restrictions which prevented non-conformists from holding teaching posts and other positions at the universities of Oxford and Cambridge. As a result, it ended the Anglican dominance of Oxbridge. Many aristocrats supported special privileges for Anglicans.

3. Army Reforms, 1868-74
Under the guidance of Edward Cardwell,the Minister of War, a number of Acts and reforms were passed that led to a substantial reorganisation of the army. Among the most important were:
- abolition of the purchase of commissions
- abolition of flogging as a military punishment in peacetime
- the Army Enlistment (Short Service) Act which reduced the standard term of 12 years in active service to six in active service and six in reserves
- reorganisation of the War Office
- provision of more modern weapons, such as the breech-loading rifle
- reorganisation of infantry regiments, linking them to counties.

4. The Ballot Act, 1872
As a result of this Act, the secret ballot replaced open voting at elections (see Unit 2, Section 3.1).
Adapted from Cooper 1995 and Lee 1994.

'The answer was not to try to prohibit alcohol altogether since this would constitute an attack on the individual's freedom of choice. He aimed, rather, to induce [encourage] a more responsible social attitude.' (Lee 1994, p.166)
By adopting such an approach, however, not only did the Act alienate non-conformists, but it also greatly annoyed those involved in the drink trade and many drinkers. Watts argues that this Act was targeted at members of the working class (who were regarded as being irresponsible about drink) and, therefore, alienated many of those given the vote in 1867.

Reforms which alienated the aristocracy
Lee argues that:
'One of Gladstone's priorities was to remove inefficiency and its partner, inequality of opportunity.' (Lee 1994, p.165)
This involved a number of measures which could be interpreted as attacks upon the aristocracy and the 'old system'. These are outlined in Box 1.6 below.

The two measures which particularly upset aristocrats were the introduction of civil service examinations and the abolition of the purchase of army commissions. Watts argues that the concerns expressed over these measures related to the outcry from landowners over Gladstone's Irish Land Act (see above):
'Within the Establishment, there were again fears that the government was interfering with property rights for the aristocracy whose members tended to view senior positions in the civil service and the army as their monopoly.' (Watts 1995, p.87)
Such measures were of particular concern to the Whig element in the Liberal Party which, Parry (1993) argues, remained an important section within the party:
'Jonathan Parry....considers the Whigs - rather than Gladstone - to be central to the development of the Liberal tradition. The "Whig-Liberals" (Parry's term) sought to maintain the rule of a propertied but educated and conscientious élite who would govern in the best interests of the nation.' (Jenkins 1996, p.11)
Reforms like those described in Box 1.6 (left) made it more difficult for this élite to maintain its hold on power.

Reforms which alienated members of the working class
It has already been noted that the Licensing Act of 1872 was unpopular with members of the working class. Two other Acts were passed which directly concerned members of the working class - the Trade Union Act (1871) and the Criminal Law Amendment Act (1871). Both Acts are described in detail in Unit 4, Section 1.3. While the Trade Union Act was broadly welcomed, the Criminal Law Amendment Act was bitterly opposed. Cooper argues:
'The trade union legislation doubtless cost working-class votes in the 1874 election.' (Cooper 1995, p.267)

Assessments of Gladstone's first administration
The standard view is that Gladstone's first administration started brightly, introducing a number of important reforms, and then ran out of steam. Many historians quote Disraeli who said, in 1872, that the Liberal front bench in the Commons was, by then, a 'row of exhausted volcanoes'. As Watts points out, this was an unintended compliment:
'[The government] was exhausted because ministers had completed a major programme of reform which, until it petered out in 1872-73, had transformed important aspects of life.' (Watts 1995, p.93)
A number of historians point out that the reforms of the first administration fit within the framework of a laissez-faire approach, though Feuchtwanger suggests

that, ironically, the overall result was a willingness to accept that the state had a greater role to play:

'In its broad tenor, this legislation kept within the limits set by the canons [laws] of laissez-faire to the sphere of the state. Nevertheless, this great spate of activity was bound to create the impression and expectation of widened responsibilities of government, which in due course eased the transition to a more collectivist view of the state.' (Feuchtwanger 1985, p.62)

Gladstone's motives

There is some debate about Gladstone's motives. Bentley (1996) argues that, rather than pacifying Ireland, his key aim in focusing on Ireland was to 'pacify the Liberal Party'. Similarly, Cooke and Vincent (1974) argue that Gladstone was a devious politician, motivated by political ambition rather than religious or moral considerations. Other historians (for example Matthew 1986 and 1995) dispute this, arguing that Gladstone genuinely was motivated by moral considerations. Cooper argues:

'We must, however, be careful before assuming that political calculations and ambitions can fully explain what Gladstone was about. If the quest for power and power alone, was the fundamental driving force behind Gladstone, his determination to continue his mission with the Irish Land Act

and especially the Irish Universities Bill becomes hard to understand. For, as Gladstone knew very well, land and education were issues which would aggravate the stresses within the Liberal Party as surely as the disestablishment of the Irish Church had soothed them.' (Cooper 1995, p.258)

The downfall of Gladstone's first administration

When, in 1873, the government's Irish Universities Bill was defeated, Gladstone resigned. Most historians agree that, following the pattern of previous Parliaments, he hoped that Disraeli would form a minority Conservative government, giving the Liberal Party time to regroup before fighting a general election. Disraeli refused, however, and so Gladstone continued as Prime Minister for a further 11 months before calling a general election in 1874. Rubinstein describes this period as follows:

'In March 1873, despite its large majority in Parliament, the government actually lost an important vote in the Commons...Gladstone resigned suggesting that Disraeli form a minority government. He refused and Gladstone was back in office for another 11 months. The government lost an unusual number of by-elections, showed signs of increasing strain, and Gladstone called a general election in January 1874.' (Rubinstein 1998, p.166)

MAIN POINTS - Section 1.3

- Some historians claim that Gladstone's first administration was a 'great reforming ministry'. Others argue that the measures were unplanned and it alienated supporters.
- Gladstone said that his 'mission' as Prime Minister was 'to pacify Ireland'. But, the steps that were taken raised rather than lowered the political temperature in Ireland.
- Although Gladstone's first administration passed a large number of reforms, important sections of the electorate were alienated.

- The measures taken by Gladstone's government alienated religious groups, the aristocracy and the working class.
- The standard view is that Gladstone's first administration started brightly, introducing a number of important reforms, and then ran out of steam.
- There is a debate about Gladstone's motives. Some historians argue that Gladstone was devious and motivated by political ambition. Others argue that Gladstone genuinely was motivated by moral considerations.

Activity 1.2 Gladstone's first administration

ITEM 1 The key reforms

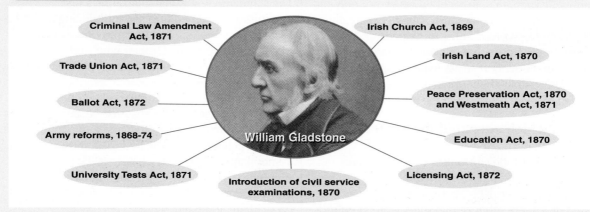

Criminal Law Amendment Act, 1871

Trade Union Act, 1871

Ballot Act, 1872

Army reforms, 1868-74

University Tests Act, 1871

Introduction of civil service examinations, 1870

William Gladstone

Irish Church Act, 1869

Irish Land Act, 1870

Peace Preservation Act, 1870 and Westmeath Act, 1871

Education Act, 1870

Licensing Act, 1872

ITEM 2 An assessment of Gladstone's first administration

Forster's 1870 Education Act was the first major measure of state education and one which brought about a national system. In terms of long-term significance, it was the greatest reform of Gladstone's first administration. The Act addressed many of the things that mattered to Gladstone - a concern for the work of the Church in education and for freedom of voluntary action, as well as a distrust of compulsion. It was typical of Gladstonian Liberalism in its scale, ambition and political courage. It met the responsibility of the government to serve the national interest, however difficult the task. Although it was only a stage in the extension of educational provision (elementary education was not made compulsory until 1881 and was not free until 1891), it was a vital step since the state had come near to recognising a duty to provide some education for all. Clearly, this was a principle which would have dramatic social consequences. It advanced the great Liberal aim of empowering individuals to make more of themselves and their talents. The assault on privilege also had important long-term effects, The reform of the civil service, for example, replaced aristocracy (gaining a position through birth or favours) with meritocracy (gaining a position through merit). This established a new civil service tradition which lasted well into the 20th century. The struggle over the abolition of privileges - especially, over the abolition of the purchase of commissions in the army - marked a turning point for Gladstone's relations with the upper classes. Gladstone was appalled by the 'folly and selfishness' which was displayed over this issue and, from that point on, showed an increasing readiness to side with the people against the aristocracy. But that did not mean that he was prepared to favour one group over another - as his trade union legislation showed. On the other hand, restrictions on picketing had a certain Gladstonian logic since they fitted with his dislike of any form of coercion or pressure on the freedom of the individual from any group.

Adapted from Lee 1994, Watts 1995 and Cooper 1995.

ITEM 3 Forster's Education Act

THE THREE R's; OR, BETTER LATE THAN NEVER.

This cartoon shows William Forster (seated at the front) telling a group of poor children that they will now be able to have an education (he was the author of the 1870 Education Act). The cartoon was published in *Punch* magazine in August 1870. The 1870 Education Act was, in many ways, the most typical piece of Liberal legislation. First, its consequences were immense, yet it was still within the sphere of self-help. The state intervened but did not take over. Second, it was an attack on privilege - on the right of the Church to control education. But, rather than being revolutionary, it was full of compromise. Forster pointed out that the aim was to 'fill up gaps' rather than to destroy the existing system or to introduce a new one. It was hoped that the Act would not only provide an efficient system of education, but also a cheap one. And third, despite all the opposition, the government insisited on pressing ahead with the measure.

Adapted from Abbott 1972.

Questions

1. a) What does Item 1 tell us about the nature of Gladstone's first administration?
   b) What do you think each of the measures was designed to achieve?
2. a) Using Items 1-3, explain why Gladstone's first administration has been described as a 'great reforming ministry'.
   b) To what extent should credit be given to Gladstone for the achievements of his government?
   c) Given the achievements of Gladstone's government, why do you think the Liberals lost the 1874 general election?
   d) Describe what might be meant by the term 'Gladstonian Liberalism'.
3. a) Using Items 2 and 3 and your own knowledge, explain why the 1870 Education Act was a controversial measure.
   b) Why do you think the 1870 Education Act is regarded as an important reform?

2 Disraeli's government of 1874-80

Key questions

1. What was Disraeli's position in 1874?
2. What were the key political and social issues in Disraeli's government of 1874-80?

2.1 What was Disraeli's position in 1874?

Disraeli's early career

Like Gladstone, Benjamin Disraeli first became an MP in the 1830s (he became MP for Maidstone in 1837). Disraeli's background was very different from that of Gladstone, however, and his climb to power was much more difficult than that of Gladstone. His early years are outlined in Box 1.7.

1846 - a turning point

As was the case with Gladstone, the downfall of Peel in 1846 was an important turning point in Disraeli's political career. Between 1844 and 1846, Disraeli took a leading part in the attacks on Prime Minister Peel, accusing him time after time of betraying his party. Machin argues that his part in Peel's downfall was crucial:

Without the confidence and morale derived from Peel's opponents from Disraeli's fearless and continuous attacks on him since 1844, the resistance in 1846 would have been much weaker...The events of that year would probably have been far different without Disraeli's crucial contributions. There is no doubt that Disraeli was the virtual Leader of the Opposition in 1846.' (Machin 1995, p.56)

Walton agrees, arguing:

'Perhaps the most important turning point in Disraeli's career came in the debate...on 22 January 1846, when...his eloquent, witty, angry and highly personal attack on Peel rallied the...country gentlemen on the Conservative back benches...It was this intervention that confirmed Disraeli's reputation as a formidable parliamentary orator, drove a wedge between Peel's followers on the front bench and the backbench squires, and set in motion the chain of events which culminated in the splitting of the Conservative Party and the secession [withdrawal] of most of its established, and potential, ministerial talent. Disraeli could not have risen to the party leadership without this upheaval.' (Walton 1990, pp.12-13)

Disraeli's rise to power 1846-68

Although the split in the Conservative Party over free

BOX 1.7 Benjamin Disraeli (1804-81) - early years

Benjamin Disraeli was born into a Jewish family living in London. His paternal grandfather, Benjamin D'Israeli had come to Britain from Italy in 1748 to sell straw hats and had made a fortune on the stock exchange. His father, Isaac D'Israeli, then gained a reputation as a historian and writer on Judaism. Through him, Benjamin met Canning and other Tory politicians, though Isaac does not seem to have had political ambitions himself or for his son. Although brought up in a Jewish family and influenced by his Jewish origins, Benjamin was baptised into the Church of England in 1817 (along with his brothers and sisters). He remained a Christian, but rather unattached to the religion (his friend Edward Stanley - Lord Derby - claimed he was sceptical about it in private). He then went to a minor public school, leaving after three years without going on to university. In the early 1820s, Benjamin considered careers in the law and journalism and speculated on the stock market. By 1825, he was in massive debt after his stock-market speculation failed and a newspaper he launched collapsed. He remained in debt for most of the rest of his life. Along with indebtedness went literary activity. His first novel was published in 1826 and most of his novels completed by the time he entered Parliament in 1837. By 1837, Disraeli had stood as a candidate five times (and had stood and then stood down before the election twice). He stood first as a radical unattached to a party and then as a Conservative. When the Conservatives came into power in 1841, Disraeli hoped Peel would bring him into government, but Peel did not do so (though he sent Disraeli an encouraging letter). The following year, Disraeli set up a loose reforming group known as 'Young England' which began to criticise the government. This group became the focus of opposition to Peel and, in 1846, helped to engineer his downfall.
Adapted from Machin 1995.

Biography Box

trade in 1846 was electorally damaging (the party did not win an overall majority again until 1874), Disraeli benefited personally. He moved from the back benches to the opposition front bench and when the Conservatives formed minority governments - in 1852, 1858-59 and 1866-67 - he became Chancellor of the Exchequer. Although the Conservative Leader throughout this period remained Lord Derby, from 1851 Disraeli was sole Conservative Leader in the Commons (between

February 1849 and 1851, Lord Derby attempted to organise a trio of Leaders in the Commons - Disraeli, Herries and Granby - but Disraeli easily outmanoeuvred the others - see Cavendish 1999). It is generally agreed, however, that Disraeli's position was not secure at first:

'Plenty of reservations were still being expressed about his personality and attitudes. He continued to depend upon the legitimacy which was conferred by Derby's overlordship of the party as a whole, and his position was never to be secure until the 1874 election had been won.' (Walton 1990, p.14)

Most historians argue that this insecurity had four main sources:

- disapproval of Disraeli's colourful past
- disapproval of his lack of 'pedigree' (he was not an aristocrat)
- distrust of his personal ambition
- disapproval of his Jewish background.

Despite the reservations many Conservatives had about Disraeli as a person, however, he proved himself to be an invaluable asset for his party - see Box 1.8.

BOX 1.8 **Disraeli's rise to power**

Interpretation

Disraeli possessed many disadvantages. Victorian England was a status-ridden society and governments were dominated by gentlemen of great wealth. He appeared to lack most of the obvious qualifications for leadership of a party which numbered so many titled names among its members. He certainly lacked rank, but was able to buy himself into the landowning fraternity by purchasing a manor house in 1848. Similarly, baptism into Christianity gave him religious respectability. However, his Jewishness was still a barrier at a time when anti-semitism (hatred of Jews) was common. It was no mean feat for Disraeli to reach the top because there is no doubt that he arrived there against the wishes and despite the prejudices of many in his party. That he did so was partly a matter of ability. He was a superb parliamentarian - skilful and courageous. He was often opposed by many great performers in the Commons, but invariably countered their oratory with resourcefulness, ingenuity and eloquence. But his rise to power was also due to the absence of any real competition. The longer the party remained in the wilderness, the more it was apparent that there was nobody else with Disraeli's quality. He was still not liked by many Conservatives and was seen as an outsider, but, despite this, his qualities were such that they accepted him as Leader.

Adapted from Watts 1994.

Disraeli becomes Party Leader

Disraeli's parliamentary skills were displayed most obviously during the period 1866-67 when he managed to defeat Gladstone's Reform Bill and then pilot through his own (see Unit 2, Section 1.3 and Activity 2.1). By 'dishing the Whigs' (the phrase used at the time to mean out witting them), Disraeli secured his position as Conservative Leader in the Commons and ensured that, when Lord Derby retired in February 1868, he was invited to succeed him as Party Leader and, briefly, as Prime Minister at the head of a minority government (he remained Prime Minister until the general election was held in December 1868). Jenkins (1997) argues that, in opposition again after defeat in the 1868 general election, Disraeli's strategy had two strands:

- not to attack the government in the hope that splits within the governing party would widen
- not to take office again while in a minority position in the Commons (to ensure that the splits that emerged within the governing party did not have time to heal).

In 1872, he made two key speeches - in Manchester and London - outlining his vision. While many historians have argued that these outlined his vision of 'One Nation' Conservatism (see below), Jenkins argues that their aim was to heighten popular unease with the Liberal government:

'Arguably, the real significance of these speeches lay in the way Disraeli sought to heighten the growing sense of public unease about the (apparently) destructive propensities [tendencies] of the Gladstonian Liberal Party.' (Jenkins 1997, p.19)

According to Jenkins, therefore, Disraeli's tactics in opposition were an important factor in the Conservative election victory in 1874.

Disraeli's political beliefs

Disraeli claimed that during the 'wilderness years' (the period 1846-74 when the Conservatives failed to win an overall majority), he was the 'educator' of his party. It was he who pushed the party into abandoning protectionism (the policy was finally abandoned in 1852), he claimed, and he who revived the party's fortunes by broadening its appeal. By making these claims, Disraeli suggested that he had a carefully worked out set of political beliefs that gradually came to be accepted by the majority of his party. This, however, has been the subject of debate among historians.

One Nation Conservatism

Some historians accept that Disraeli did indeed play the role of 'educator' of his party and argue that he developed a new form of Conservatism. This is sometimes described as 'Tory democracy' or 'One Nation' Conservatism. One Nation Conservatism has been defined as follows:

'Keen to broaden support for the Conservative Party,

Disraeli argued that, despite class differences, the interests uniting the British people were of far greater significance than those dividing them. It was true that some were more privileged than others, but it was the duty of the more privileged to look after those in need.' (Roberts 1999, p.28)

Lee argues that Disraeli had come to the conclusion that Britain was dominated by a small group of Whig families whose chief concern was their own status and wellbeing. These Whigs had widened the gap between the top and bottom of society, dividing Britain into two nations:

'With the right approach, the Conservatives could bridge the gap between the two nations. It would, of course, be necessary to entrust Britain's cohesion to its natural guarantors - the aristocracy, gentry, Church and monarchy...He believed that "the Tory Party in this country is the national party; it is the really democratic party of England". The way in which the support of the working classes would be guaranteed would be a steady stream of social reform.' (Lee 1994, p.150)

Ghosh (1987) argues that this justification of support for social reform had a long tradition in the Conservative Party and it was upon that tradition that Disraeli was building.

A pragmatic and a moral strand

Heywood (1992) notes that Disraeli's argument had both a pragmatic and a moral strand. On the one hand, Disraeli realised that growing social inequality in Britain had the potential to lead to violent uprisings like those that had taken place in Europe in 1789, 1830 and 1848. Reform was, therefore, necessary on practical grounds because it would protect the long-term interests of the wealthy by ensuring that revolution was avoided. On the other hand, Disraeli argued that reform was necessary on moral grounds. This argument was based on the traditional Conservative belief that society was naturally arranged in a hierarchy. Since those at the top of the hierarchy had more wealth and privileges than those at the bottom, those at the top had a greater responsibility to consider the needs of those less fortunate than themselves. In other words, in return for their privileged position, those at the top of the hierarchy had a moral obligation to alleviate the suffering of those at the bottom of the hierarchy.

The slogan 'one nation' was given to this type of conservatism because of Disraeli's emphasis on the unity between classes. The British people, the term suggested, all belonged to one happy family, each with a particular role to play and each with a particular place within the family hierarchy.

Arguments against this view

Some historians, however, dismiss the view that Disraeli had a carefully worked out set of political beliefs, arguing that, at decisive moments in his career, Disraeli's primary concern was his own and his party's advantage. This was a view that became popular in the 1960s when Smith (1967) and Blake (1969) published books on Disraeli. They argued that, in the field of social reform, Disraeli had no clearly worked out programme. He had some general ideas, but the real work was done by the Home Secretary, Richard Cross. Besides, they argue, much of the legislation could have been passed by either main party, there was nothing distinctive about it. Smith concludes:

'Disraeli's popular Toryism, in short, was an idea, an attitude, not a policy and what its [supporters were] calling for was a regeneration, not a reconstruction of society.' (Smith 1967, p.17)

Walton (1990) goes as far as to talk of the 'Disraelian myth' that grew up after his death and argues that what became known as 'Tory Democracy' or 'One Nation Conservatism' was an attempt, after the event, to provide a sympathetic explanation of Disraeli's actions.

It is important to bear in mind these different interpretations when considering the action taken when Disraeli was Prime Minister between 1874 and 1880.

2.2 What were the key political and social issues in Disraeli's government of 1874-80?

Disraeli's aims as Prime Minister

There is good evidence to show that, when he became Prime Minister in 1874, Disraeli did not have a set plan of action in mind. Disraeli's Home Secretary, Richard Cross, recorded in his memoirs that the Cabinet had difficulty framing a legislative programme for the 1874 Queen's Speech (the Queen's Speech outlines the Bills which the government intends to introduce in the forthcoming session of Parliament):

'When the Cabinet came to discuss the Queen's Speech, I was, I confess, disappointed at the want of originality shown by the Prime Minister. From all his speeches, I had quite expected that his mind was full of legislative schemes, but such did not prove to be the case; on the contrary, he had to rely on the various suggestions of his colleagues, and as they themselves had only just come into office...there was some difficulty in framing the Queen's Speech.' (quoted in Blake 1969, p.543)

Feuchtwanger, however, argues that it is not at all surprising that Disraeli did not have a set plan of action in mind. In part, this was a matter of personality (Disraeli was a 'big ideas' person rather than somebody who enjoyed the details) and, in part, it was a matter of political calculation:

'Not only was Disraeli disinclined and ill-equipped to hatch such a design, he knew that his victory owed much to a desire in the country for a quiet life and he was not disposed to repeat his adversary's [ie Gladstone's] mistake of alarming all and sundry by his restlessness.' (Feuchtwanger 1985, p.85)

Just because Disraeli did not have a specific programme in mind, it does not mean that he did not have specific aims about what his government should achieve. The main aims that have been suggested are summarised in Box 1.9.

BOX 1.9 Disraeli's aims on becoming Prime Minister

What Disraeli was prepared to do when he came to power was to deal with problems on which government action had become inescapable. One reason for doing this was to broaden the appeal of the Conservative Party by appealing to important groups of voters who had not necessarily voted Conservative in the past - such as trade unionists. It should be remembered that Disraeli's government was the first Conservative government with an overall majority since Peel's in 1841-46. The Liberal Party, rather than the Conservative Party, therefore, seemed to be the 'natural' party of government - something which Disraeli hoped to reverse. Second, he and his ministers were prepared to amend recent Liberal reforms in the light of Conservative interests and ideas. Rather than trying to turn the clock back by repealing Liberal legislation, they decided that a better strategy was to adapt the reforms in a way which suited them. Third, Disraeli and his colleagues were as reluctant as any Liberal to encourage state intervention. Their actions were bound by a belief in the laissez-faire approach. Fourth, Disraeli was sensitive to public opinion and anxious to take action when there was an outcry. He did not want the government to acquire a reactionary, or in the jargon of the time a 'retrograde' appearance. And finally, anything that was done could not be allowed to put an undue burden on the public revenue or go against the Tory aim of reducing local taxation.
Adapted from Feuchtwanger 1985.

Interpretation

Despite the lack of a set plan of action and despite the constraints imposed by some of the aims outlined in Box 1.9, Disraeli's government passed what Smith (1967) described as 'eleven major Acts' between 1874 and 1876. These eleven Acts and other, more minor, pieces of legislation attempted to address a variety of domestic social problems.

1. Measures concerned with living conditions

Between 1874 and 1876, five pieces of legislation aimed to improve people's living conditions.

i. The Licensing Act, 1874

This Act, introduced by Home Secretary Richard Cross, altered the licensing hours that had been introduced by the Liberal government's 1872 Act. Machin (1995) argues that this Act was designed to appeal to brewers who had voted Conservative in large numbers in 1874. Walton agrees and adds that:

'The Licensing Act of 1874 was intended as a sop to the brewers, but in some areas it actually curtailed licensing hours still further, as eventually passed, and it ultimately satisfied nobody.' (Walton 1990, p.52)

ii. The Artisans Dwelling Act, 1875

This Act, also designed by Home Secretary Richard Cross, allowed local authorities to buy up areas occupied by very poor 'slum' housing, to clear the slums and then to rebuild on the cleared site. Disraeli described the Act as 'our chief measure'. Watts, however, notes that:

'Cross met with intense pressure from within his own party to a measure which was seen as an infringement of the rights of private property, and because of this he did not make the measure compulsory.' (Watts 1994, p.97)

The Act, therefore, was a piece of 'permissive legislation' - it allowed local authorities to take action if they chose to do so, but it did not force them to take action. Because of this, and because slum clearance schemes were expensive to implement, the Act made little impact. A few cities undertook major redevelopment, notably Birmingham under Joseph Chamberlain, but most towns did nothing. Blake (1969) claims that, by 1881, the powers permitted by the Act had been taken up by only 10 out of 87 towns in England and Wales.

iii. The Public Health Act, 1875

This Act gathered together previous laws concerned with this area into one Act and imposed certain duties on local authorities:

'Among other things, nuisances were to be removed, contaminated food safely destroyed and infectious diseases notified. Other items covered ranged from street lighting to burials, and it remained the basis for legislation until 1929.' (Watts 1994, pp.97-98)

iv. The Sale of Food and Drugs Act, 1875

This Act aimed to improve the standards of purity of food and drugs by laying down standards about adulteration. Its effectiveness was limited, however, because local authorities did not have to employ food analysts. It was, in other words, another piece of permissive legislation.

v. The Rivers Pollution Act, 1875
This Act was designed to reduce the pollution of rivers, but historians agree that it made little impact. Lee's comment is typical:

'The Rivers Pollution Act of [1875] was designed to prevent the flow of poisonous liquids into rivers and streams. But this had totally inadequate definitions of pollution and, in any case, was applied with notorious inconsistency against offending factories.' (Lee 1994, p.154)

2. Measures concerning working conditions
Between 1874 and 1878, six main pieces of legislation aimed to improve people's working conditions.

i. The Factory Act, 1874
The main provisions of the 1874 Factory Act were as follows:
- the maximum working day for women and children was ten hours
- no child could be employed until they were ten (rather than eight)
- no child could work full-time until they were 14 (rather than 13).

Pearce and Stewart note that:

'Men's hours were, in theory, not regulated, as this was feared to be a breach of the principle of free contract. In effect, men's hours were reduced as well and the "week-end" with its Saturday afternoon football match became an integral part of the English way of life.' (Pearce & Stewart 1992, p.76)

ii. The Conspiracy and Protection of Property Act, 1875
This Act largely reversed the 1871 Criminal Law Amendment Act. It ended the special criminal legislation relating to the trade unions, putting them under the ordinary law of the land. Also, it legalised peaceful picketing. See also, Unit 4, Section 1.3.

iii. The Employers and Workmen Act, 1875
This Act abolished the Master and Servant Act by which employees, but not employers, could be treated as criminals and sent to prison for breach of contract. Under the new Act, employees and employers were equal parties to a contract and breaches of that contract were civil, not criminal, offences. See also, Unit 4, Section 1.3.

iv The Merchant Shipping Act, 1876
This Act was promoted by the Liberal MP, Samuel Plimsoll and reluctantly adopted by the government. The Act was designed to protect sailors by preventing the overloading and undermanning of ships. Plimsoll wanted a line to be painted on each boat to show the maximum loading point. The 1876 Act accepted the need for a line but allowed shipowners to decide where it should be painted on the ship. Cooper argues that the government's

decision to promote this legislation was due to a combination of popular pressure and pressure in Parliament:

'Conservative MPs representing ports warned [Disraeli] that working-class feelings were running high, and a furious protest in the Commons by the Liberal MP Samuel Plimsoll, the leading campaigner for sailors' interests, focused much sympathetic attention on the issue.' (Cooper 1995b, p.354)

v. The Trade Union Act Amendment Act, 1876
This Act extended the protection of funds to all trade unions, not just to those protected by the Trade Union Act of 1871. See also, Unit 4, Section 1.3.

vi. The Factory and Workshops Act, 1878
This Act was one of the few reforms to be passed after 1876. According to Watts:

'The Factory and Workshops Act (1878) distinguished between a factory and a workshop, but ensured that both types of premises should be brought under governmental inspection. This was an important advance in the rights accorded to industrial workers.' (Watts 1994, p.98)

3. Education and religious affairs
It was pointed out in Section 1.3 above that religion and education were closely intertwined in the 19th century. Between 1874 and 1876, two main pieces of legislation aimed to reform educational and religious affairs.

i. The Public Worship Regulation Act, 1874
This was a controversial Act which nearly split the Conservative government. The Act was designed to outlaw the adoption of Catholic forms of worship in the Church of England. It was opposed both by Gladstone and by 'High Anglicans' in the Cabinet (such as Salisbury). Machin notes:

'The Act caused controversy for many years and its attempt to enforce a strict observance of the Prayer Book was unsuccessful. Recalcitrant [stubborn] clergy who refused to abandon illegal ritual were imprisoned over the next eight years. But, coercion failed and their movement spread.' (Machin 1995, p.131)

ii. The Education Act, 1876
This Act set up School Attendance Committees in places where there were no School Boards. The job of these committees was to ensure that children up to the age of ten received an adequate education. Under the Act, the committees could help poor parents by paying school fees and they could force parents to ensure that their children attended school. Cooper argues that:

'[The Act] had the effect of making compulsory the education of children up to the age of ten: a marked increase of state power at the expense of

parental freedom.' (Cooper 1995b, p.354)
The reasons why this interventionist measure was introduced are explored in Box 1.10.

BOX 1.10 The 1876 Education Act

The 1876 Education Act is an example of apparently progressive social policy which was, in reality, motivated by narrow political calculations. The aim was not to create an educational ladder helping ambitious members of the working class to rise to the rank of the middle class. Rather, in Cross's words, the aim was to make the masses 'more fit to do their duty in that station of life to which they are called'. What motivated the Conservatives to take action was the effect of the 1870 Education Act on Anglican schools. The new Board Schools were widely hated by Conservatives because their teaching was not specifically Anglican and because they were often controlled by non-conformists. In addition, Board Schools had a financial advantage because they were paid for out of the rates. Voluntary (Anglican) Schools depended on fees paid by pupils. Since many Voluntary Schools were too poor to provide the 'efficient' education demanded by the 1870 Act, there was a danger of Board Schools taking over. In such circumstances, giving School Attendance Committees the power to pay for poor pupils was the easiest way of guaranteeing the Voluntary Schools an adequate income and, as a result, of staving off the threat from the Board Schools. Preserving the Voluntary School system would also save rate-payers' money. The Voluntary Schools would remain a great source of strength to the Church of England and to the Conservative interest in general.

Adapted from Cooper 1995b.

---

4. Other social reforms

Three other Acts from the period 1874 to 1876 should be mentioned.

i. The Friendly Societies Act, 1875

This Act was the product of the report of a Royal Commission set up by the previous Liberal government. The aim of the Act was to reduce the risk of members of Friendly Societies (these are defined in Unit 4, page 113) losing their money. The Act set up a register of Friendly Societies, but the government refused to take any responsibility for the way in which they managed their funds.
Feuchtwanger argues:
'The Friendly Societies Bill well illustrates that Conservative ministers were no less reluctant than any member of the Manchester School [Liberal free-traders] to countenance more than a minimum

of state intervention.' (Feuchtwanger 1985, p.87)

ii. The Agricultural Holdings Act, 1875

This Act was introduced by Disraeli himself and was influenced by Gladstone's 1870 Irish Land Act:
'This [Act] was very dear to Disraeli and through it he attempted to do something for tenant farmers on the lines of Gladstone's Irish Bill of 1870.' (Pearce & Stewart 1992, p.79)
The Act allowed tenants in mainland Britain who moved or were evicted from their farms to claim compensation for the improvements they had carried out. Like the Artisans Dwelling Act, this Act was permissive rather than compulsory. In other words, landlords could choose to ignore tenants' claims for compensation.

iii. The Enclosures Act, 1876

The aim of this Act was to protect common land:
'The Enclosure Act protected the public's right to use common pasture land by stopping landlords from absorbing it into their estates. Under this legislation, Epping Forest was saved for the people of London two years later.' (Watts 1994, p.98)

A distinctive approach?

Examination of the key social reforms introduced by Disraeli's government raises the question as to whether, taken as a whole, these reforms provide evidence of a distinctive approach. As Walton puts it:
'How much of this legislation was window dressing, and how much of real value? How far was it distinctively Conservative and how far the product of something that might be more specifically labelled Disraelian Conservatism? Do these measures embody the realisation of long-held and deeply-felt "One Nation" ideals on Disraeli's part, or should we see them as pragmatic responses to immediate circumstances and opportunities?' (Walton 1990, pp.49-50)
Walton favours the view of Smith (1967) and Blake (1969) who are both sceptical of the One Nation interpretation. The main arguments are:
- some of the issues that were addressed were inherited from the previous administration
- some of the issues were forced on the government by pressure from outside
- policies were the work of individual ministers and emerged piecemeal
- most measures had the support of the Liberals
- the Conservatives believed in the laissez-faire approach just as strongly as the Liberals did (which explains why they introduced permissive rather than compulsory legislation)
- the Conservatives were more concerned with broadening their support and proving they were capable of governing than with a particular set of ideas
- domestic social reform was not considered to be special or important - it only took centre stage

when more important matters (such as foreign policy) were not of concern (the government's record of social reform was not even mentioned in the 1880 general election campaign).

Not all historians are convinced by these arguments, however. Cooper (1995b), for example, argues that Disraeli's trade union legislation was a genuine attempt to build one nation:

'The excitement Disraeli expressed at the passing of his trade union legislation, and the centrality which he accorded it in securing the Conservatives' future successes can perhaps be explained if Disraeli is seen as fulfilling in his own mind the desire to make one nation of England's rich and poor which he had expressed 30 years earlier in [his novel] *Sybil* and which remained,

for Disraeli, the great mission and opportunity of Conservatism.' (Cooper 1995b, p.356)

Disraeli's government after 1876

While the first three years of Disraeli's second administration were preoccupied with domestic social reforms, the remaining years were dominated by foreign affairs. Watts argues that:

'In the last years of the ministry, dogged as it was by growing trade depression, Irish obstructionism in the House of Commons [see pages 26-27] and colonial problems, the impetus to reform drained away. Disraeli became ever more immersed in matters of foreign policy, and ministers and backbenchers were pleased to have a respite from further change.' (Watts 1994, p.99)

MAIN POINTS - Part 2

- Like Gladstone, Benjamin Disraeli first became an MP in the 1830s. His background was very different from that of Gladstone, however, and his climb to power was much more difficult. Between 1844 and 1846, Disraeli took a leading part in the attacks on Prime Minister Peel. This made him the virtual Leader of the Opposition in 1846.
- When the Conservatives formed minority governments in 1852, 1858-59 and 1866-67, Disraeli became Chancellor of the Exchequer. He did not become Party Leader until February 1868, after his success over the second Reform Act and Derby's retirement.
- Some historians argue that Disraeli had a carefully worked out set of political beliefs ('Tory Democracy'

or 'One Nation' Conservatism). Others argue that his only concern was personal and party advantage.
- There is good evidence to show that, when he became Prime Minister in 1874, Disraeli did not have a set plan of action in mind. Nevertheless, his government passed a large number of significant reforms.
- These reforms tackled (1) living conditions (2) working conditions (3) education and religious affairs and (4) other social problems. Some historians argue that Disraeli's reforms add up to a distinctive approach. Others argue that there was nothing really distinctive about the reforms. From 1876, the programme of social reform was abandoned in favour of foreign policy initiatives.

Activity 1.3 Disraeli's second administration

ITEM 1 An assessment of Disraeli's second administration

Disraeli produced a range of social legislation which equalled or even surpassed those of other governments of the period. But, to what extent did all this involve a distinctly 'Conservative' approach? Was Disraeli developing his earlier ideas? Was Disraelian Conservatism now a deliberate party policy, the first perhaps in modern British history? Disraeli's words suggest so - he seemed to place social reform firmly on the party agenda - and that was the approach taken by historians before World War II. More recent opinion, however, is generally against the notion that Disraeli was giving Conservatism a blueprint of social reform for the following reasons. First, there was an underlying continuity of social legislation in the late 1860s and 1870s which transcended party differences. There were, in fact, precedents in most previous governments for Disraeli's measures, preventing them from being distinctively Conservative. For example, the Liberals had proposed the Torrens Bill in 1868 and, if it had not been rejected by the Lords, it would have made the same provisions as the Artisans Dwelling Act. Similarly, the Gladstone government had set up a Royal Commission to look at Merchant Shipping in 1873, anticipating Disraeli's reforms. Second, and arising from this argument, it is possible to see 'Conservatism' as heavily diluted by a bi-partisan (joint party) approach to social reform. There was a surprising degree of cooperation between Conservatives and Liberals over key measures and the Liberals often applied the necessary pressure for measures to be passed. For example, the Liberal, Robert Lowe, argued strongly in favour of the clauses making picketing legal. Both parties supported the measures relating to the working class, public health and factory reform. Third, this cooperation between the two parties meant that there was no need for Disraeli to identify a specific programme and force it through Parliament against strong opposition. Indeed, there is some question as to whether Disraeli exerted strong overall leadership anyway. Much of the initiative came from individual ministers. What Disraeli actually did was to make it acceptable for the Conservatives to introduce social reforms after a long period spent resisting them. His aim was to revive his party by moving towards the centre ground of politics. He provided an environment in which reform could emerge, not a systematic programme for change.

Adapted from Lee 1994.

ITEM 2 Disraeli's speeches in 1872

(i) In attempting to legislate upon social matters the great object is to be practical - to have before us some distinct aims and some distinct means by which they can be accomplished. Gentlemen, I think public attention as regards these matters ought to be concentrated upon sanitary legislation. That is a wide subject and, if properly treated, comprises almost every consideration which has a just claim upon legislative interference. Pure air, pure water, the inspection of unhealthy habitations, the adulteration of food, these and many kindred matters may be legitimately dealt with by the legislature....Gentlemen, it is impossible to overrate the importance of the subject. After all, the first consideration of a minister should be the health of the people....if the population every ten years decreases and the stature of the race every ten years diminishes, the history of that country will soon be the history of the past.
Extract from Disraeli's speech in Manchester on 3 April 1872.

(ii) Gentlemen, the Tory Party, unless it is a national party is nothing...Now I have always been of opinion that the Tory Party has three great objects. The first is to maintain the institutions of the country...The principles of liberty, of order of law, and of religion are not to be entrusted to individual opinion or to the caprice [whims] and passion of multitudes, but should be embodied in a form of permanence and power. We associate with the monarchy the ideas which it represents - the majesty of law, the administration of justice, the fountains of mercy and of honour...Gentlemen, there is another and second great object of the Tory Party...to uphold the Empire of England...Another great object of the Tory Party and one not inferior to the maintenance of the Empire, or the upholding of our institutions is the elevation of the condition of the people...It must be obvious to all who consider the condition of the multitude with a desire to improve and elevate it that no important step can be gained unless you can effect some reduction of their hours of labour and humanise their toil...I ventured to say a short time ago, speaking in one of the great cities of this country, that the health of the people was the most important question for a statesman. It is, gentlemen, a large subject. It has many branches. It involves the state of the dwellings of the people...It involves their enjoyment of some of the chief elements of nature - air, light and water. It involves the regulation of industry, the inspection of their toil...Upon you depends the issue...You have nothing to trust to but your own energy and the sublime instinct of an ancient people.
Extract from Disraeli's speech at Crystal Palace, London on 24 June 1872.

ITEM 3 Disraeli's programme

This cartoon was published in *Punch* magazine on 6 July 1872. It was entitled 'The Conservative Programme' and shows (on the right) the Leader of the Conservatives, Benjamin Disraeli, being approached by a Conservative peer, Lord Abercorn (he is carrying a crown to show that he is a Lord). Beneath the cartoon appeared the following caption:

'Deputation below, Sir - want to know the Conservative programme. Rt Hon Ben. Diz: 'Eh?-Oh!-Ah!-Yes!-Quite so!' Tell them, my good Abercorn, with my compliments that we propose to rely on the sublime instincts of an ancient people!'
(See speech at Crystal Palace).

Part of the speech that Disraeli delivered at the Crystal Palace in June 1872 is reproduced in Item 2 (ii) above. Before making that speech (and the speech in Manchester in April), Disraeli's position as Leader of the Conservative Party had been under attack from his colleagues, led by Lord Cairns. According to Machin, Cairns and others were concerned that Disraeli's leadership was not active and determined enough. The two speeches, however, reassured them and cemented Disraeli's position as Party Leader:

> 'Disraeli's speeches had been concerned not so much with underlying realities as with making political statements to aid his party. The effect was considerable. His two memorable orations helped to restore Conservative morale and strengthened Conservative unity behind him. After he had delivered them, there was no further hint of replacing him as Leader'. (Machin 1995, p.121)

Questions

1. a) Using Item 1 and your own knowledge, compare and contrast Disraeli's second administration with Gladstone's first administration.
   b) 'The main aim of Disraeli's second administration was to secure the future of the Conservative Party.' Give arguments for and against this view.
2. Look at Items 2 and 3.
   a) What was the significance of the two speeches made by Disraeli in 1872?
   b) Did Disraeli have a political programme?

c) What do these items tell us about Disraeli's character and beliefs?
3. a) To what extent did Disraeli's second administration follow the model outlined by Disraeli in Item 2?
   b) Would you agree that Item 2 provides evidence that Disraeli had developed a distinctive brand of Conservatism which shaped his second administration? Explain your answer.

3 Gladstone's second administration

Key questions

1. Why did Gladstone become Prime Minister for a second time?
2. What were the main domestic, social and political issues in Gladstone's second administration?

3.1 Why did Gladstone become Prime Minister for a second time?

Retirement and re-emergence
Gladstone was 65 years old at the time of the 1874 general election. Following the Liberal Party's defeat, he resigned from the Liberal leadership, though he retained his seat in Parliament:

'Turning his back on an ungrateful nation, Gladstone retired as Leader of the Liberal Party in 1875, determined to spend his remaining years in theological study and reflection...Lord Hartington was elected Leader in the Commons and Lord Granville continued as Leader in the House of Lords.' (Adelman 1997, p.46)

Gladstone's retirement did not last for long, however. In 1876, concern over events in Bulgaria (where the Turks were alleged to have committed large-scale atrocities against Christians) brought him back to the national political stage as leader of the 'Agitation' (as the campaign against Disraeli's foreign policy became known):

'Gladstone was not at first at the forefront of the Agitation, but he soon saw its potential...In September, he published a pamphlet on *The Bulgarian Horrors and the Question of the East* which burned with righteous anger at the Turks' crimes and at Disraeli's complicity in them. Within a month, it had sold over 200,000 copies and made Gladstone the effective leader of the Agitation.' (Cooper 1995a, p.272)

Cooper argues that, for Gladstone, opposition to the Turks' atrocities was a question of morality and, once he realised that he had public support for his stance, he decided to launch another of his 'moral crusades' (earlier 'crusades' being his financial mission to free trade in the 1850s and 1860s and his mission to pacify Ireland in his first administration).

The importance of the Agitation
Since the Liberals were out of power, Gladstone's opposition to Disraeli's imperial policies had little practical effect. The Liberal front bench was reluctant to criticise Disraeli. Disraeli did not alter his policies. He was then able to present the Congress of Berlin of June-July 1878 as a great triumph for Britain and public opinion seemed to be generally supportive (Pearce & Stewart 1992 note that an anti-Russian mob broke the windows in Gladstone's house at this time). The Agitation did, however, re-establish Gladstone's links with grass-roots Liberals:

'The Agitation did have a dramatic impact on the fortunes of Gladstone and the Liberal Party. Over its course, Gladstone had reforged the links with militant non-conformity and radicalism which had been eroded by the disappointments of his first ministry.' (Cooper 1995a, p.272)

Adelman suggests that the campaign also had an important effect on Gladstone's attitudes towards members of his own party:

'He soon found, sadly, that his own front bench and official Anglicanism were lukewarm in support, whereas many radicals and the whole of non-conformity were solidly behind him. This impressed Gladstone profoundly; he never forgot what he called their "noble support" and in an article published a few months later, he described non-conformists - in the famous phrase - as the "backbone of the Liberal Party".' (Adelman 1997, p.47)

By attending the inaugural meeting of the National Liberal Federation (NLF) in Birmingham in May 1877 (see Unit 2, page 50), Gladstone strengthened his links with non-conformists and radicals and made a bid for the leadership of the Liberal Party:

'His visit to Birmingham in 1877 is, in a sense, a public gesture of support and appreciation of English non-conformity which did much to heal the rift that had developed between them over his earlier education policy. It is also something more. It is...in its attempt to rebuild that moral rapport with the masses that had been broken in 1874, a stage on the road to Midlothian and the resumption of the Liberal leadership.' (Adelman 1997, p.47)

The Midlothian campaigns

Having launched a moral crusade, Gladstone appears to have become determined to see it through to a conclusion:

'If Gladstone's opponents in the Liberal Party had hoped that Disraeli's apparent triumph in 1878 would force Gladstone into retirement again, they were to be disappointed. In fact the practical failure of the Bulgarian Agitation made it essential, in Gladstone's own eyes, that he stand his ground until other means could be found of vanquishing the abominable Disraeli.' (Cooper 1995a, p.273)

The 'other means' that Gladstone found of publicising his cause became known as the 'Midlothian campaigns' of 1879-80.

In January 1879, Gladstone agreed to put himself forward as candidate for a new constituency - Midlothian, south of Edinburgh - in the forthcoming general election. In the run-up to the election (held in March 1880), he then embarked on two 'whirlwind tours' which generated enormous publicity both for himself and for his message - see Box 1.11.

The significance of the Midlothian campaigns

The significance of the Midlothian campaigns was not just that they helped the Liberals to win the general election (most historians agree that they were not in themselves decisive), but rather that, by appealing to supporters directly, Gladstone strengthened his own position to such an extent that he was then invited to become Prime Minister even though he was not officially Leader of his party:

'The Liberals' rather unexpected landslide victory in the election of 1880 probably owed more to the poor state of trade, agricultural depression and, possibly, improved party organisation than to the "Midlothian campaign". What this did mean, however, was that it was impossible for either Hartington in the Commons or Earl Granville in the Lords to consider forming a government with Gladstone on the backbenches or even as a subordinate colleague. Reluctantly, Victoria was obliged to ask him to form the next government.' (Winstanley 1990, p.53)

BOX 1.11 The Midlothian campaigns

Interpretation

The two Midlothian campaigns took place in November-December 1879 and March 1880. On both occasions, Gladstone travelled up to Scotland by train, stopping at stations along the way to make speeches to the crowds that had gathered there in anticipation. Then there were processions through the streets of Edinburgh and whistle-stop tours of the countryside, with speech after speech to the thronging thousands. In the first campaign, the first week was spent in the constituency of Midlothian while the second was spent touring Scottish towns by train and making major speeches on arrival. Throughout Britain, newspapers carried four or five columns reporting on each major speech. This meant that, although unprepared in detail, each of the speeches had to be different from the others in theme and had to use language which would not put off voters who absorbed the words not in the emotional atmosphere of a mass meeting but in the more critical calm of their breakfast rooms. The target of these speeches was 'Beaconsfieldism' - Gladstone's name for the policies pursued by Disraeli (who had become the Earl of Beaconsfield in 1876). Never had British politics been so theatrically exciting and never had one man so impressed himself on a wider constituency. It is remarkable that Gladstone, who celebrated his 70th birthday in the middle of the campaign, should have seen so clearly the means by which the wider electorate created by the second Reform Act could be mobilised and given a sense of direction.

Adapted from Jenkins 1995 and Cooper 1995a.

Gladstone becomes Prime Minister

When the result of the 1880 general election became known, Queen Victoria sent for Lord Hartington and asked him to form a government:

'The Queen accepted Disraeli's resignation on 21 April 1880 and the next day she sent for Hartington to form a government. He explained that this was impossible without Gladstone accepting to serve under him, as Gladstone had played the role of Leader during the election campaign. The former Prime Minister had also made it clear to Hartington and Granville that he would accept no such position. It seems that he had become convinced that he alone embodied the natural will to banish Beaconsfieldism for ever.' (Pearce & Stewart 1992, p.44)

Given Gladstone's stance, Queen Victoria had no choice but to invite him to form a government.

3.2 What were the main domestic, social and political issues in Gladstone's second administration?

An overview

Most historians agree that Gladstone's second administration was less successful than his first. One reason for this is that Gladstone kept giving the impression that he was on the verge of retiring and the administration lurched from crisis to crisis:

'Gladstone's second government has often been seen as a disappointment compared with his first. Now over 70, he regarded his return to office as temporary, limited to the reversal of the most obnoxious features of "Beaconsfieldism". He was often on the point of retirement, but unforeseen crises, above all over Ireland, kept him "chained to the mast". The Liberal Party was still divided into many sections and Gladstone seemed to be the only man able to unite them.' (Feuchtwanger 1996, p.24)

Watts (1995) points out that, although there were 'high expectations' in 1880 that Gladstone's second administration would achieve as much as his first, the position in 1880 was very different from that in 1868. In particular, the Liberal Party was split in 1880 between the radical wing and the Whig wing.

The radical/Whig split

Watts argues that the divisions within the party were only made worse by the appointment of a Whig-dominated Cabinet:

'Gladstone had appointed a conservative Cabinet at a time when the party was becoming more radical and the divided team was unable to prove an effective instrument of government.' (Watts 1995, p.99)

Adelman points out that the NLF (which supported a radical programme) was considered to have played an important part in the Liberal success in the 1880 general election. This gave radicals the hope that their programme would be adopted. Gladstone, however, ensured that this did not happen:

'The enormous prestige he had built up since 1876 allowed him to bypass the radical programme and bend the party to his own will. This was something which Lord Hartington would never have had the strength to do if he had remained Party Leader; and Gladstone's triumph was, therefore, in Shannon's phrase "the ruin of radicalism".' (Adelman 1997, p.48)

Other problems

It was not just the radical/Whig split that made progress on domestic reform difficult for Gladstone's second administration. The government faced four further significant difficulties.

1. Lack of a coherent programme

Historians agree that, apart from combating Beaconsfieldism, Gladstone's second administration did not have a coherent programme:

'Apart from divisions at the top, the new Liberal government suffered from the fact that the party had no definite political philosophy or agreed programme. The ministry gained power largely because of the depression and the reaction against Beaconsfieldism...It was united only on the negative issue of denouncing Disraeli's foreign and imperial policies.' (Watts 1995, p.98)

2. The Bradlaugh case

In the 1880 general election, a well-known atheist, republican and supporter of birth control, Charles Bradlaugh, was elected MP for Northampton. Since he was an atheist and a republican, Bradlaugh refused to take the parliamentary oath and requested that he be allowed to affirm his allegiance instead. This set in train a series of events which, historians agree, took up a great deal of parliamentary time and distracted the government from other, more important, business. In short, Bradlaugh agreed to take the oath, but made public his contempt for it. When he came forward to take it, objections were made and he was unable to take his seat. He stood in the by-election which resulted and was re-elected, but he was then expelled twice more and re-elected twice more. The matter was only resolved in 1886 when Bradlaugh was finally allowed to take the oath of allegiance. In the meantime, the government introduced an Affirmation Bill in 1883 in an attempt to resolve the matter, but this was defeated despite Gladstone's strong support for it. Feuchtwanger concludes:

'The Bradlaugh case was sheer agony for the Liberal Party. Liberalism meant nothing if it did not mean that the rights of citizens should not be subject to any religious tests. The views of Bradlaugh were, however, so repugnant that even for many Liberals, non-conformist as well as Anglican, the preservation of a Christian Parliament against atheist defilement outweighed all other considerations.' (Feuchtwanger 1985, p.164)

The case put Gladstone in a difficult position since he found Bradlaugh's views repulsive, but he supported his right to hold them:

'Gladstone was at his best in that he forsook any opportunity to seek popularity or party advantage and stressed the cause of religious liberty to which over the years he had become deeply committed.' (Watts 1995, p.99)

3. The Fourth Party

The Bradlaugh case was exploited by the so-called 'Fourth Party' - a group of four Conservative MPs who did their best to obstruct government business during the period 1880-85. The members of the

Fourth Party were Lord Randolf Churchill, Henry Drummond Wolff, John Gorst and Arthur Balfour. According to Watts, Churchill, in particular, was able make life difficult for ministers:

'Bitingly sarcastic, he was able to goad Gladstone into losing his temper so that the Prime Minister seemed not to be in control of events. Gladstone took Churchill's antics seriously and recognised him as a formidable opponent. Over the five years of its existence, opportunities were effectively used by the Fourth Party and whether it was over Ireland or some colonial problem, the government front bench was much harassed and embarrassed.' (Watts 1995, pp.99-100)

4. Ireland

Winstanley argues that Gladstone's 'hopeless obsession with Ireland' ensured that the government's opportunity for success was limited:

'The record of his second administration of 1880-85 was dominated by the Irish Question which Gladstone had optimistically assumed had been solved by earlier legislation.' (Winstanley 1990, p.61)

The Irish Question and its impact on the British government is considered below.

Domestic legislation 1880-85

Historians agree that three significant measures were passed in Gladstone's second administration:

- the Irish Land Act, 1881 (see below)
- the Corrupt and Illegal Practices Act, 1883 (see Unit 2, Section 3.1)
- the Third Reform Act, 1884 and Redistribution Act, 1885 (see Unit 2, Section 3.3).

Obstruction (from the Irish MPs and the Fourth Party) and distraction (due to concerns with foreign policy, Irish affairs and the Bradlaugh case) ensured that little domestic legislation was passed in the early years of the administration. McCord suggests that:

'While Irish affairs were taking up a great deal of government time, the government's record in domestic reform seemed modest. Reforming legislation was finding its way onto the statute book, but much of it was not very controversial.' (McCord 1991, p.374)

The few significant reforms which were passed are outlined in Box 1.12.

The Irish Question

There is a consensus among historians that Gladstone's second administration was dominated by the 'Irish Question'. It was during the 1880s that an effective movement began to campaign for Irish Home Rule (self-government) both inside and outside of Parliament. During the 1880s, this movement was led by Charles Stewart Parnell - see Box 1.13 on page 26.

The Land War

At the time of the 1880 general election, Ireland was

BOX 1.12 | Domestic reforms 1880-85

1. Burial Act, 1880
This Act allowed non-conformists to bury their dead in parish churchyards

2. The Ground Game Act, 1880
This Act allowed tenants to kill vermin (such as rabbits and hares) on their land. Previously, all game had belonged to the landowner.

3. Education Act, 1880
This Act made attendance at school compulsory for children up to the age of 13.

4. The abolition of flogging in the army and navy
Flogging in the army and navy was abolished in 1881.

5. The Settled Land Act, 1881
This Act allowed tenants the power to grant leases.

6. The Employers' Liability Act, 1881
This Act was the first to make employers liable for injuries that occurred on their premises. It had many loopholes, but was important as it allowed the state to interfere in the law of contract between employer and employee.

7. The Married Women's Property Act, 1882
This Act extended the scope of the 1870 Married Women's Property Act - see Unit 3, page 69.

---

in the midst of what became known as the 'Land War'. By 1879, an economic crisis had developed in Ireland. Cheap grain flooding in from the USA had produced falling prices. The summer of 1877 was extremely wet and a poor harvest led to a serious rise in evictions as well as raising the serious possibility of famine:

'The number of evictions more than doubled in 1878 to the highest figure for over a decade. By 1880, they had more than doubled again and literally half the population of Ireland was living on private charity, with the proportion in the South-West of the country as high as nine-tenths.' (Kee 1972, p.70)

The Land League

In April 1879, Michael Davitt, a Fenian, organised a protest meeting in Irishtown, County Mayo. Tenant farmers from the local estate (which was owned by an Irish Catholic priest) attended the meeting, demanding the reduction of rents and the end of the landlord system. In response, the priest reduced his rents by 25%. This set a precedent and Davitt set out to extend the Irishtown model into a national campaign. The result, in October 1879, was the launch of the Irish National Land League. For three years, the Land League targeted estates and fought for tenants' rights.

BOX 1.13 Charles Stewart Parnell (1846-91)

Biography Box

Parnell was the son of a substantial Protestant landowner. He was educated in England and went to Cambridge University where he refused to complete his degree after being suspended following a street brawl. He entered Parliament at a by-election in 1875, not, it appears, because of any great interest in politics, but because he was at a loss for any alternative career. Although coming from the landowning Protestant gentry, Parnell was related, on one side, to Sir John Parnell who bitterly opposed the Union and, on the other side to a famous American general, Charles Stewart who had fought against the British in the war of 1812. This anti-British background expressed itself most forcibly in a sympathy for Fenianism (Fenians were revolutionaries who believed that Ireland should break all ties with Britain - see Section 1.3 above). Parnell was not himself a Fenian, but long afterwards he claimed that Fenianism had first turned him towards politics. But, this does not explain fully why he became an active nationalist. Beneath everything was a feeling very characteristic of the Anglo-Irish stock to which he belonged - an angry reaction against the air of superiority so many Englishmen adopted towards Ireland. 'These Englishmen', he once said to his brother, 'despise us because we are Irish, but we must stand up to them. That's the only way to treat an Englishman - stand up to him'.
Adapted from Lyons 1971.

This became known as the 'Land War':

'The Land League used...mass meetings, brass bands and...quieter forms of social combination and pressure. Its policy was to select estates especially notorious for rack-renting [charging excessive rents] and eviction; concentrate public attention on these estates by means of mass meetings; and then, by pressure of social ostracism [refusing to deal with landlords and their agents] and refusal of services, render life as difficult as possible for the landlord (if resident) or his agent, and especially for "grabbers" - those who rented land from which the previous tenants had been evicted and which the Land League had placed under a ban. The spectacular application of these methods in the 1880s against a Mayo estate for which a certain Captain Boycott was the agent, gave the word "boycott" to the English language.' (O'Brien & O'Brien 1985, pp.109-110)

The New Departure
As early as July 1877, Parnell and leading Fenians had begun talking about a new approach which would combine mass agitation with protest within

Parliament. The result was the so-called 'New Departure'. This was an informal agreement made at a meeting in Dublin between Davitt, John Devoy, an American Fenian, and Parnell in June 1879. The New Departure was a particularly significant development since it was the first time that the revolutionary strategy of the Fenians had been combined with the constitutional strategy (ie working for change within Parliament):

'The phrase a "new departure" was coined to describe a formidable alliance. This would consist of three strands - an independent, disciplined Irish party speaking as one voice on Irish matters in the House of Commons, a popular mass nationalist movement at home and the support of the influential Clan-na-Gael, the Irish-American organisation.' (Hodge 1998, p.15)

It was the Land League which fused the links between the three strands, not least because Parnell agreed to serve as the Land League's President. As Roy Foster notes:

'For a parliamentarian like Parnell, his involvement in the Land League meant riding a tiger. But it also provided him with the base he needed to overcome the moderate majority in his party.' (Foster 1988, p.405)

Obstructionism and non-cooperation
Following the 1880 general election, the Land War continued to rage, with violence increasing substantially in the second half of 1880:

'In the summer of 1880, a Bill to award compensation to certain classes of evicted tenants out of the Irish Church surplus actually succeeded in passing the House of Commons. It was then promptly rejected by the House of Lords, with the natural and inevitable consequence that the agitation in Ireland began ominously to boil once more.' (Lyons 1971, p.170)

The Liberal government's response was to draw up two tough Coercion Bills which the Home Rulers opposed fiercely using the obstructionist tactics they had been applying since 1875.

Obstructionism
Starting in 1875, two Irish MPs had adopted a new tactic which became known as 'obstructionism'. By making long speeches on the Irish Question and deliberately wasting parliamentary time, these MPs aimed to annoy the government into considering their demands:

'In 1875, J.C. Biggar and John O'Connor Power, both Fenians, began to apply the tactic of "obstruction" in the House of Commons. This involved interminable speeches on Irish affairs whatever subject was being debated at the time in order to disrupt parliamentary business and to focus the attention of the House on Irish grievances.' (Adelman 1996, p.81)

Once Parnell became Leader of the pro-Home Rule MPs in Parliament in May 1880, the tactic became party policy. The result was complete disruption of Commons business - see Box 1.14.

BOX 1.14 Obstructionism and the Coercion Bills

Source Box

The House was still sitting - it had been sitting without a break for over 40 hours. I shall never forget the appearance the Chamber presented. The floor was littered with paper. A few dishevelled and weary Irishmen on one side of the House, about 100 infuriated Englishmen on the other...Mr Parnell was upon his legs with pale cheeks and drawn face, his hands clenched behind his back, facing without flinching a continuous roar of interruption. It was now about eight o'clock. Half of Mr Parnell's followers were out of the Chamber snatching a few minute's sleep...Those who remained had each a specified period of time allotted to him to speak and they were wearily waiting their turn...Here then was the great Parliament of England. Of intelligent debate there was none. It was one unbroken scene of turbulence and disorder. The few Irishmen remained quiet...It was the Englishmen...who howled and roared and almost foamed at the mouth with rage at the calm and pale-faced young man who stood patiently facing them...No-one knew what was going to happen. There was no power under the rules of the House to stop the debate, it had resolved itself into a question of physical endurance...The end came suddenly and expectedly. At eight o'clock Mr Speaker Brand, from a sense of duty, as he said, and acting on his own responsibility and in defiance of the Rules of the House, ordered the debate to end [ie he imposed a 'guillotine' - see below]...The Irish members endeavoured to protest by speech against this proceeding and, failing in the attempt, they rose in their seats and left the Chamber in a body shouting 'privilege', a cry not heard in that place since Charles I attempted to invade the liberty of Parliament.

From a lecture delivered by John Redmond, a nationalist Irish MP, on 29 November 1896. In the extract, Redmond recalls the debate which lasted from 31 January to 2 February 1881.

One consequence of the battle over the Coercion Bills was that, in 1881, Parliament approved the Speaker's decision to impose a 'guillotine' (the ruling that the debate must end at a particular point - see Box 1.14). By approving this device, Parliament effectively ended the tactic of obstructionism since, if Home Rulers tried to use delaying tactics, the Speaker could impose a guillotine and then call for a vote.

Gladstone's second Irish Land Act, 1881

Gladstone's second Land Act, which passed through Parliament several months later, placed Parnell in a difficult position. The terms of the Act satisfied those moderates who had campaigned for the 'three Fs' (see Box 1.15) but did not go far enough for those on the extreme wing of the nationalist movement who wanted to convert the agrarian struggle into a campaign for independence and self-government. Parnell's dilemma was solved in October 1881 when his fiery speeches convinced the government that he was out to wreck the Land Act and he was arrested and sent to Kilmainham jail in Dublin. A week after Parnell's arrest, using its powers under the Coercion Acts, the government closed down the Land League.

BOX 1.15 Gladstone's second Land Act, 1881

Interpretation

In effect, the second Land Act of 1881 introduced the 'three Fs' - fixity of tenure throughout Ireland (which meant that tenants could not be evicted if they paid their rent), free sale (the right to compensation for improvements made on a holding when a tenant sold the tenancy to a new tenant) and, above all fair rents. In addition, the government again included a land purchase scheme. This time it was rather more favourable to the tenant since the state agreed to loan three-quarters of the purchase price (rather than two-thirds). The Act laid down that the definition of a fair rent no longer rested ultimately with the landlord but with a government Land Court. Given views on the rights of property which existed at the time, it was perhaps the most revolutionary social legislation any British government had ever introduced. There was, however, a practical problem not solved by the Act - it made no adequate allowance for tenancies which had built up considerable rent arrears.

Adapted from Kee 1972.

The Kilmainham Treaty

Parnell's imprisonment brought renewed violence in Ireland. Gladstone's government responded by entering into secret negotiations with Parnell. These negotiations resulted in the so-called Kilmainham Treaty - an informal agreement:

'The terms were that, in return for legislation to protect tenants with heavy arrears from eviction and a repeal of the Coercion Act together with the release of Parnell and his fellow detainees, Parnell should call off the agitation on the land and cooperate in the working of the Land Act. The further implications of the understanding were that Parnell would in future use his strength in Ireland and in the House of Commons to collaborate with the Liberals in continuing Gladstone's whole policy of "justice to Ireland".' (Kee 1972, p.86)

On learning that Parnell and his colleagues were to be released, the Chief Secretary for Ireland, William Forster (the main architect of the 1880 Coercion Acts) resigned.

The Phoenix Park murders

On 6 May 1882, a few days after Parnell and his colleagues were released from prison, the new Chief Secretary for Ireland, Lord Frederick Cavendish, and his under-secretary, Thomas Burke, were murdered while strolling in Phoenix Park on their first evening in Dublin (see Box 1.16). Those responsible for the murders belonged to a group called 'The Invincibles' - an extreme republican group.

The Phoenix Park murders made a profound impact on public opinion and on Parnell:
'The deed so shocked Parnell that he actually proposed to Gladstone that he, Parnell, should resign from public life. The Prime Minister declined to accept this offer (there was indeed no technical sense in which he could accept it) but the force of English public opinion drove him into a further Coercion Act for Ireland.' (Lyons 1972, p.175)

The Irish Question 1882-85

Parnell's release from prison was marked by a distinct change in approach, a change noted by Gladstone:
'Before long, there were reports of Gladstone's dinner-table conversation to the effect that the events of April and May [1882] "had completely changed, as by a religious conversion, the character and view of the Irish leader. This faith that Parnell really had been converted...remained until 1890 the prime bearing on Gladstone's Irish compass.' (Shannon 1999, p.300)

Between 1882 and 1885, Parnell set out to build a disciplined and effective parliamentary party (known

BOX 1.16 The Phoenix Park murders.

Source Box

This drawing shows Lord Frederick Cavendish being confronted by his murderers. Thomas Burke lies dead on the grass.

as the 'Irish Parliamentary Party' or 'IPP') which was backed by a strong network of local organisations in Ireland (the IPP was also known as the Irish Nationalist Party). Parnell's strategy was to pursue an independent line in Parliament, supporting whichever major party seemed likeliest to make moves towards Home Rule. At first and in line with the Kilmainham Treaty, the IPP supported the Liberals. But Joseph Chamberlain's idea of a 'Central Board' (the setting up of an Irish council with limited powers) was rejected by Cabinet and was unacceptable to Parnell anyway. As a result, the IPP moved towards the Conservatives who had begun to make encouraging signs that they would support an Irish Home Rule Bill. In June 1884, the IPP voted with the Conservatives to bring down the Liberal government.

MAIN POINTS - Part 3

- Gladstone retired as Leader of the Liberal Party in 1875, but began a campaign against Disraeli's foreign policy in 1876. This campaign culminated in the Midlothian campaigns of 1879-80. By appealing to supporters directly, Gladstone so strengthened his own position that he became Prime Minister in 1880 even though he was not officially Party Leader.
- Most historians agree that Gladstone's second administration was less successful than his first because (1) Gladstone kept indicating he was on the verge of retiring and the administration lacked stability (2) there was a split between the radical wing and the Whig wing (3) the government did not have a coherent programme (4) the Bradlaugh case (5) the Fourth Party and (6) the administration was forced to focus on the 'Irish Question'.
- Historians agree, however, that three significant measures were passed in Gladstone's second

- administration (1) the Irish Land Act, 1881 (2) the Corrupt and Illegal Practices Act, 1883 and (3) the Third Reform Act, 1884 and Redistribution Act, 1885. Other domestic reforms were introduced but they were neither controversial nor particularly significant.
- Gladstone's second administration was dominated by the 'Irish Question'. It was during the 1880s that an effective movement began to campaign for Irish Home Rule (self-government) both inside and outside Parliament.
- Although the 1881 Irish Land Act ended the Land War, the imprisonment and then the release of Parnell ensured that the Home Rule movement remained strong. Parnell cleverly adapted his tactics to ensure that his demands remained high on the political agenda.

Activity 1.4 Gladstone's second administration

ITEM 1 The Colossus of Words

THE COLOSSUS OF WORDS.

This cartoon shows Gladstone as the Colossus of Rhodes (a colossus is a statue of very great size). The Colossus of Rhodes was one of the seven wonders of the ancient world. The cartoon was published in *Punch* magazine in 1879. The cartoon makes reference to the key elements of 'Gladstonian Liberalism'.

ITEM 2 Gladstone's Cabinet in 1880

Gladstone never referred to his Cabinet of 1880 by any phrase approximating to that which he had applied to his first Cabinet - 'one of the best instruments for government that was ever constructed'. Indeed, compared to that of 1868, the 1880 Cabinet was a poor vessel for the weathering of storms. The fault for this was almost entirely Gladstone's own. Admittedly, the Queen was tiresome in her reaction to his suggested appointments. But these were time-consuming and temper-trying diversions. Of the ten points listed, she got her way only on two minor appointments. For the rest, Gladstone got his own way. Gladstone may have designed the Whig bias in the Cabinet partly to reassure Queen Victoria. But, it also fitted in well enough with his own instincts, even if not with his interests. The real distinction between the government of 1868 and that of 1880 went beyond the make-up of the two Cabinets. The 1868 government, because it had a legislative programme relevant to dominant issues, was able to make the political weather. The 1880 government not only lacked a structured programme, but it also had little idea in advance of the main issues with which it would have to deal. As a result, it was always the creature rather than the creator of the circumstances in which it operated. The Prime Minister who had grandly said in 1868 that it was his mission to pacify Ireland had hardly mentioned that unhappy island during the Midlothian campaigns. Yet, Irish issues were still more dominant in the Parliament elected in 1880 than they had been in 1868. The difference was that the first Gladstone government thrust them before Parliament whereas the second had them thrust down its own throat by deteriorating circumstances on the ground.

Adapted from Jenkins 1995.

ITEM 3 Assessment of Gladstone's second administration

The election of 1880 provided Gladstone with the opportunity to undo as quickly as possible the moral harm of Beaconsfieldism. But Irish problems, both in Ireland and in the person of Parnell in Westminster, dominated Parliament. By taking on the post of Chancellor of the Exchequer in addition to that of Prime Minister, Gladstone once again became bogged down in the petty details of government expenditure. In addition, the issues of radical reform, the Bradlaugh case and Ireland produced factions once again within the Liberal Party. It is not surprising that such difficulties put an almost complete stop to controversial domestic legislation (at least for the first half of the government's term). If, however, the reforms introduced in Gladstone's second administration are taken in conjunction with those introduced in the first administration, the effect of the changes was a concerted attack on prejudice. This was the essence of Gladstonian Liberalism. Gladstone's support for, among other things, the Disestablishment of the Church of Ireland, two Land Acts, civil service reform, the extension of the franchise and the elimination of electoral abuses aroused the hostility of the propertied classes. He was seen as an ogre who attacked the very fundamentals of society as they knew it. The reforms, therefore, indicate the extent to which the Liberals under Gladstone were ceasing to be the party of the Establishment. In the second administration, the amount of reform was not inconsiderable, but most of the changes were small-scale, useful but not far-reaching. There were exceptions, however. The extension of the franchise to agricultural workers was an important step. That measure and the Corrupt Practices Act moved the country substantially forwards on the road to becoming a political democracy.

Adapted from Abbott 1972 and Watts 1995.

Questions

1. a) Using Items 1-3 and your own knowledge, describe the main characteristics of Gladstone's second administration.
   b) How did it compare with his first administration?
2. a) Using Items 1 and 3, describe the main features of Gladstonian Liberalism.
   b) What does the cartoon in Item 1 tell us about Gladstone's public image in 1879?

c) Explain how Gladstone managed to become Prime Minister for a second time in 1880.
3. a) Using Items 2 and 3 and your own knowledge, describe the problems facing Gladstone's government in 1880-85.
   b) To what extent was Gladstone responsible for the problems his government faced in the years 1880-85?

4 The political rivalry of Gladstone and Disraeli

Key questions

1. What were the origins of the political rivalry between Gladstone and Disraeli?
2. How big were the differences between the two men?

4.1 What were the origins of the political rivalry between Gladstone and Disraeli?

Backgrounds and personalities

It was indicated in Parts 1 and 2 of this Unit that Gladstone and Disraeli had very different backgrounds and personalities. Gladstone came from a wealthy family, was educated at Eton and Oxford and married into an aristocratic family. As a young man, he was intensely religious and, according to Jenkins:

'He was tortured and he was somewhat awkward, both in movement and word.' (Jenkins 1995, p.42)

Jenkins claims that Gladstone was particularly awkward in the company of women and was a virgin when he married. Watts says that he had a 'towering personality' but was 'a mass of contradictions':

[He was] the deeply God-fearing person who anguished over his own sexual desires, the Flintshire landowner and self-confessed inequalitarian who nonetheless believed in opening opportunities for everybody, the committed Anglican who won the acclaim of English non-conformity, the cautious Conservative with a reverence for tradition who ended his career with a bold and risky attempt to resolve the Irish problem.' (Watts 1995, p.118)

Disraeli, on the other hand, came from a Jewish background, attended a minor public school but not university and, although his family was wealthy, accumulated large debts before settling down. His life before he married was 'colourful' - Machin (1995), for example, describes the affairs he had with two married aristocratic women in the 1830s - Clara Bolton and Henrietta Sykes. According to Watts:

'He had abundant charm, and women found him particularly attractive. His conversation was witty and sparkling, and he was a romantic, with a past reputation as a roué [an immoral person]. The hint of disrepute made him all the more interesting, and his pleasing manner, with its lack of pomposity, was enough to beguile [win over] many. He was also an arch flatterer who told women in particular what they were pleased to hear.' (Watts 1994, p.90)

Despite these differences in background and personality, both men became Conservative MPs in the 1830s (Gladstone in 1832 and Disraeli in 1837). They first met in 1835:

'The two men first met in 1835 at a dinner party given by Lord Lyndhurst. Disraeli was still not a Member of Parliament, whilst Gladstone was already a Junior Lord of the Treasury, if only briefly, in Peel's first government. Disraeli noted in a letter to his sister the presence of Gladstone as a "swan", who was the best company there. Gladstone, however, took no special notice of Disraeli, though later he recalled that Disraeli had been dressed foppishly and was very dull.' (Abbott 1972, p.11)

The roots of future rivalry

It was in Peel's second administration of 1841-46 that the roots of future rivalry first began to grow. Whereas Gladstone remained loyal to Peel over the repeal of the Corn Laws and followed him out of the Conservative Party, Disraeli led the attacks on Peel and used the crisis to catapult himself onto the Conservative front bench (see Section 2.1 above). Watts argues that, later:

'Gladstone could never forgive the cruel vindictiveness of [Disraeli's] earlier attacks on Peel.' (Watts 1994, p.81)

Disraeli's 1852 Budget

Much of the rivalry between Gladstone and Disraeli was played out on the floor of the House of Commons. Historians (and contemporaries) agree that both men were superb public speakers, able, on occasion, to sway the Commons to their point of view.

The first major confrontation in the Commons came in December 1852 when Disraeli presented his Budget (as Chancellor in a minority Conservative government). Jenkins shows that Gladstone had planned his response in some detail and argues that the speech he delivered on the morning of Friday 17 December 1852 was calculated to steal Disraeli's thunder:

'There can be little doubt that [Gladstone's] deliberate intention had been to trump Disraeli's ace and to seize from the government its normal right to the last word...He gradually built up a picture of Disraeli as a frivolous fellow who lacked clarity of execution, consistency of purpose or the honesty to admit that his [Budget] surplus was fictitious...When Gladstone left the House of 4 o'clock in the morning...he had destroyed the only flicker of a Conservative government between 1846 and 1858.' (Jenkins 1995, pp.142-43)

When, at the beginning of 1853, Gladstone replaced Disraeli as Chancellor there was a rather petty squabble between the two men about who should pay for some furniture in the Chancellor's residence in Downing Street and over the Chancellor of the Exchequer's robes. In the end, Gladstone paid Disraeli some money and had new robes made. The dispute, however, suggests that relations between the two men were far from cordial.

Gladstone, Disraeli and Derby's 1858 government

Nevertheless, although there is no doubt that there was genuine hostility between the two men at certain points in their career, it is important not to exaggerate their enmity. Jenkins points out, for example, that:

'Disraeli and Gladstone were never colleagues, although the margin by which they missed being so was at times narrow.' (Jenkins 1995, p.157)

This was particularly the case in the 1850s when Gladstone had not completely cut himself off from his Conservative roots. In 1858, for example, Disraeli wrote to Gladstone urging him to join Lord Derby's second administration.

There are two ways of looking at this offer. First, as Jenkins points out, although Gladstone eventually refused to join Derby's administration, he only did so after consulting other Peelites. This suggests that he seriously considered the offer and was not opposed, in principle, to serving in a government which included Disraeli. Alternatively, the episode could be seen as a power play between the two men. Machin admits that Gladstone replied to Disraeli's letter in a 'fairly friendly fashion denying that he had ever felt any enmity towards Disraeli', but points out that:

'As a career politician, Gladstone was well aware that the Liberal Leaders (Palmerston and Russell) were older than the Conservative ones (Derby and Disraeli), and that his chances of becoming Leader of a party would be more promising in this respect if

he joined the Liberals. He would also avoid the frustration which was likely to arise from the internal rivalry with Disraeli.' (Machin 1995, pp.90-91)

The second Reform Act

It is the battle over the second Reform Act (see Unit 2, Section 1.3) which ensured that the rivalry between Gladstone and Disraeli became intense - as Box 1.17 explains.

BOX 1.17 **The impact of the second Reform Act**

The battle over reform in the years 1866-67 was crucial to both Gladstone and Disraeli. The loss of the Liberals' 1866 Reform Bill ensured that Russell resigned and was succeeded by Gladstone (in December 1867), while, for Disraeli, the passage of the 1867 Reform Act was a key event. Until then, he was not regarded as a certain successor to Derby. His skill in manoeuvring through the Commons a Bill which enlarged the franchise far more than the Liberals wanted or the Conservatives originally intended, and keeping the initiative in government hands, was widely admired. When Derby resigned through ill health early in 1868, he had no hesitation in recommending that Disraeli should replace him. It is from this point onwards that the famous duel between Gladstone and Disraeli can be dated. For the first time, they faced each other as Leaders of their parties not simply in the House of Commons, but in the country as a whole. This direct personal confrontation on the floor of the House of Commons lasted until the end of 1874 when Gladstone resigned the Liberal leadership.

Adapted from Blake 1994.

4.2 How big were the differences between the two men?

A similar approach to policy

Many historians point out that, in many ways, there was not a huge difference in the sort of policies pursued by Gladstone and Disraeli when they were in power. In particular, both men were constrained by their belief in laissez-faire economics (Disraeli abandoned his support for protectionism before 1852):

'Throughout his ministerial career, Gladstone tried to reduce taxation, cut government spending and restrict defence expenditure which could otherwise upset the best-laid Budget plans...Disraeli lacked Gladstone's passion for finance and his belief in the moral importance of low taxes, but he too tried to keep down taxation and defence spending when he was Chancellor.' (Willis 1989, p.5)

They were also both reluctant to support reforms which allowed or encouraged state intervention (again in line with the laissez-faire beliefs which dominated Parliament in the mid-Victorian period). Indeed, in terms of their outlook, Blake argues:

'There was still a large measure of agreement. Disraeli and Gladstone believed in government by an upper-class élite."I am an out and out inegalitarian", Gladstone once said...As for Disraeli, he had long ago dropped protection, and when agriculture really did slump in the last years of his second administration, he made no attempt to revive it. He believed as much as Gladstone did in low taxation, Treasury economy and minimal state intervention.' (Blake 1994, p.59)

Policy differences

It was over foreign policy and imperial policy that Gladstone and Disraeli did have fundamental differences. These differences are summed up in Box 1.18.

It is the difference in attitude towards foreign affairs that explains Gladstone's re-entry into politics in 1876, following his brief retirement (see Section 3.1 above). Blake (1969, p.603) argues that Gladstone's pamphlet on the Bulgarian atrocities genuinely angered Disraeli and 'injected a bitterness into British politics which had not been seen since the Corn Law debates'. Jenkins claims:

'With their utterly conflicting styles, Gladstone's pulsating moral indignation and Disraeli's sardonic cynicism, they each infuriated the other, and increased the mutual hostility.' (Jenkins 1995, p.400)

It is important that Jenkins should refer to the two men's 'styles' since there is an argument that their rivalry owed more to style than to substance. Even though most historians agree that Gladstone and Disraeli genuinely had different attitudes towards foreign policy and towards the British Empire, in fact there was little difference in the actions they took. With reference to Gladstone's second administration (which came to power after Gladstone's campaign against Beaconsfieldism - see Section 3.1 above), Feuchtwanger says:

'Once burdened with the responsibilities of office, the Liberals had to practise continuity to a much greater extent than the pronouncements of Gladstone and others in opposition would have led one to expect.' (Feuchtwanger 1985, p.151)

Did the two men really hate each other?

While there is a consensus that Gladstone and Disraeli did not get on well, there is a debate about the extent to which they disliked each other. Cooper argues that there was real hatred between the two men:

'Gladstone loathed Disraeli, believing his influence on public life had been wholly bad.' (Cooper 1995b, p.363)

Jenkins, on the other hand, suggests that, although there may have been public rivalry between the two men, this did not necessarily extend to personal hatred. He notes, for example, that, shortly after becoming Prime Minister for the first time in 1868, Disraeli held a party:

'The party was a dazzling symbol of Disraeli's rise...There were present princes and princesses,

---

BOX 1.18 Disraeli, Gladstone and foreign and imperial policy

In foreign policy there was a clear divide between Gladstone and Disraeli - in theory at least. Disraeli's aim was to increase Britain's power and greatness. His attitude was that foreign crises should be handled according to what was in Britain's interest. For Gladstone this was not adequate. He condemned the way in which action under Disraeli's government was determined by whatever the government decided was in Britain's interests without any consideration of whether a course of action was right or wrong morally. Disraeli thought in terms of great power politics. Gladstone thought in terms of the values of Christian civilisation and sympathy with oppressed peoples. In other words, he believed in the rule of international law and the cause of nations struggling to be free - though he was also concerned with European stability and British interests. Gladstone and Disraeli also had strongly contrasting views of Empire. Disraeli was very concerned about routes to India and took great pride in purchasing Suez Canal shares in 1875 and in gaining control of Cyprus three years later. Gladstone thought that Disraeli's obsession with the route to India was absurd and he bitterly attacked the acquisition of Cyprus.
Adapted from Willis 1989.

Interpretation

---

dukes and duchesses, ambassadors and prelates - and the Gladstones.' (Jenkins 1995, p.276)

Given that this party took place shortly after Disraeli's great victory over Gladstone (he had outwitted Gladstone over the second Reform Act and, by doing so, beat Gladstone to the premiership), Gladstone's attendance suggests that the relationship between the two men had not soured completely. It should be noted, however, that Jenkins goes on to argue:

'It is much more doubtful whether, had a similar celebration taken place nine of ten years later, [Gladstone would have attended] or would indeed have been welcome.' (Jenkins 1995, p.276)

Nevertheless, when he comes to assess the relationship between Gladstone and Disraeli at the time of Disraeli's death, Jenkins argues that it was based on 'something totally different from personal hatred' and concludes:

'Above all, it was incomprehension which characterised [Gladstone's] attitude to Disraeli.' (Jenkins 1995, p.459)

Blake agrees with this conclusion, arguing that:

'It is seldom in history that two Party Leaders have so deeply [divided] politics. One can only explain it by one of those mysterious aspects of personal chemistry which are themselves inexplicable.' (Blake 1994, p.59)

MAIN POINTS - Part 4

- Gladstone and Disraeli had different backgrounds and personalities. Gladstone came from a wealthy family, was educated at Eton and Oxford and married into an aristocratic family. He was earnest and moralistic. Disraeli had a Jewish background and did not go to university. He had a colourful early life and was outgoing and charming.
- The roots of the rivalry between Gladstone and Disraeli began to grow in Peel's second administration of 1841-46. Whereas Gladstone remained loyal to Peel over the repeal of the Corn Laws and followed him out of the Conservative Party, Disraeli led the attacks on Peel and was rewarded by a place on the Conservative front bench.
- Much of the rivalry between Gladstone and Disraeli was played out on the floor of the House of Commons. Both men were superb public speakers. Their first

major confrontation in the Commons came in December 1852 over Disraeli's Budget. It was followed by a childish dispute over furniture and robes.
- In 1858, Disraeli wrote to Gladstone encouraging him to join Derby's government. This may suggest relations were not too bad, or it may have been an example of power play between the two.
- There was not a huge difference in the sort of policies pursued by Gladstone and Disraeli when they were in power. In particular, both were constrained by their belief in laissez-faire economics. It was over foreign and imperial policy that the two men differed in principle (though, in reality, the action taken by each was not so different).
- While there is a consensus that Gladstone and Disraeli did not get on well, there is a debate about the extent to which they disliked each other.

Activity 1.5 The rivalry between Gladstone and Disraeli

ITEM 1 A historian's assessment (1)

According to Gladstone, Disraeli had corrupted his party until it was no longer capable of speaking with the voice of true Conservatism. Disraeli had also tried to corrupt the public by appealing to their patriotic feelings, encouraging reckless imperialist adventures and being extravagant in his public spending. Even in death, Gladstone could not extend charity to his foe. Disraeli's preference for a modest private funeral was judged by Gladstone to be contrived - he commented that 'as he lived, so he died - all display, without reality and genuineness'. In the speech he delivered in remembrance of Disraeli, Gladstone identified three qualities - his understanding and control of his party, his genius as a parliamentarian and his immense political courage. This courage, he suggested, had sustained him as he battled against hopeless odds in the 1850s, helping him to the striking, but morally dubious, triumphs of 1867 (when he piloted the second Reform Bill through Parliament) and 1877-78 (when he forced Russia to back down and to give up much of the territory it had gained in its war against Turkey). The implication of such an analysis is obvious. Disraeli mastered the baser arts of politics but did not have the moral vision or intellectual integrity statesmen need to make good use of power (unlike Gladstone). It is striking how, until recently, historians have accepted Gladstone's assessment. The trouble is that Disraeli's concept of the function of government is difficult for modern commentators to understand. Today, legislation is the natural outcome of political activity. Disraeli's objectives were different. In 1874, he believed, the country had had enough of big Bills. Such an attitude might be unheroic, but it is unhistorical to condemn it as selfish or backward-looking.

Adapted from Cooper 1995b.

ITEM 2 A historian's assessment (2)

Gladstone was conscientious in his enquiries and calls at Curzon Street (where Disraeli was staying). When news of Disraeli's death reached him, he wrote in his diary: 'It is a telling, touching event. There is no more extraordinary a man surviving him in England, perhaps none in Europe. I must not say much, in presence, as it were, of his urn'. To the Queen, he wrote that he would not make false claims about 'the amount or character of the separation' between Disraeli and himself. But, he pointed out, that did not make him blind to Disraeli's 'extraordinary powers' and 'remarkable qualities'. To his son Harry, he wrote of a man 'whose rival some call me, much against my will or intention'. Always on good terms with Disraeli's wife, Gladstone felt that there was something 'very touching' in Disraeli's determination to be buried by her side - 'his devoted and grateful attachment to her was, I think, the brightest spot in his whole life'. Gladstone also wrote in his diary that he had been 'most widely and sharply severed' from Disraeli 'by something totally different from personal hatred' and he was 'bound to say' he did not think Disraeli 'felt any hatred' towards himself. It was undoubtedly true that Gladstone's feelings were quite distinctly different from personal hatred. But, Disraeli was much more conventionally resentful at what he felt to be Gladstone's persecution of him. Gladstone found it impossible through prior engagements to attend Disraeli's 'private' funeral. He hoped 'on some future day, if it is not asking too much, to visit the spot in a private manner'. But it does not appear that he ever did so. He was criticised for not attending the funeral and this may have provoked his much less generous remarks to Edward Hamilton about Disraeli's 'pose' of simplicity in wanting a private funeral - 'as he lived, so he died - all display, without reality and genuineness', he wrote.

Adapted from Shannon 1999.

ITEM 3 A bad example

A BAD EXAMPLE.

Dr. Punch. "WHAT'S ALL THIS? YOU, THE TWO HEAD BOYS OF THE SCHOOL, THROWING MUD!
YOU OUGHT TO BE ASHAMED OF YOURSELVES!"

This cartoon was published in *Punch* magazine on 10 August 1878. It shows
Gladstone and Disraeli as schoolboys throwing mud at each other.

Questions

1. a) Using Items 1-3 and your
   own knowledge, explain why
   the rivalry between Gladstone
   and Disraeli developed.
   b) What were the main
   characteristics of this rivalry?
   c) Give arguments for and
   against the idea that too
   much has been made of the
   personal relationship between
   Gladstone and Disraeli.
2. a) Using Items 1 and 2,
   explain the significance of
   Gladstone's comment on
   Disraeli: 'as he lived, so he
   died - all display, without
   reality and genuineness'.
   b) Compare and contrast the
   two passages.
   c) What do the two passages
   tell us about the rivalry
   between Gladstone and
   Disraeli?
3. a) What point is being made
   by Item 3?
   b) Would you say that it is an
   accurate reflection of the
   rivalry between Gladstone
   and Disraeli? Explain your
   answer.

References

- **Abbott (1972)** Abbott, B.H., *Gladstone and Disraeli*, Collins, 1972.

- **Adelman (1996)** Adelman, P., *Great Britain and the Irish Question 1800-1922*, Hodder & Stoughton, 1996.

- **Adelman (1997)** Adelman, P., *Gladstone, Disraeli and Later Victorian Politics* (3rd edn), Longman, 1997.

- **Behagg (1995)** Behagg, C., 'Victorian values' in *Scott-Baumann (1995)*.

- **Belchem (1990)** Belchem, J., *Class, Party and the Political System in Britain 1867-1914*, Basil Blackwell, 1990.

- **Bentley (1996)** Bentley, M., *Politics without Democracy*, Fontana, 1996.

- **Blake (1969)** Blake, R., *Disraeli*, Eyre and Spottiswoode, 1969.

- **Blake (1985)** Blake, R., *The Conservative Party from Peel to Thatcher*, Fontana, 1985

- **Blake (1994)** Blake, R., 'Disraeli: political outsider' in *Catterall (1994)*.

- **Burn (1968)** Burn, W.L., *The Age of Equipoise*, Allen & Unwin, 1968.

- **Catterall (1994)** Catterall, P. (ed.), *Britain 1867-1918*, Heinemann, 1994.

- **Cavendish (1999)** Cavendish, R., 'Disraeli and the Conservative Party leadership', *History Today*, Vol.49.2, February 1999.

- **Cooke & Vincent (1974)** Cooke, A.B. & Vincent, J., *The Governing Passion: Cabinet Government and Party Politics in Britain, 1885-86*, Harvester Press, 1974.

- **Cooper (1995)** Cooper, D., 'Gladstone part I: from Tory to Liberal' in *Scott-Baumann (1995)*.

- **Cooper (1995a)** Cooper, D., 'Gladstone part II: politics as crusade' in *Scott-Baumann (1995)*.

- **Cooper (1995b)** Cooper, D., 'Disraeli, Salisbury and the Conservative Party' in *Scott-Baumann (1995)*.

- **Feuchtwanger (1985)** Feuchtwanger, E.J., *Democracy and Empire: Britain 1865-1914*, Arnold, 1985.

- **Feuchtwanger (1996)** Feuchtwanger, E.J., 'Gladstone and the rise and fall of Victorian Liberalism', *History Review*, No.26, December 1996.

- **Foster (1988)** Foster, R.F., *Modern Ireland 1600-1972*, Penguin, 1988.

- **Gardiner & Wenborn (1995)** Gardiner, J. & Wenborn, N., *The Companion to British History*, Collins and Brown, 1995.

- **Ghosh (1987)** Ghosh, P.R., 'Style and substance in Disraelian social reform' in *Waller (1987)*.

- **Heywood (1992)** Heywood, A., *Political Ideologies: an Introduction*, Macmillan, 1992.

- **Hodge (1998)** Hodge, T., *Parnell and the Irish Question*, Longman, 1998.

- **Jenkins (1995)** Jenkins, R., *Gladstone*, Macmillan, 1995.

- **Jenkins (1996)** Jenkins, T.A., 'The non-conformist Anglican', *Modern History Review*, Vol.8.2, November 1996.

- **Jenkins (1997)** Jenkins, T.A., 'Disraeli and the art of opposition', *Modern History Review*, Vol.8.3, February 1997.

- **Jenkins (1998)** Jenkins, T., 'Parties, politics and society in Mid-Victorian Britain', *Modern History Review*, Vol.10.1, September 1998.

- **Kee (1972)** Kee, R., *The Green Flag Volume 1: The Most Distressful Country*, Penguin, 1972.

- **Lee (1994)** Lee, S.J., *British Political History 1815-1914*, Routledge, 1994.

- **Lyons (1971)** Lyons, F.S.L., *Ireland since the Famine*, Fontana, 1971.

- **Machin (1995)** Machin, I., *Disraeli*, Longman, 1995.

- **Matthew (1984)** Matthew, H.C.G., 'The Liberal Age' in *Morgan (1984)*.

- **Matthew (1986)** Matthew, H.C.G., *Gladstone 1809-74* (introduction to the diaries), Oxford University Press, 1986.

- **Matthew (1987)** Matthew, H.C.G., 'Gladstonian finance', *History Today*, Vol.37, July 1987.

- **Matthew (1995)** Matthew, H.C.G., *Gladstone 1809-74* (introduction to the diaries), Oxford University Press, 1995.

- **McCord (1991)** McCord, N., *British History 1815-1906*, Oxford University Press, 1991.

- **Morgan (1984)** Morgan, K.O. (ed.), *The Oxford Illustrated History of Britain*, Oxford University Press, 1984.

- **O' Brien & O' Brien (1985)** O' Brien C.C. & O' Brien, M., *Ireland: a Concise History*, Thames & Hudson, 1985.

- **Parry (1993)** Parry, J., *The Rise and Fall of Liberal Government in Victorian Britain*, Yale University Press, 1993.

- **Pearce & Stewart (1992)** Pearce, M. & Stewart, G., *British Political History 1867-1990: Democracy and Decline*, Routledge, 1992.

- **Roberts (1999)** Roberts, D. (ed.), *British Politics in Focus* (2nd edn), Causeway Press, 1999.

- **Rubinstein (1998)** Rubinstein, W.D., *Britain's Century: a Political and Social History 1815-1905*, Arnold, 1998.

- **Scott-Baumann (1995)** Scott-Baumann, M., *Years of Expansion: Britain 1815-1914*, Hodder and Stoughton, 1995.

- **Shannon (1999)** Shannon, R., *Gladstone: Heroic Minister 1865-1898*, Allen Lane, 1999.

- **Smith (1967)** Smith, P., *Disraelian Conservatism and Social Reform*, Routledge, 1967.

- **Waller (1987)** Waller, P.J. (ed.), *Politics and Social Change in Modern Britain*, Harvester Press, 1987.

- **Walton (1990)** Walton, J.K. (ed.), *Disraeli*, Routledge, 1990.

- **Watts (1994)** Watts, D., *Tories, Conservatives and Unionists, 1815-1914*, Hodder and Stoughton, 1994.

- **Watts (1995)** Watts, D., *Whigs, Radicals and Liberals 1815-1914*, Hodder and Stoughton, 1995.

- **Willis (1989)** Willis, M., *Gladstone and Disraeli: Principles and Policies*, Cambridge University Press, 1989.

- **Winstanley (1990)** Winstanley, M., *Gladstone and the Liberal Party*, Routledge, 1990.

- **Woodward (1938)** Woodward, E.L., *The Age of Reform*, Oxford University Press, 1938.

UNIT 2 Parliamentary reform

Timeline - Parliamentary reform 1832-85

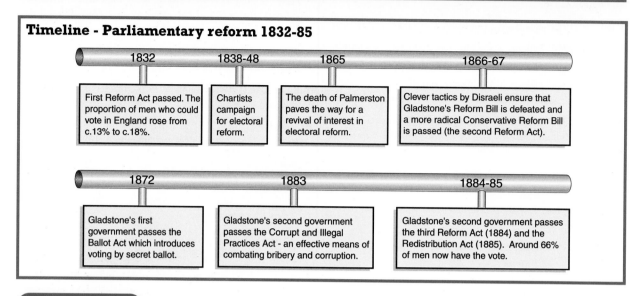

1832
First Reform Act passed. The proportion of men who could vote in England rose from c.13% to c.18%.

1838-48
Chartists campaign for electoral reform.

1865
The death of Palmerston paves the way for a revival of interest in electoral reform.

1866-67
Clever tactics by Disraeli ensure that Gladstone's Reform Bill is defeated and a more radical Conservative Reform Bill is passed (the second Reform Act).

1872
Gladstone's first government passes the Ballot Act which introduces voting by secret ballot.

1883
Gladstone's second government passes the Corrupt and Illegal Practices Act - an effective means of combating bribery and corruption.

1884-85
Gladstone's second government passes the third Reform Act (1884) and the Redistribution Act (1885). Around 66% of men now have the vote.

Introduction

Consider the following two statements: 'democracy is the best form of government' and 'every adult should have the right to vote'. Today, neither statement would be regarded as controversial. If there is one thing that all politicians from the main political parties can agree on, it is that democracy is the best form of government. Similarly, the idea that every adult should have the right to vote is something that is taken for granted. In the mid-19th century, however, Britain was not a democracy and the majority of politicians in the main political parties did not support democratic values. Furthermore, voting was not seen as a right, but as a privilege. In 1850, only a small percentage of the adult population (roughly 5%) had the right to vote. That right was based on the property that the voter owned and on gender (no women were allowed to vote - see Unit 3). The idea that all adults should be allowed to vote had little support in a Parliament which was dominated by landowning aristocrats.

While the 1832 Reform Act broadened the franchise (the right to vote) and modified the voting

system, it had been designed to ensure that members of the working class remained disenfranchised (unable to vote). It had also been designed to be a permanent settlement. Between 1867 and 1885, however, a number of further laws were passed which modified the electoral system and broadened the franchise so that it included a large proportion of working-class voters. During this period, views on democracy and on the right to vote began to change. Most politicians did not yet accept that voting should be a universal birthright, but they did accept that representatives should be chosen by a mass electorate.

This unit considers why changes were made to the electoral system in the period 1867 to 1885 and examines the impact of these changes. It pays particular attention to the impact of parliamentary reform on the development of the Liberal Party and the Conservative Party. For information on the development of the franchise between 1885 and 1918, see Units 3 and 8.

UNIT SUMMARY

Part 1 focuses on the second Reform Act of 1867. It considers why the issue of electoral reform revived in the 1860s and how historians have explained the passing of the Act. It also looks at the terms of the Act.

Part 2 examines the impact of the second Reform Act both on the political system and on the

development of the main political parties - the Liberal Party and the Conservative Party.

Part 3 begins by looking at the steps that were taken to deal with electoral corruption after 1870. It then considers why and how the electoral system was changed in 1884-85.

1 The second Reform Act of 1867

Key questions

1. What was the electoral system like before 1867?

2. Why did the issue of electoral reform revive in the 1860s?

3. How have historians explained the passing of the second Reform Act?

1.1 The electoral system before 1867

Introduction

The electoral system which existed in 1867 was that created by the 1832 Reform Act (also known as the 'first' and sometimes as the 'Great' Reform Act). That Act, passed by a reluctant Parliament in an atmosphere of great popular unrest, attempted to remove some of the obvious failings of the system known as 'Old Corruption', while ensuring that the aristocracy still retained its grip on power. The Whigs who passed the 1832 Reform Act argued that it was intended to be a final solution rather than the first step on the road to universal suffrage (suffrage is another word for 'vote'):

> 'If any persons suppose that this reform will lead to ulterior measures, they are mistaken; for there is no-one more decided against annual Parliaments, universal suffrage and secret ballots than I am. My object is not to favour, but to put an end to such hopes and projects. The principle of my reform is to prevent the necessity for revolution - reforming to preserve and not to overthrow.' (Part of a speech made by the Prime Minister, Earl Grey, in the House of Lords in November 1831)

'Old Corruption'

The unreformed (ie pre-1832 Reform Act) electoral system was termed 'Old Corruption' by the groups calling for its reform because bribery and corruption were the principal means of both securing and retaining power. The two most striking features of the electoral system were, first, the virtual monopoly of political power and influence held by the landed élite and, second, the lack of uniformity in the organisation of parliamentary constituencies and elections. There was, in reality, very little that was actually 'systematic' about the system.

The franchise

Under the unreformed system, historians estimate that less than 5% of the total population qualified to vote. The franchise (right to vote) and the right to stand for election were restricted to adult males and depended upon various forms of property qualification. For the most part, this effectively limited the electorate to the country's wealthy landowners. O'Gorman (1989) calculates that, in 1831, something like 400,000 men had the right to vote (it is difficult to be sure of the exact figure because records are inadequate and some voters had more than one vote). The total population was 13.89 million people. In other words, just 2.9% of the population as a whole and 12.7% of men had the right to vote.

Constituencies

Those who qualified to vote could vote in two types of constituency - counties and boroughs.

Counties

Whatever the size of its population, a county could send two MPs to Parliament. In this type of constituency, the franchise was standard across the country. Those who qualified were men who lived on land whose rental value was at least 40 shillings per year. Although obviously subject to variation due to regional differences in property values, this was as near to a standard franchise as existed in Britain before the 1832 Reform Act.

Boroughs

The situation in the other type of constituency - the boroughs - was much more confused. Boroughs were towns which had, at some point in their history, been granted a Royal Charter. Both the number of MPs returned to Parliament and the voting qualification varied greatly from borough to borough, depending upon local custom. Many boroughs were settlements which had been important in Medieval times, but, by 1832, had decayed and declined. Some remained small villages. Some were almost completely depopulated. Despite this, as many as four MPs were returned to Parliament from each borough (such boroughs became known 'rotten' or 'pocket' boroughs). By way of contrast, the process of industrialisation created new and economically powerful urban centres with large populations. And yet, these areas remained totally unrepresented in Parliament. As the Whig politician Lord John Russell put it in a speech to the House of Commons on 1 March 1831:

> 'Allow me to imagine, for a moment, a stranger from some distant country, who should arrive in England to examine our institutions...He would have been told that the proudest boast of this celebrated country was its political freedom...What then would be his surprise, if he were taken by this guide...to a green mound and told that this green mound sent members to Parliament...But, his surprise would increase to

astonishment if he were carried into the North of England, where he would see large flourishing towns, full of trade and activity... and were told that these places had no representatives in the Assembly which was said to represent the people.'

The organisation of elections

The organisation of elections themselves bore very little resemblance to anything we would recognise today. First, it has been estimated that around two-thirds of elections were uncontested - nobody stood against the successful candidate. Second, elections were not, as they are today, concluded on a single day. The proceedings could take several weeks and the overall result (for the country as a whole) might not be known for up to two months. And third, in constituencies where contested elections did occur, there was no secret ballot. Voting took place publicly on a platform (called the 'Hustings') in an atmosphere which mixed drunken carnival with sometimes violent intimidation. The fact that people voted openly in public meant that corruption was rife. 'Treating', where candidates would pay for their supporters' food, drink and accommodation during the election, was common practice as was the hiring of 'lambs' (gangs of armed thugs) and 'cooping' (the kidnapping of rivals' supporters until after the election).

The terms of the 1832 Reform Act

The 1832 Reform Act contained two essential elements:
- the redistribution of seats
- the remodelling and systematising of the franchise.

Both elements of reform accepted the principle that the franchise should still be based on a property qualification. The terms of the Act are outlined in Box 2.1 (it should be noted that many constituencies returned more than one MP).

The position after 1832

According to O'Gorman (1989), the percentage of men who could vote in England rose in 1832 to 18%. In Scotland, the figure was 12% and, in Ireland, it was 5%. Most of these new voters were middle-class:

'The £10 householder franchise made middle-class men the majority of the electorate. Shopkeepers replaced skilled craftsmen as the largest occupational group in the boroughs.' (Pearce & Stearn 1994, p.45)

In addition to increasing the number of voters, some of the failings of the unreformed system were addressed:

'By disenfranchising the rotten boroughs and redistributing seats, the [1832] Reform Act made the electoral system correspond more closely to the distribution of population and wealth in the country. It reduced the over-representation of the

---

BOX 2.1 The 1832 Reform Act

Summary Box

1. Redistribution

The 1832 Reform Act made the following provisions:
- 56 boroughs (with less than 2,000 inhabitants) were completely disenfranchised. This released 111 seats.
- 30 boroughs (with less than 4,000 inhabitants) lost one of their MPs.
- The borough of Weymouth and Melcombe Regis lost two of its four members.

This released a total of 143 seats for redistribution. Mostly, these seats were assigned to the English counties and to the new industrial towns:
- 62 seats were redistributed to English counties
- 22 new two-member boroughs were created
- 19 new single-member boroughs were created
- five new seats went to Wales
- eight new seats went to Scotland
- five new seats went to Ireland.

2. Remodelling the franchise

a) Boroughs

The older franchise systems were replaced by a new, uniform property qualification - the £10 householder franchise:
- every male over age 21 who occupied, either as owner or tenant, property with an annual value of £10 was entitled to vote so long as he had been living in the property for at least one year, paid taxes on the property and had not received any poor relief during the previous year
- any man who had been entitled to vote before 1832 retained the right to vote if he lived within seven miles of the borough in which he voted
- borough voters were no longer allowed to vote in county elections.

b) Counties

The county franchise remained largely as it was. Those owning land or property worth 40 shillings - 40 shilling freeholders - could vote. The Act also extended the vote to:
- £10 copyholders and leaseholders of long residence (ie tenants who lived in certain types of property).
- any tenant who rented property worth at least £50 per year - the so-called 'Chandos amendment' named after the Tory MP who proposed it as the Bill went through Parliament.

Other provisions in the Act

The 1832 Reform Act made two further important innovations. First, the Act required an official register of voters to be made and kept up-to-date. And second, polling was limited to two days.

Adapted from Cook and Stevenson 1996.

boroughs relative to the counties, of agriculture relative to industry, of the South relative to the North, and of England relative to the rest of the United Kingdom.' (Pearce & Stearn 1994, p.43) Although the Act reduced imbalances in the system, by no means did it remove them. Most historians accept that there were important continuities after 1832. These are summarised in Box 2.2.

BOX 2.2 Continuities after 1832

1. After 1832, overall control of the political system was still exercised by the landed aristocracy. Pearce and Stearn (1994) note that the first election under the new rules produced nearly 500 landowning MPs (out of a total of 658).

2. The costs of standing for election remained very high.

3. Deference (feeling obliged to obey a 'superior') continued to determine how many voters voted. Indeed, the 'Chandos Amendment' may have increased deferential voting as tenant farmers generally obeyed the wishes of landlords.

4. Voting itself remained a public act and the continued absence of the secret ballot (until 1872) meant that bribery and intimidation could continue unchecked. Also the new procedure of registering provided new opportunities for bribery and intimidation.

5. The size of constituencies continued to vary significantly. O'Gorman (1997) points out that 73 of the borough constituencies which survived the 1832 Reform Act had fewer than 500 electors and 31 possessed less than 300. This was largely because property rather than population had been the principal feature of electoral recalculation in 1832.

6. The South was still over-represented while the industrial North and Midlands were under-represented.

7. The varying levels of rents around the country worked against the creation of what was, in theory, a uniform borough franchise. Where rents were low - as in the many industrial centres - relatively few achieved the £10 qualification. For example, it is estimated that in Leeds only 5,000 people qualified to vote from a total population of 125,000 in 1832.

8. Willis (1999) notes that the background of MPs did not change markedly. Although there was a steady growth in the number of middle-class MPs from the 1840s onwards, they were not in a majority until the end of the century. Stewart (1989) shows that, of the 103 men who served in Cabinets between 1830 and 1866, only 14 could be said to be 'nouveaux riches'.

9. Despite changes in name, the same two political parties continued to contest power.

Summary Box

The impact on political parties

One important consequence of the passing of the 1832 Reform Bill was the growth of party organisation:

'The extension of the franchise meant a larger electorate to be won over, and the reduction of the nomination boroughs [ie the rotten boroughs] increased the number of constituencies where genuine elections would have to be held. These two changes forced the parties to organise themselves more effectively and to compete more openly against each other to register the new voters.' (Lee 1994, pp.61-62)

Willis notes that the two main parties developed along similar lines:

'They had a central organisation in London with a political agent or manager, committees and a club for wealthy politicians in the capital - the Carlton Club for the Conservatives and the Reform Club for Liberals. The central organisation managed funds and made contact with local agents and associations who would put up candidates, register voters and run campaigns.' (Willis 1999, p.11)

While it was between 1832 and 1867 that these basic party structures developed, the strength of party structures should not be exaggerated in this period. Purdue (1987, p.33) argues, for example, that party loyalties in the Commons were 'loose and fragmented' in the middle decades of the 19th century, while Willis points out that political parties did not organise in some boroughs until the 1860s.

1.2 Why did the issue of electoral reform revive in the 1860s?

Attempts to revive the issue before 1866

Chartism

The 1832 Reform Act made no concessions to members of the working class who had been demanding the vote. Disappointment with the Act, in part, explains the growth of the Chartist movement. This was a working-class movement which grew rapidly after the publication of the 'People's Charter' in 1838 and remained sporadically an important force until 1848. The People's Charter made the six demands outlined in Box 2.3 on page 40.

The Chartists' demands were rejected by Parliament on three occasions (in 1839, 1842 and 1848) and the movement lost momentum after the 'Kennington Common fiasco' (see also Unit 3, page 73). Some historians (such as Gash 1976 and Cunningham 1994) argue that Chartism frightened MPs, making them less, rather than more, likely to support further electoral reform. But, other historians (such as Thompson 1984 and Royle 1996) argue that the movement helped to

BOX 2.3 The People's Charter

Summary Box

The six points of the People's Charter were as follows:

1. Universal manhood suffrage - a vote for every man over the age of 21.

2. A secret ballot - to protect the voter so that employers and landlords could no longer influence voting behaviour.

3. Annual Parliaments - a general election every year to ensure that MPs kept in close touch with the needs and demands of their constituents.

4. Abolition of property qualifications for MPs - to enable representatives from the working class to stand for election.

5. Payment of MPs - to enable working men to give up their jobs in order to stand for election in the first place.

6. Constituencies of equal size (in terms of population) - to tackle the continued problem of the under-representation of industrial areas after the 1832 Reform Act.

develop hope and confidence within working-class communities which, in turn, inspired further and ultimately more successful attempts at protest towards the end of the 19th century.

Attempts to introduce reform, 1850-60

On five occasions in the period 1850-60, Electoral Reform Bills were drawn up and then rejected. On four of these occasions (in 1851, 1852, 1854 and 1860), the sponsor of the Bill was Lord John Russell, the man who had steered the 1832 Reform Act through Parliament (and who later served as Prime Minister in 1846-52 and 1865-66). Russell had announced in 1837 that he was against further reform, earning himself the nickname 'Finality Jack'. Later, however, he changed his mind. Lee argues that his aim in introducing these Bills was as follows:

'By 1851, he considered it necessary to extend the franchise into at least the upper level of the working class, as a means of preventing the revival of popular radicalism.' (Lee 1994, p.137)

The other Reform Bill introduced in this period was that put forward in 1859 by the Conservative Leader, Lord Derby, and the Conservative Leader in the Commons, Disraeli. Walton argues that:

'The Conservative proposal of 1859 was purely a matter of political expediency. It aimed at equalising the county and borough franchises, and compelling voters living in urban constituencies to vote in their borough rather than their county, in an attempt to make the county seats safer for rural Conservatism.' (Walton 1983, p.7)

This Bill, like the others, was defeated by a combination of Whigs and radicals. Lang argues that, by 1859:

'The problem was that the consensus that was beginning to emerge was in favour of reform as a general principle; but as soon as discussion progressed to specific detail, it fell apart. There was general agreement, for example, that the post-Chartist groups like Friendly Societies and trade unions had demonstrated that there was a responsible, politically literate and active section of the working class who deserved, in Gladstone's phrase, to come within the pale of the constitution...On the other hand, a great mass of the working population was unskilled, illiterate, uneducated and decidedly not respectable.' (Lang 1999, pp.70-71)

Walton (1983), however, notes that there were few signs of popular support for electoral reform in the 1850s and, as a result, little pressure on MPs to take action. Lee agrees:

'A number of factors contributed to the failure of any attempt to secure further reform during the 1850s. Perhaps the greatest of these was indifference. The collapse of Chartism was followed by a period of greatly reduced activism for parliamentary reform.' (Lee 1994, p.137)

The other factors mentioned by Lee are:

- the economic prosperity of the 1850s - which may have convinced people that there was no need for electoral reform
- events abroad, such as the Crimean War - which distracted people from domestic concerns.

Why did parliamentary reform become an issue after the 1865 election?

Historians have argued that six main factors led to the revival of parliamentary reform as an issue after the 1865 general election. These factors were as follows.

1. The death of Palmerston

Lord Palmerston sat in the Commons for 58 years and held office for 48. He served as Foreign Secretary between 1846 and 1851 and as Home Secretary between 1852 and 1855 before serving as Prime Minister for two terms in 1855-58 and 1859-65. Lee argues that, as Prime Minister, he was extraordinarily dominant:

'Palmerston established a personal ascendancy between 1855 and 1865 which no other political leader was able to threaten.' (Lee 1994, p.135)

Palmerston was a strong opponent of parliamentary reform. His death in 1865, therefore, removed an important obstacle to the issue.

2. Gladstone's views on parliamentary reform

Palmerston's death brought Gladstone, who had served as Palmerston's Chancellor, to the centre stage. Gladstone had been 'converted' to the cause of parliamentary reform in 1864. Walton argues that this was a particularly significant development in ensuring the revival of the issue:

'With hindsight, the most important development might seem to be Gladstone's conversion to a much fuller, though subtly qualified, extension of the working-class electorate in May 1864, at a time when he was becoming an increasingly popular politician and an obvious candidate to the highest office.' (Walton 1983, p.9)

Walton argues that, although parliamentary reform was not an important issue in the 1865 general election (which brought the Liberals to power under Lord John Russell, with Gladstone as Chancellor and Liberal Leader in the Commons), Gladstone's support for the issue ensured that it rose up the political agenda after the election.

3. The Conservatives' electoral position

It was noted above that both main parties had put forward Electoral Reform Bills in the period 1850-60 and that a consensus in favour of the principle that there should be reform had emerged. Between 1841 and 1865, the Conservatives failed to win an overall majority in Parliament. This encouraged the leadership to support reform:

'Conservatives felt, with some justice, that the 1832 settlement loaded the dice against them. Calculations made in the mid-1860s showed that 11.5 million lived in county constituencies in England and Wales which returned 162 MPs (recently increased from 159); only 8.5 million lived in boroughs which nevertheless returned 334 MPs. Worse, Tory chances were marred since many county seats included a substantial electorate drawn from town-dwellers who qualified via the 40-shilling freehold and voted in the counties. Conservatives did much better in county seats where "urban" voters were sparse.' (Evans 1996, p.360)

4. Party political considerations

There is an argument that, once the Liberals brought forward a Reform Bill in 1866, the leading Conservatives, Lord Derby and Disraeli, saw opportunities to split the Liberal Party over the issue. They knew that not all Liberals shared Gladstone's new enthusiasm for reform, especially the more conservative Whig element of the Liberal Party. At the same time, they knew that the radical wing of the Liberal Party would campaign for a wider electorate than the leadership was prepared to concede. As Walton (1983, p.15) puts it, 'short-term calculations of party political advantage' ensured that parliamentary reform remained high on the political agenda.

5. Popular agitation

Some historians, notably Harrison (1965), argue that the revival of extra-parliamentary agitation in support of parliamentary reform in the mid-1860s explains why the issue moved to centre stage in Parliament. It was in 1864-65, for example that the

National Reform Union and the Reform League were set up (see Box 2.4).

BOX 2.4   The National Reform Union and the Reform League

Interpretation

The National Reform Union, founded in 1864, was Liberal, predominantly middle-class and led by wealthy Manchester merchants, manufacturers and radical MPs. Establishing branches throughout the country and especially in the industrial towns, it aimed to produce political cooperation between the middle and working classes. Liberals in the industrial areas were often the strongest supporters of electoral reform. They knew that those working-class men who did have the vote tended to vote Liberal and hoped that, if they broadened the franchise, the Liberal Party would benefit. Their message was, therefore, that members of the middle class and working class shared a common interest against that of the landowning class which dominated Parliament. The demands of the National Reform Union included an extension of the franchise, secret voting and an even distribution of seats. The Reform League, founded the following year, was a predominantly working-class organisation and a good deal more radical. It was supported by various left-wing organisations, including Karl Marx's 'First International' and the Social Democratic Federation (see Unit 5, Section 1.1). The League called for the extension of the franchise to 'every resident and registered male person' but did not include the very poor, vagrants and women. The Union had more money and the League more members. In 1866, they worked together, both contributing to the growth of popular pressure. At a meeting held in Hyde Park in July 1866, around 100,000 demonstrators clashed with the police.

Adapted from Pearce and Stearn 1994.

---

6. Developments abroad

Some historians claim that developments in Italy and the USA encouraged demands for greater democracy at home. Pearce and Stearn, for example, claim that:

'British interest in foreign affairs - particularly the movement for Italian unification and in the American Civil War, both of which were interpreted as popular struggles for freedom - increased demands for change at home.' (Pearce & Stearn 1994, pp.54-55)

1.3 The second Reform Act

The 1866 Reform Bill

There is a consensus among historians that the Electoral Reform Bill introduced into the Commons in 1866 by Gladstone, on behalf of the Liberal government, was a modest Bill. It would have added around 400,000 new voters to the electorate, about half from the working class. Walton (1983) says that its proposals included:

- lowering the borough qualification for householders from £10 to £7
- giving the vote to lodgers in boroughs who paid £10 or more per year
- lowering the county qualification for tenants from £50 to £14
- giving the county vote to men who had £50 or more in a savings bank.

Despite the modest nature of the Bill, it was too radical for a group of Whigs led by Robert Lowe. With the help of the these MPs, the Conservatives were able to defeat the Bill. Russell resigned in June 1866 and the Conservatives formed a minority government.

The second Reform Act

The second Reform Act was the work of a Conservative government and yet, historians agree, it was a far more radical Act than that proposed by the Liberals in 1866 (the terms of the Act are outlined in Box 2.5).

The Act that was finally passed was the result of what Pearce and Stearn (1994) describe as 'a series of extraordinarily complex political manoeuvres' in Parliament. These can be summarised as follows.

The Bill that Disraeli originally drafted and presented to Cabinet in February 1867 proposed very modest change, but it was quickly withdrawn. Lee (1994) argues that this happened because it had become clear that the Liberals would not support the Bill (the Conservative government was a minority government and, therefore, needed the support of at least part of the Liberal opposition to pass measures). Walton (1983) suggests that the Bill was withdrawn because there was opposition to it in Cabinet, with one member, Peel (Robert Peel's brother), threatening to resign. Machin (1995) argues that it was dropped after Conservative MPs rejected it at a meeting at the Carlton Club.

When it became clear that a more radical Bill was going to be introduced, three members of the Cabinet resigned (on 2 March). But, the government went ahead and introduced its Bill. According to Pearce & Stearn:

'It was a more moderate package of proposals than Gladstone's, one which the bulk of Tory backbenchers and the Adullamites [those Liberals who had rejected the 1866 Bill on the grounds that it went too far] might well accept.' (Pearce & Stearn 1994, p.57)

That Bill, however, was then transformed during its passage through Parliament. Amendments suggested by the Liberal leadership were blocked by Disraeli, but a series of amendments proposed by radical Liberals was accepted:

BOX 2.5 The second Reform Act of 1867 (including the Scottish Reform Act of 1868)

1. Disenfranchisement clauses
A total of 53 seats were made available for redistribution as follows:
- six two-member boroughs and five one-member boroughs were disenfranchised
- 35 two-member boroughs lost one member
- Peeblesshire and Selkirkshire which had returned two members would return one.

2. Redistribution
The Act redistributed the 53 seats as follows:
- nine new boroughs were created, returning one member each
- Chelsea and Hackney became two-member seats
- one seat went to London University
- 25 seats went to counties
- one extra seat went to the following boroughs - Birmingham, Manchester, Salford, Liverpool and Leeds
- one extra seat went to Wales
- five extra seats for Scottish boroughs
- three extra seats for Scottish counties.

3. Voting qualifications
The Act broadened the franchise as follows:
- it extended the borough franchise to all male householders who paid rates directly and to lodgers who paid £10 or more a year in rent, so long as they had been living at the same address for at least one year
- it extended the county franchise to occupiers of property rated at £12 per year and to copyholders and leaseholders whose land was worth £5 a year.

As a result, the electorate now contained a majority of working-class voters - though most of the new voters were concentrated in boroughs and cities.

Minority clause
The Act also contained the 'minority clause' which stated that, where a borough or a county constituency returned three MPs, no voter could vote for more than two candidates - the aim being to allow strong minority interests to be represented in Parliament.

Adapted from Pearce & Stearn 1994 and Cook & Stevenson 1996.

'Radical amendment after radical amendment was accepted, usually with minimal debate or time for Tory backbenchers to catch their breath and reflect where Disraeli was leading them.' (Evans 1996, pp.364-65)

One exception was John Stuart Mill's amendment proposing that women be given the vote - see Unit

3, page 74. Nevertheless, the Act that was finally passed went much further than the Bill of 1866 and much further than that originally put forward by Disraeli.

At first sight, Disraeli's behaviour seems surprising.

Why would a Conservative government make so many concessions to radical Liberals and take a significant step towards democracy when the heart of Conservatism was the preservation of privilege? Activity 2.1 explores this question.

MAIN POINTS - Part 1

- The electoral system before 1832 was known as 'Old Corruption' by the groups calling for its reform because bribery and corruption were the principal means of both securing and retaining power. Around 13% of men could vote.
- The 1832 Reform Act redistributed 143 seats and remodelled the franchise. Afterwards, around 18% of men could vote. Most new voters were middle-class. Many of the imbalances in the pre-1832 system remained.
- Six factors made reform a live issue after 1865 - (1) Palmerston's death (2) Gladstone's conversion (3) Conservative lack of electoral success (4) party political considerations (5) popular agitation and (6)

developments abroad.
- The modest Bill presented by the Liberal government in 1866 was defeated by an alliance of Whigs and Conservatives. The result was the resignation of the Prime Minister, Russell, and a minority Conservative government under Lord Derby (Party Leader) and Disraeli (Leader in the Commons).
- The Bill that was finally passed was the result of a series of complex political manoeuvres in Parliament. Disraeli first proposed a very modest Bill, but then replaced it with a more radical Bill (though one which fell short of the 1866 Bill). This Bill was then transformed as the government accepted a number of radical amendments.

Activity 2.1 Disraeli and the 1867 Reform Act

ITEM 1 Why did Disraeli act as he did?

(ix) 'To argue that Disraeli had a vision of "Tory democracy" towards which he had been "educating" his party for years or to suggest that he had deliberately reached downwards to catch a hidden stratum of deferential working-class Tory voters is to mistake subsequent self-justificatory rhetoric for current policy.' (Walton 1983, p.20)

(i) 'Disraeli's concern was not principle but parliamentary arithmetic. A Conservative Reform Act would only reach the statute book if most Tory backbenchers could be kept in the fold and enough Liberal radicals could be induced to vote for the worthwhile reform they had been denied in 1866.' (Evans 1996, p.364)

(ii) Disraeli had to keep [the Liberals] split and stop them uniting behind Gladstone…The only way to do this was to work with radicals by supporting more drastic reform proposals than the Liberal leaders themselves wanted.' (Willis 1999, p.20)

(viii) 'Disraeli started to claim that he had "educated" his party and that what he had done with the Reform Bill was consistent with his life-long convictions on the relationship of classes.' (Feuchtwanger 1985, p.46)

(iii) 'Disraeli…made spectacular concessions by allowing far more voters in the boroughs, but the boroughs were largely Liberal anyway…Conservatives did best in the counties...Here Disraeli's Bill… strengthened the Tory position by ensuring more town residents voted in the boroughs rather than the counties.' (Willis 1999, p.20)

(vii) 'It was by concentrating the minds of his followers on the humiliation of Gladstone that Disraeli succeeded in driving them along behind the Bill.' (Feuchtwanger 1985, p.46)

(iv) 'If he could succeed where his detested rival Gladstone...had just failed, and in the process divide the Liberals, he would achieve a tremendous political victory...Failure might harm his career, but success would guarantee him the leadership of the party when Derby resigned.' (Pearce & Stearn 1994, p.57)

(vi) 'Popular pressure was certainly a factor in the passage of reform legislation. It convinced many MPs that the reform issue had to be settled. To Disraeli, it provided an additional motive to press ahead.' (Pearce & Stearn 1994, p.57)

(v) 'The Conservatives were undoubtedly gambling. No-one could be certain what effect the newly enfranchised would have on British politics. Disraeli hoped that, although the skilled workers were tied to the Liberal Party, the less skilled would vote Conservative. (Pearce & Stearn 1994, pp.58-59)

ITEM 2 Why did Disraeli act as he did? (2)

Having turned out Russell and Gladstone in 1866, the Conservatives had no option but to introduce their own measure of electoral reform. Disraeli understood the lesson of 1832 - that the party taking the initiative could choose who should gain the vote whereas the party opposing reform could only expect a period of political exile. But he could hardly expect the Liberals to support a Bill along the same lines as that of 1866. A new Bill would have to go substantially above or below the Liberal baseline. Since the Conservatives were in a minority (290 to 360), Disraeli had to keep his own party together and, in addition, gain some support from the Liberals. A modest Bill would keep the Conservatives together. But, Disraeli quickly realised that such a Bill would gain no support from the Liberals. Any backing would only come from the radicals, and then only if the proposals were sufficiently progressive. Disraeli, therefore, opted for a bold stroke to take the old enemy completely by surprise. This was, above all, a matter of political tactics, although Disraeli did have some sense of the electoral implications. He knew that the Liberals were reluctant to lower the property qualification below £6. This was probably because they were confident of the well-to-do workers but considered the next layer down as an unknown quantity. Disraeli saw no reason why this section might not be captured by the Conservatives. There would, after all, be no secret ballot and the influence of masters could be brought to bear. Also, the redistribution of seats would, to some extent, neutralise the borough franchise extension. At best, therefore, the Conservatives would gain, at worst they would not lose. All this was, of course, taking a calculated risk, but that was in Disraeli's political nature.

Adapted from Lee 1994.

ITEM 4 The general elections of 1865 and 1868

	1865		
Party	**Votes**	**%**	**MPs**
Conservative	346,035	39.8	289
Liberal	508,821	60.2	369
Others	-	-	-
	1868		
Party	**Votes**	**%**	**MPs**
Conservative	903,318	38.4	271
Liberal	1,428,776	61.5	387
Others	1,157	0.1	0

BALLOT BOX

Adapted from Craig 1989.

ITEM 3 The leap in the dark

A LEAP IN THE DARK.

This cartoon was drawn in response to Lord Derby's comment on the passing of the 1867 Reform Act. Derby said: 'No doubt we are making a great experiment and "taking a leap in dark", but I have the greatest confidence in the sound sense of my fellow countrymen and I entertain a strong hope that the extended franchise which we are now conferring upon them will be the means of placing the institutions of this country on a firmer basis'. The face on the horse is that of Disraeli. The rider is the Goddess Britannia (Britain). John Bull (the average Englishman) is in the background.

Questions

1. a) Using Items 1 and 2, make a list of the different ways in which Disraeli's actions have been explained.
   b) Rank the explanations in order of importance and explain why you have chosen this order.
   c) What do these items tell us about Disraeli's personality and political approach?
   d) Write your own explanation of Disraeli's actions in 1867
2. a) What do you think Lord Derby meant when he described the second Reform Act as a 'leap in the dark' (Item 3)?
   b) Was it an accurate description of the Act? Explain your answer.
   c) What advantages do you think Disraeli expected from passing the Act?
3. a) What does Item 4 tell us about (i) what changed and (ii) what stayed the same immediately after the second Reform Act was passed?
   b) Explain how the electoral system differed in the two elections.

2 The impact of the 1867 Reform Act

Key questions

1. What impact did the 1867 Act make on the political system?

2. What impact did the 1867 Act make on the Liberal Party and the Conservative Party?

2.1 What impact did the 1867 Act make on the political system?

Problems with the new system

Feuchtwanger (1985, p.47) points out that, although the 1867 Reform Act created around 100 constituencies with an electorate over 6,000, 140 constituencies remained with an electorate of under 2,000. Most of the constituencies with small electorates were county constituencies. Walton argues:

'The difference between the county and borough franchises was now the cause of visible and glaring anomalies [irregularities], with people living in identical houses having the vote if they lived on the borough side of a boundary road, but being left in the cold if they lived on the county side.' (Walton 1983, p.36)

A second problem was that there were still regional imbalances:

'Rural areas were still over-represented relative to industrial, and the South and West of England relative to the rest of the country. Whereas the South West of England had 45 MPs, for instance, the North East, despite a population three times as large, had only 32.' (Pearce & Stearn 1994, p.61)

A third problem was the position of tenants in boroughs who did not pay their rates in person - the so-called 'compound-ratepayers'. Compound-ratepayers paid a sum to their landlord which included payment for both the rent and the rates and the landlord then paid the rates to the council. An amendment to the 1867 Reform Act outlawed the practice of compounding, but this proved difficult to implement. Tenants simply refused to pay their rates in person. The result was that:

'In some boroughs, compounders were allowed on the electoral register in 1868, but in others they were excluded.' (Walton 1983, p.33)

The problem was solved in 1869, however, when the Liberal government passed legislation allowing compound-ratepayers to vote on the same basis as those who paid their rates in person.

Changes to the British constitution

There is a debate about whether and to what extent the 1867 Reform Act changed the British constitution. Some authors (for example, Walton 1983) argue that the 1832 Reform Act was the crucial Act in this regard and suggest that, in constitutional terms, the 1867 Act made little difference. Others, however, argue that there were important constitutional developments. Dunbabin (1988), for example, argues that, after 1867, the power of choosing the government passed from the Commons to the electorate. Governments, Dunbabin argues, were brought down by parliamentary votes much less after 1867 than had been the case before. In part, this was because the view emerged that it was the function of elections to put questions to the country to decide. And in part, it was because MPs began to vote more solidly along party lines than they had done before. Feuchtwanger, on the other hand, argues that, while the balance of the constitution as a whole was little altered, the role of the monarch was affected:

'After 1868 there were no occasions when the monarchy could influence the composition of ministries in the way it had done in the 1850s...[The Queen's] opinions still carried weight; a Prime Minister like Disraeli who had her on his side could derive much advantage from the fact, while her relentless hostility became a heavy burden for Gladstone. Nevertheless, the monarchy in its public face became more fully a constitutional monarchy after 1867 than it had been before.' (Feuchtwanger 1985, pp.53-54)

The development of a two-party system?

Some authors argue that the 1867 Reform Act produced a two-party system:

'After 1846, the fluidity of the party situation and the instability of governments had given individual MPs considerable independence...After the second Reform Act, many MPs were more dependent on party support and increasingly party discipline became tighter. For 20 years, there was a clearer two-party system.' (McCord 1991, p.260)

Others, however, dispute this. Lang (1999), for example, suggests that:

- there never were just two parties - the Irish Nationalists were a substantial third party in the period 1874-84, for example
- there were important splits within the two main parties - the Liberal Party split over electoral reform in 1866 and Gladstone's leadership style was so divisive in 1874 that Liberal candidates stood against each other in Sheffield and Bradford.

He concludes:

'Although politics had come a long way from the patronage politics of Pitt's day, it was not yet in the age of huge, monolithic parties imposing their wills on all their MPs.' (Lang 1999, p.98)

The new electorate

As noted in Box 2.5, the 1867 Reform Act ensured that, for the first time, the majority of voters in electorate as a whole came from the working class. Working-class voters, however, were concentrated in the boroughs - see Box 2.6.

BOX 2.6 | **Results of the second Reform Act**

Around 1.1 million new voters were added to the previous total of about 1.4 million. About one in three adult men could vote, instead of one in five. Given that the Census of 1861 put the total population of the UK at 29 million, around 8% of the total population had the vote after 1867 (up from c.5%). The greatest increase was in the boroughs, where the total number of voters rose by 135%, and in some industrial cities, the figures were much higher. For example, Birmingham's electorate rose from 8,000 to 43,000. As a result, boroughs had a majority working-class electorate after 1867. However, the increase in the counties was only 45%, with the result that county constituencies remained middle-class.

Adapted from Pearce & Stearn 1994.

It was noted in the introduction to this Unit that, in the 19th century, voting was regarded as a privilege rather than a right. In the debate over reform in 1866-67, the Liberal leadership's stance was that the vote should be extended, but it should only be extended to 'respectable', 'deserving' workers - not to those who were 'undeserving':

> 'Those Gladstone wished to enfranchise were those who had proved themselves to be rational and prudent citizens. They were the working men who led respectable lives, sent their children to school, invested in savings banks and Friendly Societies (which had together expanded spectacularly since the mid-century) and joined sensible and moderate trade unions. He and other liberals had grave doubts about the wisdom of giving the vote to a wider section of the working classes.' (Purdue 1987, p.40)

1867 - a turning point?

In 1867, however, the vote was extended to a wider section of the working class than that considered wise by the Liberals. Willis argues that this was a turning point:

> 'Before 1867, the vote was given very much as a privilege, though there were many ways in which men might qualify. Leading politicians began the reform debate by arguing about who was rich, virtuous or educated enough to vote; they ended by giving the right to all borough householders.

The vote now looked more like a general right than a special privilege.' (Willis 1999, p.22)

This helps to explain why the campaign for women's suffrage gained momentum after 1867 (see Unit 3, Part 2). After all, if 'undeserving' working-class men were allowed to vote why should 'respectable' middle-class women be excluded from the vote?

Voting behaviour after 1865

There were fears among MPs before the passing of the 1867 Reform Act that the enfranchisement of members of the working class would result in class-based voting. This, however, did not happen:

> 'After 1867, as before, class divisions as such were far from being central to voting behaviour. This is not surprising as there was no specifically working-class party, while the Conservatives were no longer identified solely with the interests of agriculture and the landed gentry.' (Walton 1983, p.39)

Walton argues that, in part because of the registration process (see below), most voters were party loyalists. There were few 'floating voters' and few 'well-informed, independent-minded working-class voters'.

Pressure on voters

Feuchtwanger agrees, adding that voters continued to be subject to a great deal of pressure and that voting behaviour was, to a large extent, determined by 'influence':

> 'Influence remained the major factor determining the allegiance of voters; influence could have its basis in natural deference, in corrupt practices of various kinds, in intimidation, open or implied, or in a combination of these.' (Feuchtwanger 1985, p.53)

This influence, Feuchtwanger argues, came from landowners who expected their tenants to follow their lead and from employers who expected employees to vote for the party they favoured. While Walton accepts that some employers put pressure on their employees to vote a particular way, he argues that this idea should not be overstated:

> 'The employer's scope for extending their control beyond the workplace was really very limited...To account effectively for the voting behaviour of the new electors, we must take into account other social influences which sometimes came partially within the orbit of the factory, but which had for the vast majority an independent existence of their own.' (Walton 1983, p.42)

Religion and voting behaviour

One of these 'other social influences' was religion. Feuchtwanger emphasises the importance of religious affiliation in determining voting behaviour:

> 'Between the second and third Reform Bills...non-conformity and dissent still supplied much of the rank and file of the Liberal Party. The late 1860s were, perhaps, the heyday of non-conformism as a political force.' (Feuchtwanger 1985, p.52)

Summary Box

Walton disagrees with this. He argues that:

'Some of the new voters were non-conformists, but in general Protestant non-conformity drew its active support from rather higher in the social scale...[In the boroughs], the chapel-going tradesmen and artisans, previously numerically important among the voters, were swamped by working-class abstainers from organised religion.' (Walton 1983, pp.42-43)

Most historians agree, however, that much of the Conservatives' support came from Anglicans, especially those living in the rural counties of England. Their allegiance to the Conservative Party helps to explain why it won around three-quarters of English county seats in all three general elections held between 1867 and 1884.

2.2 What impact did the 1867 Reform Act make on the Liberal Party and the Conservative Party?

The changing role of parties

There is a consensus amongst historians that the broadening of the franchise forced the main political parties to change. As Lang puts it:

'A substantial section of the urban working class was now enfranchised and each party was keen to capture these new votes. Doing so required a much greater degree of organisation at local level than the parties had been used to.' (Lang 1999, p.88)

Garrard (1991) argues that, after 1867, the two main political parties performed seven main functions. Some of these had been performed before 1867, but some were new or required party members to use new techniques if they were to be performed successfully.

1. Registering voters

As a number of authors have pointed out, it was one thing to have the right to vote and quite another matter to exercise that right. To be able to vote, voters' names had to appear on the register. But, for their names to appear, the voters had to be able to prove that they qualified. This was not always easy. As Garrard points out:

'In a world where only some could vote...and where there was a host of possible qualifications on the basis of which individuals might claim a vote, compilation of the electoral register was a highly complex process.' (Garrard 1991, p.35)

The political parties realised that elections could be won or lost depending on whether their supporters were registered and, as a result, they helped their supporters to register and challenged the qualification of known opponents and even of waverers. This had been a function of political parties before 1867, but it became a more important function after 1867 - see Box 2.7.

BOX 2.7 | Registration of voters in the late 1860s

Interpretation

By the late 1860s, there were party workers in most urban constituencies who devoted their time and expertise to the protection of voting rights for the supporters of their party. They also sought the removal from the register of opponents, or even waverers. Each year thousands of claims were challenged in local registration courts, with most of the work being done by agents from the main parties. This made a particular impact on working-class voters. Without the backing of the local party, a would-be working-class voter was unlikely to be included on the electoral register because hearings took place in working hours. In reality, therefore, too much time and trouble were involved for most working-class lodgers to be able to qualify. Also, because of the registration process, the result of elections was often known in advance. As a result, on many occasions, one party did not put forward a candidate, allowing the other party to win the seat uncontested. In many areas, therefore, parties became the means by which people, even if the registration game permitted them to become voters, were denied effective electoral choice.

Adapted from Walton 1983 and Garrard 1991

---

2. Spreading the message

The broadening of the electorate meant that parties had to devise new ways of communicating their message to potential supporters since they could no longer rely on personal contact. At a local level, therefore, constituency and ward parties distributed leaflets and canvassed supporters, as well as organising meetings and social events. Also, Lang notes that local newspapers began to play an important part in communicating information to voters:

'[The] growth of interest and participation in political activity was helped by - indeed it could hardly have happened without - a big increase in the number and circulation of local newspapers which would carry long and detailed descriptions of political meetings and marches, and verbatim reports of major speeches.' (Lang 1999, p.99)

At the national level, the party leadership learned to communicate via the press. Gladstone, in particular, became skilled at launching high-profile campaigns - the obvious example is the Midlothian campaigns of 1879-80 (see also Unit 1, page 23) when he toured the country by rail, stopping to make speeches which were then recorded word-for-word in the press. Biagini argues that:

'Gladstone always spoke for two audiences: the one physically present at the "mass meeting" and the nationwide readership of the daily and weekly press. Hundreds of thousands of people all over the country read verbatim versions of Gladstone's speeches only a few hours after their original deliverance.' (Biagini 1994, p.30)

3. Selecting candidates

It had always been the function of the local party to find candidates to stand for Parliament or as councillors. In addition, local parties had to find people willing to stand for election as Poor Law Guardians and, after the passage of the 1870 Education Act, as members of Education Boards. It should be noted that, unlike today when the party headquarters may exercise control over the selection of candidates, local parties were left to their own devices in the late 19th century.

4. Organising election campaigns

The organisation of election campaigns had, of course, always been a primary function of political parties. Indeed, before 1867, it was only at election time that anything resembling a party structure materialised in some constituencies. According to Dunbabin:

'The normal mid-19th century electoral organisation consisted between elections of an informal committee of the MP/candidate and other large subscribers that hired a solicitor to "work" the electoral register. During contests, this expanded into a central committee to supervise his management of the campaign, supported (where appropriate) by ward committees and secretaries. Such organisation was both ephemeral [short-lived] and candidate-centred.' (Dunbabin 1988, p.115)

While, in some constituencies, more permanent party structures had evolved before 1867, it was only after 1867 that permanent party structures grew up all over the country (see page 49 below). A key function of these new permanent party structures was to organise election campaigns.

5. Exerting pressure on the leadership

There is a debate about whether or not it became a function of ordinary party members to exert influence over the party leadership after 1867. Garrard argues that this function did develop as a result of party members' work in elections:

'Parties put up rival candidates, organised election meetings, distributed propaganda and...got voters to the polls. In performing this role, they became also, however much the parliamentary leaderships might dislike the fact, a means whereby voters' policy preferences achieved a degree of political relevance.' (Garrard 1991, p.34)

But, he points out that there was little attempt to influence policy directly:

'Although government policies were often discussed in wards and constituencies, there was little open criticism - except of course where the opposite party was in charge...[Local parties] largely contented themselves with resolutions expressing unlimited confidence in the national

leadership.' (Garrard 1988, p.130)

Lang admits that Joseph Chamberlain, who built a formidable local Liberal party in Birmingham in the 1870s (see page 50 below), did this in order to exert pressure on the Liberal leadership to adopt his programme. But, he argues, far from reducing the power of Party Leaders, the passing of the 1867 Reform Act increased it - see Box 2.8.

BOX 2.8 Party Leaders after 1867

The modern role of Party Leader, with a strong hold on the party, can be dated from the period of Gladstone and Disraeli. Their colourful personalities, their skill at public speaking and the personal hatred each felt for the other lent them a sort of 'star quality' and helped to personalise politics for the electorate and newspaper readers. Their features were well-known and their names became almost shorthand terms for their parties. Later Leaders adopted different styles, but their hold on their parties was no less secure. Although parties had splits and factions within them and could, on occasion, cause their Leaders serious trouble, Party Leaders proved capable of overcoming this trouble. In both main parties, the leadership was usually able to keep the grass-roots party out of policy and decision making.

Adapted from Lang 1999.

6. Integrating groups into the political system

Garrard argues that a particularly important function of political parties after 1867 was to make new and potentially hostile groups feel at home in the political system:

'Parties were an important means whereby groups were "integrated" into the political system - giving those groups a stake in its continuation by demonstrating its sensitivity to at least some of their desires and prejudices.' (Garrard 1991, p.34)

He emphasises that political parties were not just electoral machines. They also played an important part in the political education of their members and they provided social and leisure facilities which encouraged members to adopt the (mainly middle-class) values the main parties supported. This function, Garrard argues, arose from the debate (outlined above) about the 'political fitness' of certain groups to be given the vote:

'By this phrase, contemporaries primarily meant two things. Firstly, they were worried whether potential voters were sufficiently well informed on the great issues of the day, and sufficiently free from influences like drink and bribery, to exercise mature political judgement. Secondly, they worried whether those they might enfranchise had sufficiently absorbed the social and economic values of, and had come to have a sufficient "stake" in, the surrounding capitalist industrial society - so as not to disrupt it when they and their demands became politically relevant.' (Garrard 1991, p.36) By providing political education and encouraging party members to adopt the party's values, political parties hoped to build up a loyal following which would not challenge the system by making extremist demands.

7. Providing facilities for leisure activities

As indicated above, political parties had a social side. They provided facilities for members to use in their leisure time and they organised leisure activities designed to encourage loyalty as well as to provide enjoyment. Lang argues that:

These social functions were always secondary to the clubs' [ie the local party groups'] prime purpose: to mobilise support at election times.' (Lang 1999, p.99)

Garrard (1991), however, disagrees, arguing that the leisure activities played an important part in the process of integration mentioned above. He argues that leisure activities were intended:

- to keep party activists happy
- to encourage non-members to join
- to 'elevate and improve' working-class members by exposing them to middle-class values
- to keep young people away from 'bad' influences.

Party structure

To perform the functions mentioned above, the two main political parties required a new, permanent structure. This developed in the years following 1867. Feuchtwanger (1985) argues that the new structures which emerged marked the origins of party organisation in its modern form. This, he says, has three strands:

- local party associations in each constituency
- national federations of constituency associations
- central party bureaucracy.

It was after 1867, Feuchtwanger claims, that both main parties developed structures which followed this pattern.

1. The Conservative Party

The Conservative Party was the first to develop the three strands mentioned above:

'A group of younger politicians...some of them actively committed to giving the party a more popular base...in 1867, began to promote a movement for the formation of Conservative working men's associations and clubs in borough constituencies. Such bodies came into being alongside and overlapping with existing Conservative and Constitutional Associations. In the same year a national federation of these organisations was started and acquired the name of National Union of Conservative and Constitutional Associations [NUCCA].' (Feuchtwanger 1985, p.47)

The new local bodies and the NUCCA account for

the first two strands mentioned above.

A central bureaucracy

The third strand - a central bureaucracy - materialised after John Gorst was appointed Party Agent in 1870:

'Disraeli effectively created the role of full-time Party Agent to keep an eye on the growing number of local associations and, in 1870, he appointed an efficient and methodical MP, John Gorst, to the post. Gorst established a Central Office for the party and also became Secretary of the NUCCA, which promptly moved into the same building as Gorst's Central Office.' (Lang 1999, p.101)

Adelman argues that the NUCCA and Central Office were 'top-down' organisations and that, when, in 1871, Gorst transferred NUCCA to the same building as Central Office:

'The National Union became in practice what it had always been in theory, the propaganda arm of the Conservative Central Office.' (Adelman 1997, pp.35-36)

Adelman also argues that Gorst's top-down initiatives were successful:

'By the end of 1873, Gorst was able to report to Disraeli that 69 new Conservative Associations had been founded and that more than 400 were in existence...By the time of the 1874 general election, a Conservative candidate had been found for every reasonable constituency.' (Adelman 1997, p.35)

2. The Liberal Party

Walton argues that the Liberal Party moved more slowly towards a 'modern' party structure:

'The Liberals were slightly slower into the field, and they suffered from inhibitions about allowing drink and billiards into their clubs, which made it difficult for them to reach out to the apathetic masses of the working class.' (Walton 1983, p.45)

The Central Office

Like the Conservatives, the Liberals set up a Central Office at the beginning of the 1870s. In its early years, this was controlled by the Chief Whips (the Party Agent remained a minor figure until the late 1880s). Feuchtwanger argues that:

'The diversity of the party, the existence of many national organisations within the spectrum of Liberal politics, as well as Gladstone's inspirational leadership reduced the scope and the need for central organisation.' (Feuchtwanger 1985, p.50)

He also points out that the work that the Reform League did in the 1868 general election (supplying the Chief Whip with information, finding candidates and encouraging working-class men to vote Liberal) was similar to the work done by the Conservative Party Agent, Gorst, in 1870-74. Adelman agrees that the Liberal Central Office was less important than its Conservative counterpart, but argues that this did not matter:

> 'The fact that there was no great change in either the machinery or the personnel of the Liberal Central Office was relatively unimportant since the real changes in party organisation came not from above but from below: it was the changes at grass-roots that were of major importance.' (Adelman 1997, p.39)

In particular, developments in Birmingham before the 1868 general election started a trend which would gain great importance in the Liberal Party. It should be noted that, before 1867, there was little in the way of democracy at local level in the Liberal Party.

The Birmingham Caucus

The Birmingham Liberal Association was set up in 1865. Pearce and Stewart argue that, from the start, its organisation was rather different from that of other Liberal organisations:

> 'William Harris, the Association's first secretary, created a powerful structure with elected ward committees at the bottom level, a central committee of 600, and the Council of Ten at the top - nicknamed the "Caucus". It was these ten who took the vital decisions, much like the parliamentary Cabinet, but the overall democratic nature, combined with a centralised leadership proved highly effective in winning elections.' (Pearce & Stewart 1992, p.41)

When the 1867 Reform Act was passed, Birmingham became a three-member borough and so the 'minority clause', allowing voters to vote for only two members, applied (see Box 2.5). In theory, that meant that the Liberal Party could only expect to win two seats, but the superior organisation of the Caucus ensured that it won all three:

> 'The Caucus showed that it controlled its voters so tightly that it could win all three seats in Birmingham in 1868, in spite of the limited vote introduced by the Bill. In each ward, voters were instructed which two of the three Liberal candidates they should support.' (Feuchtwanger 1985, p.48)

The success of the Birmingham Caucus ensured that it became a model which other local Liberal organisations followed. It also helped to launch Joseph Chamberlain's parliamentary career (see Box 2.9).

The National Liberal Federation

As Box 2.9 suggests, Joseph Chamberlain was the chief architect of the formation of the National Liberal Federation (NLF). The NLF was an umbrella organisation which aimed to bring together all the local Liberal associations organised along the same lines as the Birmingham Caucus. It held its first conference in May 1877 at Bingley Hall in Birmingham. Pearce and Stewart (1992, p.42) describe this as 'the first of the modern party conferences'. Feuchtwanger notes that most Liberal associations in the boroughs soon joined the NLF and followed the Birmingham model, but he points out that:

BOX 2.9 Joseph Chamberlain (1836-1914)

Biography Box

Joseph Chamberlain's parents owned a small business in South London. He left school at 16 and did not go to university. At 18, his father sent him to Birmingham to represent the family's business there and he became a commercial success. In the late 1860s, he became a leading light in the National Education League (NEL) and a local Liberal councillor (thanks to the Caucus). In 1873, he became Lord Mayor of Birmingham and, over the next three years, transformed the city into a model for the country. The local gas company was bought by the council and its profits ploughed into improvement schemes. The water company was bought and improvements made. The centre was rebuilt. Slums were torn down and new houses built, together with an art gallery and museum. Chamberlain differed from many older radicals. He was a new breed of politician - a programme rather than a single-issue campaigner. He favoured dissolving the NEL and transforming it into a broader National Liberal Federation (NLF). The machinery and headquarters of the NEL were placed at the disposal of the NLF and Chamberlain became its President. Via the NFL, Chamberlain hoped to unify radicalism, transform the Liberal Party and provide a launch pad for his own race to the top.

Adapted from Pearce and Stewart 1992.

> 'The aims of those who promoted the Federation went far beyond the objective of an organisational tidying up. They wanted to capture the whole of the Liberal Party for the radical cause and programme and reduce to naught what remained of Whig and right-wing power and influence in the party. The origins and purposes of the National Liberal Federation were, therefore, very different from those of its Tory counterpart.' (Feuchtwanger 1985, p.49)

In fact, Chamberlain failed to gain control of the Liberal Party. He was outmanoeuvred by Gladstone who accepted an invitation to speak at the NLF's inaugural conference and used the opportunity to launch his 'crusade' against Turkish atrocities in Bulgaria - a crusade which led to Gladstone's re-emergence as Liberal Leader (see also Unit 1, Section 3.1):

> '[Gladstone and other Liberal leaders] rightly predicted that such a formidable political machine [as the NLF] would not be content with producing voters for other people's policies, but would want a say in drawing those policies up. Gladstone launched into his vigorous Midlothian Campaigns at least partly in order to seize the initiative back from Chamberlain.' (Lang 1999, p.100)

Significantly, when Chamberlain broke with Gladstone over Irish Home Rule in 1886 and left the party together with 78 Liberal MPs (see also Unit 6, page 181), the NLF remained loyal to Gladstone. As Pearce and Stewart note when discussing Chamberlain's decision to invite Gladstone to the first meeting of the NLF:

'Little did Chamberlain appreciate that it was Gladstone who was to hijack the National Liberal Federation rather than vice versa.' (Pearce & Stewart 1992, p.42)

The Liberal Party - a broad church

The NLF was by no means the only national organisation aiming to influence the Liberal leadership:

'Advanced Liberals of differing persuasions, with various special interests or "faddists", such as the United Kingdom Alliance, pressing for temperance [avoidance of alcohol], or the Liberation Society, pressing for disestablishment [the separation of the Church of England from the state] - all these had to be accommodated.' (Feuchtwanger 1985, p.49)

In addition, the Liberal Party 'hijacked' the Reform League, which had campaigned for electoral reform before 1867. As Harrison (1965) points out, the League was in a strong position to push for the selection of working-class candidates since, in July 1867, it had 600 branches and c.65,000 members. But, rather than pushing the Liberal Party into accepting working-class candidates, its leadership gave in to Liberal demands:

'The League was short of money and the enlarged electorate made election organisation even more expensive than hitherto. So, its political activity was dependent on largesse [money] from middle-class Liberals...[In practice], its influence (and its paymasters' money) was consistently used to deter radical and working-class candidates from coming forward if there was any possibility of their threatening an established MP or mainstream candidate.' (Walton 1983, p.44)

Nevertheless, the fact that the Liberal Party found a way to work with the League and other semi-detached organisations shows that it was a broad church with many competing interests pushing for support.

Political activism

There is a consensus among historians that the last quarter of the 19th century was a time of great political activism. Much of this political activism was channelled through the party organisations which began to develop after 1867:

'By the 1880s, any sizeable town would have its local Liberal Association, often a local Women's Liberal Association and, in university towns there would be a University Liberal Association too. On the Conservative side, as well as the local Conservative or Constitutional Club, there would be...the Primrose League [see also Unit 6, page 185] which had 2,300 branches and over 1.5 million members by 1900.' (Lang 1999, p.99)

Garrard argues that the main parties aimed to give people - especially the new working-class voters - a 'sense of participation' in the political process:

'This helps explain the vast number apparently involved in running the new constituency party machinery.' (Garrard 1991, p.36)

Garrard cites the example of the Liberal constituency associations designed along the lines of the Birmingham Caucus. The fact that 600 people were elected to the constituency's General Committee, he argues, indicates the huge scale of participation. He also mentions the annual constituency outings where 'many hundreds or even thousands' of party members would go out on a trip.

MAIN POINTS - Part 2

- Three main problems remained after the passing of the 1867 Reform Act - (1) the different property qualifications for counties and boroughs (2) regional imbalances and (3) the problem of compound-ratepayers (which was solved in 1869).
- As a result of the 1867 Reform Act, a majority of voters came from the working class - though most of the new voters were concentrated in the boroughs.
- After 1867,the two main parties performed seven main functions - (1) registering voters (2) spreading the message (3) selecting candidates (4) organising election campaigns (5) exerting pressure on the leadership (6) integrating groups into the political system and (7) providing facilities for leisure activities.
- Party structure and organisation changed after 1867. In both main parties three strands emerged - (1) local constituency organisations (2) national federations representing local constituency organisations and (3) a central party bureaucracy.
- The Conservative Party set up local clubs, the NUCCA and the Central Office. Top-down initiatives had paid dividends by the time of the 1874 general election.
- The Liberal Party also set up a Central Office, but initiatives tended to come from below, not from the centre. Many Liberal associations followed the model of the Birmingham Caucus and, later, joined the National Liberal Federation (NLF).

Activity 2.2 Which party benefited most from the 1867 reform?

ITEM 1 Election results 1868-84

Party	1868			1874			1880		
	Votes	%	MPs	Votes	%	MPs	Votes	%	MPs
Conservative	903,318	38.4	271	1,091,708	43.9	350	1,426,351	42.0	237
Liberal	1,428,776	61.5	387	1,281,159	52.7	242	1,836,423	55.4	352
Home Rule	-	-	-	90,234	3.3	60	95,535	2.6	63
Others	1,157	0.1	0	2,936	0.1	0	1,107	0	0

BALLOT BOX

Adapted from Craig 1989.

ITEM 2 Who benefited from the 1867 Reform Act?

(i) To some extent, the hopes of both of the major parties were realised. Immediately, the Liberals seemed to have benefited from the second Reform Act, in their clear victory in the general election of 1868. In the longer-term, however, the Conservatives proved the gainers. In the general election of 1874, the Conservative Party won its first overall majority since 1841. In addition, after 1867-68, there were already signs of increased Conservative voting strength in the larger urban centres, especially in the London area. The 1867 Act increased the number of Catholic voters, especially in constituencies with large numbers of Irish immigrants. While most immigrants voted Liberal, there was an anti-Irish, anti-Catholic backlash which explain why Lancashire became an important centre of Conservative strength in the late 19th century.
Adapted from McCord 1991.

This cartoon was published in *Punch* magazine on 25 May 1867.

THE DERBY, 1867. DIZZY WINS WITH "REFORM BILL."
Mr. Punch. "DON'T BE TOO SURE; WAIT TILL HE'S WEIGHED."

(ii) The direct party-political effects were limited. The 1868 elections certainly saw more contests and changes of seats than any since 1832. Both parties made important gains, some of which (like the Conservative breakthrough in Lancashire) may have been facilitated by enfranchisement or boundary changes. But the net effect in England was neutral. Conservative gains from the increased number of county constituencies offset Liberal ones in the boroughs. The next election, 1874, saw the first Conservative majority since 1841. The most interesting development was the Conservative gains in suburban areas. This was largely unexpected. It is natural to explain this and the 1880 Liberal recovery as chiefly shifts in opinion.
Adapted from Dunbabin 1988.

(iii) Electoral figures do not support the view that the Tories gained. The Liberals won landslide majorities at two of the three general elections held under the 1867 electoral system. Indeed, in 1880, they did well in regions in which they had traditionally been weak, such as Ulster and the English counties. It is significant that, at a time when in most other European countries the Liberals were being displaced from their traditional position of the main party of 'the left' by either socialism or radical nationalism, in the United Kingdom Gladstone's party grew from strength to strength. This happened because the Liberal leadership was able to communicate with the new electorate and absorb the left. It was, in other words, successfully able to adapt itself to the new requirements of mass politics.
Adapted from Biagini 1994.

ITEM 3 Party organisation

Political parties, if they are to win elections, require not only policies but organisation. Before 1867, with a small electorate, the problem was not so urgent. The central organisation of the parties was in the hands of the Whips whose main task (outside Parliament) was to raise money for the election fund and obtain candidates. The only practical help the whips obtained was from a part-time party agent. In the counties and boroughs, party affairs were in the hands of virtually self-appointed and self-perpetuating committees of local bigwigs. They ran the constituency with the help of a registration agent for day-to-day business and advice and, at election time, a paid election agent. The links between local and national party organisers were loose and were conducted mainly through the London political clubs - the Conservatives' Carlton Club and Liberals' Reform Club. The second Reform Act had a decisive effect on party organisation. The period 1867-86 was essentially a transitional period in party organisation. It was during this period that both main parties set up central party offices. This raised the fear of 'caucus control' - dictation to Parliament by outside irresponsible bodies. By the end of the century, however, the Leaders of both parties had 'shackled the monster they had created'.

Adapted from Adelman 1997.

Questions

1. a) Using Items 1-3 and your own knowledge, describe the problems the two main parties faced after the passing of the 1867 Reform Act.
   b) How did they deal with these problems?
2. Look at Item 2.
   a) Was the cartoonist right to suggest that Disraeli had won or was Mr Punch right to suggest that such a conclusion was in doubt? Explain your answer.
   b) What does Item 2 tell us about the state of the current debate over the impact of the 1867 Reform Act?
   c) Which passage is most convincing? Explain why.
3. Item 3 says that the 1867 Reform Act had 'a decisive effect on party organisation'.
   a) Why did it have a 'decisive' effect?
   b) Describe what actions the main parties took to ensure their future success.
4. What was the significance of the 1867 Reform Act for (a) the Liberal Party and (b) the Conservative Party?

3 The third Reform Act

Key questions

1. What steps were taken to deal with electoral corruption after 1870?

2. Why was the electoral system changed in 1884-85?

3. How did the electoral system change in 1884-85?

3.1 What steps were taken to deal with electoral corruption after 1870?

The problem of corruption

It was noted above that supporters of reform in the late 1820s often described the unreformed pre-1832 electoral system as 'Old Corruption'. But, the 1832 Reform Act did not bring electoral corruption to an end. Indeed, Hoppen argues that there was actually a growth in corruption after the passing of the 1832 Reform Act:

'The reports of election committees and commissions and other sources reveal how common the coin of corruption became not only before but even after the second Reform Act...Two committees - in 1835 and 1868 - examined the electoral system throughout the whole of the United Kingdom and found that no deep trawling was needed to show that corrupt practices had expanded rather than contracted since 1832.' (Hoppen 1996, p.559)

An example of the sort of corrupt practice which was common in the mid-19th century is given in Box 2.10 on page 54.

Violence

In addition to bribery and 'treating' many electoral contests descended into violence, sometimes violence of serious proportions. Pearce and Stearn, for example, note that 'between 1865 and 1885, there were at least 71 incidents of serious disorder'. Often this violence was the by-product of bribery and 'treating' with drunken supporters of the different candidates clashing around the Hustings. On occasion, however, the violence was planned, with candidates hiring people to intimidate voters. O'Leary notes that, between 1832 and 1868:

'Violence or intimidation at elections was also common at this period. In most of the large urban constituencies the more genteel electors were sometimes terrorised on polling day by gangs of

BOX 2.10 Electoral corruption

The kinds of bribery and 'treating' of voters which marked the Maldon election of 1852 were typical. Money was handed out by mysterious strangers, groups were entertained in dozens of pubs, bills were presented to candidates listing the gallons of beer that had been drunk. In 1837, boatloads of Hull electors, after sailing across the Humber, were met by coaches at the pier and whisked to a tavern. There they were provided with large amounts of food and drink. They were then taken to cast their votes and, following that, provided with yet more food and drink before being shipped back home that night. Hull was a comparatively large borough, but it had a reputation for corruption. After the 1852 election (which cost the four candidates at least £9,200), a Royal Commission found that a third of the 3,983 people who voted had been bribed. That this continued after the second Reform Act was passed is shown by an investigation in 1880. This found that a third of voters in Chester and two in five voters in Gloucester had accepted bribes. Of 32,401 voters in eight boroughs examined by special commissioners, a quarter fell into the corrupt category. In one case (Macclesfield), no fewer than 55% did so.
Adapted from Hoppen 1996.

hired bullies and deterred from voting. Sometimes the candidates encouraged this.' (O'Leary 1962, pp.15-16)

Less corruption in county constituencies

Hoppen argues that most corruption took place in borough constituencies. There was less corruption, he claims, in county constituencies because they were largely rural. Many voters were deferential (they believed that they should obey their 'superiors') and did not need to be bribed to vote according to the wishes of the local landowners. Nevertheless, there is evidence of landowners using threats to persuade voters to support a particular candidate (threatening to evict them if they did not vote a certain way, for example). Since voting was a public act until 1872 (people had to stand on the Hustings and declare who they were voting for and their vote was then recorded), such threats had a bearing on how some people voted.

The Ballot Act of 1872

It was noted above that, before 1872, voting was a public act. As Willis points out, one reason for this was the idea that those given the privilege of voting were somehow the representatives of all the people living in their community and, as a result, everybody in the local community had the right to know how each voter had voted:

'One of the arguments for open voting was that the electors were voting on behalf of the whole community as some sort of trustees and everyone should see their choice.' (Willis 1999, p.22)

Open voting, however, allowed and sometimes encouraged intimidation and opponents argued that it should be replaced by the secret ballot. As O'Leary points out, these opponents had been arguing their case for some time before 1872:

'The Ballot Act of 1872 differed from the other stages in the improvement of electioneering morals in that it was not so much an ad hoc [spur of the moment] measure as the culmination of a long reformist struggle.' (O'Leary 1962, p.58)

Pearce and Stearn agree, noting that:

'Radicals had been calling for a secret ballot since the 1770s. An attempt had been made to include such a provision in the 1831 Reform Bill, and it had figured among Chartist demands.' (Pearce & Stearn 1994, p.62)

Why was the Ballot Act introduced?

Historians agree that there was little interest in the secret ballot in Parliament until after the 1868 general election. O'Leary, for example, argues that:

'The peculiar features of the 1868 election, the long campaign leading to excessive canvassing and expenditure, the rowdiness and rioting, the flood of petitions [protesting that bribery had taken place in particular constituencies], and the trials in open court, caused the new Liberal government a good deal of heart-searching.' (O'Leary 1962, pp.58-59)

Pearce and Stearn agree that the 1868 general election was important, but they suggest that there was a further reason why the Liberal government was prepared to take action on this matter - namely, because it needed the support of radical MPs and the promise of a secret ballot would be enough to ensure that leading radical, John Bright, joined the Cabinet:

'[John Bright] had been calling for this measure ever since the 1830s; now the politicians listened. Gladstone wished to increase radical support for his new government by including Bright within the Cabinet, but the price of his participation was the introduction of secret ballot legislation. Gladstone personally disliked the proposal.' (Pearce & Stearn 1994, p.62)

The terms of the Ballot Act

Following the 1868 general election, a Select Committee was set up to investigate conduct at elections and it was specifically asked to examine whether a secret ballot should be introduced. When this committee published its report in 1871, it recommended that a secret ballot should be introduced. The government took up the recommendations of the Select Committee and, after a battle in Parliament, the Ballot Act became law in 1872. As a result:

'Electors were to vote by secretly marking a printed ballot paper with a cross and placing it in a sealed ballot box. If an elector was illiterate or blind, the election official was to mark the paper for him. Votes were to be counted in the presence of the candidates' agents.' (Pearce & Stearn 1994, pp.63-64)

An amendment made by the House of Lords - the 'Beauchamp amendment' - made this a temporary arrangement for eight years. After that period had ended, however, it became a permanent arrangement.

Consequences

The 1872 Ballot Act was a significant step because it reflected a change in attitude towards the vote:

'It was on the issue of the ballot that the Liberal Party as a whole came round to the radical view that the vote was a right, not a trust or a privilege.' (O'Leary 1962, p.73)

O'Leary also points out that, by replacing the Hustings with the polling booth, the Act ensured that voting came to be seen more as 'a political act rather than as a social occasion'.

In addition, the Act was constitutionally important since it was an important step on the path to democracy:

'By enabling electors to vote as they chose rather than as others commanded, it made the electoral system more representative and democratic.' (Pearce & Stearn 1994, p.64)

Historians agree that the amount of violence and intimidation during election campaigns was reduced as a result of the introduction of the secret ballot. But, they also agree that the Act did little to reduce bribery:

'[The Ballot Act] did much to reduce the violence and street theatre associated with elections. It probably also stopped employers and landlords threatening their workers and tenants, although some doubts remained about how secretly the votes were counted. It did not stop bribery.' (Willis 1999, p.22)

Consequences in Ireland

In Ireland, the Act ensured that landlords no longer had such strong control over their tenants, allowing tenants to vote for pro-Home Rule (Irish Nationalist) candidates for the first time. This was of great importance since parliamentary arithmetic ensured that the small group of pro-Home Rule MPs was then able to put governments under a great deal of pressure after 1872. This, together with Gladstone's 'conversion' to Home Rule (and the consequent split in the Liberal Party in 1886), ensured that the issue of Irish Home Rule came to dominate British politics in the late 19th and early 20th century (see Unit 6, Part 4).

The Corrupt and Illegal Practices Act of 1883

It was noted above that the 1872 Ballot Act failed to end bribery. Indeed, Lang suggests that bribery may have increased as a result of the Ballot Act:

'Some thought the Ballot Act made [elections] more corrupt rather than less since the more [grasping] voters could now accept bribes from both parties without either knowing how they actually voted.' (Lang 1999, p.88)

Box 2.11 shows the sort of corrupt practices which were commonly used in elections as late as 1880. Just as the 1868 general election was the turning point which led to the secret ballot, the 1880 general election led to the Corrupt and Illegal Practices Act. O'Leary argues that the 1880 general election was, in some senses, the first of a new style since it was the first in which the Leaders of the main parties organised national campaigns and the first with two mass party organisations. On the other hand, the sort of electoral practices which had been common in previous elections continued to be practised. As a result:

'The general election of 1880 marked a transition: it was the first general election fought on the national level; it was the last to be disgraced by widespread

---

BOX 2.11 The Sandwich by-election of 1880

After the Liberal victory in the 1880 general election, the MP from Sandwich was promoted to the Lords and a by-election was held. The Conservative agent's first move was to hire 88 pubs as 'committee rooms' at £5 a piece. Only 17 were ever used. All that the innkeepers did for their money was to post up a few posters. The agent then divided the constituency up into districts and appointed 42 canvassers at £6 a day. He spent nearly £350 on rosettes for the wives and children of voters. Thousands of yards of bunting and ribbon was bought from local traders (all of whom were voters) and, on the day before the election, cards were sent in Conservative colours to all inhabitants, allowing them to use the Deal pier free of charge. The Conservative agent spent £6,500 on the election, but could only account for £5,600 (which probably means that £900 was spent on direct bribes). Meanwhile, the Liberal candidate spent £2,000 partly on direct bribery, partly on flags and banners, and partly on dubious employment. For example, an enormous flagstaff was put up in front of his house with 20 flags and 'no end of men to watch it'. The result gave the Conservatives 1,145 votes and the Liberals 705. When the Royal Commission that had been set up to investigate electoral practices published its report, it found that 1,005 people had accepted bribes (127 from both sides) and that both sides were guilty of corrupt practices.

Adapted from O'Leary 1962.

Interpretation

corrupt practices.' (O'Leary 1962, p.158)
Following the election, the government set up the Royal Commission referred to in Box 2.11 and then introduced a Bill designed to put an end to the sort of corrupt practices which the Royal Commission had uncovered. This Bill became law in August 1883.

Pearce and Stearn argue that it was experience of elections under the secret ballot that persuaded the majority of MPs to support further measures to counter corruption:

'Politicians disliked heavy election costs, especially since the secret ballot meant that those who accepted [bribes] would not necessarily do the honourable thing and vote for their benefactor. Some electors might even take bribes from both candidates.' (Pearce & Stearn 1994, p.65)

The main provisions of the Corrupt and Illegal Practices Act are outlined in Box 2.12 below.

The impact of the Corrupt and Illegal Practices Act

The Corrupt and Illegal Practices Act was by no means the first piece of legislation designed to eliminate electoral corruption. But, its penalties were much more severe than those imposed by previous legislation and historians agree that, in the long term, it was a success. O'Leary describes it as a 'landmark in the struggle for electoral purity' and says:

'Its effect was to transform the whole character of British electioneering within a generation.' (O'Leary 1962, p.175)

Willis, however, notes that, although there was less corruption, it did not completely disappear:

'Violent habits continued to the end of the 19th century. When Rider Haggard stood as a Conservative candidate in East Norfolk in 1895, opposition went beyond the heckling he expected. Three of his meetings broke up in disorder. At one village he was pelted with eggs and he and his wife got used to coming out of village halls to booing and occasional stone throwing.' (Willis 1999, p.23)

Pearce and Stearn (1994) note that other consequences of the Act were:

- a stimulation of local party organisation (since candidates had to rely on volunteers rather than paid workers)
- corrupt practices outside election time (some rich candidates 'nursed' constituencies by spending money there between elections)
- difficulties for poorer voters (since the Act prevented candidates paying for transport, making it difficult for some voters to cast their vote)
- less drunkenness and disorder at election time (since 'treating' was illegal).

Certainly, the number of election petitions significantly decreased after the Corrupt and Illegal Practices Act was passed (election petitions were legal challenges against an election result based on the allegation that illegal actions had taken place). The impact of the Act in terms of average election expenditure per candidate is shown in Box 2.13 on page 57.

BOX 2.12 The Corrupt and Illegal Practices Act

Summary Box

The Corrupt and Illegal Practices Act had three parts which contained the following provisions:

1. Penalties

Anyone found guilty of corrupt practices:
- could face up to a year's imprisonment (with hard labour) and a fine
- would be banned for life from standing in the same constituency
- lost their right to vote and their right to stand for office for seven years.

Anyone found guilty of illegal practices:
- could face a fine
- lost their right to vote and their right to stand for office for five years
- was banned from standing in the same constituency for seven years.

2. Definition of corrupt and illegal practices

Corrupt practices were defined as 'bribery, treating, undue influence, assaulting or abducting [taking hostage] a voter, personation, perjury and a false statement in the return of expenses'. 'Personation' means pretending to be somebody else for a fraudulent purpose.

Illegal practices were:
- spending more than the maximum legal election expenses
- payment for transporting voters to the poll
- employment of voters
- failure to arrange expenses as required by law (eg paying all accounts within four weeks of the election and listing every item of expenditure separately)
- failure to limit the number of paid workers to two for every 500 voters.

3. Expenses

The Act laid down how much a candidate could spend in an election campaign. This varied according to the type of constituency and number of voters in it. For example, a candidate in an English county constituency with less than 2,000 voters could spend £650 while a candidate in an English borough constituency with less than 2,000 voters could spend only £350.

Adapted from O'Leary 1962.

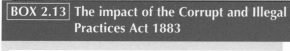

BOX 2.13 The impact of the Corrupt and Illegal Practices Act 1883

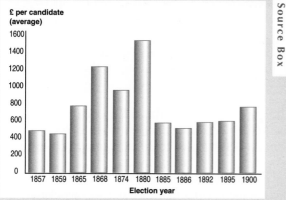

Source Box

This chart shows the average election expenditure per candidate in elections between 1857 and 1900.

3.2 Why was the electoral system changed in 1884-85?

Why 1884-85?
Historians agree that there was no burning public desire for electoral reform in the early 1880s:

'The 1884 Act was not - as in 1832 or 1867 - the culmination of a generation of political and intellectual ferment; nor was it a response to the irresistible "pressure from without" of the rural masses.' (Adelman 1985, p.24)

In order to explain, therefore, why the electoral system was changed again in 1884-85, historians give five main reasons.

1. Experience of the 1867 electoral system
The general election of 1880 brought the Liberals back to power after six years of Conservative rule. By then, it was clear that both main parties could win overall majorities under the system introduced in 1867. It was also clear, however, that the post-1867 electoral system was flawed. It was noted in Section 2.1 above that the 1867 Reform Act produced three main problems:

- irregularities between electorates in different constituencies (especially between county and borough constituencies)
- regional imbalances
- the position of compound-ratepayers.

While the third problem was solved in 1869 when compound-ratepayers were given the same right to vote as direct ratepayers, the other two problems remained:

'The great towns and cities still lacked their rightful number of MPs in terms of population; and the rural areas - where there still existed scores of small boroughs returning two MPs each - remained heavily over-represented in the House of

Commons. Two-thirds of MPs were, therefore, elected by about a quarter of the electorate. The anomalies [irregularities] relating to the franchise system were even more absurd. Since the vote had been granted only to urban householders, this meant that industrial workers living outside the borough boundaries - the half million or so miners, for example - were denied the vote...[This contrast] was too stark to be tolerable for long.' (Adelman 1985, p.25)

2. Continued corruption, 1867-83
It was noted in the previous section that the introduction of the secret ballot made an impact after 1872. In particular, it raised the possibility that rural working-class voters (those living in county constituencies - which were Conservative strongholds) might not vote Conservative in such large quantities:

'The Ballot Act of 1872 made it possible for all men to vote freely and there were soon signs of untapped Liberal support in the counties, especially among coal miners.' (Pearce & Stearn 1994, p.68)

In addition, the outcry about corruption after the 1880 general election and the government's decision to pass legislation against it helped to focus MPs' minds onto the issue of electoral reform:

'The passing of the first effective anti-corruption Act in 1883, with virtually all-party support, could be seen as a prelude to a further assault on the system of 1867.' (Adelman 1985, p.26)

3. Pressure from the radicals
Pressure for electoral reform within the Liberal Party came from the radical wing. From 1872, for example, the radical Liberal G.O. Trevelyan regularly raised in the Commons the matter of broadening the vote in the counties. Electoral reform was also supported by radicals Joseph Chamberlain and Charles Dilke, both of whom had posts in the Cabinet by 1884.

While the radicals had played an important part in the Liberal victory of 1880 (Joseph Chamberlain's NLF had played a particularly important part), there was a great deal of disharmony within the party after the election because the Whigs (led by Lord Hartington, who was also a member of the Cabinet) competed for control against the radical wing. In a bid to set the agenda, Chamberlain launched a national campaign in 1883 to revive radicalism. This campaign put electoral reform as the top priority:

'[Chamberlain] was worried by the disillusionment of the radical forces in the country with the dismal record of the government of which he was a notable member. In [1883], therefore, he launched a national campaign to revive the flagging spirit of radicalism...The basis for such a revival now lay, he believed, in parliamentary reform.' (Adelman 1985, p.25)

This campaign, Adelman argues, was an important

factor in the government's decision to support an Electoral Reform Bill.

4. Gladstone's support for change

Some historians argue that Gladstone's support for electoral reform was a crucial factor. According to Jenkins, Gladstone had supported electoral reform for some time and he deliberately kept back the issue until late in the life of the government elected in 1880:

'During the run-up to the 1883 session when Gladstone was recovering from his insomnia at Cannes, his mind and those of the radicals were turning towards franchise reform. It had always been part of his strategy that the extension of household suffrage from the towns to the countryside should be the major task for the government in the second half of its life.' (Jenkins 1995, p.485)

Many historians point out that the Liberal government was at a low ebb in 1884 (see also Unit 1, Section 3.2) and suggest that Gladstone calculated that electoral reform would be an issue around which the party could unite. The view of Pearce & Stewart is typical:

'To rouse and rally the disparate forces of the Liberal Party, the Cabinet decided in 1884 to go for one of the major political issues of the day, the reform of Parliament itself. Such a measure would rally the radicals and persuade special-interest groups like Wilfred Lawson's for temperance reform and James Stansfield's contagious diseases lobby to forgo their fads for the greater good. Many Whigs were dubious, but Hartington reluctantly accepted that a Franchise Bill was inevitable and the prospect of succeeding Gladstone kept him in the Cabinet.' (Pearce & Stewart 1992, p.48)

5. Changing attitudes

Some historians argue that in Parliament there was a change of attitude towards democracy after 1867:

'The first and second Reform Acts had shifted ruling-class political attitudes in Britain. After 1867, most politicians of all parties, whether they wanted it or not, accepted that further extensions of the franchise were inevitable sooner or later.' (Pearce & Stearn 1994, p.67)

As a result of this change of attitude, Pearce and Stearn argue, electoral reform became a matter of party advantage rather than a matter of principle. The Conservatives calculated in 1874-80 that it suited their party not to make changes, while the Liberals calculated in 1884 that change would benefit them.

Adelman argues that this change of attitude was a key reason why demands for electoral reform were made in the 1880s:

'The major factor was the increasing "democratisation" of English political life in the

1870s and, therefore, the growing recognition by all shades of opinion of the indefensible anomalies [irregularities] contained within the electoral system created by the second Reform Act.' (Adelman 1985, p.24)

3.3 How did the electoral system change in 1884-85?

The passing of the third Reform Act

The Reform Bill introduced by Gladstone in February 1884 aimed to create a uniform franchise in both boroughs and counties. It did not contain any clauses redistributing seats. This Bill passed through the Commons easily, but was blocked by Conservatives in the Lords. The result was a constitutional crisis (see Box 2.14) which Adelman (1985) describes as a 'dress rehearsal' for the struggle between the Commons and the Lords in 1909-11 (see Unit 6, Part 3).

BOX 2.14 **The crisis over the 1884 Reform Act**

Interpretation

In the House of Lords, Lord Salisbury, the Conservative Leader, was determined to fight the Reform Bill for strictly party reasons. He believed, probably correctly, that the extension of household suffrage into the counties without any redistribution of seats would give the Liberal Party considerable electoral advantages since the old constituencies would be swamped with new Liberal voters. What the Conservative Leader aimed at, therefore, was to use the in-built Conservative majority in the Lords to prevent the passing of the Reform Bill until he obtained firm guarantees from Gladstone that it would be accompanied by a redistribution measure. Alternatively, if the government refused to compromise, then Salisbury hoped that his tactics would result in a general election - which the Tories might win. Radicals like Chamberlain welcomed the confrontation. They wanted to use the crisis to rouse the country against the (unelected) Lords and to fight a general election on the issue of 'The Peers against the People'. Their hope was that this would result in the Lords being reformed or even abolished - 'mended or ended'. But, the crisis failed to enthuse people. All that happened was that a few feeble demonstrations took place. Gladstone was not at all impressed with the radicals' campaign. Nor were the Whigs. The last thing they wanted was the mobilisation of the people. Nor did they support the abolition of the House of Lords. Like Salisbury (and Queen Victoria), they wanted compromise.

Adapted from Adelman 1985 and Pearce & Stearn 1994.

The Arlington Street Compact

Since both Salisbury and Gladstone wanted a compromise, they (and their deputies) met secretly and worked out a deal:

'These secret talks were in fact unprecedented, for never before had rival Party Leaders discussed the details of a measure to be introduced into Parliament.' (Pearce & Stearn 1994, p.69)

The deal was finalised at a meeting between the two Party Leaders in November 1884. This meeting was held in Salisbury's London home in Arlington Street and, as a result, is known as the 'Arlington Street Compact'. The deal was as follows - Salisbury would instruct the Conservative majority to allow the Reform Bill to pass through the Lords and, in return, Gladstone would introduce a separate Redistribution Bill.

The terms of the Redistribution Bill

The terms of the Redistribution Bill, drawn up by the radical Liberal Charles Dilke, were acceptable to both Party Leaders and were agreed by them before the Bill was introduced into Parliament. Dilke's scheme was based on two main principles:

- all constituencies should have an electorate of roughly the same size
- the vast majority of constituencies should return a single MP.

Adelman argues that, at first sight, Salisbury's acceptance of Dilke's scheme is surprising:

'The attitude of Gladstone and Dilke was not unexpected: it was the outlook of Lord Salisbury that was remarkable.' (Adelman 1985, p.28)

But, he explains, Salisbury was prepared to accept a radical redistribution of seats because it would ensure not only that the Conservatives retained their domination in the counties, but also because there was a good chance of them winning seats in the new middle-class constituencies which would be created. As Jenkins observes:

'The counties and towns were all divided into single-member districts. This was the real gain for the Tories. It laid the foundation of "Villa Conservatism" [Conservative support from the lower middle-class] and the safe Tory seats of the Home Counties and the prosperous suburbs in and around the big provincial cities.' (Jenkins 1995, p.498)

As a result of the deal, the third Reform Act was passed in December 1884 and the Redistribution Act was passed in June 1885.

The third Reform Act, 1884

The third Reform Act created a uniform franchise in both boroughs and counties and, unlike previous Reform Acts, it applied to the UK as a whole. In addition to those who already had the vote, the Bill enfranchised:

- all male householders who paid rates and had lived in the house for at least one year
- all male lodgers who occupied lodgings worth £10 a year and had lived there for at least one year
- all those who had land or property worth £10 a year.

It should be noted that:

'After 1884, it was still possible for a voter to amass plural votes by acquiring several property qualifications such as 40 shilling freeholds in different county constituencies.' (McCord 1991, p.376)

Also, university graduates continued to have two votes. Nevertheless, the Act enfranchised a significant number of voters:

'The legislation added more voters than either of the earlier Reform Acts. It increased the number of those eligible to vote from 3 million to nearly 6 million. Henceforth, approximately two in three adult men could vote, instead of one in three.' (Pearce & Stearn 1994, p.70)

The Census of 1881 gave the population of the UK as a whole as 34.9 million. The proportion of adults with a vote, therefore, rose from c.8% to c.18%.

The Redistribution Act, 1885

According to Cook and Stevenson (1996), under the terms of the 1885 Redistribution Act:

- boroughs with a population under 15,000 lost their MPs and merged with the counties
- boroughs with a population under 50,000 lost one of their two MPs.

As a result, 138 seats were made available for redistribution. In addition, existing constituencies were broken up so that 647 constituencies out of a total of 670 became single-member constituencies. Lee notes that the new distribution of seats tackled the North-South imbalance:

'Cornwall's seats, for example, were now reduced from 44 to seven; Lancashire, by contrast, increased its representation from 14 to 58.' (Lee 1994, p.146)

Similarly, large cities gained considerably more seats. Cook and Stevenson note, for example, that London gained 40 new MPs, a rise from 22 to 62. Pearce and Stearn conclude that:

'The Redistribution Act brought the most thorough redistribution of seats in the whole of the century... The old county divisions were cut into single-member constituencies, and indeed, most constituencies henceforth had only a single Member of Parliament; as a result, they were no longer historic communities but artificial units based approximately on numbers.' (Pearce & Stearn 1994, p.70)

MAIN POINTS - Part 3

- There was a growth in electoral corruption after the passing of the 1832 Reform Act. In addition to bribery and 'treating' many electoral contests descended into violence. There was more corruption in boroughs than counties.
- Before 1872, voters voted openly in public. But this sometimes encouraged intimidation. The 1868 election was a turning point both because there was a great deal of corruption and because the winner - Gladstone - needed support from the radical wing. The result was the 1872 Ballot Act which introduced voting by secret ballot.
- The Ballot Act reduced intimidation, but it failed to prevent bribery and other illegal activities. The extent of bribery in the 1880 general election led to the Corrupt and Illegal Practices Act of 1883 - the first effective measure to combat corruption. Bribery petered out after 1883.
- Historians agree that there was no burning public desire for electoral reform in the early 1880s. They give five main reasons why the electoral system was changed again in 1884-85 -(1) experience of the 1867 electoral system (2) continued corruption 1867-84 (3) pressure from radicals (4) Gladstone's support for change and (5) changing attitudes.
- The Liberal government introduced a Reform Bill creating a uniform franchise in both boroughs and counties. When the Conservatives blocked this in the Lords, the two Party Leaders negotiated a deal. The result was the passing of both the Reform Bill and a Redistribution Bill which made single-member constituencies the norm.

Activity 2.3 The impact of the electoral reforms passed between 1872 and 1885

ITEM 1 The electoral impact of the third Reform Act

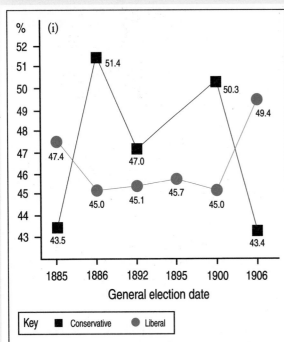

This graph shows the percentage of the vote won by the two main points in general elections held between 1885 and 1906.

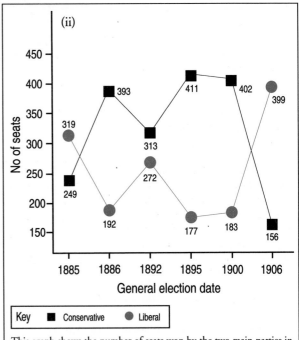

This graph shows the number of seats won by the two main parties in general elections held between 1885 and 1906.

(iii)

Party	1885	1886	1892	1895	1900	1906
Conservative	2,020,927	1,520,886	2,159,150	1,894,772	1,767,958	2,422,071
Liberal	2,199,998	1,353,581	2,088,019	1,765,266	1,572,323	2,751,057
HR/Nat	310,608	97,905	311,509	152,959	91,055	35,031
ILP/Lab	-	-	-	44,325	62,698	321,663
Others	106,702	1,791	39,641	8,960	29,448	96,269

This table shows the number of votes won by the parties in the general elections held between 1885 and 1906. 'HR/Nat' stands for Home Rule/Irish Nationalist. 'ILP/Lab' stands for Independent Labour Party/Labour Party.

ITEM 2 The impact on the Conservative Party

(i) By limiting election expenses the Corrupt and Illegal Practices Act transformed the character of electioneering since it allowed poorer men to stand for election and made voluntary work essential. It was this that led to the setting up of the Conservative Party's Primrose League (see also Unit 6, page 185). After 1884, the Primrose League became a shrewd and effective political organisation. In particular, its recruitment of women (see Unit 3, pages 81-82) and its emphasis on entertainment and social activities gave it enormous appeal without it being a threat to the party leadership (it focused on Tory beliefs - in religion, monarchy, Empire - rather than on party policy). The League took off in 1885 and had half a million members by 1887 and 1.5 million by 1900. The electoral reform of 1884-85 also had an important effect on party organisation. The increase in the unity and standardisation of the electoral system, accompanied as it was by the rise of national leaders and national issues enlarged the influence of the parties' central offices. From 1885, every Conservative association was automatically affiliated to the National Union - which became a truly national organisation. In the following year, ten Provincial Unions were set up. Any attempts by the Union conferences to influence policy, however, were ignored by the party leadership. In the late 19th century, the Conservative Party was run by three men - Lord Salisbury (Prime Minister), Akers Douglas (Chief Whip) and Captain Middleton (Party Agent and Secretary of the National Union). By linking up the two principal sections of party organisation with the parliamentary party, Conservative organisation reached virtually technical perfection. Also, strong leadership ensured the principle of 'authority' triumphed.

Adapted from Adelman 1997.

ITEM 3 The redistributed MP

" EVICTED "!

REDISTRIBUTED M.P. *(soliloquises sadly).* "FOR THE LAST FIFTEEN YEARS I'VE SUBSCRIBED TO THE INFIRMARY, AND THE CRICKET AND FOOTBALL CLUBS; I GAVE 'EM A DRINKING-FOUNTAIN; I'VE OPENED A BAZAAR; I'VE LAID SIXTEEN FOUNDATION-STONES; I'VE FOUNDED ALMSHOUSES; I'VE BECOME AN ODD-FELLOW; I'VE HUNTED THE COUNTY FOR 'EM; THEY'VE RAISED ME A STATUE, AND I BUILT 'EM A LIGHT-HOUSE. THERE'S NO COMPENSATION FOR DISTURBANCE! AND——*WHERE AM I NOW?*"

This cartoon appeared in *Punch* magazine on 13 December 1884.

(ii) The first-past-the-post electoral system distorts the majorities of winning parties. During the 1880s and 1890s, this worked in favour of the Conservatives and against the Liberals. In 1900, for example, the Conservatives and Liberal Unionists (the group which split from the Liberal Party over Home Rule in 1886 and then worked closely with the Conservatives) secured 50.3% of the vote for 402 seats while the Liberals secured 45.0% for their 183. The reform measures of the 1880s also worked in favour of the Conservatives. It has been estimated, for example, that, at any one time, over 1 million men did not appear on the electoral register because their changes of jobs or residence meant they could not meet the 12-month residence qualification. It would be safe to assume that the majority would not have voted Conservative. On the other hand, those higher up the social scale benefited from plural votes. At least 7% of voters had more than one vote and the majority voted Conservative. In addition, the Conservatives gained considerably from the 1885 Redistribution Act since single-member constituencies allowed them to make inroads into Liberal-held boroughs. The Conservative Party also changed its character as the middle classes gained greater influence. MPs with a background in industry and the professions increased significantly between 1868 and 1900, while landed Tory MPs declined. This helped the party to appeal to those who had reluctantly voted Liberal because they considered the Conservative Party to be dominated by the landed gentry.

Adapted from Lee 1994.

ITEM 4 The impact on the Liberal Party

(i) The Liberal Party developed along similar lines to the Conservative Party. The National Liberal Federation (NLF) remained loyal to Gladstone when the party split over Home Rule in 1886. Francis Schnadhorst then combined the posts of Secretary of the NLF and of the Liberal Central Office. Until his retirement in 1894, he did much to bring Liberal central and local organisations closer together. At the same time, the split in 1886 removed many of the Whigs, allowing radicalism to flourish. This was reflected in the growing attempt by the NLF to formulate and commit the leadership to a definite programme. The result was the 'Newcastle Programme' of 1891 - a list of measures which the NLF wanted the next Liberal government to implement. When a minority Liberal government came to power in 1892 (Gladstone's fourth administration), it did legislate on

The issue of reform united the Liberal Party in 1884-85, but afterwards divisions arose about the direction the party should take. This cartoon shows Liberal MPs hunting for new policies. Gladstone is on the horse in the foreground. The hounds have the faces of prominent Liberal MPs.

some of the proposals in the Newcastle Programme. But, Gladstone finally retired in 1894 and his successor, Rosebery, denounced and dropped the programme, even blaming it for the downfall of the government in 1895. For the remainder of the 19th century, while altering the rules of the NLF to give it the pretence of greater power, the Liberal leadership secured its control over the party.

Adapted from Adelman 1997.

(ii) The most distinctive feature of the internal development of the Liberal Party after the split over Home Rule in 1886 was the growth of influence within the party of the NLF whose offices moved to London (from Birmingham) in October 1886. Having given important support to Gladstone against Chamberlain in 1886, the NLF saw itself as a power to be reckoned with. This trend culminated in the declaration of the Newcastle Programme - a bold attempt to commit the Liberal Party to a designated plan of reform proposed and supported by the grass-roots of the party and constructed with an eye on electoral advantage. The tone of the programme and its apparent acceptance by the party leadership suggested that Gladstone's personal obsession with Home Rule had not restricted the instincts of the party for domestic reform. Never before in British politics had the lower ranks of an organised political party claimed such a positive role in decision making, with such apparently effective results. Significantly, however, Gladstone himself never fully endorsed the Newcastle Programme. Lack of progress in 1892-95 and then defeat in the general election of 1895 marked a watershed in the development of the Liberal Party. The defeat marked the beginning of a reaction against the power of the NLF. By 1898, the NLF was ready to accept that it did not have any claim to be the policy-making centre of the party. Its resolutions recognised that the NLF was not 'to interfere with the time or order in which questions are taken up'. Similarly, the NLF agreed that its relationship with the official leadership was purely advisory. There were no more 'omnibus' resolutions proposing specific measures for a Liberal government to undertake. The heyday of the Caucus was over.

Adapted from Cook 1998.

Questions

1. a) Using Items 1-4, describe the impact of the electoral reforms of 1884-85 on the two main parties.
   b) What evidence is there to suggest that the Conservatives benefited from the changes more than the Liberals?
2. a) Using Items 2 and 4, describe the way in which the main parties responded to the electoral reforms

   of 1884-85.
   b) Why did they respond in this way?
3. a) Explain the political context in which the cartoon in Item 3 was drawn.
   b) How did the electoral system in operation after the passing of the 1885 Redistribution Act differ from that in operation in 1867?

References

- **Adelman (1985)** Adelman, P., 'The Peers versus the People', *History Today*, Vol.35, February 1985.

- **Adelman (1997)** Adelman, P., *Gladstone, Disraeli and Later Victorian Politics* (3rd edn), Longman, 1997.

- **Biagini (1994)** Biagini, E.F., 'Liberalism and the new electorate after 1867', *History Review*, No.19, September 1994.

- **Catterall (1994)** Catterall, P. (ed.), *Britain 1815-1867*, Heinemann, 1994.

- **Cook (1998)** Cook, C., *A Short History of the Liberal Party 1900-1997* (5th edn), Macmillan, 1998.

- **Cook & Stevenson (1996)** Cook, C. & Stevenson, J., *The Longman Handbook of Modern British History 1714-1995* (3rd edn), Longman, 1996.

- **Craig (1989)** Craig, F.W.S., *British Electoral Facts 1832-1987*, Gower Publishing Ltd, 1989.

- **Cunningham (1994)** Cunningham, H., 'The nature of Chartism' in *Catterall (1994)*.

- **Dunbabin (1988)** Dunbabin, J.P.D., 'Electoral reforms and their outcome in the United Kingdom 1865-1900' in *Gourvish & O'Day (1988)*.

- **Evans (1996)** Evans, E., *The Forging of the Modern State: Early Industrial Britain 1783-1870*, Longman, 1996.

- **Feuchtwanger (1985)** Feuchtwanger, E.J., *Democracy and Empire: Britain 1865-1914*, Arnold, 1985.

- **Garrard (1988)** Garrard, J., 'Parties, members and votes after 1867' in *Gourvish & O'Day (1988)*.

- **Garrard (1991)** Garrard, J., 'Educating the masters: urban political parties and the new voters after 1867', *History Sixth*, No.9, March 1991.

- **Gash (1976)** Gash, N., *Peel*, Longman, 1976.

- **Gourvish & O'Day (1988)** Gourvish, T.R. & O'Day, A. (eds), *Later Victorian Britain 1867-1900*, Macmillan, 1988.

- **Harrison (1965)** Harrison, R.J., *Before the Socialists: Studies in Labour and Politics 1861-88*, Macmillan, 1965.

- **Hoppen (1996)** Hoppen, K.T., 'Roads to democracy: electioneering and corruption in 19th century England and Ireland', *History*, Vol.81, 1996.

- **Jenkins (1995)** Jenkins, R., *Gladstone*, Macmillan, 1995.

- **Lang (1999)** Lang, S., *Parliamentary Reform 1785-1928*, Routledge, 1999.

- **Lee (1994)** Lee, S.J., *British Political History 1815-1914*, Routledge, 1994.

- **Machin (1995)** Machin, I., *Disraeli*, Longman, 1995.

- **McCord (1991)** McCord, N., *British History 1815-1906*, Oxford University Press, 1991.

- **O'Gorman (1989)** O'Gorman, F., *Voters, Patrons and Parties: the Unreformed Electoral System of Hanoverian England 1734-1832*, Oxford University Press, 1989.

- **O'Gorman (1997)** O'Gorman, F., *The Long Eighteenth Century: British Political and Social History 1688-1832*, Arnold, 1997.

- **O'Leary (1962)** O'Leary, C., *The Elimination of Corrupt Practices in British Elections 1868-1911*, Oxford University Press, 1962

- **OU (1987)** Open University, *The Representation of the People: Town and Country*, A102, Units 27-30, Open University Press, 1987.

- **Pearce & Stewart (1992)** Pearce, M. & Stewart, G., *British Political History 1867-1900: Democracy and Decline*, Routledge, 1992.

- **Pearce & Stearn (1994)** Pearce, R. & Stearn, R., *Government and Reform 1815-1918*, Hodder & Stoughton, 1994.

- **Purdue (1987)** Purdue, B., 'The passing of the Reform Act of 1867' in *OU (1987)*.

- **Royle (1996)** Royle, E., *Chartism* (3rd edn), Longman Seminar Studies, 1996.

- **Stewart (1989)** Stewart, R., *Party and Politics, 1830-52*, Macmillan, 1989.

- **Thompson (1984)** Thompson, D., *The Chartists: Popular Politics in the Industrial Revolution*, Aldershot, 1984.

- **Walton (1983)** Walton, J.K., *The Second Reform Act*, Routledge, 1983.

- **Willis (1999)** Willis, M., *Democracy and the State 1830-1945*, Cambridge University Press, 1999.

UNIT 3 Votes for women to 1914

Timeline - Votes for women to 1914

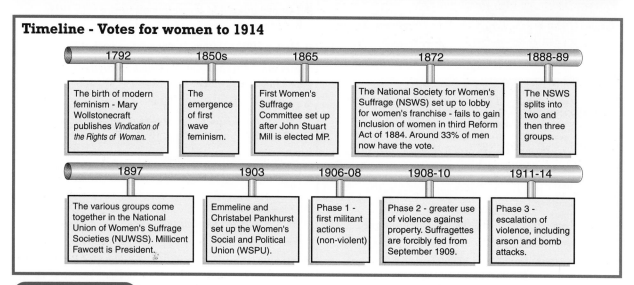

1792	1850s	1865	1872	1888-89
The birth of modern feminism - Mary Wollstonecraft publishes *Vindication of the Rights of Woman*.	The emergence of first wave feminism.	First Women's Suffrage Committee set up after John Stuart Mill is elected MP.	The National Society for Women's Suffrage (NSWS) set up to lobby for women's franchise - fails to gain inclusion of women in third Reform Act of 1884. Around 33% of men now have the vote.	The NSWS splits into two and then three groups.

1897	1903	1906-08	1908-10	1911-14
The various groups come together in the National Union of Women's Suffrage Societies (NUWSS). Millicent Fawcett is President.	Emmeline and Christabel Pankhurst set up the Women's Social and Political Union (WSPU).	Phase 1 - first militant actions (non-violent)	Phase 2 - greater use of violence against property. Suffragettes are forcibly fed from September 1909.	Phase 3 - escalation of violence, including arson and bomb attacks.

Introduction

Before the 1960s, most historians focused almost exclusively on the actions of men. For example, a standard school textbook in use from the mid-1920s to the 1950s was G.M. Trevelyan's *History of England* (first published in 1926). The 1952 edition covered English history from prehistoric times to 1919 in 732 pages. Of these 732 pages, just six pages contain references to women's position in society. For Trevelyan, history was about high politics, war and 'big' events. Because women were mainly excluded from high politics, war and 'big' events, they hardly featured. Since the emergence of a 'second wave' of feminism in the 1960s, however, historians have begun to reassess women's place in the past (feminism is a political theory which suggests that women should have the same rights and opportunities as men). Feminist historians believe that gender is an important, if not the most important, factor in explaining historical developments. By starting from this viewpoint, they have shed new light on old historical issues as well as examining new areas that historians had previously neglected.

One area of particular concern to second wave feminist historians is the emergence and development of first wave feminism, a development which occurred in the middle of the 19th century. It was out of the non-militant campaigns of mainly upper- and middle-class first wave feminists in the second part of the 19th century that the militant campaign for women's suffrage developed in the early part of the 20th century. But, were the militant campaigners for women's suffrage (the so-called 'suffragettes') right to justify their militant campaign by arguing that 40 years of non-militant campaigning had achieved nothing?

This unit examines the debate surrounding that central question and then goes on to look at the structure and organisation of the main militant organisation - the Women's Social and Political Union (WSPU) - the way in which the militant campaign evolved and reactions to the campaign for women's suffrage among different political and social groups. The impact of the First World War on the campaign for women's suffrage is examined in Unit 8.

UNIT SUMMARY

Part 1 looks at the position of women in the mid-19th century. It then goes on to explore the emergence of first wave feminism in the period c1850-80.

Part 2 examines the development of the campaign in support of women's suffrage in the period c1865-1903.

Part 3 focuses on the Pankhurst family and the Women's Social and Political Union (WSPU). In particular, it considers why militant tactics were adopted and what forms militancy took.

Part 4 analyses the reactions to the campaign for women's suffrage among political and social groups in the period 1903-14.

1 The emergence of first wave feminism

Key questions

1. What was the position of women in the mid-19th century?

2. Why did a women's movement emerge in the 1850s?

1.1 The position of women in the mid-19th century

The birth of feminism

The term 'feminism' was not coined until the 1890s and was not used widely until the First World War. But, that does not mean that feminism did not exist before the 1890s. Indeed, feminist ideas can be traced back to at least the 17th century. Most historians, however, follow Ray Strachey who argued in 1928 that the year 1792 marked the birth of feminism in Britain (Strachey's book was republished in 1979):

'The real date for the beginning of the [women's] movement is 1792. In that year, Mary Wollstonecraft, inspired by thoughts of "Liberty, Equality and Fraternity", wrote and published her great book *A Vindication of the Rights of Woman*. In this book, the whole extent of the feminist ideal is set out and the whole claim for equal human rights is made; and, although at the time it was little noticed, it has remained the text of the movement ever since.' (Strachey 1979, p.12)

Mary Wollstonecraft argued that women should have the same rights as men. Although her writing never gained a popular following, it continued to be central to all the criticisms of male domination that were made in the 19th century.

Women's legal position

Before 1850, political rights and individual rights more generally were allowed only to men from the wealthier sections of society. The basis for these rights was the individual's claim to have 'reason'. Women, it was thought, were incapable of rational thought. From the mid-18th century, women belonging to the wealthier sections of society were increasingly excluded from the public world of . work, political debate and economics and expected to behave as 'ladies' (ie to be respectable, refined, beautiful and above reproach):

'According to one estimate, in early 18th century London no fewer than a third of all women of property ran some sort of business. That figure declined steeply in subsequent decades... Increasingly women were found to lack the professional training and other forms of specialised knowledge required...Prospering merchants and retailers tended to move their homes away from their place of work, leaving their wives (and often their daughters) to play domestic roles.' (O'Gorman 1997, p.347)

Women's lack of legal rights

Before 1850, women, especially married women, had few legal rights. May notes that:

'When Queen Victoria came to the throne [in 1837] all women, of whatever class were subject to laws which put them on a par with male criminals, lunatics and minors. Under the Common Law, a married woman had no identity apart from that of her husband...A husband assumed legal possession or control of all property that belonged to his wife upon marriage and of any property that might come to her during marriage. The law distinguished between real property (mainly freehold land) which the husband could not dispose of without his wife's permission (although he could control it and its income) and personal property which passed into his absolute possession and which he could dispose of in any way he chose.' (May 1996, p.284)

It was not just property that men gained on marriage. Under the law, they also gained considerable power over their wife:

'Husbands had the right to decide where to live and how to live, they were legally entitled to, and sometimes did, beat their wives and could, and sometimes did, lock them up. Once divorced, husbands gained custody of all children.' (Bartley 1996, p.11)

The doctrine of coverture

In legal terms, the position of women was defined by the 'doctrine of coverture'. This was the doctrine that:

'The legal existence of a woman is suspended during marriage, or at least incorporated and consolidated into that of the husband, under whose wing, protection and coverage she performs everything.' (Bolt 2000, p.39)

One of the few advantages this legal status brought married women was that they could not be sued. As a result, husbands were liable for any debts built up by their wives, even if they were built up without the knowledge of the husband. In addition, since husband and wife were one body under the law, a wife could not be convicted of stealing from her husband or of destroying his property.

'Angel in the House'

With some notable exceptions, the Victorian upper- and middle-class male's ideal of womanhood was that of the 'Angel in the House' (the title of a poem by Coventry Patmore which was published in 1854).

Men and women were seen to occupy separate spheres of activity - public for men and domestic for women:

'The public world of politics, the market and the workplace was the location of rough, competitive male activities, while the private world of home and family encapsulated the Christian virtues and the morality of personal relationships.' (Thompson 1993, p.8)

A typical account of the way in which middle-class men viewed women can be found in Box 3.1. It is important to note that the ideal woman was a married woman. Single women, especially older single women, could not meet the ideal.

BOX 3.1 Men and women in the mid-19th century

Source Box

The separate character of men and women are these. The man's power is active, progressive, defensive. He is the doer, the creator, the discoverer, the defender. His intellect is for speculation and invention; his energy for adventure, for war, and for conquest. But the woman's power is for rule, not battle - and her intellect is not for invention or creation, but for sweet ordering, arrangement and decision. Her great function is praise. By her office and place, she is protected from all danger and temptation. The man, in his rough work in the open world, must encounter all peril and trial. He guards the woman from all this; within his house, as ruled by her, need enter no danger, no temptation. This is the true nature of the home - it is the place of peace, the shelter from all terror, doubt and division. Within the home, the woman is the centre of order, the balm of distress.

This account appeared in 'Sesame and Lilies' by John Ruskin, published in 1865. Ruskin was a leading art critic, writer and socialist.

Married women were not entirely confined to their homes. They were allowed to take on (unpaid) work with charitable or religious organisations. But, the basic role of women was seen as a domestic one. In other words, married women should be, and should be seen to be, 'leisured'.

Did women accept this division of life?

How far women accepted this division of life into two spheres is difficult to assess. Some women clearly did accept the notion:

'By the middle years of the century, there seems to have been a remarkable degree of acceptance of the separate spheres ideology among all strata of the upper classes, at least until the emergence in the last decades of the "new woman".' (Thompson 1993, pp.8-9)

But, there were always strong-minded women who did not accept this view even among the upper classes:

'There were those, bolder or more fortunate,

pushed out into the fray. They carried with them the early Victorian flavour - it was in black silk gowns, corsets, crinolines and elastic-sided boots that these intrepid ladies began to turn society inside out.' (Strachey 1979, p.80)

Single women

In the mid-19th century, there was a rapid growth in the number of single women. May (1996) records that the number of single women between the ages of 15 and 45 rose by 72% - from 2.76 million to 3.29 million - in the 20 years between 1851 and 1871 with the result that:

'For every three women over 20 who were wives, there were two who were widows or who had never married.' (May 1995, p.290)

May suggests that there were three main reasons for this. First, more males died at birth or in childhood than females. Second, more men emigrated than women (over 100,000 men in 1861, for example, compared to 40,000 women). And third, men married later than they had in the past.

The 'surplus women problem', May argues, was a particular problem for the middle class because, in middle-class eyes, a single woman was a woman who had not fulfilled her proper role in life as wife and mother. For single middle-class women, there were few paid jobs that were 'respectable'. Teaching was one possibility and many single women worked as teachers or governesses and some even set up their own schools. Most teaching posts, however, were poorly paid and work as a governess might mean a loss of social status. Many single middle-class women ended up living with married relatives:

'Unmarried women were marginalised in Victorian and Edwardian England and often faced an isolated and somewhat lonely existence in the households of a relative where they were expected to help with the management of the household.' (Bartley 1996, p.9)

Working-class women in the mid-19th century

In recent years, many historians have concentrated less on 'intrepid ladies' and have begun to uncover a broader picture of women's history. Working-class women had to serve both as homemakers and contributors to the family income. As a result, the lives of the majority of women in the 19th and early 20th century remained limited by economic circumstances.

D'Cruze points out that running a home in the mid-19th century was a difficult job in itself:

'In the 19th century, domestic work was arduous, physically demanding and time consuming. This was true whether it was done by servants in a middle-class or upper-class household or by wives, mothers and daughters without cash payment in working-class or lower middle-class homes.'

(D'Cruze 1995, p.66)

Bartley (1996) points out that, throughout the 19th century, many houses were without running water and cooking was done on an open fire. Cleaning products were expensive and less efficient than they are today. The washing of clothes was often done communally in the local stream.

Working-class women and separate spheres

There is a debate among historians about the extent to which the ideology of separate spheres applied to working-class women. Thompson, for example, argues that:

'The ideology of separate spheres was very much that of an influential section of middle-class opinion. The option of so dividing their lives was rarely open to working people. (Thompson 1993, p.8)

Behagg, on the other hand, argues that the ideology applied equally to working-class women:

'In fact, domestic ideology defined the boundaries of all women's lives, irrespective of class. For the working-class woman it meant that her role as a wage earner was seen as subsidiary to that of a man's. Employers argued that women in the workplace had stepped outside their "proper sphere" and were therefore simply transitory [temporary] workers on their way to fulfilling their true destinies as wives and mothers. As such it was perfectly legitimate to pay them less than men. They were also excluded from certain jobs that were considered unfit for women.' (Behagg 1995, pp.208-09)

Clark points out that when, in the 1820s, men who worked as mule spinners began to earn high wages, their wives stopped going to work:

'Mule spinners adopted the breadwinner ideal as early as the 1820s when high wages enabled them to keep their wives at home instead of sending them to the factories.' (Clark 1995, p.20)

The 1842 Mines Act and Factory Acts

The 1842 Mines Act was the first piece of legislation to regulate women's work. The Act had severe long-term effects on the position of women economically and socially. By viewing women in a similar way as children, it, in effect, classified them as minors - dependents who were incapable of looking after themselves - rather than as mature adults. Later regulatory legislation (for example, the Factory Act of 1844) continued to classify women in this way. This may have helped to spark the growth of feminism in the 1850s.

1.2 Why did a women's movement emerge in the 1850s?

The emergence of 'first wave feminism'

Most historians agree that it was in the 1850s that 'first wave feminism' emerged. It was in that decade that a small number of mainly upper- and middle-class women began to rebel against their exclusion from the public sphere and to campaign for greater equality with men. Between 1850 and 1880, a number of significant battles were fought and won on issues of concern to female activists. Before the 1880s, however, the focus was not on winning the vote:

'The demand for parliamentary suffrage was only one of a range of campaigns. Some of these sought access to the public sphere, which was clearly defined as "the universities, the professions, central and local government". Others aimed to improve women's legal and economic position within marriage...These varied campaigns were seen by contemporaries as forming a women's (or a women's rights) movement that was particularly active between the late 1850s and the 1880s.' (Hannam 1995, p.220)

Not all historians agree that it is accurate to talk about a 'women's movement' in the period 1850-80, however. Bassnett, for example, points out that the women involved in the various campaigns focused on single issues and some did not necessarily support feminism (ie they did not believe that they should have the same rights and opportunities as men):

'They were individualists, often individualists who rejected any [connections] with feminism, who used their class position to exert influence on the system.' (Bassnett 1986, pp.145-6)

Bassnett does concede, however, that, alongside the individualist tradition, feminism was developing and feminist activity was beginning to take place.

What led to first wave feminism?

Historians have suggested a number of reasons why first wave feminism emerged in the 1850s. Alexander (1994) argues that the key was the growth of a 'sense of grievance'. This, she argues, was stimulated by a number of factors. These are outlined in Box 3.2.

BOX 3.2 The emergence of first wave feminism

Interpretation

The following factors help to explain the emergence of first wave feminism:

- resentment at the 1832 Reform Act which prevented women from voting
- disappointment at the failure of Chartism
- concern about the 'surplus women problem'
- frustration at the lack of educational and work opportunities
- a growing awareness of the lack of legal rights
- a realisation that Parliament could be pressured into passing reforms (eg the 1842 Mines Act)
- the support of some men (especially the fathers of a number of leading early feminists who ensured their daughters were unusually well-educated and had a social conscience).

Adapted from Alexander (1994).

Pugh (1994) claims that it was the debates over divorce reform in the mid-1850s which were the main stimulus. May (1996) suggests that Caroline Norton's campaigning in the 1830s (see below) inspired other women to set up their own campaigns. Bedarida (1991) argues that the emergence of the women's movement was a response to social changes stimulated by industrialisation.

Caroline Norton's campaign

In the 1830s, married women's lack of legal rights was drawn to public attention by the case of Caroline Norton, a rich upper-class woman who had married a barrister, but then separated from him. After the separation, Caroline's husband, Richard, took their three children away from Caroline and refused to let her see them. He refused to give Caroline an allowance and took away from her any money that she earned from writing. He also sued the Prime Minister, Lord Melbourne, for 'criminal conversation' (adultery) with his wife:

'As wives were considered the property of their husbands, jealous spouses were able to sue other men for trespass. By committing adultery, defendants had used the body of a wife and had thus damaged the property of husbands.' (Bartley 1996, p.15)

Although Richard Norton's court action was unsuccessful, Caroline was unable to defend herself:

'For she found that in this trial which concerned her honour and her good name, she had no standing at all. Being a married woman, she could neither sue nor be sued and could not be represented by counsel in the trial. Legally, it was no affair of hers, for legally she could have no affairs, if she was a virtuous and a married woman.' (Strachey 1979, p.35)

After the trial, Caroline Norton embarked on a campaign to improve women's legal status. She wrote pamphlets and lobbied MPs and peers. Largely as a result of her efforts, the Infants' Custody Act was passed in 1839. This allowed divorced or separated women access to their children up to the age of seven, provided they had an 'unblemished character'.

The Marriage and Divorce Act, 1857

Caroline Norton also played a part in the passage of the Marriage and Divorce Act in 1857. This Act abolished the need for a private Act of Parliament to obtain a divorce and set up a civil divorce court with the authority to grant judicial separations and divorces. Also, women were permitted to sue for divorce if they could prove two of three charges - cruelty, desertion or adultery (men had to prove one charge). Caroline Norton suggested an amendment that women who separated from their husbands should resume possession of their own property and be able to keep their future inheritance and earnings (the amendment was taken up by an MP and passed).

While some historians have claimed that this Act was a turning point in legal history, Bartley points out that:

'This reform did not introduce any new principles of divorce but just altered the way in which the law was administered as it really only benefited wealthy men and continued to reflect the gender and class inequalities of 19th century England.' (Bartley 1996, p.16)

The Married Women's Property Act of 1870

Strachey (1979, p.72) records that, as early as 1854, Barbara Leigh Smith (a cousin of Florence Nightingale and the daughter of an 'enlightened' radical MP) began a campaign to change the laws on property. Her first steps were to write a pamphlet which made the case for a change in the law and to set up the 'first regular feminist committee'. The ideas in the pamphlet were taken up by the Law Amendment Society, a petition containing 26,000 signatures was presented to Parliament, and a Bill was drawn up proposing that married women be given property rights. The Bill, however, was withdrawn in favour of the Marriage and Divorce Bill (see above). Following this, it was not until the second Reform Act had been passed in 1867 that the law was changed.

The 1870 Married Women's Property Act (MWPA) allowed married women to keep up to £200 in earnings and personal property. The Act, therefore, was a move away from the idea that married women were simply the property of their husband. The reasons why this law was passed and its importance are outlined in Box 3.3.

BOX 3.3 Why the MWPA was passed and its importance

Interpretation

There were three main reasons why the MWPA was passed. First, cases like that of Caroline Norton had shown that the law was unsatisfactory and there was support for reform. Second, Parliament was under pressure for reform (from feminist groups and their male supporters). And third, many Liberal MPs supported the MWPA because they believed it might compensate for not giving women the vote - they believed women wanted the vote to press MPs into changing the property laws. Once the property laws had been rationalised in favour of all women, it was thought that the demand for women's suffrage might disappear. The Act gave women greater independence and modified the marriage relationship. But, it reflected rather than promoted changes in women's position. It was passed at a time when women were beginning to make inroads into the masculine world of work and politics. This gave them the confidence to demand more equal treatment in law.

Adapted from Bartley 1996

The second MWPA, 1882

The 1870 Act was followed in 1882 by a second Married Women's Property Act. This gave married women control of all money and property they brought into a marriage and allowed them to carry on trade and business using their property. Despite this, the 'doctrine of coverture' continued to exist:

'The campaign to secure for married women control over their property and earnings did achieve important victories in 1870 and 1882; but it was hard fought and...with regard to property rights, full equality between married and single women was achieved only in 1935.' (Bolt 2000, p.39)

The Langham Place Group

It was noted above that, during the period 1850-80, feminists began to fight battles on many fronts. It was during this period that significant reforms or breakthroughs were made in the following areas:

- education
- local government
- the medical profession
- sexual morality.

Much of the work in these areas was pioneered by women associated with the 'Langham Place Group'. This group, which developed out of Barbara Leigh Smith's campaign for married women's property rights, met in Langham Place in London:

'The ladies of Langham Place in the late 1850s set up a reading room, an employment register, an emigration society and housed the Society for the Promotion of Women's Employment and a school for industrial training (as clerks, cashiers and book-keepers) as well as the *English Women's Journal*. Limited, financially pressed, sustained through determination and private donation and always fraught with internal political and personal conflict, Langham Place women strove for knowledge, for enlightenment, for the transformation of women's lives through work.' (Alexander 1994, p.139)

Apart from Barbara Leigh Smith, the women associated with Langham Place included Emily Davies, Elizabeth Garrett, Dorothea Beale and Frances Buss - all of whom made important breakthroughs in their chosen fields (see below).

1. Education

Education was an area of particular concern to feminists in the mid-19th century since there were few educational opportunities for girls, especially in secondary and higher education. Between 1850 and 1880, a number of significant advances were made, though it should be emphasised that these advances mainly benefited a small number of upper- and middle-class girls. The mass of working-class girls continued only to have access to a basic elementary education. Following the passage of the 1870 Education Act, working-class girls did gain access to schools in all parts of the country (before, they did

not). But, Bartley points out that:

'Gender divisions were fundamental after 1870 when newly-built Board Schools offered a different curriculum to girls and boys.' (Bartley 1996, p.29)

Secondary and higher education

In the mid-19th century, the ideology of separate spheres ensured that very few girls received an academic education:

'It was believed that too much education could result in infertility through overstraining the delicate female constitution.' (McDermid 1995, p.108)

The work of three pioneers helped to change this attitude. First, in 1850, Frances Mary Buss opened the North London Collegiate School. This offered girls a broader secondary education than other schools (and made students take the equivalent of GCSEs),while simultaneously encouraging 'ladylike' behaviour. It became the model which other schools followed. Second, when Dorothea Beale became head teacher at Cheltenham Ladies College, she transformed the curriculum, introducing subjects such as Latin which previously were considered only to be suitable for boys and placing great emphasis on exam results. Other exclusive girls schools followed Beale's example. For example, when Roedean was set up in 1885, it set very high academic standards. And third, Emily Davies successfully campaigned for women to be able to take the Oxford and Cambridge University local and entrance examinations and, in 1869, she set up a women's college at Hitchen. In 1873, she moved this college to Girton, near Cambridge, and, although the University did not allow students to take degrees, it allowed them to sit the same examinations as male students sat.

2. Local government

Positions in local government were considered to be suitable for women:

'Positions in local government (on School Boards, as Poor Law Guardians or as local councillors) could be interpreted as an extension of women's familial caring role and remained less prestigious than similar work done by men.' (D'Cruze 1995, p.72)

But, it was only in 1875 that the first woman served as a Poor Law Guardian (even though women had been eligible to hold such a post since 1834) and it was only in the 1890s that legislation was passed allowing women to serve as councillors (the 1894 Local Government Act). Nevertheless, in 1869, single and widowed women who paid rates were given the right to vote in local elections (married women were excluded until the 1894 Local Government Act was passed) and there is evidence that women became increasingly active in local politics. By 1900, for example, there were c.1,000 female Poor Law Guardians.

3. The medical profession

Following her work tending wounded soldiers in the Crimean War (1853-56), Florence Nightingale transformed the image and practice of nursing in Britain. In 1860, she set up a training college for nurses and introduced professional practices. By the end of the century, nursing throughout Britain had been reformed along the lines she laid down.

While it was acceptable for women to be nurses, the assumption, until the 1850s, was that doctors should be men. This assumption was first challenged by Elizabeth Blackwell. She was born in Bristol, but brought up in the USA and gained a medical degree there. She returned to Britain to complete her studies and, early in 1859, her name was placed on the British Medical Register. In March 1859, Elizabeth Blackwell gave a lecture on the suitability of the medical profession for women. This struck such a chord with one member of the audience, Elizabeth Garrett, that she decided she would do all she could to qualify as a doctor herself. Elizabeth Garrett Anderson (as she became after her marriage) did become the first woman to qualify in Britain as a doctor, but she had to overcome a great many obstacles, as Box 3.4 suggests.

Elizabeth Garrett Anderson's success, however, was followed by a backlash. British medical schools either refused to accept female medical students or, in the case of Edinburgh (where five female medical students were admitted), placed great obstacles in their way. In 1875, however, an Act of Parliament was passed making it lawful for universities to accept female students and several medical schools opened their doors to women for the first time.

4. Sexual morality

In 1864, 1866 and 1869, Parliament passed three Contagious Diseases Acts which gave police and magistrates in military and naval bases the power to order any woman suspected of having venereal disease to be medically inspected, by force if necessary. There were no provisions making the same demands of men who might have venereal disease. According to Trevor Fisher:

'The government saw the Acts as a step towards

BOX 3.4 **The obstacles faced by Elizabeth Garrett**

When in 1860, Miss Garrett desired to enter the profession, she applied for admission to one college and school after another, but with no success, until at last she discovered that the Company of Apothecaries were unable to refuse to examine any candidate who complied with their conditions. She accordingly went through a five year apprenticeship, attended all the needful lectures and passed all the prescribed examinations and, at length received the licence to practice, in virtue of which she was admitted to the [medical] register. In order, however, to observe the regulations of Apothecaries' Hall, she was obliged to attend the lectures of certain specified teachers. In some cases she was admitted to ordinary classes, but in others she was compelled to pay very heavy fees for separate and private tuition.
Part of an account written in 1873 by Sophie Jex-Blake, the first woman doctor to practise in Scotland, and quoted in McDermid 1995.

maintaining military efficiency in the teeth of a worrying venereal epidemic.' (Fisher 1996, p.33) The passage of the 1869 Act sparked the formation of the Ladies' National Association (LNA) to campaign against the Acts. The LNA launched its campaign in 1870 under the leadership of Josephine Butler who was from a Liberal upper-class family and related to the former Prime Minister Lord Grey. Butler and the LNA campaigned for 17 years and were finally successful in 1886. Fisher argues that Butler has been 'feminism's neglected pioneer', claiming that:

'Josephine Butler fundamentally changed the terms of women's political lives. She not only challenged the Victorian taboo that sexual matters were unmentionable, but, by taking a dominant role in a major pressure group, permanently destroyed the notion that women could not take a leading part in politics.' (Fisher 1996, p.32)

MAIN POINTS - Part 1

- The Victorian middle-class male's ideal of womanhood was that of the 'Angel in the House'. Men and women were seen to occupy separate spheres of activity - public for men and domestic for women.
- Most historians agree that it was in the 1850s that 'first wave feminism' emerged. Groups of women (mainly upper- and middle-class women) began to rebel against their exclusion from the public sphere and to campaign for greater equality with men.
- Reasons for the emergence of first wave feminism in

the 1850s include - (1) the growth of a sense of grievance (2) the debate over divorce (3) reaction to the case of Caroline Norton and (4) changes resulting from industrialisation.
- Between 1850-80, women's legal position changed. The key laws were the 1857 Marriage and Divorce Act and the 1870 Married Women's Property Act.
- Significant reforms or breakthroughs were made in the following areas in 1850-80 - (1) education (2) local government (3) the medical profession and (4) sexual morality.

Activity 3.1 Feminism 1850-80

ITEM 1 The legal position of women

His latest purchase.

This picture was produced in the 1890s. It was painted by Martin Anderson (also known as 'Cynicus'). Anderson (1854-1932) was born in Scotland and moved to London in 1891. He opened a studio in Drury Lane, selling satirical pictures, postcards and books.

ITEM 2 The background of early first wave feminists

The feminists who emerged in the period 1850 and 1880 generally came from a privileged background and they were usually well-educated. Many had experienced a religious crisis during their adolescence. Many came from non-conformist families (non-conformists were Protestants who did not belong to the Church of England). In particular, many came from Unitarian reforming families (there was a long tradition of Unitarians being involoved in radical causes). Many were brought up in an environment where there was support for political reform. The new religions of the age challenged orthodox Christianity's claim to truth. Identification with these religions enabled women to break out of silence and submission. It also added a keen sense of the suffering and oppression of other peoples and the duty of the educated to help others. Barbara Leigh Smith Bodichon (as she became after she was married), for example, was brought up in a radical household. Her father gave her an allowance of £300 a year when she came of age. The roots of her radicalism lay in her education in family and school and also in her parental history. She was an illegitimate child and only her father's affection and honour stood between her and being cast out or reduced to poverty. Other feminists admired and identified with those fathers who had supported their education and instilled in them a need for social reform. Josephine Butler, for example, wrote: 'My father was a man with a deeply rooted fiery hatred of all injustice. The love of justice was a passion with him. Probably, I have inherited from him this passion'.

Adapted from Alexander 1994.

ITEM 3 Women and education

THE HIGHER EDUCATION OF WOMEN.
Dora (consulting a Playbill). "ONLY FANCY! 'AS YOU LIKE IT' IS BY SHAKSPEARE!"

This cartoon was published in *Punch* magazine in 1885. The cartoonist was George du Maurier (1834-96).

ITEM 4 Women doctors

THE COMING RACE.   1872.

Dr. Evangeline. ⬜BY THE BYE, MR. SAWYER, ARE YOU ENGAGED
TO-MORROW AFTERNOON? I HAVE RATHER A TICKLISH
OPERATION TO PERFORM - AN AMPUTATION, YOU KNOW⬜
Mr. Sawyer. ⬜I SHALL BE VERY HAPPY TO DO IT FOR YOU.⬜
Doctor Evangeline. ⬜O, NO, NOT THAT! BUT WILL YOU KINDLY
COME AND ADMINISTER THE CHLOROFORM FOR ME?⬜

This cartoon was published in *Punch* magazine. The cartoonist was George du
Maurier. Du Maurier had a French father and English mother. He settled in
London in 1860 and joined *Punch*'s staff in 1864.

Questions

1. a) Take Items 1, 3 and 4 and
   explain what point is being
   made in each.
   b) What does each cartoon tell
   us about changes that had taken
   place in the position of women.
   c) What does each cartoon tell
   us about attitudes towards the
   women's movement?
   d) Give arguments for and
   against the view that the
   position of women changed
   dramatically in the period 1850-
   80.
2. a) What do Items 1-4 tell us
   about the nature of the women's
   movement in the period 1850-
   80?
   b) Would it be correct to
   describe the women's movement
   as a 'top-down' rather than a
   'bottom- up' movement?
   Explain your answer.
3. a) What does Item 2 tell us
   about the origins of the
   women's movement?
   b) Why do you think women
   like Barbara Leigh Smith
   Bodichon developed a sense of
   grievance about the position of
   women?
   c) To what extent do you think
   the background of leading first
   wave feminists determined their
   strategy?

2 Early women's suffrage movements

Key questions

1. Why did women's suffrage come onto the
   political agenda in the 1860s?

2. What was the nature of the women's
   franchise movement 1866-80?

3. Was the period 1880-1903 one of failure
   for the suffragists?

2.1 Why did women's suffrage come onto the political agenda in the 1860s?

The first parliamentary debate
Women were not formally prohibited from voting
until the 1830s:
   'The 1832 Reform Act and the 1835 Municipal

Corporations Act stated that only men could vote,
specifically excluding women from local and
national elections.' (Willis 1999, p.13)
The first debate in the House of Commons on
women's right to vote came just after the 1832
Reform Bill had been passed. The case of a wealthy
single woman, Mary Smith, was put to the Commons
by the radical MP Henry 'Orator' Hunt. He argued
that, since Mary Smith was a single woman, she was
subject to the law but had no say in making it. As
she had sufficient property to qualify for the vote,
he asserted, and seeing that she paid taxes, she should
be allowed to vote. Hunt's arguments, however,
were dismissed.

Chartists and the vote for women
Chartism was the mass movement (the first 'working-
class' mass movement) which grew up in the late
1830s around the demands made in the six-point

'People's Charter'. The 'People's Charter', which was published in 1838, made the demands outlined in Box 3.5.

BOX 3.5 The People's Charter

The six points of the People's Charter were as follows:

1. **Universal manhood suffrage** - a vote for every man over the age of 21.
2. **A secret ballot** - to protect the voter so that employers and landlords could no longer influence voting behaviour.
3. **Annual Parliaments** - a general election every year to ensure that MPs kept in close touch with the needs and demands of their constituents.
4. **Abolition of property qualifications for MPs** - to enable representatives from the working class to stand for election.
5. **Payment of MPs** - to enable working men to give up their jobs in order to stand for election in the first place.
6. **Constituencies of equal size** - to tackle the continued problem of the under-representation of industrial areas after the 1832 Reform Act.

There is some evidence that William Lovett, one of the authors of the People's Charter, wanted to include a demand for women's suffrage in the Charter, but was persuaded to drop it on the grounds that including it would delay the implementation of the Charter as a whole.

The Chartist movement had mass support throughout the decade 1838-48. On three occasions, huge petitions were collected nationally and delivered to Parliament in the hope that the government would be pressed into implementing the Chartists' demands. On all three occasions, however, the demands of the Chartists were rejected. In 1839 and 1842, rejection was followed by an upsurge of violent protest.

The Kennington Common fiasco

In April 1848, the government provoked a confrontation with the Chartist leadership. It allowed Chartists to meet on Kennington Common, but refused them permission to march in a procession to Parliament to present the third petition. Since the Chartist leadership seemed to back down because it ordered the crowd to disperse peacefully rather than to defy the authorities, this was presented as a great triumph for the government. Although there were threats of violence and further demonstrations following the 'Kennington Common fiasco' (as the incident in April 1848 became known), the authorities managed to prevent any serious outbreaks and, after 1848, Chartism faded as a mass movement.

Chartism's social side

Chartists did not just collect petitions. There was also a social side to the movement. Chartist libraries, Chartist schools and Chartist Churches all flourished during the decade 1838-48. There was even a Chartist 'Land Plan' - a scheme to resettle industrial workers on smallholdings purchased by a Chartist land company. This, however, was not a great success. Although there were 70,000 subscribers (see Brown 1998), only 250 people were ever actually settled in new houses.

Chartist women

Traditional accounts tended to overlook women's participation in the Chartist movement. Since the publication of Dorothy Thompson's research (Thompson 1984), however, more attention has been paid to female Chartists. While historians now accept that women were involved in Chartist activity, most (for example, Thomis & Grimmett 1982 and Clark 1995) agree that the majority of women Chartists campaigned for universal manhood suffrage rather than for votes for themselves. One theory is that many women supported the Chartist movement because they believed that gaining universal male suffrage would result in higher pay and better working conditions which, in turn, would lead to better living standards. In other words, they were prepared to campaign for an extension to the male vote in the hope that the family as a whole would benefit.

Nevertheless, there is evidence that, during the years of Chartist activity, some women did argue that women should have the right to vote. Schwarzkopf notes that over 150 female radical associations are known to have been set up in the early 1840s and that:

'In June 1838, a woman weaver from Glasgow, dubbing herself a "real democrat", addressed the women of Scotland through the columns of the *Northern Star*, calling on them to join the Chartist struggle. She maintained that it was "the right of every woman to have a vote in the legislation of her country". In England, the Chartists of Ashton, considering intelligence irrespective of sex the only precondition for the right to vote, expected female suffrage to follow automatically from the enactment of the Charter. More self-consciously, Helen Macfarlane...maintained in one of her contributions to the Chartist press that granting women the franchise was the touchstone of any true democracy.' (Schwarzkopf 1991, p.90)

Similarly, McDonald (1989) notes that a Sheffield Association for Female Franchise was in existence in 1847 and that one of its members, Anne Knight, published a pamphlet that year arguing that women should be treated equally with men.

Male Chartists and women's suffrage

There is, in addition, evidence that some Chartist

men were sympathetic to the idea of women's suffrage. Thomis and Grimmett note that John Watkins spoke publicly in support of women's suffrage in April 1841, though he argued that only single women and widows should have the vote - a view supported by R.J. Richardson who published *The Rights of Women* around this time. They also point out, however, that:

'The championship of such men as Julian Harney, who believed that women should participate as fully as men in society, or Bronterre O'Brien, who believed that women had the same inherent rights as men...still left women without a substantial base of...support for their own political enfranchisement.' (Thomis & Grimmett 1982, p.134)

The Chartist legacy

Furthermore, Hannam argues that, in the long term, Chartism discouraged working-class women from becoming involved in political activity. This was because Chartist leaders promoted the traditional view that women should be dependent on men:

'Leading male Chartists encouraged and valued women's support, but the aim of the movement was to restore the traditional division of labour and sexual power between men and women in the family which, it was argued, had been disrupted by industrialisation. The ideal of a working-class family in which a male breadwinner supported his dependent wife and children, which subsequently became entrenched in the labour movement, was, therefore, encouraged by Chartism.' (Hannam 1995, p.219)

Taylor (1983) suggests that this ideal of domesticity discouraged working-class women from becoming involved when new opportunities arose for them to take part in politics in the 1880s.

John Stuart Mill's election in 1865

Following the decline in Chartist activity after 1848, the issue of parliamentary reform in general and of women's suffrage in particular died away and it was not until the mid-1860s that the issue re-emerged. A breakthrough came in 1865 when John Stuart Mill (see Box 3.6) agreed to stand for Parliament on a platform which placed women's suffrage at the top of his agenda. He refused to canvass, but made an election address which made it clear that he supported women's suffrage and intended to press for it if he was elected. According to Strachey, this was the signal for the Langham Place Group to spring into action:

'The workers of Langham Place were, of course, among the first to be active and Mme [ie Barbara Smith Leigh] Bodichon, who always proposed innovations, hired a carriage and covered it with placards, and in this carriage Emily Davies and Bessy Parkes and Isa Craig drove about Westminster, testing the novel joys of election

---

BOX 3.6 John Stuart Mill (1806-73)

Biography Box

John Stuart Mill was the son of the philosopher James Mill. His father gave him a 'hot house' education - he began to read Greek at the age of three and had studied philosophy, logic and calculus before he was 12. He later studied under the philosopher Jeremy Bentham. Mill developed a humanised version of the philosophy supported by his father and Bentham. He also believed in 'the complete equality in all legal, political, social and domestic relations which ought to exist between men and women'. When he married Harriet Taylor in 1851, Mill drew up and signed a statement voicing his opposition to 'the whole character of the marriage relation'. He described the powers it gave the husband as 'odious' and he added that 'I feel it my duty to put on record a formal protest against the existing law of marriage in so far as conferring such powers; and a solemn promise never in any case or under any circumstances to use them'. Mill believed in the extension of the franchise, a system of proportional representation and workers' involvement in decision making. In 1869, he published *The Subjection of Women*, an influential work which has been described as 'a founding text of feminism'. Mill worked as a civil servant in the India Office for most of his life. He served as an MP between 1865 and 1868. His works on political philosophy and his principled stance earned him great respect from his contemporaries.
Adapted from Gardiner & Wenborn 1995.

---

excitement. "We called it giving Mr Mills our moral support", wrote Emily, "but there was some suspicion that we might rather be doing him harm, as one of our friends told us he had heard him described as 'the man who wants to have girls in Parliament'".' (Strachey 1979, pp.102-03)

In fact, Mill was elected and, as a result, he was an MP in the run-up to the second Reform Act (for details on the run-up, see Unit 2, Part 1).

The first Women's Suffrage Committee

According to Strachey (1979), Mill's election was the catalyst for the formation, in London, of the first Women's Suffrage Committee. After Mill's election in 1865, a Ladies Discussion Society (set up by the Langham Place Group) debated the question 'Should women take part in public affairs?' and found that nearly all 50 present agreed that they should. Barbara Leigh Smith Bodichon then suggested that a suffrage society be set up, but no action was taken because Emily Davies argued that such an organisation would be taken over by 'extremists'. The following year, however, when it became clear that a Reform Bill would be put before Parliament, Bodichon approached Mill and asked him whether he would present a petition in support of female suffrage to Parliament. Mill agreed, but warned that less than 100 signatures might do more harm than good. Bodichon then formed the first Women's Suffrage Committee which, within a fortnight, had collected 1,500 signatures. Mill then presented the petition:

'Mill presented the petition on 7 June [1866] and on 17 July asked for a return of the number of women householders who would qualify if not excluded by sex. He spoke briefly and cautiously and was heard with respect...He had succeeded in this session in getting women's suffrage onto the parliamentary agenda and had avoided undue ridicule. But, the Liberal government had fallen and women's suffrage had to await new developments.' (Rendall 2000, p.59)

2.2 What was the nature of the women's franchise movement 1866-80?

The second Reform Bill

The next major development was the second Reform Bill which was put before Parliament in February 1867 (see also Unit 2, Part 1). By this time, a second Women's Suffrage Committee had been set up in Manchester. The Manchester Suffrage Committee's first Secretary was Lydia Becker (see Box 3.7). She communicated closely with the London group, organised the collection of more signatures, wrote an article putting the case for women's suffrage in the *Spectator* (a national magazine) and wrote to the Prime Minister, Benjamin Disraeli. During the debate over the Bill, several petitions supporting women's suffrage were presented to Parliament by sympathetic MPs (including Mill) and, on 20 May, Mill proposed an amendment - to substitute 'person' for 'man' in the clause which dealt with occupation qualification. This amendment was defeated by 196 votes to 73, but Rendall notes that:

'In spite of the failure of the amendment, it was pointed out in subsequent debates that in this area as in many others, the Bill had been drafted so hastily that the legal implications were unclear and it could be argued that the Act already included women. An Act of 1850...had very specifically prescribed that the term "man" should also incorporate women and that "male persons" should be used in all legislation where the intention was gender-specific. That requirement was ignored [in the second Reform Bill] and the term "man" used throughout.' (Rendall 2000, p.61)

The London committee's split, June 1867

The second Reform Bill became law in August 1867. By then, a split within the London committee in June

---

BOX 3.7 Lydia Becker (1827-90)

Biography Box

The Becker family moved from Germany to Manchester a generation before Lydia was born there in 1827. The daughter of a manufacturer, she was educated at home and in Germany, with a short spell at boarding school in Liverpool. Convinced that women should study science, she gave talks at local girls' schools and wrote two textbooks. She also founded the Manchester Ladies Literary Society to which Charles Darwin sent a paper in 1867. It was Barbara Leigh Smith Bodichon's paper on the enfranchisement of women which encouraged Lydia Becker to campaign for the vote. She was a founder and first Secretary of the Manchester Women's Suffrage Committee in early 1867. In April 1868, she became the first British woman to speak publicly on women's suffrage at the Free Trade Hall, Manchester and, from 1869, lectured throughout the North. In 1870, she became one of the first women elected to serve on School Boards in Manchester. From 1870 to her death, she edited the *Women's Suffrage Journal* which reported on all parliamentary speeches and events relating to women's suffrage. A clear thinker, she was a crucial figure in the campaign for the vote, although her acceptance of a Suffrage Bill which excluded married women caused controversy.
Adapted from Uglow 1998.

---

had led to its dissolution and reformation. Strachey says that this split was 'political' and points out that:

'[it] was due to the first appearance of an internal difficulty which was to recur again and again during the course of the movement.' (Strachey 1979, p.110)

In part, the split was a matter of party allegiance and, in part, it concerned tactics. Some suffragists (as women campaigners for the vote came to be called) were Conservatives (notably Emily Davies) while others were Liberals (such as Helen Taylor, John Stuart Mill's daughter). Emily Davies argued that Conservative support was essential and that cautious tactics should be adopted 'so as not to alarm public opinion' (Strachey 1979, p.110). Others, such as Helen Taylor, disagreed. As a result, the committee was dissolved and Helen Taylor invited activists who shared her approach to form a new committee - which was named the London National Society for Women's Suffrage. This committee immediately worked on building links with the parallel groups which had emerged in Manchester and Edinburgh. Rendall argues that the effect of this early split in the movement was long-lasting:

'The schism had a lasting effect on the movement in that it left an executive that was subject to weak and often absent leadership, with many formerly active women channelling their energies elsewhere. It allowed the more dynamic, though politically less radical, Lydia Becker to play the major organisational role in the first years of the women's suffrage movement.' (Rendall 2000, p.62)

Lily Maxwell

In a by-election held in Manchester in November 1867, the name of Lily Maxwell, a shopkeeper whose house and shop had a ratable value high enough for her to qualify to vote, was included on the electoral register by mistake (she was a single woman and the person drawing up the electoral register assumed that her name was that of a man). When she turned up at the Hustings to vote, she was allowed to do so:

'The most detailed contemporary account is in the *Manchester Guardian* which described her as casting her vote for Jacob Bright, in public, at Chorlton Town Hall, accompanied by ladies, to a round of applause.' (Rendall 2000, p.71)

Lydia Becker (who had encouraged Lily Maxwell to use her vote) followed up this success with a campaign which encouraged other women in Lily Maxwell's position to vote. In this, she had some success. In Manchester nine out of 13 women on the electoral register voted in the 1868 general election. Also, over 5,000 women householders in Manchester applied to join the register.

The application of these women householders led to a test case in the High Court in 1868. In the so-called Chorlton v Lings case, however, the argument that women had the right to vote under ancient English law was dismissed on the grounds that custom overruled this. One of the lawyers who argued the case on behalf of Lydia Becker was Richard Pankhurst, the husband of Emmeline (who was to make such an impact on the women's suffrage movement later - see Part 3 below). In 1870, Richard Pankhurst drafted the first Women's Suffrage Bill. It was introduced into the Commons as a Private Members' Bill (see Box 3.8) and passed its first and second readings, but it was defeated when the Prime Minister, Gladstone, made it clear that the government was opposed to it.

The 1870s

It was in the 1870s that the women's suffrage movement developed into a national movement. Following the defeat of the first Women's Suffrage Bill, the Manchester and London committees attempted to build wider support while, at the same time, lobbying MPs:

'They sent platform speakers into the provinces, extended their network of branches, printed quantities of pamphlets, organised petitions and cultivated sympathetic MPs.' (Pugh 1994, p.10)

The main focus was on parliamentary lobbying, the idea being to persuade sympathetic MPs to introduce

---

BOX 3.8   Private Members' Bills

Definition

Most proposals for legislation ('Bills') are introduced into Parliament by the government. Private Members' Bills, however, are proposals for legislation introduced into the House of Commons by MPs who are not members of the government (ie they are private members). While governments sometimes support Private Members' Bills and provide them with the parliamentary time and backing necessary for them to succeed, they do not do so very often. Most Private Members' Bills fail because they lack support in the Commons. Even if a Bill gains a majority, however, that does not mean it will succeed. If the government opposes the Bill, then it can put pressure on backbenchers to vote against it at later stages in the legislative process or it can ensure that the Bill runs out of time. On the few occasions when Private Members' Bills proposing women's suffrage did gain a majority in the Commons between 1870 and 1914, the government ensured that they did not pass into law.

Private Members' Bills in support of women's suffrage. Lewis (1987) notes that such Bills were introduced every year in the 1870s except 1875. She also points out that:

'Reliance on Private Members' Bills was unlikely to meet with success, but this, together with petitioning and parliamentary lobbying constituted the bulk of the activity of the early suffragists.' (Lewis 1987, p.3)

The National Society for Women's Suffrage (NSWS)

In 1872, the local groups joined together into a single organisation - the National Society for Women's Suffrage (NSWS). This was strictly a non-party organisation (it aimed to encourage MPs from all parties to support women's suffrage). Its Central Committee was based in London. Billington notes that, between 1872 and 1888:

'The Central Committee and the Manchester Society organised most of the parliamentary business of the movement, but the local societies remained autonomous [free to act as they pleased]. Cooperation [was] achieved by the existence of a single clearly defined aim for the movement and the structural limitation...on the type of tactics available to pursue this aim.' (Billington 1985, p.5)

As with the London Committee in June 1867, however, the NSWS suffered splits in the 1870s. Historians have identified three main causes of these splits. First, the campaign against the Contagious Diseases Acts divided suffragists. Some suffragists worked closely with Josephine Butler, while others argued that the two campaigns should be completely separate. Second, there was a reluctance in the provinces to accept leadership from London. And third, suffragists were divided on whether or not they should support legislation which gave single women the vote, but excluded married women.This dispute came to a head in 1874. The problem was that, despite the passage of the 1870 Married Women's Property Act, the doctrine of coverture (the doctrine that the legal existence of a women is suspended during marriage - see page 65) continued to exist. Some suffragists argued that, given that this was the case, it was best to campaign for the vote for single women, while others argued that all women should be enfranchised. In the 1874 general election, Jacob Bright, who had led the group of MPs who supported women's suffrage, was defeated and replaced by Conservative MP, William Forsyth. When Forsyth argued that, because a Conservative government was in power, suffragists should limit their demand to votes for single women, Lydia Becker reluctantly agreed. This, however, alienated more radical suffragists.

MAIN POINTS - Sections 2.1 - 2.2

- The first parliamentary debate on women's suffrage came just after the passage of the 1832 Reform Bill. Although there is some evidence of support for women's suffrage over the next 30 years, it was only in the 1860s that a campaign for women's suffrage began.
- An important breakthrough came in 1865 when John Stuart Mill was elected on a platform in support of women's suffrage. A year later, the first Women's Suffrage Committee was set up.
- Mill raised the issue of women's suffrage in Parliament, but his amendment to the 1867 Reform Act failed and, following a test case in 1868, it was confirmed that women were excluded from voting.
- The women's suffrage movement developed into a national movement in the 1870s. Following the defeat of the first Women's Suffrage Bill in 1870, the main tactic was to lobby MPs, hoping to persuade sympathetic MPs to introduce Private Members' Bills in support of women's suffrage.
- The NSWS suffered splits in the 1870s over (1) the campaign against the Contagious Diseases Acts (2) whether or not the London group was in charge and (3) whether or not to campaign for the vote for married women.

Activity 3.2 Early suffragist activity

ITEM 1 John Stuart Mill and women's suffrage

MILL'S LOGIC ; OR, FRANCHISE FOR FEMALES.

"PRAY CLEAR THE WAY, THERE, FOR THESE—A—PERSONS."

This cartoon was published in *Punch* magazine in 1867. John Stuart Mill is the man in the centre with a balding head. The man in the top hat is John Bull (the average Englishman).

ITEM 2 Suffragist activity in 1869

'Our movement is now in a stage to demand greater effort than we have hitherto been able to accomplish ' wrote Miss Becker...This was undoubtedly true...The first step must be to spread the organisation over the country, they felt, and make their principles known. Mrs M'Laren and Miss Mair in Edinburgh. Mrs Osler in Birmingham, the Misses Priestly in Bristol and a dozen more began to work in earnest. Over 18,000 pamphlets were issued, but they soon realised that something more direct was required and the question of meetings arose. Up to that date hardly any women had spoken in public at all. A few bold spirits had given 'lectures'...and Miss Becker had arranged a real public meeting in the Free Trade Hall in Manchester the year before, at which the Mayor had taken the chair and she herself had been among the speakers. But even she, intrepid as she was, had admitted to being 'unnerved'... Drawing room meetings were the first step and these were alarming enough, but public meetings were soon to follow and, in July 1869, the first London one was held...Mrs Peter Taylor was in the chair - the presiding of a woman was another startling novelty...It all went off splendidly and everyone was thoroughly pleased. The new campaign was launched...It was far more difficult to go out into country places and break new ground. This, however, had now to be undertaken and a number of volunteers came forward for this unwelcome task...There was no fear of meetings failing for lack of audience, for everyone crowded to see the novel sight of a woman speaking in public...Nervous and anxious chairmen found it necessary to assure their audiences that the ladies were quite respectable...The impromptu votes of thanks at the end were often a little curious. They frequently referred to the 'heroism' of the speakers and were sometimes extended to include the husbands who had been so good as to spare their wives to come away and speak.

From Strachey 1979, pp.117-19.

ITEM 3 Why women desire the franchise

During the last five years the proposal to give votes to women has very distinctly grown. Few [supporters] would have ventured in 1865 to hope that by the close of 1872 it should stand where it most obviously does in public opinion or that 335,801 persons should have petitioned on its behalf. The last Reform Bill, by lowering the franchise for men, has affected the claims of women in several indirect ways. In the first place by admitting to the exercise of political judgement a class whose education is confessedly of the narrowest and whose leisure to study politics extremely small, it has virtually silenced for all future time the two favourite arguments against the claims of women: that their understandings are weak and their time too fully occupied by domestic cares. The most strenuous asserter of the mental and moral inferiority of women cannot urge that the majority of the new voters have more power to understand, or more leisure to attend to, public affairs than even the inferior class of female householders...On the contrary, may it be maintained that the picked class of women who would be admitted...to the franchise are needed to restore the just balance of an educated constituency against the weight of the illiterate male voters now entrusted with the suffrage...By identifying the duty of ratepaying with the right of voting in the case of men, the Reform Bill has made more glaring than before the inconsistency of enforcing rates upon women while refusing to them the [vote]. At the present moment our proper course appears to be this: to form committees in every town in England for the purpose of directing attention to the subject...Local petitions as numerous as possible will afford the best machinery for carrying on such a plan...It is just possible that keeping the peace and signing petitions to Parliament may eventually be thought...to prove their [ie women's] fitness for a voice in the legislature.

From 'Why Women Desire the Vote', a pamphlet by Frances Power Cobbe, published in 1874.

Questions

1. a) Write a caption for Item 1, explaining the context in which the cartoon was drawn.
   b) Why was John Stuart Mill's election an important breakthrough for the women's movement?
2. a) Using Items 2 and 3 describe the tactics that the early suffragists used.
   b) What do these items tell us about the nature of the movement?
3. a) What does Item 2 tell us about the difficulties that early suffragists faced?
   b) Using Item 3 explain how the passing of the second Reform Act affected the arguments used by suffragists in support of the vote for women.

2.3 Was the period 1880-1903 one of failure for the suffragists?

The historical debate

Between the setting up of the first Women's Suffrage Committee in 1866 and the formation of Emmeline Pankhurst's Women's Social and Political Union (WSPU) in 1903, suffragists followed the 'constitutional' path to reform (ie they acted within the commonly accepted boundaries of law and convention). As the historian Jane Lewis has pointed out, the early suffragists took the view that they had to proceed cautiously if they were to be taken seriously:

'The early women's rights campaigners...stressed they were law abiding. As Frances Cobbe remarked in 1874, it was something of a triumph to make votes for women a public question at all: when the issue was first raised in the Commons, it was treated as a great joke. The suffragists chose their ground carefully and argued their claim as tightly as possible in order that they might be taken seriously.' (Lewis 1987, p.3)

By 1903, however, suffragists had been campaigning for nearly 40 years without winning the vote. For Emmeline Pankhurst and her followers (who became known as 'suffragettes'), it was this apparent lack of progress which justified the adoption of the militant tactics which dominated the period 1903-12 (see Part 3 below). From the Pankhurst point of view, therefore, the period 1880-1903 was one of failure. This point of view has coloured later accounts:

'Traditionally, perceptions have been dominated by the Pankhursts. Their view - essentially propagandist it should be remembered - held that militancy became a necessity in the early 1900s because decades of campaigning by the non-militants had been a failure. Some historians, while not necessarily endorsing all the Pankhursts' claims, have suggested that, after an initial upsurge during the 1860s and 1870s, the suffrage movement suffered a period of decline in the later 1880s and 1890s.' (Pugh 1994, p.20)

The Pankhurst approach, however, is only one of several. Sandra Holton (2000) suggests that it is possible to identify four different approaches to the history of the suffrage movement:

1. The constitutionalist approach
Historians who follow this approach tend to be sympathetic to suffragists (those who used constitutional tactics) and they are critical of the militants. Ray Strachey's *The Cause* (first published in 1928) is an example of this approach.

2. The militant approach
Historians who follow this approach tend to accept the Pankhursts' view (as described above). They tend to focus on the Pankhursts at the expense of other campaigners and to dismiss or minimise the 19th century campaigns. Sylvia Pankhurst's *The Suffragette Movement* (published in 1931) and Christabel Pankhurst's *Unshackled: the Story of How We Won the Vote* (published in 1959) are examples of this approach. Sylvia and Christabel were daughters of Emmeline Pankhurst and active in the suffragette movement.

3. The masculinist approach
Male historians who criticise the tactics adopted by suffragists or suffragettes or who minimise the impact made by women who campaigned for the vote are described by Holton as 'masculinists'. A number of these writers, she says, emphasise:

'The otherness, the strangeness, the difference and ultimately the ridiculousness of women in pursuit of their own political and personal ends.' (Holton 2000, p.24)

While George Dangerfield's *The Strange Death of Liberal England* (published in 1935) became the model for this approach, Holton includes Brian Harrison and Martin Pugh in this category. She does so on the grounds that Harrison (1983, for example) 'lets off the hook' the male electorate and male politicians (because he argues that lack of progress in the years 1880-1903 was due to suffragist tactics), while Pugh (in his early work - 1974, for example) argues that 'the women's movement had little to do with the eventual enfranchisement of women in 1918' (Holton 2000, p.25).

4. The new-feminist approach
New-feminist historians emphasise the achievements of all those involved in the suffrage campaigns (whether constitutionalists or militants) and move away from the 'great woman' approach which was found in both constitutionalist and militant accounts. The struggle for the vote is seen as part of a broader struggle in which conventional views about the role of women were challenged and overturned, and new feminised approaches to politics and protest were developed. The first full new-feminist interpretation was Marian Ramelson's *The Petticoat Rebellion: a Century of Struggle for Women's Rights* (published in 1967).

It should be clear from this summary that it is possible to make very different assessments of the campaign for women's suffrage in the period 1880-1903 according to which of the four approaches is taken. Constitutionalist and new-feminist writers tend to be positive about developments in this period, while militant and masculinist authors tend to support the view that the suffrage movement went into decline and achieved little.

The third Reform Act
The dilemma that suffragists faced was that women had to rely on Parliament to pass legislation giving women the vote, but there were no women in Parliament to ensure that this happened. It was noted in Section 2.2 above that, since there was no sign of the government proposing legislation in the 1870s, the suffragist tactic was to encourage MPs into proposing Private Members' Bills. But, as Billington points out:

Such a radical reform [as giving women the vote] was unlikely to be achieved through a Private Members' Bill, so the women's movement needed a government-, or at least, a party-sponsored Bill - or majority support for an amendment to a general franchise reform Bill.' (Billington 1985, p.2)

It was only in 1880, with the election of a Liberal government, that this became a realistic possibility:

'At the 1880 general election, the Liberals were returned and, with them, so suffragists thought, a majority in favour of female suffrage. The work of the suffrage societies was bearing fruit and at the Liberal Party conference there had been a large vote in favour of further constitutional reform which included votes for women.' (McDonald 1989, p.21)

Woodall's equal franchise amendment

During the debate in the Commons over the third Reform Bill (see also Unit 2, Section 3.2), an amendment was included proposing that women should have the vote on an equal basis to men (Woodall's equal franchise amendment). But, that amendment was defeated when the Prime Minister, William Gladstone, made it clear that he did not support it (Gladstone did not make his views on women's suffrage clear until 1892 - see Box 3.9). McDonald (1989) argues that there were three main reasons for Gladstone's opposition:

- his attitude towards women's suffrage (although not openly hostile at the time, in 1892 he eventually admitted publicly that he was against it)

BOX 3.9 Gladstone's views on women's suffrage

In 1892, Gladstone wrote a letter to Samuel Smith MP in which he outlined his views on women's suffrage in some detail. This was the first occasion on which he had come out against women's suffrage in principle. Previously, he had suggested that it was impractical to enfranchise women at that time (which suggested that he supported it in principle). The following extract gives some of the arguments he used:

'A permanent and vast difference of type has been impressed upon women and men respectively by the Maker of both [ie God]. Their differences of social office [ie the ideology of separate spheres] rest mainly upon causes, not flexible and elastic like most mental qualities, but physical and in their nature unchangeable. I for one am not prepared to say which of the two sexes has the higher and which the lower province. But, I recognise the subtle and profound character of the differences between them...I am not without the fear lest, beginning with the state, we should eventually be found to have intruded into what is yet more fundamental and more sacred, the precinct of the family, and should dislocate, or injuriously modify the relations of domestic life. As this is not a party question or a class question, so neither is it a sex question. I have no fear lest the woman should encroach upon the power of the man. The fear I have is lest we should invite her unwittingly to trespass upon the delicacy, the purity, the refinement, the elevation of her own nature which are the present sources of its power...My disposition is to...take no step in advance until I am convinced of its safety.'

Quoted in Lewis 1987.

Source Box

- concern that the Bill as a whole would be defeated if such a controversial clause was included (he argued that the House of Lords was much more likely to reject the Bill if the Woodall amendment was included)
- fear that, if women were given the vote, most would vote Conservative, reducing the Liberals' chance of forming future governments .

Harrison (1983) argues that suffragists had simply not made sufficient headway in converting Liberals to their cause for Gladstone to be able to include them in the legislation:

'Suffragists in 1912 were still claiming that [Gladstone] had "thrown overboard" the women to lighten the ship in 1884; in reality, the women had never even embarked...Mid-Victorian suffragists never converted enough Liberals to the equal franchise for any other course to be feasible for Gladstone in 1884.' (Harrison 1983, pp.97-98)

Consequences

Historians agree that failure to achieve the vote in 1884 was a blow to the suffragist movement. Billington, for example, argues that:

'Once the women's suffrage amendment to the 1884 Reform Bill was clearly lost and "the bright hopefulness of earlier times had gone out of the movement", there was dissension within it over tactics, principles and leadership.' (Billington 1985, p.5)

Harrison agrees, stating that:

'The defeat of Woodall's equal franchise amendment in 1884 accentuated the suffragist decline.' (Harrison 1983, p.98)

In an analysis of the annual income of women's organisations from 1866-1939, he shows clearly that there was a marked decline in income between 1884 and 1900, suggesting a significant loss of support.

The political parties and women's suffrage

It was pointed out in Section 2.2 above that the NSWS adopted a strictly non-party approach when it was set up in 1872. It did this on the assumption that support could be built up in both the main parties in much the same way as support had been built up against the Corn Laws during the period of Anti-Corn Law activity (in which some suffragists had participated) in the early 1840s.

The Liberals

Although suffragists aimed to build support for their cause in both main parties, Hirshfield points out that:

'Liberals pioneered the concept of women's suffrage and the writings of John Stuart Mill, Jacob Bright and the Fawcetts - Henry and Millicent - established a firm intellectual basis for the cause. The extension of the vote conformed to progressive Liberal principles and was probably favoured by a majority of the party's male office holders. In each of the 15 woman suffrage votes in the Commons that occurred between 1867 and 1886, Liberals and radicals accounted for more than two-thirds of affirmative [ie pro-women's suffrage] totals.' (Hirshfield 1990, pp.174-75)

This explains the optimism when the Liberals replaced the Conservatives in government in 1880 - though the government's subsequent opposition shows that the Liberal leadership was less sympathetic than backbenchers and party workers. Billington (1985) argues that the Liberal leadership's opposition to women's suffrage was not simply a matter of 'anti-feminism'. Rather, she argues, it was a reflection of the problems facing the Liberal Party. In order to deal with what the party regarded as the 'great problems' of the day - imperialism, poverty and Ireland - the leadership focused either on a single issue (eg Ireland in Gladstone's first administration of 1868-74) or on the party's programme:

'Since women were not defined as a politically important group and had no political power, women's suffrage was not included in official Liberal Party aims. It was neither a "great" issue nor part of the changing Liberal "programme".' (Billington 1985, p.3)

Billington also points out that, once the Liberal Party had split over Home Rule for Ireland in 1886, there was little likelihood of it being distracted from that by the women's issue. Hirshfield (1990), on the other hand, emphasises that the Liberals were responsible for the legislation which allowed single women to vote in local government elections and to join School Boards. This allowed them to participate in the public domain and, as a result, encouraged attitudes towards them to change.

The Conservatives

The position in the Conservative Party was almost the reverse. At first, in general terms (and there were exceptions), leading Conservatives tended to be more favourable to the idea that (some) women should be given the vote than their backbenchers were. This, however, did change, to some extent, after the third Reform Act was passed:

'Whereas from 1867 to 1884 a majority of Conservatives who voted had opposed the suffrage, between 1884 and 1908, a majority of those voting came out in support. Taking the Commons as a whole, there was a definite trend in favour of the female franchise.' (Pugh 1994, p.22)

One reason for this change was the calculation that women - especially middle-class women (who would be the majority to qualify if they were given the vote on the same basis as men) - would be likely to vote Conservative:

'Conservative proponents of women's suffrage...claimed that women were naturally more religious than men and would consequently support Conservative causes such as an Established Church and religious education, in addition to

private property, the monarchy and the Union with Ireland.' (Pugh 1994, pp.16-17)

Billington (1985), however, points out that although Conservative Leaders supported extending the vote to women in opposition, they did little to put it into effect when in government:

'When in power they gave "all aid short of help" to the movement, despite their support for it in opposition. Unfortunately for the movement, there was a Conservative government in power from 1886 to 1905, except for a brief period of Liberal rule between 1892 and 1895 when, in fact, the Conservatives held the balance of power.' (Billington 1985, p.3)

The growth of women's political organisations

One consequence of the widening of the franchise was the rapid growth in the number of women's political organisations. Historians have often pointed out that, because the third Reform Act substantially increased the number of voters and led to a restructuring of constituencies, some form of new political organisation was necessary to ensure that parties could manage to maintain the support of the voters. In addition:

'Since Gladstone's legislation against corrupt electoral practices set limits on campaign expenditures, volunteers were needed to supplement the services of paid agents. Thus a perfect opportunity was at hand to engage the legions of women eager to help friends and relatives campaigning for office.' (Hirshfield 1990, p.174)

It was in the 1880s that the main political parties began to make use of the time and energy that women who supported them were prepared to donate.

The Primrose League

The Conservative Party's Primrose League was set up in 1883 to promote the sort of Conservative values supported by Disraeli (see also Unit 6, page 185). The organisation was hierarchical, offering one class of membership to the upper classes (at a high subscription rate) and associate membership to the lower classes (at a lower rate). It was immediately very popular, especially with women. Pugh has analysed membership records and argues that:

'They obviously corroborate the impressionistic evidence of the Primrose League as an organisation which catered to women: but what is more striking is that they show the League as a body which incorporated men and women rather than segregating them. Moreover they suggest that the Primrose League - uniquely for a Victorian political institution - must have included hundreds of thousands of women in its ranks.' (Pugh 1985, pp.50-51)

Women's role in the Primrose League is outlined in Box 3.10 on page 82.

BOX 3.10 Women and the Primrose League

Local groups of the Primrose League were called 'habitations' and full members were called 'Dames' (males were called 'Knights'). While Dames were heavily involved in the social side (organising tea parties, fetes and so on), they also played a political role. Primrose Dames routinely convened political meetings, brought voters to the polls on election days, and distributed campaign literature to small and remote villages, in support of fathers, husbands and brothers. 'Women whether they like it or not, are born members of the state', a prominent Dame noted. While she was careful to insist that 'we don't wish to govern the country', she nonetheless noted how important it was to 'assist in placing men in government who will lead our country in the paths of peace and prosperity'. The League did not campaign in favour of women's suffrage (although some Dames were suffragists). Rather, the Ladies Grand Council made it clear that, although members were free to support women's suffrage, it was not one of the League's goals and the League would, therefore, not take part in the campaign.
Adapted from Hirshfield 1990.

The Women's Liberal Associations (WLA)

The first Women's Liberal Association (WLA) was formed in Bristol in 1881. But, it was only after the formation and rapid success of the Conservatives' Primrose League that the growth in WLAs accelerated. Billington (1985) suggests that the early WLAs were set up to combat many Liberals' indifference to women's suffrage, but those that were set up later did not necessarily have a suffragist agenda. These organisations operated separately from the all-male local associations and, in 1887, came under the control of the Women's Liberal Federation (a council of 500 delegates elected by the local associations with an executive committee of 30, chosen by the council). The experience women gained from the WLAs is outlined in Box 3.11.

Divisions within the movement

Shortly after the third Reform Bill had been passed, Gladstone's 'conversion' to Home Rule split the Liberal Party (see Unit 6, page 181). A group of Liberals - the so-called 'Liberal Unionists' left the party and sat as an independent group in the House of Commons. This split also produced divisions within the women's suffrage movement:

'While the main body of Liberal women suffragists remained staunch Gladstonians, other such as Millicent Garrett Fawcett opposed Home Rule and became Liberal Unionists.' (Holton 1995, p.284)

These divisions were then intensified in 1888 when a group of Liberal women on the central committee of the National Society for Women's Suffrage

(NSWS) attempted to change the way in which the organisation was structured. Until 1888, the NSWS had followed a strictly non-party policy. In 1888, however, it was proposed that:

1. The NSWS executive committee should have the power to make decisions that were binding on local societies.
2. The number of delegates which societies affiliated to the NSWS could send to the central committee should be determined by the number of members in the local society.
3. Any society which included women's suffrage as one of its aims should be able to affiliate.

The third proposal was the most controversial because it would end the non-party basis of the organisation. Because of this, two leading suffragists - Lydia Becker and Millicent Fawcett (see Box 3.12) - opposed it:

'The Becker-Fawcett group pointed out that there were only eight independent suffrage societies, but probably 200-300 women's political organisations. If only 50 of these were to join the Central Committee of the NSWS, the provincial suffrage societies would be outnumbered. Since Primrose habitations were prohibited from outside affiliations, the organisations joining the NSWS would be Liberal or Liberal Unionist.' (Billington 1985, p.5)

In other words, if these rules were adopted, they would effectively end the NSWS's non-party approach since the movement would be dominated by the Liberal Party. The debate over the new rules ended with the NSWS splitting into two separate groups, one supporting the new rules and one sticking to the old rules:

- the Parliament Street Society - officially, the

BOX 3.11 The experience women gained from the Women's Liberal Associations (WLAs)

The main function of WLAs was to carry out canvassing and other political work (such as leafleting and encouraging voters to register). Although it was usually the wives, mothers and daughters of prominent politicians who established local Liberal associations, the Women's Liberal Federation attempted from the start to broaden its membership base, often seeking to enlist professional women and veterans of the temperance (anti-alcohol) and moral reform movements. As a result, WLAs often provided grass-roots support for people ambitious to seek office at both the local and national level. Liberal women learned not only to face the general public in door-to-door canvassing, but to confront male politicians in local meetings. Inevitably, they were introduced to the techniques of practical electioneering, and many learned their lesson well.
Adapted from Hirshfield 1990.

BOX 3.12 | Millicent Garrett Fawcett (1847-1929)

(i) Millicent Fawcett was the younger sister of Elizabeth Garrett Anderson, the first woman to qualify in Britain as a doctor (see Section 1.2 above). They were the daughters of an East Anglian merchant. Millicent's only formal schooling was at Blackheath in London (1859-62). In 1867, she married Henry Fawcett, professor of politics at Cambridge from 1863 and an MP from 1865. His blindness led her to act as his political secretary. She was on the first Suffrage Committee in 1867 and worked for the Married Women's Property Act. She published *Political Economy for Beginners* in 1870 and was also active in the campaign for university education. After Henry Fawcett's death in 1884 she became more active. In 1886, she formed a separate non-party suffrage society with Lydia Becker (who died in 1890). Then, in 1897, she reunited the movement, becoming President of the National Union of Women's Suffrage Societies (NUWSS). In 1890s, she became a national political figure. She broke away from the Liberal Party over Home Rule for Ireland and became a frequent visitor and speaker against Home Rule. She was also leader of a women's commission to investigate concentration camps in South Africa in the Boer War. She remained a convinced constitutionalist after Emmeline Pankhurst's militant campaign began and remained President of the NUWSS throughout the period 1903-14.

Adapted from Uglow 1998.

Millicent Fawcett

(ii) There is a story...which may not be true in fact...Emily [Davies], the story runs, went to stay with the Garretts at Aldburgh and at night, the two friends [Emily Davies and Elizabeth Garrett] sat up talking together by Elizabeth's bedroom fire. Millicent Garrett, then [in the 1850s] quite a small girl sat nearby on a stool, listening, but saying nothing. After going over all the great causes they saw about them, and in particular the women's cause, to which they were burning to devote their lives, Emily summed the matter up. 'Well Elizabeth', she said, 'It's quite clear what has to be done. I must devote myself to securing higher education, while you open the medical profession to women. After these things are done', she added, 'we must see about getting the vote'. Then she turned to the little girl who was still sitting on her stool and said, 'You're younger than we are, Millie, so you must attend to that'.

From Strachey 1979, p.101.

Central National Society for Women's Suffrage - ie the group which accepted the new rules
- the Great College Street Society - officially, the Central Committee of the National Society for Women's Suffrage - ie the group which refused to accept the new rules.

The Women's Franchise League

Holton (1995) claims that the Parliament Street Society attracted the bulk of existing members and became the main body. She also notes that the split in 1888 was not just over the new rules, it was also over the question of whether the organisation should support Bills which excluded married women from voting. While the Great College Street Society was prepared to accept such legislation, the Parliament Street Society remained divided over the issue:

'[The Parliament Street Society] attempted to hold its members together by deciding to support both suffrage Bills which excluded married women and suffrage Bills framed in terms of equal rights [ie Bills which gave women the same voting rights as men]. But it opposed the most radical formulation of the demand - which expressly included married women.' (Holton 1995, p.284)

The Parliament Street Society's stance over this issue led to a further split. In July 1889, a third group was set up - the Women's Franchise League (WFL). The WFL argued that, because the Married Women's Property Act of 1882 gave married women the ownership of their property, they should be included in any legislation giving women the vote. In addition, the WFL had a wider agenda:

'The WFL also had wider "women's rights" objectives and attracted a more radical membership than other suffrage organisations.' (Billington 1985, p.6)

The group's first leader was Elizabeth Wolstenholme Elmy, but she was soon replaced by Ursula Bright and Emmeline Pankhurst.

The Women's Emancipation Union

When Elizabeth Wolstenholme Elmy was ousted from the leadership of the Women's Franchise League, she set up yet another group - the Women's Emancipation League. This campaigned to improve the position of married women and, in particular, launched a campaign against rape within marriage.

From division to reconciliation

While there is little doubt that the splintering of the movement in the late 1880s did not increase the suffragists' chance of success, the divisions within the movement should not be exaggerated. Billington argues that:

'Wherever a Woman's Liberal Association existed which was affiliated to the "new" Central Committee, there were in effect two women's suffrage organisations, but nowhere do there appear to have been two organisations actually calling themselves specifically suffrage societies. This points to a basic unity of purpose in the movement. The desire behind many suffragists to avoid public disagreement was probably behind the decision of societies such as Birmingham to remain separate from either of the central organisations for a time.' (Billington 1985, p.5)

This view is confirmed by the fact that both the Parliament Street Society and the Great College Street Society were able to cooperate in the build-up to the 1894 Local Government Act which gave married women the same rights as single women to vote in local government elections, to become Poor Law Guardians and to join School Boards. The 1894 Local Government Act was a significant advance for married women (see page 69) and it removed a source of division between suffrage societies:

'The way was now clear for suffragists to work together for a measure which all societies could now agree on - equal rights in the parliamentary franchise for women, both single and married.' (Holton 1995, p.285)

Greater cooperation after 1894

Following the passage of the Local Government Act, suffragists from all the groups set about gathering a petition in support of the franchise. To coordinate

this, a special committee was set up which included representatives from the Parliament Street Society, the Great College Street Society, the Primrose League, the Women's Liberal Federation, the Women's Liberal Unionist Federation and the Women's Franchise League. A conference of all women's suffrage societies was then called in Birmingham in 1896:

'The organisation set up following the conference was similar to that which had existed prior to 1888, with a more systematic effort to cover all areas, but the movement had also learned from its members' involvement with local political party organisations. Each society was to cover a specified area. Paid organisers were to operate in small towns and villages without sufficient voluntary workers, but larger towns and cities would be worked through big meetings. Speakers at the Birmingham Conference stressed that the "political difficulty" within the movement need not divide it since women's suffrage was a non-party issue. Political associations were to remain affiliated to the movement but were not part of its regional organisation.' (Billington 1985, p.9)

In the following year, 1897, the petition was presented to Parliament. It contained over 250,000 signatures. The petition was presented in support of the Women's Suffrage Bill which was introduced by Faithfull Begg (a Conservative MP). This Bill passed its second reading, the first Bill to have done so since 1870, though, like other Private Members' Bills it did not become law. This success, Strachey argues, was the catalyst for the formation of the National Union of Women's Suffrage Societies (NUWSS):

'The societies, which had already been moving towards reunion, now took the matter up in real earnest. The two London societies became one central society and, with the 18 provincial ones, grouped themselves in a national organisation of which Mrs [Millicent] Fawcett was the President, and adopted a regular democratic constitution under the the name of the National Union of Women's Suffrage Societies.' (Strachey 1979, p.287)

The work of the NUWSS is outlined in Box 3.13 on page 85.

Who were the early suffragists?

It is difficult to know exactly how many suffragists there were at any one time in the 19th century. Nevertheless, there is a consensus among historians that, throughout the period 1866-1903, the battle to gain the vote for women was fought mainly by a small group of predominantly upper- and middle-class women:

'Research suggests that, in the early years of the suffrage movement, the campaign was dominated by middle-class women...When all the small local

Interpretation

BOX 3.13 | The NUWSS 1897-1903

Between 1897 and 1903 (the year in which Emmeline Pankhust set up her, more militant, organisation, the WSPU), the NUWSS coordinated the campaign for women's suffrage and it remained the focus of the constitutionalist approach after 1903. Millicent Fawcett continued to promote her non-party approach and she urged women in all parties to work for MPs or candidates who supported women's suffrage and to refuse to work for those who did not (a strategy she had devised and promoted in 1892). As a result of the formation of the NUWSS, many new local and regional societies were formed and, although there was continuity with the 19th century movement, the 20th century 'constitutional' suffrage movement, as the NUWSS became known, owed more to the organisational patterns of the major political parties.

Adapted from Billington 1985.

organisations joined together to form the National Union of Women's Suffrage Societies (the NUWSS) in 1897 it was comprised, at least at leadership level, of women from notable families. These were exceptional political activists, many of whom had been involved in other middle-class campaigns.' (Bartley 1996, pp.111-12)

Working-class suffragists

Bartley goes on to point out that, although the campaign for women's suffrage was, in its early years, exclusively an upper- and middle-class campaign, by the end of the century, there is evidence of working-class participation. Ray Strachey notes, for example, that:

'In the North of England at this time [1898], a movement in favour of the suffrage arose among the mill hands and textile workers.' (Strachey 1979, p.288)

The growth of working-class support for the suffrage movement coincided with the growth of support for working-class representation in Parliament (see Unit 5). In 1895, the Independent Labour Party voted to give both men and women the vote and some of the leading figures in the labour movement (such as Keir Hardie and, before 1905, Ramsay MacDonald) were strong supporters of women's suffrage (though many were not). Liddington and Norris (1978) have shown that many working-class women with experience in the trade unions and labour movement joined the women's suffrage movement in the early 1900s (women's participation in trade unions is examined in more detail in Unit 4, Section 2.3). They describe such women as 'radical suffragists' and argue that:

'The radical suffragists wanted more than an abstract right; they were not merely interested in the possession of the vote as a symbol of equality. They wanted it in order to improve conditions for women like themselves. The majority of working-class men had won the vote in the electoral reforms of 1867 and 1884, and by 1900 had begun to send their own representatives to Parliament. But working-class women had no such rights.' (Liddington & Norris 1978, p.25)

The radical suffragists, therefore, had a different agenda from the middle-class suffragists who had dominated the movement before 1900. They also used different tactics - such as holding meetings outside factory gates. Rather than relying on 'discreet lobbying' they 'aimed to build a mass movement' (Liddington & Norris 1978, p.26). This soon brought tensions within the movement.

Other working-class groups

Two other working-class suffragist groups that should be mentioned are the Women's Trade Union League (WTUL) and the Women's Cooperative Guild (WCG). While, according to Pugh (1985) the WTUL 'played down' suffragism to win support within the trade union movement, the WCG campaigned for women's suffrage. The WCG was formed in 1883 and gained a membership of c.30,000 in the early 1900s. It supported women's suffrage rather than adult suffrage.

MAIN POINTS - Section 2.3

- Between 1866 and 1903, suffragists followed the constitutional path to reform. In order to justify their later militant campaign the Pankhursts argued that the period 1880-1903 had been one of failure. There is a debate between historians about whether this is an accurate view.

- While the suffragist tactic of promoting Private Members' Bills was unlikely to succeed, the 1884 Reform Bill provided a real chance of women's suffrage. Woodall's equal franchise amendment was defeated, however. This was a major blow for the suffragists.

- It was during the 1880s that political parties began to encourage the participation of women - through the Women's Liberal associations and the Primrose League.

- There were further splits in the women's suffrage movement in the 1880s over (1) the non-party approach and (2) whether or not to campaign for the vote for married women.

- Suffragists worked together in the 1890s and, in 1897, the various groups came together in the NUWSS whose President was Millicent Fawcett.

- Although, in the early years, the battle to gain the vote for women was fought mainly by a small group of upper- and middle-class women, there is evidence of working-class women becoming involved in the 1890s.

Activity 3.3 Women's suffrage 1880-1903

ITEM 1 'An ugly rush'

AN "UGLY RUSH!"

This cartoon appeared in *Punch* magazine on 28 May 1870. John Bull (the average Englishman) leans against the door as women try to force their way in.

ITEM 3 A historian's view (2)

In the period 1880-1903, the suffragists made a number of tactical errors. First, before 1884, they failed to convert enough Liberal MPs to the cause of women's suffrage. This allowed Gladstone to go ahead with a Reform Bill which excluded women. Second, they failed to change their non-party strategy after 1884. This was a serious mistake because the 1884 Reform Act meant that progressive Liberals would prefer democracy to equality - ie they would be more likely to listen to demands for universal franchise than to demands for women to gain the vote on the same basis as men. What the suffragists should have done is to have accepted the Liberal connection and campaigned with the Liberals for universal suffrage. In principle, this should not have been too difficult. The campaign for women's suffrage had, after all, been launched by Liberals. In only three of the 17 votes on women's suffrage in the Commons between 1867 and 1904 did Conservatives and Unionists contribute a higher percentage of the suffragist vote than Liberals and radicals. As it was, after 1884 suffragists provided behind-the-scenes resistance against proposals for universal suffrage and insisted that women should get the vote before any further extension of the male franchise took place. The suffragists' tactical conservatism helps to explain why several mid-Victorian radicals - such as John Bright and Joseph Chamberlain - did not support the suffragists. The third error was that suffragists underestimated the scale of the difficulties politicians faced. They underestimated the importance of Home Rule for Ireland, for example - one of those Liberal causes which dwarfed all other issues and obstructed women's suffrage. And they campaigned for equal franchise (ie women gaining the right to vote on the same basis as men) without realising that this was impossible for the Liberals because it would damage their electoral interests (on the other hand, women's suffrage as part of an adult suffrage measure was equally impossible because the House of Lords would delay it).

Adapted from Harrison 1983.

ITEM 2 A historian's view (1)

In several ways, the period 1880-1903 proved to be a period of very advantageous change for women, though some developments made an indirect impact which is hard to measure. For example, the introduction of the secret ballot in 1872 and legislation against electoral corruption in 1883 made elections more civilised and better suited for women's participation. It was in this period that women first began to play a part in local government activity. By 1895, for example, 128 women had been elected to School Boards and 893 as Poor Law Guardians. By demonstrating they were able to handle public affairs, this changed attitudes and encouraged women to raise their sights. Some women who became MPs in the 1920s served their apprenticeship in local politics. An even more significant development in this period was the extensive female participation in party political work. The legal restrictions on expenditure at elections imposed in 1883 obliged all parties to rely heavily on volunteer activities. Many women canvassed, organised functions and spoke on public platforms. In this way, they moved decisively beyond the conventional female sphere and, by the end of the century, politicians on both sides had accepted the necessity of women's participation. The Conservatives adopted women's suffrage resolutions in 1887, 1889, 1891 and 1894. When the Liberal leadership refused to support women's suffrage, the Liberal women's organisation split in 1892 - a minority of branches withheld support from anti-suffragist Liberal candidates. Such friction shows how far attitudes had moved since 1867. And finally, the most obvious measurement of progress made by the suffragist cause was the shift by Conservative MPs (no doubt sensitive to the help women gave them) in favour of women's suffrage. Whereas from 1867 to 1884 a majority of Conservatives opposed women's suffrage, between 1884 and 1908, a majority of those voting came out in support. Taking the Commons as a whole, there was a definite trend in favour of the female franchise.

Adapted from Pugh 1994.

Questions

1. a) 'Item 1 was drawn in 1870, but it could equally well have been drawn in the 1880s'. Give arguments for and against this statement.
   b) Would you expect the attitudes expressed in the cartoon still to be widely held in the period 1880-1903? Explain your answer (use Item 2 to help answer the question).
2. Judging from Items 2 and 3, what tactics did women use to campaign for the vote in the period 1880-1903?
3. a) Using Items 2 and 3 and your own knowledge, give arguments for and against the view that the women's suffrage movement was in decline in the period 1880-1903.
   b) What problems did the movement face?
   c) How did it deal with them?
4. a) What do Items 2 and 3 tell us about the debate over the state of women's suffrage in the period 1880-1903?
   b) Which of the arguments is most convincing? Explain your answer.
   c) Brian Harrison (Item 3) has been described as a 'masculinist'. Using Item 3, explain why.

3 The Pankhursts and the WSPU

Key questions

1. What led the Pankhursts to begin the militant campaign?
2. What were the structure and organisation of the WSPU?
3. What tactics were used by the WSPU and were they a success?

3.1 What led the Pankhursts to begin the militant campaign?

Introduction

It was noted in Section 2.3 above that the Pankhurst view of history has coloured some later accounts. So has their actions. Ever since the WSPU came to national prominence in 1905, Emmeline Pankhurst and her three daughters, Christabel, Sylvia and Adela, have been surrounded by controversy. Not only did they provoke fierce opposition both within and outside the suffragist movement at the time, but ever since they called a halt to militancy in 1914, their actions have provoked lavish praise or hostile criticism. Much of this hostile criticism has focused on the suffragettes' militancy. This section will consider why the WSPU decided to use militant tactics (women using militant tactics became known as 'suffragettes' whilst those using non-militant tactics are generally called 'suffragists').

The Pankhurst family before 1903

By the time that Emmeline Pankhurst set up the Women's Political and Social Union (WSPU) in October 1903, she was a veteran political campaigner. Emmeline Goulden (her original name) was born in 1858:

'She was the eldest of ten children of a prosperous Manchester calico printer. Her parents were radical reformers and she attended her first suffrage meeting at the age of 14.' (Uglow 1998, p.416)

After being educated in Manchester and Paris, Emmeline, aged 21, married Richard Pankhurst, the (older) radical barrister who had drafted the first Women's Suffrage Bill in 1870. Based in Manchester between 1879 and 1885, the Pankhursts worked for the Manchester Women's Suffrage Committee and the Married Women's Property Committee (Richard Pankhurst drafted the 1882 Married Women's Property Bill). Emmeline also worked as a Poor Law Guardian. Davis (1999) claims that Emmeline's work as a Poor Law Guardian convinced her of the need for women to have the vote. Their three daughters were born in this period - Christabel in 1880, Sylvia in 1882 and Adela in 1885 (they also had two sons, one of whom died in childbirth and the other of whom died in 1910).

Political allegiance in the 1880s

Richard Pankhurst stood unsuccessfully as a Liberal parliamentary candidate in 1883 and 1885. Following the Gladstone government's refusal to include women's suffrage in the 1884 Reform Bill, however, the Pankhursts lost faith with the Liberal Party and became involved, first, with the Fabian Society and, in 1893, with the Independent Labour Party (see Unit 5, Parts 1 and 2 for more information on these groups). In 1895, Richard Pankhurst ran (again unsuccessfully) as the Independent Labour candidate for Gorton in Manchester.

The move to Manchester

After spending some time in London in the mid-1880s (Richard's legal career was not successful and so Emmeline ran a shop to supplement their income), they then spent the 1890s in Manchester where the three daughters were educated first at home and then at Manchester High School. Purvis notes:

'Both Emmeline and Richard were members of the newly formed Independent Labour Party and their children often accompanied their parents to political and social events that the ILP organised...Emmeline was elected to the National Executive Council (NEC) of the ILP in 1897.' (Purvis 2000, p.110)

The following year, Richard died and Emmeline temporarily retired from political activity - not least because there were many debts to pay and she had to devote her time to providing for her family. The family moved to a smaller house and Emmeline resigned as a Poor Law Guardian and took a salaried job as Registrar of Births and Deaths. Purvis argues that it was this work which convinced her of the need to secure the vote:

'In this work, she met many despairing working-class women, burdened with over-numerous families; in particular, she was especially moved by the plight of single mothers, some of them as young as 13, who, having been seduced by a father or close male relative, came to register the birth of their babies. Her conviction grew that, if women were to progress then they had to lift themselves out of their subordinate position and campaign for the parliamentary vote.' (Purvis 2000, p.110)

The formation of the WSPU

According to Bartley, dissatisfaction with the Independent Labour Party and the NUWSS was behind the Pankhursts' decision to set up a separate organisation to campaign for women's suffrage:

'The decision to form a new association was prompted by dissatisfaction with both the Labour Party (which was seen to be too lukewarm in its support of women's suffrage) and the NUWSS (which was seen to be too cautious).' (Bartley 1998, p.35)

Purvis (2000), however, argues that the formation of the WSPU was the direct consequence of Richard Pankhurst's death. When he died, a radical newspaper launched a campaign to provide financial support for the Pankhurst family (since the family's debts were, in part at least, a consequence of their political activity). Emmeline, however, refused to accept money to pay for her children's schooling (on the grounds that the money was being raised by people who could not themselves afford school fees) and asked for it to be used to build a socialist meeting hall in Richard's memory. When this hall was completed in 1903, Emmeline discovered that the ILP branch which was to use the hall would not allow women to join. This infuriated her and, as a result, she invited to her house the wives of a number of ILP men. They, together with Emmeline and her oldest daughter Christabel decided to set up a new organisation:

'It was in October 1903 that I invited a number of

women to my house in Nelson Street, Manchester, for the purposes of organisation. We voted to call the new society the Women's Social and Political Union, partly to emphasise its democracy and partly to define its object as political rather than propagandist. We resolved to limit our membership exclusively to women, to keep ourselves absolutely free from any party affiliation, to be satisfied with nothing but action on our question [ie the question of women's suffrage]. Deeds not words, was to be our permanent motto.' (Pankhurst 1914, p.38)

It was this reliance on action rather than dialogue which ensured that the WSPU became a very different kind of suffrage society from those which had been set up before. This only became apparent two years later, however, when the first militant acts took place.

Why did the WSPU adopt militant tactics?

It is important to emphasise that the term 'militancy' is rather a vague term. As Holton (1986) points out, action that was termed 'militant' in the 1860s (women speaking in public, for example) was no longer regarded as being militant at the beginning of the 20th century because people had become used to it. It is also important to point out that the WSPU did not just rely on militant tactics. In the first phase of militant action especially, the NUWSS often cooperated with and supported the WSPU in part because many of the events organised by the WSPU were perfectly peaceful and not militant at all.

Nevertheless, the WSPU did, eventually, turn to violence (violence directed against property not people) and it was the first women's suffrage society to use disruptive and confrontational tactics to draw attention to its demands. The reason why the WSPU did this has been the source of debate. Early (male) historians tended to argue that suffragettes were mentally unbalanced:

'The first historians to write about the suffragettes...emphasised the psychological weaknesses of the suffragettes and decried militancy as the action of a few demented spinsters.' (Bartley 1998, p.54)

More recent historians have accepted that the use of militant tactics was an understandable response to the failure of the authorities to accept suffragette demands:

'Over the years non-militant methods had failed and attempts to promote backbench Bills seemed futile. Instead, women should attack the government of the day until it agreed to introduce its own legislation for women's suffrage. A militant campaign would push suffrage up the agenda and, by rousing the country, force the Cabinet to back down.' (Pugh 1994, p.24)

Bartley's explanation of the adoption of militant tactics is outlined in Box 3.14.

BOX 3.14 **Why did the WSPU adopt militant tactics?**

Bartley argues that the WSPU used militant tactics:

- because women had been demanding votes since the 1860s but had been constantly disappointed
- because the Liberal government elected in 1906 excluded suffragettes from meetings and refused to meet them or to discuss the issue
- because the government used violence against suffragettes (suffragette hunger strikers were forcibly fed, for example)
- because suffragettes considered themselves to be following a long tradition in which violent protest had resulted in electoral reform (there had been violent clashes in 1831-32 and 1866-67, for example)
- because suffragettes believed that the government would not concede women's suffrage until they were forced to do so.

Adapted from Bartley 1998.

Interpretation

The first militant acts

Although the WSPU adopted a non-party approach, Emmeline Pankhurst initially remained a member of the ILP and was elected to its NEC again in 1904 (she eventually resigned her membership in 1907). Her resolution at the ILP's 1904 conference that the ILP should sponsor a Private Members' Bill proposing women's suffrage was passed and an MP was found to introduce the Bill. When, in May 1905, this Bill was talked out, what Emmeline Pankhurst described as the 'first militant act' took place:

'As the news reached the crowd of nearly 300 suffragists waiting in the Strangers' Lobby, the more placid representatives of the NUWSS left. Emmeline Pankhurst, on the other hand, instantly decided that the time had come for a demonstration such as "no old-fashioned suffragists had ever attempted". Thus, she called upon the women to follow her for a protest against the government...The aged suffragist, Elizabeth Wolstenholme Elmy began to speak and the police rushed into the crowd of women, ordering them to disperse. The WSPU Leader...helped the women to regroup as they demanded government intervention to save the talked-out Bill while the police took the names of the offenders.' (Purvis 2000, p.112)

The WSPU gains national coverage

If the first militant act took place in May 1905, the spark which ignited the suffragette movement took place five months later in October (the term 'suffragette' was first used in 1906 to describe militant suffragists by the, hostile, *Daily Mail*).

On 13 October, two members of the WSPU, Christabel Pankhurst and Annie Kenney (a working-class member from Oldham), attended a meeting held in the Free Trade Hall in Manchester. The main speakers were leading Liberals, Winston Churchill (a member of the Liberal Party at this early stage of his career) and Edward Grey. Grey's speech outlined the Liberal programme to be put to the electorate in the forthcoming general election. At question time, the two WSPU members stood up and repeatedly asked whether a Liberal government would introduce women's suffrage, but the men on the platform refused to answer. When Annie Kenney shouted out her question again as people were beginning to leave, there was uproar and she and Christabel Pankhurst were ejected by stewards. This, it appears, was all part of the plan:

'The women were roughly handled and dragged outside by stewards where Christabel deliberately committed the technical offence of spitting at a policeman in order to be arrested. In court the next day, Christabel and Annie refused to pay the fines imposed on them and were sentenced to one week and three days imprisonment respectively.' (Purvis 2000, p.112)

The result (as planned) was a mass of publicity. Much of the publicity was hostile, but, as Strachey observes, it still bore fruit for the WSPU (see Box 3.15).

BOX 3.15 **The impact made by Christabel Pankhurst and Annie Kenney**

Here was news, thrilling news, involving a future Cabinet minister, and a cause about which ridicule and cheap joking were easy. With one accord, the brawling and wickedness of the women were deplored and the leader-writers lamented with sham regret that their cause was put back for ages and that women had now proved themselves forever unfit for enfranchisement. Manchester University (where Christabel Pankhurst had already been troublesome by insisting on being a law student) threatened to expel her, and the whole affair was the great preoccupation of the city. Already, by this one act, hundreds of people who had never thought about women's suffrage before, began to consider it and, though the vast majority of them deplored what had been done, this did not make the result any the less important. A wonderful new weapon, the weapon of publicity and advertisement, was put in the hands of the Women's Social and Political Union and the leaders at once saw its value.

From Strachey 1979, pp.294-95.

Interpretation

Once it had started, the militant campaign went through three phases. These are described in Section 3.3 below.

3.2 Structure and organisation

The leadership

Following the success of the first militant actions and

the election of the first Liberal government for 20 years, the WSPU began campaigning in London. Sylvia Pankhurst was already studying art in London. In January 1906, she was joined by Annie Kenney and, by August, Christabel Pankhurst had moved there, becoming the WSPU's 'Chief Organiser'. Money for the campaign was raised by, amongst others, the Labour MP Keir Hardie and, on his recommendation, Emmeline Pethick Lawrence was appointed Treasurer (her husband, Frederick, was a lawyer and he also became closely involved in the campaign). In March 1907, Emmeline Pankhurst resigned from her Registrar post (relying on the money that the WSPU paid her) and, in April, she sold her house in Manchester:

'By now, Emmeline was travelling around the country, speaking in endless meetings and leading the by-election campaigning...From now until the end of the militant campaign she had no settled home but stayed in a number of rented flats, hotels or homes of friends.' (Purvis 2000, p.117)

An autocratic structure

One of the criticisms of the WSPU made by many historians is that it had an autocratic (non-democratic) structure. This was a criticism made by Ray Strachey in 1928 and repeated many times since:

'The Women's Social and Political Union adopted a purely autocratic system and entrusted all decisions to their leaders - Mrs Pankhurst and her daughter Christabel, and Mr and Mrs Pethick Lawrence. These people alone decided what was to be done; the others obeyed and enjoyed the surrender of their judgement, and the sensation of marching as an army under discipline.' (Strachey 1979, p.310)

The WSPU never had a formal constitution and all decisions of any importance were made by the leadership and then communicated to the membership. In this sense, the WSPU was truly a top-down organisation:

'From 1906, policies were decided by an unelected Central Committee with Sylvia Pankhurst as Secretary, Emmeline Pethick Lawrence as Treasurer and Annie Kenney as paid Organiser. This Central Committee was assisted by a sub-committee which consisted of family and friends such as Mary Clarke (Emmeline Pankhurst's sister). Members did not participate in decision making but were informed of new policies and strategies during the "At Home" sessions which were held each Monday afternoon at the headquarters in Lincoln Inn's Field, London. The leadership controlled their own publications, appointments to paid positions and, of course, the finances of the organisation.' (Bartley 1998, p.35)

The historical debate

Historians hostile to the WSPU have used terms such as 'dictatorship' or 'tyranny' to describe this structure and suggest that it was hypocritical to demand greater democracy from the government while not using democratic methods within the organisation itself. Historians sympathetic to the Pankhursts, however, make a number of counter-arguments. Purvis (2000), for example, points out that Emmeline Pankhurst never apologised for setting up an autocratic structure because, as far as she was concerned, it was the most effective structure to achieve the organisation's goals. Bartley (1998), on the other hand, points out that there is evidence of greater democracy in WSPU branches outside London and she gives four other reasons not to condemn the structure of the organisation out of hand:

- much criticism has come from constitutionalists who have an axe to grind
- the organisation, at first at least, attempted an 'informal approach to politics' - members could always leave if they did not support the WSPU's approach
- a democratic structure would not have worked - especially when the WSPU's activities became illegal
- the leadership by no means ignored the membership - they took great pains to educate and involve them.

Splits within the leadership

Between 1903 and 1914, there were a number of splits within the WSPU leadership. Historians agree that three were particularly important, although they differ over how to interpret the splits.

1. The 1907 split

The first of these splits occurred in the summer of 1907. According to Holton (1995), the cause of the split was Christabel Pankhurst's move to London:

'Christabel Pankhurst had introduced a change of policy without any consultation of the WSPU's membership in August 1906, one which caused some unease among socialist suffragists because it saw the WSPU attacking Labour and Liberal candidates equally at by-elections.' (Holton 1995, p.291)

These 'socialist suffragists', for example Teresa Billington-Grieg and Charlotte Despard drew up a written constitution (giving the membership a greater say in decisions) which they hoped would be accepted at the annual conference planned for October. Emmeline Pankhurst was aware of this plan as early as June 1907 and she wrote to Sylvia:

'As for the TBG [Teresa Billington-Grieg] affair, we have just to face her and put her in her place.' (part of a letter written on 22 June 1907)

At the annual conference, Emmeline Pankhurst dramatically ripped up the proposed constitution and made a speech appealing for members to follow her. The majority did. The minority followed Teresa Billington-Grieg and Charlotte Despard out of the WSPU and into a new, democratic version of it - the Women's Freedom League (WFL).

While historians hostile to the Pankhursts cite this as

an example of their dictatorial methods, Bartley (1998) notes that the WFL (a militant group) 'fell between the law-breaking suffragettes and the law-abiding suffragists'. It also suffered from internal divisions.

2. The October 1912 split

In October 1912, Emmeline and Christabel Pankhurst expelled Emmeline and Frederick Pethick Lawrence from the organisation following differences over tactics (the Pankhursts favoured greater militancy while the Pethick Lawrences did not). This split was particularly traumatic because the two families had been very close. Christabel had lived with the Pethick Lawrences when she moved to London, for example. While critics have cited this as a further example of the Pankhurst's dictatorial tendencies, Bartley says:

'If the Pankhursts were criticised, friendship ties were swiftly broken...The Pethick Lawrences had not only questioned the escalation of violence, but Fred, as the only man ever to take a large part in the running of the WSPU, was seen increasingly as a social embarrassment.' (Bartley 1998, p.40)

3. The January 1914 split

Even Pankhurst family members were not secure within the organisation. Purvis notes that, in 1912, Adela suffered a breakdown and was sent by Emmeline to Australia. Then, in January 1914:

'Sylvia was told by Christabel, with Emmeline's support, that her East London Federation must be separate from the WSPU since it was allied with the Labour Party, contrary to WSPU policy.' (Purvis 2000, p.127)

Bartley explains that:

'Christabel disliked her sister's emphasis on class politics. In concentrating her energies in the East End of London, in conducting the campaign for votes for women along class lines and in forming a "People's Army" to fight against class oppression, Sylvia Pankhurst was thought to have discredited the WSPU.' (Bartley 1998, p.40)

For historians hostile to the WSPU, this is further evidence that the organisation was élitist. Those sympathetic to the organisation, however, accept the argument that its strength was a central leadership following a single approach. Since Sylvia refused to follow that approach, it was right to eject her.

Membership

Unlike the NUWSS, the WSPU did not publish records of its membership and so it is difficult to be sure about the extent of support at any one time. In general terms, however, there seems to have been growing support until at least 1910 and a decline in 1913-14 - see Box 3.16.

The NUWSS and the WSPU

The growth in support of the WSPU was accompanied by a big growth in support of the NUWSS, especially after 1909. Pugh claims that this was because the NUWSS allowed women to express their support for the vote while, at the same time, showing their disapproval of suffragette tactics:

'From 1909 onwards, militancy appears to have had an important indirect effect on the membership of the NUWSS which rose from 12,000 to over 50,000. The explanation is that many women who had no wish to be associated with the suffragettes could not help being moved by their example and, therefore, chose to express their feelings by joining the non-militants.' (Pugh 1994, p.26)

Though critical of the NUWSS's tactics, Harrison confirms that support grew and argues that the NUWSS was more successful than the WSPU in several ways:

'The non-militants remained organisationally, numerically and educationally superior throughout the period [1903-14] and maintained their growth rate more successfully...The number of NUWSS branches rose from 33 in October 1907 to 70 in March 1910 and to 478 in February 1914. Membership grew accordingly - from 22,000 in January 1911 to 52,000 by February 1914. If local and national funds are aggregated, the non-militant total had reached about £45,000 in the financial year 1913-14.' (Harrison 1983, p.114)

Working-class support for the WSPU

One of the main criticisms made of the WSPU by hostile historians on the left is that the WSPU abandoned the Labour Party and became an élite, predominantly middle-class organisation. This argument is made strongly by Martin Pugh:

'After their move to London in 1906, the Pankhursts abandoned any attempt to mobilise the Lancashire cotton textile girls. However, they took care to retain one, Annie Kenney, whose function was to prove that working-class women wanted the vote...The Pankhursts threw their energies into cultivating the Conservative leaders and tapping the funds and support of metropolitan [ie London] society.' (Pugh 1985, p.241)

BOX 3.16 | **WSPU membership**

Historians have reached the following conclusions about the WSPU's membership:

- WSPU funds continued to grow until 1914, but the pace of growth slowed after 1909 and income from new members declined after 1910
- in 1913-14, the WSPU raised £37,000.
- the WSPU was able to employ 98 women office workers and 26 officers in the regions
- at their height, 'At Home' sessions in London were attended by c.1,000 people per week
- at the WSPU's height, it had 88 branches, 34 of them in London
- the circulation of the WSPU newspaper *Votes for Women* reached 30,000-40,000 copies per issue.

Adapted from Harrison 1983 and Bartley 1998.

Interpretation

This point of view has been rejected by Bartley (1998 and 1999). She argues that:

'[The WSPU] was set up specifically for working-class women and, between 1903 and 1906, did valuable propaganda work in the textile towns. Even when the WSPU headquarters moved to London, it targeted working-class women. When Annie Kenney...and Sylvia Pankhurst were sent to London to organise the campaign in the capital, most of their energies were spent in working-class districts.' (Bartley 1998, p.38)

Bartley admits that, when Christabel Pankhurst arrived in London, 'working-class women receded into the background'. Nevertheless, in her 1999 article, she claims that:

'The WSPU remained committed to working-class women in spite of the fact that women from a wide variety of social backgrounds played leading parts in its development.' (Bartley 1999, p.41)

The evidence in support of this claim is outlined in Box 3.17.

Propaganda

Since the WSPU's key aim was to draw attention to the issue of women's suffrage, the organisation developed into a formidable propaganda machine. Successful fund-raising drives allowed the organisation to buy property in London and the provinces. In London, the WSPU set up its headquarters at Clement's Inn and, in May 1910, opened a shop in Charing Cross Road - the Women's Press. As well as earning money for the WSPU, the shop publicised the cause:

'The shop itself is a blaze of purple, white and green...Just now, the Women's Press is showing some beautiful motor and other scarves in various shades of purple as well as white muslin summer blouses and among the almost unending variety of bags, belts etc are the noticeable "The Emmeline" and "The Christabel" bags and "The Pethick" tobacco pouch. In addition to books, pamphlets and leaflets, stationery, games, blotters, playing cards and indeed almost everything that can be produced in purple, green or white, or a combination of all three, is to be found here.' (extract from *Votes for Women*, July 1910)

Clement's Inn

Suffragette campaigns and activities were organised and coordinated from Clement's Inn. Diane Atkinson notes that:

'From here, the plans of the WSPU were turned into direct action...The daring "Pestering the Politicians" campaign, which targeted Cabinet ministers when they were "off duty" was arranged. The huge set-piece demonstrations...were also planned in detail in these offices. As well as these major ventures, the less prestigious but equally significant everyday activities of the campaign were coordinated on the premises too.' (Atkinson 1996 , p.42)

BOX 3.17 The WSPU and working class women

Interpretation

In support of the claim that the WSPU remained committed to working-class women, Bartley notes that:

1. Annie Kenney was not the only leading member of the WSPU to have a working-class background - so did Jessie Stephens (a leading Scottish suffragette), Emma Sproson (imprisoned in 1907) and Mary Leigh (the first suffragette to break windows).

2. Many working-class women were recruited in London - not just to the East London Federation of Suffragettes (which remained part of the WSPU until 1914) but also to branches in Woolwich, Lewisham and Greenwich.

3. Some of the WSPU's paid officers were working-class women.

4. Working-class women took part in many WSPU demonstrations (often wearing their working clothes - as many photographs show).

5. Many of the WSPU activists who were imprisoned, went on hunger strike and were forcibly fed were working-class women.

6. The WSPU supported working-class women's issues - eg the WSPU campaigned for women chain-makers and barmaids when their jobs were threatened and, in 1911, they led the campaign against legislation which would have banned women from working above ground in coal mines ('pit brow' workers). The campaign was a success.

Bartley's conclusion

Bartley concludes that the struggle in support of pit-brow women shows that the WSPU remained committed to working-class women. Women from all social classes were involved in the campaign for the vote. Many suffragettes continued to ally themselves with radical politics and involved themselves in working-class struggles.

Adapted from Bartley 1999.

These 'less prestigious' activities included:

- organising meetings and rallies
- producing and circulating leaflets and tickets for indoor meetings
- organising volunteers to chalk pavements to advertise meetings
- sending out suffragette scouts on cycles to rally support
- designing and marketing goods to be sold in suffragette shops.

In addition, the suffragettes' newspaper *Votes for Women* was written and produced in Clement's Inn. This was sold by volunteers (who often dressed in suffragette colours) and via 'press carts' (horse-drawn wagons decorated with WSPU propaganda) as well as in newsagents.

Non-militant tactics

As well as using militant tactics (see Section 3.3 below), the WSPU used a range of innovative non-militant tactics to draw attention to their cause:

- two suffragettes were posted as 'human letters' addressed to 10 Downing Street and were led there by a telegraph boy
- suffragettes hired a boat on the Thames and sailed to Parliament to shout at MPs taking tea on the terrace
- suffragettes flew a kite with the slogan 'Votes for Women' above the pitch at the 1908 FA cup final
- around 200,000 demonstrators simultaneously shouted 'Votes for Women' at a parade in Hyde Park in June 1908 (the so-called 'Great Shout') and most dressed up in WSPU colours
- suffragettes made floats and dressed up in national costume or as famous women in the Women's Coronation Procession of June 1911.

MAIN POINTS - Sections 3.1-3.2

- By October 1903, Emmeline Pankhurst was a veteran political campaigner. Reasons given for the formation of the WSPU include dissatisfaction with (1) the Independent Labour Party in general (2) the local ILP in particular and (3) the NUWSS.
- Although the term 'militancy' is rather vague and the WSPU did not just rely on militant tactics, it was the first women's suffrage society to use violence and confrontation.
- While some historians have argued that suffragettes were 'unbalanced', Bartley argues they used militant tactics because - (1) no progress had been made since the 1860s (2) the Liberal government ignored their demands (3) the authorities used force against them (4) there were precedents and (5) they believed it would work.
- The WSPU has been criticised for its autocratic (non-democratic) structure. In defence, it has been pointed out that (1) it was effective (2) branches were more democratic than the centre (3) hostility reflects authors' prejudices (4) members were free to leave if they disagreed and (5) the leadership by no means ignored the membership.
- There were three important splits in the WSPU - (1) in 1907 when Teresa Billington-Grieg and Charlotte Despard left after failing to democratise the group (2) in 1912 when the Pethick Lawrences were expelled after disagreements over tactics and (3) in 1914 when Sylvia Pankhurst was expelled for being too close to the Labour movement.
- The growth of the WSPU stimulated the growth of the NUWSS. Although many of its leaders were upper- and middle-class, the WSPU also retained its links with working-class women.

Activity 3.4 The Pankhursts

ITEM 1 Adela Pankhurst

In 1906, Adela Pankhurst gave up her job as an elementary school teacher in Manchester to become a WSPU organiser in Lancashire and Yorkshire. During the general election campaign of 1905, she repeatedly questioned Winston Churchill at large public meetings and was 'ejected night after night'. She served several short prison sentences for interrupting Liberal meetings and for participating in marches on the House of Commons. Adela's left-wing views, however, were not shared by her mother and sister Christabel. In 1911, she lost her voice, caught pleurisy (an illness which affects the lungs) and was urged to give up public speaking. Emmeline and Christabel used this as an excuse to end her career in the WSPU. Adela accepted the offer of going on a gardening course, but after failing to find work when she had finished the course, emigrated to Australia in 1912 where she lived for the rest of her life. June Purvis describes her illness as a 'breakdown' and says that she was 'shattered' when she realised that her mother (to whom she was devoted) thought her a failure. To avoid a clash, Purvis says, she accepted Emmeline's 'well-meaning' plan to give her a fresh start in Australia.

Adapted from Atkinson 1996.

VOTES FOR WOMEN.

Miss ADELA PANKHURST,

Organiser, National Women's Social and Political Union, 4, Clement's Inn, Strand, W.C.

ITEM 2 Emmeline and Christabel

The day after the meeting at the Free Trade Hall in October 1905, an anxious Emmeline Pankhurst hurried into the room into which Christabel and Annie Kenney were ushered and pleaded with Christabel, 'You have done everything you could be expected to do in this matter. I think you should let me pay your fines and take you home'. But her daughter was resolute, replying: 'Mother, if you pay my fine I will never go home'. Emmeline did not insist. Believing that Christabel had the finest political instinct, she accepted the new tactics completely - evidence not only of her perception, but also of her perfect understanding with Christabel. Sylvia Pankhurst claimed that, from the day of Christabel's first imprisonment, their mother proudly and openly declared her eldest daughter, her favourite child, to be her Leader. Although Christabel always denied this, she and her mother were seen as two sides of the same coin. This is important to understanding the WSPU since it was Emmeline and Christabel who decided policy. According to Frederick Pethick Lawrence, Christabel was left to deal with day-to-day business and to devise short-term strategy while Emmeline usually got her own way when it came to long-term aims. Following the 1907 split, Emmeline did not exercise any direct personal control. Although she was consulted on all major policy issues, she had absolute confidence in Christabel's judgement. An example of their absolute loyalty to each other came in 1912 when the two decided to expel the Pethick Lawrences. Emmeline informed them in October. Shattered by such news, they insisted that Christabel (who was in exile in France) come to London to debate the matter. Travelling in disguise, Christabel emphasised that she and her mother were 'absolutely united in this matter'.

Adapted from Purvis 2000.

ITEM 3 Emmeline, Christabel and Sylvia

I did not meet Christabel until several months after I had been working with Sylvia and Annie [Kenney]...She was cut out for public life...She possessed the gifts necessary to succeed. Like all the Pankhursts, she had great courage. She had a cool logical mind and a quick ready wit. She was young and attractive, graceful on the platform, with a singular clear and musical voice. She had none of Sylvia's passion or pity - on the contrary, she detested weakness, which was discouraged in her presence. Although to all the Pankhursts the cause of women's suffrage was a religion that demanded from them everything that they had to give, the approach of each one was different. As to Sylvia...she has never wavered in her loyalty to the victimised and oppressed in every part of the world. Although in comparison with many who took the lead in the suffrage movement, she was not considered as conspicuously popular or conspicuously effective, yet she, with her devoted following in the East End, was the first (in 1914) to break Mr Asquith's resistance and to win from him the admission that the vote must be granted to working women like those she had sent to him...To her, the vote meant the amelioration [improving] of the lot of the workers. Christabel was not inspired by

This photograph was taken on 4 October 1911 at Waterloo station. It shows Emmeline Pankhurst (left) with her daughters Christabel (centre) and Sylvia. Emmeline was about to embark on a fund-raising lecture tour of the USA and Canada. Women in some states in the USA had already won the right to vote.

pity but by a deep secret shame - shame that any woman should tamely accept the position accorded her as something less than an adult human being - a position half way between the child and the citizen. Christabel cared less for the political vote itself than for the dignity of her sex...She never made any secret of the fact that to her the means were more important than the end. Militancy to her meant putting off the slave spirit. To Mrs Pankhurst, the appeal was different again. She was, as she instinctively knew, cast for a great role...Left a widow with a family to educate...the fire in her had been damped down. But the smouldering spark leapt into flame when her daughter Christabel initiated militancy. It was fed by a passion for her first-born. Once years later...she dwelt upon the name of her daughter 'Christabel the Anointed One', the young deliverer who was to emancipate the new generation of women.

Extract from Emmeline Pethick Lawrence's autobiography, 'My Part in a Changing World', published in 1938.

Questions

1. a) 'The Emmeline and Christabel Pankhurst show'. Is this an accurate description of the WSPU? Use Items 1-3 in your answer.
   b) What leadership qualities did the Pankhursts have?
2. a) What does Item 1 tell us about relations between members of the Pankhurst family?
   b) What sort of a mother was Emmeline Pankhurst?
3. a) What do Items 2 and 3 tell us about the WSPU leadership?
   b) Why do you think there were tensions between Christabel and Sylvia?
   c) How might a historian hostile to the Pankhursts respond to the view of the Pankhursts given in Items 2 and 3?

3.3 The WSPU and militant tactics

Militant tactics

It is possible to identify three distinct phases in the WSPU's campaign to win the vote during the period 1905-14. In each phase, the tactics adopted by the WSPU became more militant, but it should be remembered that non-militant tactics were also used throughout the period.

According to Jane Marcus, behind the many different types of action performed by the suffragettes, there was a central theme. The suffragettes aimed to 'interrupt male political discourse'. Marcus points out that, at the beginning of the 20th century:

'[Women were] trained in silence and good behaviour to modestly listen to the men, to a role, whatever her class, of "she who may be interrupted", whose work or speech is always subservient to the male's.' (Marcus 1987, p.9)

Throughout the period 1905-14, however, suffragettes refused to perform the role expected of them. Instead, they would not be quiet. They started asking questions and heckling at political meetings, demanding to be heard and not giving way until they were heard or were forcibly removed. Marcus argues that what was at stake here was more than just winning the right to vote. Suffragettes, she says, were 'taking one of the most important steps in the history of women' - they were finding their political voice.

Looking back from 21st century Britain when it seems natural for women to have their say in political debates, it is difficult to appreciate just how shocking for some men the suffragette's interventions were. Box 3.18 provides an passage to illustrate this point.

Arguments against Marcus' view

While Purvis (2000) describes Marcus' interpretation as 'apt', Bartley disputes Marcus' theory. She argues:

'Of course, this is historical speculation: the WSPU perhaps had more pragmatic reasons for interrupting the government. Indeed, they were possibly more influenced by Parnell's obstructionist tactics in the Irish Home Rule campaign of the 1880s than in interrupting men to make a feminist point.' (Bartley 1998, p.62)

Bartley notes that, between 1882 and 1885, Charles Stewart Parnell and his supporters in the Irish National League campaigned against all Liberal candidates at elections whether or not they supported Home Rule in order to put pressure on the government to propose a Home Rule Bill (see Unit 1, Section 3.2). Similarly, between 1905 and 1914, suffragettes opposed all Liberal candidates at by-elections whether or not they supported women's suffrage to put pressure on the government to propose a Women's Suffrage Bill. Bartley also notes

BOX 3.18 Sylvia Pankhurst and Winston Churchill, 1905

I was at Churchill's meeting in a schoolroom in Cheetham Hill, Manchester. There was a running fire of questions of all sorts. Churchill answered them as they came. I put mine as soon as he gave me an appropriate cue. He attempted to ignore me, but my brother and some ILP men at the back of the hall led the audience in demanding that I should be answered. Such a clamour was raised that Churchill could not proceed. As soon as I stood up again, there was complete silence, but when my question was put and again ignored, the din began once more. This continued for some time. To end the deadlock the chairman asked me to put my question from the platform. I did so and turned to go, but Churchill seized me roughly by the arm and pushed me into a chair at the back of the platform, saying: 'No, you must wait here until you have heard what I have to say'. Then, turning to the audience, he protested that I was 'bringing my disgrace upon an honoured name' by interrupting him, and added, 'Nothing would induce me to vote for giving women the franchise; I am not going to be henpecked into a question of such importance'. I would have gone then, but in a scuffle, during which all the men on the platform stood up to hide what was happening from the audience, I was pushed into a side room. I was left there, the door being locked on the outside, but not before I had opened the window and called to the people in the side street to witness the conduct of an enthusiastic Liberal who was jumping around like a madman and threatening to scratch my face. It appeared that I was a prisoner, for the windows were barred, but the people who had gathered outside called to me that a window at the other end of the room had a couple of bars missing. They helped me out and called for a speech. Someone brought me a chair and I had a rousing time of it.

From Pankhurst 1931, pp.193-94.

that Richard Pankhurst had stood as a Liberal candidate and failed to gain election in 1885 - in part, perhaps, due to opposition from the Irish National League. In other words, Emmeline Pankhurst may have learned from this experience and, later, discussed it with her daughters (Christabel was only five in 1885).

Whether Bartley is right to assert that the suffragettes did not want to make a 'feminist point' is debatable. Certainly, this appears to have been the aim of Christabel Pankhurst (Item 3 in Activity 3.4 above certainly suggests that this was the case). Besides, Marcus' point is that, whether it was a deliberate aim or not, the militant campaign raised the possibility of women entering 'the space of male political debate' and was, therefore, an important influence on the feminism which emerged later (from the 1960s).

Phase 1 - April 1906-June 1908

While the first militant acts took place in the run-up to the 1906 general election, it was after the election that the campaign began in earnest. As McDonald points out, the election result raised suffragists' hopes that progress would be made:

'The women's hopes must have been sky-high when the election results were announced in January 1906. The Liberals swept in with one of the largest ever majorities - 399 seats to 156 for the Conservatives - and with Labour increasing their share from two to 29. Surely there must now be a majority for women' suffrage?...[But] it soon became apparent that the election had brought no fundamental change.' (McDonald 1989, pp.34-35)

The first phase of the militant campaign was a response to this lack of progress. In this phase of their militant campaign, the suffragettes broke with convention and encountered violence from others, but they did not use violence themselves. This phase had two main strands.

1. Confronting Parliament and ministers

As with the constitutionalists, Parliament and government was the focus of a great deal of WSPU activity. WSPU activity, however, was different from that of the constitutionalists in several ways.

First, in April 1906, a group of suffragettes who had been admitted to the Ladies' Gallery in the House of Commons caused a great deal of outrage when they attempted to intervene in a Parliamentary debate on Keir Hardie's resolution in support of women's suffrage. When an anti-suffragist MP attempted to talk out the resolution, the women in the gallery started heckling, shouted 'divide, divide' and brandished banners marked 'Votes for Women'. The police were called and the women ejected. This action was condemned by Keir Hardie and the constitutionalists, but gained a great deal of publicity.

Second, while the constitutionalists did organise demonstrations and lobby MPs, they did not confront the authorities. The NUWSS's first procession, for example, was organised in February 1907. Because of the bad weather, it became known as the 'Mud March'. The procession was orderly and peaceful and was followed by a rally in which supporters such as Keir Hardie made speeches. The WSPU, on the other hand, deliberately set out to confront the authorities even if that meant rough treatment, arrest and imprisonment. The first confrontation came on the day of the King's Speech (which announced the government's forthcoming programme) in February 1906 when Emmeline Pankhurst led a group of around 300 suffragettes to the House of Commons to protest at the lack of reference to a Bill on women's suffrage. It was the first of many such 'raids'. The common pattern which emerged is described in Box 3.19

| BOX 3.19 | WSPU 'raids' on Parliament |

Interpretation

A meeting in the neighbourhood would be the first step; at this meeting a deputation would be appointed and eight, ten, 50 or 100 women would then file out either in procession or in small groups and proceed to Westminster. As they neared Palace Yard they would be met by cordons of police, sometimes as many as 1,000 strong, on foot and on horseback. They would then be ordered to turn back, and would refuse. The crowds which had been following them would close in and a sort of confused scuffle would follow in which the women were usually knocked about, sometimes pretty severely. They would do no violence themselves, but merely persist in their attempt to go on, and finally, after varying periods of time, they would be arrested. *From Strachey 1979, p.312.*

And third, suffragettes targeted Cabinet ministers, organising sit-down protests in Downing Street and chaining themselves to railings there so that they could not be evicted so easily, or heckling them at public meetings. As Christabel Pankhurst explained in a speech delivered on 15 October 1908, there were two reasons for heckling Cabinet ministers:

'We do it, in the first place, to draw attention to our grievance and educate the public. Cabinet ministers will not do this for us - they shirk the question - we have got to do it ourselves. In the second place, we know it to be an excellent way of harassing Cabinet ministers. It is nothing to us to be interrupted, but to them it is a serious matter... Cabinet ministers think their own speeches of vast importance. They like to deliver those speeches to a unanimous and enthusiastic audience...On the day following their meeting they like to read in the press verbatim [word-for-word] accounts of what they said and it makes them a bit sore when they find there is more in the newspapers about what the women have said than what they have said themselves.' (quoted in Marcus 1987, pp.46-47)

2. Campaigning at by-elections

In August 1906, Christabel Pankhurst announced that the WSPU would be adopting a new policy - namely, in order to put pressure on the government to support a Women's Suffrage Bill, they would oppose Liberal candidates in any by-elections which took place. Emmeline Pankhurst's explanation of this is provided in Box 3.20 on page 97.

It is difficult to be sure how effective the suffragettes were in their by-election campaign. The Liberals claimed that they made little impact, while the suffragettes claimed the opposite. Purvis (2000, p.115 and p.118) notes that when the Conservative candidate won the Cockermouth by-election of

BOX 3.20 The WSPU's by-election policy

Source Box

Our by-election work was such a new thing in English politics that we attracted an enormous amount of attention wherever we went. It was our custom to begin work the very hour we entered a town. If, on our way from the station to the hotel, we encountered a group of men, say in the market place, we either stopped and held a meeting on the spot, or else we stayed long enough to tell them when and where our meetings were to be held, and to urge them to attend. The usual first step after securing lodgings was to hire a vacant shop, fill the windows with suffrage literature and fling out our purple, white and green flag. Meanwhile some of us were busy hiring the best available hall. If we got possession of the battle ground before the men, we sometimes "cornered" all the good halls and left the candidate nothing but schoolhouses for his indoor meetings. Truth to tell, our meetings were so much more popular than theirs that we really needed the larger halls.

From Pankhurst 1914, p.87.

August 1906, the result was 'blamed on the WSPU', and she also notes that Emmeline Pankhurst claimed the WSPU was responsible for pulling down the Liberal vote in nine by-elections held in 1908. She also notes, however, that suffragettes sometimes encountered great hostility and even violence:

'Often Emmeline [Pankhurst] became a target for rough treatment and violence, as in January 1908 when the by-election result was announced at Newton Abbot in favour of the Conservative candidate. She and her co-worker, Nellie Martel, were attacked by a group of young male clay-cutters who had supported the ousted Liberal candidate, whom the women had opposed. While Emmeline was running to the haven of a grocer's shop, a staggering blow fell on the back of her head, rough hands grasped the collar of her coat and she was flung to the muddy ground.' (Purvis 2000, pp.117-18)

Phase 2 - June 1908 to the truce of January 1910

The second phase of militant tactics was characterised by a greater willingness to use violence against property, and 'technical' violence against the authorities to provoke arrests. It was also during this period that the first cases of hunger striking and forcible feeding took place.

The turning point was a rally organised by the suffragettes in June 1908. By then, Herbert Asquith, was Prime Minister (he took over in April 1908 when Henry Campbell Bannerman was forced to resign through ill health). Asquith had the reputation for being hostile towards women's suffrage. As Bartley puts it:

'Asquith, although married to a very shrewd political operator, was unchanging in his implacable opposition to votes for women. In his first major speech on suffrage in 1892 Asquith gave four reasons why he was against women's suffrage. Firstly he argued that the vast majority of women did not want the vote, secondly that women were not fit for the franchise, thirdly that women operated by personal influence, and finally that it would upset the natural order of things. Asquith believed that woman's place was in the home rather than in what he termed the "dust and turmoil" of political life.' (Bartley 1998, pp.68-69)

The rally of 21 June 1908 - 'Women's Sunday'

The suffragette rally of 21 June was organised in response to an announcement made by Asquith that the government would back an Electoral Reform Bill that would be worded in such a way as to allow an amendment introducing women's suffrage provided that:

- the amendment was on democratic lines
- the amendment had the support of the women of the country
- the amendment had the support of the electorate.

In order to demonstrate that the women of the country supported such an amendment, the WSPU organised a mass rally. According to the *Daily Chronicle* (22 June 1908), a crowd of over 300,000 people gathered, with WSPU members all dressed in their uniform of purple, white and green (these colours had been chosen by Emmeline Pethick Lawrence as the WSPU's because purple symbolised dignity, white purity and green hope). Holton (1996) and Purvis (2000) agree that this was a turning point:

'This colourful, peaceful demonstration was a watershed in the development of militancy for the WSPU since Asquith remained unmoved by the scale of support; from this time, militancy, conceived as the heckling of Liberal MPs, civil disobedience and peaceful demonstrations, was gradually replaced by the organisation of more threatening demonstrations and acts of violence.' (Purvis 2000, p.119)

Purvis points out that Emmeline Pankhurst supported the new forms of militancy, but there is a debate as to whether she or Christabel initiated them.

The militant tactics used in the second phase include the following.

1. Stone throwing

On 30 June 1908, Emmeline Pankhurst led a group of suffragettes to Parliament. As usual, the group was dispersed by the police. On this occasion, however, two suffragettes - Mary Leigh and Edith New - went on to throw stones at the windows of 10 Downing Street in protest. They were arrested and sentenced to two months in prison. In prison, the two women contacted Emmeline Pankhurst accepting that they had acted without orders and, as a result, expecting her to criticise them. Purvis records that:

'Far from repudiating [criticising] them, Emmeline went at once to see them in their cells and "assured them" of her approval.' (Purvis 2000, p.119)

From this point, stone throwing became part of the suffragette's armoury, though Bartley points out that:

'Window smashing became part of a well-orchestrated campaign, with suffragettes travelling down from as far as Scotland to take part. Even so, window smashing generally occurred not haphazardly but as a consequence of alleged government double dealing.' (Bartley 1998, p.56)

2. Technical offences

The arrest and imprisonment of suffragettes did not have the effect the government intended. There is evidence that many people were shocked at the harsh sentences and no sign that the suffragettes were deterred by this treatment. As a result:

'Orders were accordingly issued that the suffragettes were not to be arrested, or if they had to be arrested, they were not to be charged.' (Strachey 1979, p.312)

The suffragette response was to commit 'technical' violent offences to ensure that the police had no option but to arrest them. For example, on 29 June 1909, Emmeline Pankhurst went with eight women to the Commons. When they were confronted by the police, Strachey records that:

'Mrs Pankhurst herself led the way by striking Inspector Jervis upon the face at the door of the House of Commons. Her victim perfectly understood why she did this and admitted it as he arrested her; but from the press a howl of indignation arose. Screaming scratching, biting and yelling were attributed to the militants.' (Strachey 1979, p.313)

3. Hunger striking

Just as stone throwing was the initiative of ordinary WSPU members, rather than an initiative of the leadership, so too was hunger striking. On 24 June 1909, an artist, Marion Wallace Dunlop, was arrested and imprisoned after painting an extract from the 1689 Bill of Rights on the wall of the Commons. Like other suffragette prisoners, Wallace Dunlop was refused political status in prison and, on 5 July, she began a hunger strike in protest. After 91 hours of fasting, she was released. Other suffragettes followed her example and were also released. But, from September 1909, the government introduced forcible feeding (see Box 3.21).

Phase 3 - From November 1911 to August 1914

The second phase ended when the WSPU announced a suspension of militant action, following the promise of a 'Conciliation Bill', at the end of January 1910. A general election had been held in early January 1910, resulting in a Liberal government

BOX 3.21 Forcible feeding

Source and interpretation

(i) The doctor and four wardresses came into my cell. I decided to save all my resistance for the actual feeding and, when they pointed to my bed on the floor, I lay down, and the doctor did not even feel my pulse. Two wardresses held my hands and one my head. Much as I had heard about this thing, it was infinitely more painful than I had expected. The doctor put the steel gag in somewhere on my gums and forced my mouth until it was yawning wide. As he proceeded to force into my mouth and down the throat a large rubber tube, I felt as though I was being killed - absolute suffocation is the feeling. You feel as though it would never stop...It irritates the throat, it irritates the mucous membrane as it goes down, every second seems an hour and you think they will never finish putting it down. After a while, the sensation is relieved, then the food is poured down and then again you choke, and your whole body resists and writhes under the treatment; you are held down and the process goes on and finally, when the vomiting becomes excessive, the tube is removed.
Part of a speech recorded in 'Votes for Women' in January 1910.

(ii) Historians are divided over the significance of force-feeding. Some justify its use because it saved the lives of hunger strikers. Roger Fulford, for example, dismisses it as a harmless procedure that had been in use for years with 'lunatics'. Historians hostile to the suffragettes tend to downplay the brutality of the government. On the other hand, much suffragette propaganda portrayed it as oral rape and many feminist historians agree with such an interpretation. Over 1,000 women endured what Jane Marcus describes as 'the public violation of their bodies'. Sometimes the tubes used were not even sterile and had been used before. The use of force-feeding may suggest the government was deeply hostile to suffragettes or it may suggest that it was alarmed at the prospect of women dying in prison. But, there is also a class aspect. Influential women like Lady Constance Lytton (see page 106) were released while working-class women were treated brutally.
Adapted from Bartley 1998.

without an overall majority. This new government immediately set up a cross-party 'Conciliation Committee' to draft an Electoral Reform Bill acceptable to all parties. In the hope that the Conciliation Bill would mean the implementation of women's suffrage, Emmeline Pankhurst announced that the WSPU was calling a truce - all militant action was to be suspended.

'Black Friday'

This truce lasted initially until November 1910. On Friday 18 November, Asquith failed to mention the Conciliation Bill when outlining the government programme (making it clear that the Bill would fail because the government would not allow it any time). In protest, groups of suffragettes marched to Parliament. There, the police used unexpected violence against them:

'The police, instructed not to arrest the suffragettes, forced the women back, kicked them, twisted their breasts, punched their noses and thrust knees between their legs. All the 135 statements made by the suffragettes testify to the violence.' (Bartley 1998, p.73)

One woman, Ellen Pitfield, died of the injuries she received on 'Black Friday', as this event became known. A further 'raid' on Parliament then took place on 22 November and there was a renewed outbreak of stone throwing.

A second general election was held in December 1910, with Asquith's minority government returning to power. When it was announced that a revised Conciliation Bill would be introduced, the WSPU truce was restored. It lasted until November 1911.

In November 1911, Asquith announced that he preferred a Manhood Suffrage Bill (which could be amended to include women's franchise) to the second Conciliation Bill (which, like the first, had passed it second reading but was allowed to proceed no further). In response to what the WSPU saw as a betrayal, the truce was lifted and militant action began again. In this, third phase, however, suffragettes went much further than they had done before.

The militant tactics used in the third phase include the following.

1. Window breaking on a larger scale

The first response to Asquith's 'betrayal' was a renewal of window breaking, but on a larger scale. On 1 March 1912, for example, Emmeline Pankhurst and two others broke windows in 10 Downing Street while, at the same time, around 150 other suffragettes smashed shop windows on a large scale in the West End of London. Further window breaking then took place on the next two days. On 4 March, the Pethick Lawrences were arrested. They and Emmeline Pankhurst (who was already in custody) were charged with conspiracy. The warrant included Christabel Pankhurst, but she escaped into exile in France.

2. Mass hunger strike

Emmeline Pankhurst was released from prison on 15 March, but faced the conspiracy trial in May 1912. Following the trial (they were found guilty and sentenced to nine months), Emmeline Pankhurst and the Pethick Lawrences threatened to go on hunger strike unless they were granted status as political prisoners. They were, but other suffragette prisoners were not. As a result, a mass hunger strike began (on 19 June):

'Holloway became a place of "horror and torment", recollected Emmeline, as she listened to cries of women undergoing instrumental invasion of the body. When her own cell door was opened, she picked up a heavy earthenware jug and, with an air of authority, cried to the doctors and wardresses 'if any of you dares so much to take one step inside this cell, I shall defend myself'. They all retreated. Two days later, both Emmeline Pankhurst and Emmeline Pethick Lawrence were released on medical grounds.' (Purvis 2000, p.125)

As the number of suffragette prisoners rose and suffragette propaganda continued to make capital out of forcible feeding, the government changed its strategy. In April 1913, the Prisoners' Temporary Discharge for Ill-Health Act was passed. This allowed the authorities to temporarily discharge prisoners and rearrest them at a later date. As a result, hunger strikers could be released and, once they had recovered, be rearrested. This was soon described as the 'Cat and Mouse' Act.

3. Arson

Like window breaking and hunger striking, arson was the initiative of an ordinary WSPU member rather than the leadership. The first arson attack took place in December 1911 when Emily Davison set fire to the letters in a pillar box. Other attacks on pillar boxes followed (in some cases, the letters were destroyed by pouring chemicals through the letter box rather than burning them). In 1913, arson attacks escalated. A number of houses, including David Lloyd George's country house in Surrey, were fire bombed and destroyed. Bartley points out that:

'Many of the arson attacks were, like window smashing, a response to particular political events. At least four of the major acts of arson committed in March 1914 were precipitated by the arrests of Emmeline Pankhurst.' (Bartley 1998, p.57)

4. Other violence against property

In addition to arson attacks, suffragettes:
- slashed works of art in art galleries
- poured acid on golfing greens, burning messages such as 'No Vote, No Golf'
- cut messages into the turf on race courses
- destroyed plants at Kew Gardens
- cut telegraph wires.

One of the most notorious attacks occurred in March 1914 when Mary Richardson attacked a painting of the goddess Venus by Velasquez in the National Gallery - see Box 3.22 on page 100.

5. Emily Davison

In June 1913, Emily Davison rushed on to the race course as the Derby race was in progress and

Interpretation

BOX 3.22 | Mary Richardson's attack in the National Gallery

The WSPU's newspaper reported the incident on 13 March 1914 as follows: 'The first warning the attendant in charge had was the crash of breaking glass and turning round he saw a woman raining blows on the Velasquez with a small axe. He and a policeman, who was also on watch, made a dash at her, but before they could reach her she had struck the picture seven blows.' Richardson explained that she did this to draw attention to Emmeline Pankhurst's poor health (she was very weak at this time as a result of hunger striking): 'I have tried to destroy the picture of the most beautiful woman in mythological history as a protest against the government for destroying Mrs Pankhurst who is the most beautiful character in modern history'.

Adapted from McDonald 1989.

grabbed the reins of the King's horse. The horse turned a complete somersault and she received fatal head injuries, dying a short time later in hospital. Davison instantly became a suffragette martyr. Her funeral was a great showpiece, attended by vast crowds and a suffragette guard of honour.

Was militant action a success?

When the First World War broke out in August 1914, Emmeline and Christabel Pankhurst called a truce for its duration. This truce became permanent since, at the end of the war, women were enfranchised for the first time. The extent to which militancy helped or hindered the campaign for women's suffrage has been a matter of debate.

While some historians (for example, Marcus 1987 and Purvis 2000) are sympathetic to the use of militant tactics, few have argued that they were successful. An early view was that such tactics actually delayed the granting of women's suffrage:

'The first influence of militancy was stimulating. Later the hostilities it aroused put the clock back. Had it not been persisted in, some kind of Women's Suffrage Bill would probably have passed the Commons between 1906 and 1914.' (Ensor 1936, p.398)

Some more recent accounts (such as Rosen 1974 and Liddington & Norris 1978) have argued that the role of the Pankhursts in the struggle for women's suffrage has been exaggerated. Others (such as Harrison 1990 and Pugh 1994) argue that, despite the suffragettes' abilities to mobilise thousands of supporters on occasion, they never really managed to gain popular support. The general consensus is that militancy was an irritation for the government rather than a real threat. It lost the WSPU sympathy while providing the government with an excuse not to make concessions.

MAIN POINTS - Section 3.3

- Jane Marcus argues that there was a central theme behind the many different types of action performed by the suffragettes - they aimed to 'interrupt male political discourse' and find their political voice. Paula Bartley disagrees, arguing that they were more influenced by Parnell's obstructionist tactics in the 1880s.
- Phase 1 of militancy (May 1906-June 1908) was a response to lack of progress after the 1906 general election. It was characterised by (1) confronting Parliament and ministers and (2) campaigning at by-elections.
- Phase 2 of militancy (June 1908-Jan 1910) was characterised by a greater willingness to use violence.

- The main tactics were (1) window breaking (2) technical offences and (3) hunger striking.
- Phase 3 of militancy (Nov 1911-Aug 1914) followed a truce while the two Conciliation Bills had a chance of becoming law. The failure of the second Bill led to an escalation in violence. The main tactics were (1) window breaking on a larger scale (2) mass hunger striking (3) arson attacks (4) other attacks on property.
- While some historians are sympathetic to the use of militant tactics, few have argued that they were successful. The consensus is that militancy lost the WSPU sympathy while providing the government with an excuse not to make concessions.

Activity 3.5 Militant tactics

ITEM 1 An incitement to militancy

Those of you who can express your militancy by facing party mobs at Cabinet ministers' meetings when you remind them of their falseness to principle - do so. Those of you who can express your militancy by joining us in our anti-government by-election policy - do so. Those of you who can break windows - break them. Those of you who can still further attack the secret idol of property so as to make the government realise that property is as greatly endangered by Women's Suffrage as it was by the Chartists of old - do so. And my last word to the government: I cite this meeting to rebellion. You have not dared to take the leaders of Ulster (see Unit 6, Part 4) for their incitement to rebellion, take me if you dare.

Part of a speech delivered by Emmeline Pankhurst in the Albert Hall in October 1912.

ITEM 2 Emmeline Pankhurst and militant action

When Asquith announced on 27 January 1913 that the Manhood Suffrage Bill was dropped for that session, Emmeline immediately declared war on the government. Over the next 18 months, the WSPU was increasingly driven underground. Emmeline Pankhurst frequently stressed that she took full responsibility for all acts of militancy, as at a meeting on 30 January 1913 - 'I want to say that, placed as I am in a responsible position, with others, of guiding the movement, that for all the women have done, and for what all the women are doing, I take full responsibility'. Now regarded as a dangerous subversive, she was watched by the police. On 2 April, she was sentenced to three years in prison, but she served less than six weeks of her sentence between the time of her conviction and the suspension of militancy. Using the 'Cat and Mouse Act', she was repeatedly in and out of prison (whenever she was imprisoned she went on hunger strike). Never once did she hesitate to share with her followers that which they too experienced. She saw herself in a historic role as an individual who brought about radical change through political action. After spending January 1914 in Paris with Christabel, she returned to England where her recently formed bodyguard was waiting to protect her from arrest. Like a fugitive, she seldom stayed in one place for long, but was sheltered by a network of supportive and devoted friends. On 10 February, she spoke from the second-storey window of a house, challenging the government to re-arrest her and accusing them of cowardice in forcibly feeding suffragettes whom she had incited to militancy while not daring to force-feed her. As she left surrounded by 20 women, there was a fierce conflict with the police who had surrounded the house. A black-veiled woman was arrested but turned out to be a decoy. Emmeline was arrested again on 9 March and released in a state of utter exhaustion after five days of hunger and thirst strike. In total, she was arrested nine times between April 1913 and August 1914.

Adapted from Purvis 2000.

Emmeline Pankhurst was arrested at Buckingham Palace as a group of suffragettes attempted to petition the King on 21 June 1914 (the right to petition the monarch was explicitly included in the Bill of Rights of 1689). As the arresting officer lifted her into a waiting car, she shouted 'That's right! Arrest me at the gates of the Palace. Tell the King'.

ITEM 3 An arson attack

This house, belonging to Lady White (a well-known opponent of women's suffrage), was burned down on 20 March 1913. The WSPU claimed that all arson targets were carefully checked to ensure that no people or animals would be in danger.

About 1.20, the constable on duty in the district was informed that the house was on fire. He ran to the telephone and summoned the Egham Volunteer Fire Brigade, but, by the time of their arrival, with their manual engine, the flames had obtained a firm hold. As the building stood on a hill, a great length of hose had to be unspun and the pressure of the water was inadequate. It was impossible, therefore, for the firemen to cope with the flames...Underneath the rockery at the back of the house, police discovered pieces of paper upon which were written the sentences - 'Votes for Women' and 'Stop torturing our colleagues in prison'...It is believed that, before applying the match to the pile which would set the house on fire, the central staircase was soaked in oil and the windows unlatched and fixed open so that the fire could be fanned by the draught...Nothing was found which would give the slightest clue to the actual perpetrators of the deed.

Extract from 'The Suffragette', 28 March 1913.

ITEM 4 The government and militancy

The response of the government to women who broke the law certainly suggests that it was hostile to votes for women. There was a decided contrast between the treatment of law-breaking Ulster Unionists (who made inflammatory speeches and smuggled in guns - see Unit 6, Part 4) and law-breaking suffragettes. A blind eye was turned to the gun smuggling. Ulster rebels were not arrested. But, they were consulted by the government. The suffragettes, on the other hand, were first ignored, then harassed, arrested, imprisoned and force-fed. When the WSPU began its illegal activities, the government reacted by denying them democratic forms of protest. Women were forbidden to attend Liberal meetings unless they had a signed ticket. The government refused to meet delegations or accept petitions. It banned public meetings and censored the press in an attempt to silence the WSPU. The Commissioner of the Police (directed

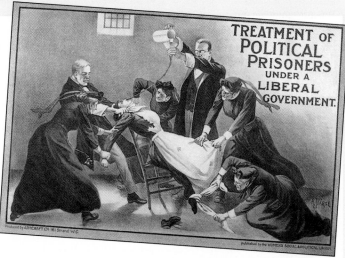

This poster was produced as propaganda for the suffragette cause. A great deal of suffragette propaganda focused on the government's treatment of hunger strikers.

by the Home Office) refused to allow suffragettes to meet in parks in London. Eventually, the management agreed not to hire the Albert Hall out to the WSPU. When the WSPU found a different venue, the police threatened to remove the owner's licence. The government also prosecuted the *Suffragette*'s printer and raided the offices and homes of WSPU members.

Adapted from Bartley 1998.

Questions

1. a) Using Items 1-4, explain what is meant by 'militant action'.
   b) Why do you think the WSPU adopted militant tactics?
   c) Did the adoption of militant tactics help or hinder the women's suffrage movement?
2. a) What do Items 1 and 2 tell us about Emmeline Pankhurst's leadership style?
   b) Would you agree that she was a dynamic leader? Explain your answer.
3. a) Judging from Item 4 how well did the authorities handle the suffragette challenge?
   b) What does the government's response tell us about its attitude towards the WSPU?
4. Why do you think that historians have tended to focus on the Pankhursts rather than on constitutional suffragists?

4 Reactions to the suffrage campaigns

Key questions

1. Who opposed the women's suffrage movement?
2. How did different political and social groups respond to the women's suffrage movement 1903-14?

4.1 Who opposed the women's suffrage movement?

The arguments against women's suffrage

Pugh (1994) suggests that the arguments made by those opposed to women's suffrage fall into five categories:

1. The 'separate spheres' argument

According to this argument, the role played by men is different (and should be different) from that played by women. While the masculine public sphere is for men, the feminine domestic sphere is for women. Giving women the vote, therefore, would damage their femininity.

2. The 'different biology and psychology' argument

According to this argument, women are physically and mentally weaker than men. They are less rational and more emotional and are, therefore, unfit to take on the responsibility of voting.

3. 'Physical force' arguments

Pugh suggests that there were a number of variants on the basic argument which claimed that, because women could not fight in defence of their country, they did not deserve full citizenship. Some opponents of women's suffrage pointed out that the maintenance of the British Empire required a large army - an army to which women did not contribute. Because women did not contribute to the Empire's defence, they should not have the vote. Others suggested that giving women the vote would put the whole British Empire in danger because Britain would lose the respect of those it ruled in the colonies or because women would oppose wars against foreign states. A further variant was the idea that, since women could not physically enforce the laws they made, men might simply refuse to accept them, leading to a breakdown of the rule of law.

4. Women did not really want the vote

Some opponents of women's suffrage argued that the majority of women did not want the vote (or, at least, did not care one way or another whether they had it). Suffragists, they claimed, were an unrepresentative but vocal minority.

5. Fears about the practical effects

Pugh also suggests that some opponents of women's suffrage were worried about the practical consequences of women's enfranchisement. Some were worried that women would vote as a single bloc or in support of issues opposed by most men. Others were worried that the enfranchisement of women would lead to universal suffrage and women entering Parliament. There were also concerns that women would use their new political power to improve their position in the labour force or that they would neglect their domestic duties.

Other anti-suffragist arguments are outlined in Box 3.23.

BOX 3.23 | Other anti-suffragist arguments

Two further (and somewhat contradictory) lines of argument which can be added to Pugh's list are as follows:
1. The argument that women were already represented in Parliament by the men in their family. Also, women already exercised some control over political decision making since leading politicians listened to the views of their wives, mothers and other female acquaintances.
2. The argument that women were incapable of making decisions and would do what the men in the family told them to do. This would result in some men, in effect, having several votes more than others.

Adapted from Bartley 1998.

Interpretation

Opposition to the suffragists before 1908

Throughout the period 1867 to 1914, opposition to women's suffrage (like support for it) was not confined to any single group. Some women, as well as men, opposed women's suffrage, and opposition (as well as support) could be found in all classes and

in all political parties. The nature and extent of the opposition to the suffragists has been studied by Brian Harrison (1978). The details and figures which follow come from this study.

It has already been noted (in Part 2) that the idea that women should have the vote was alien to most politicians in the 1860s, but had gained ground by 1903. As support for women's suffrage gained ground, those opposed to it - the 'Antis' - also began to mobilise both inside Parliament and outside. Harrison argues that it was in the 1870s that anti-suffragist MPs first developed the arguments outlined above. He notes that, in 1875, a Parliamentary Committee for Maintaining the Integrity of the Franchise was set up, though it became redundant after 1877 as the threat of proposals for women's suffrage melted away. It was not until the late 1880s that the prospect of women's suffrage again became a realistic possibility. In response, the 'Appeal against Woman's Suffrage' was published in a journal called the *Nineteenth Century* in June 1889. This was largely the work of the novelist Mrs Humphry Ward and contained the signatures of 104 prominent women (prominent mainly because their husbands were prominent). According to Harrison, this appeal made a big impact on decision makers. Indeed, it may have persuaded Gladstone to reveal that he was opposed to women's suffrage in 1892. But, the appeal did not result in the setting up of an organisation to fight the growing popularity of the suffragist movement. That did not happen until 1908.

The Anti-Suffrage League

The Anti-Suffrage League was set up in 1908 after an exchange of letters in the *Times* (the *Times* was consistently opposed to women's suffrage). A number of women wrote to the *Times* expressing their concern about the growing activity of the suffragists and suffragettes, arguing that it was time for the Antis to become active in response. The result was the Women's National Anti-Suffrage League whose first meeting took place on 21 July, with Lady Jersey in the chair. Then, in December, male Antis launched their Men's Committee for Opposing Female Suffrage.

Membership

The Women's League expanded rapidly, soon setting up branches throughout Britain. By October 1909, it had around 10,000 members. By April 1910, there were 104 branches and, by April 1912, 235 branches:

'Analysis of branch distribution shows that London and the South East contributed most to the anti-suffrage effort - these areas giving 42% of the total between 1908 and 1914. When discrepancies in population are borne in mind, the branches were relatively prevalent [numerous] in the West of England and relatively weak in the North; nor it there much of a Celtic fringe.' (Harrison 1978, pp.122-23) While the Men's Committee was skilled at fund-raising, it failed to gain popular support:

'The Men's Committee was more a collection of major public figures than a nationwide movement, for the Antis' major strength was always the list of great names they could parade.' (Harrison 1978, p.120)

Both groups were set up on a non-party basis and had members belonging to all parties (Harrison shows that, although the Conservative Party was the 'natural home' of the Antis, people opposed to women's suffrage could be found right across the political spectrum). It was a frequent charge, however, that the groups were dominated by rich and titled people. In January 1913, for example, Millicent Fawcett obtained a copy of letter sent to business leaders in October 1910 asking for money:

'Mrs Fawcett pointed out that only a quarter of the 293 subscribers mentioned in the letter were women; they had contributed only 7.1% of the £19,265 subscribed. Of the 220 male subscribers, 85 were titled and of these 51 were peers [members of the House of Lords]. Of the 75 women, 21 were peeresses or titled.' (Harrison 1978, p.137)

Amalgamation in 1910

In 1910, negotiations between the two groups led to an amalgamation of the two groups under the title the National League for Opposing Women's Suffrage. At the national level, the league was controlled by an executive committee made up of seven men and seven women with a male President, Lord Cromer (until 1912 when the Conservative Lord Curzon and Liberal Lord Weardale took over jointly), and a female Deputy President, Lady Jersey.

Aims and tactics

The Anti-Suffrage League's main aim was twofold. First, it aimed to ensure that there was sufficient opposition in Parliament to prevent any proposals in favour of women's suffrage being passed. And second, it aimed to counter the suffragists' argument that a majority of people favoured women's suffrage. It should be noted that there were no opinion polls in the early 20th century and it was, therefore, difficult to gauge public opinion. The Antis argued that there was a 'silent majority' on their side of the argument and, significantly, when an anti-suffrage petition was launched in 1908, the Antis collected 337,018 signatures - more than had been collected on any suffragist petition since 1874. In addition, the Anti-Suffrage League paid for surveys ('canvasses'), the results of which were published in their journal the *Anti-Suffrage Review*:

'The complete results were published in the *Review* for April 1912: in a poll of 72,301 women municipal electors, reply-paid postcards produced 20,915 Antis, 11,896 suffragists and 2,120 neutral. In a poll of 66,171 women municipal electors, anti-suffragist or paid canvassers on house-to-house

visits produced 27,235 Antis, 10,409 suffragists and 7,358 neutral. The survey of 94 districts revealed suffragist majorities in only five - Sheffield and four divisions of Liverpool.' (Harrison 1978, p.157)

It should be noted that, when suffragists conducted similar exercises, they produced completely different results. Nevertheless, Harrison suggests that, despite its rather élitist leadership, the Anti-Suffrage League appealed widely, especially to conservative working people.

The tactics adopted by the Anti-Suffrage League are outlined in Box 3.24.

BOX 3.24 | Tactics adopted by the Anti-Suffrage League

As might be expected, the Anti-Suffrage League adopted a non-party stance and constitutional tactics. It worked behind the scenes, lobbying waverers in the Commons and maintaining the pressure on known Antis in all parties. More publicly, it produced anti-suffrage propaganda and held meetings to publicise its point of view. The style was very different from that of the suffragists. The Anti-Suffrage League could offer none of Mrs Pankhurst's drama and flamboyance, none of Mrs Fawcett's intelligent perception of women's problems, none of the imaginativeness and inventiveness in campaigning methods which lent such panache to Edwardian suffragism. On the other hand, Antis did not want these things. They wanted a well-organised, discreet and politically informed leadership which could work successfully within the political élite and mobilise already existing anti-suffrage sentiment in the country at large. There were, however, a number of ways in which the Anti-Suffrage League was less efficient than the suffragists:

- the Antis found it difficult to recruit young women
- Anti-Suffrage League meetings were drab and uncolourful
- the Antis lacked the international contacts that the suffragists had
- the Anti-Suffrage League's press office was less effective than that of the WSPU.

Despite this, the Anti-Suffrage League did have the majority of the press on its side and this ensured that it was able to communicate its message effectively. It was also very skilful at working behind the scenes in Parliament.

Adapted from Harrison 1978.

4.2 How did different political and social groups respond to the women's suffrage movement 1903-14?

Some general points

Between 1903 and 1914, no political party in Parliament adopted women's suffrage as part of its official programme. Yet, within all of the main parties there was at least some support for women's suffrage - though this was counterbalanced by support for the Antis and fears about the consequences of giving women the vote. The increasingly militant activity of the WSPU tended to be viewed with outrage by those already opposed to women's suffrage. While there is also evidence that some supporters of women's suffrage were irritated by the WSPU's militancy, it has already been noted that membership of the NUWSS rose rapidly during this period (see above, page 91). The fact that those who were sympathetic to women's suffrage but disapproving of the WSPU's tactics had a non-militant alternative is important. It ensured that women's suffrage had a 'respectable' side and prevented moderate supporters becoming alienated. So, while WSPU activity brought the women's suffrage movement great publicity and ensured that the issue remained in the public eye, the existence of the NUWSS ensured that the issue was not written off as something that could only appeal to extremists. How to respond to women's suffrage campaigns was something which taxed all political parties, but especially the Liberal Party since it was that party which formed the government between 1906 and 1914.

1. The Labour Party

It was in the period 1903-14 that the Labour Party emerged as a force in British politics (see Unit 5). Although it might be expected that the new party and the women's suffrage movement would have been natural allies, Martin Pugh points out that this was not the case. The only group within the party to support and promote women's suffrage was the Independent Labour Party (ILP). As a result:

'As the women's question grew more acute, Labour's approach to it repeated that of the older parties. One sees a similar display of male prejudice, a similar reluctance to divide the party by giving priority to the women, similar calculations of party advantage and a similar fragmentation of the suffragist forces themselves.' (Pugh 1985a, p.233)

Pugh does accept that the Labour Party was less divided than the other parties over the issue and he points out that the small group of Labour MPs consistently voted for women's suffrage as a group. Nevertheless, he argues, if the party had been united over women's suffrage:

'It would have been quicker to seize the opportunity to outflank the other parties on the issue. Not until the eve of the First World War can it plausibly be argued that Labour was on the verge of accomplishing this.' (Pugh 1985a, p.234)

Negative reaction to the suffrage campaigns

Some leading members of the early Labour Party were hostile to suffragists because suffragists were campaigning for the 'equal franchise' (the vote on the same basis as men) rather than for the 'universal franchise' (votes for all). Socialists who did not believe in property qualifications were suspicious of a campaign which was led by middle-class women who had little in common with, and little apparent interest in, working-class men. Indeed, some suffragists argued that they should have the vote on the grounds that they were superior to members of the working class. As a result, women's suffrage was dismissed as a middle-class concern or as something that would be achieved as a matter of course once socialism was introduced.

Some individuals were particularly hostile to women's suffrage. Pugh cites comments made by John Bruce Glasier:

'A weary ordeal of chatter about women's suffrage from 10 pm to 1.30 am - Mrs and Christabel Pankhurst belabouring me as Chairman of the Party for its neglect of the question. At last get roused and speak with something like scorn of their miserable individualist sexism...Really the pair are not seeking democratic freedom, but self-importance...Christabel paints her eyebrows grossly and looks selfish, lazy and wilful. They want to be ladies not workers and lack the humility of real heroism.' (cited in Pugh 1985a, p.236)

Pugh also notes that Ramsay MacDonald, who was a lukewarm suffragist, was alienated by the WSPU's militant campaign.

It was not just individuals who were alienated by the WSPU's militancy. In 1909, the Women's Cooperative Guild changed its demand for women's suffrage to a demand for universal adult suffrage because it disliked the WSPU's approach.

Positive reaction to the suffrage campaigns

On the other hand, some leading members of the Labour Party were close supporters of the suffragists and reacted positively to militancy. Keir Hardie, for example, was close to the Pankhursts and supported the militant campaign:

'According to Sylvia Pankhurst, he collected funds, wrote leaflets, taught the suffragettes parliamentary procedure, introduced them to influential people, visited them in prison and even condoned their violent tactics.' (Bartley 1998, p.70)

Similarly, the Labour MP George Lansbury was an enthusiastic supporter of the WSPU:

'On one occasion, he rushed across the House of Commons floor, shook his fist at Asquith and shouted: "You'll go down in history as the man who tortured innocent women" in objection to the force-feeding of the suffragettes.' (Bartley 1998, p.70)

In 1912, Lansbury proposed that Labour MPs vote against the government on all Bills until a Women's Suffrage Bill was passed (the NEC overruled him). He then resigned his seat, hoping to gain the backing of the local electorate for his pro-suffragist stance. Despite, or because of, support in the by-election campaign from the NUWSS and WSPU, he lost.

In addition to individual Labour MPs' support, the women's suffrage movement gained the active support of some Labour branches:

The Woolwich Labour Party, for example, consistently supported the aims and methods of the WSPU because they realised that even a limited extension of the franchise would enfranchise a respectable number of working-class widows and spinsters.' (Bartley 1998, p.71)

Two developments in 1912
In 1912, two significant developments suggest that the party as a whole was becoming more inclined to give priority to women's suffrage. First, at the annual conference in January, Arthur Henderson's proposal that the Labour Party should only support an Adult Suffrage Bill if it included women's suffrage was passed. Pugh claims:

'Henderson, a consistent if phlegmatic [unenthusiastic] suffragist, was ideally placed to bring the two sides together and, from 1912 to 1917 when women's suffrage was finally written into a government Bill, he played the key role on the Labour side.' (Pugh 1985a, p.246)

And second, the NUWSS dropped its non-party stance and made an election pact with the Labour Party:

'Essentially, they were offering to raise a special fund and designate election organisers to assist Labour MPs and candidates in seats held by anti-suffragist Liberals.' (Pugh 1985a, p.247)

2. The Conservative Party

Although, as Harrison (1978) points out, the Conservative Party was the 'natural home' for Antis, that does not mean that the party's reaction to the campaigns for women's suffrage was wholly negative. On the contrary, there is good evidence to show not only that a number of individuals prominent in the campaigns for women's suffrage were Conservatives, but also that Conservative Party organisations, notably certain 'habitations' of the Primrose League (see Section 2.3 above), actively supported the campaigns.

Perhaps the best known Conservative suffragette was Lady Constance Lytton - see Box 3.25.

Conservative Party organisations
In his study of women in the Conservative Party, Martin Pugh argues that the party's reputation for anti-suffragism needs reconsideration:

'The hostility of party activists and the MPs has been exaggerated, while conversely the sympathy of Party Leaders has been overestimated.' (Pugh 1985, p.59)

Pugh points out that, on seven occasions between 1887 and 1910, the National Union of Conservative

---

BOX 3.25   Lady Constance Lytton

Interpretation

Constance Lytton was born in 1869 in Vienna. She was the daughter of the Earl of Lytton, who once served as Viceroy of India. She lived a retired life with her mother until, in 1906, an inheritance brought them independence. In 1908, Lytton had a chance meeting with Emmeline Pethick Lawrence and Annie Kenney and they fired her interest in the cause of women's suffrage. She joined the WSPU in 1909 and was imprisoned a number of times for militant protests. On each occasion, however, she was released without being forcibly fed. Believing that she was being given special treatment because of her aristocratic background, she decided to test her theory. In 1911, she dressed as a working-class woman and ensured that she was arrested in a protest outside Walton Gaol in Liverpool. She gave her name as 'Jane Wharton', was passed fit after a cursory medical examination, forcibly fed and became so ill that she suffered a stroke that partially paralysed her. After her release, her story generated a great deal of publicity for the WSPU. Constance Lytton received public support from her brother Lord Lytton, another Conservative.
Adapted from Uglow 1998 and Mulvey-Roberts 2000.

Associations voted in favour of women's suffrage at its annual conference. The decisions were not binding, but they did indicate that there was a significant degree of support for women's suffrage.

Pugh also argues that the work of the Primrose League encouraged support for women's suffrage:

'In the long run, the Primrose League surely assisted rather than retarded the cause of women's enfranchisement, in spite of not being a suffragist organisation, indeed perhaps because of it; for the League steadily undermined assumptions about political inertia [inactivity] and ignorance of women without driving men as a whole into opposition...An apprenticeship in organisations like the League was for many British women a precondition for their subsequent suffragism. ' (Pugh 1985, p.66)

Nevertheless, it should also be remembered that many of those most strongly opposed to women's suffrage were active members of the Conservative Party - not least Lord Cromer and Lord Curzon, the Presidents of the Anti-Suffrage League.

3. The Liberal Party

Part 3 above makes it clear that it was because of the Liberal government's unwillingness to respond positively to demands for women's suffrage that the WSPU's militant campaign escalated. In other words, the government's reaction to women's suffrage campaigns was negative. Throughout the period

1903-14, the suffragists never managed to convince the government that it should set aside sufficient parliamentary time to ensure the passage of a Women's Suffrage Bill.

What were the Liberal government's aims?

This, however, is by no means the full story. As Box 3.18 on page 95 above makes clear, senior politicians hoped that, by ignoring the issue, it would go away (this may also explain why, as Prime Minister, Asquith refused to meet suffragist delegations). The issue did not go away, however. On the contrary, it gained ever greater urgency - which suggests that the women's suffrage campaigns did make an impact on the government. This is confirmed by the fact that the government was forced to make concessions (or at least the promise of concessions) which raised women's hopes - as in June 1908, for example. That Asquith, an anti-suffragist, should promise a women's suffrage amendment if certain conditions were met shows that the suffrage campaigns were making an impact.

In addition, since the WSPU's militant campaign involved breaking the law, the government was obliged to respond (otherwise the rule of law might break down). Some authors (for example, Vicinus 1972 and Kingsley Kent 1987) have suggested that the use of force against suffragette demonstrators (for example, on Black Friday - see pages 99 and 109) was excessive and included sexual harassment, and that the adoption of a policy of forcible feeding had symbolic as well as practical intentions. In other words, it can be argued that government's response was more than a simple attempt to maintain law and order. It was also an attempt to 'put women in their place'. It was, therefore, the knee-jerk reaction of a patriarchal (male-dominated) society which felt itself to be under threat.

The reaction of party members

Like the other parties, the Liberal Party was divided on the issue of women's suffrage. Nevertheless, there is good evidence to show that the women's suffrage campaigns made an important impact in the period 1903-14. By 1903, the Women's Liberal Federation (see Box 3.11 on page 82) had passed a resolution in support of women's suffrage. In the 20 by-elections in the period May 1904 to November 1905, the Federation demanded pro-suffrage pledges from Liberal candidates and refused to work for them if they were not provided. It also worked closely with the NUWSS 'in rallies, demonstrations and educational efforts' (Hirshfield 1990, p.180). Following the 1906 general election, at first:

'The majority of [the Federation's] Executive Committee viewed WSPU tactics with distaste and clung to the hope that the Liberal government would honour its obligations to loyal women workers.' (Hirshfield 1990, p.181)

Within two years, however, disappointment at the lack of progress led several members of the Executive Committee to resign their positions and share platforms with the WSPU. What began as a trickle of resignations, became a significant stream after 1912 with 68 branches of the Federation collapsing between 1912 and 1914. Many of the women left to join the Labour Party, seeing it as a better prospect for progress on women's suffrage. In other words, the reaction of many Liberal suffragists to the failure of the suffrage campaigns to achieve their goals under a Liberal government was to leave the Liberal Party. The suffrage campaigns raised their hopes and then provoked disillusion in their party.

Social groups

1. Social classes

It was noted in the discussion on the Anti-Suffrage League at the beginning of this section that, although the organisation was dominated by members of the aristocracy at the top, it aimed to appeal to the 'silent majority'. Indeed, Harrison (1978) provides evidence to suggest that there was a great deal of anti-suffragist feeling among the working class. On the other hand, Liddington and Norris (1978) have shown that, in some parts of the country (especially in the North West), there was a great deal of evidence of pro-suffragist working-class feeling. Reactions to the suffrage campaigns, in other words, were mixed. They did not depend on class or, more precisely, they were not necessarily determined by class.

2. Gender

The same point can be made about gender. There were female members of the Anti-Suffrage League and, conversely, male organisations were set up to campaign for women's suffrage:

'The first male-only organisation, the Men's League for Women's Suffrage, was established in 1907 and numbered among its members men from all shades of political opinion. Any man, whatever his political or religious persuasion was welcome to join. It formed branches all over Britain.' (Bartley 1998, p.81)

Men could and did belong to the NUWSS and, although the WSPU was supposed to be a women-only organisation, Frederick Pethick Lawrence worked for the organisation, was imprisoned along with other suffragettes and was forcibly fed like them. Besides, the Men's Federation for Women's Suffrage (set up in 1910) adopted WSPU-style tactics. As with class, therefore, reactions to the suffrage campaigns were not necessarily determined by gender.

3. Trade unions

Although the trade unions were, in general, hostile to women's suffrage, there were some women trade unionists (see Unit 4, Section 2.3). Pugh argues that the unions were reluctant to support women's suffrage because of 'pride and fear':

'This was the pride of men for whom the franchise was one element in their improved status which they could not easily share. Their fear was the fear of the skilled for women as unskilled workers who would hold down wages and inhibit union agreements in an overstocked labour market.' (Pugh 1985, p.238)

Nevertheless, in 1913, the TUC followed the Labour Party and made its support for any government-supported Adult Suffrage Bill dependent on the inclusion of women. In general, therefore, the unions' reaction to the suffrage campaigns was negative in the period 1903-14.

The press

It was noted above that the *Times* was particularly hostile to women's suffrage. The same was true of most national and regional newspapers, especially once the militant campaign began. On the other hand, militancy did encourage newspapers to print stories about suffragettes, providing them with the 'oxygen' of publicity.

The suffragists produced their own newspapers - *Common Cause* (NUWSS), *Vote* (the Women's Franchise League) and *Votes for Women* (the WSPU). *Votes for Women* played a central part in the WSPU's campaign. It was often sold by women wearing the purple, green and white uniform of the WSPU.

Religious groups

Bartley (1998) points out that the WSPU condemned the Church of England because it did not speak out in favour of women's suffrage and because its bishops did not oppose the Cat and Mouse Act in the House of Lords. Nevertheless, some individual clergymen spoke out in favour of votes for women and a large number spoke out against forcible feeding. As might be expected, given the traditional links between non-conformity and radicalism, there was greater support for the women's suffrage campaigns from non-conformists.

MAIN POINTS - Part 4

- The main arguments against women's suffrage were based on the idea of (1) separate spheres (2) different biology and psychology (3) physical force (4) a majority of women not wanting the vote (5) fear about the practical effects (6) men already representing women and (7) women giving men extra votes by voting as they were told.
- Despite the influential 'Appeal against Women's Suffrage' of 1889, it was only in 1908 that a formal organisation was set up to oppose women's suffrage.
- The women's part of the Anti-Suffrage League expanded rapidly into a national organisation. The men's part concentrated on fund-raising. The two parts amalgamated in 1910. The League lobbied MPs and put

the case that a 'silent majority' opposed women's suffrage. It adopted a non-party stance and constitutional tactics.
- There was at least some support for women's suffrage in all the main parties in 1903-14 - though this was counterbalanced by support for the Antis. By 1914, the Labour Party was committed to women's suffrage while many Liberals had become disillusioned with their party's reaction to the women's suffrage campaign.
- Reactions to the suffrage campaigns did not depend on class or gender. Trade unions, the national press and the Church of England reacted in a largely negative way, though individual examples of a positive reaction can be found.

Activity 3.6 Reactions to the suffrage campaigns 1903-14

ITEM 1 Anti-Suffrage League propaganda (1)

The woman voter would be pernicious [ruinous] to the state not only because she could not back her vote by physical force, but also by reason of her intellectual defects. Woman's mind...is over-influenced by individual instances, arrives at conclusions on incomplete evidence; has a very imperfect sense of proportion; accepts the congenial [agreeable] as true and rejects the uncongenial [disagreeable] as false; takes the imaginary which is desired for reality and treats the undesired reality which is out of sight as non-existent - building up for itself in this way...a very unreal picture of the external world...The failure to recognise that man is the master and why he is the master lies at the root of the suffrage movement. By disregarding man's superior physical force, the power of compulsion upon which all government is based is disregarded. By leaving out of account those powers of the mind in which man is the superior, woman falls into the error of thinking she can really compete with him and that she belongs to the self-same intellectual caste [class]. Finally, by putting out of sight man's superior money-earning capacity, the power of the purse is ignored.

From A.E. Wright's 'The Unexpurgated Case Against Women's Suffrage', published in 1913.

ITEM 2 Anti-Suffrage League propaganda (2)

This postcard is typical of the sort of propaganda produced by the Anti-Suffrage League before the First World War.

ITEM 3 Women's Sunday, 21 June 1908

This photo shows supporters of women's suffrage marching past Parliament on 21 June 1908.

(i) I am sure that a great many people never realised until yesterday how young and dainty and elegant and charming most leaders of the movement are. And how well they spoke - with what free and graceful gestures; never at the loss for a word or an apt reply to an interruption; calm and collected; forcible, yet, so far as I heard, not violent; earnest, but happily humorous as well.' (Daily Mail, 22 June 1908)

(ii) The dignity, the grace, the beauty, the courage of the processionists carried conviction everywhere. Scoffers were converted. Some who had evidently come to jeer stayed to cheer. The good-humoured London crowd was not without its banter here and there; but the genuine outbursts of cheering, the waving of handkerchiefs, the crying out of words of encouragement, must have been very gratifying to those among the processionists who have withstood harshness and insults.' (Daily News, 22 June 1908)

ITEM 4 Black Friday, 18 November 1910

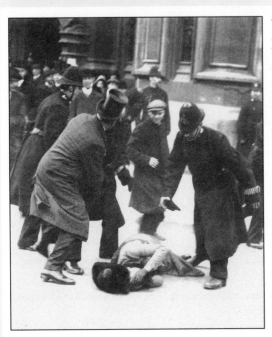

This photo was taken on 18 November 1910, 'Black Friday'. An eyewitness recalled that the police picked out a suffragette called Ada Wright: 'She was treated in the most violent way. They knocked her down two or three times. When she came to, another lady and myself helped her on to her feet and then two policemen dragged her up and she fell on her back on the ground'. At this point, a bystander in a top hat stepped forward to prevent further violence. As Ada Wright lay on the ground with this man shielding her, a number of press photographers, including Victor Consolé, recorded the scene. Consolé submitted his picture to the editor of the Daily Mirror and it was chosen for the front cover. The editor submitted a copy to the Commissioner of the Police who argued that, since one of the onlookers was smiling, it seemed likely that Ada Wright had simply sunk to the floor exhausted with struggling against the police. Privately, the Commissioner was concerned about so controversial an image and later that night an attempt was made to stop publication. When it was discovered that production was already underway, a desperate attempt was made to buy up all the copies that had so far been produced. This failed, however, and 750,000 copies were circulated. This helped turn criticism away from the suffragettes and towards the Home Secretary, Winston Churchill.

Adapted from Hiley 1993.

ITEM 5 The range of pro-suffrage organisations

It is important to remember that the NUWSS and WSPU were not the only organisations which demanded the vote. It is true that they probably represented the largest numbers of women and were the most visible, but they worked alongside a variety of other groups which included:

- the Friends' League for Women's Suffrage
- the Conservative and Unionist Women's Franchise Association
- the Artists' Suffrage League
- the Men's League for Women's Suffrage
- the Men's Federation for Women's Suffrage
- the Women's Freedom League
- the Actresses' Franchise League
- the Scottish University Women's Suffrage Union
- the Church League for Women's Suffrage

- the People's Suffrage Federation
- the Men's Political Union for Women's Enfranchisement
- the Women's Tax Resistance League
- the Catholic Women's Suffrage Society
- the Irish Women's Suffrage Federation
- the Civil Service Women's Suffrage Society
- the Women Teachers' Franchise Union
- the Forward Cymric Suffrage Union
- the Jewish League for Woman Suffrage.

The suffrage movement may have gained support from men who joined organisations supporting women's suffrage, but it seems to have been less successful in convincing a majority of British men. The evidence that is available - the comments made by famous individuals, popular music hall songs, the banning of women from certain places and the growing violence against suffragettes when members of crowds clashed - points to a generally hostile response. It is tempting to suggest that most men were apathetic or impartial, but it is difficult to be sure. Certainly, there are isolated incidents of male violence against suffragettes and their property. In Glasgow in March 1912, 200 men broke up the WSPU shop. At the Eisteddfod in Wales (an annual festival) in the same year, suffragettes who heckled the local hero, Lloyd George, were seriously assaulted, their hair pulled and clothing ripped. But, men who assaulted women were very much in the minority.

Adapted from Atkinson 1996 and Bartley 1998.

Questions

1. a) What do Items 1-5 tell us about the ways in which people reacted to the campaigns for women's suffrage in the period 1903-14?
   b) How did the reactions of different groups help or hinder the groups campaigning for women's suffrage?
2. Look at Items 1 and 2.
   a) Why do you think the Anti-Suffrage League was set up?
   b) What sort of organisation was it?

c) Make a list of the arguments which are made against women's suffrage.
d) 'In the period 1903-14, most men would have agreed with the arguments expressed in Items 1 and 2'. Give arguments for and against this statement.
3. a) Using Items 3-5, explain why it is difficult to generalise about the attitudes of different social groups towards women's suffrage.
   b) Why do you think the authorities tried to prevent the publication of the photo in Item 4?

References

- **Alexander (1994)** Alexander, S., *Becoming a Woman: and Other Essays in 19th and 20th Century Feminist History*, Virago, 1994.

- **Atkinson (1996)** Atkinson, D., *The Suffragettes in Pictures*, Sutton Publishing, 1996.

- **Bartley (1996)** Bartley, P., *The Changing Role of Women 1815-1914*, Hodder and Stoughton, 1996.

- **Bartley (1998)** Bartley, P., *Votes for Women 1860-1928*, Hodder and Stoughton, 1998.

- **Bartley (1999)** Bartley, P., 'Suffragettes, class and pit-brow women', *History Review*, No.35, December 1999.

- **Bassnett (1986)** Bassnett, S., *Feminist Experiences*, Allen and Unwin, 1986.

- **Bedarida (1991)** Bedarida, F., *A Social History of England 1851-1990* (2nd edn), Routledge, 1991.

- **Behagg (1995)** Behagg, C., 'Victorian values' in *Scott-Baumann* (1995).

- **Bentley & Stevenson (1983)** Bentley, M. & Stevenson, J. (eds), *High and Low politics in Modern Britain*, Clarendon Press, 1983.

- **Billington (1985)** Billington, R., 'Women, politics and local Liberalism: from "female suffrage" to "votes for women", *Journal for Regional and Local Studies*, Vol.5, 1985.

- **Blackburn (1970)** Blackburn, H., *Women's Suffrage: a Record of the Suffrage Movement in the British Isles*, Source Book Press, 1970 (first published in 1902).

- **Bolt (2000)** Bolt, C., 'The ideas of British suffragism' in *Purvis & Holton* (2000).

- **Brown (1985)** Brown, K.D. (ed.), *The First Labour Party: 1906-14*, Croom Helm, 1985.

- **Brown (1998)** Brown, R., *Chartism*, Cambridge University Press, 1998.

- **Clark (1995)** Clark, A., *The Struggle for the Breeches: Gender and the Making of the British Working Class*, University of California Press, 1995.

- **Davis (1999)** Davis, J., *A History of Britain, 1885-1939*, Macmillan, 1999.

- **D'Cruze (1995)** D'Cruze, S., 'Women and the family' in *Purvis (1995)*.

- **Ensor (1936)** Ensor, R.C.K, *England 1870-1914*, Oxford University Press, 1936.

- **Fisher (1996)** Fisher, T., 'Josephine Butler: feminism's neglected pioneer', *History Today*, Vol.46.6, June 1996.

- **Gardiner & Wenborn (1995)** Gardiner, J. & Wenborn, N., *The Companion to British History*, Collins and Brown, 1995.

- **Hannam (1995)** Hannam, J., 'Women and politics' in *Purvis (1995)*.

- **Harrison (1978)** Harrison, B., *Separate Spheres: the Opposition to Women's Suffrage in Britain*, Holmes & Meir Publications, New York, 1978.

- **Harrison (1983)** Harrison B., 'Women's suffrage at Westminster 1866-1928' in *Bentley & Stevenson (1983)*.

- **Harrison (1990)** Harrison, J.F.C., *Late Victorian Britain 1875-1901*, Fontana Press, 1990.

- **Hiley (1993)** Hiley, N., 'The candid camera of the Edwardian tabloids', *History Today*, Vol.43, August 1993.

- **Hirshfield (1990)** Hirshfield, C., 'Fractured Faith: Liberal Party women and the suffrage issue in Britain, 1892-1914', *Gender and History*, Vol.2.2, Summer 1990.

- **Holton (1986)** Holton, S.S., *Feminism and Democracy*, Cambridge University Press, 1986.

- **Holton (1995)** Holton, S.S., 'Women and the vote' in *Purvis (1995)*.

- **Holton (1996)** Holton, S.S., *Suffrage Days: Stories from the Women's Suffrage Movement*, Routledge, 1996.

- **Holton (2000)** Holton, S.S., 'The making of suffrage history' in *Purvis & Holton (2000)*.

- **Kingsley Kent (1987)** Kingsley Kent, S., *Sex and Suffrage in Britain 1860-1914*, Routledge, 1987.

- **Lewis (1987)** Lewis, J. (ed.), *Before the Vote was Won: Arguments for and against Women's Suffrage*, Routledge, 1987.

- **Liddington & Norris (1978)** Liddington, J. & Norris, J., *One Hand Tied Behind Us: the Rise of the Women's Suffrage Movement*, Virago, 1978.

- **Marcus (1987)** Marcus, J., *Suffrage and the Suffragettes*, Routledge & Kegan Paul, 1987.

- **May (1996)** May, T. *An Economic and Social History of Britain 1760-1970* (2nd edn), Longman, 1996.

- **McDermid (1995)** McDermid, J., 'Women and Education' in *Purvis (1995)*.

- **McDonald (1989)** McDonald, I., *Vindication! A Postcard History of the Women's Movement*, Deirdre McDonald Books, 1989.

- **Mulvey-Roberts (2000)** Mulvey-Roberts, M. 'Militancy, masochism or martyrdom? The public and private prisons of Constance Lytton' in *Purvis & Holton (2000)*.

- **O'Gorman (1997)** O'Gorman F., *The Long Eighteenth Century British Political & Social History 1688-1832*, Arnold, 1997.

- **Pankhurst (1914)** Pankhurst, E., *My Own Story*, Eveleigh Nash, 1914.

- **Pankhurst (1931)** Pankhurst, S., *The Suffragette Movement: an Intimate Account of Persons and Ideals*, Longman, 1931.

- **Pugh (1974)** Pugh, M., 'Politicians and the women's vote', *History*, Vol.59, 1974.

- **Pugh (1985)** Pugh, M., *The Tories and the People: 1880-1935*, Blackwell, 1985.

- **Pugh (1985a)** Pugh, M., 'Labour and women's suffrage' in *Brown (1985)*.

- **Pugh (1994)** Pugh, M., *Votes for Women in Britain 1867-1928*, Historical Association, 1994.

- **Purvis (1995)** Purvis, J. (ed.), *Women's History: Britain 1850-1945*, UCL Press, 1995.

- **Purvis (2000)** Purvis, J., 'Emmeline Pankhurst (1858-1928) and votes for women' in *Purvis & Holton (2000)*.

- **Purvis & Holton (2000)** Purvis, J. & Holton, S.S. (eds), *Votes for Women*, Routledge, 2000.

- **Rendall (2000)** Rendall, J., 'Who was Lily Maxwell? Women's suffrage and Manchester politics, 1866-67' in *Purvis & Holton (2000)*.

- **Rosen (1974)** Rosen, A., *Rise up Women! The Militant Campaigns of the Women's Social and Political Union*, Routledge, 1974.

- **Schwarzkopf (1991)** Schwarzkopf, J., *Women in the Chartist Movement*, MacMillan, 1991.

- **Scott-Baumann (1995)** Scott-Baumann, M. (ed.), *Years of Expansion: Britain 1815-1914*, Hodder and Stoughton, 1995.

- **Strachey (1979)** Strachey, R., *The Cause: a Short History of the Women's Movement in Great Britain*, Virago, 1979 (first published in 1928).

- **Taylor (1983)** Taylor, B., *Eve and the New Jerusalem: Socialism and Feminism in the 19th Century*, Virago, 1983.

- **Thomis & Grimmett (1982)** Thomis, M.I. & Grimmett, J., *Women in Protest 1800-50*, Croom Helm, 1982.

- **Thompson (1984)** Thompson, D., *The Chartists: Popular Politics in the Industrial Revolution*, Aldershot, 1984.

- **Thompson (1993)** Thompson, D., *British Women in the Nineteenth Century*, The Historical Association, 1993.

- **Uglow (1998)** Uglow, J., *The Macmillan Dictionary of Women's Biography* (3rd edn), Macmillan, 1998.

- **Vicinus (1972)** Vicinus, M., *The Widening Sphere*, Methuen, 1972.

- **Willis (1999)** Willis, M., *Democracy and the State 1830-1945*, Cambridge University Press, 1999.

UNIT 4 — Trade unions 1850-1914

Timeline - Trade unions 1850-1914

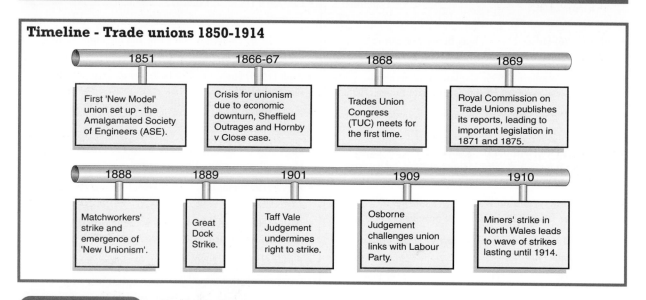

1851 — First 'New Model' union set up - the Amalgamated Society of Engineers (ASE).

1866-67 — Crisis for unionism due to economic downturn, Sheffield Outrages and Hornby v Close case.

1868 — Trades Union Congress (TUC) meets for the first time.

1869 — Royal Commission on Trade Unions publishes its reports, leading to important legislation in 1871 and 1875.

1888 — Matchworkers' strike and emergence of 'New Unionism'.

1889 — Great Dock Strike.

1901 — Taff Vale Judgement undermines right to strike.

1909 — Osborne Judgement challenges union links with Labour Party.

1910 — Miners' strike in North Wales leads to wave of strikes lasting until 1914.

Introduction

For many years, the broad outlines of trade union history were those laid down by Beatrice and Sidney Webb in their *History of Trade Unionism* (first published in 1894 and revised in 1920). Their view was that the history of the union movement could be divided into a series of distinct phases. First, there was the attempt to achieve 'general unionism' in the 1830s when unions representing workers from different trades joined together in larger federations than had existed before. John Doherty's National Association for the Protection of Labour and Robert Owen's Grand National Consolidated Trade Union (GNCTU), which recruited unskilled as well as skilled workers, are examples. Then, after a period of decline following the failure of the GNCTU, trade unionism was revived in the 1850s by the development of 'New Model unions' - élite craft unions which looked after the needs of certain groups of skilled workers. And third, following a series of strikes in 1889-90, 'New Unions' emerged - unions which catered for semi-skilled and unskilled workers and which adopted an approach which was much more militant than that favoured by the New Model unions.

In recent years, however, the Webbs' version of the history of the trade union movement has been increasingly disputed. Whilst historians accept that New Model unions and New Unions did develop, many argue that there was a great deal more continuity between the different phases than the Webbs allow. In addition, historians have begun to ask questions that were ignored by the Webbs. For example, a debate has emerged about whether or not a so-called 'labour aristocracy' developed after 1850 and historians are divided about why a period of industrial unrest broke out between 1910 and 1914.

This unit considers how far the Webbs' view of trade union history stands up to scrutiny and examines the questions that have engaged historians in recent years. For information on relations between the trade unions and political parties see Unit 5.

UNIT SUMMARY

Part 1 examines the emergence of New Model unions in the 1850s and considers how 'new' they were. It also looks at the debate between historians about whether or not a so-called 'labour aristocracy' developed after 1850.

Part 2 looks at the events which led to the development of New Unionism. It considers how 'new' New Unionism was and how successful the New Unions were. It also focuses on women's participation in trade unionism after 1850.

Part 3 focuses on the period of industrial unrest which broke out between 1908 and 1914. It examines the causes of unrest and analyses the contribution of syndicalism.

1 Trade Unions, 1850-80

Key questions

1. What was the position of trade unions in the mid-19th century?

2. How new were the 'New Model' unions?

3. What led to the burst of trade union legislation in 1867-75?

4. Why was the TUC set up?

1.1 The position of trade unions in the mid-19th century

A definition

Trade unions have been defined as:

'Associations of wage earners which exist to maintain or improve the conditions of work and rates of pay of their members.' (Gardiner & Wenborn 1995, p.752)

Whereas, individually, employees have little chance of persuading employers to improve pay or conditions, collectively, workers have a great deal of bargaining power. If all the workers in a factory withdraw their labour in protest by going on strike in support of higher pay, for example, this puts the employer under a great deal more pressure to make concessions than if only a single worker takes such action. Going on strike is a union's main weapon of last resort. For a strike to be effective, workers need to ensure that production is stopped. The easiest way to do this is to blockade or 'picket' the workplace. It was only in the late 19th century that striking and peaceful picketing became legal activities.

In addition to bargaining with employers on behalf of employees, unions also developed other functions. They organised social functions for members, for example, and used subscriptions to set up funds to provide members with sickness benefit or to pay members' funeral expenses.

Unions' potential to damage the interests of employers (by striking or by stirring up discontent) ensured that there was a constant struggle between unions and governments since governments throughout the 19th century were more inclined to protect the interests of employers than workers.

Between 1800 and 1850, the legal position of unions changed, but laws continued to restrict unions' freedom of action.

The legal position of unions, 1799-1850

The Combination Acts, 1799 and 1800

At the beginning of the 19th century, it was illegal to belong to a trade union. The Combination Acts of 1799 and 1800 banned any organisation which acted 'in restraint of trade'. The Combination Acts meant, therefore, that it was illegal for groups of workers to combine together to demand wage rises, shorter hours or better working conditions, or to go on strike. Previous laws had banned combinations of workers in individual trades, but the Combination Acts were the first laws to apply to all workers.

Despite the fact that unions were illegal and workers could face imprisonment for joining them, they continued to exist in the first quarter of the 19th century:

'The Combination Acts...did not prevent the spread of unionism. Paradoxically, unions of skilled workers gained strength during the 25 years of blanket illegality.' (Evans 1996, p.167)

Many of these unions posed as 'Friendly Societies'. Friendly Societies were organisations which provided members with benefits such as unemployment benefit, sickness benefit and funeral expenses in return for a regular subscription. Unlike unions, however, Friendly Societies did not have any role to play in the workplace.

The Master and Servant Act, 1823

In 1823, a further piece of legislation was designed to restrict union activity - the Master and Servant Act. According to Behagg, this was a particularly important piece of legislation:

'This codified previous Master and Servant Acts, and was probably the most significant single piece of trade union legislation before 1875. Under its provisions, employees who broke their contract of work (either written or verbal) could be imprisoned. A strike which resulted in work not being completed could be deemed a breach of contract...Between 1857 and 1875 (the period for which figures are available) there were, on average, 10,000 prosecutions of workers per year in England and Wales.' (Behagg 1991, pp.78-79)

Repeal of the Combination Acts, 1824-25

Following a long campaign, the Combination Acts were repealed in 1824. A new Act allowed combinations of workers (unions) to be set up, but picketing still remained an offence. Some historians (for example, Evans 1996) have argued that the main reason why the Combination Acts were repealed was that members of the government were persuaded that unions would lose their appeal if they were legal and legalising them would reduce or even end strikes. As soon as the Acts were repealed, however, a wave of strikes broke out. In response to this, the government passed a second Act in 1825, the Combination of Workmen Act, which amended the terms of the 1824 Act. Unions remained legal, but members could be prosecuted for 'molestation, intimidation and obstruction' and it was illegal for workers to encourage colleagues to break their contracts by striking:

'Unions were forbidden to pressurise fellow workers to join their organisations or their strikes, such pressure constituting [adding up to] "molestation". Over the next 50 years, courts interpreted this clause pretty loosely, with cases even recorded of fellow workers imprisoned for throwing "black looks" at non-cooperative fellow workers. After 1825, trade unions were legal but it was difficult to see how a strike could be organised without breaking the law.' (Behagg 1991, p.79)

Behagg describes the status of unions between 1825 and 1875 as 'quasi-legal'. In other words, it was perfectly legal to belong to a union, but, in practice, if members of a union took collective action to put pressure on employers, they risked prosecution. Evans points out that:

'The 1825 Act remained the basic legal statement on trade unionism for half a century, but it did not remove the other legislation which could be invoked. When the famous agricultural labourers of Tolpuddle (Dorset) were organised into a Friendly Society by the Methodist local preacher George Loveless in 1833, for example, they were transported [sent to Australia] under legislation against the administration of forbidden oaths. Miners suffered under the "Master and Servant" Acts under which the breaking of contracts by workers was a criminal offence while similar breaches by employers were deemed civil offences only.' (Evans 1996, p.171)

Unions before 1850

There has been a historical debate about the nature of unions in the period 1825-50. According to the Webbs and others (for example, Thompson 1980), there was a burst of important union activity followed by a lull. The burst of activity came in the period 1829-34 when there was an attempt to create national unions (unions whose membership came from many different parts of the UK, not just one area) and general unions (unions whose members came from many trades, not just a single trade). This burst of activity, these authors claim, had revolutionary potential since the new national and general unions raised working-class consciousness and had political as well as economic goals (inspired by Robert Owen's ideas that people should work cooperatively in the workplace). According to this viewpoint, the burst of union activity came to an end with the collapse of Robert Owen's Grand National Consolidated Trades Union (GNCTU) in 1834. There then followed a lull in trade union activity (with the exception of the 'Plug Plot' - a general strike which affected much of industrial Britain - in July/August

1842) until the setting up of the first 'New Model' union in 1851.

Other historians, however, believe that such a viewpoint is distorted. Laybourn, for example, argues that the idea that trade union history can be divided into neat and separate phases is unhelpful:

'Such divisions might be convenient, but they do not represent what really happened. They tend, on the whole, to exaggerate the importance of rapid change in trade union development...Although there was change, trade unionism developed more steadily than the Webbs first suggested through patient organisation and the improvement in working and social conditions.' (Laybourn 1992, p.23)

Laybourn points out that the number of national and general unions set up in the period 1829-34 was small and they were all short-lived (see Box 4.1).

BOX 4.1   National and general unions, 1829-34

The following national and general unions were set up and collapsed in the period 1829-34:

1. John Doherty's Grand General Union of Operative Cotton Spinners (set up in 1829) was defeated in a series of strikes in 1830-31.

2. The collapse of the Grand General Union of Operative Cotton Spinners led to the collapse of the National Association for the Protection of Labour (a union which was meant to protect the interests of workers from different trades) after only a year in existence.

3. Attempts to set up a national and general trade union for workers in the building industry resulted in the Grand National Guild of Builders (set up in June 1833). This, however, lost strikes in Manchester and Liverpool at the end of 1833 and collapsed in '1834 or 1835'.

4. Robert Owen's GNCTU was essentially a London-based organisation and it, too, only survived for a few months (it was set up in February 1834, but had effectively collapsed by August).

Adapted from Laybourn 1992.

Interpretation

The Tolpuddle Martyrs

As noted above, it was in 1833 that six agricultural workers from Tolpuddle in Dorset were prosecuted after setting up a union and sentenced to transportation for seven years. This sentence provoked a great deal of protest, including a mass demonstration in London organised by the GNCTU on 21 April 1834. This union-inspired protest, however, provoked a backlash against the unions, with a number of attempts being made to prevent union activity. In Oldham, for example, two trade union leaders were arrested and a union member shot when union members clashed with employers at a mill.

According to the Webbs, the failure of general unionism and the controversy surrounding the transportation of the Tolpuddle Martyrs in 1834 ended the 'militant' phase of union activity and led to a lull. Laybourn (and others), however, argue that this was not the case:

'More recent assessments tend to suggest that the importance of the events of the early 1830s was exaggerated by the Webbs, that the campaign to release the "Tolpuddle Martyrs" helped to unify trade unionism, and that there was some success - the sentences of the Dorset labourers being remitted in 1836 and they being returned home in 1838. Even more to the point...trade unions were in no way halted by the events of 1834 and "business as usual" continued between then and the 1850s.' (Laybourn 1992, p.30)

The nature of unions before 1850

Behagg (1991) points out that, in the first half of the 19th century, most unions were loosely-knit groups of workers from a particular area who supported one another at times of confrontation with employers. Such organisations were temporary and informal:

'In studying the building trades, historian Richard Price has argued that before 1850 it was considered more important among workers that they were "in union" (with one another) than that they were "in the union".' (Behagg 1991, p.80)

Leeson (1984) argues that it was in the period 1834-50 that unions became more formal in their structure and more permanent. They also became bigger, with a number of amalgamations resulting in unions that had between 20 and 80 branches and between 500 and 2,000 members. Such amalgamations were not as ambitious as the experiments with national and general unions in the period 1829-34, but they proved to be longer-lasting. Leeson claims:

'There were some 14 amalgamations or attempts at such, during the late 1830s and 1840s. The 1851 Amalgamated Society of Engineers [ASE] and the Boilermakers and Iron Shipbuilders' amalgamation which followed in 1852 thus, in a way, crowned a development rather than gave rise to one.' (Leeson 1984, p.16)

Laybourn agrees that unions became more formal in their structure, pointing out that:

'The movable head office, whereby various branches shared the role of running the union in order to avoid cliquism began to be replaced in the 1830s and 1840s by the appointment of permanent national officers. In the late 1840s, the masons appointed a paid General Secretary and, in 1845, the boilermakers also elected their first full-time General Secretary.' (Laybourn 1992, p.32)

1.2 How new were the 'New Model' unions?

What were the 'New Model' unions?

In 1851, a new trade union was set up exclusively for workers in the engineering industry - the Amalgamated Society of Engineers (ASE). As the name suggests, the ASE was the fusion of a number of smaller (locally-based) unions which represented skilled engineers. Around 75% of members of the ASE came from the Society of Journeymen Steam Engine Makers, a union which had been set up in 1826:

'The resulting Amalgamated Society of Engineers (ASE) was larger than any other union. It started with only 5,000 members, but had 12,000 at the end of its first year.' (Fraser 1999, p.26)

It was the Webbs who described unions like the ASE as 'New Model' unions, though how 'new' they were is a matter of debate (see below). Since these New Model unions were set up to represent groups of skilled workers who worked in a particular industry or craft, they are sometimes called 'craft unions' or 'craft societies'. A number of such unions were set up in the 1850s:

'From 1850, it is possible to trace the steady growth of the major craft societies: the ASE grew from 5,000 in 1851 to 54,000 in 1888. Similar patterns of growth were achieved by the Society of Ironfounders, the United Society of Boilermakers and Iron and Steel Shipbuilders, the Amalgamated Society of Carpenters and Joiners, the London Society of Compositors, and the Society of Operative Stonemasons.' (Clegg et al. 1964, p.3)

It should be noted that some authors argue that the number of New Model unions was small, that not all New Model unions were organised in the same way, and that the extent and influence of the New Model unions has been exaggerated (see Laybourn 1992, pp.39-50). Despite these reservations, it is possible to make a number of generalisations.

1. Selective and exclusive membership

New Model unions all represented a particular craft and the basis for membership was:

'A sharp distinction between qualified and unqualified workers, with qualification defined primarily in terms of a formal apprenticeship.' (Clegg et al.1964, p.4)

In other words, these unions were selective in their membership. Qualified workers could join, whereas unqualified workers could not. This meant that skilled workers were represented and protected whilst unskilled workers were not. Indeed, the primary aim of such unions was to protect the privileged position of their members:

'The aim of the amalgamated societies was to improve the conditions for their members by restricting entry to the trade and ensuring that work was spread evenly. They invariably resisted the employment of unskilled labour, insisting on the use of skilled union men for particular jobs. They also opposed the use by employers of systematic overtime and piecework, both of which tended to increase the pressure on the individual worker to be more productive, and thus decrease the total amount of work available.' (Behagg 1991, p.82)

2. Friendly Society-style benefits

Fraser argues that, as well as being selective, the New Model unions aimed at stability and permanence:

'The history of many of the early unions had been brief, with workers flocking to them at times of industrial unrest and flocking out of them when the moment of confrontation had passed. The much more successful models of stability were the Friendly Societies where workers subscribed for future benefits and where failure to pay dues would result in loss of savings. Those organisations which managed to combine Friendly Society benefits and industrial activities were the survivors.' (Fraser 1999, pp.27-28)

The New Model unions learned from this experience and offered benefits to their members in return for subscriptions. For example, members of the ASE who paid a subscription of one shilling a week could then claim ten shillings a week for 26 weeks and seven shillings for the next 12 weeks, if they became unemployed. Those who paid a higher subscription could claim sickness benefit, a lump sum if they became permanently disabled, a funeral allowance and emigration assistance. It should be noted that the payment of benefits by unions had precedents. For example, the Society of Journeymen Steam Engine Makers Society (which, at first, made up the bulk of the ASE) paid similar benefits to those listed above. What was new, Fraser (1999) argues, was the size of the New Model unions, the range of benefits offered and the efficiency of the running of the new organisations. He also notes, however, that the number of unions offering the full range of benefits was small. The vast majority of unions continued to offer limited benefits (death benefit and strike pay only, for example) or none.

The links between the New Model unions and the Friendly Societies were close. Following the passage of the 1855 Friendly Societies Act, several of the New Model unions deposited their rules with the Registrar of Friendly Societies, assuming that this would protect their funds. In fact, the Hornby v Close case of 1866-67 showed that it did not do so (see pages 121-22 below).

3. National organisation

Whereas other unions tended to be regionally or locally organised, New Model unions were nationally organised with headquarters usually in London, a centralised Executive Committee and paid officials (a Secretary and staff) who worked full-time. This new central organisation was partly a result of advances in transport. By the late 1850s, the new rail network was well enough developed for people to travel and to communicate over long distances with relative ease. This allowed a centrally-based organisation to function smoothly. Unions also set up their headquarters in London in order to make contact with politicians and journalists. This 'pressure group' approach was a new development (see point 5 below).

According to Laybourn (1992), the strength of the New Model unions' central organisation should not be exaggerated. He shows that many decisions were made at branch rather than national level and that power struggles between branches and the national leadership sometimes resulted in breakaways. For example, the National Association of Operative Plasterers was formed in 1860, but most of its London branches broke away to form a Metropolitan Association in 1870.

4. A moderate image

In general, officials in the New Model unions tried to cultivate a moderate, non-militant image, not least because the build-up of funds could be threatened by long, wasteful strikes. William Allan (Secretary of the ASE) even said in 1867:

'We believe that all strikes are a complete waste of money.'

It should be noted, however, that Allan made this comment when appearing before a Royal Commission which had been set up to 'inquire into the organisation and rules of trade unions' and he was clearly anxious to present union activity in the least threatening light. In reality, the New Model unions certainly did not reject the use of strikes as a last resort. The ASE itself was involved in a long dispute with the engineering employers just after its formation, in 1852 and, in 1859-60, it made three separate donations of £1,000 in support of strike action by builders' unions. Robert Applegarth, Secretary of the Amalgamated Society of Carpenters and Joiners (ASCJ), best summed up the view of the craft unions:

'Never surrender the right to strike, but be careful how you use a double-edged weapon.' (quoted in Pelling 1987, p.49)

When the New Model unions did strike, it was as a national union. They only supported and financed strikes that were officially recognised by the union's Executive Committee.

5. A high public profile

Fraser (1999) argues that what was new about the New Model unions was their high public profile. Unlike other unions, he argues, the New Model unions were able and prepared to manipulate the press and they set out to win friends in high places in the hope of countering anti-union publicity:

'Probably the really new feature of the ASE was its high public profile. Partly, this was from choice, partly from force of circumstances. Inevitably, a new organisation of the size of the ASE was going to attract attention. It emerged at a time when the press was expanding and strikes were news. But, it also courted publicity deliberately.' (Fraser 1999, p.39)

Fraser suggests that the ASE chose to have its headquarters in London to gain 'power and influence' and he points out that the leadership deliberately set out to make contacts with 'journalists, lawyers and civil servants' as well as with politicians. By making these contacts and moving in such circles, New Model union leaders hoped to improve the image of unions and to gain more favourable reports in the press. This also helps to explain why New Model unions presented themselves as the moderate voice of unionism.

Challenges to the Webbs' view

A number of historians have challenged the Webbs' view that there was a lull in union activity between 1834 and 1850 and then a dramatic leap forward with the formation of the New Model unions in the 1850s. Musson, for example, argues that the Webbs exaggerated both the importance of the GNCTU and the difference between New Model unions and those in existence before 1850. He claims that the craft unions of the 1850s were not radically different from those of earlier periods and that:

'There is little if any justification for the term "New Model".' (Musson 1972, p.50)

Behagg agrees, suggesting that there was little about the New Model unions that was genuinely new:

'In fact, the New Model unions inherited much of their organisation and strategy from earlier unions. For example, they emphasised their role as Friendly Societies...Unions had always attempted to do this, although never with great success...Even the idea of paid full-time officials was not a new departure. The stonemasons had applied this in 1834, as had the miners in 1842. All that was really new about these New Model unions was their effectiveness in applying these strategies and their ultimate success in persuading employers of their acceptability.' (Behagg 1991, p.82)

Pelling, on the other hand, accepts that the New Model unions did draw on the past but argues that they still represent a landmark in trade union development:

'Although many of the apparently novel characteristics of the ASE were borrowed from the "Old Mechanics" (Journeymen Steam Engine Makers, founded 1826)...yet the foundation of the new society in 1851 is rightly regarded as a landmark in the history of trade unionism.' (Pelling 1987, p.40)

A 'labour aristocracy'?

The debate about the novelty of the craft unions of the 1850s has wider implications because it raises questions about what these unions represented. Harrison (1965), Hobsbawm (1968) and other historians saw the New Model unions as representing a shift of union power into the hands of the 'labour aristocracy'. Marx's collaborator, Friedrich Engels, had written in 1844 of a 'trade union aristocracy' whose members were more prosperous than the majority of the working class. Hobsbawm saw the period 1840 to 1890 as the 'classical period' of this aristocracy. Members of the labour aristocracy, he argued, represented about 10% of the working class and could be identified by 'the level and regularity of their earnings'. The New Model unions were very much the unions of this group. Their most important feature was their desire to gain acceptability by collaborating with, rather than opposing, the capitalist system. The New Model unions, therefore, represent one strand of union history, while the other is represented by the more militant, mass membership unions of the 1830s and those which became active in the late 1880s.

The views above have been challenged for a number of reasons. First, the supposed docility of the New Model unions is disputed. It has been pointed out that they were not completely opposed to strike action. Indeed, they were involved in strikes. Besides, the New Model unions (like their predecessors) faced a formidable range of legal obstacles to strike action. Their caution, therefore, can be explained by the circumstances in which they had to work. It is not necessarily best explained by the fact that they represented a privileged minority of working-class people. And second, historians like Musson (1972) and Pelling (1987) have attacked the idea that a labour aristocracy dominated the trade union movement in the period 1850-90. They point out that many unions existed outside the tightly-knit group of New Model unions - the miners, textile workers, railway workers, agriculture labourers and many other small groups, for example. The leaders of the New Model unions, they claim, were influential but not as dominant as some have argued. The Trades Union Congress (TUC - see pages 125-26 below), they note, was set up by trade unionists mainly from the provinces, without any support from the New Model unions. It was only later that the New Model unions joined forces with the TUC.

Different ideological positions

The different views outlined above reflect the ideological position of the various authors. Some, like Clegg et al. (1964) and Musson (1972), see the development of the unions in the 19th century as a process of moderate, cautious attempts at improvement. They emphasise (and approve of) continuity and the non-revolutionary and non-militant approach of the New Model unions. More radical historians like Harrison (1965) and Hobsbawm (1968), on the other hand, acknowledge the cautious route taken by many trade unionists, but they see it as alternating or interweaving with a more militant tradition (of which they approve). This more militant tradition, so they argue, revived in the 1880s and 1890s.

Other unions after 1850

It is important to note that the New Model unions made up only a part of the trade union movement after 1850:

'Trade unionism in the craft industries was built on apprenticeship and on customs inherited from before the Industrial Revolution. In industries created by the Industrial Revolution, like the railways, there were none of these customs. Other

industries, notably coal, iron, cotton and wool, were so profoundly altered that any protective customs were swept away.' (Clegg et al. 1964, p.15)

In the coal mining and cotton industries, district unions remained strong:

'Centralised activity in the miners' and cotton unions was mostly confined to efforts at obtaining mines and factory legislation - ie it was political, not industrial.' (Musson 1972, p.53)

These unions lacked the strong central direction of the New Model unions, but they were more representative in their structures, with local delegates having a say in policy. There are many examples of industrial disputes affecting the coal, cotton and other industries, but generally little violence or militancy:

'One of the most striking characteristics of industrial bargaining from the 1840s was the increasing emphasis placed by union leaders on "respectability" and non-violence.' (Pimlott & Cook 1982, p.21)

MAIN POINTS - Sections 1.1-1.2

- The Combination Acts of 1799 and 1800 banned any organisation which acted 'in restraint of trade'. A new Act repealed them in 1824, but an amendment to it in 1825, and the Master and Servant Act of 1823, ensured that union activity remained restricted.
- According to the Webbs, there was a burst of militant union activity in the period 1829-34, followed by a lull until New Model unions were set up in the 1850s. Some contemporary historians dispute this, arguing that the importance of the national and general unions of 1829-34 has been exaggerated and that there was steady union

development after 1834.
- The term 'New Model' union was coined by the Webbs. New Model unions are also known as craft unions. The first New Model union - the ASE - was set up in 1851.
- New Model unions had five main characteristics - (1) a selective and exclusive membership (2) Friendly Society-style benefits (3) a national organisation (4) a moderate image and (5) a high public profile.
- There is a debate about how new the New Model unions were and whether New Model unions developed in response to the growth of a moderate 'aristocracy of labour'.

Activity 4.1 The New Model unions

ITEM 1 A historian's view (1)

The Webbs, having inflated the 'revolutionary' aspects of the trade union movement of 1829-34, created a 'New Model' of trade unionism dating from the formation of the ASE in 1851. But, what occurred in the 1850s and 1860s was not a 'New Model' but a strengthening of the old. There was no radical change in organisation. The movement towards amalgamation had begun earlier. The so-called 'New Model' unions maintained the traditional characteristics of the old skilled unions - restriction of membership to apprenticed craftsmen, high subscription and the sort of benefits provided by Friendly Societies. Nor was there any change of objectives. These unions had policies regarding wages, hours, apprenticeship and the closed shop. Concern with these practical affairs gives a basic continuity to trade unionism between the 1820s and the 1870s. Also, a 'labour aristocracy' was not a new feature of trade unionism between 1850 and 1875. The extent to which there was a loss of 'class consciousness', a narrowing of trade union horizons, a retreat from wider political and social aims, has been grossly exaggerated. Trade societies had almost always been composed of 'labour aristocrats' and they had always been exclusive. These fundamental characteristics had always been far stronger than any emergent class consciousness.

Adapted from Musson 1972.

ITEM 2 An ASE membership certificate

The membership certificate (left) is typical of those produced by the New Model unions. The two engineers at the top (1) are idealised, as is the industrial landscape in the background with its clean factory, river, steamer and train. Heroes are identified and claimed for the ASE - Crompton (2) who invented the spinning mule - a machine which combined the spinning jenny and water frame and greatly speeded up textile production, Watt (3) who invented the steam engine and Arkwright (4) who invented the water frame. All three, significantly, were of humble origin. The themes of the text ('Be united and industrious') are clearly illustrated. War (5 - the god Mars) is being refused (to emphasise the moderate image of the union). Abundance comes from peaceful production (6). The kneeling figures (7) emphasise strength through unity (a single stick can be broken, but a bundle cannot). The pictures on the base (8) illustrate the five different names which make up the full title of the Society. The phoenix rising from the ashes (9) refers to the ASE's origins (one union reborn from many). The certificate has several functions: proof of membership; a work of art to be hung on the wall; a utopian vision of working life which emphasises dignity and the social importance of the skilled worker and offers a vision of noble morals where skills can create abundance; and, a statement to the world outside the union.

Adapted from Bellamy 1990.

ITEM 3 A historian's view (2)

Socially speaking, the best paid stratum of the working class merged with what may loosely be called the 'lower middle class'. Indeed, the term 'lower middle class' was sometimes used to include the aristocracy of labour. But, if the boundaries of the labour aristocracy were fluid on one side, they were precise on another. An 'artisan' or 'craftsman' was not under any circumstances to be confused with a 'labourer'. The Secretary of the Boilermakers' Union, for example, was appalled at the thought of a labourer being allowed to do a craftsman's work as 'it would not be desirable for a man of one class to go to another class'. Also, before the 1890s, the boundaries of the labour aristocracy and of trade unionism were believed to coincide - as the following quote from *A Working Man* (a book published in 1879) shows: 'As his title of unskilled implies, he has no handicraft and no union'. In fact, it was commonly believed that unions did not make groups of workers strong so much as indicate that they already were strong.

Adapted from Hobsbawm 1968.

Questions

1. What, if anything, was new about the New Model unions? Use Items 1-3 in your answer.
2. a) How do Items 1 and 3 differ in their viewpoints?
   b) 'The development of New Model unions is evidence of the development of a labour aristocracy'. Using Items 1-3 give arguments for and against this view.
3. a) What does Item 2 tell us about the nature of New Model unions?
   b) Explain what impression the artist was aiming at and whether it was successful.

1.3 What led to the burst of trade union legislation in 1867-75?

Trades Councils

Trades Councils have been defined as:

'Local organisations of trade unions representing the major unions in particular areas. They have usually acted as spokespersons for the workers' side of local industry against local chambers of commerce.' (Gardiner & Wenborn 1995, p.756)

In general terms, Trades Councils would be made up of delegates from the main local unions. Fraser (1999) argues that they had two main aims:

- to coordinate support for disputes involving workers (both local and non-local disputes)
- to improve the public image of unions amongst the local population.

So, for example, striking workers from one town who aimed to raise funds to continue a strike would approach Trades Councils in other towns. These Trades Councils would then put the strikers in touch with local union branches. Equally, when a dispute arose in a particular town, the Trades Council in that town would put across the workers' case.

Although a few temporary Trades Councils had been set up before 1850 (see Fraser 1999, pp.36-37), Fraser argues that it was only at the end of the 1850s that permanent Trades Councils began to be set up:

'Between 1855 and 1866 at least 24 Trades Councils had come into existence and, although some of them did not survive into the 1870s, in most of the main cities these became permanent organisations.' (Fraser 1999, p.37)

Perhaps the most important of these Trades Councils was that set up in London in July 1860 on the initiative of William Allan, Secretary of the ASE. It was the setting up of the London Trades Council that led to the formation of what the Webbs described as the 'Junta'.

The 'Junta'

According to the Webbs, the key to the shape of the trade union movement which developed in the period 1850-80 was a group of five men - the so-called 'Junta':

- William Allan, Secretary of the ASE
- Robert Applegarth, Secretary of the Amalgamated Society of Carpenters and Joiners
- Edwin Coulson, Secretary of the Operative Bricklayers Society
- George Odger, Secretary of the London Trades Council
- Daniel Guile, Secretary of the Friendly Society of Ironfounders.

The Webbs claimed that, from the early 1860s to 1871, these five men met weekly as a 'Conference of Amalgamated Trades', making decisions which determined the approach and policies adopted by the union movement as a whole:

'The Junta, apparently, encouraged trade unionism to [oppose] industrial action, fostered Friendly Society benefits and centralised union funds in an attempt to control strike action. It was the Junta who shaped the whole trade union movement into a pressure group to extend trade union rights.' (Laybourn 1992, p.39)

According to the Webbs, the Junta was progressive and forward-looking, while its main opponent, George Potter (see Box 4.2) was the opposite.

BOX 4.2 George Potter

The main opposition to the Junta came from George Potter. He was a joiner who had shot to fame during the London building trades dispute in 1859-60. Building workers demanded a nine-hour, rather than a ten-hour, working day and employers responded by attempting to employ non-union workers. The dispute ended in a compromise in February 1860 with the employers agreeing to employ workers who belonged to unions in return for the unions dropping their demand for a nine-hour day. From 1859-61, Potter was Secretary of the Committee of London Building Trades' Workers. His fame spread as a result of the publication of the *Bee-Hive*, a working-class newspaper which he owned and edited. He used the *Bee-Hive* to put forward his beliefs in the need to reject the ideas of the Junta and to set up an independent political party for the working class. He formed the London Working Men's Association as a counter to the London Trades Council (to which he and some supporters were delegates). Potter constantly challenged Applegarth on the London Trades Council in 1864-65, drew support from many of the small London societies who had lost members to the Amalgamated Carpenters, and presented an alternative to the rule of the New Model unions. Potter's support was widespread, with many of the provincial trade unions supporting him.

Adapted from Laybourn 1992.

Interpretation

Fraser, however, argues that the Webbs' interpretation is quite wrong:

'The Webbs painted [the members of the Junta] as enlightened modernisers against the backward-looking George Potter. Others have accepted the argument that the so-called "Junta" provided a national leadership. But, this is grossly to exaggerate both their unity of purpose and their influence. Few wanted to get caught in the personal animosity which existed between Applegarth and Potter and at no time, other than in the Conference of

Amalgamated Trades, did these leaders act effectively as a "joint committee of the officers of the national societies".' (Fraser 1999, p.44)

According to Fraser, it was only in January 1867 that the Conference of Amalgamated Trades first met and it was only in 1867 that the five members of the Junta seriously attempted to provide national leadership. That, he argues, was in response to the crisis which developed in 1866-67 and threatened the very existence of trade unionism.

The crisis of 1866-67

According to Pelling (1987), the crisis which arose in 1866-67 had three main causes:

- the economic downturn of 1866-67
- the Sheffield Outrages of 1866
- the Hornby v Close case.

1. The economic downturn of 1866-67

Pelling claims that the economic downturn of 1866-67 was the result of a 'banking panic in the City' (Pelling 1987, p.53). In a sense, the cause is unimportant. What matters is the response of employers and politicians. The economic downturn, it seems, triggered a great deal of anti-union feeling amongst both employers and politicians, with employers in some parts of the country taking steps to break the grip that unions had over workers in certain trades. Fraser (1999, p.44) claims that unions were described by employers and politicians as 'violent and dangerous class conspiracies' and Pelling suggests that:

'[The downturn] provided an opportunity for a number of publicists to denounce the unions for weakening the competitive position of British goods by their insistence on higher wages than foreign workmen obtained.' (Pelling 1987, pp.53-54)

2. The Sheffield Outrages of 1866

The 'Sheffield Outrages' (see Box 4.3) were a series of acts of violence committed by members of unions based in Sheffield, culminating in the use of gunpowder to blow up the house of a man who had not paid his union subscription:

'The small unions in the Sheffield cutlery trades depended for their survival on being able to keep a tight control of entry into the trade and, to do this, they used funds to pay people not to work at under the acceptable rate. They could only pursue this policy effectively if all dues were paid.' (Fraser 1999, p.42)

Attacks of the sort described in Box 4.3 had been common for some time. Fraser points out that relations between employers and workers in Sheffield were poor because employers hoped to restructure the cutlery industry but workers were resisting. But, the reports of violence provided useful ammunition for those politicians, journalists and employers mentioned above who wanted to use the economic downturn as

an opportunity to campaign for action to be taken against the unions. The result was a great deal of hostile publicity in the national press:

'Immediately, the newspapers of the whole country were attributing this crime, not so much to a special local situation at Sheffield, but to the institution of trade unionism generally.' (Pelling 1987, p.54)

Significantly, calls for a public inquiry into trade unionism (which came as a result of the Sheffield Outrages) were supported both by those who were opposed to unions and by trade union leaders who hoped to use such an inquiry to improve unions' image with the public.

BOX 4.3 The Sheffield Outrages

Strikes were by no means the only form of industrial conflict available. The sabotage of equipment and intimidation were not uncommon. Indeed, the events of the early 1860s provide some of the strongest evidence of the way in which trade unions were prepared to be aggressive in their pursuit of control of the labour market. The Sheffield Outrages of the 1860s reflect the willingness of trade unions to use a variety of techniques to control those who would not follow union policies. 'Rattening' - the practice of removing wheel-bands from grinding machines or other tools - was a common method of disciplining workers. And, there was other, more violent, activity such as the Hereford Street Outrage of 8 October 1866 when the house of Thomas Fearnehough was blown up. In order to secure information, those guilty of this and other offences were promised that they would not be prosecuted if they provided a full account. These accounts revealed just how far William Broadhead of the Grinder's Union had been prepared to go to enforce the will of the union. Broadhead had employed Samuel Crooks to enforce the union's power on several occasions for a sum of £15. This, it was alleged, was 'about the regular sum'. *Adapted from Laybourn 1992.*

3. The Hornby v Close case, 1866-67

The Hornby v Close case of 1866-67 was an important setback for unions because it raised a question mark over both their legal status and their ability to protect their funds. The case was brought by the Boilermakers Union against a branch treasurer who had stolen union funds. The union argued that unions had the same status as Friendly Societies (the funds of Friendly Societies were protected by the Friendly Societies Act of 1855). But, in January 1866, the judges rejected the union's argument, ruling that the union was not covered by the Friendly Societies Act of 1855 because unions were organisations with an illegal purpose and their rules were 'in restraint of trade' (since they included the calling of strikes). As a result, they had no right to recover their funds if they were misused by an official. This ruling was then confirmed on appeal in 1867, making it clear that, in the eyes of the law:

'All trade unions, although they had a Friendly Society side to their activities, were inherently in restraint of trade and, therefore, illegal.' (Fraser 1999, p.42)

This judgement threw doubt, therefore, on the legal status of unions. It was of particular concern to the New Model unions because they had substantial funds which, as a result of the ruling, were no longer protected. Also, by raising doubts about the legal status of unions, it added to the pressure for a government inquiry into trade unionism.

The Junta's response to the crisis of 1866-67

There is a consensus among historians that members of the Junta, particularly Robert Applegarth, played an important role in the period 1867-69 - the period between the announcement that a Royal Commission would be set up to inquire into trade unionism and the publication of its two reports.

The Royal Commission on Trade Unions, 1867-69

The Royal Commission on Trade Unions was set up to examine the rules and organisation of trade unions and to consider whether the law should be changed in any way. The Junta's first demand was that two union members should sit on the Commission (which was to have 11 members). The government refused this demand, but it did allow the Junta to nominate one commissioner. The Junta chose a sympathetic barrister, Frederic Harrison. A second commissioner, Thomas Hughes (an MP), was also sympathetic. In addition, Applegarth attended the Commission as the expert trade unionist and other members of the Junta appeared as witnesses before the Commission.

The Junta's strategy

From the outset, the Junta's strategy was to influence the Commission by presenting a picture of responsible unionism:

'The main strategy of Applegarth and Harrison was to concentrate the attention of the Commission on the large amalgamated unions of which Applegarth's own was a conspicuous example. He himself appeared as the first witness and did much to present unionism in a favourable light. He, Allan and Coulson [all members of the Junta] in their evidence built up a picture of the unions as sober insurance societies whose affairs were business-like and entirely respectable.' (Pelling 1987, p.56)

The union leaders argued that, far from provoking strikes, their unions were a restraint on them. In other words, they 'presented themselves as Friendly Societies rather than strike-mongering trade unions' (Laybourn 1992, p.56). Fraser, however, notes that:

'The immediate concern of Applegarth and the amalgamated unions was to get protection for those unions who, like themselves, were registered under the Friendly Societies Act. There is little doubt that they saw their interests as different from those of the smaller societies.' (Fraser 1999, p.44)

The Conference of Trades, March 1867

The approach of the Junta was not popular with some smaller and provincial unions since many of these unions had no interest in registering as Friendly Societies and some were resentful at the London leadership's domination. As a result, George Potter organised a conference which was open to all groups not represented by the Conference of Amalgamated Trades (30 provincial unions and nine Trades Councils attended). As a result of this conference, a committee was set up:

'This committee was allowed to nominate a representative to attend the hearings of the Royal Commission, but the unionist nominated was excluded after a brief period of service because he made a public attack on one of the commissioners.' (Pelling 1987, p.56)

As Pelling observes, the result of this was that the Junta was able to dominate proceedings.

The Commission finally published its reports in 1869. The two commissioners sympathetic to unionism, Harrison and Hughes, and a peer, the Earl of Lichfield, refused to sign the Majority Report on the grounds that it did not go far enough. Instead, they published their own, Minority Report.

The Majority Report

The main recommendations in the Majority Report are outlined in Box 4.4.

BOX 4.4 **The Majority Report, 1869**

The Majority Report made the following recommendations:
- trade unions should be legalised
- legal unions should register their rules with the Registrar of Friendly Societies
- the Registrar should have the power to reject rules that included 'objectionable' clauses
- unions should separate their strike and benefit funds.

By 'objectionable' clauses, the report meant clauses which placed restrictions on:
- the employment of apprentices
- the use of machinery
- the introduction of piecework.

Adapted from Pelling 1987.

Summary Box

Although the Majority Report did not go as far as the Minority Report, it recognised and accepted that unions could play a legitimate role - as the conclusion of the report suggests:

'With regard to the general question of the right of workmen to combine together for determining and stipulating with their employer the terms on which only they will consent to work for him, we think that, provided the combination be perfectly voluntary and that full liberty be left to all other workmen to undertake the work which the parties combining have refused, and that no obstruction be placed in the way of employers resorting elsewhere in search of a supply of labour, there is no ground of justice for withholding such a right from workmen.'

The Minority Report

The main recommendations in the Minority Report are outlined in Box 4.5.

BOX 4.5 **The Minority Report, 1869**

Summary Box

The Minority Report made the following recommendations:
- trade unions should be legalised and there should be a repeal of the criminal sections of the 1825 Act
- trade unions should have the protection of the Friendly Societies Act
- unions should register their rules with the Registrar of Friendly Societies
- the Registrar should not have the power to reject rules unless they were incomplete or fraudulent.

Adapted from Pelling 1987.

Laybourn argues that, if the recommendations of the Minority Report had been implemented, the unions would have benefited in two ways:

'If this had been accepted, unions would have been able to protect their funds and would not have been subject to legal action.' (Laybourn 1992, p.56)

Fraser (1999) points out that it was the Minority Report rather than the Majority Report which shaped future legislation (which is outlined in Box 4.6 on page 124).

The impact made by the Royal Commission

There is a consensus amongst historians that the work of the Royal Commission transformed people's attitudes towards trade unions. Trade unions gained greater public sympathy than they had ever gained before and pressure grew for legislation giving them greater legal protection. As Pelling puts it:

'The publication of the Commission's reports resulted in a remarkable change in the public attitude to trade unionism. People recognised that the great bulk of the work done by unions was of

a character that was entirely beneficial. A leader in the *Times* in July 1869 acknowledged the transformation of opinion and declared that it could not be due to anything but the work of the Commission.' (Pelling 1987, p.58)

The transformation in the press's attitude towards unions is documented by Fraser. He shows that newspapers which would previously have automatically supported employers actually criticised them when engineering workers in Newcastle upon Tyne campaigned for a nine-hour day in 1870-71:

'The *Times* denounced the employers' resistance as "imprudent and impolitic"; the *Spectator* declared that there could be little sympathy for "masters who reply cavalierly by lawyer's letters to their men's demands". The *Pall Mall Gazette* found the union demand "perfectly reasonable".' (Fraser 1999, pp.46-47)

This turnaround, however, should not be exaggerated. As Behagg (1991) points out, a great deal of resentment towards unions remained after 1869, especially amongst the middle classes. The press's sympathy towards the union's demands in 1870-71 was the exception rather than the rule. It did, however, show that, on occasion, the press would support the workers' case - provided it was 'just' and the union's behaviour was 'respectable'.

Trade union reforms 1867-76

Between 1867 and 1876, seven Acts of Parliament affected the legal position of trade unions (see Box 4.6 on page 124). While it was the Royal Commission which provided the initial impetus for legislation, the reform process gained a momentum of its own which was fuelled by the campaigning of trade unionists.

The Acts of 1871

Whilst, according to Fraser (1999), the Acts of 1868 and 1869 were 'stopgap' measures, the Liberal government (Gladstone's first administration) published a government Bill on trade unions in February 1871. This Bill was opposed by the unions:

'[The Bill] protected the funds of registered unions, without limiting the content of their rules other than if they had criminal intent, and freed unions from criminal conspiracy because they were in restraint of trade. Yet it retained the special offences of "molestation", "obstruction", "intimidation" and "threat" by workmen during strikes, which led to a trade union protest.' (Laybourn 1992, p.57)

This protest was led by the parliamentary committee of the TUC (see Section 1.4 below). All that the TUC's lobbying achieved, however, was the division of the Bill into two parts (the first part being the Trade Union Act, the second being the Criminal Law Amendment Act). By the time that the Criminal Law Amendment Act became law, it included two new

BOX 4.6 Trade union reforms, 1867-76

1. Russell Gurney's Act, 1867
Although this Act did not mention trade unions, it provided a way for trade unions to take legal action in cases where officials stole or embezzled funds.

2. Trade Unions' Funds Protection Act, 1869
This was a temporary measure which allowed societies to take legal action, even if they were judged to be in restraint of trade.

3. The Trade Union Act, 1871
This Act was welcomed by the unions since it allowed unions previously defined as being illegal to register their rules with the Registrar of Friendly Societies. As a result of this Act, registered unions were able to protect their funds. Not all unions were covered by this Act, however.

4. The Criminal Law Amendment Act, 1871
This Act was opposed by the unions. It codified previous laws on 'coercion, threats, intimidation molestation and obstruction', restricting picketing. As a result, strikes could be judged to be 'criminal conspiracies'.

5. The Conspiracy and Protection of Property Act, 1875
This Act was welcomed by the unions as it largely reversed the Criminal Law Amendment Act. It ended the special criminal legislation relating to the trade unions, putting them under the ordinary law of the land. Also, it legalised peaceful picketing.

6. The Employers and Workmen Act, 1875
This Act was welcomed by the unions. It abolished the Master and Servant Act by which employees, but not employers, could be treated as criminals and sent to prison for breach of contract. Between 1858 and 1875, 6,000 working people had been convicted of offences under this law. Under the new Act, employees and employers were equal parties to a contract and breaches of that contract were civil, not criminal, offences.

7. The Trade Union Act Amendment Act, 1876
This Act extended the protection of funds to all trade unions, not just to those which were protected by the 1871 Trade Union Act.
Adapted from Fraser 1999.

offences in addition to those mentioned above - the offences of:
- persistently following
- watching and besetting.

The Criminal Law Amendment Act then became the main focus of union discontent:

'Almost every trade union expressed its opposition to the new legislation. Their antagonism increased when, in December 1872, five leaders of the London gas stokers who had gone on strike and caused a blackout in parts of London, were sentenced to a year's hard labour by Mr Justice Brett...There was a mammoth demonstration of trade unionists in Hyde Park on 2 June 1873 and further agitation when 16 farm labourer's wives...were sentenced under the Criminal Law Amendment Act for hooting at and, therefore, "intimidating" blacklegs [strike breakers].' (Laybourn 1992, pp.57-58)

The 1874 general election
The general election of 1868 was the first to be held after the 1867 Electoral Reform Act had been passed and was, therefore, the first election in which many trade unionists could vote (see also Unit 2, Parts 1 and 2). Pelling notes that:

'The only practicable policy in the hurried election of 1868 had been the support of Liberals who were friendly to the unions - a policy which had its successes here and there, for instance in the replacement of Roebuck [an MP who was very hostile to unions] at Sheffield by the friendly A.J. Mundella.' (Pelling 1987, p.63)

The passage of the Criminal Law Amendment Act and the refusal of the Liberal government to make any further concessions to the trade unions, however, brought a change of approach:

'What the separation of the criminal clauses from the [1871] Trade Union Act did do, however, was to permit a focused campaign for repeal of the Criminal Law Amendment Act. Over the next three years, there was a demand for equal treatment before the law, something which had been a persistent trade union demand.' (Fraser 1999, p.48)

During the 1874 general election campaign, trade unionists adopted a neutral stance. They submitted a questionnaire to candidates and, if the Conservative candidate gave more favourable answers than the Liberal, they campaigned and voted for the Conservative. Pelling also notes that:

'About ten distinctively working-class candidates stood in various constituencies against both Liberal and Conservative opposition and, although none was elected, several secured good polls.' (Pelling 1987, p.63)

In addition, two trade unionists were adopted as Liberal candidates and elected - Alexander McDonald and Thomas Burt. These were the first men to be elected as Lib-Lab MPs (see also Unit 5, Part 1).

The Disraeli government and trade unions
For Gladstone's Liberal government of 1868-74 it was a matter of principle to refuse to make concessions to trade unionists. The Liberals supported free trade and the freedom of the individual. Trade unions, it was argued, prevented free trade (since, by taking action to improve pay and conditions, they

interfered with market forces) and were an attack on the freedom of the individual (since unions campaigned as a group for a group). Disraeli's Conservative government, however, had a different point of view (see Unit 1, Section 2.1 for the debate about Disraeli's beliefs):

'Keen to broaden support for the Conservative Party, Disraeli argued that, despite class differences, the interests uniting the British people were of far greater significance than those dividing them...Reform was necessary on practical grounds because it would protect the long-term interests of the wealthy by ensuring that revolution was avoided. On the other hand, Disraeli argued that reform was necessary on moral grounds...In return for their privileged position, those at the top of the hierarchy had a moral obligation to alleviate the suffering of those at the bottom of the hierarchy.' (Roberts 1999, p.28)

Pelling points out that the Home Secretary under Disraeli, Richard Cross, had responded favourably to the trade union questionnaire. His support, combined with Disraeli's desire to broaden support for the Conservative Party, helps to explain why the Conservative government steered the three Acts mentioned in Box 4.6 through Parliament in 1875-76.

1.4 Why was the TUC set up?

The birth of the Trades Union Congress

It was while the Royal Commission was sitting between 1867 and 1869 that a key union organisation was set up - the Trades Union Congress (TUC). According to Pelling (1987), the origins of the TUC lie in the publication of the National Social Science Association's Annual Report for 1865. The National Social Science Association was an organisation which arranged 'congresses' (meetings) in which guest speakers delivered papers on subjects of interest to its mainly middle- and upper-class membership. In 1865, the National Social Science Association had examined trade unionism and included in their annual congress a paper which was delivered by William Dronfield who was Secretary of the Sheffield Association of Organised Trades. Pelling claims that Dronfield was 'bitterly disappointed' when he discovered that his paper was not mentioned in the National Social Science Association's Annual Report and his disappointment led his friend, Sam Nicholson, who was President of the Manchester and Salford Trades Council, to suggest that they should organise a congress of their own along the lines of that organised by National Social Science Association. The following year, Dronfield did organise a congress which resulted in the formation of the United Kingdom Alliance of Organised Trades. But, Dronfield hoped this organisation would be able to raise funds to support members involved in disputes and, when it

failed to raise sufficient funds, it collapsed. In 1868, Sam Nicholson organised a further congress along less ambitious lines. He followed the model of the National Social Science Association, inviting speakers to read papers on topics of concern to trade unionists. It was this meeting which was the founding meeting of the TUC.

The first Congress

The first meeting of the TUC took place in June 1868 in Manchester and was attended by 34 delegates, 11 of whom were from Trades Councils and only two of whom were from London (including George Potter - see Box 4.2 on page 120). The London Trades Council did not send a delegate. Pelling claims that 'no formal organisation' was set up at this initial meeting, but Fraser contradicts him, claiming:

'The initial structure was modelled on the National Social Science Association whose annual conferences discussed presented papers, but there was an immediate decision by the 34 delegates to turn it into an annual meeting which could act as a pressure group on Parliament and encourage collaboration between unions.' (Fraser 1999, p.45)

Fraser also claims that it was because Sam Nicholson was 'impressed by the effective publicity' of the Conference of Trades organised by George Potter that he decided to organise the congress.

The second Congress

The second meeting of the TUC took place in Birmingham in 1869, with 40 delegates attending (representing a total union membership of c.250,000). On this occasion, a delegate did come from the London Trades Council. Pelling claims that:

'The novelty of the occasion was a decision to appoint a committee to "prepare a statement to go out to the world, to the trade unions and legislators, as to the reasons why we hold the opinions therein contained". Yet, this committee was still not a permanent body and again the arrangements for summoning the next congress were left to local unionists.' (Pelling 1987, p.61)

The third Congress

The third meeting of the TUC did not take place until 1871. The delay was tactical - it was decided to wait until the government had finalised its legislation (see Box 4.6) before meeting. By March, it was clear that the proposed legislation did not meet the needs of the unions, and so the third Congress was held in London and a Parliamentary Committee set up to lobby MPs.

Fraser (1999, p.45) argues that, by March 1871, the Junta and George Potter had joined forces and agreed to support a Bill which implemented the recommendations of the Minority Report of the Royal Commission. The result, he claims, was that national leadership of the unions passed to the TUC's Parliamentary Committee. Pelling agrees that national leadership of the unions passed to the TUC in 1871, but his chronology is slightly different. He claims that this happened once the Liberal government had passed the 1871 Acts, not before:

'The passing of the Liberal government's legislation, in spite of its shortcomings, was the signal for the dissolution of the Junta. Clearly an important phase in relations between the unions and Parliament had ended. The Parliamentary Committee appointed by the Trades Union Congress could provide a more truly representative leadership; and furthermore, the driving force of the Junta, Robert Applegarth, was lost in May 1871 when he resigned.' (Pelling 1987, p.62)

The TUC's role

The Parliamentary Committee of the TUC became a permanent institution. Members of the committee lobbied Parliament, pressing for changes in the law. Representatives of all types of trade unions (not just the New Model unions) sent delegates to the annual congress and, there, elected the members of the Parliamentary Committee. The TUC, therefore, was more representative than the Junta and campaigned on behalf of unions as a whole, not just on behalf of the bigger unions (whose interests did not necessarily coincide with those of the smaller unions). The TUC developed into the unions' main mouthpiece and campaigning organisation. It played a particularly important part in the campaigns which led to the 1876 Trade Union Act Amendment Act (see Box 4.6 on page 124).

MAIN POINTS - Sections 1.3-1.4

- The Webbs claimed that, between 1860 and 1871, the Junta (a group of five leading trade unionists) met weekly and made decisions which determined the approach and policies adopted by the union movement as a whole. Fraser argues, however, that the influence of the Junta has been exaggerated.
- According to Pelling (1987), the crisis for trade unions which arose in 1867 had three main causes (1) the economic downturn of 1866-67 (2) the Sheffield Outrages of 1866 and (3) the Hornby v Close case.
- From the outset, the Junta's strategy was to influence the Royal Commission of 1867-69 by presenting a picture of responsible unionism. The union leaders argued that, far from provoking strikes, their unions were a restraint on them.

- There is a consensus amongst historians that the work of the Royal Commission transformed attitudes towards trade unions. Unions gained greater public sympathy than ever before. Pressure grew for legislation giving them greater legal protection.
- Between 1867 and 1876, seven Acts of Parliament affected the legal position of trade unions. Whilst it was the Royal Commission which provided the initial impetus for legislation, the reform process gained a momentum of its own which was fuelled by the campaigning of trade unionists.
- The TUC was modelled on the National Social Science Association. Its first meeting was held in 1868. It was only in 1871 that it appointed a parliamentary committee and became a permanent mouthpiece for trade unions.

Activity 4.2 Trade Union reforms 1867-75

ITEM 1 A historian's view (1)

The two Acts of 1871 - the Trade Union Act and the Criminal Law Amendment Act - reveal Gladstone's ignorance of working-class conditions. The ban on picketing was clearly an error of judgement, though Gladstone believed that decisions should be freely arrived at by both employers and employees. Coercion of an individual's opinions, even for the good of a group, was repugnant to him. As a result, the main focus of trade unions' campaigns became repeal of the obnoxious Act. Nevertheless, at a time when official opinion was still strongly opposed to trade unionism, it was Gladstone's government which first brought to the attention of Parliament a national problem which had long been neglected. Disraeli's response to the unions' hostile reaction to the Criminal Law Amendment Act was to take the opportunity to woo the unions to the Conservative Party. Cross's Conspiracy and Protection of Property Act in 1875 repealed the Criminal Law Amendment Act, expressly permitted peaceful picketing and, for the first time, permitted trade unions to do as a group whatever was lawful for an individual without fear of being charged with conspiracy. Cross also introduced the Employers and Workmen Act. At last, the trade unions had become a recognised element of the capitalist society which, in the eyes of many unionists, had at one time sought to enslave them. Disraeli took a keen interest in this legislation and supported Cross against the more faint-hearted members of the Cabinet. He told Lady Chesterfield that the legislation 'will gain and retain for the Conservatives the lasting affection of the working classes'.

Adapted from Abbott 1972.

ITEM 2 A historian's view (2)

The two Acts of 1875 - the Employers and Workmen Act and the Conspiracy and Protection of Property Act - settled the position of labour for a generation - until judges began to reinterpret them systematically in the employer's favour. Unions were no longer to be vulnerable to prosecutions for conspiracy or to the prohibition of peaceful picketing whenever a dispute occurred. Organised labour obtained all the major concessions it had been seeking. Disraeli was firmly behind this measure. He realised its importance to working men and supported it in a generally hostile Cabinet. His aim was to redress the visible unfairness of legislation which restricted employees more than employers. Disraeli's legislation should not, however, be seen as a move away from free-trade 'laissez-faire' economics (see page 3 for a definition of laissez-faire). It is now clear that the Liberals in 1871 had intended to reach much the same position and had been frustrated by the insufficiently precise language used by their parliamentary draftsmen which had enabled judges and magistrates to interpret the legislation more favourably to employers than had been planned. In November 1873, Gladstone's Cabinet agreed to prepare a Bill which would have been very similar to Disraeli's legislation. Also, the impetus for peaceful picketing came from Robert Lowe and other Liberals after the Conservative leadership had dragged its feet.

Adapted from Walton 1990.

ITEM 3 Striking in the mid-19th century

EFFECTS OF A STRIKE

This cartoon appeared in *Punch* magazine in 1852.

Questions

1. a) Using Items 1 and 2, explain why there was a burst of legislation affecting trade unions in the period 1867-75.
   b) How did the various pieces of legislation affect the position of trade unions?
   c) Why do you think the Criminal Law Amendment Act of 1871 was the focus of a trade union campaign?
2. a) What do Items 1 and 2 tell us about the motives behind the burst of trade union legislation in 1867-75?

   b) What does the legislation tell us about the nature of Gladstone's and Disraeli's governments?
   c) Give arguments for and against the view that Gladstone should be given credit for tackling the position of trade unions rather than Disraeli.
3. Look at Item 3.
   a) How did the law on striking change between 1852 (when the cartoon was drawn) and 1875?
   b) What point is being made by the cartoon?
   c) Was the point still valid in 1875? Explain your answer.

2 'New Unionism', 1888-1910

Key questions

1. What do historians mean by 'New Unionism'?

2. How new were the 'New Unions'?

3. Did women share in the New Unionism?

4. How successful were the trade unions between 1890 and 1910?

2.1 What do historians mean by 'New Unionism'?

Origins of the term

It was noted in the introduction to this Unit that the traditional view of 19th century unionism is derived from the work of Sidney and Beatrice Webb. It was the Webbs who coined the phrase 'New Model' unions and it was the Webbs who detected the development of a 'New Unionism' in the late 1880s. They argued that a series of events in 1888-89 led to a new and distinct type of union in the 1890s which presented a major challenge to the ideas and methods of the New Model unions of the 1850s and 1860s. These 'New Unions' were, according to this view, fundamentally different in terms of their membership, organisation, ideology and tactics. Their characteristics were:

- a membership of unskilled, low-paid labourers
- an open recruitment policy
- a militant outlook
- a readiness to use force against non-unionists and 'blacklegs' (strike breakers)
- low subscriptions allowing for the payment only of 'fighting' benefits (ie no Friendly Society functions such as sickness benefit and pensions)
- an acceptance of socialist ideas.

These characteristics can be grouped under three headings.

1. Membership

There was a major extension of union membership between 1889 and 1893 with many previously unorganised and unskilled workers joining unions. Between 1888 and 1892, total trade union membership increased from 750,000 to 1.5 million. New Unions did not seek to exclude workers (unlike the New Model unions) and were organised across whole industries rather than individual crafts (for example, the General Railway Workers Union recruited casual railway labourers who had been excluded from membership of the Amalgamated Society of Railway Servants). Minimal subscriptions were charged.

2. Militant tactics

There was a marked readiness to use the strike weapon in the late 1880s and early 1890s, particularly in 1888-89. Unions representing unskilled workers faced particular dangers from the drafting in of non-unionised 'blackleg' labour and so aggressive picketing was often a feature of disputes.

3. Ideology

Support of socialism is seen as one of the clearest distinguishing features of New Unionism. A number of prominent leaders of the New Unions were socialists - for example, Will Thorne (Gasworkers), Ben Tillett and Tom Mann (Dockers), Annie Besant (Matchworkers) and Tom Maguire (Leeds Builders' Labourers) were all involved in socialist organisations. Also, it was in the early 1890s that political activists like Keir Hardie encouraged the unions to support the formation of an independent working-class (labour) party (see Unit 5, Section 1.2).

Nevertheless, there is a debate on how 'new' these unions actually were (see Section 2.2. below).

Why did New Unionism emerge in the late 1880s?

Three main reasons have generally been given to explain the emergence of the New Unions in the late 1880s. First, economic conditions improved in the late 1880s with an upturn in trade:

'Rates of industrial growth were clearly important, since it is easier for a union to organise effectively in an expanding industry than in one which is on the decline. Most of the industries from which the new unions drew their strength were expanding rapidly.' (Clegg et al. 1964, p.88)

Second, a more general reason was the decline of faith in the ability of laissez-faire capitalism to create a fair society. The confidence of the mid-Victorian period had disappeared. The idea of collectivism (namely, that the power of the state could be used to promote general wellbeing) was becoming more acceptable. The acute poverty of the time was revealed in surveys like Charles Booth's *Life and Labour of the People in London* (1889). When the dockers went on strike, their campaign brought to light social conditions which ensured much public sympathy for the strikers. And third, there was a revival of socialism in the late 1880s. Numerically, socialist groups remained small (see Unit 5, Section 1.1), but their members were often good organisers. They played an important part in the Great Dock Strike (see below) and they also played a very important role in the provinces - socialists were active in the Gas and General Labourers Union (GGLU) which was strong in Yorkshire, for example.

Key events

There were three main events which sparked the development of New Unionism.

1. The matchworkers' strike, 1888

First, there was the matchworkers' strike in July 1888 when c.1,400 women working at the Bryant and May factory in East London came out on strike against dangerous working conditions and low pay. The socialist journalist Annie Besant publicised the womens' cause and helped them to organise a Match Makers Union. After two weeks and much bad publicity, the employers conceded better pay and conditions.

2. The Gasworkers and General Labourers Union

Second, the London gasworkers formed a union in 1889 under the leadership of Will Thorne (a former navvy from Birmingham) and Eleanor Marx (the daughter of Karl Marx). Both Thorne and Marx were members of the Social Democratic Federation (SDF), one of several socialist groups to emerge in the 1880s (see Unit 5, Section 1.1). The Gasworkers and General Labourers Union quickly attracted 20,000 members. The main cause pursued by the union was the reduction of hours of work - from 12-hour shifts to eight-hour shifts:

> 'The men's demands were ambitious. The Gas Light and Coke Company estimated their annual extra costs at £50,000. To grant such demands, put forward by a body of unskilled men who had never before formed a stable union, seemed grotesque. Yet, between June and December 1889 most of the important gasworks gave in, hardly even tasting the men's strength.' (Hobsbawm 1968, p.165)

The increasing competition of electricity had made the gas industry vulnerable to determined action by its workers.

3. The London dock strike

It is the London dock strike (later known as the 'Great Dock Strike') which began in August 1889 that has attracted most attention from historians. The strike generated tremendous publicity and the victory of the dockers encouraged other unorganised workers to form unions.

The dockers went on strike in the hope of improving their conditions of employment. These conditions are described in Box 4.7.

Factors leading to the strike

By 1889, some dockers had gained experience of what unions could achieve. This was due to a number of factors. First, since dock work was seasonal, many worked in the gasworks in the winter. As a result, some dockers were involved in the setting up of the new Gasworkers and General Labourers Union. Second, in 1887, Ben Tillett (a former sailor who was working as a tea porter and, like Thorne and Marx, a member of the SDF) had formed the Tea Operatives and General Labourers Union. And third, the matchworkers' strike made a huge impact on the dockers. The fact that the matchworkers were women (and supposedly more docile than men) made an impression, as did the fact that many of the dockers were married to matchworkers and, therefore, heard about the strike first-hand.

In August 1889, Tillett put forward the dockers' demands to the employers:

- abolition of the present contract system
- a guaranteed minimum of four hours' employment per day instead of the current one hour
- men should be hired on two set occasions each day instead of whenever a ship docked
- wages should be six pence an hour (the famous 'docker's tanner'), with eight pence an hour for overtime.

The employers refused these demands and the strike began.

BOX 4.7 Dockers' conditions of employment, 1889

Interpretation

While the stevedores supervised the loading of ships and the lightermen transferred the cargo from the ship to the quayside, the bulk of the heavy, manual work was done by dockers. This was thought of as unskilled work - a job which any strong man could do. The work, however, required an expertise which only came with experience - a badly placed hook could rip open a sack of grain, pouring its contents into the docks, and carrying a heavy load up a narrow plank placed at a sharp angle was not easy. Different cargoes needed different handling and, once the men became experts in handling a particular type of cargo, they tended only to seek work at the docks which handled it. There was no standard way of getting work. Some of the men worked for the wharf owners, some for the ship owners and some for dock companies. The largest of the employers, the dock companies, had amalgamated to form the Joint Dock Company (JDC) earlier in 1889. The men also worked for contractors paid by the ship owners or JDC. In order to make a good profit, the contractors hired as few men as possible for the shortest possible time. When a ship arrived, the men were herded into an enclosure known as the 'cage'. Only those with the loudest voices or who were strong enough to push their way to the front, or who could afford to 'treat', or bribe, the hirer were taken on. They might only work for one or two hours before being dismissed, to rejoin the other men who still milled outside the dock gates.

Adapted from Howson 1996.

Support for the strikers

A number of other leading unionists came to help during the strike, including Eleanor Marx, Tom Mann and John Burns. Mann and Burns are often cited as typical New Union activists. Like Tillett, they both had working-class backgrounds and were members of the SDF. Both were also members of the ASE. In the late 1880s they spent a great deal of their time working on political and union campaigns. As well as being active in the dockers' strike, for example, they also helped to organise the campaign fought by the gasworkers.

The dockers were further supported by Herbert Champion, another member of the SDF. He publicised the dockers' case in his paper the *Labour Elector*. The strikers also gained publicity by holding daily marches through the City of London:

'The sight of this orderly host of determined men, walking five abreast, impressed public opinion, and won many generous contributions to the strike funds.' (Pelling 1987, p.89)

The most significant financial aid came from trade unionists in Australia who contributed £30,000.

The outcome of the strike

By the middle of the second week of the strike, over 100,000 dockers were on strike, the ports were at a standstill and cargoes had begun to rot.

The employers remained unmoved by the dockers' campaign but eventually (after five weeks), with the intervention of Cardinal Manning and the Mayor of London, a settlement was reached. The dockers got their 'tanner' and their eight pence overtime and a new union was set up - the Dock, Wharf, Riverside and General Labourers Union - under the leadership of Tillett and Mann. Within two months, it had 30,000 members.

2.2 How new were the 'New Unions'?

Criticisms of the term 'New Unionism'

Just as the labels applied to earlier phases of trade union development have been challenged, so too has 'New Unionism' come under scrutiny on almost all counts. First, as is the case with the New Model unions, historians have differed in their views over the aims of New Unionism:

'Some historians, identifying with the socialists, exaggerate the coherence and ambition of the mass labour movement that emerged. Others, more sympathetic to the pragmatic behaviour of trade union officials, see only sectionalism and a readiness to settle for modest gains.' (Hinton 1982, p.21)

Second, there were trade unions which included semi-skilled or unskilled workers well before the late 1880s:

- Joseph Arch's Agricultural Labourers Union - which had 100,000 members in 1873, before the economic depression hit agriculture
- 'general unions' were formed for railway workers, gas workers, dockers and other low paid workers in the 1870s
- the National Federation of Labour which was founded on Tyneside in 1886
- the Sailors and Firemen's Union - set up by Joseph Havelock Wilson - had 60,000 members by 1889.

And third, if, as some historians argue, New Model unionism was in some sense a betrayal of earlier trade union trends and represented the conservative and 'class collaborationist' aims of the labour aristocracy, then there is a good case for arguing that New Unionism did indeed represent a fundamental break with New Model unionism. If, on the other hand, it is argued that there was a great deal of continuity in trade union development up to the 1880s, that New Model unions only made up a small part of the union movement as a whole and that, anyway, they were capable of militant action on occasions, then there is a good case for arguing that the New Unions were not actually as significant as has sometimes been suggested.

How important was the role played by socialism?

Hobsbawm (1968) emphasises the role played by socialism in the New Unions. He argues that it was the relevance of socialism to the contemporary industrial situation that appealed to a new generation of trade union leaders. These new leaders, he claims, had lost faith in the 'economic liberalism' in which the older leaders still believed. He does, however, concede that the rank and file members of the new unions had less clear-cut aims than the socialist leadership:

'By the late 1880s a body of socialist organisers and propagandists was once again available in Britain. One may, however, guess that the large national and regional general unions of 1889 (the New Unions) were the offspring of a marriage between the class unionism of the socialists and the more modest plans of the unskilled themselves.' (Hobsbawm 1968, p.182)

Some historians, like Clegg et al. (1964) and Lovell (1977), have suggested, however, that the socialist influence in New Unionism has been exaggerated:

'The extent of socialist involvement in the general unions is not in doubt, but involvement is not the same thing as influence. It is true that contemporary socialists like to think of the New Unions as militant, free from Friendly Society benefits, open, class-conscious and socialist. But some were led by socialists, others were not. Some adopted militant postures, others pursued conciliatory policies from the beginning. Some introduced Friendly Society benefits at the outset,

others later on.' (Lovell 1977, pp.22-4)
These historians see trade unions developing in a way which is very different from that seen by historians like Hobsbawm. They take what Hobsbawm calls an 'industrial relations' approach. In other words, they argue that effective trade union policy had nothing to do with ideological views. Rather, policy was based on the calculation of tactical possibilities and bargaining strengths. Trade union leaders played the game. They did not aim to change the rules of the game.

Recent contributions to the debate

This debate was broadened in the 1980s and 1990s. In his account of New Unionism, for example, Keith Laybourn (1992) agrees with the conventional picture of a surge of union activity from 1889 into the 1890s. He also emphasises, however, the limitations of this New Unionism, pointing to the lack of progress among the very poor and women workers. He doubts the emergence of a 'homogenous' (undivided) working class:

'The fact is that the variety of experiences of work, education, housing and other factors, ensured that throughout this period the working class continued to be divided in numerous ways.' (Laybourn 1992, p.77)

The development of the New Unions has also been more closely linked with changes in workplace technology. In gasworking, for example, the introduction of new retorts (equipment used to generate gas) changed the work pattern. While fewer workers were employed, those who retained their jobs had the chance of more settled employment and, therefore, the chance to establish strong unions.

Changes in working practices were partly the result of the growing foreign competition facing British industry from the 1870s:

'The challenge of foreign competition forced employers to speed up existing machinery, to reduce labour costs, to introduce new machinery, and to gain increasing control over their factories and mills.' (Laybourn 1992, p.68)

As a result of these changes, the unskilled and the semi-skilled needed to organise unions and the skilled often had to broaden the membership of their previously more exclusive unions. At the same time, the unions began to look to the emerging political labour movement for the protection that no longer seemed to materialise from the existing political parties.

MAIN POINTS - Sections 2.1-2.2

- The Webbs argued that a series of events in 1888-89 led to a new and distinct type of union in the 1890s. These 'New Unions' were fundamentally different in terms of their membership, organisation, ideology and tactics.
- The main characteristics of these New Unions were (1) a membership of unskilled, low-paid labourers (2) an open recruitment policy (3) a militant outlook (4) a readiness to use force against 'blacklegs' (5) low subscriptions but no Friendly Society functions and (6) an acceptance of socialist ideas.
- New Unionism developed for three main reasons -

(1) there was an economic upturn at the end of the 1880s (2) there was a decline in faith that laissez-faire capitalism would deliver a fair society and (3) there was a revival of socialism.
- The three key factors which sparked New Unionism were (1) the matchworkers strike of 1888 (2) the formation of the Gasworkers and General Labourers Union and (3) the London dock strike of 1889.
- Some historians have argued that there was little that was new about New Unionism. There is a debate about the extent to which socialist ideas fuelled New Unionism.

Activity 4.3 The Great Dock Strike and the New Unions

ITEM 1 The Great Dock Strike (1)

The men who had been earning four or five pence an hour before the strike now earned an estimated five pence a day extra but, as the men were no longer paid for their meal breaks, those who had been earning six pence an hour before the strike were worse off. And because the men were guaranteed a minimum of four hours work, many who might have been given the occasional hour were no longer taken on. Trade became depressed after 1890 and, once again, many men found themselves at the dock gates looking for work. Once again, the employers were able to exploit them. So, what little was gained by the strike was soon lost. If the dock strike benefited only a small minority of the men, it was, however, a great victory for unskilled workers. Following the dockers' example, other casual workers organised themselves and, by mid-1890, there were unions for, among others, railwaymen, seamen and farm labourers. These new unions were called general unions because they were open to anyone within the industry, regardless of their job. Because of the dock strike, workers who did the unskilled back breaking jobs that were essential to every industry were finally recognised as people worthy of respect and consideration.

Adapted from Howson 1996.

ITEM 2 The Great Dock Strike (2)

This picture was specially commissioned to commemorate the dock strike of 1889. The leading organisers are pictured at the top. John Burns (standing) and Tom Mann (sitting) are pictured on the top left whilst Ben Tillett (standing) and Henry Champion (sitting) are pictured on the top right (Champion was a former army officer who owned a printing press which was used to print leaflets in support of the dockers. He also worked with Burns and Mann, organising spectacular parades and demonstrations). The three men in the centre at the top represent, on the left, Australian dockers (who donated £25,000 to the strike fund), in the middle the British dockers themselves and, on the right, members of engineering trade unions (which had supported the strike). Despite playing a leading part in the strike, Eleanor Marx is not pictured (see Section 2.3 below).

Questions

1. How new were the New Unions? Use Items 1-3 in your answer.
2. a) Using Items 1 and 2, explain why the Great Dock Strike was an important event in the development of trade unionism.
   b) How far do you agree with the view that the Great Dock Strike was a great success?
   c) Give arguments for and against the view that the Great Dock Strike marked the beginning of New Unionism.
3. a) List the key arguments made by Mann and Tillett in Item 3.
   b) How did their approach differ from that adopted by the New Model unions?

ITEM 3 New Unionism

It is quite true that most of the newly formed unions pay contributions for trade purposes only, leaving sick and funeral benefits to be dealt with by sick and insurance societies. The work of the trade unionist is primarily to obtain such a readjustment of conditions between employers and the employed as shall secure to the latter a better share of the wealth they produce in the form of reduced working hours and higher wages; and our experience has taught us that many of the older unions are very reluctant to engage in a labour struggle, no matter how great the necessity because they are hemmed in by sick and funeral claims so that, to a large extent, they have lost their true characteristics of being fighting organisations. The sooner they revert to their original programme, the better for the wellbeing of the working masses. In conclusion, we repeat that the real difference between the 'new' and the 'old' is that those who belong to the latter and delight in being distinct from the policy endorsed by 'new' do so because they do not recognise (as we do) that it is the work of the trade unionist to stamp out poverty from the land. They do not **contend** (as we contend) that existing unions should exert themselves to extend organisations where they do not exist. Our ideal is a **cooperative commonwealth**, the abolition of systematic overtime, material reductions of working hours, elimination of **sweaters**, an ever-increasing demand for a more righteous share of the wealth created by labour.

From Mann & Tillett 1890.

Glossary

- **contend** - argue
- **cooperative commonwealth** - a state where people would work in cooperatives (organisations where all members have the same rights and make decisions on pay and working conditions collectively).
- **sweaters** - people who worked in the 'sweated industries' (industries where people had to work long and hard for little pay).

2.3 Did women share in the New Unionism?

Women trade unionists in the 1870s

Another legacy of the Webbs' domination of trade union history is the silence in most accounts on the role played by women workers. As Sally Alexander points out:

'[The Webbs] told the story, gave it its heroic cast, largely created its conceptual architecture and their history is indeed peopled with men...[Their] portrait of the male trade unionist is deliberately seductive. They wrote to convince the British governing class that representatives of labour with their long tradition of self-government should be allowed to join them.' (Alexander 1994, pp.57-58)

From the early 1870s, however, women began to set up their own organisations and to play a part in the trade union movement - albeit a small part initially and a part that was resented by many male trade unionists.

According to Alexander (1994), only around 19,000 women belonged to unions in the 1870s - a tiny percentage (about 0.47%) of all working women over the age of 10. By 1896, the number had risen to c.142,000 which might, at first sight seem to be a substantial increase. It should be noted, however, that, by the turn of the century, women made up 30% of the workforce but they still only made up 7.5% of trade unionists.

Why were there so few women trade unionists?

Two main reasons have been suggested to explain why the number of women trade unionists remained so low.

1. The jobs women did

Women often worked in jobs where union organisation was difficult:

'Trade unionism made little headway in such personalised employment situations as domestic service - and, in 1911, 39% of all employed women were domestic servants. The large number of women employed in outwork or in small workshops in dressmaking, millinery, tailoring, or the light metal trades, women who often worked on a part-time or seasonal basis, were almost equally difficult to organise.' (Hinton 1982, p.28)

Women in more secure and regular jobs were more likely to join unions. Nearly half the women in trade unions by 1914, for example, worked in the cotton industry. Unions were also more successful in some of the new areas into which women's work was expanding. In the so-called 'white blouse' jobs, such as shop assistants, clerks, secretaries and elementary school teachers, some progress was made.

2. Attitudes towards women

There was widespread suspicion of women in the trade unions from working-class men. The reasons were partly economic and partly cultural. Indeed, Box 4.8 reveals how economic factors reinforced culturally determined attitudes. As Box 4.8 suggests, the view that 'the woman's place was in the home' was widely held. This put particular pressure on married women:

'Given large numbers of children and the labour-intensive character of housework, the fulfilment of the domestic ideal required the full-time labour of housewives. Better-off workers preferred their wives to stay at home. The notion of the "family wage" - that a man's wage should be sufficient to keep his wife and children out of the labour market - was an important element in late 19th century working-class respectability.' (Hinton 1982, p.28)

BOX 4.8 Men and women at work

Interpretation

The legal position of women workers, although it is the easiest to explain, is not by any means the most important of the factors governing their working lives. Customary restrictions and the subdivision of industry into men's and women's work is a far more considerable matter, and on this complex and difficult ground, the feminists dared to tread [in the period 1870-90] - only to be warned off with indignation by the spokesmen of the men's trade unions...[Men] regarded women as necessarily unskilled, almost casual labour, and believed them to be a menace to their own precarious standard of life and a dangerous class of 'blacklegs' whose whole industrial existence was a mistake...So long as conditions remained unchanged, the women would refuse to do 'men's' jobs or, if they were willing, the men would refuse to work beside them. But when the job itself changed, when new machinery, new subdivision of processes and new objects of manufacture were introduced, the employer was able to put in an entering wedge and the custom was circumvented. And in most cases the employer was eager to do this because of the immediate reduction in the wages bill which he could thus ensure...The certainty of undercutting was so terrible and the economic pressure so great that [men] opposed the employment of females as much as they could, refused to work with them...and tried to drive them down to a small number of trades...Instead of justifying themselves by their own needs, they sought for a moral justification and ardently preached that women 'ought not' to be in industry at all and that their 'proper place' was at home. *From Strachey 1979, pp.238-40.*

Laybourn (1992) notes that, if employers did recruit women to do 'men's jobs', the unions (especially the craft unions) often demanded that the employers pay the women at the same rate as men in the hope that this would discourage them from recruiting women.

Such attitudes help to explain why, when a commemorative drawing of the docker's strike was commissioned (see above Activity 4.3, Item 2), Eleanor Marx did not appear on it (even though she had been one of its leading organisers). They also help to explain why less than 10% of married women were in paid employment by 1910. Indeed, it is ironic that the first of the wave of strikes which launched 'New Unionism' in 1888-89 was of women workers (the matchworkers) and was led by a woman, Annie Besant.

The WPPL

Developments in the 1870s were not just a response by women to economic expansion and the growth of male trade unionism. Working men living in towns had won the right to vote in 1867 and women were angered by the rejection of women's suffrage (see Unit 3, Section 2.2). In 1874, the Women's Provident and Protection League (WPPL) was set up:

'To encourage the growth of women's trade unions in the belief that combination was the first step towards the alleviation of women's "disgracefully low" rate of wages.' (Alexander 1994, p.62)

The WPPL also campaigned for admittance to existing unions and it lobbied the TUC, civil servants and ministers. Emma Paterson, founder of the WPPL, saw the separate unions as a temporary expedient until women were more generally accepted by the trade union movement. She also saw clearly the link between women's rights as workers and their need for political rights. Isabel Ford, a radical suffragist (campaigner for women's right to vote), agreed:

'Trade unionism means rebellion, and the orthodox teaching for women is submission. The political world preaches teaching woman submission so long as it refuses them the parliamentary franchise and, therefore, ignores them as human beings.' (quoted in Alexander 1994, p.72)

The WTUL

In 1889, campaigning within the TUC finally paid off when the TUC agreed to help the women to organise and the WPPL became the Women's Trade Union League (WTUL). There certainly was no sea change, but the women began to make some headway:

'New agreements were now made, to which the women had some slight chance of being parties, by which the work in several of the trades was parcelled out; and though in these arguments the women invariably got the worst of it, still they got a trifle more than they would have had alone. They entered upon the path of collective bargaining and here and there, as a crisis arose, a union would spring up, a fight would be fought and a little advance recorded.' (Strachey 1979, p.244)

Nevertheless, the predominant view remained that of Will Thorne, socialist leader of the gasworkers:

'Women do not make good trade unionists and for this reason, we believe that our energies are better used towards the organisation of male workers.' (quoted in Hinton 1982, p.30)

2.4 How successful were the trade unions 1890-1910?

Membership in the 1890s

The success of New Unionism in 1889-90 depended on:

- full employment
- the readiness of the police to tolerate vigorous picketing
- the absence of concerted opposition from employers.

None of these conditions lasted long. In 1890, the New Unions had about 300,000 members, but the membership had dropped to 130,000 in 1892 and to 80,000 in 1896. This was largely due to the fact that the unskilled were the most vulnerable to unemployment and to employers' attacks. During the same period, however, trade unions of the skilled and semi-skilled continued to increase in membership and there was an increase in membership of trade unions as a whole from 1.5 million in 1892 to just over 2 million in 1900.

Unions under attack in the 1890s

Despite the overall increase in membership in the period 1892 to 1900, trade unions in general became concerned at what they saw as a counter-attack on their position after the successful strikes of 1889. This counterattack took two main forms.

1. Attacks led by employers

From 1890, the employers began to set up new organisations which deliberately began or widened trade disputes in the hope of reducing the unions' power. In the docks, for example, the shipping owners formed the Shipping Federation in September 1890, a year after the dock strike. The Shipping Federation then fought union strikes with 'free' (or, from the union view, 'blackleg') labour. In 1893, a National Free Labour Association was set up to supply such workers to strike-breaking employers. The result was a decline in membership of the dockers' union - from 56,000 members in 1890 to under 14,000 by 1900.

Lockouts and collective bargaining

The tactic used in other industries was the lockout. In 1891, employers in the textile industry formed the Federation of Master Cotton Spinners (FMCS). When, in 1892, the FMCS cut wages by 5%, workers refusing the pay cut were locked out. The dispute continued until the 'Brooklands Agreement' was made in 1893. Under this agreement, a joint committee of employers and union representatives was set up to determine wage levels. In other words, it was agreed that wage levels should be decided by 'collective bargaining procedures'.

The same pattern was then followed by mine owners. In July 1893, they cut wages and locked out workers who refused to accept the pay cut. After a series of clashes between strikers and troops (including the death of two miners at Featherstone Colliery in Yorkshire), the government intervened and a Conciliation Board (a committee which included both employers and union representatives) was set up to decide wage levels - another example of collective bargaining.

Then, in 1896, employers set up the Employers' Federation of Engineering Association (EFEA) to challenge the power of the ASE. When some members of the ASE in London demanded an eight-hour day and went on strike, the EFEA began a national lockout which lasted for six months and ended in defeat for the union. The ASE was forced to give up its demands for an eight-hour day, employers were to decide which workers were to work on new machinery and all decisions to take strike action were, in future, to be agreed by the ASE's national executive.

Employers' aims

According to Behagg, these events show that employers aimed to reduce rather than destroy the power of unions:

'Historians have sometimes argued that, by consolidating their own organisations, the employers were clearly bent on the destruction of trade unions. This is too simplistic a view...After all, it had been demonstrated earlier in the century that compliant [obedient] unions, who were prepared to discipline their members, were useful to employers. It was in the employers' interests to have strong, centralised unions with an acknowledged but restricted role in the workplace. Thus, most of the disputes where unions were defeated resulted not in the eradication [destruction] of the unions but rather in the establishment of collective bargaining procedures for those unions.' (Behagg 1991, p.112)

Both Pelling (1987) and Laybourn (1992) argue that the lesson learned from the defeat of the ASE was that unions had to work together. As a result, attempts were made to form federations of unions.

2. Unfavourable judgements

A second form of attack against the unions came through the law:

'In 1875, Disraeli's ministry had put through legislation which seemed to allow trade combinations to declare strikes without fear of legal reprisals. In the 1890s, however, the courts began to curtail this immunity, by pronouncing

that certain sorts of stoppage were not to be permitted.' (Phillips 1992, p.8)

A number of cases went against the interests of the unions - for example, the Lyons v Wilkins case of 1899 which limited the unions' right to picket. But, it was the Taff Vale Judgement (1901) that was the most important legal decision faced by the unions since it appeared to undermine the right to strike - see Box 4.9.

BOX 4.9 The Taff Vale Judgement of 1901

The dispute

The Taff Vale Railway Company in South Wales refused to grant wage increases requested by the Amalgamated Society of Railway Servants (ASRS) despite increased profits from transporting coal during the Boer War. When the company refused to recognise the right of the ASRS to bargain for a wage increase, the union called a strike. The company called in 'blackleg' labour from the National Free Labour Association (an organisation set up in 1893 to break strikes by providing non-union labour to employers) and took out an injunction preventing the union from picketing. The dispute ended in the complete defeat of the union.

The court case

The company sued the union for damages to compensate for the loss of revenue during the strike. The case went to the House of Lords which awarded in favour of the company. The ASRS was ordered to pay £23,000 in compensation plus costs.

The significance of the case

The right to strike was undermined. Any union was now liable to pay unlimited damages for losses caused by a strike in which it took part. This judgement convinced many trade unionists of the need for a political party to represent working people. Many unions affiliated with the newly formed Labour Representation Committee (see Unit 5, Section 2.2) and the reversal of Taff Vale became a major issue at the 1906 election. *Adapted from Laybourn 1992.*

It was only when a Liberal government was elected in 1906 that the law was changed. The new government passed the Trade Disputes Act in 1906. This Act protected the unions' right to strike, even if, by striking, the union caused a breach of civil (as opposed to criminal) law. Peaceful picketing was also clearly legalised.

The Osborne Judgement, 1909

A further major legal challenge to the unions came with the Osborne Judgement of 1909 and it came this time from within the unions. Walter Osborne, a member of the Amalgamated Society of Railway Servants (ASRS), objected to paying the political levy because part of his union subscription went to provide funds for the Labour Party. The case went to the House of Lords where Law Lords ruled in 1909 in Osborne's favour. This hit the Labour Party hard since Labour MPs relied on the funds raised by trade unions to pay their salaries (MPs were not paid a state salary until 1911). After pressure from the Labour Party, the Liberal government eventually reversed the Osborne Judgement when it steered the Trade Union Act of 1913 through Parliament.

The Trade Union Act, 1913

The Trade Union Act of 1913 allowed unions to divide their subscriptions into a political fund and a social fund after a ballot of members. Any member not wishing to pay into the political fund (the political levy) could 'contract out'.

The passing of this Act made a big impact on the fortunes of the Labour Party. The Osborne Judgement had led to a dramatic drop in Labour Party funds, threatening the party at both national and local level. In the ballots that followed the 1913 Act, however, the majority of trade unionists voted to support the political levy and the Labour Party's financial position improved.

Unions and party politics 1890-1910

In 1900, a group of unions agreed to join the Labour Representation Committee (the LRC developed into the Labour Party - see Unit 5, Section 2.2). Most historians agree that this decision was linked to the feeling of insecurity which developed as a result of the employers' counterattack. There is, however, debate about the extent to which support for socialism was a factor in the unions' decision to join the LRC. Clearly, socialist trade unionists, especially those in the New Unions, supported the idea of joining an independent political party whose aim was to provide a voice for the working class. But, many trade unionists remained wedded to the Liberal Party. Throughout the 1890s and early 1900s, trade union MPs continued to sit as Lib-Labs (ie working-class MPs sponsored and supported by the Liberal Party - see Unit 5, Part 1) and to remain distant from the Labour Party. In addition, the powerful Miners' Federation did not decide to affiliate to the Labour Party until 1909. Further, there is evidence that rank and file members were opposed to links with the Labour Party. Walter Osborne is the obvious example:

'Walter Osborne provides the most obvious example of a determinedly non-Labour Party trade unionist of the 1900-1914 period. For Osborne, and those Liberal trade unionists whose views were akin to his, the committing of the unions to socialism seemed likely to undermine their ability to carry out collective bargaining effectively.' (Phelps Brown 1959, pp.133-4)

Throughout the period 1900-14, trade unions, like the Labour Party in which they became such an important force, continued to contain a mixture of socialists and Lib-Labbers, with the divide largely following industrial lines. Workers in heavy industries were likely to be socialists whilst those in the old light craft industries were likely to be Lib-Labbers. During this period, there was a struggle between the two groups at both local and national level. Yet, in spite of their differences, both groups managed to stay together in the new Labour Party. The industrial unrest of the period 1908 to 1914, however, put considerable strain on this relationship (see Part 3 below).

MAIN POINTS - Sections 2.3-2.4

- Although the Webbs are quiet on the subject, from the early 1870s women began to play a part in the trade union movement.
- Two main reasons have been suggested to explain why the number of women trade unionists remained so low - (1) the jobs women did and (2) attitudes towards women - there was widespread suspicion of women in the trade unions from working-class men.
- In 1874, the Women's Provident and Protection League (WPPL) was set up. In 1889, the TUC agreed to help the women to organise and the WPPL became the Women's Trade Union League (WTUL).
- In 1890, the New Unions had about 300,000 members, but the membership had dropped to 80,000 by 1896 as unskilled union members were vulnerable to unemployment and there was an economic recession. Overall membership of unions increased from 1.5 million in 1892 to just over 2 million in 1900.
- After the successful strikes of 1889, unions became concerned at a counterattack on their position. This took two main forms - (1) attacks led by employers (eg lockouts) and (2) unfavourable judgments (eg Taff Vale and the Osborne Judgement).
- Although some unions joined the LRC in 1900, unions continued to contain a mixture of socialists and Lib-Labbers throughout the period 1900-14.

Activity 4.4 Pressures on the unions 1890-1910

ITEM 1 The Taff Vale Judgement

The substantial question...is this. Has the **Legislature** authorised the creation of numerous **bodies of men**, capable of owning great wealth and of acting by agents, with absolutely no responsibility for the wrongs they may do to other persons by the use of that wealth and the employment of those agents? In my opinion Parliament has done nothing of the kind...It is perhaps satisfactory to find that nothing of the sort was contemplated by the minority of the members of the Royal Commission on Trade Unions whose views found acceptance with the Legislature...It would seem to follow that it was intended by the strongest **advocates** of trade unionism that persons should be **liable** for concerted as well as for individual action...And when I find that an Act of Parliament actually provides for a registered trade union being sued in certain cases for penalties by its registered name, as a trade union, and does not say that the cases specified are the only cases in which it may be so sued, I can see nothing contrary to the principle, or contrary to the provisions of the Trade Union Acts, in holding that a trade union may be sued by its registered name. I am therefore of the opinion that the appeal should be allowed and the judgement...restored with costs.

The judgement on the Taff Vale case delivered by Lord MacNaughten in 1901.

Glossary
- **Legislature** - Parliament
- **bodies of men** - ie trade unions
- **advocates** - supporters
- **liable** - open to being sued

ITEM 2 Capital and labour

WHIPS FOR LABOUR'S BACK.

This cartoon was drawn in response to the Taff Vale case. It shows a judge handing whips to an employer for use on his worker.

ITEM 3 The views of W.V. Osborne

In view of the present fierce world competition, trade union leaders bear an almost appalling responsibility. The only road to real advancement lies through higher wages and greater purchasing power. The application of science and machinery has both increased and cheapened output. Good work adds to the wealth not merely of one class but of the nation, and the duty of the unions is to see that workmen get their full share of the fruits of their labour. Just as national peace is necessary for national advancement, so is industrial peace essential for industrial progress. Every day lost by a strike is a loss to the nation. When the unions confined themselves to purely industrial affairs, they could meet the employers on an equal footing - their bargain being merely for the rightful division of the profits of the two partners - capital and labour. When the unions openly proclaimed that it was no longer their policy to bargain as between the employer and the employed, but rather to exterminate the former, who were recognised as the natural enemy of the worker, then an atmosphere was created which tended to make the true functions of the trade unions difficult if not impossible.

This passage was written by W. V. Osborne in 1913.

Questions

1. What do Items 1-3 tell us about the pressures on unions between 1890 and 1910?
2. Look at Item 1.
   a) Describe the issues at stake in the Taff Vale case.
   b) What was the judge's view?
   c) What was the significance of this judgement for unions?
3. a) What point is being made by the cartoon in Item 2?
   b) Is it an accurate illustration of the position of trade unions in the period 1900-14?
4. Compare Item 3 with Item 3 in Activity 4.3.
   a) On what points do the authors agree and disagree?
   b) How far would you agree that the two passages reveal divisions within the trade union movement between 1890 and 1910?

3 Industrial unrest 1908-14: the rise of syndicalism?

Key questions

1. What was the nature of industrial unrest 1908-14?

2. Why was 1910-14 a time of widespread industrial unrest?

3. What is syndicalism and how important was it?

3.1 What was the nature of industrial unrest 1908-14?

Industrial peace 1899-1907
The industrial strife of the years immediately before the First World War was in marked contrast to the previous decade:

'The opening years of the new century were ones of industrial peace. The years 1899-1907 were the quietest in the whole period from 1891 to the 1930s.' (Lovell 1977, p.41)

Some authors - for example, Clegg et al. (1964) - argue that this period of calm was the result of the development of collective bargaining procedures - see Section 2.4 above. Among the main areas covered by collective bargaining agreements were the cotton, boot and shoe, engineering, building and shipbuilding industries. These agreements did not prevent all disputes, but there was generally an atmosphere of industrial peace during this period.

Industrial strife, 1908-14
In 1908, the number of working days lost through strikes grew significantly and, although there was less strike action in 1909, a period of major unrest began in 1910 and continued until the outbreak of the First World War in August 1914 (see Box 4.10 below):

'The first sign of the malaise occurred in the cotton textile industry, the scene of relative industrial harmony since 1893 when the Brooklands collective bargaining machinery had been established. In 1908, the industry suffered a seven week strike when the employers lowered wages. This was an indication of things to come and, in 1910, a strike wave broke on British industry.' (Behagg 1991, pp.130-31)

The miners' strike in South Wales, 1910-11
The 'strike wave which broke on British industry' in 1910 was marked by bitterness and violence on a much larger scale than had occurred before. The first dispute involved miners in South Wales. It lasted from September 1910 to August 1911 and involved, at its height, 30,000 miners. Significantly, the strike began when miners refused new wage rates offered by the Conciliation Board (in other words, collective bargaining procedures broke down). As the strike spread, there were frequent clashes between strikers and troops or police officers. During a battle at Tonypandy on 7-8 November 1910, one striker died and over 500 were injured.

Further violence, 1911
There were further violent incidents. In August 1911, sailors and then dockers and railway workers came out on strike. On 13 August, troops and police officers clashed with strikers at the Liverpool docks. In the battle, one police officer died and many strikers were injured. Two days later, two Liverpool dockers were shot dead as they were being taken to prison. Then, four days after that, two railway workers were shot dead in Llanelli, South Wales, and five other people died after a van exploded in a goods yard which was being looted. The result of all this was an atmosphere of crisis, typified by the following extract from the *Times*:

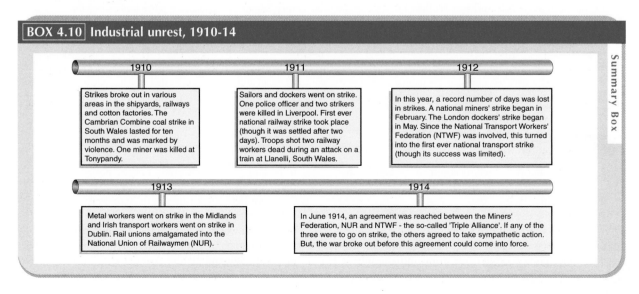

BOX 4.10   Industrial unrest, 1910-14

Summary Box

1910
Strikes broke out in various areas in the shipyards, railways and cotton factories. The Cambrian Combine coal strike in South Wales lasted for ten months and was marked by violence. One miner was killed at Tonypandy.

1911
Sailors and dockers went on strike. One police officer and two strikers were killed in Liverpool. First ever national railway strike took place (though it was settled after two days). Troops shot two railway workers dead during an attack on a train at Llanelli, South Wales.

1912
In this year, a record number of days was lost in strikes. A national miners' strike began in February. The London dockers' strike began in May. Since the National Transport Workers' Federation (NTWF) was involved, this turned into the first ever national transport strike (though its success was limited).

1913
Metal workers went on strike in the Midlands and Irish transport workers went on strike in Dublin. Rail unions amalgamated into the National Union of Railwaymen (NUR).

1914
In June 1914, an agreement was reached between the Miners' Federation, NUR and NTWF - the so-called 'Triple Alliance'. If any of the three were to go on strike, the others agreed to take sympathetic action. But, the war broke out before this agreement could come into force.

'These trade unionists in their crazy fanaticism or diseased vanity are prepared to starve the whole population. This is the greatest labour upheaval this country has ever seen.' (*Times*, August 1911)

National strikes and government interventions, 1911-12

The railway workers' strike in August 1911 was the first ever national railway strike. As with the miners' strike, it was called after workers became frustrated with the failure of their Conciliation Boards to meet their demands. In the case of the railway workers, however, the government intervened and the strike was settled in the union's favour after just two days (largely due to the negotiating skills of David Lloyd George).

The railway workers' success led the Miners' Federation to call a national strike in February 1912 in the hope of winning a minimum wage. Again the government intervened and a settlement was reached - the principle of a minimum wage was accepted, though its rate was not what the miners had campaigned for.

The government intervened in a third dispute - the national dock strike that was called in May 1912. On this occasion, however, it was unable to find a solution.

The government intervened in these disputes mainly because they were national disputes with the potential to cause major disruption. This was a new phenomenon. The railway dispute was resolved quickly as a result of government intervention. The dock strike suffered because the dockers in different ports had little sense of national solidarity (the strike collapsed in August 1912). But, despite attempts by the government to intervene, the impact of the national strike called by the Miners' Federation was great:

'The strike had shown the disruptive effect on the nation's whole industrial life which a miners' general stoppage could cause - hundreds of thousands of other workers were thrown out of work - but it also suggested that there were limits to the extent to which, in the face of public opinion, any one union could extort concessions from their employers by putting pressure on the government.' (Pelling 1987, p.127)

Why were the strikes on a larger scale?

The larger scale of these strikes was due in part to the tendency of unions to amalgamate into federations - a tendency which had begun in the 1890s. It was also due to the growth in union membership which picked up after the fall resulting from the Taff Vale Judgement in 1901. Between 1900 and 1910, union membership grew from c.2 million to 2.5 million. Then, between 1910 and 1914, union membership grew very rapidly - from 2.56 million to 4.14 million. Many of the new members were unskilled or semi-skilled workers. The recruitment of these groups led

to some massive gains. For example, the Workers' Union (which had been set up by Tom Mann in 1898 for the semi-skilled in engineering) increased its membership from 5,016 in 1910 to 159,000 in 1914.

Were the strikes any different from previous strikes?

Contemporary observers and some historians have suggested that the wave of strikes which broke out in the period 1910-14 was significantly different from previous waves of strikes. While earlier strikes were called in response to specific grievances, many of the strikes in the period 1910-14 appear to have been less focused and, perhaps, more 'political' in the sense that they sometimes appeared to be a means of expressing discontent with authority as much as concern about pay or conditions. It could be argued, therefore, that the wave of strikes in 1910-14 was 'qualitatively' different - different in nature - from earlier strikes and that this was a problem both for union officials and for the Labour Party (which aimed to represent workers in Parliament):

'Many observers noted that these strikes seemed qualitatively different to earlier disputes, in that grievances were often imprecisely spelled out, strikers frequently took action and decided afterwards what the dispute was actually about. In this way, the period represented a crisis for the unions, confronting them with the problem of how to control the actions of their members. It also created difficulties for the Labour Party since the focus of action now shifted from Westminster to the workplace, away from reformism and towards direct action.' (Behagg 1995, p.443)

3.2 Why was 1910-14 a time of widespread industrial unrest?

Dangerfield's thesis

The reasons for the change from a period of relative calm in industrial relations to this wave of violent unrest in the years before the First World War have been the subject of debate. One explanation was most forcibly expressed in 1935 by George Dangerfield in *The Strange Death of Liberal England*. He linked the industrial unrest to the militant tactics of the suffragettes (see Unit 3, Part 3), the problems of Ireland (see Unit 6, Part 4), the conflict with the House of Lords (see Unit 6, Part 3) and other issues which, he believed, were bringing about the collapse of 'Liberal England'.

Other explanations

In the 1950s and 1960s, historians such as Phelps Brown (1959) and Pelling (1987) argued against this idea of instability. Since then, however, opinions have become divided. Some historians - such as Price (1986) - support Dangerfield's viewpoint, whilst others - such as Read (1982) and Laybourn (1992) argue that, although British society came under strain during this period, there was no serious threat to its stability.

The economic context

More specific economic and social factors have also been examined in the search for an explanation of the unrest of the period. Some historians have argued, for example, that the state of the trade cycle was an important reason for unrest. In 1908, they argue, unemployment was very high and the strikes in that year appear to have been a defensive reaction to wage cuts. By 1910, however, unemployment was low, prices had been rising for some time and inflation was increasing as real wages fell. The unions were, therefore, anxious to catch up ground lost in previous years. According to this view, there was a parallel with the economic circumstances which had led to the outbreak of strikes in 1888-90:

'The unrest was of a more opportunist character. There were more strikes each year and many were quickly settled by higher wages. The labour market was sufficiently tight for newly organised (or even unorganised) workers to take part and for strife to occur alongside very rapid increase in union membership. The strikes of 1910-14 had much in common with those of 1888-91.' (Hunt 1981, p.322)

Box 4.11 (below) shows that the evidence in support of this theory is not clear-cut. Contemporary statistics have been questioned by modern economists.

The growth of working-class consciousness

A second root cause of the unrest in the period 1908-14 may have been a growth in working-class consciousness. Some historians point to an increasing awareness of and resentment against inequalities of incomes in this period. This was something commented upon by contemporaries. Seebohm Rowntree, writing in the *Contemporary Review* in 1911, for example, noted that:

'The working classes read in the papers that imports and exports have exceeded all previous records, and that never have railway returns been so high. They have been like men watching a rich feast, in the provision of which they had played an important part but in which they might not share.'

BOX 4.12 The labour unrest

The first thing that has to be realised if the labour question is to be understood at all is this, that the temper of labour has changed altogether in the last 20 or 30 years. Essentially, that is a change due to **intelligence not merely increased but greatly stimulated**, to the work, that is, of the board schools and of the cheap press. The outlook of the workman has passed beyond the works and his beer and his dog. He has become, or rather has been replaced by, a being of eyes, however imperfect, and of criticism, however hasty and unjust...The old workman might and did quarrel very vigorously with his specific employer, but he never set out to **arraign** all employers. He took the Church and statecraft and politics for the higher and noble things they claimed to be. He wanted an extra shilling or he wanted an hour of leisure and that was as much as he wanted. The young workman, on the other hand, has put the whole social system upon its trial and seems quite disposed to give an **adverse verdict**. He looks far beyond the older conflict of interests between employer and employed.
From Wells 1912.

Glossary

- **intelligence not merely increased but greatly stimulated** - ie workers were better educated
- **arraign** - find fault with
- **adverse verdict** - a hostile judgement

H.G. Wells, in particular, made the link between better education and industrial unrest in this period, - as Box 4.12 illustrates.

One of the reasons for this growing awareness of inequality between the classes was the publication of two important reports which examined the extent of poverty that existed at the end of the 19th century. Charles Booth's 17 volume survey of the condition of people living in London, *Life and Labour of the People in London*, was published between 1889 and 1903 and Seebohm Rowntree's study of poverty in York, *Poverty: a Study of Town Life*, was published in 1901. The impact of these surveys was heightened by newspaper reports that many working-class men who hoped to fight in the Boer War were being rejected by the army on the grounds that they were not fit enough (because of poor diet and lack of resistance to disease - see also Unit 6, page 195). This brought home to many people just how much genuine poverty there was:

'Education was by this time probably more influential in sharpening critical faculties and raising expectations rather than in instilling deference. The poverty surveys and disclosures of the alarmingly high proportion of Boer War recruits that had been found to be medically unfit were among other causes of the increase in "felt poverty".' (Hunt 1981, p.322)

BOX 4.11 Real wages, 1900-14

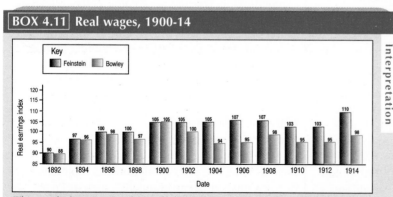

This graph shows two analyses of how real wages changed during the period 1892-1914. The findings of Bowley (who used contemporary statistics) have been challenged by Feinstein (a modern economist).
Adapted from Johnson 1994.

The increase in 'felt poverty', it is argued, helped to produce a climate in which workers became more militant.

Problems with collective bargaining

Another factor which needs to be taken into account when explaining the growth in industrial strife after 1910 is the fact that, in practice, collective bargaining arrangements had two important shortcomings. First, Lovell (1977) points out that the trouble with national agreements was that discontent could build up locally. Shop stewards (union officials in the workplace) were often at odds with the national leadership of the union. As a result, local discontent often led to workers taking unofficial action. This is what happened in engineering, shipbuilding and the cotton industry in the period 1910-14. And second, collective bargaining arrangements were limited in terms of coverage. Union membership in 1910 was about 2.56 million (17% of the workforce). This meant that most workers were outside the collective bargaining system. Between 1910 and 1914, however, unions recruited many members from outside the collective bargaining system and this had a significant effect on the number of strikes:

'This explosion of trade unionism was essentially a movement of the rank and file, with strikes growing directly from the shop floor. Even where the established unions were involved, many of the strikes consisted of "unofficial" action by rank and file unionists acting without the consent of their central union leadership. Union officials often complained that they were the last to know that a strike was taking place.' (Behagg 1991, p.131)

In such circumstances, even where collective bargaining arrangements existed, they were bypassed - which suggests that there was discontent with this way of resolving disputes.

Other factors

Three other factors need to be taken into account when explaining the growth of industrial unrest after 1910. First, Church (1987) places great emphasis on regional differences. In some areas (such as South Wales) miners were very militant, for example, while in other areas they were not. Local circumstances and the local political culture, therefore, need to be taken into account. Second, Pelling argues that:

'There was also the fact that many workers were disillusioned by the failure of the Labour Party in Parliament.' (Pelling 1987, p.129)

It was difficult for the small group of Labour MPs to make any impact after the 1906 general election because the Liberal government had such a big majority (see Unit 5, Part 3). Disillusionment because of lack of progress in Parliament encouraged workers to take direct action. And third, there was an increasing willingness on the part of the Liberal government to intervene in industrial disputes - both by mediating between employers and unions when national strikes broke out and by sanctioning the use of police and troops to combat strikes. By showing that it would respond to industrial action, the government encouraged action to be taken.

Conclusion

It is clear that there is no simple explanation as to why 1910-14 was a time of industrial unrest. The economic climate played a part, as did longer-term developments such as better education for workers and a growth in class consciousness. According to Behagg, however, the most important factor was discontent with the system of collective bargaining and a growing disillusionment with elected representatives:

'Above all the strike wave was an expression of discontent with the existing strategies for advancing labour's case - collective bargaining in the industrial sphere and parliamentary support for moderate social reform in the political sphere. The promised benefits of these two strategies had not materialised. Neither had been able to prevent the fall in real wages and the deterioration of working conditions. In the main, working people were unimpressed by the Liberal reforms. Declining wages and increasing job insecurity seemed to outweigh the benefits of any welfare legislation.' (Behagg 1991, p.132)

MAIN POINTS - Sections 3.1-3.2

- Following a period of industrial peace in the years after 1900, the number of working days lost through strikes grew significantly in 1908. A period of major unrest then began in 1910 and continued until the outbreak of the First World War in August 1914.
- The key characteristics of this period of industrial strife were (1) there were violent clashes between strikers and the authorities (2) there were national strikes for the first time (3) the government was prepared to intervene and (4) the strikes were less focused and more 'political' than previous waves of strikes.
- The larger scale of these strikes was due in part to the tendency of unions to amalgamate into

federations and also to the growth in union membership (especially after 1910).
- Dangerfield argued that the growth in industrial unrest was linked to the militant tactics of the suffragettes, the problems of Ireland, the conflict with the House of Lords and other issues which were leading to the collapse of 'Liberal England'.
- Other factors that should be taken into account include - (1) the economic context (2) the growth of working-class consciousness (3) flaws in the collective bargaining system (4) local circumstances and local political culture (5) disillusion with Labour and the Liberals and (6) the willingness of government to intervene.

Activity 4.5 Industrial unrest 1910-14

ITEM 1 Union membership and strikes 1900-14

Year	Number of Trade Unions (thousands)	Total membership (millions)	Number of stoppages (hundreds)	Number of working days lost in year through strikes (millions)
1900	1.32	2.02	6.33	3.09
1901	1.32	2.02	6.31	4.13
1902	1.29	2.01	4.32	3.44
1903	1.28	1.99	3.80	2.32
1904	1.25	1.96	3.46	1.46
1905	1.24	1.99	3.49	2.37
1906	1.28	2.21	4.79	3.02
1907	1.28	2.51	5.85	2.15
1908	1.26	2.48	3.89	10.79
1909	1.26	2.47	4.22	2.69
1910	1.27	2.56	5.21	9.87
1911	1.29	3.14	8.72	10.16
1912	1.25	3.41	8.34	40.89
1913	1.27	4.13	14.59	9.80
1914	1.26	4.14	9.72	9.88

Adapted from Pelling 1987.

ITEM 2 The miners' strike of 1910 - a newspaper account

The effect of the presence of the cavalry in Tonypandy - the scene of five hours' continuous rioting and looting last night - has been to restore comparative peace and order. There is still, however, the danger of a renewed outbreak of violence. Tonight the streets are being patrolled by a squadron of the 18th (Queen Mary's Own) Hussars with their carbines (firearms), and bodies of the London police are marching slowly up and down through dense masses of strikers who, up to 8 o'clock, were quite orderly. The looted shops, and those which escaped damage, have been barricaded with wooden shutters and corrugated iron and the whole of the main street is fortified against any further attack...Tonypandy this morning presented the appearance of a town that had been bombarded by guns. Stone walls had been overthrown, and the roadway leading to the Glamorgan pit gates was bespattered with blood. There were bloodstains on the walls in the town and even inside looted shops...All day long the streets have sounded with the tramp of soldiers and police.

From the 'Daily Mail', 10 November 1910.

ITEM 3 The first national strikes, 1911-12

In the railway strike of 1911, the government was faced with a totally new situation of a strike covering the whole railway network and not one confined to one area or local authority. The Home Secretary, Winston Churchill, put large areas of the country under martial law and mobilised all available soldiers for duty in protecting the railway lines and stations. This approach came under strong attack in the Commons. The Chancellor, David Lloyd George, met both directors and union leaders separately and managed to reach a compromise after only two days' stoppage. The dispute had arisen because the employers refused to recognise union representatives on the Conciliation Boards. Lloyd George promised to set up a Royal Commission to examine the Conciliation Boards. After it reported later in the year, a new scheme was introduced, with employers agreeing to union representation on the Boards. In the next national strike, the coal strike which began in February 1912, the Home Office told the mine and railway owners who asked for military aid that they must not expect the government to repeat the steps taken in the rail strike. Instead, with a million miners on strike and with the owners resisting the miners' demand for a national minimum wage, the government tried to settle the dispute by mediation. When this failed, Parliament passed a Bill which set up local boards to establish district minimum wages. Although this met the demands of neither side, it established the principle of a minimum wage - which was of great importance to the miners. The miners went back to work in April. The strike showed that a national miners' strike could disrupt the nation's whole industrial life, but it also suggested that there were limits to the extent to which any one union could force concessions from employers by putting pressure on the government.

Adapted from Pelling 1987 and Weinberger 1987.

ITEM 4 The dock strike in Liverpool, 1911

Over 50,000 troops were sent to keep order in Liverpool in August 1911, during the dock strike.

Questions

1. a) Judging from Items 1-4, what was new about the wave of strikes which broke out in 1910-14?
   b) Suggest reasons why these strikes broke out.
2. a) Using Item 1, describe the development of industrial relations between 1900 and 1914.
   b) Suggest reasons for these developments.
3. What do Items 2-4 tell us about the nature of industrial unrest 1910-14?

3.3 What is syndicalism and how important was it?

What is syndicalism?

Between the 1890s and 1920s, a new and distinctive political philosophy gained popularity in many parts of Europe, the USA, Latin America and Australia. This philosophy is termed 'syndicalism':

'[It was the aim of syndicalists] to overthrow capitalism through revolutionary industrial class struggle and to build a new social order free from economic or political oppression.' (Holton 1976, p.17)

In other words, syndicalists were revolutionary socialists. They hoped and believed that a revolution would bring about socialism. But, unlike many early socialists who looked to Parliament and the state to bring socialism (see Unit 5, Section 1.1), syndicalists looked to the trade unions. The trade unions, they argued, had the potential to bring about a revolution because trade unionists had the power to bring down their employers. The key to this revolution was the use of industrial action and, ultimately, a general strike (a strike in which all workers in all industries stopped work at the same time). A general strike, they argued, would lead to workers' control over the economy and society.

A contemporary description of the syndicalists' aims is provided in Box 4.13.

Syndicalism in Britain

In Britain, syndicalist ideas developed in the early years of the 20th century. In 1903, Sam Mainwaring, formerly a member of the Socialist League (a Marxist splinter group - see Unit 5, Section 1.1) started a short-lived journal called the *General Strike*. E.J.B.Allen, a

BOX 4.13 Syndicalism

Source Box

We shall unite all the workers in any one industry, and unite all industries. We will build a 'state within a state', a workers' democracy in opposition to the capitalist **oligarchy**. The existing unions must be united, strengthened and enlightened as to the real purpose that a labour union should be formed for - to teach their members to think every time they enter the yard, mill or mine: 'This is the place where my fellow workmen and I are robbed. This is the place that we keep going. This is the place we ought to own and control.'...Let us think and act as a class. The industrial union is destined to become the most powerful instrument in the class struggle by showing the working class how to hold in check the **rapacity** of their masters and the tyrannies of the state by direct pressure of their collective economic strength which power reaches its highest expression in the complete paralysis of the whole of the normal functions of capitalist society by means of a general strike. The use of a general strike must be amplified and extended, embracing a larger number of workers in the actual combat; evolving that unity of action and sameness of inspiration which will make them think and act as a class, for the direct and forcible **expropriation** of the capitalists.

From 'Working class socialism', an article written by E.J.B. Allen in the *Industrial Syndicalist* (a journal set up by Tom Mann), in November 1910.

Glossary
- **oligarchy** - rule by the few
- **rapacity** - greed
- **expropriation** - overthrow

former Social Democratic Federation (SDF) member (another Marxist splinter group), then set up the Industrialist League in 1908 and wrote *Revolutionary Unionism* in 1909. The ideas in this book influenced the trade unionist Tom Mann (one of the leaders in the dock strike of 1889 - see Section 2.1 above). Laybourn (1992) explains how, on returning from Australia in 1910, Mann aimed to use the existing trade union structure to unite the working class and then to organise a general strike which would win control of the state:

'It was Tom Mann, returning from Australia in April 1910 who was, for a couple of years, to dominate the direction which the syndicalist movement took...He was attracted to the ideas of winning industrial unionism, "boring from within" the existing trade union structure, uniting the working class, and of using the general strike to win control of the state.' (Laybourn 1992, pp.100-01).

Together with Guy Bowman, Mann launched a newspaper, the *Industrial Syndicalist*, and he helped to set up the Industrial Syndicalist Education League, an organisation devoted to the spreading of syndicalist ideas.

Syndicalism and industrial unrest 1910-14

While there were many reasons for the industrial unrest of 1910-14 (see Section 3.2 above), some historians have argued that the increased militancy of the unions was related to the growth of syndicalism:

'It was left to the rank and file and to various militants to articulate a new philosophy of mass unionism and direct action. Whether a great many workers grasped the key tenets of syndicalism or not, the syndicalist approach resonated well with the mood of the men and helped to express its central thrust.' (Cronin & Schneer 1982, p.90)

Evidence in support of syndicalist influence

Historians have pointed to a number of pieces of evidence which suggests that syndicalism did play a part in the industrial unrest of 1910-14. First, particular areas and particular strikes have been seen as examples of syndicalist influence. Pelling, for example, notes that:

'Many of the members of the Plebs League [a syndicalist organisation set up in 1908] belonged either to the South Wales Miners Federation or to the Amalgamated Society of Railway Servants - and these men were largely responsible for the aggressive tactics of their respective unions in 1911-12.' (Pelling 1987, p.130)

And Laybourn adds that:

- Tom Mann encouraged Ben Tillett, leader of the dockers union, and Havelock Wilson, leader of the National Sailors' and Firemen's Union, to set up the National Transport Workers' Federation in November 1910

- Mann and other syndicalists were active in the miners' strike in South Wales in 1910-11
- Mann and local syndicalists organised the dock strike in Liverpool in 1911
- Mann and Bowman were supported by many unions after being imprisoned for publishing the *'Don't Shoot'* leaflet (see below) in 1912 and this support secured their early release
- The South Wales miners produced *The Miners' Next Step*, a pro-syndicalist document, in early 1912
- a syndicalist called Leonard Hall was active among engineers in the Midlands
- a syndicalist called Jim Larkin was active in Ireland.

In addition to setting up the National Transport Workers' Federation, syndicalists also played a part in bringing about the merger of unions in two other important areas - the railways (forming the National Union of Railwaymen in 1913) and the Triple Alliance of 1914 (an alliance between the miners, railway workers and transport workers - see below).

The *'Don't Shoot'* leaflet

In January 1912, an article which had first been published in the *Irish Worker* in July 1911, was republished in the *Industrial Syndicalist*. Entitled 'Open Letter to British Soldiers', this article called on British soldiers not to use force against striking workers and was judged to be an incitement to mutiny. As a result, the editors of the *Industrial Syndicalist*, Tom Mann and Guy Bowman were arrested, tried and sentenced to six and nine months in jail respectively. Following protests and demonstrations by unionists, however, the two men were released after seven weeks.

The Triple Alliance

In 1914, the Miners' Federation, the National Union of Railwaymen and the National Transport Workers' Federation agreed that, in the event of an industrial dispute involving any one of their members, the other two unions would take sympathetic action in support of the union in dispute. This was a particularly significant development because the miners and railway workers had already organised national strikes that had prompted government intervention and the National Transport Workers' Federation had caused disruption in the various disputes that had taken place in the docks in 1911-12. If the three organisations came out on strike together, they had the potential to bring the country to a standstill.

How important was syndicalism?

While accepting that some syndicalists played an active role in the industrial unrest of the period before 1914, many historians reject the view that syndicalist ideas spread either widely or deeply among working people. Pelling, for example, stresses the moderation of most trade union leaders:

'The idea of "direct action" for revolutionary political purposes might influence some Welsh miners; it had little appeal to the great bulk of British union leaders, whose respect for parliamentary methods was yet too deeply ingrained to be easily lost.' (Pelling 1987, p.132)

More recently, Laybourn (1992) has played down the importance of syndicalism. He supports the view of Clegg et al. (1964) that only four out of 14 major strikes involved syndicalists. His own conclusion is that:

'It is difficult, if not impossible, to believe that syndicalism was in any sense pervasive among the British working class. Active syndicalists seem to have established themselves in a few small areas, as in Liverpool and South Wales, but to have been rather thin on the ground elsewhere.' (Laybourn 1992, p.104)

This is a view supported by Behagg:

'It is easy to exaggerate the importance of the syndicalists. Their direct influence was less than they would have wished. The labour unrest in these years grew from the grass roots...The syndicalists simply tried to harness this movement.' (Behagg 1991, pp.133-34)

So, while it is important to emphasise that syndicalism did play a part in the industrial unrest of 1910-14, it is equally important not to exaggerate the part that syndicalists played.

MAIN POINTS - Section 3.3

- Between the 1890s and 1920s, syndicalism - a new and distinctive political philosophy - gained popularity in many parts of the world, including Britain.
- Syndicalists were revolutionary socialists who believed that the trade unions had the potential to bring about a revolution. The key to this revolution was a general strike which would lead to workers' control over the economy and society. An important step towards a general strike was the amalgamation of unions into larger federations.
- There is a debate about whether the increased militancy of the unions in 1910-14 was related to the growth of syndicalism.
- There is evidence that syndicalists were active in some unions and helped to organise some strikes. Also, some unions amalgamated, forming national unions, and, in 1914, the Triple Alliance was formed.
- Many historians, however, reject the view that syndicalist ideas spread either widely or deeply among working people. Most union leaders remained moderate and most strikes in 1910-14 had no syndicalist involvement. Rather than being responsible for the industrial unrest, there is an argument that syndicalists tried to take advantage of it.

Activity 4.6 Syndicalism

ITEM 1 *The Miners' Next Step*

We cannot get rid of employers and slave-driving in the mining industry until all other industries have organised for and progressed towards the same objective...All we can do is set an example and the pace...Our objective begins to take place before your eyes. Every industry thoroughly organised, in the first place, to fight, to gain control of, and then to administer that industry. The coordination of all industries on a Central Production Board who, with a statistical department to ascertain the needs of the people, will issue its demands on the different departments of industry, leaving the men themselves to determine under what conditions and how the work should be done. This would mean real democracy in real life, making for real manhood and womanhood. Any other form of democracy is a delusion and a snare.

From 'The Miners' Next Step', a pamphlet produced by syndicalist miners in South Wales in 1912.

ITEM 2 A historian's assessment

As Professor Clegg has noted, there is little evidence that the industrial disputes of 1910-14 had much to do with syndicalism - in the sense of challenging capitalism and the state in the way which syndicalists urged. Whilst noting the impossibility of examining the 4,000 strikes of 1911-14, Clegg stresses that, by examining the 14 major disputes which account for 51 million of the 70 million working days lost through strikes, a fair reflection of the period can be gained. Examining each of these disputes and analysing the overall pattern of events, he notes that only four of the disputes involved syndicalists and that, apart from the Liverpool dock strike, these 14 major disputes involved relatively small numbers of workers but contributed to a large number of days lost because they were drawn out. Clegg is at pains to stress that syndicalism was a relatively minor factor in the industrial conflict of the pre-war years and that nearly all the major strikes could be accounted for by two factors - first, the boom in union organisation and, second, the poor financial position of some groups of employers, mainly the mine owners and railway companies, who were forced to reject what might otherwise have been considered reasonable demands.

Adapted from Laybourn 1992.

ITEM 3 The 'Triple Alliance' - two cartoons

(i)

THE PROBLEM-PICTURE OF 1921.
HOW TO MAKE THE TAIL WAG.

(ii)

UNION OF TRADES UNIONS IS STRENGTH

In this cartoon (produced in 1921), the Triple Alliance is portrayed as a figure from Greek mythology - the three-headed dog Cerberus who guarded the entrance to the underworld (Hell).

In this cartoon, the Triple Alliance is portrayed as a bundle of sticks. The man in the top hat symbolises capitalism. He cannot break the bundle because it is too thick. He would probably be able to break each stick, however.

Questions

1. a) Using Item 1, explain what is meant by 'syndicalism'.
   b) Assess the significance of the document quoted in Item 1.
2. a) Describe the view being put forward in Item 2.
   b) What counter-arguments might be used to challenge their view?
   c) Assess the importance of syndicalism in the period 1910-14.
3. a) What point is being made by each of the cartoons in Item 3?
   b) Is either cartoon supportive of the Triple Alliance? Explain your answer.
   c) Why was the formation of the Triple Alliance significant?

References

• **Abbott (1972)** Abbott, B.H., *Gladstone & Disraeli*, Collins Educational, 1972.

• **Alexander (1994)** Alexander, S., *Becoming a Woman and Other Essays in 19th and 20th Century Feminist History*, Virago Press, 1994.

• **Behagg (1991)** Behagg, C., *Labour and Reform: Working-Class Movements 1815-1914*, Hodder and Stoughton, 1991.

• **Behagg (1995)** Behagg, C., 'Trade unions and the rise of Labour 1885-1914' in *Scott-Baumann (1995)*.

• **Bellamy (1990)** Bellamy, J., 'Trade Union Imagery' in *OUP (1990)*.

• **Church (1987)** Church, R.T., 'Edwardian labour unrest and coalfield militancy 1890-1914', *Historical Journal,* Vol.30.4, 1987.

• **Clegg et al. (1964)** Clegg, H.A., Fox, A. & Thompson, A.F., *A History of British Trade Unions since 1889*, Vol.1, Oxford University Press, 1964.

• **Cronin & Schneer (1982)** Cronin, J.E. & Schneer, J., *Social Conflict and the Political Order in Britain*, Croom Helm, 1982.

• **Dangerfield (1935)** Dangerfield, G., *The Strange Death of Liberal England*, Paladin, 1970.

• **Evans (1996)** Evans, E., *The Forging of the Modern State: Early Industrial Britain 1783-1870*, Longman, 1996.

- **Fraser (1999)** Fraser, W.H., *A History of British Trade Unionism 1700-1998*, Macmillan, 1999.

- **Gardiner & Wenborn (1995)** Gardiner, J. & Wenborn, N., *The Companion to British History*, Collins & Brown, 1995.

- **Harrison (1965)** Harrison, R., *Before the Socialists*, Macmillan, 1965.

- **Hinton (1982)** Hinton, J., 'The rise of a mass labour movement: growth and limits' in *Wrigley (1982)*.

- **Hobsbawm (1968)** Hobsbawm, E., *Labouring Men: Studies in the History of Labour*, Weidenfeld and Nicolson, 1968.

- **Holton (1976)** Holton, B., *British Syndicalism 1900-14: Myth and Realities*, Pluto Press, 1976.

- **Howson (1996)** Howson, J., 'The dock strike of 1889', *Modern History Review*, Vol.7.3, February 1996.

- **Hunt (1981)** Hunt, E.H., *British Labour History 1815-1914*, Weidenfeld and Nicolson, 1981.

- **Johnson (1994)** Johnson, P. (ed.), *Twentieth Century Britain: Economic, Social and Cultural Change*, Longman, 1994.

- **Laybourn (1992)** Laybourn, K., *A History of British Trade Unionism c.1770-1990*, Alan Sutton, 1992.

- **Leeson (1984)** Leeson, R.A., 'Business as usual - craft union development 1834-51, *Bulletin of the Society for the Study of Labour History*, Vol.49, 1984.

- **Lovell (1977)** Lovell, J., *British Trade Unions 1875-1933*, Macmillan, 1977.

- **Mann & Tillett (1890)** Mann, T. & Tillett, B., *The 'New' Trade Unionism*, 1890.

- **Musson (1972)** Musson, A.E., *British Trade Unions 1800-1875*, Macmillan, 1972.

- **OUP (1990)** Open University Arts Foundation Course Team, *Culture: Production, Consumption and Status* (2nd edn), Open University, 1990.

- **Pelling (1987)** Pelling, H., *A History of British Trade Unionism*, Pelican, 1987 (first published in 1963).

- **Phelps Brown (1959)** Phelps Brown, P.E.H., *The Growth of British Industrial Relations*, Macmillan, 1959.

- **Phillips (1992)** Phillips, G., *The Rise of the Labour Party 1893-1931*, Routledge, 1992.

- **Pimlott & Cook (1982)** Pimlott, B. & Cook, C., *Trade Unions in British Politics*, Longman, 1982.

- **Price (1986)** Price, R., *Labour in British Society: an Interpretative History*, Croom Helm, 1986.

- **Read (1982)** Read, D., *Edwardian England*, Harrap, 1982.

- **Roberts (1999)** Roberts, D. (ed.), *British Politics in Focus* (2nd edition), Causeway Press, 1999.

- **Scott-Baumann (1995)** Scott-Baumann, M. (ed.), *Years of Expansion: Britain 1815-1914*, Hodder and Stoughton, 1995.

- **Strachey (1979)** Strachey, R., *The Cause: a Short History of the Women's Movement in Great Britain*, Virago, 1979 (first published in 1928).

- **Thompson (1980)** Thompson, E.P., *The Making of the English Working Class*, Pelican, 1980 (first published in 1963).

- **Walton (1990)** Walton, J.K., *Disraeli*, Routledge, 1990.

- **Weinberger (1987)** Weinberger, B., 'Keeping the peace?' Policing Strikes 1906-26, *History Today*, Vol.37, December 1987.

- **Wells (1912)** Wells, H. G., *What the Worker Wants*, Hodder and Stoughton, 1912.

- **Wrigley (1982)** Wrigley, C. (ed.), *A History of British Industrial Relations 1875-1914*, Harvester, 1982.

UNIT 5 — The birth of the Labour Party to 1914

Timeline - The birth of the Labour Party to 1914

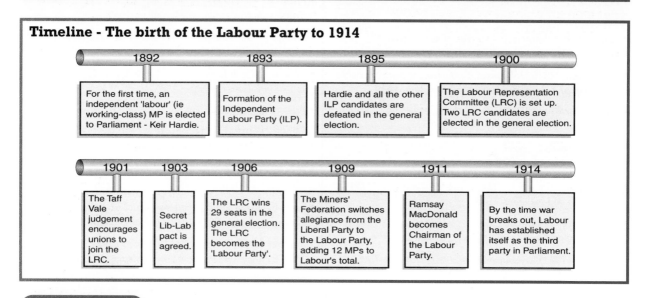

1892 — For the first time, an independent 'labour' (ie working-class) MP is elected to Parliament - Keir Hardie.

1893 — Formation of the Independent Labour Party (ILP).

1895 — Hardie and all the other ILP candidates are defeated in the general election.

1900 — The Labour Representation Committee (LRC) is set up. Two LRC candidates are elected in the general election.

1901 — The Taff Vale judgement encourages unions to join the LRC.

1903 — Secret Lib-Lab pact is agreed.

1906 — The LRC wins 29 seats in the general election. The LRC becomes the 'Labour Party'.

1909 — The Miners' Federation switches allegiance from the Liberal Party to the Labour Party, adding 12 MPs to Labour's total.

1911 — Ramsay MacDonald becomes Chairman of the Labour Party.

1914 — By the time war breaks out, Labour has established itself as the third party in Parliament.

Introduction

Although the second and third Reform Acts (see Unit 2) meant that more working-class men were able to vote, the number of working-class MPs remained very small right until the end of the 19th century. With the exception of Keir Hardie and two other 'independent' MPs (who were elected in the general election of 1892), the only members of the working class to be elected to Parliament before 1900 were 'Lib-Lab' MPs - working-class MPs sponsored and supported by the Liberal Party. Nevertheless, the idea that an independent working-class (or 'labour') party should be set up to promote working-class interests and provide working-class representation in Parliament gained momentum in the 1880s and the Independent Labour Party (ILP) was set up in 1893. The ILP remained weak without the support of the unions, however, and it was only in 1900 when a number of unions agreed to set up the Labour Representation Committee (LRC) that an independent labour party with a real chance of gaining electoral success was born. The LRC

(renamed 'Labour Party' in 1906) had some success in the period 1900-14, but then grew in spectacular fashion after the First World War had ended. In 1924, it won enough seats to form the first Labour government and, from that point on, remained one of the two main parties (at the expense of the Liberal Party).

Historians who have examined the rapid rise of the Labour Party and equally rapid decline of the Liberal Party have found much to disagree about. First, there is a debate about the Labour Party's origins. To what extent was it a socialist party and what factors prevented it being formed earlier? Second, there is a debate about how much progress the Labour Party had made by 1906 and whether the 1906 general election was a turning point. And third, there is a debate about the progress made by the Labour Party in the period 1906-14. To what extent were the seeds of the party's later success sown then? This unit examines each of these debates in turn.

UNIT SUMMARY

Part 1 examines the origins of the Labour Party. Why were the 1880s particularly important? What obstacles stood in the way of the creation of an independent labour party?

Part 2 focuses on the part played by the ILP and the trade unions in setting up the Labour Representation Committee (LRC) in 1900. It then considers the

progress made by the LRC up to 1906.

Part 3 deals with the question of whether the Labour Party's success (and Liberal Party's decline) was inevitable. It looks at the Labour Party's record in the period 1906-14 and considers the extent to which developments before 1914 explain the party's success after 1918.

1 The origins of the Labour Party

Key questions

1. Why were the 1880s particularly important in the development of the Labour Party?

2. What obstacles stood in the way of the creation of an independent labour party?

3. What role did Keir Hardie play in the labour movement before 1893?

1.1 Why were the 1880s particularly important in the development of the Labour Party?

The key historical questions

The Labour Party came into existence in February 1900 when a conference attended by representatives from trade unions and socialist groups agreed to set up the Labour Representation Committee (LRC). The LRC remained the party's official title until 1906 when it formally adopted the title 'Labour Party'. The historical debate surrounding the emergence of the Labour Party focuses on a number of questions:

'The first is to account for the creation of a new and separate party to represent labour [ie the working class]. Who felt it necessary to establish such a political organisation and why? In answering this question we must, of course, consider the timing of the enterprise: what particular conditions prevailed at the birth of the Labour Representation Committee in 1900 and what had delayed its introduction at an earlier juncture?' (Phillips 1992, p.1)

Most historians who have examined these questions begin their accounts in the 1880s, arguing that it was in this decade that four key developments began to take shape. This section examines these key developments and then considers the obstacles that had to be overcome before an independent labour party (ie a party which supported the interests of members of the working class) could be set up.

1. The end of mid-Victorian economic confidence

Although free-market capitalism remained the dominant ideology in Britain throughout the 19th century, some people looked for alternatives. In the early part of the 19th century, there were experiments with forms of socialism. These experiments, however, did not catch on:

'Britain had been one of the main centres of early socialism but, by mid-century, little of this remained. It was not until the 1880s that socialism

began to revive.' (Thorpe 1997, p.9)

By the 1880s, mid-Victorian confidence in an ever-increasing prosperity was giving way to fears of foreign competition, and rates of economic growth had begun to slow down. The use of the term 'Great Depression' to describe the last 20 years of the 19th century may be an exaggeration, but more people were beginning to question the workings of the free-market economy:

'The 1880s was a watershed decade in British social history. It was a period when Britain was experiencing economic depression and deflation, unemployment marches in London, social surveys which highlighted the blight of poverty and when a range of radical and Liberal opinion was asking what could be done to improve the quality of life for the working classes.' (Laybourn 1997, p.2)

2. The extension of the franchise

The passage of the third Reform Act in 1884-85 broadened the franchise, giving more working-class men the vote (see Unit 2, Section 3.3). Although most working-class men and all women still could not vote, there was scope for mobilising the working-class vote in some constituencies. While, at first, the Liberal Party tried to take advantage of this (see point 3 below), the broader franchise and working-class dissatisfaction with the Liberals helped to create a climate favourable to calls for an independent party to be set up to meet the needs of the working class. Between 1885 and 1910, in England and Wales:

'It is possible to distinguish 89 constituencies, electing 95 MPs, which were predominantly working-class in character.' (Pelling 1967, pp.419-20)

An important characteristic of these 89 constituencies was that they were not safe seats. Sometimes they returned Liberal MPs and sometimes Conservative MPs. It was in constituencies like this that a political party which represented labour issues might prosper (so long as it could persuade members of these constituencies to vote along class lines).

3. New Unionism

Following the passage of the second Reform Act in 1867, the Liberal Party began to build ties with the trade unions. The most important development was the practice of selecting union leaders as Liberal parliamentary candidates in constituencies with a large working-class vote. In the 1870s and 1880s, a number of these 'Lib-Lab' candidates were elected (the first two were elected in 1874 and 12 were elected at the 1885 general election). It is important to note that the Lib-Lab MPs were a distinct grouping within the Liberal Party, conscious of their special role in forwarding working-class interests on any issues concerning labour. Support for close ties with the Liberal Party was particularly strong in the TUC.

While the ties between the old unions and the Liberal Party continued to be close during the 1880s, at the end of the decade a new phase of trade union activity began - so-called 'New Unionism' (see Unit 4, Part 2). Although there is a debate over the extent to which socialist ideas inspired New Unionism and although the rapid growth of New Unions slowed in the early 1890s, many of the leaders of the New Unions belonged to socialist groups and New Unions tended not to be as close to the Liberal Party as the old unions.

4. New socialist groups in the 1880s

By the 1880s, also, the work of Karl Marx and Friedrich Engels was becoming influential. Their *Communist Manifesto* was first published in 1848 and translated into English in 1850. Their other major works were written in the years between 1848 and Marx's death in 1883 (Marx's *Das Capital* was translated into English in 1887).

First and foremost, Marx and Engels criticised free-market capitalism. They argued that workers (those without capital) were being exploited by capitalists (property owners) and that, once the workers realised the extent to which they were being exploited, they would rise up and overthrow the capitalists in a revolution (ie they would take control of the state). This revolution would lead to a new way of organising society - socialism. In a socialist society, people would share property and work cooperatively. Although Marxism had a greater appeal and made a greater impact on politics in other European countries, it informed the development of socialist thought in Britain.

Socialist groups in Britain

In Britain in the 1880s, several new socialist groups were set up. While none of these groups would disagree with Marx and Engels that capitalism was exploitative or that a society in which people shared property and worked cooperatively was desirable, not all of these new groups agreed with Marx and Engels about how such a society could be realised. In fact, ideas about the nature of socialism and how it might be implemented varied quite dramatically from group to group.

Furthermore, it should be noted that membership of these groups was small - a minute proportion of the population of Britain. Despite this, these groups made an important contribution to the political debates which took place in the late 19th century. Indeed, they made a contribution which was out of proportion to their size:

'The socialists were only a small body - probably no more than 2,000 in the 1880s and perhaps

20,000 or 30,000 by 1900 - but their influence was widespread. Their activities, and above all their propaganda, set up a ferment of social ideas which captivated a whole generation of young people in the 1890s.' (Harrison 1984, p.338)

Three main groups were set up in the 1880s - the Social Democratic Federation (SDF), the Socialist League and the Fabian Society.

A. The Social Democratic Federation (SDF)

One of the most important of the new socialist groups formed in the early 1880s was the Social Democratic Federation (SDF). It started life as the Democratic Foundation in March 1881, changing its name in 1884 under the influence of its leading figure, Henry Mayers Hyndman (see Box 5.1).

BOX 5.1   Henry Hyndman and the SDF

Hyndman was rather an eccentric figure. His family was wealthy and he was educated at Eton and Trinity College, Cambridge. He had a private income which he increased by speculating on the stock market. In addition, he was always conscious of his status as a gentleman and normally wore a top hat and frock coat - the 'uniform' of the upper classes in Victorian society. Moreover, he was a strong supporter of the British Empire and British naval power. And yet, he was a convinced Marxist. Hyndman had read Karl Marx's *Das Capital* while on a business trip in 1881 and, under his influence, the SDF became a Marxist party. The origins of the SDF, however, lie not in Hyndman's Marxism, but in his opposition to Liberalism. In June 1881, a number of working men from the London radical clubs, together with Hyndman and a group of prominent left-wing Liberals, held a meeting in London 'to unite, if possible, all societies willing to adopt a radical programme with a powerful democratic party'. As a result, the Democratic Federation was born - a radical rather than a socialist body whose interests lay primarily in Irish policy and land reform. But, Hyndman's increasingly outspoken criticisms of Gladstone led to the withdrawal of most of the group's radicals and, in 1883, Hyndman was able to convert it into a purely socialist body. It was renamed the Social Democratic Federation in 1884, by which time it had recruited a number of socialists including Eleanor Marx (Karl Marx's daughter) and William Morris.
Adapted from Adelman 1986.

Interpretation

The SDF's stance

Members of the SDF accepted Marx's idea that the key to politics was a continuous struggle between the classes and that, ultimately, this class struggle would lead to a revolution which would overthrow the capitalist system. The SDF was, therefore, a revolutionary socialist group, which, at first, opposed the parliamentary route to socialism. The SDF was also suspicious of trade unions - for two reasons. First, it was argued that unions were élitist - they campaigned on behalf of a small group of privileged workers rather than for all workers. And second, it was argued that unions had formed an alliance with capitalists (since they were prepared to negotiate and deal with employers):

> 'The SDF followed the Hyndman line of reasoning published in the manifesto it published in *Justice* on 6 September 1884, accusing the trade unions, not unreasonably, of having concluded an alliance with capitalism, forgetting the existence of the class struggle and catering to the needs of a few favoured workers rather than the masses who lived in misery. The trade unions were urged to understand that it was revolution, not reform, that was required.' (Laybourn 1997, p.9)

Hyndman also believed that strikes were a waste of time and that strike pay could be better spent on socialist propaganda. On this, as on many other matters, however, Hyndman was criticised by some SDF members. The trade unionists Tom Mann (Dockers), Ben Tillett (Dockers), John Burns (Engineers) and Will Thorne (Gasworkers) - see Unit 4, Section 2.1 - were all members of the SDF at some time.

'Bloody Sunday' and its aftermath

The SDF never became a mass movement. The only time it seemed near to that was in 1886-87 when it launched campaigns on behalf of the unemployed and in support of popular control of the Metropolitan Police. These campaigns culminated in a mass meeting held in Trafalgar Square on 13 November 1887 - 'Bloody Sunday'. Violence broke out at the meeting and two demonstrators were killed by the police and troops. The following Sunday, 40,000 demonstrators attended a meeting in Hyde Park. At that meeting, mounted police charged the crowd and another man was fatally wounded. Over 120,000 people attended his funeral. Despite this, the SDF was unable to maintain any momentum and, by 1890, its membership was in decline. Laybourn (1997, p.49) estimates an average membership of around 9,000 between 1890 and 1914.

The SDF - failings and successes

Many historians have been very critical of Hyndman's leadership:

> 'Hyndman's personality made it difficult for him to collaborate except with inferiors. He cannot escape blame for the failure of the SDF to exploit its unique position as the pioneer socialist organisation in Britain.' (Hobsbawm 1964, pp.234-35)

Yet, despite Hyndman's authoritarian leadership, as Hobsbawm also shows, the party often ignored Hyndman and, at the grass-roots, the SDF became an important agent for the spread of socialism. A recent study of the SDF argues:

> 'The SDF was far less dogmatic than is often supposed and it acted as an important training ground for socialists.' (Crick 1994, p.296)

B. The Socialist League

On 30 December 1884, the majority of the SDF's executive committee - including Eleanor Marx and William Morris - split away from the party and set up a new one - the Socialist League. Apart from personal dislike of Hyndman and his authoritarian style of leadership, the main reason for the split was Hyndman's decision that SDF candidates should stand in the general election of 1885.

Just as the SDF was dominated by Hyndman, the Socialist League was dominated by William Morris, a well-known artist and writer - see Box 5.2.

BOX 5.2 William Morris and the Socialist League

Rather like Hyndman and the SDF, William Morris dominated the Socialist League until the late 1880s and offered politics which were distinctively his own (he communicated his views via the group's newspaper, the *Commonweal*). He and his colleagues set up the Socialist League in order to overthrow the existing system by force. The idea was that their organisation would be 'a body of able, high-minded, competent men who should act as instructors of the masses and as their leaders during critical periods of the movement'. The League saw its task as being to encourage a revolutionary situation to develop rather than simply idling and awaiting a spontaneous revolution.
Adapted from Laybourn 1997.

Interpretation

The League remained, however, a tiny organisation with only about 700 members at its peak in the 1880s. It made no headway with the mass of working people, remaining overwhelmingly middle class.

The contribution of William Morris

Although the League made little practical impact on British politics, historians such as Thompson (1977) and McCarthy (1994) have argued that Morris was an important figure in the development of socialist ideas. This is a view shared by Andrew Thorpe:

> 'Morris wrote a series of utopian works describing what a socialist society could be like. These showed a spiritual side of socialism, a vision of a free and equal society. He inspired many, particularly younger people, to work for the movement.' (Thorpe 1997, p.10)

C. The Fabian Society

The Fabian Society was set up in 1884. The group was named after the Roman general Fabius Cunctator who defeated Hannibal by using delaying tactics and by avoiding a set-piece battle against Hannibal's troops. Like Fabius, members of the Fabian Society believed that their enemy (capitalism) could be defeated by taking patient, gradual steps and by avoiding direct confrontation. Although they were highly critical of capitalism, Fabians, therefore, were reformists not revolutionaries. Indeed, they were totally opposed to the Marxist belief in revolutionary socialism. Instead they believed in an evolutionary socialism engineered by state enterprise and municipal reform. The emphasis on local action led to the phrase 'gas and water socialism' to describe the Fabian position.

Membership

Membership of the Fabian Society was almost exclusively middle class. It included some of the leading writers of the period (such as George Bernard Shaw and H.G.Wells) as well as the journalist Annie Besant, famous for her support of the match girls in their strike (see Unit 4, Section 2.1). In fact, writers and journalists made up 10% of the membership of the Fabians with the result that:

'They have always been strong on public relations. They have never required others to blow their own trumpet.' (Hobsbawm 1964, p.250)

The Fabians were certainly good at promoting their ideas. Fabian essays and pamphlets poured out on a huge range of topics. Two of the most influential thinkers in the movement were Beatrice and Sidney Webb who wrote on topics like the reform of the Poor Law and local government. *Fabian Essays* (published in 1889) sold 27,000 copies in two years.

The role played by Fabians

The Fabians later claimed to have played a major role in defining socialism and the way it developed in Britain. Several historians (for example, McBriar 1962, Hobsbawm 1964, Thompson 1967), however, have played down their role, pointing out how little contact they had with the working class (usually less than 10% of their membership) and particularly with the trade unions. Their failure to decide on how best to put their ideas into practice has also been highlighted. Until the First World War, they wavered between supporting the Independent Labour Party (ILP - see Section 2.1 below), the Labour Party and the Liberals. Their hope that their ideas would 'permeate' the Liberal Party was an illusion. Similarly, the claim that they saved British socialism from Marxism has also been dismissed. It is as a think-tank that their contribution to socialism best holds up.

1.2 Obstacles to an independent labour party 1880-1900

What obstacles have historians identified?

Historians have identified six main obstacles that needed to be overcome before an independent party catering for the needs of the working class could stand a realistic chance of success.

1. The Lib-Labs

While some working-class political activists in the 1880s joined socialist groups, many others tried to work through the established Liberal Party which, it was argued, could be used as a vehicle to bring change. The idea was that, by joining the Liberal Party, working-class men would gain a real chance of standing for Parliament in a seat that they could win. Once elected, these men could then champion labour issues in Parliament. The logical conclusion of this argument was that there was simply no need for a separate party.

The existence of the Lib-Labs was a real problem to supporters of a separate and independent labour party in the period 1880-1900. The Lib-Labs had very strong influence in the Trades Union Congress (TUC) and, throughout the 1890s, they vetoed any attempt to encourage TUC involvement in setting up a separate and independent party. Also, on occasions when independent labour candidates were put up for election against Liberal candidates, the anti-Tory vote was split. Sometimes, working-class activists and trade unionists even worked for a Liberal candidate against an independent labour candidate on the grounds that the independent candidate had no hope of election. The result was often tension between independent labour leaders like Keir Hardie (see Section 1.3 below) and Lib-Labs like Henry Broadhurst. The clash of personalities further delayed the founding of a separate and independent Labour Party.

2. The narrowness of the franchise

The narrowness of the franchise remained an obstacle even after the passing of the third Reform Act - see Box 5.3 on page 153.

3. The problem of finance

There were certain practical problems that made it difficult for members of the working class to play an effective part in parliamentary politics. An obvious problem was finance. A party needed funds to campaign effectively and this was a special problem for a party that represented the poorest sections of society. In 1895, for example, the Independent Labour Party (ILP - see Section 2.1 below) put 27 candidates up for election. None was successful in a campaign obviously run on a shoe string:

'Nothing was so remarkable as the wonderful self-sacrifice which, in a period of trade depression, led a small section of the working class to raise an ILP election fund of nearly £6,000 at few weeks' notice.' (comment made by Keir Hardie in 1896)

If a working man was elected, then funds had to be found to support him in Parliament. It was not until 1911 that MPs were paid.

Interpretation

BOX 5.3 The franchise and an independent labour party

Many working men still had no vote - and of course no women at all could vote. Between 1885 and 1910, there were 89 constituencies which were predominantly working-class in character. That means that the vast majority of constituencies were not. In addition, there was the difficulty of staying on the electoral register. If working men lived in lodgings, went on poor relief or moved house (as they often did to follow work opportunities), then they often lost their right to vote. Further, there were practical problems that made it difficult for working men to use their newly acquired votes. For example, polling stations were sparse and polling hours rather inconvenient (8 am to 8 pm after 1884), so that most men were at work when the booths opened in the morning and had to hurry in to vote in the last half hour at night.
Adapted from Pugh 1993.

4. Lack of cohesion

As well as practical problems, there were more fundamental obstacles to overcome for those who were trying to form a separate labour party. The working class was by no means a cohesive force with a clearly defined set of aims. Working-class voters generally gave their support to one of the two main parties and had to be convinced that a new third party could be an effective vehicle for promoting their interests. Like other voters, they did not just focus on class issues and Liberal and Tory politicians were not slow to exploit their conflicting interests and prejudices. Some working-class voters would vote on religious or nationalist grounds. The Irish immigrant vote in Lancashire, for example, switched from Conservative to Liberal in 1886 when the Leader of the Irish Nationalists, Charles Stewart Parnell, urged voters to support Liberal candidates because the Liberal Party had promised to introduce an Irish Home Rule Bill (see Unit 6, pages 213-14). Others were deferential voters (they felt obliged to vote according to the wishes of their social 'superiors' - for example, many tenant farmers felt obliged to vote according to the wishes of their landlord) or were influenced by the policies offered by the main parties. McKenzie and Silver (1968) show that, between 1885 and 1918, the Conservative Party won substantial support from working-class voters.

5. The theory of removable inequalities

A further obstacle to support for a separate labour party was what the historian Geoffrey Best (1979) calls 'the theory of removable inequalities'. This was an attitude born of the very real mid-Victorian prosperity which stretched from the 1850s to the

1870s. It was a belief, carefully fostered by the governing classes, that, by hard work and self-help, anyone could rise up the social scale. Marxist historians have seen the same idea in rather different terms - they talk of an 'aristocracy of labour' aspiring to a bourgeois (middle-class) style of life (see Unit 4, Section 1.2). While this was an obstacle until the 1880s, there is the argument that, as the confidence in ever-increasing prosperity and economic and social advancement began to decline in the last two decades of the century, the policies of the two main parties began to look less appealing to trade unionists and other working people.

6. A suspicion of state intervention

Finally, there was the suspicion among some working people of state intervention. A key feature of socialist thought in Britain in the late 19th century was the belief that the capitalist system could only be changed radically through political action by the state. But, this did not always appeal to members of the working class. In the 19th century, there had been some steps away from liberal individualism. The social reforms of both Liberal and Conservative governments showed some acceptance of the need for state action to remedy grievances. Such action was, however, not always popular with those it was supposed to benefit - and for good, practical reasons. The Poor Law of 1834, for example, stood, from poor people's point of view, as a monument of inhumanity. Other, supposedly beneficial, social legislation also had serious side effects for poor people. These side effects made some working people suspicious of socialist views promoting state action, although, in the second half of the 19th century, attitudes did slowly begin to change.

1.3 What role did Keir Hardie play in the labour movement before 1893?

Keir Hardie's contribution

There is a consensus amongst historians that Keir Hardie played a key role in the development of an independent labour party. As one of his biographers puts it:
'Keir Hardie is, by any test, a decisive figure in the making of 20th century Britain. More than any other man, he was the maker of the modern Labour Party.' (Morgan 1975, p.viii)
Another biographer notes:
'He participated in what turned out to be every important event in Labour's official life: the strikes of the new unionism in the 1880s, the founding of the Scottish Labour Party in 1888, of the Independent Labour Party in 1893 and of the Labour Representation Committee (LRC) in 1900. He was there during the LRC's transformation in 1906 into the Labour Party in Parliament, when he acted briefly as Leader.' (Benn 1992, p.xvii)

Keir Hardie's early life

James Keir Hardie (1856-1915) was born the illegitimate son of a farm servant, Mary Keir, in Lanarkshire, Scotland in 1856. He took the name Keir (by which he is generally known) from his mother and his surname from the man his mother later married, a ship's carpenter called David Hardie. Historians agree that his upbringing was hard. Box 5.4 provides a typical account.

BOX 5.4   Keir Hardie's childhood

'As a child, he worked in the coal-pits near Hamilton. His education was extremely rudimentary. His mother taught him to read using scraps of newspaper she picked up in the street. He taught himself to write using a pin to scratch a stone blackened with the smoke of his pit lamp. As an adult, he became a skilled face worker and a leading trade unionist among Ayrshire miners. He was also a non-conformist, a teetotaller and a Liberal, working hard to persuade miners to vote Liberal when they were enfranchised in 1884.'

(Behagg 1991, pp.114-15)

Interpretation

Hardie's biographers (for example, Morgan 1975 and Benn 1992) agree that Hardie's religious conversion in 1877 (when he joined a non-conformist church), his dedication to self-education and his active support for temperance (avoidance of alcohol) were important in his early life, as was his early experience as a trade unionist. Hardie first became involved in trade union activity in 1878. The following year, he was sacked and 'blacklisted' (banned from working in all mines in the area) because of his union activity. But, he continued to work as a paid union official until 1881 (when the union collapsed after a series of unsuccessful strikes). Between 1881 and 1886, he worked as a journalist on a local newspaper. Then, in August 1886, he was appointed as Secretary of the newly-formed Ayrshire Miners' Union and, in October 1886, he became Secretary of the new Scottish Miners' Federation (which campaigned on behalf of miners' unions throughout Scotland).

The Mid-Lanarkshire by-election, 1888

In the early 1880s, Hardie supported and campaigned for the Liberals. In 1888, however, he made his first move away from the Liberal Party. According to Behagg (1991) and Benn (1992), two key factors explain this move:

1. When, in 1887, troops used a great deal of violence to break up a strike in which Hardie was involved, the Liberal press did not condemn the use of violence.

2. In 1887, Hardie visited Parliament and lobbied

for a Bill introducing an eight-hour working day. While he was there, he witnessed Lib-Lab MPs speaking in the Commons and became disillusioned at their lack of support for his campaign and at their apparent indifference to working-class concerns.

This disillusionment with the Liberal Party intensified after a by-election was called in Mid-Lanarkshire in 1888. Hardie's name was put forward as the miners' choice for Liberal candidate, but he was passed over in favour of a middle-class candidate. In response, he stood as an independent against the Liberal and Conservative candidates. Although he failed to be elected - he polled 617 votes, 8.3% of the vote - he claimed he had won a great victory. Morgan claims that the importance of the by-election was that:

'It riveted national attention on the theme of working-class representation as no previous contest had quite done.' (Morgan 1975, p.31)

The by-election also 'riveted national attention' on Keir Hardie himself and helped to launch his career as a national politician.

The Scottish Labour Party

A few weeks after the by-election, Hardie was involved in the setting up of the Scottish Labour Party - the first party in Britain to call itself a 'Labour Party'. Its aims were as follows:

'[The Scottish Labour Party] exists for the purpose of educating people politically and securing the return to Parliament and all local bodies of members pledged to its programme. If, therefore, anyone, peasant or peer is found willing to accept the programme and work with the party, his help will be gladly accepted.' (Keir Hardie writing in the *Miner*, September 1888)

Hardie was the Scottish Labour Party's Secretary. The party put forward five candidates in the general election of 1892 (none was elected) and, by 1893, had 23 branches. Benn notes:

'[The party] promoted Hardie's conviction that parties should have programmes and only those who support the programmes should stand in their name. It also forwarded the idea of independence from other parties.' (Benn 1992, p.62)

Although it remained weak, the Scottish Labour Party was a step towards a national independent labour party.

The 1892 general election

Following the Mid-Lanarkshire by-election, Keir Hardie became active outside Scotland. He toured the country speaking (he gained a great deal of publicity from his outspoken attacks on Lib-Lab MPs - see Activity 5.1 below) and spent a great deal of time in London. In 1890, he was persuaded to put his name forward as a candidate in West Ham. When the Liberal candidate was found dead in January 1892 (he committed suicide), the Liberal Party decided not to put up another candidate in the forthcoming general election, but to leave Hardie to fight the Conservative candidate. Hardie fought the election as candidate who had close ties with, but was independent from, the Liberal Party. He won the election, becoming the first independent working-class (labour) MP. Behagg notes that:

'Hardie's supporters in West Ham, largely New Unionists from the East End, sent him to Parliament in a two-horse charabanc [carriage] with a trumpeter to announce his progress. The Lib-Lab MPs had always been careful to appear in the House "properly" dressed in top hat and tails, but Hardie wore his ordinary clothes - a deerstalker hat and tweed suit...Hardie was simply making the point, that he was to stick to throughout his career, that independent labour MPs should retain their independence inside the House of Commons.' (Behagg 1991, p.115)

MAIN POINTS - Part 1

- The historical debate surrounding the emergence of the Labour Party focuses on three key questions - (1) who felt it necessary to establish a separate labour party and why? (2) what particular conditions existed at the birth of the LRC in 1900? and (3) what had prevented the party from emerging earlier?
- Most historians who have examined the Labour Party's origins begin their accounts in the 1880s, arguing that it was in this decade that four key developments took place - (1) the end of mid-Victorian economic confidence (2) the extension of the franchise (3) New Unionism and (4) the emergence of new Socialist groups.
- Three key socialist groups emerged in the 1880s - the Social Democratic Federation, the Socialist League

and the Fabian Society.
- Historians have identified six main obstacles to the setting up of an independent labour party - (1) the Lib-Labs (2) the narrowness of the franchise (3) finances (4) lack of cohesion in the working class (5) the theory of removable inequalities and (6) working-class suspicion of state intervention.
- Historians agree that Keir Hardie made an important contribution to the development of an independent labour party. By the time he gained election in 1892, he had reached the conclusion that working-class interests could only be promoted by independent labour MPs. Lib-Lab MPs, he argued, lacked sufficient independence.

Activity 5.1 Keir Hardie and the Lib-Labs

ITEM 1 Why the working class is divided

Keir Hardie

What keeps the workers divided? They are at one on labour questions. They all want to enjoy the full fruits of their toil. Many of them are good trade unionists and stand together when on strike. What is it that divides them at the poll? One goes to Church on Sunday and one goes to Chapel. That and nothing more. The chapel-goer wishes for **disestablishment**, the church-goer does not. Or one is a member of a **temperance society** and the other isn't. Or one is a North of Ireland Protestant and the other a South of Ireland Catholic. The questions which divide them are rarely matters of principle, being nearly always matters of personal opinion or belief. But the **politician on both sides** sees his chance therein, and fans the flames of religious bigotry. By thus keeping the workers divided against themselves, they ensure the perpetual rule of the landlord and the employer. Before the workers can conquer political power, they must cease fighting each other.

Adapted from an article by Keir Hardie in the journal 'Labour Leader', November 1896.

Glossary

- **disestablishment** - the removal of the ties between the Church of England and the state
- **temperance society** - society which promoted the avoidance of alcohol
- **politician on both sides** - ie belonging to the Conservative Party or Liberal Party

ITEM 2 An attack on Henry Broadhurst, a leading Lib-Lab MP

It is difficult to write calmly of a man like Mr Broadhurst. Whatever power he may have had in the political world has come solely from the belief that he was a representative of labour. As one who was a worker, he might be expected to know something about the needs of workers. The other day Mr Broadhurst had a motion before the House of Commons on the condition of the poor. When he came to put forward his remedies, he had nothing to propose except free education and one free meal a day for the poor children. What a proposal for such a serious problem. Little wonder members [MPs] laughed. Mr Broadhurst totally lacks qualification for the position he holds. So long as he holds the position of Secretary to the Parliamentary Committee of the TUC, he will be seen as the spokesman of trade unionists. I put it to members of our leading unions. Can they afford to pay a man £200 a year for misrepresenting their views?

Adapted from an article by Keir Hardie in the journal 'Labour Leader', April 1889.

ITEM 3 A by-election in Halifax, 1897

The Independent Labour Party, in conjunction with the Trades Council in Halifax, fixed upon Tom Mann as a candidate. There were two courses open to the Lib-Lab MPs - they could abstain from taking any part in the contest or they could support Tom Mann, the trade union nominee. But, they preferred a third course. The Lib-Lab MPs Henry Broadhurst, John Wilson and Charles Fenwick, together with some smaller fry, all took part in the contest in support of the Liberal lawyer and company owner, Mr Billson. They glorified him as the 'true friend of the worker'. As a result of their efforts, Tom Mann was defeated. Some say they supported Mr Billson because Mann had no chance of winning. Others say Mann would have been powerless as an independent labour member. But, he reserved to himself a freedom to fight for labour - against both parties if necessary. The Lib-Labs put the interests of a political party before the interests of labour. What is the explanation of it all? If the workers allow their representatives to be returned as the nominees of any political party, the price will be the betrayal of the cause of labour when that conflicts with the claims of party.

From a speech made by Keir Hardie after the Halifax by-election in 1897.

Questions

1. a) What do Items 1-3 tell us about Keir Hardie's views?
   b) Using Items 1-3, give the arguments for and against setting up a separate and independent labour party.
2. Why did no separate and independent labour party

   exist before 1900? Use Items 1 and 2 in your answer.
3. What do Items 1 and 3 tell us about voting behaviour in the late 19th century?
4. How might Henry Broadhurst have replied to the attack made on him by Keir Hardie in Item 2?

2 From Independent Labour Party to Labour Party

Key questions

1. What role did the ILP play in the 1890s?

2. Why did union opposition to a separate labour party soften after 1895?

3. What progress had the LRC made by 1906?

4. Did the 1906 general election establish Labour as a distinctive third party in British politics?

2.1 What role did the ILP play in the 1890s?

The Independent Labour Party (ILP)

Of all the socialist organisations to emerge after 1880, the Independent Labour Party (ILP), founded in 1893, was the one which pushed hardest to set up a separate parliamentary party to represent the labour movement. Members of the ILP were socialists, but they had no time at all for the revolutionary path supported by Marx and Engels. There is even a debate as to whether Keir Hardie (who became President of the ILP) can accurately be described as a socialist (see Box 5.5).

The ILP was formed as a result of a growing feeling of frustration at the inability of the established parties (especially the Liberal Party) to take up and address labour (ie working-class) concerns. The main pressure for a separate labour party, however, came from below:

'The ILP grew from the bottom upwards. It was not

BOX 5.5 Keir Hardie and socialism

Whether or not Keir Hardie can be described as a socialist in the 1890s has been much debated. Some authors (such as, Morgan 1975 and 1992) argue that he remained, at heart, a radical Liberal who learned to cooperate with socialists without ever becoming completely convinced by socialism. Others (such as Reid 1978), however, argue that he genuinely did become a socialist and did so because of his experience of attempting to work with Liberals. This experience showed him that working-class concerns would never be resolved by Liberalism.
Adapted from Benn 1992.

the creation of a few would-be leaders. It was the result of a range of initiatives taken in communities by men and women, in each case responding to the opportunities and difficulties posed by their local environment.' (Howell 1994, p.93)

David Howell has traced these local pressures from Scotland in 1888 to the Yorkshire woollen towns and Lancashire cotton areas in the early 1890s. Such initiatives were encouraged by Joseph Burgess, a cotton worker turned journalist, in his weekly paper the *Workman's Times*.

Collaboration with trade unions

The key to the eventual success of the drive for an independent party was the collaboration between socialists and trade unionists. In the early 1890s, circumstances ensured that this collaboration should become established. An important spark was the Manningham Mills strike in Bradford in 1890-91. This is described in Box 5.6.

BOX 5.6 The Manningham Mills strike

When the employers at the mills imposed wage cuts of 25%, the workers went on strike. The employers, however, were supported by Liberals on the local council and it was they who attempted to prevent the strikers holding public meetings in the town. The lessons learned from this strike were spelled out by Fred Jowett in 1892 (Jowett later became the first Labour MP for Bradford in 1906 and was a minister in the first Labour government of 1924): 'In the strike, the people of Bradford saw plainly, as they have never seen before, that, whether their rulers are Liberal or Tory, they are capitalists first and politicians afterwards'. As a consequence of the strike, a Labour Union was set up in Bradford, followed by many others throughout the North and Scotland in 1891-92. These Labour Unions then organised campaigns for local and, in 1892, parliamentary seats.
Adapted from Laybourn 1997.

Interpretation

The general election of 1892

The first national breakthrough came when Keir Hardie was elected as the first ever independent Labour MP in the 1892 general election (see Section 1.3 above). Two other 'independent' Labour MPs were elected (John Burns in London and Joseph Havelock Wilson in Middlesbrough), but they both received help from the Liberals. Also in the 1892 general election, the trade union leader, Ben Tillett, narrowly lost to the dominant Liberal figure in Bradford, gaining 2,749 votes (he came third, but only 500 votes separated the top three candidates).

Pelling argues that the election of independent labour candidates provided an important opportunity:

'Discounting Wilson [who became, in effect, a Liberal], the leadership of the independent movement rested on Burns and Hardie. The parliamentary limelight was on them, and the development of a national organisation in time for the next election depended on their initiative.' (Pelling 1965, p.107)

Inside Parliament, however, this opportunity was not taken. There appears to have been a clash of personalities between Hardie and Burns and a difference of approach. Moore says that Burns became 'to all intents and purposes a Lib-Lab' (1978, p.50) while Pelling notes that, unlike other independent MPs, 'Hardie became more independent instead of less so after his election' (1965, p.109). Benn argues:

'Before the three-year term was out, it was particularly clear that the 'labour' contingent of 15 [12 Lib-Labs and three independent labour MPs] had lost any coherence. Hardie did not expect anything from the 12 Lib-Labs, but he did from the two elected as independents, John Burns and J. Havelock Wilson. Wilson was still pursuing trade union causes outside Parliament and Burns still considered himself a leader of labour inside. Yet there was increasingly less cooperation with Hardie and Hardie made little attempt to coordinate his own activity with theirs.' (Benn 1992, p.123)

Outside Parliament, however, Hardie worked closely with those who supported the formation of a national party which would promote working-class representation in Parliament. It is from this work that the ILP emerged.

The formation of the ILP, 1893

Benn (1992) claims that, in 1888, a number of delegates (possibly including Keir Hardie) had discussed the setting up of a national independent labour party at the annual TUC conference, but the decision had been made that the time was not right. The initiative which actually led to the setting up of the ILP was made by Joseph Burgess:

'On 30 April 1892, he invited all readers [of the *Workman's Times*] who wished to join to send their names and addresses. The names, he promised, would be sorted by constituencies and local sympathisers would be put in touch with one another with a view to the formation of branches. By the middle of September, over 2,000 names had been sent in and the process of forming local branches was well advanced.' (Pelling 1965, p.109)

At the TUC annual conference held in September 1892, a preliminary meeting was held of independent labour supporters and Keir Hardie was elected to the chair. It was at this meeting that a decision was made to call a conference in Bradford in January 1893. Bradford was chosen because:

- W.H. Drew, an activist from Bradford, had written to Burgess warning him that supporters in the provinces would not accept a national organisation dominated by London and suggested that, instead, supporters come to Bradford (Pelling 1965)
- it was a 'natural venue' because it was an independent labour stronghold (Morgan 1975).

Pelling argues that Hardie's role was crucial in shaping the new organisation:

'The national conference was at last arranged, principally as the result of the work of Burgess, Hardie and Drew. Although Hardie had no direct part in the work of the provisional committee, his views were given full weight and the structure of the party was largely built on the lines he envisaged....

He argued that it should be built on the model of the TUC - there should be a National Executive, to correspond to the TUC parliamentary committee and it should be charged with the duty of carrying out the decisions of conference.' (Pelling 1965, p.113)

Delegates were invited from the local branches set up as a result of Burgess's initiative, the Fabian Society and other socialist societies:

'In total there were about 120 delegates who came mainly from the industrial North of England and Scotland and there were no delegates from Ireland, Wales and from the southern part of England except for London, Chatham and Plymouth.' (Laybourn 1997, p.31)

Keir Hardie was the only MP present and he was elected to chair the conference by 54 votes to 27. The contents of his keynote speech are described in Box 5.7.

BOX 5.7 Keir Hardie's keynote address, January 1893

Interpretation

Hardie demanded the formation of an independent party drawn from the ranks of the working class. Its object should be 'economic freedom - the natural outcome of political enfranchisement'. A socialist resolution calling for a programme of state ownership was adopted almost unanimously. On the other hand, the programme as a whole did not exclude radical Liberals and trade unionists. The overwhelming majority of the items on the new party programme were part and parcel of the standard advanced radicalism of the day:

- social policies, such as the eight-hour working day and the abolition of piecework, sweated and child labour
- political policies, such as the payment of MPs, shorter Parliaments, universal adult suffrage and the use of referendums
- economic policies, such as the introduction of a system of graduated income tax and the abolition of indirect taxation.

On all the key decisions of the conference, Hardie's influence was decisive. He took the lead in demanding that local groups should be able to become affiliated to the national organisation, allowing a wide range of groups to be embraced in the ILP. He also successfully argued against the proposal that ILP members be prevented from voting for sympathetic (ie working-class Liberal) candidates in local elections. He successfully ensured that the title Independent Labour Party was adopted rather than the Socialist Labour Party. At the second annual ILP conference, he was elected President of the ILP by an overwhelming majority and retained the position for six years.
Adapted from Morgan 1975.

The ILP's 'socialism'

Behagg (1991) suggests that, although the ILP had a socialist programme, the brand of socialism it promoted was distinctively British. This, he argues, was due to three key influences:

- the Liberal Party - many of the ILP's leaders were former Liberals who had become disillusioned with the Liberal Party (James Ramsay MacDonald, the future first Labour Prime Minister, is an example - he spent four years working as private secretary to a Liberal MP before joining the ILP)
- the trade unions - many of the ILP's leaders had trade union experience
- the non-conformist churches - many of the ILP's leaders had a background in the non-conformist churches.

The result, Behagg claims, was a type of socialism which:

- rejected the revolutionary 'class war' approach
- supported the parliamentary route to socialism
- developed a programme with practical, realistic aims
- stressed its moderation in the hope of appealing to the trade unions
- drew heavily on Christian values and biblical references
- generated an almost religious enthusiasm amongst its grass-roots supporters.

This British version of socialism was promoted by the *Clarion*, a newspaper set up by Robert Blatchford in 1891. By the end of the 1890s, the *Clarion* had become the voice of the ILP and was selling around 80,000 copies per issue. In addition, a Clarion movement (see Box 5.8 on page 159) developed to spread the 'religion of socialism':

'They constructed their own world, now sadly gone for ever, of socialist Sunday Schools, labour churches and Clarion Cycling Clubs...An early member of the Clarion Cycling Club, Tom Groom, recalled many years later: "The *Clarion* had made socialists of us all; it was the *Clarion* which brought us all together; it was the *Clarion* which had inspired the socialist movement with that spirit of cheerfulness and fellowship which was so badly needed."' (Fowler 1997, p.25)

This cultivation of socialism at the grass roots was an important part of the work of the ILP. It ensured that ordinary members of the party - whatever the views expressed by the leadership - supported a socialist line. Although some historians (notably Tanner 1990) have argued that this made little impact on the development of the labour movement, others claim that the contribution of the ILP was crucial:

'The ILP was far more important in the growth of socialism in Britain and in the emergence of the Labour Party than has often been supposed...The ILP played a vital role in the early development of the Labour Party, even though its importance diminished rapidly after 1914.' (Laybourn 1997, pp.36, 38)

BOX 5.8 The Clarion movement

This photo shows one of the ILP's Clarion vans that toured round Britain promoting socialism.

Despite early setbacks (for example, Keir Hardie losing his seat in the 1895 general election), the distinctive grass-roots socialism of a third party developed, as E.P. Thompson put it, 'amongst the mills, brickyards and gasworks of the West Riding'. Like the suffragettes of the same period, the early ILP members were keen on using state-of-the-art communication techniques. The gospel of labour was preached from touring Clarion vans (named after the ILP's newspaper) with Clarion cyclists riding on ahead to give advance notice. There was the socialist Sunday School movement where members learnt a socialist version of the Ten Commandments including 'Love learning which is the food of the mind'. There was also the Masses Film and Theatre Guild and a stream of books, pamphlets and summer schools. By means such as this, the ILP sought to bolster electoral activity with 'comradeship, commitment and fun'. One early ILP activist, Stella Davies, wrote in her memoirs: 'There was a tradition that one Clarion group had pasted some posters on a herd of cows in a field...We scrawled slogans in chalk on barns and farmhouse walls and sang "England, arise, the long, long night is over" outside pubs and on village greens.'
Adapted from ILP 1993.

Membership of the ILP

Membership of the ILP grew rapidly between 1893 and 1895. Laybourn (1997) claims that the 200 clubs and branches in 1893 had risen to over 400 in 1894 and the total number of members grew to 35-50,000 in 1895. The ILP directory published in early 1895 (and, therefore, showing the position in 1894) shows that, of 300 branches listed:

- 100 were in Yorkshire
- over 70 were in Lancashire and Cheshire
- 40 were in Scotland (the Scottish Labour Party dissolved itself into the ILP in 1894)

- 30 were in London
- the vast majority of those remaining were in the Midlands and North East.

Since Wales, Ireland, the South East and South West had very few branches, Pelling concludes:

'The party had its upper- and middle-class members, who might belong to any part of the country; but primarily it was an industrial party with a definite local bias - first of all in the woollen areas, then in the cotton towns, and thirdly, to some extent, in the more scattered engineering districts of England.' (Pelling 1965, p.163)

It was, therefore, a provincial rather than a national party. It differed from other socialist groups because it was a genuinely working-class party which did not have the core of its support in London.

Women supporters

It should be noted that the ILP had many women supporters. Laybourn notes that:

'Women were allowed to be full members of ILP branches, which was not the case in the Tory and Liberal Party branches at that time.' (Laybourn 1997, p.35)

But, he also points out that the extent to which the ILP supported first-wave feminism has been questioned. Emmeline Pankhurst and her daughters, for example, left the ILP after becoming disillusioned with it (see Unit 3, Section 3.1).

Drawbacks

Although the ILP grew rapidly between 1893 and 1895 and, although expectations were high when the 1895 general election was called, the party suffered from two key drawbacks:

- many of its supporters were too young to vote or did not qualify to vote
- without the formal backing of the trade unions, it lacked resources and faced the opposition of Lib-Labs.

The general election of 1895

In the general election of 1895, the ILP experienced a major setback. It put up 28 candidates, but all were defeated (including Keir Hardie). The new party did not have the resources to fight a successful campaign and disappointed members drifted away.

The poor performance of ILP candidates in 1895 underlined the view of leaders like Keir Hardie that it was essential for the future of labour politics that an alliance be formed with the trade unions. Keir Hardie's point of view was clear and consistent:

'It must be evident to everyone that no labour movement can ever hope to succeed in this country without the cooperation of the trade unions...Some of us have held the opinion from the beginning that it was possible to make trade unionism and ILPism interchangeable terms for electoral purposes.' (Keir Hardie writing in 1897, quoted in Phillips 1992, p.6)

2.2 Why did union opposition to a separate labour party soften after 1895?

Opposition from Lib-Lab trade unionists

The biggest problem for the ILP in the period 1895-1900 was the opposition of the Lib-Lab leaders of the trade unions. Far from cooperating with the ILP, the 'old guard' leaders actively tried to keep socialist influences out of the TUC (many of the 'old guard' were supporters of, or members of, the Liberal Party). In 1894, the union leader and leading member of the ILP, Tom Mann, stood for the post of Secretary of the TUC. He failed to be elected, but gained around a third of the total votes. This showed that the ILP was making headway in the TUC, The response of the TUC was to introduce a block vote system, designed to strengthen the power of large unions (such as the coal and cotton unions) which were opposed to a separate labour party (see Box 5.9).

BOX 5.9 | The introduction of block voting in the TUC

Interpretation

A large number of TUC delegates who supported the ILP in 1894 were the delegates of Trades Councils (see Unit 4, page 120 for a definition). It could be argued, however, that Trades Councils had no right to be represented at Congress. To allow them at all was to duplicate the representation of their members since members of Trades Councils were also members of trade unions. To exclude them would be to sacrifice little (as far as the 'old guard' was concerned) since the Trades Councils had virtually no financial strength of their own. In 1894, therefore, a group on the TUC's Parliamentary Committee, alarmed by the growing strength of the socialists, drew up new standing orders. The new orders introduced a new voting system. This gave delegates from the unions votes proportional to the number of their members - the so-called 'block vote'. In addition, the Trades Councils were excluded altogether, and no delegate was admitted who was not either a working trade unionist or an official of a union.
Adapted from Pelling 1965.

The acceptance of this rule-change in 1895 meant that:

- the number of socialist delegates to the TUC dropped by a quarter
- an ILP member, Ben Tillett, lost his place on the TUC's Parliamentary Committee (he was voted off the Committee by the big unions' block vote)
- Keir Hardie was prevented from attending the TUC since he was no longer a union official (he never attended the TUC after 1895)

- the TUC was dominated by the massive card votes of the Miners' Federation and the cotton unions - which opposed a separate labour party.

Yet, in spite of such opposition to the ILP in the mid-1890s, the 1890s ended with a proposal coming from the TUC that a special conference be held for the purpose of securing 'a better representation of the interests of labour in the House of Commons'. Historians argue that this change of heart resulted from four key developments.

1. Setbacks for the unions in the 1890s

During the 1890s, employers launched an onslaught on the unions, forming associations and federations which were strong enough to take them on (see also Unit 4, Section 2.4). The defeat of the Amalgamated Society of Engineers (ASE) after a lockout was organised in 1897-98 by the Federation of Engineering Employers, for example, was a great shock to the union movement:

'It was a humiliating set-back for a union which was still regarded as the foremost in the country.' (Pelling 1963, p.113)

In addition, the unions suffered a series of legal setbacks. These threatened two areas which trade unionists thought had been settled in the 1870s:

- the liability of their funds for damages arising out of industrial action
- the right to peaceful picketing.

Conservative governments between 1885 and 1905 positively encouraged such legal challenges against the unions and played up the threat of militant socialism.

2. Lack of support in Parliament

As well as their industrial vulnerability, the unions' political weakness was exposed. The Liberals were out of power for all but three years between 1886 and 1905 and labour's voice in Parliament was feeble. The number of Lib-Lab MPs remained small in number - there were 13 after the 1892 election and only 11 after 1898. A Labour Electoral Association (LEA), set up by the TUC in 1887 to increase the number of Lib-Lab trade union MPs, made little progress:

'The LEA met with little success in attempting to get support for Lib-Lab candidates at both municipal and parliamentary elections. The Liberal Party would not respond to the challenge...The fact is that the LEA got nowhere and the organisation and its members were accused of not being truly representative of the working classes.' (Laybourn 1997, p.27)

3. Growing annoyance with the Liberals

The Liberal Party's reluctance to back working-class candidates became an increasing source of annoyance to the growing number of trade unionists with political ambitions. By the mid-1890s, over 600 trade unionists sat on local councils or other bodies, yet the number of Lib-Lab MPs rose slowly:

'The Liberal Party was patently unwilling to adopt parliamentary candidates from a working-class background. The objections arose, not from the party's national organisers, but from its constituency associations, usually dominated by middle-class clientele and preferring to put forward someone who had money to spend on elections and other political activities.' (Phillips 1992, p.9)

4. Divisions in the Liberal Party

In 1886, a group of Liberal MPs led by Joseph Chamberlain left the Liberal Party and joined the Conservatives in protest at Gladstone's support for Home Rule for Ireland. This was a blow for working-class Liberals because, a year previously, Chamberlain had launched a radical programme designed to encourage working-class voters to vote Liberal. By the time that Gladstone resigned in 1894, the split in the Liberal Party had not healed:

'After Gladstone's retirement as premier in 1894, his party had entered a period of internal dissension. It was heavily beaten in the election of 1895 and there seemed no prospect of it recovering a parliamentary majority in the foreseeable future. It could thus do little practically to further the interests of the unions whether in the field of labour law or social policy.' (Phillips 1992, p.9)

The ILP, on the other hand, had a programme of welfare reform designed to appeal to trade unionists who had previously supported the Liberal Party. The old ties with the Liberals were hard for many trade unionists to break, but an increasing number began to consider the possibility of a separate labour party.

Keir Hardie and the ILP 1895-1900

The years 1895-1900 were difficult for both the ILP and for Keir Hardie. Out of Parliament and out of the TUC, Hardie made his living and tried to maintain the campaign for an independent labour party which had close ties with unions through his speaking tours and journalism. Within the ILP, there was a struggle between those who supported closer cooperation with the SDF and those (including Hardie) who opposed such a strategy - a struggle which Hardie's faction won in 1897. In addition, Moore (1978) shows that, while membership of the ILP grew between 1896 and 1898 (after declining rapidly in 1895), it then declined rapidly after 1898. Hardie's biographer, Caroline Benn (1992) describes the period from the 1895 general election to the formation of the LRC in 1900 as years of 'defeat and depression'.

The formation of the LRC

The campaigning of Keir Hardie and other leading ILP members made some impact on some unions. Morgan (1975) notes, for example, that support for

the ILP grew in the Amalgamated Society of Railway Servants (ASRS) and the National Union of Boot and Shoe Operatives. But, historians agree that it was the legal and other attacks on the trade unions outlined above that were decisive in the conversion of the trade unions to the idea of an independent labour party. In 1899, the ASRS put forward a proposal to the TUC proposing that 'all cooperative, socialistic, trade union and other working organisations' should attend a special conference to 'secure a better representation of the interests of labour in the House of Commons'. The proposal was passed by a narrow

BOX 5.10 The LRC

The 129 delegates who met in February 1900 in response to the TUC's resolution came from the socialist societies and 67 trade unions representing about a quarter of total trade union membership at the time. The conference was a resounding success for the ILP. It was able to steer the delegates between the 'class war' supported by the SDF and the desire of some trade unions to limit the parliamentary actions of working-class MPs to particular issues. Keir Hardie's resolution to create an organisation that would support a 'distinct Labour group in Parliament who shall have their own whips and agree upon their own policy' was accepted. He would have liked this to be called the 'United Labour Party' but the conference opted for 'Labour Representation Committee'. An ILP man, Ramsay MacDonald, was elected Secretary. There were a number of characteristics in its origins which determined the sort of party it would be. First, it had emerged from a trade union initiative and union support would be important in the future. Second, it contained within it socialist organisations of various kinds, but its manifesto was not openly socialist. A new word began to be used - 'socialistic', meaning generally sympathetic to the broad aims of socialism but not too firm in support of state ownership. The LRC was socialistic and Hardie was prepared to accept this compromise in order to retain union support. This was too much for the SDF which soon left. And third, many LRC activists had close links with the Liberal Party and the LRC was open to any political alliance that would assist the election of its candidates without compromising their independence. So, the LRC was drawn from groups which were prepared to sink their differences and achieve a common goal. But, while there were links between these different groups, there were also tensions which would not go away.
Adapted from Behagg 1991.

majority - 546,000 votes to 434,000. Seven major unions and many smaller ones supported the motion, while two of the largest unions, the miners and cotton workers, opposed it.

The TUC resolution of 1899 led to a conference being held in London in February 1900. A total of 129 delegates attended, representing:

- some trade unions
- the ILP
- the Fabians
- the SDF.

It was at this conference that the Labour Representation Committee (LRC) was set up (see Box 5.10 on page 161).

Hardie, MacDonald and the LRC

There is a tradition (stemming from Philip Snowden who later became Chancellor of the Exchequer in the first Labour government - see Snowden 1934) that Keir Hardie and Ramsay MacDonald drafted the ASRS motion which resulted in the formation of the LRC. Most contemporary historians deny this, however, accepting that it was drawn up by Thomas R. Steels, a member of the union's Doncaster branch as well as being a member of the ILP.

Hardie and MacDonald may not have been responsible for drawing up the resolution, but they played an important part in the conference which followed. MacDonald (with Hardie's agreement) drew up proposals for the conference which, Benn (1992) argues, were difficult for the unions to disagree with:

- unions were to run and pay for their own candidates, as were other groups such as the ILP, SDF and Fabians
- the only two things that any union had to agree in return were that such candidates would stand independently of all other parties and that the LRC would have a political committee.

These proposals were accepted at the conference.

There is general agreement among historians (as suggested in Box 5.10) that the conference was a triumph for the ILP in general and for Keir Hardie in particular. Faced with an SDF motion binding the conference to socialism and 'class war', Hardie proposed a compromise amendment which was accepted. This, it is often said, was the most important of the conference. The key passage was that which stated there should be:

'A distinct Labour group in Parliament, who shall have their own whips and agree upon their policy, which must embrace a readiness to cooperate with any party which, for the time being may be engaged in promoting legislation in the direct interests of labour, and be equally ready to associate themselves with any party in opposing measures having an opposite tendency.'

A further 'triumph' for the ILP was the decision to reduce the size of the LRC's executive committee from 18 to 12, made up of:

- seven trade union delegates (down from the 12 delegates originally proposed)
- two ILP delegates
- two SDF delegates
- one Fabian delegate (down from the two originally proposed).

This reduction ensured that, if two or more trade unionists were socialists, then the socialists would have a majority on the committee. This suited the ILP:

'As [the Fabian, George Bernard] Shaw noted later with his usual mischievous eye, "if the LRC had been democratically established", the trade unions "would have swept out all the socialists and replaced them with...Conservative or Lib-Lab members". But, it was not. Warring trade union and socialist interests were resolved by reducing both TUC and Fabian representation, leaving the ILP with more places than before.' (Benn 1992, p.157)

MAIN POINTS - Sections 2.1-2.2

- Of all the socialist organisations to emerge after 1880, the Independent Labour Party (ILP), founded in 1893, was the one which pushed hardest for an independent parliamentary party which had close ties with the unions.
- The Manningham Mill strike of 1890-91 and Keir Hardie's election to Parliament in 1892 paved the way for the formation of the ILP in 1893. The first national conference of the ILP was held in Bradford.
- Keir Hardie played a key role in the ILP. He shaped its organisation and approach and remained its Leader throughout the 1890s.
- Although the ILP had a socialist programme, its brand was distinctively British because many of the ILP's leaders - (1) were former Liberals (2) had trade

union experience and (3) had a background in the non-conformist churches. As a result, their socialism was moderate and heavily influenced by Christianity.
- Union opposition to an independent labour party softened at the end of the 1890s because of - (1) attacks on unions' legal status (2) lack of union support in Parliament (3) growing annoyance with the Liberal Party and (4) splits in the Liberal Party.
- Following the passing of an ASRS proposal at the 1899 TUC, a special conference was held in London in February 1900. This was attended by some trade unions, the ILP, the Fabians and the SDF. It was at this conference that the Labour Representation Committee (LRC) was set up.

Activity 5.2 The ILP

ITEM 1 The ILP's viewpoint

Liberalism, even in its most advanced form, is a quarter of a century in the rear of the requirements of the times. It is not true, as has been asserted, that **Liberation** has been achieved and that a period of building up has set in. The cry is still for freedom. Men are conscious of being **held in thrall** by an iron set of circumstances which **fell them** at every turn. They are free to hold any or no religious belief. They are free to vote or abstain from voting. But, they are not free to labour. They are not free to live the life they feel stirring within. The means of existence are owned by others and are used to add to the wealth of the nation at the expense of the life of the people. The ILP is the outcome of all this. It

An ILP membership certificate signed by Keir Hardie.

sees and **chafes at the impotency** of Liberalism either to deal in drastic fashion with political reforms, or even to understand the new desire for economic freedom. Its members look on the untilled land and the unemployed and ask: 'Why are these **complements** not brought together? They see their aged poor suffering the indignities of our inhuman Poor Laws and themselves hurrying on to a like fate, and Liberalism has no word of hope or cheer. They are impatient of injustice and wrong. They feel that, were they in power, these things would cease. The aim of the ILP is to create a genuinely independent party in politics to take charge of the revolution which economic conditions are leading us toward; and its object is to build up an **industrial commonwealth** in which none will suffer want because of the over-abundance of others.

> ### Glossary
>
> - **Liberation** - freedom
> - **held in thrall** - enslaved
> - **fell them** - knock them down
> - **chafes at the impotency** - is annoyed at the powerlessness
> - **complements** - ie two parts of a whole
> - **industrial commonwealth** - ie economic system

Part of an article written by Keir Hardie and published in the 'New Review' in March 1893.

ITEM 2 The ILP's early years (1)

By 1893, Hardie's long-term ambition was the formation of a broad-based labour alliance which brought the socialists and trade unionists together in the promotion of labour causes. But, in the frustrating years 1896-98, nothing seemed less likely to emerge. Later, Hardie and his followers gave the impression that there was something inevitable about coalition which emerged and many historians have followed this line. In fact, the idea of a labour alliance made only halting progress until the end of 1898 and Hardie's erratic efforts to promote an alliance made slight impact. He himself was now almost wholly detached from the trade union world. He was pleasantly surprised when he saw a genuine worker reading his journal *Labour Leader* on Preston railway station. He had resigned as Secretary of the Ayrshire Miners in 1891 and did not attend the TUC after 1895. He himself was suspect in some trade union circles. After all, as manager of the *Labour Leader*, he was something of a capitalist employer himself. Opponents in the SDF in West Ham campaigned against his candidature forcing him, eventually (in April 1899), to withdraw in favour of Will

This photograph shows the ILP's executive council in 1899. From left on the front row - J. Bruce Glasier, J. Keir Hardie (Chair), H. Russell Smart, P. Snowden. From left on the back row - J. Ramsay MacDonald, J. Burgess, J. Parker, J. Penny (Secretary), F. Littlewood (Treasurer).

Thorne (leader of the Gasworkers and a member of West Ham council for several years). If Hardie was isolated at this time, so in many ways was the ILP. By 1898, the revolutionary passion of its early years was waning. It was losing its capacity to reflect working-class opinion, despite the growth of ILP representation amongst unions such as the Railway Servants and Boot and Shoe Operatives. The key figures on the executive were not workers - John Bruce Glasier, an unsuccessful artist and designer; Philip Snowden, once a minor civil servant; Ramsay MacDonald, who had begun a course at university (something which only upper- or middle-class people generally did - see Box 5.11 below). All were basically journalists. None was in a union. The ILP's membership was in decline. Its by-election record was disappointing. What provided the key to the new political transformation and suddenly lent relevance to Hardie's tireless crusading was the embittered industrial climate of the late 1890s.

Adapted from Morgan 1975.

ITEM 3 The ILP's early years (2)

The ILP was a cultural as well as a political movement. Indeed, the importance of club life can never be overestimated since, as the *Bradford Labour Echo* put it on 1 January 1898, it 'awakened and developed the self-governing powers of the members'. Club activities were regarded as a 'way of life'. Many clubs ran Sunday lectures and classes in singing, dancing, elocution and political economy. The Labour Church movement overlapped with the club life of many ILP supporters. About 80 Labour churches emerged, though most were small and short-lived. Many socialist Sunday schools also emerged. These were seen as training schools for the future generation of socialists and they developed the 'Socialist Ten Commandments' which focused on respect for all. The fourth commandment was 'Honour good men, be courteous to all men, bow down to none'. Underpinning the ILP clubs, the Labour churches and the socialist Sunday schools was the Clarion movement. Some leading members of the ILP were critical of clubs and social organisations which appeared to spend little time on political activity. The *Labour Leader* of 3 June 1894 reports that Keir Hardie, speaking to the new Labour Club in Leicester 'warned them against turning the club into a lounge for loafers' as was likely to be the case 'when liquor was sold'. Similarly, John Bruce Glasier was critical of the Darwen Club and suggested in his diary that 'some of the men obviously are members merely for the "booze" and have a bad reputation as fathers and husbands'. Yet, there is no doubting that the Clarion movement added to the general mood of debate about socialism in the 1890s.

Adapted from Laybourn 1997.

Questions

1. a) What do Items 1-3 tell us about the nature of the ILP in the late 1890s?
   b) Why did the ILP fail to make an electoral breakthrough before 1900?
   c) What part did the ILP play in the birth of the Labour Party?
2. a) Using Item 1, explain why the ILP was set up in 1893.
   b) What does this item tell us about the views and approach of Keir Hardie?

3. a) Judging from Item 2 and your own knowledge, what problems did Keir Hardie face after his defeat in the general election of 1895?
   b) What happened to change his political fortunes?
4. Look at Item 3
   a) Why do you think ILP clubs organised cultural and social activities?
   b) What does this item tell us about the type of socialism promoted by the ILP?

2.3 What progress had the LRC made by 1906?

Two key factors
In order to explain the LRC's electoral breakthrough in 1906, historians point to two main factors:
- the impact of the Taff Vale Judgement
- the secret Lib-Lab Pact of 1903.

1. The impact of the Taff Vale Judgement
Before the Taff Vale Judgement, the LRC was very weak. In 1901, those trade unions which did affiliate with it represented only 17% of all trade unionists, with about 350,000 members in total. The Cooperative Movement decided not to join and, in 1901, the SDF withdrew. Funds were practically non-existent and affiliated unions were under no obligation to provide financial aid:

'The organisation formed in February 1900 was weak and impoverished..Even the unions which had voted for its formation in 1899 were in some cases slow to attach themselves. The new party of labour seemed to represent only a small and marginal element of the labour movement as a whole. It began life without accommodation or paid officials.' (Phillips 1992, p.11)

Thorpe (1997) suggests that the LRC's first Secretary, Ramsay MacDonald (see Box 5.11 below), was appointed partly because he was a good organiser, but also because his wife was wealthy and so he was able to work for nothing.

Moore, however, suggests that the appointment of MacDonald was an important factor in the LRC's subsequent success. He says that MacDonald performed 'very real and vital services to the infant Labour Party' and 'provided a very necessary element of subtlety and finesse'. MacDonald's approach was different from that of Keir Hardie, but the two men had similar goals:

'Hardie had all along sought to secure the position of Secretary for MacDonald and invariably backed him to the hilt in his determination to establish the LRC on a firm basis. Apart from the maintenance of independence, this was to be achieved in two ways: first by winning over the large sections of the trade union world that were still sceptical about the new party; secondly, by opening up some line of communication with the Liberals. Although Hardie insisted on independence, he had been particularly careful not to close the door on the idea of cooperation, while MacDonald saw it was essential to secure some working arrangement if the LRC were to make headway.' (Moore 1978, p.84)

BOX 5.11 **Ramsay MacDonald (1866-1937)**

Biography Box

Like Keir Hardie, James Ramsay MacDonald was a Scot whose mother was unmarried when she gave birth to him. His mother worked as a domestic servant and then as a dressmaker. MacDonald was educated first at home and then at school. Scholastic success - in biology - brought him to London and he started a course at Birkbeck College before dropping out and moving to Bristol. He worked as a clerk and then as an agent for a Liberal MP, hoping to become a Liberal-backed MP. At first, he did not join the ILP. But, the Liberal Party choice of a middle-class manufacturer rather than a trade unionist (as promised) for the Attercliffe by-election in 1894 was the final straw. MacDonald realised that he would never be chosen as a candidate and he decided to leave the Liberal Party and join the ILP. The following year, he met and married Margaret Gladstone, daughter of a Liberal professor of Chemistry - an educated, middle-class socialist with an independent income. Margaret gave MacDonald emotional and financial security. MacDonald built up a reputation for being a good organiser and was elected to the ILP executive. Then, in 1900, he became the first Secretary of the LRC. He became an MP in 1906 and Leader of the Parliamentary Labour Party in 1911. He resigned the post in 1914 because he opposed Britain's involvement in the First World War and he lost his seat in 1918. Nevertheless, he returned to Parliament in 1922 and regained the leadership of the party. In 1924, he became the first Labour Prime Minister. *Adapted from Benn 1992 and Gardiner & Wenborn 1995.*

The 1900 general election

The 'weak and impoverished' state of the LRC helps to explain the difficulties it faced at the general election which was called just eight months after its formation in October 1900. The LRC had no time to prepare a proper campaign. Labour issues were not prominent in an atmosphere of flag-waving patriotism whipped up over the Boer War. Also, there was virtually no money with which to fight the campaign:

'The total LRC expenditure on the 1900 general election amounted to only £33.' (Pelling 1991, p.10)

The LRC put up 15 candidates. Two were victorious - Keir Hardie and Richard Bell, the ASRS Leader. Moore (1978) notes that both candidates had the advantage of extra funds from private sources (Bell spent £900 in his campaign, while Hardie was given a donation of £150 by the chocolate manufacturer George Cadbury). Also, Keir Hardie's election - to the constituency of Merthyr Tydfil - was by no means a victory for labour politics. Rather, it was a reflection of the strong anti-Boer War feeling amongst the miners in that constituency (see also Unit 7, Section 1.2 for attitudes towards the Boer War). Hardie, like other members of the LRC, was strongly opposed to the war:

'Hardie himself felt very dubious about his chances in South Wales and had in fact let his name go forward for the Preston constituency where he spent almost all his time and energy...He spent only "eleven waking hours" in Merthyr Tydfil, yet secured election in the double-member seat along with the Liberal coal-owner David Thomas. The fact was that the third candidate, Pritchard Morgan, was a Liberal Imperialist [ie a supporter of the Boer War]...[Hardie] undoubtedly received a good deal of support from anti-war Liberals who were strong in the area and could not stomach Morgan at any price.' (Moore 1978, p.81)

Nevertheless, some historians do not regard the 1900 general election as a failure for the LRC. Phillips, for example, argues that:

'The start was not as unpromising as might at first appear. The LRC had achieved an average poll of over 4,000 (15 candidates gained 62,698 votes). This compared favourably with the results obtained by the ILP in 1895 - its 28 candidates had each attracted 1,400 votes.' (Phillips 1992, p.11)

The results, however, did show that the LRC had a huge task ahead of it. The eight Lib-Lab MPs outnumbered those of the LRC, and Lib-Lab supporters in the TUC worked hard to stifle the infant labour organisation. Also, on many major political issues, like free trade or Irish Home Rule, it was difficult to distinguish LRC views from those of Liberals.

The Taff Vale Judgement

In 1901, the Taff Vale Judgement in the House of Lords (see also Unit 4, page 135) gave the infant LRC a defining labour issue:

'On 1 August 1901, MacDonald issued a circular to the unions in which he argued: "The recent decisions of the House of Lords should convince the unions that a labour party in Parliament is an immediate necessity".' (Moore 1978, p.87)

Although the Liberals showed the unions some sympathy over Taff Vale, they were out of power and so could do nothing to help. The Lib-Lab MPs made little impact in the House of Commons and so many trade unionists came to see a separate labour party as their best hope. There was a massive increase in union affiliations to the LRC. Pelling notes that the number of members in affiliated unions increased from c.350,000 at the beginning of 1901 to c.861,000 by the end of 1902:

'The largest reinforcements came from the adhesion [ie the joining] of the Textile Workers - a group of unions with altogether more than 100,000 members...The Textile Workers early in 1903 joined the LRC in a body. The Engineers had also joined in the course of 1902...As a result, the only large unions not yet in the LRC were those of the miners, whose success in electing their own members as "Lib-Labs" continued to inhibit their enthusiasm for joining in with the other unions or abandoning the Liberal Party.' (Pelling 1991, p.12)

By-election gains 1902-03

Between August 1902 and July 1903, three more LRC MPs were elected in by-elections:

- in August 1902, David Shackleton, a textile union official, was elected unopposed in Clitheroe (see Box 5.12)
- in March 1903, Will Crooks, a member of the London County Council, won a straight fight against a Conservative in Woolwich
- in July 1903, Arthur Henderson, Leader of the Ironworkers Union, beat both a Conservative and a Liberal candidate to win at Barnard Castle.

In addition, Philip Snowden won substantial support, but lost, a by-election in Wakefield and John Hodge of the steel smelters' union almost won a by-election in Preston.

While these by-election gains (and near misses) were significant (not least because they showed the Liberals that the LRC was capable of winning seats), the LRC group found it difficult to assert its independence in Parliament. Moore points out that:

'Shackleton's views were very close to Liberalism. Will Crooks was conscious that a significant proportion of his majority at Woolwich was due to Liberal support. Henderson, as an ex-Liberal Party worker, undoubtedly felt the pull of Liberalism.' (Moore 1978, p.83)

And Pelling suggests that:

'As none of the recently elected trio was a socialist or a keen independent, MacDonald and Hardie had a good deal of difficulty in keeping them on the narrow line of political separation from the Liberals.' (Pelling 1991, p.14)

In addition, since joining Parliament in 1900, Richard Bell had moved steadily towards the Liberals:

'It rapidly became apparent that Bell saw the LRC as a pressure group and no more. He pugnaciously [strongly] resisted the idea of an independent party and actively advocated open by-election pacts with the Liberals. By the start of 1903 he was urging working-class voters to support Liberal candidates at Newmarket and Liverpool.' (Morgan 1975, p.127)

Constitutional changes, 1903

The third annual conference of the LRC was held in Newcastle in February 1903. This conference made two decisions of great importance:

BOX 5.12 David Shackleton's election

Interpretation

In June 1902, the Liberal MP for Clitheroe was elevated to the Lords and a by-election was called. Aware of this in advance, a conference of trade unionists, ILP and SDF delegates met in early 1902 and decided to adopt an independent candidate. At this meeting, an ILP motion proposing that a socialist candidate be adopted was heavily defeated. But, the ILP still hoped that Philip Snowden (a socialist and a member of the ILP) would be chosen since he had local connections and some support among the delegates. In the months after the meeting, it became clear, however, that the majority of delegates supported David Shackleton, Vice President of the Northern Weavers' Union (who was not a socialist). The ILP's parliamentary committee then made the decision that Snowden should withdraw, provided that Shackleton agreed to act independently if elected (Shackleton was a non-conformist with close ties to the Liberals - he had once been Secretary of a Liberal ward party). By stepping down gracefully, the ILP calculated that it would gain the confidence and respect of union leaders who were still suspicious of it. Also, it was known that the local Liberal association was willing to back the candidature of Philip Stanhope if he chose to stand. Stanhope supported Lib-Labism, but announced he would only stand if a socialist was put forward by the LRC. Snowden's candidature might, therefore, split the Labour vote. As a result, Snowden stood down and Shackleton was chosen. The result was his election unopposed (the Conservatives were prepared to put up a candidate if Stanhope stood against the LRC candidate because they had a chance of benefiting from the split vote, but realised it was pointless to oppose Shackleton). The ILP's patience and willingness to compromise paid handsome dividends. Shackleton's election marked an almost revolutionary change in the textile unions' attitudes towards political representation. In the summer of 1902, ballots showed large majorities in favour of joining the LRC and affiliation was completed in January 1903.

Adapted from Moore 1978.

- the annual subscription rate was raised from a nominal ten shillings per 1,000 members to one pence per member
- a parliamentary fund was set up to support MPs during their term in Parliament.

The parliamentary fund had a political purpose. By paying MPs, the LRC would be able to exercise greater control over them. In other words, it was a response to the difficulties within the parliamentary group outlined above. One consequence was the expulsion of Richard Bell in 1905.

As for the purpose behind the rise in annual subscriptions, Ramsay MacDonald said:

'Hitherto, Labour war chests have been left in the possession of the unions which filled them and were only used for candidates connected with those unions. Now we are to have a common fund and Labour candidates - not necessarily trade unionists - run from that fund.' (Ramsay MacDonald quoted in Phillips 1992, p.13)

The decisions made at the 1903 conference, therefore, ensured that the LRC gained some financial independence, allowing it to build the machinery necessary to convert it into a significant political force. Adelman argues that this, together with the growth in support for the LRC among the unions meant that:

'The year 1903 marks the real turning point in the history of the Labour Representation Committee. For the LRC not only vastly increased its membership and, as [a result] its income also, but it gained considerably in prestige and self-confidence.' (Adelman 1986, p.33)

2. The Lib-Lab Pact of 1903

A second extremely significant development for the LRC was the electoral pact made with the Liberal Party in 1903 - see Box 5.13.

BOX 5.13 The Lib-Lab Pact of 1903

After secret negotiations between Herbert Gladstone (the Liberal Chief Whip) and Ramsay MacDonald, it was agreed that the Liberals would not oppose LRC candidates in 30 constituencies in England and Wales. These were seats where it was thought that a LRC candidate was more likely than a Liberal to defeat the Conservatives. In return, the LRC would restrict the number of candidates elsewhere. The clear purpose of the pact was to prevent, as far as possible, three-cornered contests in which the anti-Conservative vote was split. The terms of the pact presented MacDonald's organisation with a priceless gift. In effect, the LRC was promised the extensive support of Liberal votes to defeat Conservative opponents. This gave it the opportunity to secure a level of parliamentary representation far above what it could hope for without the agreement.

Adapted from Phillips 1992.

Why did the Liberals agree to a pact?

Historians have suggested that there were seven main reasons why the Liberals agreed to a pact.

1. Fear of splitting the 'progressive' vote

Adelman (1986) notes that Herbert Gladstone spoke of making some kind of agreement as early as 1901, after the North East Lanark by-election. In this by-election, the LRC and Liberal candidates had split the 'progressive' vote, allowing in the Conservative. Fear that the progressive vote would be split in three-way contests in other constituencies was, therefore, a reason for making a pact. Moore (1978) suggests that Arthur Henderson's victory in a three-way contest in July 1903 was a decisive last straw in persuading Gladstone to make a pact.

2. The LRC's consolidation

Pelling (1991) suggests that the growth in support for the LRC and the changes made at its 1903 conference encouraged Gladstone to 'come to terms with the LRC'. By 1903, in other words, the LRC had become strong enough to be taken seriously as an electoral threat.

3. The LRC's moderate stance

Phillips argues that Liberals on the progressive wing of their party had no difficulty in allying themselves with people like MacDonald. There seemed to be nothing very revolutionary or even socialistic in the LRC's aims. Gradual reform and the safeguarding of workers' rights seemed quite in line with progressive liberalism:

'The negotiations of 1903 would not have succeeded if the Liberals had thought the new party likely to do harm to a Liberal government. It was because the LRC was manifestly not a socialist organisation - because most of its affiliates and candidates were trade unionists whose opinions were indistinguishable from the Liberals' own - that the Chief Whip felt so complacent.' (Phillips 1992, p.14)

4. Common causes

Thorpe (1997) emphasises the importance of Joseph Chamberlain's decision to announce his support for protection (see also Unit 6, pages 190-91). For members of the LRC, like Liberals, free trade was a key policy:

'Free trade meant cheap food, but was also seen as the key to other classic tenets of British radicalism, notably international peace, clean government and fair play. Protection had its working-class supporters, of course, but it was an issue that united most socialists and trade unionists.' (Thorpe 1997, pp.15-16)

Thorpe argues that, since both the LRC and the Liberal Party were fundamentally opposed to protection, their common cause brought them closer together. Pelling (1991) adds that there were several other issues on which the LRC and Liberal Party were united. They both campaigned against the 1902 Education Act, for example, and against 'Chinese slavery' in South Africa (see Unit 6, page 192).

5. The LRC's appeal to working-class Conservatives

Tanner (1990) argues that there were two main strands of socialism within the LRC:

- a moderate, moral strand supported by people like Keir Hardie and Ramsay MacDonald
- a more radical 'dissenting' strand supported by people like George Lansbury and Fred Jowett.

The first strand (the predominant strand within the party), Tanner argues, appealed to working-class Liberals. The more radical strand, on the other hand, appealed to working-class Conservatives (even though few of the ideas proposed by the 'dissenters' were adopted by the party). Since the LRC appealed to working-class Conservatives, this opened the way to the 1903 pact since the Liberal Party was unable to appeal to this group.

6. The views of Herbert Gladstone

Adelman (1986) argues that the views of Herbert Gladstone were of particular importance. A different Liberal Chief Whip might not have been so keen to make a deal with MacDonald.

7. The Liberal Party's finances

Adelman (1986) also argues that one motive for making the pact was to save money in the forthcoming general election. Gladstone knew, he argues, that the LRC had an election fund of £150,000. By making the pact, the Liberals would not have to spend large sums countering LRC opposition.

Greater cooperation with the Lib-Labs

Moore (1978) argues that, in the run-up to the 1906 general election, relations improved between the LRC and the Lib-Labs. In the Monmouth by-election of 1904, the LRC agreed to support the Lib-Lab candidate because he had stated that:

'He was the labour candidate only and that if returned to the House of Commons, he would work with the labour group.' (quoted in Moore 1978, p.97)

Although, Moore points out, this statement was misleading since the candidate had already been adopted by (and was supported by) the local Liberal association, it was a sign of changing attitudes. In February 1905, the so-called 'Caxton Hall Concordat' followed - see Box 5.14 above.

2.4 The LRC and the 1906 general election

The 1906 general election

Organisation

By 1906, Ramsay MacDonald (the Secretary) and Arthur Henderson (Chair) had 'created at least the skeleton of a national political machine' (Moore 1978, p.99). From 1900, local LRC constituency branches were encouraged, but, at first, no uniform model was imposed from the centre. In 1903, MacDonald and Henderson produced an agent's handbook which provided guidance for the setting up of new constituency branches based on the

---

BOX 5.14 The Caxton Hall Concordat

Interpretation

In February 1905, delegates from the LRC and from the TUC's Parliamentary Committee met at in Caxton Hall in London. At this meeting, it was agreed that each group would support the other's candidates. Following this agreement, there was much closer cooperation between the two groups in Parliament. Indeed, there was something of a honeymoon period between the Lib-Labs and the LRC members in the Commons. The two groups drew closer together and, in the last months of the dying Parliament, the 'labour' members sat as one group in the Commons under the chairmanship of John Burns.

Adapted from Adelman 1986.

---

structure of MacDonald's local branch in Leicester (MacDonald stood as a candidate and was elected in Leicester in 1906). But, as Moore points out:

'The peculiar thing was that the local LRCs were not directly affiliated to the national LRC.' (Moore 1978, p.99)

In other words, a newly formed local constituency branch had no automatic right to send delegates to the annual LRC conference or to participate in decision making at a national level. In some constituencies, the Trades Council was affiliated to the national LRC and these Trades Councils became, in effect, the local constituency branch. In other constituencies, however, new local LRCs remained unaffiliated. This problem was solved at the LRC's 1905 annual conference. A resolution was passed which laid down that, in constituencies where there was no affiliated Trades Council, the local LRC should be eligible for affiliation. Moore estimates that, by the time of the 1906 general election 70-100 of these branches had affiliated to the national LRC.

Policy

Ramsay MacDonald and Arthur Henderson were also key players in the development of a national policy programme. Moore (1978) notes that, in April 1904, they called a meeting of prospective parliamentary candidates who agreed to support a particular stance on a number of issues. When the 1906 general election was called, it was Ramsay MacDonald who drew up the LRC's manifesto (see Activity 5.3, Item 1). Moore argues that:

'The election manifesto eventually drawn up by MacDonald turned out to be a rather nebulous [vague] document, particularly when compared with that issued by the [TUC] Parliamentary Committee on behalf of the Lib-Labs. Basically, it was simply an appeal for more labour members and...there was no specific programme of legislation outlined for the electorate's consideration.' (Moore 1978, p.99)

The election result

In the 1906 general election, the LRC put up 50 candidates and won 29 seats (the Liberals gave them a clear run in 30 constituencies). This parliamentary group increased to 30 MPs when a Durham miners' MP joined Labour immediately after the election. The average vote of Labour candidates rose from about 4,000 to 7,500. The pact with the Liberals had worked well:

'Of the 29 victories, 24 were achieved in straight fights with the Conservatives. The willingness of the Liberals to withdraw their candidates, under the terms of the 1903 understanding, thus played a vital part in Labour's success.' (Phillips 1992, p.14)

The significance of the election is described in Box 5.15.

BOX 5.15 | **The significance of the 1906 election**

Interpretation

The success of the LRC in the 1906 general election caused a sensation at the time. The defeated Conservative Leader, Arthur Balfour, went so far as to suggest that the new Liberal Prime Minister, Campbell Bannerman was 'a mere cork dancing on a current which he cannot control'. But, the opposite was really true. The Labour members were swept into the House of Commons on a tidal wave of Liberalism that gave the Liberal Party 399 seats and a majority of 130 over all the other parties combined. Nevertheless, Balfour was not far wrong in seeing something especially significant about the results of the 1906 election. For, partly as a result of the Gladstone-MacDonald agreement, the LRC now had an independent political power of its own. This was indicated by its members sitting on the opposition benches when Parliament reassembled on 12 February 1906, and electing their own officers and whips. On that day, 30 LRC MPs decided that they should adopt the simple title of - the Labour Party.

Adapted from Pelling 1991 and Adelman 1986.

Composition of the Parliamentary Labour Party

The composition of the Parliamentary Labour Party following the 1906 general election was as follows:

'Of the 29 LRC men, seven, including Hardie, MacDonald and Snowden, were sponsored by the ILP. The rest, although sponsored by trade unions or local labour bodies, also contained a good many members of the ILP, and one (Will Thorne of the Gasworkers Union) was a member of the SDF. It was equally significant, however, that, of the successful 29, only five were elected against Liberal opposition...All of the 29 new MPs were of working-class origin.' (Pelling 1991, pp.15-16)

Was the LRC a socialist party?

Historians are divided over the question as to whether the LRC can be described as a socialist party. Some accounts (for example, McKibbin 1974) downplay the importance of socialism in the early development of the Labour Party while others (for example, Laybourn 1997) argue that socialist ideas played an important part in the party's development. The question is complicated by the fact that the LRC was an umbrella organisation, a loose coalition of independent groups with very different identities (the ILP, the unions, the Fabians). It was also complicated by the fact that the main aim of the organisation was to win the support of the trade unions which backed the Liberals and, to do this, it needed to present a moderate image.

Liberalism and the leadership

To some extent this debate depends on whether an examination is being made of the leadership of the LRC or ordinary members. As far as the leadership is concerned, there is good evidence that Liberalism rather than socialism was often the main inspiration. The ideology of the Labour MPs elected in 1906 has been examined by David Martin, for example. He points out that most of them were middle-aged and so:

'[Most] had formed their views when socialism in Britain was almost unknown. Consequently, many had first entered politics via the radical wing of the Liberal Party.' (Martin 1985, pp.17-18)

Pelling, however, points out that all 29 LRC candidates elected in 1906 had a working-class background and asserts that:

'Many of them were under a vague socialist influence, but only one or two were Marxists.' (Pelling 1991, p.16)

A distinctive party?

The picture which emerges is of some enthusiasm for socialism at the grass roots, but a lukewarm commitment to socialism at the leadership level. This presented the party with two main problems in its early years. First, it was difficult to keep the support of more radical supporters - especially those who belonged to the ILP. And second, it was difficult to see, in policy terms, how the Labour Party differed from the radical wing of the Liberal Party. The Liberal government's adoption of a programme of social reform made it even harder for the Labour Party to be distinct:

'The new party found it very difficult in these early years to establish itself as offering something very different from the Liberals. This difficulty was exacerbated by the Liberals' new commitment to social reform...In fact, up to 1914, there was little to distinguish the policy of the Labour Party from that of the Liberals. This was hardly surprising since many of the Labour leaders had supported the Liberal Party until fairly recently. This, and the importance to the young party of retaining the support of moderate trade unionists, militated against the adoption of overtly socialist policies.

Labour distinguished itself from the Liberals, not so much by its policies, but rather by its ability to see things from a distinctly working-class perspective.' (Behagg 1995, pp.438-39)

MAIN POINTS - Sections 2.3-2.4

- In order to explain the LRC's electoral breakthrough in 1906, historians point to two main factors - (1) the impact of the Taff Vale Judgement and (2) the secret Lib-Lab pact of 1903.
- Before the Taff Vale decision, the LRC was very weak, though it did manage to win two seats in the general election of 1900.
- The Taff Vale decision and the LRC's moderate approach (engineered particularly by Ramsay MacDonald) ensured a rapid growth in union support and some significant by-election victories. Constitutional changes in 1903 strengthened the party.
- Historians have suggested seven reasons why the Liberals agreed to an electoral pact in 1903 - (1) fear of splitting the 'progressive' vote (2) the LRC's consolidation (3) the LRC's moderate stance (4) common causes (5) the LRC's appeal to working-class Conservatives (6) Herbert Gladstone's viewpoint and (7) financial concerns.
- The 1906 general election was significant because 29 LRC candidates were elected. The LRC group then sat in the Commons as an independent opposition group with its own whips.
- Historians are divided over the question as to whether the LRC can be described as a socialist party. Some accounts downplay the importance of socialism while others argue that socialist ideas played an important part in the party's early development.

Activity 5.3 The Labour Party and the 1906 general election

ITEM 1   The LRC's 1906 manifesto

To the electors-
This election is to decide whether or not labour is to be fairly represented in Parliament. The House of Commons is supposed to be the people's House and yet the people are not there. Landlords, employers, lawyers, brewers and financiers are there in force. Why not labour? The trade unions ask for the same liberty as capital enjoys. They are refused. The aged poor are neglected. The slums remain. Overcrowding continues, whilst the land goes to waste. Shopkeepers and traders are overburdened with rates and taxation whilst increasing land values, which should relieve the rate-payers, go to people who have not earned them. Wars are fought to make the rich richer and underfed school children are still neglected. Chinese labour is defended because it enriches the mine owners...And now, when you are beginning to understand the causes of your poverty, the red herring of Protection is drawn across your path. Protection, as experience shows, is no remedy for poverty and unemployment. It serves to keep you from dealing with the land, housing, old age and other social problems. You have it in your power to see that Parliament carries out your wishes. The Labour Representation Committee Executive appeals to you in the name of a million trade unionists to forget all political differences which have kept you apart in the past.

Part of the LRC's 1906 general election manifesto.

ITEM 2   A historian's view (1)

What kind of party had now taken shape? Judging by its MPs, it was overwhelmingly a party of, as well as for, the working class - but it embodied that class in its most respectable and morally worthy garb. Of both its trade unionist and its socialist representatives, most were earnest, largely self-educated men. Eighteen professed to be religious dissenters and several were teetotallers. Ideologically, the party was less coherent. It was not defined by a socialist programme, though most of its MPs would have called themselves socialists of a kind. In the years after 1906, party conferences were quite willing to support resolutions proposing the public ownership of one industry or another. For most of the MPs, however, socialist causes were not matters of great urgency. It was more important for the party to protect the more immediate and tangible interests of the working class. In practice, the nature of those interests was primarily determined by the leaders of trade unions - for example, restoration of the legal protection which the Taff Vale Judgement had demolished, the improvement of working conditions and the engineering of a labour market in which wage-earners would be less insecure. This ideological position was sometimes called 'labourism'. It would be misleading to regard the party as divided into socialists and non-socialists, but it was true that some socialists within it wanted to give more attention with less delay to radical objectives. And it was also apparent that some trade unionists distrusted the intellectual tastes and refined manners of many in the ILP. These differences of temper and outlook became wider in the next few years.

Adapted from Phillips 1992.

ITEM 3 A historian's view (2)

The results were very encouraging for the LRC, although they paled somewhat at the side of the Liberals' achievement in winning almost 400 seats. Of the 30 Labour MPs, 13 came from Lancashire, four from Yorkshire and three from the North East. In other words, two-thirds sat for northern English seats. There were only three Labour MPs from the London area, two from Scotland and one from Wales. In some sense, therefore, this was hardly a great victory. Labour had made a breakthrough but was heavily dependent on the pact with the Liberals and was very much a sectional party with scarcely any presence at all outside areas of heavy industry and high levels of unionisation. Looking back with hindsight, this election can be seen as the first stage on the party's inevitable push towards power. But, even by 1914, the party's future was far from assured.

Adapted from Thorpe 1997.

ITEM 4 The 1906 election result

Party	Total votes	%	Candidates	MPs
Conservative	2,422,071	43.4	556	156
Liberal	2,751,057	49.4	536	399
Labour	321,663	4.8	50	29
Nat*	35,031	0.7	86	82
Others**	96,269	1.7	45	4

BALLOT BOX

* Nat = Irish Nationalist
** One of the four 'others' to be elected was J.W.Taylor (Durham). He was not an official LRC candidate at the time of the election, but joined the Labour Party as soon as he had been elected.

Information from Craig 1989.

Questions

1. Look at Item 1.
   a) Who do you think this manifesto is aimed at?
   b) What was distinct about the LRC's message?
   c) What does it tell us about the approach adopted by the LRC after 1900?
2. Did the 1906 general election establish Labour as a distinctive third party? Use Items 2-4 in your answer.
3. Look at Item 2.
   a) What is the difference between 'labourism' and 'socialism'?
   b) Would you say that the views expressed in Item 1 are 'labourist'? Explain your answer.
4. a) What do Items 3 and 4 tell us about the nature of the Labour Party in 1906?
   b) What difficulties did the Labour Party face in establishing itself as a mainstream political party in the period 1900-06?

3 Labour and the Liberals, 1906-14

Key questions

1. Was Labour's growth and the Liberals' decline inevitable?
2. How successful was Labour as a parliamentary party after 1906?

3.1 Was Labour's growth and the Liberals' decline inevitable?

The historical debate

Before the First World War, Labour was a minor parliamentary party. In the two general elections held in 1910 (the last before the war), it won 40 and then 42 seats. The Liberal Party, by way of contrast, won 274 and 272 seats. In the general election of 1922, however, the Labour Party won 142 seats and replaced the Liberal Party (which won 115 seats) as the main party of opposition. Then, following the general election of December 1923, the Labour Party was able to form its first government (albeit a minority government which lasted for less than a year). When a further general election was held in 1924, the Liberals won just 40 seats while Labour won 151 seats, in effect reversing the position of the two parties before the war. This dramatic change in the fortunes of the two parties has led to a sharp debate among historians as to why Labour overtook the Liberals and whether this was an inevitable process, already underway before 1914 (see also Unit 6, Part 6):

'Was the Labour Party making significant progress before 1914 as a result of rising working-class support or was its rise based on the destruction of the Liberal Party by the internal battles between Asquith and Lloyd George in 1916?' (Laybourn 1998, p.22)

Early views

One early view was that, once launched, the Labour Party made a seamless progress to power, inevitable because it coincided with the rise of working-class solidarity. As Pelling (1991) has pointed out, however, this was a political rather than historical view and was put forward by Labour leaders like Arthur Henderson and Sidney Webb. A different interpretation came from Liberal historians of the 1930s like J.A. Spender and Ramsay Muir. In their view, it was the Liberals who had torn themselves apart during the First World War. According to them, Labour made little impact between 1906 and 1914 when the great reforming Liberal ministry dominated politics. A refinement of this view came in 1936 when George Dangerfield wrote *The Strange Death of Liberal England*. He saw 1910 to 1914 as crucial years when issues like industrial unrest, Irish Home Rule, women's suffrage and the approach of war tore the Liberals apart.

The view of Wilson and Clarke

More recently, the debate has been taken further, though it does still focus on the questions raised earlier. The emphasis on the decline of the Liberals was developed by Wilson (1966) and Clarke (1971). They suggested that the period from 1906 to 1914 was one of great Liberal progress. There was impressive social legislation (see Unit 6, Part 2). This was promoted by the 'New' Liberals led by Lloyd George and it appealed to the working class. Clarke shows that this support grew in areas like Lancashire and London. He sees Labour's parliamentary performance as weak and stresses a lack of electoral success in 1910 and in subsequent by-elections. Wilson dismisses Dangerfield's view, seeing the crises of 1910-14 as an 'accidental convergence of unrelated events'. He and Clarke put the blame for the Liberals' later disasters on the split between Asquith and Lloyd George in 1916. The Liberal Party, they suggest, was like a pedestrian in an accident:

'A rampant omnibus (the First World War) mounted the pavement and ran over him. After lingering painfully, he expired.' (Wilson 1966, pp.16-18)

The view of Pelling and Martin

Other historians argue that the Labour Party made real progress in the period 1906-14 and are more sceptical about Liberal strength between 1906 and 1914. Pelling, for example, sees the basis of Labour's growing influence before 1914 as the support of the trade unions:

'The difference between the Labour Party and the other political parties was that its principal strength lay in its extra-parliamentary organisation and, in this period, that organisation was constantly being strengthened. Between 1906 and 1914 the number of affiliated trade union members rose from 904,496 to 1,572,391.' (Pelling 1968, p.117)

Another historian taking a similar view, David Martin, emphasises how, after the Osborne Judgment

was reversed (see below and Unit 4, Section 2.4), large numbers of trade unionists opted to pay the political levy. Prior to 1914:

'Despite all its limitations, it was becoming more accepted that the Labour Party had a role to play in representing the working class. An acknowledgement of this was the way in which a majority of members of almost all trade unions voted to pay the political levy.' (Martin 1985, p.30)

Pelling (along with other historians) has also emphasised that before the Representation of the People Act (1918), Labour was not able to poll its full support at elections:

'The Act of 1918 considerably improved the position of the Labour Party in the constituencies. It would result in gains in such districts as Yorkshire, North England and West Scotland.' (Pelling 1968, p.120)

In addition, Pelling sees broader factors working in Labour's favour:

'Long-term social and economic changes were simultaneously uniting Britain geographically and dividing her inhabitants in terms of class.' (Pelling 1968, p.120)

The views of McKibbin, Tanner and Laybourn

While McKibbin (1974) emphasised the importance of the growth of 'working-class consciousness' in the period 1906-14, some recent historians, notably Tanner (1990), have argued against this viewpoint. Tanner argues that Labour's position was stronger than that of the Liberals in certain areas of the country before 1914, but that the Liberals retained strong support from members of the working class as well as from sections of the middle class. In addition, the Liberal Party could rely on the rural vote while Labour support in rural areas remained very slight. In general terms, Tanner 'rejects the idea that Labour would inevitably become the sole anti-Tory party'. Instead, he believes that a three-party system was emerging but was forestalled by the chaos in the Liberal Party which resulted from the First World War. Tanner, however, has not gone unchallenged. Laybourn criticises his approach - see Box 5.16 on page 173.

3.2 Labour's record 1906-14

Problems faced by the Labour Party 1906-14

In order to form a view on which side of the historical debate described above is more convincing, it is necessary to examine the problems faced by the Labour Party in the period 1906-14 and the success (or otherwise) of the steps taken to counter them. Historians have identified four key problems facing the Labour Party in the period 1906-14.

1. Parliamentary arithmetic

If the result of the 1906 general election had been a

BOX 5.16 Laybourn's criticism of Tanner

Despite Tanner's claims to the contrary, the fact is that the thrust of his work is parliamentary in nature. The success of Labour at the local level, the most immediate source of power in municipal, board of guardians, county council, urban district council and other local elections is not examined. Between 1906 and 1914, evidence of such growth was widespread throughout England and Wales. In fact, there was significant Labour growth in many areas and little evidence that New Liberalism, with its emphasis on social harmony, was checking Labour's growth.

Adapted from Laybourn 1997.

close call between the two main parties, it is possible that the small group of Labour MPs would have been in a position of power. As it was, the Liberals won with a landslide. As a result, the Liberal government was not obliged to take much notice of the views expressed by the Labour group and, apart from in 1906 when Labour MPs persuaded the government to drop its own Trade Disputes Bill and adopt that drawn up by them (see below), it did not do so:

'Never again after the initial success of the Trade Disputes Bill was the Labour Party able to impose its will on the Liberal Party; indeed, the opposite is true. The nature and pace of legislation was thereafter determined by Liberal ministers and the members of the Parliamentary Labour Party often seemed to exist merely to provide voting fodder in support of Liberal issues - Lords reform, Irish Home Rule, National Insurance - which they had not chosen and to which they gave no high priority.' (Adelman 1986, p.39)

Even after the first election in 1910 when the two main parties won almost an identical number of seats (272 for the Conservatives and 274 for the Liberals), the balance of power was held by the Irish Nationalists (with 82 seats) rather than by the Labour Party (with 40 seats) and the Labour Party found itself in a difficult position.

Parliamentary arithmetic, therefore, made it difficult for Labour MPs to make their mark.

2. New Liberalism

Some historians argue that, by adopting a programme of social welfare - so-called 'New Liberalism' (see Unit 6, Part 2) - the Liberal Party stole much of Labour's thunder. Certainly, the social welfare programme presented the Labour group in Parliament with a dilemma. If the Labour MPs opposed the programme on the grounds that it did not go far enough, they ran the risk of being branded as extremists. If, on the other hand, they supported the programme, they ran the risk of appearing to be

an irrelevance. What was the point of a separate Labour Party when its members simply supported the Liberal government?

In addition, the great political issues which dominated Parliament in 1909 and afterwards (such as the constitutional crisis over the House of Lords and the Home Rule crisis) tended to push Labour to the political sidelines because Labour's policies on these matters were similar to those of the ruling Liberals:

'When constitutional reform or Irish affairs were under discussion, the Labour Party could only follow in the Liberals' footsteps and champion their causes.' (Phillips 1992, p.17)

3. Finances - the Osborne Judgement

In 1909, a member of the Amalgamated Society of Railway Servants objected to paying the political levy (the part of each union member's subscription which went to the Labour Party) and the courts ruled that it was illegal for unions to force members to pay the political levy - the so-called Osborne Judgement (see also Unit 4, pages 135-36). This ruling hit the Labour Party's finances very hard since Labour MPs relied on funds raised by unions to pay their salary (MPs were not paid until 1911).

4. Lack of electoral progress

Although some historians argue against the idea that the Labour Party failed to make electoral progress after 1906, others claim that this is what happened. They point out that, following the 1906 general election, there were 30 Labour MPs. In 1909, this number was artificially inflated when the Miners' Federation of Great Britain (MFGB) decided to affiliate to the Labour Party, bringing it an additional 12 MPs. Since the Labour Party won three by-elections between 1906 and 1909, that brought the total of MPs to 45 in that year. But this number actually went down after the general election of January 1910 and further by-election defeats after 1910 reduced the number to 37 MPs in 1914. These figures show that, certainly, there was no major breakthrough in parliamentary elections fought between 1906 and 1914.

The position of the Labour Party in the period 1909-14 is summarised in Box 5.17 on page 174.

Labour successes 1906-14

While those historians who argue that there was nothing inevitable about Labour's rise to power tend to emphasise the problems faced by the party in the period 1906-14, other historians have pointed to successes and signs that Labour was making progress during this period.

1. Making an impact in Parliament

Although Labour MPs found it difficult to make their mark in the Commons, there is some evidence that they did help to shape some legislation. In 1906, for

BOX 5.17 The Parliamentary Labour Party 1909-14

Interpretation

Unhappily for the Labour Party, the situation in 1910 was very different from that in 1906. Partly because the Lords rejected the 'People's Budget' of 1909, the Liberal Party had its own priorities - two general elections in 1910, the Parliament and Insurance Acts of 1911, followed by the Irish Home Rule Bill and Welsh Disestablishment Bill in 1912. As a result, the Labour Party found itself at the back of a long queue. Although the government introduced payment for MPs in 1911 in return for Labour's support of the Insurance Acts, the party had to wait until 1913 before a new Trade Union Act reversed the Osborne Judgement. Besides, the parliamentary arithmetic changed dramatically in 1910. In order to remain in office, the Liberals needed the support of Irish Nationalist and Labour MPs. Since the Labour Party (partly for financial reasons, following the Osborne Judgement) had no wish to face a third general election, it had to keep the Liberals in office, vote for their Bills and accept whatever crumbs they had to offer.

Adapted from Adelman 1986.

example, Labour pressure on the Liberals ensured that the Trade Disputes Act (1906) provided the sort of protection for trade unions that had existed before the House of Lord's Taff Vale decision of 1901:

'Partly due to the especial sympathy of the Prime Minister, Henry Campbell Bannerman, and the electoral commitments of many Liberal members, the government threw overboard its own moderate and complicated Trade Union Bill and accepted the Labour Bill...This was a major triumph for the Labour group; and in the same year they supported (and improved) a new Workmen's Compensation Act and School Meals and Medical Inspection Acts.' (Adelman 1986, p.39)

Adelman goes on to point out, however, that 1906 was an exceptional year. The next time in which Labour MPs could extract concessions was after the 1910 general elections changed the parliamentary arithmetic. The Liberal government needed Labour MPs to vote with it and, in return for Labour's support of the National Insurance Act, the government introduced payment for MPs. This eased the party's financial problems, but the Osborne Judgement was not finally reversed until a new Trade Union Act was introduced in 1913.

The difference in the way that historians have interpreted the contribution made by Labour MPs in the period 1906-14 is illustrated in Box 5.18.

2. Growing support from the unions

Union support for the Labour Party grew on a significant scale during the period 1906-14. In 1909,

the Miners' Federation of Great Britain switched allegiance from the Liberal Party to the Labour Party. This was significant not only because it brought Labour new members, but also because its 12 MPs joined the Labour group in Parliament. In addition, the rapid growth of union membership in the period 1910-14 (see also Unit 4, Part 3) benefited the Labour Party:

'The outburst of industrial conflict between 1910 and 1914, which produced national transport and mining strikes, strengthened and speeded up the process of rising trade union support for the Labour Party.' (Laybourn 1997, p.41)

3. Electoral progress

At the national level, the party's electoral fortunes fluctuated quite considerably after 1906. Although some historians (for example Tanner 1990) argue that the poor showing in 1910 and the by-election losses between 1910 and 1914 show that the Labour Party was in no position to make a serious challenge to the Liberals by the time the First World War broke out, others argue against this on a number of grounds:

'Some historians have laid much emphasis on the electoral system itself and particularly on the limited extent of the working-class franchise.

BOX 5.18 The contribution made by Labour MPs, 1906-14

Interpretation

(i) Thane's view

'Historians have, on the whole, understated the drama of the entry into the House of this first band of working-class representatives, for the first time a group large and confident enough to make an independent impact. The new Labour MPs did not underestimate the element of theatre in the events in which they were involved. Their speeches read as conscious attempts to describe the reality of the experience of the working classes to their fellow MPs, often across a gulf of evident incomprehension.'

(Thane 1985, p.188).

(ii) Adelman's view

'Some of the trouble lay with the composition of the Parliamentary Labour Party itself. Apart from a few outstanding men like Hardie...the bulk of the Labour Party members represented, in Hyndman's phrase, 'a dull and deferential respectability'. Small in numbers, hampered by financial stringency [difficulties] and the pressures of trade union business, often ill at ease and inarticulate in Parliament and ignorant of or uninterested in the wider questions of debate, they made little impact on the House of Commons.'

(Adelman 1986, p.40).

Others have stressed the failure of the party to extend its appeal to those strata of wage earners lying below the relatively secure and respectable membership of the unions and the socialist societies. Others again have shown how, in some localities, even in centres of industry, the power and influence of social élites could undermine the capacity of the working class for political action on its own behalf. Finally, historians interested in the Liberal and Conservative parties in these years have drawn attention to the strength of the opposition to Labour. The Liberal government tried energetically to sustain its electoral support in face of Labour's competition, radical ministers like Lloyd George showing much skill in cultivating their own popular following.' (Phillips 1992, pp.21-22)

Developments at local level

There were more encouraging signs for Labour outside the area of national electoral politics. In local government elections, Labour made a net gain in seats in every year between 1900 and 1913. In local elections in England and Wales, for example, Labour won 91 seats in 1906 and increased this to 171 seats in 1913. At the local level, Labour could often present a programme of social reform which was more distinct from that of its rivals than it was at national level. As a result, in some local areas, Labour was clearly beginning to take over from the Liberals by 1914. It should be noted, however, that progress at local level varied from place to place:

'While Labour was making progress on a local front, its advance was still very uneven. In some towns it had secured a substantial representation by 1913, in others it was still negligible. It had 20 members of a council of 84 in Bradford and won 14 out of 48 wards in Leicester...In Birmingham, on the other hand, it had only eight representatives among 120 councillors and in Sheffield only two among 64...Its strength was concentrated in Lancashire and Yorkshire. At the outbreak of the war, more than half its sitting town councillors

were to be found in these two counties.' (Phillips 1992, p.24)

4. Membership and party organisation

Most historians agree that the Labour Party made significant advances in both membership and party organisation in the period 1906-14. The unions were the greatest source of new recruits to the Labour Party. The decision of the Miners' Federation to affiliate to the party in 1909 brought in 550,000 new members. As the trade unions themselves experienced a major expansion of members (from 2.5 million in 1910 to 4.1 million in 1914), so Labour's membership increased accordingly (from 1.4 million in 1910 to 2.1 million in 1915). Significantly, after the 1913 Trade Union Act was passed, union members voted in support of paying a political levy to the Labour Party:

'Union after union, holding secret ballots under the Trade Union Act of 1913, voted in favour of Labour representation. By the beginning of 1914, about 420,000 trade unionists from unions with a membership of 1,208,841 had voted on the necessity of establishing political funds for the Labour Party. Of these, 298,702 voted in favour and 125,310 against. The organised trade union movement and its rank and file were overwhelmingly committed to the Labour Party before the onset of war.' (Laybourn 1997, pp.42-43)

In addition to union support, significant progress was made at the local level:

'Labour membership of local bodies more than doubled during this period, often at the expense of the Liberals, as did affiliations to the parent party from Trades Councils and local labour parties; the foundation of the London Labour Party in 1914, for example, was a major event in the party's history.' (Adelman 1986, p.45)

Support from women

Labour was also able to attract some support from another group which felt discontented with both main political parties before 1914 - women (see also

---

BOX 5.19 Ramsay MacDonald and Labour Party organisation

The increasing size of the extra-parliamentary party meant that one man could no longer effectively combine the secretaryship with major parliamentary duties. Between 1906 to 1911, Ramsay MacDonald managed to be Secretary of both the parliamentary and extra-parliamentary party; but, by 1910, it was clear that he could not do justice to both posts. The illness of George Barnes enabled MacDonald to take over as Chair of the Parliamentary Labour Party at the beginning of 1911 and, the following year, he resigned as Secretary of the external organisation. Arthur Henderson then took over this post. MacDonald was a master of organisation and strategy. Under his leadership there emerged a national organisation, with national and local officers and properly organised constituency parties. The staff at Head Office was increased, with the appointment of two national organisers and it was agreed that a separate Scottish organisation should be set up. While it would be rash to argue that these changes led inevitably to the party's post-war progress, they did suggest that Labour would be pushing the Liberals for a greater role in the not-too-distant future.

Adapted from Pelling 1991 and Thorpe 1997.

Interpretation

Unit 3, Section 4.2). Women played a role in some trade unions, although they were often treated badly by male trade unionists (see Unit 4, Section 2.3). They had also consistently played an important role in the socialist societies:

'Alongside women prominent at the national level, like Katherine Bruce Glasier, were women at the grassroots, who could and often did play a significant role. For many, socialism was the appeal; for others, Labour seemed the most likely party to push women's suffrage.' (Thorpe 1987, p.27)

Labour supported women's suffrage in 1911 and individuals in the party worked for the women's cause. The most dramatic example was that of George Lansbury who resigned and fought an unsuccessful by-election on the issue in 1912. The party also established links with the moderate National Union of Women's Suffrage Societies (NUWSS), especially during the First World War - see page 293.

Party organisation

Historians agree that the organisation of the party became more professional in the years leading up to the First World War. The parliamentary party was more effectively organised from 1911 when Ramsay MacDonald became Chair - see Box 5.19 on page 175.

Improved finances after the passage of the Trade Union Act of 1913 ensured that the party was able to employ more officials and put up more candidates for election at both local and national level:

'The party was able to add to its full-time agents and officers. It had four such senior staff in 1910, seven by 1914, and there were comparable appointments in some individual constituencies. Most important, it was in a position to field more parliamentary candidates. At the general election pending at the outbreak of the war (and cancelled because of it) Labour seemed to be preparing to fight around 150 seats, more than double the number it had ever contested previously. Though still very much a third party, it was now a far more formidable one.' (Phillips 1992, p.23)

MAIN POINTS - Part 3

- The dramatic change in the fortunes of the Labour and Liberal parties in the period 1906-24 has led to a sharp debate among historians as to why Labour overtook the Liberals and whether this was an inevitable process, already underway before 1914.
- Some historians argue that Labour had made significant gains by 1914 and was in a position to mount a serious challenge to the Liberals. Others argue that Labour's rise to power was by no means inevitable in 1914.
- Historians have identified four main problems facing

the Labour Party between 1906 and 1914 - (1) parliamentary arithmetic, (2) New Liberalism, (3) finances and (4) lack of electoral progress.
- On the other hand, historians have identified four main areas where the Labour Party made gains in the period 1906-14 - (1) Labour MPs made an impact in Parliament (2) trade union support grew (3) there was growing success in elections, especially local elections and (4) there was a growth in membership and better party organisation.

Activity 5.4 The Labour Party and the Liberals

ITEM 1   General election results 1900-24 (1)

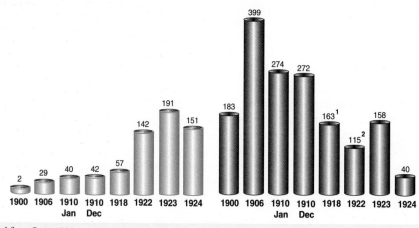

Number of Labour and Liberal MPs elected in general elections 1900-24

KEY:
- Labour
- Liberal

NOTES:
1. In 1918, 127 Coalition (Lloyd George) MPs elected and 36 Official (Asquith) MPs elected, making a total of 163.
2. In 1922, 53 National (Lloyd George) MPs elected and 62 Official (Asquith) MPs elected, making a total of 115.

Adapted from Craig 1989.

ITEM 2   General election results 1900-24 (2)

Percentage of votes won by the Labour Party and Liberal Party in general elections 1900-24

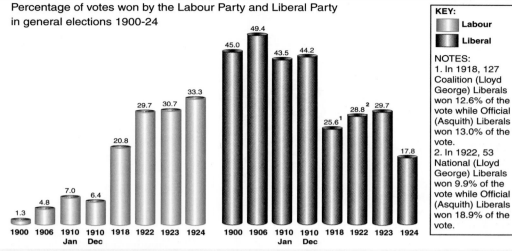

KEY:
■ Labour
■ Liberal

NOTES:
1. In 1918, 127 Coalition (Lloyd George) Liberals won 12.6% of the vote while Official (Asquith) Liberals won 13.0% of the vote.
2. In 1922, 53 National (Lloyd George) Liberals won 9.9% of the vote while Official (Asquith) Liberals won 18.9% of the vote.

Adapted from Craig 1989.

ITEM 3   How strong was Labour in 1914?

Passage A

Labour remained, at the outbreak of war, still at an infant stage of development - more than a mere pressure group but less than a mature political party. It can, however, be credited with two substantial achievements. First, it had made itself, beyond all question, the party of the trade unions. Neither the Conservatives or the Liberals could any longer maintain, however many working-class votes they attracted, that they represented organised labour. This gave the Labour Party a political identity of its own, even if it did not embrace a distinct programme or ideology. Second, Labour had built up an electoral capacity which placed it in a strong bargaining position in relation to the Liberal Party. If Labour ran 150 candidates at a general election, it would make a Liberal victory almost impossible. Whether the Labour Party knew how best to exploit this opportunity is doubtful, but the opportunity was there and was likely to become more obvious with the passage of time. As it was, the realignment of the parties and of electors was postponed by the war.
Adapted from Phillips 1992.

Passage B

The evidence suggests the rapid and dramatic rise of the Labour Party in the decade before the First World War was due to the growth of working-class support for it through the medium of trade unionism. The fact that many working men did not have a parliamentary vote might also have affected the parliamentary performance of the Labour Party. Four million or more working men were denied the vote and undoubtedly many of them would have voted Labour as they began to do in the immediate post-war years. Many regional studies show the rapid local growth of the Labour Party. New Liberalism, with its emphasis on social reform, seems to have carried little weight outside Lancashire and Westminster. Labour was doing well before 1914. Its by-election results were not bad. Then, the Liberals split as a result of the war. Given Labour's pre-war growth, it seems that the Liberal split merely speeded up the process of Labour growth and Liberal decline.
Adapted from Laybourn 1997.

Passage C

The Liberal Party's success was founded not only on New Liberal ideas but on an ability to mobilise working-class votes while retaining some middle-class support and an additional base in rural areas and market towns. Yet, the party was not without weaknesses. In particular, Labour was stronger than the Liberals in some areas where specific social, occupational and political circumstances prevailed. This base, growing before 1914, was expanded by wartime events which considerably increased Labour's credibility with the voters. By 1914, a three-party system was developing from which Labour later emerged as the dominant anti-Tory force in British politics. Labour's expansion cannot be explained by social changes. Policies and political images which varied according to local circumstances were equally important. The rise of Labour was not the triumph of class solidarity.
Adapted from Tanner 1989.

Passage D

The birth of the Labour Party and the upsurge of trade unionism were among the developments that led politicians to look more closely at the changes that were taking place in society. However, few members of the older, upper-class parties were able to understand the everyday life of the majority of the population. As Chancellor of the Exchequer, Lloyd George undoubtedly had an appeal to many of the working class. He could on occasion speak movingly of the hardships of the poor and condemn the 'idle rich' - though he confessed that he did not fully realise the nature of poverty until he came to administer the Old Age Pensions Act. While some progressive Liberals had social consciences, their knowledge of working-class life was limited. As for the average politician, the philanthropic George Cadbury was near the truth when he told a party of LRC delegates at Bournville that 'few of the present MPs knew or cared to know much about the condition of the working men of the country'.
Adapted from Martin 1985.

ITEM 4 'Then and Now'

Then and Now.

LIBERAL PARTY: My dear sir, I am delighted to give you a lift. It is quite a pleasure to have your company.

LIBERAL PARTY: Dear me! If he grows much bigger, I shall be crowded out of the trap altogether.

It has been resolved that the Miners' Federation shall join the Labour Party.

This cartoon was produced in 1909 after the Miners' Federation announced its decision to join the Labour Party.

Questions

1. Was it inevitable that the Labour Party would replace the Liberals as the second main party after 1914? Use Items 1-4 in your answer.
2. Look at Items 1 and 2.
   a) What do these items tell us about the fortunes of the two parties in the period 1900-24?
   b) What was the turning point for Labour? Explain your answer.
   c) What factors other than election results need to be taken into account when explaining the rapid rise to power of the Labour Party?
3. a) Using the passages in Item 3, make a list of factors which played a part in ensuring that Labour replaced the Liberals as the second main party after 1914. Indicate which factors, in your view, are most important and explain why.
   b) Write your own analysis of the strength of the Labour Party in 1914.
4. What point is being made by the cartoon in Item 4? How accurate do you think this viewpoint was? Explain your answer.

References

- **Adelman (1986)** Adelman, P., *The Rise of the Labour Party* (2nd edn), Longman, 1986.

- **Behagg (1991)** Behagg, C., *Labour and Reform: Working-Class Movements 1815-1914*, Hodder and Stoughton, 1991.

- **Behagg (1995)** Behagg, C., 'Trade unions and the rise of labour 1885-1914' in *Scott-Baumann (1995)*.

- **Benn (1992)** Benn, C., *Keir Hardie*, Hutchinson, 1992.

- **Best (1979)** Best, G., *Mid-Victorian Britain 1851-75*, Fontana,1979.

- **Brown (1985)** Brown, K.D. (ed.), *The First Labour Party: 1906-14*, Croom Helm, 1985.

- **Catterall (1994)** Catterall, P. (ed), *Britain 1867-1918*, Heinemann, 1994.

- **Clarke (1971)** Clarke, P.F., *Lancashire and the New Liberalism*, Cambridge University Press, 1971.

- **Craig (1989)** Craig, F.W.S., *British Electoral Facts 1832-1987*, Gower Publishing Ltd, 1989.

- **Crick (1994)** Crick, M., *The History of the Social Democratic Federation*, Keele University Press, 1994.

- **Fowler (1997)** Fowler, S., '"Building Jerusalem": the activist and the Labour Party 1900-45', *Modern History Review*, Vol.8.4, April 1997.

- **Gardiner & Wenborn (1995)** Gardiner, J. & Wenborn, N., *The Companion to British History*, Collins & Brown, 1995.

- **Harrison (1984)** Harrison, J.F.C., *The Common People*, Flamingo, 1984.

- **Hobsbawm (1964)** Hobsbawm, E.J., *Labouring Men*, Weidenfeld and Nicolson, 1964.

- **Howell (1994)** Howell, D., 'The origins of the ILP', see *Catterall (1994)*.

- **ILP (1993)** ILP, 'Challenging "common sense"', *History Today*, Vol.43, March 1993.

- **Laybourn (1997)** Laybourn, K., *The Rise of British Socialism*, Sutton, 1997.

- **Laybourn (1998)** Laybourn, K., 'The rise of the Labour Party', *Modern History Review*, Vol.10.1, September 1998.

- **MacCarthy (1994)** MacCarthy, F., *William Morris: a Life of our Time*, Faber, 1994.

- **McBriar (1962)** McBriar, A.M., *Fabian Socialism and English Politics*, Cambridge University Press, 1962.

- **McKenzie & Silver (1968)** McKenzie, R. & Silver, A., *Angels in Marble: Working-Class Conservatives in Urban England*, Heinemann, 1968.

- **McKibbin (1974)** McKibbin, R., *The Evolution of the Labour Party: 1910-1924*, Oxford University Press, 1974.

- **Martin (1985)** Martin, D., 'Ideology and composition' in *Brown (1985)*.

- **Moore (1978)** Moore, R., *The Emergence of the Labour Party*, Hodder & Stoughton, 1978.

- **Morgan (1975)** Morgan, K.O., *Keir Hardie: Radical and Socialist*, Weidenfeld and Nicholson, 1975.

- **Morgan (1992)** Morgan, K.O., 'Keir Hardie and the Rise of Labour', *History Review*, Issue 12, March 1992.

- **Pelling (1963)** Pelling, H., *History of British Trade Unionism*, Penguin, 1963.

- **Pelling (1965)** Pelling, H., *The Origins of the Labour Party*, Oxford University Press, 1965.

- **Pelling (1967)** Pelling, H., *Social Geography of British Elections*, Macmillan, 1967.

- **Pelling (1968)** Pelling, H., *Popular Politics and Society in Late Victorian Britain*, Macmillan, 1968.

- **Pelling (1991)** Pelling, H., *A Short History of the Labour Party* (9th edn), Macmillan, 1961.

- **Phillips (1992)** Phillips, G., *Rise of the Labour Party*, Routledge, 1992.

- **Pugh (1993)** Pugh, M., *The Making of Modern British Politics* (2nd edn), Blackwell, 1993.

- **Reid (1978)** Reid, F., *Keir Hardie: the Making of a Socialist*, Croom Helm, 1978.

- **Scott-Baumann (1995)** Scott-Baumann, M., *Years of Expansion: Britain 1815-1914*, Hodder & Stoughton, 1995.

- **Snowden (1934)** Snowden, P., *An Autobiography*, Vol.1, Nicolson and Watson, 1934.

- **Stedman Jones (1983)** Stedman Jones, G., *Language of Class: Studies in English Working Class History 1832-1982*, Cambridge University Press, 1983.

- **Tanner (1989)** Tanner, D., 'The rise of the Labour Party', *Modern History Review*, November 1989.

- **Tanner (1990)** Tanner, D., *Political Change and the Labour Party*, Cambridge University Press, 1990.

- **Thane (1985)** Thane, P., 1985, 'The Labour Party and state welfare' in *Brown* (1985).

- **Thompson (1977)** Thompson, E.P., *William Morris: Romantic to Revolutionary*, Merlin Press, 1977.

- **Thompson (1967)** Thompson, P., *Socialists, Liberals and Labour: the Struggle for London*, Routledge, 1967.

- **Thorpe (1997)** Thorpe, A., *A History of the British Labour Party*, Macmillan, 1997.

- **Wilson (1966)** Wilson, T., *Downfall of the Liberal Party*, Collins, 1966.

The Liberal Party 1886-1914

Timeline - The Liberal Party 1886-1914

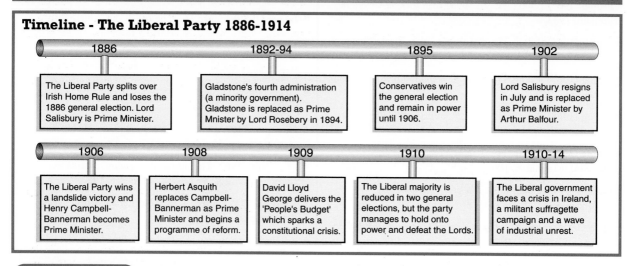

1886
The Liberal Party splits over Irish Home Rule and loses the 1886 general election. Lord Salisbury is Prime Minister.

1892-94
Gladstone's fourth administration (a minority government). Gladstone is replaced as Prime Mnister by Lord Rosebery in 1894.

1895
Conservatives win the general election and remain in power until 1906.

1902
Lord Salisbury resigns in July and is replaced as Prime Minister by Arthur Balfour.

1906
The Liberal Party wins a landslide victory and Henry Campbell-Bannerman becomes Prime Minister.

1908
Herbert Asquith replaces Campbell-Bannerman as Prime Minister and begins a programme of reform.

1909
David Lloyd George delivers the 'People's Budget' which sparks a constitutional crisis.

1910
The Liberal majority is reduced in two general elections, but the party manages to hold onto power and defeat the Lords.

1910-14
The Liberal government faces a crisis in Ireland, a militant suffragette campaign and a wave of industrial unrest.

Introduction

After dominating the British political scene between 1846 and 1886, the Liberal Party spent 17 of the following 20 years out of power. Then, in the general election of 1906, the party won a resounding victory and a Liberal government remained in power until the Prime Minister, Herbert Asquith, set up a coalition government in 1915. The Liberal government of 1906-15, however, was the last purely Liberal government to take office in the 20th century. It is true that Liberals continued to serve in the coalition governments that retained power between 1915 and 1922. But, after the First World War, the Liberal Party was never the force it had been before war broke out. Indeed, by the end of 1924, the decline in Liberal fortunes was so marked that there is good reason to describe it as a 'third party' rather

than a 'major party'. The varying political fortunes of the Liberal Party in the period 1886-1924 have given rise to a number of important historical debates. First, there is the debate over the turnaround in electoral fortunes of the two main parties in the period between 1886 and 1906. Second, there is the debate over why the Liberal Party won the 1906 general election so convincingly. Third, there is a debate about just how radical the Liberal government's social reforms were and over what motivated them. Fourth, there is a debate over the impact of the constitutional crisis which arose when the Lords rejected Lloyd George's 1909 'People's Budget'. And fifth, there is a debate about why the Liberal Party declined so rapidly after the First World War. This unit addresses each of these debates in turn.

UNIT SUMMARY

Part 1 examines the turnaround in the electoral fortunes of the two main parties in the period 1886-1906. It considers why the Unionist alliance was successful during this period and what led to the Liberals' convincing win in the 1906 general election.

Part 2 focuses on the debates over 'New Liberalism' and on the welfare reforms passed by the Liberal government in the period 1906-14. What impact did New Liberalism make on the Liberal Party? How new was 'New Liberalism'? How radical were the government's welfare reforms?

Part 3 looks at the constitutional crisis which arose after Lloyd George introduced the 'People's Budget' of 1909. How did the crisis affect the Liberal Party and the Unionist alliance? Did it

result in a triumph for the Liberals?

Part 4 assesses the way in which the Liberal government tackled the Irish Question in the period 1906-14. What was the background to the crisis of 1912-14? Why did the crisis develop? Who was to blame for the crisis?

Part 5 tackles the question of political leadership. What led to the rise to power of Asquith and Lloyd George? Why were their leadership styles so different? Who was the most effective leader?

Part 6 looks at the theories which have been developed to explain the Liberal Party's rapid decline after the First World War. Was George Dangerfield right to suggest that the party was in decline before war broke out?

1 What led to the turnaround in electoral fortunes, 1886-1906?

Key questions

1. Why were the Liberals out of power for so much of the period 1886-1906?

2. How do historians explain Conservative success in the period 1886-1906?

3. Why did the Liberals win the 1906 general election?

1.1 Why were the Liberals out of power for so much of the period 1886-1906?

1886 - a turning point
After the repeal of the Corn Laws in 1846, the Liberal Party dominated the political scene for 40 years. Between 1846 and 1886, the Conservative Party won an overall majority in just one general election (in 1874). Yet, between 1886 and 1906, the position of the two main parties was reversed (see Box 6.1). Most historians agree that the turning point was Gladstone's 'conversion' to Home Rule in 1885. Gladstone's decision to agree to put forward a Home Rule Bill quickly won the backing of the majority of Liberal MPs, but it alienated a significant minority. On the one hand, it alienated a group of conservative Whigs led by Lord Hartington. And, on the other hand, it alienated a group of radical Liberals led by Joseph Chamberlain. When Gladstone introduced the Home Rule Bill in the summer of 1886, both groups of dissidents voted

against it and then left the Liberal Party, forming a new parliamentary group and calling themselves 'Liberal Unionists'. Following this split in the Liberal Party, the Conservative Party won more seats than any other party in each of the four general elections held between 1886 and 1906 and, with the exception of 1892-95 when Gladstone was able to form a minority government, the Conservative Party was able to form the government throughout this period.

What led to the turnaround in electoral fortunes?
Historians are divided about what led to the turnaround in the electoral fortunes of the two main parties. There are three main theories.

1. The traditional view
The traditional explanation of the turnaround in the electoral fortunes of the two main parties was that the Home Rule crisis of 1886 brought to an end a process of realignment in British politics - a process of realignment which had been going on since the 1860s:

'One long-term trend was the shift of the middle class and propertied interests towards Conservatism from the 1860s, culminating in the schism [split] of 1886.' (Pugh 1993, p.5)

A number of factors are cited as contributing to this realignment:

- electoral reform in 1867 and 1884-85 changed the electoral geography, in particular, allowing Conservatives to win borough seats for the first time (previously the party's support was concentrated in rural county seats)
- the Conservative Party built a more professional party machine which enabled it to mobilise support more effectively
- there was an economic downturn after 1875, making it difficult for the Liberal government to retain support
- many members of the middle classes were afraid of the radical ideas being promoted by some Liberal MPs (notably, Joseph Chamberlain).

Before 1886, the argument goes, the Liberal Party had managed to keep together an unsteady alliance of radical reformers and conservative Whigs. In 1886, however, the conservative Whigs (and a small number of radicals) split away from the party and found their natural home in the Conservative Party.

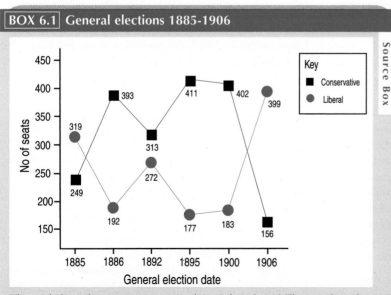

BOX 6.1 | **General elections 1885-1906**

Key
■ Conservative
● Liberal

Source Box

This graph shows changing party support in the period 1886-1906. The vertical axis shows how the number of seats won by each party in general elections changed. The horizontal axis shows the dates of the general elections.

2. The revisionist view

The traditional explanation has been challenged in two main ways. First, Cooke and Vincent (1974) argue that, rather than being the result of a long-lasting process, the political realignment was a matter of 'high politics' - the product of a power struggle which grew up in response to the 1885 general election result (when the Liberals won 319 seats, the Conservatives won 249 and the Irish Nationalists held the balance of power with 86). In other words, the personalities of the people involved and parliamentary arithmetic were more important than long-term trends.

And second, whilst Blewett (1972) and Jenkins (1988) accept that the political realignment was the product of a power struggle, they emphasise that there were serious ideological divisions between the pro- and anti-Home Rulers in the Liberal Party. These ideological divisions, they argue, had grown up over the previous 20 years, but came to a head in 1886:

'The Home Rule issue provided the opportunity for men to break with Gladstone in defence of unity, Empire and the Protestant religion. Without Home Rule, the rising stream of affluent seceders [splitters] would have continued; with Home Rule the stream became a torrent.' (Blewett 1972, p.15)

3. The Marxist view

According to Marxists, Liberalism was a set of ideas particularly suited to the earlier phases of the Industrial Revolution. By the late 19th century, the nature of industrial society had changed and, as a result, Liberalism began to lose its appeal. Three main factors account for this. First, there was a growing divide between workers and employers in the workplace, and growing class consciousness. Second, there was growing social segregation as distinct middle-class areas and working-class areas developed in industrial towns. And third, lower economic growth and greater international competition after 1875 reduced profits and increased unemployment, placing a new strain on both the working and middle classes.

The problem that Liberalism faced in the late 19th century was that it needed to appeal to those workers who had the vote (by passing reforms), but, in doing so, it risked alienating those members of the middle class who were afraid of change. In such circumstances, it was only a matter of time before the working class would abandon the Liberal Party for an independent labour party and before the middle class would abandon the Liberal Party for the Conservative Party. The Liberal Party would, therefore, have lost support with or without the crisis of 1886.

What impact was made by the Liberal Unionists?

In the revolt over the Home Rule Bill, 93 Liberal MPs voted against the government and then left the party:

'Their decision to vote against the Bill and bring down the government was made easier by the Conservative pledge not to oppose in the next election any Liberal MP who rebelled against the Gladstonian leadership. At this stage, there seemed little enthusiasm for any formal alliance between the two sides and in the election which followed the government's defeat they fought separate campaigns. The Liberal Unionists with 78 seats held the balance in the new House and generally gave their backing to what was an exclusively Conservative administration.' (Watts 1994, p.124)

The initial aims of the Liberal Unionists

The 78 Liberal Unionists elected in the 1886 general election included both conservative Whigs led by Lord Hartington (the majority) and radical reformers led by Joseph Chamberlain (see Box 2.9 on page 50 and Box 6.2 on page 183). Given that these two groups had previously been divided over almost every issue and were even divided over Home Rule (Hartington's group rejected Home Rule outright whilst Chamberlain's group opposed specific parts of the Bill), Dutton argues that, at first, Chamberlain saw the partnership as a temporary arrangement:

'With Home Rule defeated at the polls, Chamberlain imagined that Gladstone would soon resign the Liberal leadership and the party's schism [split] could be healed...With Gladstone out of the way, Chamberlain would be in a strong position to mould Liberalism along the radical paths which he had already charted in his municipal career in Birmingham.' (Dutton 1994, pp.32-33)

The Liberal Unionists move towards the Conservatives

Gladstone did not resign from the leadership of the Liberal Party in 1886. He remained Leader until 1894. By then, attempts to heal the split in the party had failed. In 1887, an attempt was made to heal the split when the so-called 'Round Table' talks were held between Liberals and Liberal Unionists. But, they ended in failure. Over the next few years, the Liberal Unionists' ties with the Liberal Party loosened and their ties with the Conservatives strengthened. While it is not surprising that the conservative Whigs were able to cooperate with the Conservative Party, it is more surprising that Chamberlain and his supporters were able to do so. Yet, Salisbury's government adopted policies which appealed to them:

'In practice, Salisbury's Conservative government showed itself an increasingly attractive bedfellow as far as Chamberlain was concerned. He and his supporters had the pleasure of seeing many of their own most cherished policies enacted by the Tory Cabinet. These included the legislation of 1888-89 creating the London County Council and elected

BOX 6.2 Joseph Chamberlain (1836-1914)

A screw-manufacturing industrialist, Joseph Chamberlain built up a political base in Birmingham. As Lord Mayor in 1873-76, he encouraged the city council to buy land and public utilities. The council then ran the public utilities and built amenities on the land, transforming the city (Chamberlain's policy is known as 'gas and water socialism'). Chamberlain was elected as Liberal MP for Birmingham in 1876, determined to do for the nation what he had done for the city. In 1885, he wrote a campaigning document outlining his main ideas. This became known as the 'unauthorised programme' since Gladstone did not adopt it. The unauthorised programme and the Liberal Party's official manifesto are summarised below:

Unauthorised Programme	Official programme
1. Reform of the Lords	1. Possible reform of the Lords
2. Parliaments to last three years	2. Reform of Commons procedure
3. Payment of MPs	3. Scheme to increase voter registration
4. Universal manhood suffrage	4. Local government reform
5. Disestablishment of the Church of England	5. Modest changes in land registration
6. Democratic local government	6. No commitment on Ireland
7. National councils for England, Scotland, Wales and Ireland	7. Vague references to tax changes.
8. Free elementary education	
9. Tax on property	
10. The 'three acres and a cow' policy - agricultural workers to be given smallholdings to farm.	

Although a radical in some respects, Chamberlain was strongly committed to the maintenance and the growth of the British Empire. It was this commitment which led to his break with Gladstone over Home Rule in Ireland.

Adapted from Watts 1995 and Gardiner & Wenborn 1995.

county councils for England, Wales and Scotland, the introduction of free education in 1891 and various measures about allotments and smallholdings.' (Dutton 1994, p.33)

By the time of the 1892 general election, Chamberlain had shared a public platform with Lord Salisbury and announced that 'I neither look for nor desire reunion' with the Liberals. In the election campaign, he campaigned on behalf of Conservative candidates. The 47 Liberal Unionist MPs elected in 1892 remained in opposition with the Conservatives throughout Gladstone's final term in office and, when Salisbury returned to power in 1895, five Liberal Unionists joined his Cabinet. Although the Liberal Unionists remained theoretically independent until 1912, in practice the two parties became indistinguishable and the term 'Unionist' is often used as an umbrella term covering both Conservatives and Liberal Unionists.

How did the Liberal Unionist split affect the Liberal Party?

Although the Liberal Party managed to recover sufficiently from the split in 1886 to form a minority government after the general election of 1892 (the 272 Liberal MPs gained the support of 81 Irish Nationalist MPs, giving them a majority over the 313 Conservative MPs), historians have identified a number of ways in which the 1886 split affected the

party. First, in the short term at least, the split damaged the reputation of the party with the electorate as a whole. It is often said that split parties do not win general elections in Britain and this was the case in the general election of 1886. Although the party recovered in 1892, the continued presence of the Liberal Unionists in Parliament was a constant reminder of the split and helps to explain why voters found the Liberal Party less attractive in the period 1885-1906. Second, the split changed the nature of the party:

'Nearly all of the Liberal aristocracy departed from the main body of the party, to become Liberal Unionists.' (Douglas 1971, p.4)

This had an important knock-on effect in terms of funding. Many of the Liberal aristocrats who split in 1886 had been generous in their donations to the party. As a result, the party suffered financially after the 1886 split.

And third, it has been suggested that the creation of Liberal Unionism affected voting behaviour. The argument is that, in some constituencies, voters had strong emotional ties with the Liberal Party and were reluctant to vote against it. Such voters were prepared to vote Liberal Unionist, however. In other words, the existence of the Liberal Unionist Party reduced the trauma of breaking long-established party loyalty:

'The traumatic break [with the Liberal Party] was eased for many by the existence of the Liberal Unionist Party, possessing many of the symbols, some of the leaders and even the name of the party they were abandoning...Thus the Liberal Unionist Party acted as a stepping-stone to the right for electors of conservative inclination but anti-Conservative prejudices.' (Blewett 1972, p.15) As a result, the Liberal Party lost seats in constituencies it would previously have expected to hold.

1.2 How do historians explain Conservative success, 1886-1906?

Conservative strengths

Historians have tended to explain Conservative success in the period 1886-1906 by examining, on the one hand, Conservative strengths and, on the other hand, Liberal weaknesses. Four key Conservative strengths have been identified.

1. A new-look party

The Conservative Party repositioned itself in the 1880s. Before 1880, the Conservative Party was closely identified with agricultural interests - the interests of the landed gentry and the 'old order':

'A Liberal MP in 1867 spoke of the two great parties, "the one which represented the agricultural and the other, the manufacturing and commercial interests of our vast community". This identification of the Conservative Party with agriculture was a pardonable exaggeration. Before the Reform Act, the Conservatives took 67% of agricultural seats, and after 1867, 77%.' (Pearce & Stewart 1992, p.69)

In the 1880s, however, the Conservative Party attempted to broaden its appeal. Although its leadership remained predominantly aristocratic, it sought and gained greater support from the urban middle classes as well as appealing to the working class - see Box 6.3.

2. The new electoral system

The electoral system which came into operation after the 1884-85 Reform Acts were passed favoured the Conservatives. In particular, the Conservatives began to win seats in industrial towns. Blewett (1972) argues that this was due to the fact that the Conservatives secured a larger proportion of the working-class vote than the Liberals. Pugh (1993) and Lee (1994), on the other hand, suggest that this was due to the creation of single-member constituencies. Single-member constituencies worked to the advantage of the Conservatives because they were smaller than multi-member constituencies. As a result, pockets of middle-class Conservatives (who tended to be concentrated in the suburbs) were not swamped by other voters as they had been previously.

BOX 6.3 Working-class Conservatism

Interpretation

The attempt to broaden the appeal of the Conservative Party among the working class had some success. Working-class Conservatism remained strong throughout the late Victorian period in Liverpool and West Lancashire, Birmingham and a number of London's East End constituencies. There were particular local factors for Conservative strength in these areas. In Liverpool, for example, a predominantly Protestant working class was hostile to Irish immigrants who were Catholics and rivals for jobs. As the Liberals moved to support Home Rule, so the Conservatives gained wider support among the working-class voters. But, historians have also seen more general factors at work in producing working-class Conservatives. One is deference, or the acceptance by working-class voters that government by their social superiors was the natural order of things. The second is the Conservative Party's success in 'wrapping itself in the flag'. In addition to a policy of cautious reform designed to consolidate middle-class support, the Conservatives were able to generate popular support by focusing on the British Empire. As in Germany and France during the same period, imperial issues were a useful means of diverting potential discontent among the working classes into surges of patriotism (see also Unit 7, Section 1.2). It should be noted, however, that working-class imperialism may have had less to do with fervent 'jingoism' and more to do with practical considerations. Members of the working class made a link between vigorous imperial policies and material wellbeing. Such a link obviously underpinned the support for Conservatism in centres like Woolwich where jobs depended on the fortunes of arms manufacturers, and also in dockyard towns like Plymouth, Chatham and Portsmouth.

Adapted from Lee 1994 and Pugh 1993.

3. The development of a professional party

It was in the 1880s that the Conservative Party developed a professional and national party machine:

'The development of a professional party structure was largely the responsibility of two gifted and dedicated lieutenants who were appointed in 1885. Richard Middleton provided an essential link with the grass roots in his dual role as Principal Agent and Secretary to the National Union of Conservative Associations. Working in close cooperation with the new Chief Whip, Aretas Akers-Douglas, he reorganised the constituency associations, encouraged the recruitment of full-time professional agents and distributed centrally-produced propaganda material.' (Goodlad 1996, p.3)

Lee (1994) points out that, by 1900, the Conservatives had 30 party agents in London while the Liberals had just three.

The Primrose League

In addition, it was in November 1883 that the Primrose League was set up (see also Unit 2, page 61 and Unit 3, pages 81-82). The Primrose League was a club whose aim was to promote the sort of Conservative values supposedly supported by Disraeli (the primrose was Disraeli's favourite flower). The club was organised in a hierarchical way, offering one class of membership to the upper classes (at a high subscription rate) and associate membership to the lower classes (at a lower rate). Although it was a political club, the Primrose League performed an important social function. It organised tea parties, fetes and other forms of entertainment which allowed members of the working class to mingle with their social superiors (often the entertainment it organised was the only available locally). It also encouraged the participation of women:

'Middle- and upper-class ladies threw themselves enthusiastically into arranging League functions, canvassing, contacting the outvoters, conveying electors to the polls in private carriages, raising funds and generally keeping the grass roots of Conservatism vigorous.' (Pugh 1993, p.56)

Membership of the League grew rapidly and reached more than a million in 1891. It then fluctuated depending on the popularity of the party nationally:

'Membership more than doubled in 1886-87 under the stimulus of the Home Rule crisis, slackened in the early 1890s as Salisbury's government ran out of steam, quickened dramatically before and during the Boer War and stagnated thereafter until 1910. By that year some 2,645 habitations [groups] existed.' (Pugh 1993, p.55)

It is important to note that there were groups in rural and industrial areas and that, according to the League, 90% of its members were from the working class.

4. The contribution of Lord Salisbury

Until recently, the view of historians was that the Conservative domination of the period 1886-1906 was due less to the actions of Lord Salisbury than to the circumstances in which he found himself. In recent years, however, Lord Salisbury's contribution has been reassessed and his reputation restored (see Box 6.4). In particular, it has been argued that he sowed the seeds of Conservative success by:

- ensuring that the electoral reform package of 1884-85 favoured the Conservatives
- adapting to the new electoral system by repositioning the party, broadening its appeal and making it more professional
- forging an alliance with the Liberal Unionists
- ensuring that the Unionist alliance presented a united front
- appointing men who shared his outlook to key ministries

- adopting a cautious approach to reform which satisfied those supporters who wanted change but did not alienate those who were afraid of change.

| BOX 6.4 | Robert Cecil, Lord Salisbury (1820-1903) |

Lord Salisbury led the Conservative Party, jointly at first and then alone, for a total of 21 years. He formed four governments (1885-86, 1886-92, 1895-1900, 1900-02), holding the premiership for longer than any individual since Lord Liverpool. He began his career in the 1850s as a fiery right-wing intellectual. By the end of the century, he had been transformed into a national institution. But, he was never taken to heart by the Conservative Party at large. Even at the peak of his career, he aroused the respect and confidence of the party faithful rather than deeper more emotional loyalty. Salisbury's deep Christian faith and firm commitment to Anglican doctrine was the sheet anchor of his life and it underpinned a fundamentally pessimistic view of the world. His view was that, in an imperfect world, all political decisions involved a choice between differing evils. Salisbury first made a serious political impact in 1867 when he resigned from Lord Derby's government rather than support electoral reform. This was consistent with his principled opposition to democracy. Popular government, he argued, involved the triumph of numbers over quality, of passion over reason. Although he never came to approve of emerging democracy, he discovered that it was possible to defend Conservative interests in a changed context. As Party Leader, Salisbury skilfully exploited the techniques of the new democratic politics. First, in the hope of winning support in the cities and suburbs, he developed an effective extra-parliamentary speaking style. He made over 70 speeches between 1881 and 1885, mostly to large audiences in industrial towns. Second, he did a deal with Gladstone over electoral reform in 1884, ensuring that Conservatives could win seats in the suburbs. Third, he encouraged the development of a professional party machine. And fourth, as well as holding his own party together, he did all he could to widen the split in the Liberal Party.
Adapted from Goodlad 1996.

Liberal weaknesses

Some historians (for example, Blewett 1972) have argued that Conservative success in the period 1886-1906 (what he calls 'Unionist hegemony') was due more to Liberal weaknesses than to Conservative strengths:

'In retrospect, the Liberals appear to have done their best to lose the elections of 1886, 1895 and 1900...The hegemony was founded and sustained

not primarily because of any positive enthusiasm for the Unionists but because the Liberals were considered "impossible"...The realignment of 1886 can be seen rather as a negative restructuring of political patterns sustained for two decades more by antipathy [hostility] to Liberalism than by enthusiasm for Unionism.' (Blewett 1972, pp.22-23)
These Liberal weaknesses can be described under the following headings.

1. Electoral weaknesses
During the period of Conservative supremacy, the Liberal Party suffered from three interrelated electoral weaknesses. First, as noted above, the split in the party in 1886 led to a financial crisis which made it difficult for the party to field candidates. In the 1886 general election, for example, the Liberal Party handed 116 seats to the Conservatives and Liberal Unionists by failing to put up a candidate of their own (the Conservatives had won just six seats in this way in 1885). While the number of unopposed seats handed to the Unionist alliance fell to 43 in 1892, it rose again to 117 in 1895 and to 149 in 1900 (figures from Blewett 1972). As Lee (1994, p.213) points out, 'this was not the way to win elections'. Second, Blewett argues that a significant number of Liberal supporters simply did not turn out to vote for the Liberals in the elections of 1886, 1895 and 1900:
'In the period 1886-1900, the Unionist achievement was essentially a negative one, based on the failure of Liberal leaders to arouse the party workers and to rally the Liberal voters.' (Blewett 1972, p.22)
And third, there was a change in the electoral geography of mainland Britain. Between 1886 and 1906, Liberal support was concentrated in Scotland, Wales and the South West:
'Increasingly it was a party of the Celtic fringe...and, therefore, increasingly wedded to politics with little relevance outside Wales and Scotland. Disestablishment of the Anglican Church in Wales might cause a waving of flags in the valleys and chapels of the Principality, but in Huddersfield, Newcastle and the East End of London it meant very little.' (Pearce & Stewart 1992, p.54)

2. Leadership
Gladstone's resignation as leader in March 1894 led to a leadership struggle within the Liberal Party:
'No-one could provide the necessary leadership to hold the diverse elements of the party together. The task was difficult for there were serious divisions within the party.' (Watts 1995, p.124)
First, Queen Victoria chose the Earl of Rosebery as Prime Minister rather than William Harcourt, the Chancellor of the Exchequer. This was resented by the radical wing in the Liberal Party because Rosebery was from the Whig side of the party. In 1896, Harcourt replaced Rosebery as Party Leader, but he failed to gain the support of sections of the party and, in turn, resigned from the leadership in 1898. He was replaced by Henry Campbell-Bannerman. As Lee points out:
'With problems as fundamental as these, it is not surprising that the Liberals were unable to hold on to power in the second half of the 1890s.' (Lee 1994, p.213)

3. A 'crisis of identity'
Lee argues that the Liberals suffered from a 'crisis of identity' in the 1890s. In addition to the problems described above, this crisis arose because the party was caught between two stools. On the one hand, it needed to gain the support of working-class voters if it was to be successful electorally. That meant supporting reforms which would appeal to such voters. On the other hand, it could not afford to ignore the interests of its sponsors (many of whom were wealthy industrialists) nor could it afford to alienate middle-class voters who were opposed to reform. This crisis of identity intensified after Gladstone's resignation.

MAIN POINTS - Sections 1.1 - 1.2

- Between 1846 and 1886, the Liberal Party dominated the political scene, with the Conservative Party winning an overall majority in just one general election (in 1874). Yet, between 1886 and 1906, the position of the two main parties was reversed.
- The three main theories on what led to this reversal are - (1) the crisis of 1886 ended a process of realignment in British politics which had begun in the 1860s (2) the crisis of 1886 was the product of a power struggle following the 1885 general election and (3) the process of industrialisation made a crisis of Liberalism inevitable.
- Although some Liberal Unionists expected the split to be temporary, it became permanent. The split injured the Liberal Party in both the short term and medium term.
- The Conservatives had four key strengths in the period 1886-1906 - (1) the party repositioned itself (2) the new electoral system favoured the party (3) a new party machine was built and (4) the Prime Minister, Lord Salisbury, skilfully exploited circumstances.
- The Liberal Party suffered from (1) electoral weaknesses (2) a leadership struggle and (3) a crisis of identity.

Activity 6.1 Conservative supremacy

ITEM 1 The voting pattern 1886-1906

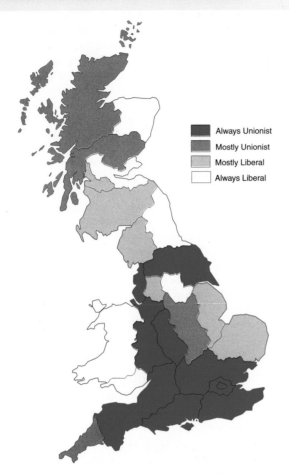

Always Unionist
Mostly Unionist
Mostly Liberal
Always Liberal

This map shows how support for the Unionists and Liberals was distributed in general elections held between 1886 and 1906.

ITEM 2 A historian's view (1)

In the past, Liberals had been able to unite against the actions of their common political enemy - the Tories. Unfortunately for them, between 1886 and 1906, the Tories refused to make it easy for their rivals by adopting a die-hard reactionary stance. Instead, under Salisbury's careful stewardship, they revealed themselves to be in tune with the new middle-class aspirations of what their Leader called 'Villa Toryism'. They were good at tapping working-class conservatism and imaginative in their handling of the Irish land question. Confident that they would win support in the cities, they willingly abandoned county seats in the Redistribution Act of 1885 in favour of single-member constituencies (see Unit 2, Section 3.2). The introduction of reforms such as democratically elected county councils in 1888 and free education in 1891 were also notable Tory coups. All this was too much for the Liberals who constantly cried foul and claimed that their policies had been hijacked by their opponents. The problem was that the Liberals no longer had anything distinctive to offer the electorate except outdated causes like disestablishment and temperance reform (which had lost both their relevance and popular appeal) and, as ever, Ireland. By the time Gladstone resigned, the Liberals still had no clear idea of what their future role would be.

Adapted from Winstanley 1990.

ITEM 3 Election results 1886-1906

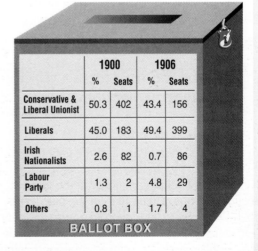

	1886 %	1886 Seats	1892 %	1892 Seats	1895 %	1895 Seats
Conservative & Liberal Unionist	51.4	393	47.0	313	49.1	411
Liberals	45.0	192	45.1	272	45.7	177
Irish Nationalists	3.5	85	7.0	81	4.0	82
Others	0.1	0	0.9	4	0.2	0

	1900 %	1900 Seats	1906 %	1906 Seats
Conservative & Liberal Unionist	50.3	402	43.4	156
Liberals	45.0	183	49.4	399
Irish Nationalists	2.6	82	0.7	86
Labour Party	1.3	2	4.8	29
Others	0.8	1	1.7	4

These tables show the general election results between 1886 and 1906.

Adapted from Craig 1989.

ITEM 4 Lord Salisbury

St. Stephen's Review Presentation Cartoon, April 25th, 1891.

ONE FLAG, ONE LEADER, ONE VOICE!

This cartoon was produced by Tom Merry and published in the *St Stephen's Review* (a magazine) on 25 April 1891.

ITEM 5 A historian's view (2)

If we examine figures in those 119 seats which were contested in both 1885 and 1886 and which were won by the Unionists from the Liberals in 1886, we can see how much impact Liberal abstention made. In these seats, the Liberal vote fell by 127,892 in 1886, yet the Unionist vote only increased by 45,735. Even allowing generously for involuntary abstention, it appears that the majority of seats fell to the Unionists not because of Liberal switches, but through voluntary abstention. So, the period of Unionist hegemony was ushered in by default rather than by conversion. In the years that followed, it was similarly maintained not by positive enthusiasm for Unionism but by the inability of the Liberals to mobilise their resources and their potential supporters. The inability of the Liberal machine to mount a wide-ranging election campaign was seen in the large number of uncontested seats in the elections held between 1886 and 1900. In both 1895 and 1900, the Unionists were well on their way to victory before polling began. Even in 1892, the most favourable election for the Liberals, Unionist candidates returned without a contest outnumbered Liberals by two to one. At root lay a lack of enthusiasm among Liberal Party members reflected in the poverty of party resources and lack of finance. Much of the wealth had gone with the Liberal Unionists and, in some cases, Liberal organisations crumbled away. Lack of enthusiasm affected voters as well as activists. Turnout remained low until 1906 and the smaller the poll, the larger the Conservative share of it. So, in the period 1886-1900, the Unionist achievement was essentially a negative one, based on the failure of Liberal leaders to enthuse party workers and rally voters.

Adapted from Blewett 1972.

Questions

1. Using Items 1-5 and your own knowledge, explain why the Conservatives enjoyed success in the period 1886-1906.
2. a) What do Items 1 and 3 tell us about the fortunes of (i) the Liberal Party and (ii) the Conservative Party in the period 1886-1906?
   b) Give reasons for these results.
3. a) Explain how the analyses in Items 2 and 5 differ.

   b) Give arguments for and against the view that 1886 marked the beginning of the Liberal Party's long-term decline.
4. a) Judging from Item 4, what image was the Conservative Party trying to promote in 1901?
   b) Why do you think it was trying to promote this image?

1.3 Why did the Liberals win the 1906 general election?

The historical debate

Although the Liberal Party lost the general elections of 1895 and 1900 by a considerable margin, they won an overwhelming majority at the general election of 1906. Given that, in the late 1890s, the Liberal Party was suffering from a crisis of identity, its leadership was divided and it lacked morale and money, this represents quite a turnaround. When exactly this turnaround took place and why it occurred are subjects that have aroused debate

amongst historians. There are four main theories.

1. The Boer War was responsible

The first theory stems from the idea that wars can be important turning points in history. Lee argues that, like the First World War later, the Boer War transformed the political climate in Britain (see also Unit 7, Section 1.2):

'At several stages in the 19th and early 20th century, Britain's domestic politics have been transformed as involvement in a foreign conflict has upset apparent equilibrium. In this case, the Boer War (1899-1902) proved the principal catalyst for change.' (Lee 1994, p.217)

Lee argues, first, that the British public was not expecting its soldiers to encounter such strong resistance from the Boers and blamed the government for what appeared to be military incompetence. Second, Lee argues that the war stimulated Joseph Chamberlain's campaign for tariffs which split the Conservative Party (see pages 190-91 below). And third, Lee argues that the war stimulated significant change in the Liberal Party:

> 'The decline of the Conservatives was paralleled by the revival of the Liberals. Again, the catalyst was the Boer War which removed the Irish shadow from the party and diverted attention from internal wrangles. By 1902, the Liberal Party had become more accommodating and less obsessive about the issues it espoused [supported]. The policy of Campbell-Bannerman was to promote the party as a "Broad Church", in which no policy or faction should be allowed to predominate.' (Lee 1994, p.218)

2. The 1902 Education Act was responsible

The second theory is that the turnaround in electoral fortunes came in 1902 when the Conservative government passed its Education Act (see Box 6.5). In order to understand this theory, it is important to be aware that, traditionally, the Liberal Party gained a great deal of support from non-conformists (Protestants who do not belong to the Church of England). Gladstone described them as the 'backbone of the party' - see Unit 1, page 22. While non-conformist support for the Liberals remained high during the period 1886-1900, there is good evidence that many thousands of non-conformists abandoned the Liberal Party during this period. The 1902 Education Act, however, was offensive to non-conformists because it allowed all schools to be funded by the rates. If non-conformists lived in an area where there was a Church of England or a Catholic school, therefore, the rates they paid would, in part, go towards the funding of that school. For many non-conformists, this was unacceptable:

> 'Here was the political sting. Schools under religious control qualified for assistance. It meant 'Rome on the rates' in those districts where Catholic schools had been set up. More important at the time, the Church of England's many thousands of elementary schools also had to be assisted by their local county councils.' (Clarke 1996, p.22)

Non-conformists (who are also known as 'dissenters') had always objected to what they saw as the privileges of the Church of England and a fierce campaign was launched against the Act. This campaign was supported by the Liberals and resulted in a Liberal revival:

> 'The Education Act (which infuriated dissenters by providing rate aid to Church Schools) undoubtedly led to thousands of dissenters who had abandoned Gladstonian Liberalism over Home Rule returning

---

BOX 6.5 The Education Act,1902

Interpretation

1. Background to the Act

Education and religion were inseparable in the minds of many Victorians and this was reflected in the national system of elementary education established by the 1870 Forster Act. There were two types of school - Voluntary Schools (Church Schools) and Board Schools (schools run by an elected School Board). Since Board Schools were only required to provide undenominational religious lessons ('simple Bible teaching'), non-conformists preferred to send their children to them (Church Schools would provide Anglican or Catholic religious lessons). The Board Schools were funded by the local rates while the Voluntary Schools were funded by the Anglican (or Catholic) Church. By 1902, more than three times as many children attended elementary school as in 1870. Church Schools taught most, but Board Schools were gaining fast. Most Board Schools were town schools and, thanks to the rates, many had better facilities than Voluntary Schools.

2. Terms of the Act

The Act had two main elements. First, it allowed Voluntary Schools to be funded by the rates. And second, it abolished School Boards. From 1902, schools were to be run by local council education committees - Local Education Authorities (LEAs). Also, whereas School Boards could only provide elementary education, the LEAs were responsible for organising secondary and higher education. *Adapted from Hill & Wright 1981.*

---

to the fold.' (Searle 1992, p.39)

Blewett's theory

According to Blewett (1972), an analysis of by-election results after 1900 shows that there was a marked increase in support for the Liberals after the passing of the Education Act. Before the Education Act was passed, the Unionist alliance had been winning by-elections (members of the Unionist alliance had won nine out of the ten contests which had been held between the 1900 general election and May 1902). After May 1902, however, they began to lose them. Blewett points out that this was at the time when the Boer War had ended in victory and at a time when economic conditions were fair (two factors that should have favoured the Conservative government). In other words, the key to the turnaround in the electoral fortunes of the Liberal Party was the Education Act:

> 'This sudden crumbling of the government's popularity at the very moment of victory in South Africa, and with the economic climate still fair, resulted apparently from the Education Bill of 1902.' (Blewett 1972, p.27)

3. Chamberlain's tariff reform campaign was responsible

The third theory is that the turnaround of electoral fortunes began in 1903 when Joseph Chamberlain launched his tariff reform campaign. This, it is argued, split the Unionist alliance and damaged its image so much that voters turned to the Liberals in the 1906 general election.

Chamberlain's speech

Between 1895 and 1903, Joseph Chamberlain served in the Cabinet as Secretary of State for the Colonies. By 1903, he had become convinced that Britain's future could only be secured if it abandoned free trade, the cornerstone of Victorian economic policy, and replaced it with a system of 'preferential tariffs' (see Box 6.6). His idea was that Britain would charge tariffs (taxes) on all imports, but imports from British colonies and dominions would be subjected to no or to lower tariffs. In this way, Britain would raise revenue which could be spent on social reforms and imperial ties would be tightened. On returning from a trip to South Africa in May 1903, Chamberlain made a public speech in Birmingham in which he outlined his plan. The speech made a significant impact:

'This speech initiated a debate which split the Unionists as a whole with both Conservatives and Liberal Unionists divided over their response...Some Unionists, including the young Winston Churchill, decided to defect to the Liberals...In September 1903, Chamberlain resigned from the government in order to carry on a full-time campaign in the country at large. Leading free traders in the Cabinet also resigned.' (Byrne 1995, pp.461-62)

The impact of the speech

Chamberlain's speech has been described as a 'radical bombshell':

'Joseph Chamberlain produced a sweeping panacea [cure-all], a radical bombshell which was to split the Tory Party and irretrievably halt the Conservative ascendancy.' (Pearce & Stewart 1992, p.102)

Its immediate impact was twofold:

'The immediate impact of his move was to rally the disunited Liberals and open a serious breach in the Conservative Party. Some government supporters such as the old Whig, Lord Hartington, now the Duke of Devonshire, were in favour of free trade. More, perhaps one-third of the parliamentary party, were in agreement with Chamberlain, and many more were in the middle.' (Watts 1994, p.137)

Chamberlain set up the Tariff Reform League to promote his message and, in September 1903, he resigned from the government to work on the campaign full-time. While protection had some appeal with some sections of British society, it was, in general, unpopular. Most people believed that free trade kept food prices low and that the imposition of tariffs would make them rise:

BOX 6.6 Tariff reform

Interpretation

(i) During the last three decades of the 19th century, many of Britain's European competitors began to place high tariffs (or 'duties') on imports. In France, a campaign against the low protection agreement with Britain began in 1860 and finally resulted in the Méline tariff of 1892. In Germany, the policy of low duties was reversed in 1879. Italy adopted high protection in 1887. Austria and Russia returned to it in 1874-75 and 1877 respectively. Spain established new rates in 1877 and 1891; and so on throughout Europe. Overseas, American import duties tended to rise with each new tariff law from the Civil War in 1861-65. Britain had been a free-trade nation since the repeal of the Corn Laws in 1846 and it remained such throughout the 19th century. In 1881, however, a group of industrialists set up the Fair Trade League to campaign for protection. This campaign was of little importance until Chamberlain's speech in 1903 moved the issue of British protectionism to the centre of the political stage.
Adapted from Landes 1969.

(ii) On 15 May 1903, Chamberlain declared his faith in 'imperial preference'. The idea was that a system of duties (taxes), lower for goods within the Empire, would tie the Empire together, raise revenue for social reform and protect British industry. Chamberlain had long been concerned with the issue of unity within the Empire. Like many others, he believed that only through the Empire could Britain survive into the 20th century as a superpower. The emotional bonds of unity fostered by the Boer War led Chamberlain to believe that the opportunity for strengthening links within the Empire had to be seized. Soon after the war, in July 1902, the fourth colonial conference was held in London. But, Chamberlain's hopes of persuading the self-governing colonies to accept some kind of imperial council proved a complete failure. On the other hand, there were some encouraging noises as far as imperial economic cooperation was concerned. Chamberlain made a lengthy visit to South Africa which ended in March 1903. This confirmed his ideas. His speech in May 1903 was a challenge which rapidly escalated into a massive political crisis. In the Commons, Chamberlain allowed himself to be drawn by Lloyd George into supporting food taxes to pay for social reforms, notably old age pensions. Protection had appeal to some manufacturers facing German competition and many farmers backed it. But to most British people, free trade meant prosperity and cheap food. Protection meant smaller loaves. Fears of dear food produced a swing against the Conservatives of devastating proportions.
Adapted from McCord 1991 and Pearce & Stewart 1992.

'Protection had appeal to some manufacturers facing German competition and this was particularly true of Chamberlain's own Midland heartland...But, to most English men and women, free trade meant prosperity and cheap food. Protection meant smaller loaves.' (Pearce & Stewart 1992, p.103)

Most historians agree that this general feeling was skilfully exploited by the Liberals. A poster campaign played on people's fears by showing two loaves that could be bought for the same money - a large one under free trade and a smaller one under protection. By presenting a united front over free trade, the Liberals were able to increase their electoral appeal.

By way of contrast, the Unionist alliance appeared divided. The Prime Minister, Arthur Balfour (who had replaced Salisbury in 1902) tried to find a middle way between the free traders and protectionists, but was unable to find a compromise which suited all sides:

'Before the [1906] election, Balfour attempted to hold a middle position between the free traders (83 out of the 392 Conservative MPs) and the protectionists on the basis of a retaliation policy, the idea being to force concessions from protectionist states and thus restore genuine freedom of trade. However tactically shrewd, this failed to satisfy the emotional forces unleashed on both sides of the debate.' (Pugh 1993, p.108)

By-election losses after May 1903 indicate that the government's image was badly bruised. Between August 1903 and January 1906 (when the general election was held), there were 17 by-elections in seats which had been won by the Conservatives in the 1900 general election. In none of these by-elections was the Conservative candidate successful (see Butler & Butler 1994, pp.234-35).

4. Balfour was responsible

The fourth theory is that the miscalculations of Arthur Balfour were responsible for the turnaround in electoral fortunes. Before Salisbury retired, it is argued, there were no signs that the Unionist alliance would lose the next general election. After his retirement, however, everything seemed to go wrong. If Salisbury had not retired, therefore, or if his successor had been someone other than Arthur Balfour, it is possible that the electoral turnaround would not have happened. Of course, given that Salisbury died in August 1903 and his health was declining in July 1902, it may not have been possible for him to continue after July 1902. Nevertheless, there are three main reasons for suggesting that, from the Conservative point of view, Balfour was a bad choice as Prime Minister.

i. Balfour and the Education Act, 1902

First, Salisbury is known to have been concerned about the political consequences of the 1902 Education Bill which was steered through Parliament by Balfour:

'Notwithstanding his personal devotion to the Church of England, Salisbury [undoubtedly] detected the political dangers which such a nakedly pro-Anglican measure entailed. The extreme unpopularity of the Bill with non-conformist Liberals bore out Salisbury's perception that a coalition ministry [ie the coalition between Liberal Unionists and Conservatives] could not afford to strain too far the loyalties of a powerful section of its followers.' (Goodlad 1996, p.5)

In other words, it could be argued that the Education Act was a mistake and, since Balfour so closely supported the Act, he can be said to be responsible for this mistake.

ii. Balfour and tariff reform

Second, as noted above, Balfour attempted to take a middle course on tariff reform. Robert Blake argues that, unlike Chamberlain, Balfour realised that the British public opinion would never accept food taxes:

'[Balfour] rightly saw that Joseph Chamberlain's campaign for imperial preference would never be accepted if it involved food taxes. "The prejudice against a small tax on food is not the fad of a few imperfectly informed theorists", he wrote to Chamberlain on 18 February 1905, "it is a deep-rooted prejudice affecting a large mass of voters, especially the poorest class, which it will be a matter of extreme difficulty to overcome". Balfour was right and the association of Chamberlain's proposals with dearer food was almost certainly a major element in the defeat of 1906.' (Blake 1985, p.171)

The implication here is that Chamberlain, rather than Balfour, was responsible for the unpopularity of the government after May 1903. Against this, however, it could be argued that, since Balfour was Prime Minister and he realised that Chamberlain's policy would be electorally damaging, he should have acted decisively to prevent this happening. Goodlad points out that:

'Tariff reform did for the Liberals what Home Rule had done for the Unionists almost 20 years earlier. The abandonment of free trade and the [populist] style of the Chamberlain campaign marked a break with the cautious, defensive Conservatism upon which Salisbury had built the Unionist alliance.' (Goodlad 1996, p.5)

In other words, since this break with 'cautious, defensive Conservatism' came under Balfour, he should be held responsible for it.

iii. Balfour and the working class

Third, it has been argued that Balfour miscalculated over two other issues - 'Chinese slavery' and Taff Vale - and, as a result, alienated many members of the working class. Given that there had been substantial support for Unionist candidates from working voters in 1900, this may have had an important bearing on the 1906 general election.

'Chinese slavery'

At the end of the Boer War a severe labour shortage arose in South Africa. To combat this, the British High Commissioner agreed to allow mine owners to import around 50,000 Chinese workers on low wages. These workers, described as 'Chinese slaves' by the Liberals, were housed in camps and suffered poor living and working conditions. News of this development caused outrage in Britain for three main reasons. First, there were humanitarian concerns. Second, there was discontent that a potential emigration route was being closed. And third, there were objections from trade unionists on the grounds that it was a practice that might be extended to Britain (in times of labour shortage in Britain, foreigners might be imported and the unions undermined). Blake claims that Balfour himself did not approve of this scheme, but allowed it to go ahead anyway. This was a mistake because there was a great deal of popular discontent as a result:

> 'The Prime Minister ought to have seen its implications, but Balfour was singularly insensitive to any save the most predictable reactions of the working class.' (Blake 1985, p.172)

Taff Vale

The second way in which Balfour managed to alienate the working class was in the government's refusal to take action to reverse the Taff Vale decision (see also Unit 4, page 135). Blewett argues that the government's refusal to act made it much easier for the LRC to make an electoral alliance with the Liberals (the so-called 'Lib-Lab Pact' of 1903 - see Unit 5, page 167). It also encouraged trade unionists and their supporters to vote Liberal rather than Conservative:

> 'Disenchantment with the Unionist failure over social reform and the obvious hostility of the Unionist Party to any amendment, yet alone reversal, of the Taff Vale judgement, led Labour to pin its hopes increasingly on a Liberal victory.' (Blewett 1972, pp.28-29)

Blake is particularly critical of Balfour on this point, arguing:

> 'Few things contributed more than Conservative

inaction in this field to the rise of the Labour Party and the alienation of the working class which had such disastrous effects on the Conservative Party in the 1906 election. It is hard to believe that Disraeli would have made a similar error.' (Blake 1985, pp.172-72)

Conclusion

While each of the four theories outlined above suggests that a slightly different date can be given for the point at which the electoral turnaround began, there is a great deal of overlap between them. A historian who argued that the turning point was the passing of the Education Act in 1902 would not deny that the launch of Chamberlain's tariff reform campaign was an important factor in explaining the outcome of the 1906 election. Equally, a historian who argued that the turning point was the launch of Chamberlain's tariff reform campaign would not deny that Balfour made miscalculations. An example of an account which links the various factors in this way is as follows:

> 'After 1902, it was the distinctive contribution of Balfour as Tory Prime Minister to pursue policies which succeeded in rallying the divided Liberal Party...All Liberal factions could agree in their denunciation of the 1902 Education Act which offended the non-conformists because it provided aid from the rates for Church schools. With even greater passion, they could campaign in defence of free trade, a traditional Liberal cause...The effect of [Joseph Chamberlain's] policy would have been to make goods from outside the Empire more expensive. Because much of our wheat was imported from America, this would have increased the price of bread. The working classes were unlikely to support the "small loaf" of the tariff reformers when they could have the larger one which Liberal policy would allow them to buy. The Liberals did themselves some good in the short term by making an electoral pact with the emerging Labour Representation Committee in 1903...and this was to contribute to the scale of the Conservative defeat when polling took place.' (Watts 1995, pp.125-26)

MAIN POINTS - Section 1.3

- Given that the Liberal Party lost the general elections of 1895 and 1900 by a considerable margin, their victory in 1906 represents quite a turnaround. There are four main theories about when exactly this turnaround took place and why it occurred.
- The first theory is that the Boer War transformed the political climate in Britain. Voters blamed the government for incompetence. The war encouraged Chamberlain to launch his tariff reform campaign and it revived the Liberal Party.
- The second theory is that the 1902 Education Act was the turning point. This united the Liberal Party and

brought non-conformist voters back to it. By-elections show that 1902 (not 1903) was the turning point.
- The third theory is that Joseph Chamberlain's tariff reform campaign was the turning point. The speech Chamberlain made in May 1903 split the Unionist alliance, damaging the image of the government in the eyes of the voters.
- The fourth theory is that Arthur Balfour's appointment as Prime Minister was the turning point. Balfour made a series of miscalculations which alienated voters from the Unionist alliance and strengthened the Liberal Party.

Activity 6.2 The 1906 general election

ITEM 1 The 1906 election result compared with that in 1900

(i)

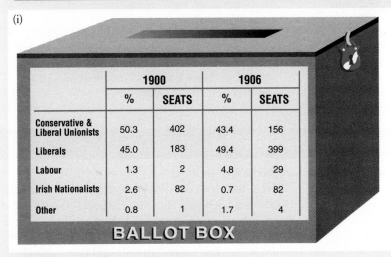

	1900		1906	
	%	**SEATS**	**%**	**SEATS**
Conservative & Liberal Unionists	50.3	402	43.4	156
Liberals	45.0	183	49.4	399
Labour	1.3	2	4.8	29
Irish Nationalists	2.6	82	0.7	82
Other	0.8	1	1.7	4

BALLOT BOX

Adapted from Craig 1989.

ITEM 2 Liberal Party poster

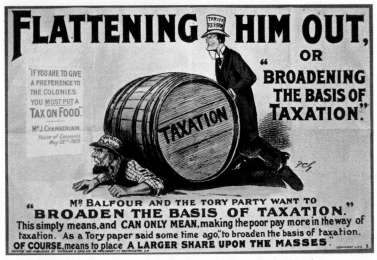

This poster was published during the 1906 election campaign by the Liberal Party. The man on the right is Joseph Chamberlain (Chamberlain's trademark was a top hat and monocle).

(ii) A significant factor in the overwhelming defeat of the Conservatives in 1906 was the ability of the Liberals and the LRC to mobilise previously untapped support. The turnout rose by 8% over 1900 and was the highest since 1885. The Liberal vote revealed extraordinary gains. The anti-Conservatives secured the bulk of former abstainers and new voters. Yet this is by no means an adequate explanation of the Conservative catastrophe. In many constituencies, particularly in London, Lancashire, Yorkshire, North-East England and Scotland, Unionist defections appear at least as important as increased turnout in explaining Conservative losses. It is plausible to argue that many thousands of Conservative voters converted to Liberalism in opposition to tariff reform. Also, particularly in the industrial areas, the presence of Labour candidates served to bring former Tory working-class voters to both anti-Conservative parties. In the residential areas of the Home Counties, the Liberals won, for the first time, seats with substantial numbers of middle-class voters. Many Conservatives, unable to support Balfour yet unwilling to vote Liberal, sought refuge in abstention. There were, in 1906, a number of factors whose anti-Conservative implications were likely to be short-term. On the other hand, the magnitude of the swing and the advent of Labour suggest fundamental and durable changes in the patterns of party identification.

Adapted from Blewett 1972.

ITEM 3 A historian's view

It is sometimes claimed that the Liberal victory of 1906 represented a popular mandate for sweeping measures of social reform. There is very little truth in this. The landslide victory swept into Parliament a motley crowd of enthusiastic reformers of one kind or another, but the frontbenchers were ominously non-committal about social reform, even about old age pensions which had been on the political agenda for nearly 20 years. The emphasis fell upon retrenchment (cutting back public spending) and economy, not on a programme of state-aided welfare that was bound to be expensive. As George Bernard Shaw correctly observed, the 1906 election was a triumph for conservatism with a small 'c'. It was quite clear what the Liberals were against. They were against tariff reform; against high arms expenditure; against 'Chinese slavery'; against the 1902 Education Act and so on. The Liberals had even promised not to introduce a Home Rule Bill within the lifetime of the forthcoming Parliament. But what were the Liberals for?

Adapted from Searle 1992.

Questions

1. a) 'It was the Conservatives who lost the election of 1906, not the Liberals who won it.' Judging from Items 1-3 would you agree with this conclusion? Explain your answer.
   b) Why was the Conservative defeat so heavy?
2. a) Using Item 1, design the front page of a newspaper which might have appeared on the day after the 1906 general election result became known.
   b) What were the main trends in the election?
3. a) Summarise the argument being made by Item 2.
   b) What contribution did Chamberlain's tariff reform campaign make to the outcome of the 1906 general election?
4. a) Item 3 refers to 'Chinese slavery' and 'the 1902 Education Act'. How did each issue affect the 1906 general election result?
   b) What do Items 2 and 3 tell us about the sort of campaign run by the Liberal Party?

2 The Liberal Party in power, 1906-14

Key questions

1. Why did 'New Liberalism' develop and what was new about it?
2. How radical were the social reforms passed in the period 1906-14?
3. To what extent did the reforms tackle poverty in Britain?

2.1 Why did 'New Liberalism' develop and what was new about it?

Why did New Liberalism develop?

Historians have suggested that five main factors led to the development of 'New Liberalism'.

First, Britain's economic position in the late 19th and early 20th century was less secure than it had been in the mid-19th century. Especially after the Boer War, there was no longer the certainty that Britain would be able to maintain its economic prosperity. This raised questions about the benefits of a laissez-faire approach:

'In the last 20 years of the century, the elements of interventionism waxed steadily stronger and not only in Liberalism. Why was this so? Undoubtedly, the perceived difficulties of the British economy, now facing severe international competition and shrinking profits, eroded the attractions of industrial growth as a panacea [cure] for society's ills.' (Lee 1994, p.114)

Second, the 1892-95 Liberal government departed from the orthodox Old Liberal position on taxation. The Chancellor, William Harcourt, drew a distinction between 'productive' and 'unproductive' wealth and used this as the basis of his taxation policy - he cut income tax on moderate incomes but introduced death duties on large incomes. This was an important departure because it sent out the signal that taxation on unproductive wealth was justified. This led some Liberals to argue that a Liberal government should finance a programme of social reforms by raising money from taxes on unproductive wealth.

Third, the work of social researchers like Charles Booth and Seebohm Rowntree proved conclusively that some people were so poor that self-help would never lift them out of poverty (see Box 6.7). These findings shocked many Liberals and encouraged them to question their values.

Fourth, socialist ideas began to gain popularity in the 1880s (see Unit 5, Section 1.1) and New Liberalism

BOX 6.7 The findings of Rowntree and Booth

Interpretation

Early in 1899, Seebohm Rowntree began an investigation of the working-class population of York, involving 46,754 people - two-thirds of the total population. He found 20,302 people living in poverty - by which he meant that they did not have enough food, fuel or clothing to keep them in good health. About one-third did not have a big enough income to live a normal healthy life even if they spent every penny wisely. Rowntree called this 'primary poverty'. All the traditional Victorian 'remedies' like thrift (careful management of money) were no use to these people. You could not be expected to save money when you did not have enough for the basic essentials. The remaining two-thirds had enough income to give them the bare necessities, but they spent some portion of it 'unwisely'. As a result, they were forced to go short on bread or clothing or both. Rowntree called this 'secondary poverty'. Rowntree's figures were very close to those arrived at by Charles Booth. He found just over 30% of people living in poverty in East London in the 1890s and early 1900s. It seems likely, therefore, that almost a third of Britain's town dwellers were forced to go without some of the necessities of a civilised life. The terrible effect of this on the health and wellbeing of the army can be seen from the fact that a third of men applying to join the army at this time were rejected as being unfit. These conditions were not just confined to towns. A few years later, Rowntree found that agricultural workers were even worse off.
Adapted from Cootes 1966.

was, in part, a response to a new political climate:

'New Liberals mixed and discussed with Labour and socialist intellectuals and sought their political and electoral cooperation.' (Tanner 1990, p.23)

Furthermore, the widening of the franchise in 1884-85 (see Unit 2, Section 3.2) ensured that the Liberal Party needed to devise new ways to attract working-class support in elections.

And fifth, experiments in local government in the late 19th century showed that, if local authorities took over public amenities and facilities, they could be run in a way that benefited the whole community. This is what happened under Joseph Chamberlain when he was Mayor of Birmingham, for example. Although such schemes are sometimes described as 'gas and water socialism', they were often set up and run by Liberals. The success of such schemes raised the possibility of similar schemes on a national scale.

The debate over 'National Efficiency'

It was in this context that the debate over 'National Efficiency' arose. Concern about poverty in Britain and anxiety that Britain was in decline as a world power led to the idea that Britain had to improve its 'efficiency' by taking steps to improve the quality of the workforce:

'If Britain was to compete and maintain its position as a world power, then it had to be run efficiently. This theory supported the belief that a strong, healthy, well-educated workforce was essential.' (Murphy 2000, pp.16-17)

One reason why this debate arose at the beginning of the 20th century was because of the difficulty of finding fit young men to fight in the Boer War:

'The Boer War left many in Britain with doubts about the quality of the working-class male - and about his ability to perform the tasks expected of him, in the workplace and on the battlefield. Almost a third of those who volunteered to fight in the conflict had to be turned away on the grounds of physical unfitness.' (Potter 2000, p.19)

In addition, as noted above, the research conducted by Seebohm Rowntree and Charles Booth revealed that poverty was more widespread than previously thought and that many poor people simply did not earn enough to escape poverty even if they spent every penny wisely. This suggested that action would have to be taken by government if such people were to make a positive contribution.

It was, in part, to address the problem of National Efficiency that Joseph Chamberlain launched his tariff reform campaign. Equally, the debate over National Efficiency made an impact on Liberal thinking both before and after the 1906 general election. In particular, it is tied in with the development of what became known as 'New Liberalism'.

New Liberalism

Some historians have argued that a new type of Liberalism had emerged by 1906 and it was this 'New Liberalism' which provided the inspiration for the reforms which were then made in the period 1906-14.

What was 'New Liberalism'?

At the heart of New Liberalism was a new attitude towards the state. 'Old' Liberalism (also known as 'Classical Liberalism' or 'Gladstonian Liberalism') was in favour of non-intervention and self-help:

'Traditionally most Liberals had started off with a presumption that state intervention in the working of the market was both futile and wrong. This particularly applied to projects of social reform which would involve public expenditure.' (Searle 1992, p.62)

The state's role, Old Liberals argued, was to allow people the greatest amount of freedom to live their lives as they thought best. If people found themselves in difficulty, it would be wrong for the state to intervene because, then, those people would have no motive to take action to improve themselves:

'If economic growth was to be secured through the creation of a climate of individual enterprise, then the role of the government had to be small, restricted to the provision of limited social services and the removal of obstacles to entrepreneurship. The state was to be feared as it threatened to choke growth through bureaucracy, corruption and tyranny and undermine the initiative and morality of the individual by doing too much for them. The catchphrase of mid-Victorian Classical Liberalism was "liberty, retrenchment and reform". In order to ensure liberty of the individual and economic progress, government spending should be pared down [cut] to the absolute minimum.' (Potter 2000, pp.18-19)

New Liberals disputed this view. They argued that there were circumstances in which it was right for the state to intervene in people's lives. Indeed, they argued, state intervention could, in certain circumstances, actually improve people's lives by providing them with the liberty self-help failed to provide:

'In the past the Liberal Party had been too concerned with individual liberty. The economic conditions which had caused a morally unacceptable degree of inequality and disadvantage had consequently not been tackled. Moreover, social conditions effectively removed the real liberty of the poorer sections of society to lead a decent life.' (Tanner 1990, p.23)

An important difference between New Liberalism and Old Liberalism was over taxation. Whereas Old Liberals believed that taxes should be as low as possible so that individuals would be free to spend their money as they liked, New Liberals argued that taxes should be raised to pay for schemes which would help those who were unable to help themselves.

The work of T.H Green was an important

inspiration for many New Liberals. His contribution is summarised in Box 6.8.

BOX 6.8 T.H Green and New Liberalism

Interpretation

Green rejected the Classical Liberal (ie Gladstonian) definition of society as a simple collection of individuals. Rather, he argued, society was 'organic', like a living creature. Individuals were the cells that made up the body. These cells were distinct, but at the same time they worked together with and in relation to others. As a result of this cooperation, society had a value of its own. Just as a human was more than the sum of their kidneys, liver and heart, so too did society have a separate identity which was more than the sum of its individual members. If society was more than the sum of its parts, then it followed that the good of society could no longer be judged purely in terms of the 'greatest good for the greatest number'. Rather, it was important to acknowledge the needs of society as a separate entity - needs which were different from, but complementary to, those of the individual. Green went on to argue that the state should monitor and regulate the behaviour of individuals. Later New Liberal thinkers built on this, arguing that the state should be allowed to correct the flaws in an economic system that placed individuals in a position of poverty from which they could not raise themselves.
Adapted from Potter 2000.

Continuities

Although there was much that was new about New Liberalism, Potter (2000) stresses that there were important continuities with Old Liberalism. He points out that New Liberals were keen to appeal to traditional Liberal supporters and not to be dismissed as socialists. There were four strands of New Liberalism, he argues, which fitted with Old Liberalism:

- like Old Liberals, New Liberals focused on the individual and individual initiative - individuals should rise to their 'proper level in society', though the state should act to remove some of the obstacles they faced before they could do this
- like Old Liberals, New Liberals preferred social services to be paid for by voluntary contributions rather than by money raised by the state
- like Old Liberals, New Liberals distinguished between 'deserving' individuals and 'undeserving' individuals
- like Old Liberals, the main goal of New Liberals was to provide members of the working class - through hard work and saving - with the opportunity of enjoying a middle-class standard of living.

Potter concludes that:

> 'In many ways, in the Edwardian period, Liberalism underwent a change of emphasis rather than of aims.' (Potter 2000, p.20)

Who supported New Liberalism?

Historians agree that support for New Liberalism mainly came from members of the middle class:

> 'The impetus behind the "New Liberalism" came from the professional middle class: from journalists, writers and lecturers, plus certain lawyers and doctors with a social conscience...From a recent study, one gets a vivid picture of these men: high-minded intellectuals, living in spacious but draughty houses in Hampstead or the Manchester suburbs (fresh air was valued as a stimulus to progressive thought), eating raw fruit and thinking ruthlessly about the political problems of their age.' (Searle 1992, pp.101-02)

Although some Liberal MPs supported New Liberalism, most did not, at least openly. Watts claims that, in 1906:

> 'No leading member of the Cabinet was at this time committed to the New Liberalism.' (Watts 1995, p.130)

Cook argues that the vast majority of Liberal MPs elected in 1906 were in the 'centre' - neither committed to Old Liberalism or New Liberalism:

> 'The Parliamentary Liberal Party was not composed of the wild radicals that its enemies sometimes supposed. Politically, the party was dominated by "centre" Liberals...The Liberals were still not a party catering to any significant degree to the parliamentary ambitions of working men...Not surprisingly, the social composition and political outlook of the parliamentary party acted as no great spur to radical reform.' (Cook 1998, p.43)

Lloyd George and New Liberalism

It has sometimes been argued that David Lloyd George - who introduced several key reforms in the Liberal administration of 1906-14 - was a New Liberal. For example, Byrne asserts that:

> 'Advocates [supporters] of New Liberalism, such as David Lloyd George, who entered the Cabinet as President of the Board of Trade in 1905, wished to see a far more interventionist (or collectivist) approach to improving life for the lower classes.' (Byrne 1995, p.463)

But, other historians deny that Lloyd George was a New Liberal - at least at first. Watts points out that:

> 'Even Lloyd George, for all his recognition of the needs of labour after the election, was still essentially committed to the old causes - temperance, Church disestablishment, local Home Rule and land reform - not a programme particularly in tune with the needs of the working-class electorate.' (Watts 1995, p.130)

Similarly, Packer argues that:

'There is very little evidence that Lloyd George was influenced by, or even much aware of, the new thinking on social reform occurring in Liberalism, even though he was a friend of the New Liberal journalist, H.G. Massingham, from the mid-1890s.' (Packer 1998, p.14)

Packer argues that, in opposition, Lloyd George's strategy was to attack the Conservatives without making firm commitments about what a Liberal government would do in power:

'The sole measure of social reform he took to including in his speeches was old age pensions, and this was largely because he could attack Chamberlain for promising them in 1895 and then reneging [backing down] on his commitment.' (Packer 1998, pp.14-15)

Once Lloyd George was in power, Packer argues that his actions were shaped as responses to circumstances rather than as attempts to put a particular set of ideas into practice. Referring to Lloyd George's 1909 Budget, he argues:

'None of these startling new developments could have been predicted from an examination of Lloyd George's previous career. They were not the outcome of long-held beliefs, but of a unique open-mindedness and daring when faced by a desperate political situation.' (Packer 1998, p.24)

Was Lloyd George converted to New Liberalism in 1908?

While Lloyd George's support of New Liberalism before 1908 has been questioned, his speeches show that, from 1908, he became committed to the need for greater state intervention to tackle social problems. Morgan (1973, p.8) talks of Lloyd George's 'conversion' to the cause of social reform after a trip to Germany in the summer 1908. In his biography of Lloyd George, he argues that:

'Lloyd George himself was greatly stirred by a visit to Germany in the late summer of 1908 and much impressed by the social insurance and labour exchanges that Bismarck had set up there...He returned from Germany fired with radical enthusiasm, immersed in practical detail about reform policies. He instructed Churchill at Criccieth in what the latter called "two days very memorable to me". They worked out a grand design for a comprehensive system for national health and unemployment insurance, and for labour exchanges. These would regenerate the nation. They would also, incidentally, regenerate the Liberal Party.' (Morgan 1974, p.66)

Pugh on the other hand, argues that since the visit was taken to find out about how existing schemes worked, this suggests that Lloyd George already supported the principle which lay behind such schemes. In other words, he had been converted to the principle some time before the summer of 1908:

'To speak of his "conversion to social reform during a visit to Germany in the summer of 1908" is surely a misrepresentation. That visit was undertaken at a time when he was devising a strategy for reform and typically wanted to learn more about the operating of existing schemes; it was more a consequence than a cause of his commitment to social reform.' (Pugh 1988, p.40)

What seems clear is that, although not a committed New Liberal at the time of the 1906 general election, Lloyd George was receptive to New Liberal ideas and, given the circumstances he faced in office and party political considerations (the need to persuade working-class voters to vote Liberal rather than Labour or Conservative, for example), he had decided to back policies which embraced New Liberalism by the summer of 1908.

MAIN POINTS - Section 2.1

- New Liberalism developed because - (1) Britain's economic position was less secure (2) Harcourt had already taxed 'unproductive' wealth (3) the work of Rowntree and Booth made an impact (4) socialist ideas gained popularity (5) local government intervention was successful.

- At the heart of New Liberalism was a new attitude towards the state. 'Old' Liberalism (also known as 'Classical Liberalism' or 'Gladstonian Liberalism') was in favour of non-intervention and self-help. New Liberals argued that there were circumstances in which it was right for the state to intervene in people's lives.

- Like Old Liberals, New Liberals (1) focused on the individual and individual initiative (2) preferred social services to be paid for by voluntary contributions not public funds (3) distinguished between 'deserving' and 'undeserving' individuals and (4) aimed to provide workers with the opportunity of enjoying a middle-class standard of living.

- Historians agree that support for New Liberalism mainly came from members of the professional middle class. Although some Liberal MPs supported New Liberalism, most did not.

- Although David Lloyd George is sometimes described as a New Liberal, some historians argue that he was not committed to New Liberalism before the 1906 general election. Circumstances, open-mindedness and concern about the Liberal Party winning working-class support pushed him into adopting policies favoured by the New Liberals.

Activity 6.3 New Liberalism

ITEM 1 Old Liberalism and New Liberalism

Old Liberalism	New Liberalism
Society is a collection of unconnected individuals.	Society is 'organic', composed of distinct parts working together.
Society is, therefore, no more than the sum of its parts.	Society is, therefore, more than the sum of its parts.
The role of the state is to ensure 'the greatest happiness of the greatest number'.	The role of the state is to judge the needs of both individuals and society itself.
The role of the state is, therefore, small. Its only job is to remove obstacles to entrepreneurship.	The role of the state is, therefore, large. The state should intervene to correct flaws in the economic system.

ITEM 3 A historian's view

In 1910, Lloyd George argued that Liberalism 'has not abandoned the traditional ambition of the Liberal Party to establish freedom...but side by side with this effort it promotes measures for [improving] the condition of life for the multitude'. The role of the state, therefore, had to be modified. Whereas Gladstone had focused on 'freedom to' and 'freedom of', the Edwardian Liberals added 'freedom from'. This required more active government intervention. It was necessary to move away from a laissez-faire approach to the economy and it was necessary to improve social conditions through a legislative programme and a redistribution of wealth by progressive taxation. Lloyd George saw this as the key task for any government and confidently predicted that 'there will soon be no civilised land in the world where proper provision for the aged, the broken and the unfortunate amongst those who toil will not be regarded as the first charge upon the wealth of the land'. To an extent this was idealistic. The Liberal Party had always been an alliance of principles and causes. It should be no surprise, therefore, that the party should also have come to accept a social role for the state. At the same time, the party clearly needed a revived image if it was to compete with the Conservatives. This meant appealing more directly to the enlarged working-class vote and preventing the Labour Party from overtaking it on the left. In addition, the party leadership had to find a national issue which would unite the sectional interests within the party. This could not be an external issue since the adoption of Irish Home Rule had done great damage. As a result, Home Rule was downgraded. Instead, the idea of progressive reform would offer something to all groups. The only danger was alienating the Whigs, but they were too few to be significant.

Adapted from Lee 1994.

ITEM 2 New Liberalism

(i) It [is] the function of the state to secure the conditions upon which mind and character may develop themselves. Similarly, we may say now that the state is to secure conditions upon which its citizens are able to win by their own efforts all that is necessary to a full civic efficiency. It is not for the state to feed, house or clothe them. It is for the state to take care that the economic conditions are such that the normal man who is not defective in mind or body can by useful labour feed, house and clothe himself and his family. The 'right to work' and the right to a 'living wage' are just as valid as the rights of person and property...Society owes to [the labourer] the means of maintaining a civilised standard of life and this debt is not adequately discharged by leaving him to secure such wages as he can in the higgling [ups and downs] of the market.

Extract from 'Liberalism' by L.T. Hobhouse, published in 1911. Hobhouse was a leading New Liberal.

(ii) The cause of the Liberal Party is the cause of the left-out millions...No man can be a collectivist alone or an individualist alone...Collectively, we have an army and a navy and a civil service; collectively, we have a post office and a police and a government; collectively, we light our streets and supply ourselves with water; collectively, we indulge in all the necessities of communication. But we do not make love collectively, and the ladies do not marry us collectively, and we do not eat collectively and we do not die collectively and it is not collectively that we face the sorrows and hopes, the winnings and losings of this world of accident and storm. No view of society can be complete which does not comprise within its scope both collective organisation and individual incentive. The very growing complications of civilisation create for us new services which have to be undertaken by the state.

Part of a speech made by Winston Churchill on 11 October 1906. Churchill became President of the Board of Trade in 1908 and worked closely with Lloyd George on the key social reforms passed by the Liberal government in 1906-14 (see Section 2.2 below).

ITEM 4 Poverty in the early 20th century

This photo shows a family living in poverty in the early 20th century.

Questions

1. a) Judging from Items 1 and 2 and your own knowledge, what were the main characteristics of New Liberalism?
   b) How did it differ from Old Liberalism?
   c) How new was New Liberalism?
2. a) Using Item 3, explain why the Liberal Party came to accept New Liberalism after 1906.
   b) What is the evidence in Item 3 to suggest that Lloyd George had come to accept a New Liberal approach by 1910?
3. a) Explain the part that poverty like that illustrated in Item 4 played in the development of New Liberalism.
   b) How would you expect New Liberalism to deal with the problem of poverty illustrated in Item 4?

2.2 How radical were the social reforms of 1906-14?

The position in 1906

The campaign fought by the Liberal Party in the run-up to the 1906 general election was largely a negative campaign. The Liberals spent a great deal of time attacking the Unionist alliance and very little explaining what they would do if they won power. In his election address (which, in effect, was a party manifesto), the Liberal Leader, Henry Campbell-Bannerman, devoted just two small paragraphs to what a Liberal government would do if it was elected (see Box 6.9). The rest of the speech attacked the Conservative government's record and gave reasons why the arguments in favour of tariff reform were flawed. In other speeches made before the election, Asquith, who became Chancellor of the Exchequer under Campbell-Bannerman, made it clear that reduction of taxation, rather than social reform, was a priority:

'The most serious burden upon the industry of Great Britain...[is] the enormous and progressive increase in what the state [is] taking by taxation and by borrowing out of pockets of the people of this country...If a Liberal government came into power, the first duty they set themselves would be a reduction in the country's expenditures.' (Part of speech made by Asquith in Cambridge in 1904)

Despite, therefore, what Searle (1992) describes as 'a mood of expectancy in the air in 1906', there was no carefully worked out blueprint for reform and little indication that the new government would be a radical reforming government.

BOX 6.9 Campbell-Bannerman's election address

Should we be confirmed in office, it will be our duty, whilst holding fast to the time-honoured principles of Liberalism - the principles of peace, economy, self-government and civil and religious liberty - and whilst resisting with all our strength the attack upon free trade to repair, as far as lies in power, the mischief wrought in recent years and, by a course of strenuous legislation and administration to secure those social and economic reforms which have been too long delayed.

As to the spirit in which foreign affairs will be conducted… the Unionist Party have made it possible for us to pursue a substantial continuity of policy without departing from the friendly and unprovocative methods which, under Liberal governments in the past, have determined the relations of Great Britain with her neighbours.
Quoted in Craig 1975.

Source Box

The Campbell-Bannerman government, 1906-08

Historians agree that, between 1906 and 1908, there was little evidence that New Liberalism had made much of an impression on the Liberal government:

'The New Liberalism was largely confined as yet to journals and the *Manchester Guardian*. It had certainly not captured the Cabinet. Campbell-Bannerman, the triumphant Prime Minister, was an old-fashioned Gladstonian in his attitudes. Asquith, his deputy, was a pragmatist from the right of the party who enjoyed the high society into which his rich second wife had introduced

him. Herbert Gladstone, the architect of victory, became Home Secretary. He was well meaning and cautious.' (Pearce & Stewart 1992, p.196)
Many historians argue that the Liberal government's first two years in power were not a success. Three main reasons are given for this.

1. Campbell-Bannerman's failings
Many historians are critical of the Prime Minister, Henry Campbell-Bannerman. He lacked strong leadership qualities, they argue, and failed to take advantage of his huge majority in the Commons:
'With Campbell-Bannerman failing to give a firm lead, the first couple of years of Liberal rule were a period of aimlessness and drift.' (Searle 1992, p.80)
Not all historians blame lack of rigorous reform on Campbell-Bannerman's personal failings, however. Some point out that he accepted the Gladstonian approach and simply was not prepared to respond to New Liberals' demands for radical reform:
'Campbell-Bannerman never thought in terms of widespread social reform, which he deemed to be too expensive, and Asquith spent his first year at the Treasury in restoring Gladstonian standards without any hint of a revolution in public finance. There were some changes...but the cause of reform did not flourish. Hence the disappointment of the New Liberals.' (Watts 1994, p.132)

2. Opposition from the Lords
Although Campbell-Bannerman had a large majority in the Commons, the Unionist alliance had a large majority in the Lords. Balfour (who had lost his seat in the 1906 general election, but regained his place in the Commons via a hastily arranged by-election) was determined to exploit this majority. He claimed that:
'The great Unionist Party should still control whether in power or in opposition the destinies of this great Empire.' (comment made in a speech delivered in Nottingham on 15 January 1906)
Between 1906 and 1908, he worked closely with Lord Lansdowne, Unionist Leader in the Lords, organising opposition to those Bills which they felt were in the interest of the Liberal Party rather than the country:
'[Lansdowne] and Balfour adopted a very simple principle: that the in-built Conservative majority in the Lords should be used in the interests of the Conservative Party. Thus, Bills that were popular, however misguided their provisions were thought by Tory peers, would be let through. Bills which simply appealed to partisan Liberals, by contrast, though they might be part of the platform on which the party won the 1906 election, were fair game for obstructive action.' (Clarke 1996, p.37)
As a result, a number of Bills put forward by the government between 1906 and 1908 had to be scrapped - for example, an Education Bill and a Licensing Bill.

3. The government was living in the past
Some historians (for example, Clarke 1996 and Cook 1998) argue that the Campbell-Bannerman government was living in the past. Clarke points out that the issues that the government chose to address - such as reform of the 1902 Education Act and a Licensing Bill (to reduce the number of places allowed to sell alcoholic drinks) - were issues which would appeal to non-conformists, but had little appeal for the mass of the population:
'The fact was that the government was in no position to fight back against the tactics employed against it because it lacked a strategy that promised popular appeal. It was living in the past, fiddling around with measures on schools and pubs that no longer seemed relevant to most of those who voted Liberal in 1906. The negative nature of that victory was belatedly revealed by the fact that its major election cry (free trade) implied no agenda for action.' (Clarke 1996, p.39)
Cook, on the other hand, argues that:
'Although Campbell-Bannerman's two years in office were in many ways important and constructive, his ministry as a whole never really constituted a real success. Whilst it had brought self-government to South Africa, initiated far-reaching army reforms, pursued a successful détente with Russia and repaired the damage done by the Taff Vale decision, it was open to fundamental criticism. Essentially, the ministry had been concerned with the issues of the past, not of the future.' (Cook 1998, p.45)

Reforms passed 1906-08
Although most historians are critical of Campbell-Bannerman's government, they do concede that some important reforms were passed during this period. The main reforms are outlined in Box 6.10 on page 201.

Impact of the reforms 1906-08
Some historians (for example, Pearce & Stewart 1992) argue that, although the Campbell-Bannerman government failed to make a popular impact at the time, a number of measures had particular significance because they showed that the government was prepared to intervene far more than had been the case in the past. They point to four initiatives in the period 1906-08:

1. The 1906 Education (Provision of Meals) Act was controversial because it raised a debate about the issue of state versus individual responsibility - the passing of the Act meant a significant advance in the role of the state.
2. In 1907, David Lloyd George, President of the Board of Trade, organised the first census of industrial production - this was indicative of the new extended role of the state since, without information, planning and government action

BOX 6.10 Reforms 1906-08

Summary Box

i. Trade Disputes Act, 1906
This Act reversed the Taff Vale Judgement (see Unit 4, page 135) by protecting the unions' right to strike and legalising peaceful picketing.

ii. Workmen's Compensation Act, 1906
This Act extended compensation for injury at work to 6 million workers, introduced new categories of injury (eg disease) and shortened the time before which compensation was paid.

iii. Education (Provision of Meals) Act, 1906
This Act allowed local authorities (on a voluntary basis) to provide free school meals for needy children.

iv. Merchant Shipping Act, 1906
This Act improved conditions for seamen and forced foreign vessels using British ports to adopt the same standards.

v. Education (Administrative Procedures) Act, 1907
This Act required medical inspections of children and permitted medical treatment.

vi. The introduction of probation
Probation was introduced in 1907 as an alternative to prison.

vii. Children's Act, 1908
This Act dealt with child neglect and abuse, set up juvenile courts and remand homes and prohibited the imprisonment of children under 14. It also banned children from pubs and from buying cigarettes.

viii. The introduction of old age pensions
A pledge was made in the 1908 Budget to introduce old age pensions. They were only to be paid to the over 70s at the single rate of 5 shillings per week to those whose incomes were less than £21 per year (those who had habitually failed to work or had been in prison would be excluded).

was impossible.

3. In 1908, a measure was passed limiting miners' working hours to 8.5 per day - many Liberal industrialists hated the idea of limiting adult male hours on the grounds that it was a dangerous interference with market forces and profitability.
4. The introduction of old age pensions in 1908 was a break with the past - for the first time, the state offered security without the stigma of the old poor law relief (when people had to go to the workhouse to receive aid).

(Adapted from Pearce & Stewart 1992, pp.198-99)

Murphy argues that it was in the context of the debate over National Efficiency (see page 195 above) that some of the measures can be explained:

'If Britain was to compete and maintain its position as a world power, then it had to be run efficiently. This theory supported the belief that a healthy, well-educated workforce was essential. [Such] ideas help explain why the Liberals introduced compulsory medical inspection and free meals in schools in 1906-07, and also why free grammar school places were introduced under the Education Act of 1907.' (Murphy 2000, p.17)

1908 - a turning point?

The standard view is that when Campbell-Bannerman ('C-B') resigned because of ill health in April 1908, the Liberal government, which had been running out of steam, was transformed into a vibrant, radical reforming government which began to put New Liberal ideas into practice (see Box 6.11 on page 202):

'The reforming impetus accelerated dramatically after 1908 when Asquith became Prime Minister, Lloyd George became Chancellor of the Exchequer and Winston Churchill became President of the Board of Trade. Under their guidance, the Liberal Party consolidated and extended its shift towards reform.' (Tanner 1990, p.25)

According to this view, therefore, Campbell-Bannerman's resignation was a turning point:

'The change came with C-B's departure in 1908. Asquith (1858-1928) became Prime Minister. He was not the man to supply new initiatives, but his arrival marked a dramatic change in the tone and approach of the Liberal administration.' (Watts 1995, p.132)

Neal Blewett, however, argues against this point of view. He claims that the departure of Campbell-Bannerman made little difference at first. For a year after Asquith took over, the fortunes of the Liberal government remained bleak:

'The winter of 1908-09 found the Liberal government at the nadir [bottom-most point] of its fortunes. The by-elections were running strongly against it. The government's legislative programme had been mutilated by the Lords; powerful interests had been alienated by its attempts at reform; and a deepening trade recession gripped the country...It appeared that the Liberal Party's tenure of power would be both short and rather barren.' (Blewett 1972, p.45)

According to Blewett, the turning point came a year after Campbell-Bannerman had resigned - in April 1909 when David Lloyd George introduced his first Budget. It was this Budget - the so-called 'People's Budget' - which led to a power struggle between the Commons and the Lords (see Part 3 below) and which, as a by-product, revived the fortunes of the Liberal Party.

How radical were Liberal reforms after 1908?

In judging how radical the Liberal government's reforms were in the period 1908-14 (the main reforms passed between 1908 and 1914 are outlined

BOX 6.11   Main reforms 1908-14

1. The People's Budget, 1909
Lloyd George's first Budget introduced a supertax on the income of the rich, a land tax and a road tax. It increased duties on petrol, tobacco and alcohol and changed the rate of income tax - reducing it for lower incomes and increasing it for high incomes. The money raised was to be used for old age pensions and armaments.

2. The Old Age Pensions Act, 1909
The pledge to introduce pensions made in Asquith's 1908 Budget was steered through Parliament by Lloyd George and became law in 1909.

3. The Labour Exchanges Act, 1909
This Act, introduced by Winston Churchill, set up a nationally-organised but regionally-operated system of Labour Exchanges (job centres), allowing the unemployed to find out about job vacancies at a central point rather than having to go from workplace to workplace seeking a job.

4. The Trade Board Act, 1909
Introduced by Churchill, this Act set up boards of officials to supervise pay and conditions and to set minimum wages in 'sweated industries' (at first, tailoring, box-making, lace-making, chain-making and, in 1913, six other industries were added).

5. The Parliament Act, 1911
The product of the constitutional crisis arising from the Lords' rejection of the People's Budget, this Act prevented the Lords from rejecting money Bills and allowed them to delay, not to reject, legislation passed by the Commons, so long as it passed in three successive parliamentary sessions.

6. The National Insurance Act, 1911
This Act had two parts, the first introducing National Health Insurance and the second Unemployment Insurance. Health cover was provided to workers in certain industries by automatically deducting 4 pence from their wages into an insurance fund (the employer then added 3 pence and the state 2 pence). Unemployment Insurance worked on the same principle. Spouses and families were not covered by the scheme.

7. Payment of MPs
Lloyd George introduced the payment of MPs for the first time in 1911. Before then, MPs had to support themselves.

8. Miners' Minimum Wage Act, 1912
This Act set up boards to grant minimum wages to miners on a district basis.

9. Trade Union Act, 1913
This Act reversed the Osborne Judgement (see Unit 4, pages 135-36) by allowing unions to divide their subscriptions into a political fund and a social fund after a ballot of members. Any member not wishing to pay into the political fund (the political levy) could 'contract out'.

Adapted from Searle 1992 and Watts 1995.

in Box 6.11 above), historians have tended to take three approaches. It should be noted, however, that the key reforms were the work of just two members of the Cabinet - David Lloyd George, the Chancellor, and Winston Churchill, the President of the Board of Trade. Their initiatives were approved by the Prime Minister and by the Cabinet and, in that sense, can be said to be government initiatives. On the other hand, there is substantial evidence to show that there was some opposition to the measures in the Cabinet. It should also be noted that other Cabinet ministers could have proposed reforms, but chose not to do so.

1. Judging the reforms in light of Victorian values
One approach is to judge the Asquith government's achievements in light of Victorian values. Historians do this in two ways.

First, some historians explain the limitations of the reforms by reference to Victorian values. Pugh, for example, points out that, although the National Insurance Act of 1911 was an innovation, the idea that only people who contributed to the scheme would benefit from it was very much a Victorian idea:

'Lloyd George's 1911 National Insurance Act reflected Victorian self-help traditions in incorporating the contributory principle and by involving existing Friendly Societies and insurance companies in the scheme.' (Pugh 1993, p.120)

Similarly, Watts argues that Victorian values prevented ministers from introducing more radical reforms:

'Ministers had not formulated a creed and a programme which could provide a comprehensive answer to the problems of society...if only because several ministers were still committed to old 19th century attitudes. They thought in terms of restraining government expenditure and, therefore, could only make a limited impact on the social problems of Edwardian England. Moreover they were constrained by their general philosophy and approach. They preferred minimum government intervention and, although they recognised that certain problems required legislative action, they were content where possible to avoid its necessity. Inevitably then, changes were often modest in scope and there was a number of areas which remained unreformed.' (Watts 1995, p.140)

A second way of judging the Asquith government's reforms in light of Victorian values is to emphasise ways in which the approach of the Asquith government contrasted to that of previous Liberal governments. Between 1908 and 1914, it is argued, Gladstonian Liberal values were replaced by New Liberal values. Some authors (such as Clarke 1971) even argue that the Liberal Party had transformed itself into a social democratic party by 1914.

Certainly, it is possible to find evidence of the state playing a new interventionist role in the period 1908-14. By 1914, the state provided old age pensions and administered sickness and unemployment benefits. State-run Labour Exchanges had been set up and the state was prepared to intervene to ensure that a minimum wage was paid in some industries. State intervention on this scale had been rejected in the past. In addition, the 'People's Budget' of 1909 marked a clear departure in terms of approach to taxation. Taxes were deliberately raised in order to pay for state-run social schemes (something which had not been done before) and there was, for the first time, an element of redistribution of wealth (since income tax was graduated and new taxes were targeted at the very rich). All this, it can be argued, added up to a radical break with the past.

2. Judging the reforms in light of later developments

The second approach is to judge the Asquith government's achievements in light of later developments. This approach focuses on the shortcomings of the Liberal government's reforms. Historians point out that, while the foundations of a welfare state were laid in the period 1906-14, much was left undone. In particular, the Liberal government did not accept that the provision of state benefits should be universal - available to anyone who happened to be old, ill or unemployed. Rather, the national insurance scheme was open only to those who worked in certain sectors and the old age pension was only provided to those who met certain criteria:

'The legislation was hardly revolutionary. The state pension was free but not universal. Only around half a million of the oldest, poorest and most sober elderly people obtained a pension which was less than a bare subsistence income.' (Tanner 1990, p.25)

Judged in terms of later developments, therefore, the reforms of 1906-14 were not radical.

3. Judging the reforms in party political terms

A third approach is to judge the Asquith government's achievements in party political terms. Searle argues that:

- the government, as a whole, does not seem to have been very committed to welfare reforms - apart from Lloyd George and Churchill, other members of the government had little interest in reform
- Lloyd George and Churchill's main concern was to capture working-class support and, by

doing so, to marginalise the Labour Party
- there was no reform programme as such - rather a series of measures based on no single principle or philosophy
- the impetus behind social reform slackened after the National Insurance Act was passed
- welfare policies disappeared from the party's political agenda during and after the First World War
- New Liberalism failed to excite party members or to break the mould at local level.
(adapted from Searle 1992)

The key argument of those who believe that New Liberalism was a major influence on the Liberal Party in the period 1908-14 is that the reforms of this period reflect a new, radical way of thinking which was widely held by party members. The reforms, in other words, reflect a realignment of the party as a whole. If, however, it is accepted that New Liberalism failed to make much of an impact on the party as a whole, it could be argued that it is wrong to look at the reforms in terms of a radical realignment. Rather, it might be better to focus on what the two main reformers - Lloyd George and Churchill - were aiming to do. Watts, for example, points out that:

'[Lloyd George and Churchill] revealed a certain skill in adapting Liberalism to the challenge of the "condition of the people" question. In so doing, they retained some middle-class support and made a bid for the loyalty of the working classes. They were working out of political necessity, for social improvement offered a route which was an alternative to the challenging creed of socialism.' (Watts 1995, p.141)

In other words, it could be argued that the reforms were Lloyd George and Churchill's response to what they saw as the challenge from the left. By stealing Labour's thunder, they hoped to capture working-class votes. By ensuring that reforms were as moderate as possible, they hoped to retain middle-class support. In other words, if the reforms are seen in terms of party political advantage, far from being radical, the reforms can be described as a conservative response to the radical threat from the left.

2.3 To what extent did the reforms tackle poverty in Britain?

The Royal Commission on the Poor Law 1905-09

In 1904, the Conservative government decided to set up a Royal Commission to examine the system of alleviating poverty that had grown up under the Poor Law Amendment Act of 1834, the last major piece of legislation in this area (see Box 6.12 on page 204). Historians argue that this Royal

BOX 6.12 The Poor Law Amendment Act, 1834

Interpretation

The Poor Law Amendment Act was designed to discipline an 'irresponsible' and fast-growing population and to moderate the rapid rise in the cost of poor relief under the old Poor Law. The Act severely restricted access to outdoor relief (ie poor people living independently could not gain relief). Instead, help was largely available through the workhouse, entry to which was only granted if the applicant could pass a test (the aim of which was to ensure that there was genuine need). Parishes were organised into Poor Law Unions under elected Boards of Guardians. These were supervised by the Poor Law Commission, a body of three, in London. The Poor Law Commission sent Assistant Commissioners around the country to assist the formation of Boards of Guardians and to advise on the construction of workhouses. The Commissioners also drew up diet sheets and rules and regulations for the workhouses. The scheme was devised by Edwin Chadwick who designed the workhouses to be, in his own words, 'uninviting places of wholesome restraint'. The idea was that conditions in the workhouse had to be less attractive than those which the poorest independent labourer would experience. In 1847, the Poor Law Commission was replaced by a Poor Law Board which, in 1871, united with the Public Health Board to form the Local Government Board.
Adapted from Gardiner & Wenborn 1995.

Commission was set up in response to:
- concerns about National Efficiency
- the reports by Charles Booth and Seebohm Rowntree on poverty (see Section 2.1 above)
- the rapid growth in unemployment in recent years.

The work of the Royal Commission
The Royal Commission first met in 1905, but did not publish its findings until 1909:

'The Commission which met [in 1905] was chaired by Lord George Hamilton, and its 20 members shared a wide range of expertise on the subject: they included Poor Law Guardians, civil servants from the Local Government Board, leading members of the Charity Organisation Society, religious leaders, trade unionists and the social investigators Charles Booth and Beatrice Webb. The detailed inquiry conducted by the Commission ran to 47 volumes and was the result of hundreds of interviews and visits.' (Murray 1999, p.103)

When the Commission did publish its findings, it was unable to produce a single report because there were major differences of opinion within the Commission. As a result, a separate Majority Report and Minority Report were published.

The Majority Report
The Majority Report did criticise some of the features of the existing system. It supported the abolition of Boards of Guardians and their replacement by Public Administration Committees (panels of local councillors and appointees). It also criticised the lack of uniformity in the provision of outdoor relief in some areas and the lack of coordination between Boards of Guardians and local charities. But, the Majority Report accepted that the Poor Law system should continue without any fundamental change and it supported the view that much poverty was 'moral' (due to idleness and bad character) rather than unavoidable.

The Minority Report
The Minority Report was supported by Beatrice Webb (a Fabian), George Lansbury (a socialist and, later, a Labour MP), Francis Chandler (a trade unionist) and Russell Wakefield (the Dean of Norwich). They did not agree that much poverty was 'moral'. Rather, they argued that poverty was 'economic' (the result of low wages or unemployment) and that the state should play a role in tackling it. In other words, the Minority Report argued for a fundamental change in the system of dealing with poverty:

'Its authors recommended that specialist committees should be set up by councils to deal with specific types of poverty: education committees to deal with issues of child poverty; health committees to deal with the sick and disabled; pensions committees to deal with the elderly poor. They believed that the problem of unemployment was beyond the capacity of local authorities and recommended the establishment of a Ministry of Labour.' (Murray 1999, pp.103-04)

This Ministry of Labour, they argued, should be responsible for setting up labour exchanges (job centres), retraining schemes and public works programmes.

Impact of the Royal Commission
By the time that the Royal Commission published its reports, the Liberal government had already taken a number of steps to tackle poverty (these are assessed below). Murray argues that the publication of two reports lessened the impact made by the Royal Commission:

'The split within the Commission was an important reason why neither report resulted in direct government action. The recommendations of the majority seemed inadequate to the New Liberals, while the enthusiastic campaigning of the Webbs seems to have alienated the government.' (Murray 1999, p.104)

Feuchtwanger, on the other hand, argues that:

'Those ministers who were looking for social reform as a means to revive Liberal fortunes were prepared to take ideas from the Webbs as well as from any other source.' (Feuchtwanger 1985, p.308)

He argues that the problem with the recommendations of the Minority Report was the cost of implementing them. He also notes that the way in which the Poor Law worked had made many generations of working-class people suspicious of government initiatives and that ministers, therefore, were reluctant to be too radical.

Even if the recommendations of neither report were adopted wholesale, the publication of the reports in 1909 ensured that the subject of tackling poverty remained high on the political agenda.

Liberal Reforms and child poverty

It was noted above that a number of the reforms passed in the years 1906-08 (see Box 6.10 on page 201) were passed in the hope of improving National Efficiency. That is another way of saying that they were designed to tackle poverty (since healthier workers would be more efficient at work and in battle). Two measures in particular were targeted at child poverty - the provision of free school meals and the provision of medical inspections. The measure to provide children with school meals was controversial. It was not, initially, a government measure. It was introduced by a Labour MP as a Private Members' Bill (see Unit 3, Box 3.8 on page 76 for a definition of 'Private Members' Bill'). But, the government took the Bill over and steered it through Parliament. Opponents argued that the state was undermining the independence of the family and providing a poor example because children would learn that they did not have to fend for themselves - the state would look after them.

Similarly, the Act which made school medical inspections compulsory was not a government initiative. It was the work of a senior civil servant who believed strongly in National Efficiency:

'Medical inspection of school children owed something to backbench pressure, but Sir Robert Morant, Permanent Secretary at the Board of Education was responsible for its introduction, hidden among the clauses of the Education (Administrative Provisions) Act of 1907.' (Hay 1983, p.44)

Historians agree that MPs simply did not pick up on the implications of the clause as the Bill went through Parliament.

Murray argues that these two measures had a significant effect:

'Both measures gradually had a major impact despite their opponents. Although the 1906 Act was at first permissive (Local Education Authorities were not compelled to supply school meals), by 1914 over 14 million meals per annum were being provided for 158,000 children. In a similar way, the 1907 Act did not compel local authorities to set up clinics, but by 1914 most were providing some medical treatment for children.' (Murray 1999, p.106)

Liberal Reforms and adult poverty

Whilst historians agree that, taken as a whole, the welfare package introduced by the Liberals in the period 1906-14 helped to alleviate poverty for those eligible for the various benefits, they also agree that many people continued to 'slip through the net':

● old people under the age of 70 did not qualify for pensions (and the pension itself was a bare minimum)

● workers outside the industries covered by the Labour Exchanges Act and Miners' Minimum Wage Act did not qualify to receive a minimum wage

● only c.13 million people out of a total population of c.45 million were included in the National Insurance scheme

● workers outside the industries covered by the unemployment benefit scheme did not receive any benefits if they became unemployed.

Murray concludes that:

'The social reforms of the pre-war Liberal government had no opportunity to make a major dent in the extent of poverty before the Great War, but there is some evidence to suggest that they (and the legislation of the 1920s which developed from them) began to make a difference in the longer term.' (Murray 1999, p.122)

Murray notes that, while Rowntree had found in his 1901 survey that 9.9% of people were living in 'primary' poverty (ie receiving too little income to buy the basic essentials of life even if every penny was spent wisely), in a follow-up survey in 1936, this figure had fallen to 3.9%. Given that the follow-up survey was conducted during the Great Depression, this indicates that significant progress had been made. It should be noted, however, that in the follow-up survey Rowntree still found that 20% of people were living in 'secondary' poverty (ie although they could afford the basic essentials, they still had to go short on food or clothing, or both). In other words, a large proportion of the population remained very poor.

MAIN POINTS - Sections 2.2-2.3

● The Liberal Party ran a negative campaign before the 1906 general election. There was no carefully worked out blueprint for reform and little sign that the new government would introduce radical reforms.

● Many historians argue that, although some important measures were taken in 1906-08, Campbell-Bannerman's government was not a success because of (1) Campbell-Bannerman's failings, (2) opposition from the Lords and (3) the government was living in the past.

● The standard view is that, when Campbell-Bannerman resigned because of ill health, the reforming impetus accelerated dramatically. All the key reforms, however, were introduced by just two members of the Cabinet - Lloyd George and Churchill.

● Some of the key measures were (1) the People's Budget (2) the Old Age Pensions Act, 1909 (3) the Parliament Act, 1911 and (4) the National Insurance Act, 1911.

● Whether or not the reforms introduced between 1908-14 are regarded as radical depends on whether they are judged (1) in light of Victorian values (2) in light of later developments or (3) in light of party political concerns.

Activity 6.4 Liberal reforms 1906-14

ITEM 1 Old age pensions

(i) The big dog and the little one

THE BIG DOG AND THE LITTLE ONE.

[From the *Westminster Gazette*]

LORD HALSBURY: I don't think much of that paltry little thing—it's a mockery of a dog.

AGED PENSIONER: Well, my lord, 'tis only a little 'un, but 'tis a wunnerful comfort to me. Us bain't all blessed wi' big 'uns!

[Lord Halsbury, in a speech at Budleigh Salterton on January 6th, spoke of the Pensions given by the Liberal Act of Parliament as " so paltry as to be all but a mockery." Lord Halsbury himself draws a State Pension of £5,000 a year, or nearly £100 a week.]

Published by the LIBERAL PUBLICATION DEPARTMENT (in connection with the National Liberal Federation and the Liberal Central Association), 42, Parliament Street, Westminster, S.W., and Printed by the National Press Agency Limited, Whitefriars House, London, E.C.

LEAFLET No. 2207.]   1/2/09.   [Price 4s. 6d. per 1000.

(ii) You have never had a scheme of this kind tried in a great country like ours, with its thronging millions, with its rooted complexities; and everyone who has been engaged in any kind of reform knows how difficult it is to make way through the inextricable [confused] tangle of an old society like ours. This is, therefore, a great experiment...We do not say that it deals with all the problems of unmerited destitution [poverty] in this country. We do not even contend that it deals with the worst part of that problem. It might be held that many an old man dependent on the charity of the parish was better off than many a young man broken down in health or who cannot find a market for his labour. The provision which is made for the sick and unemployed is grossly inadequate in this country and yet the working classes have done their best during the past 50 years to make provision without the aid of the state. But, it is insufficient. The old man has to bear his own burden while in the case of a young man who is broken down and who has a wife and family to maintain, the suffering is increased and multiplied to that extent. These problems of the sick, of the infirm, of the men who cannot find means of earning a living are problems with which it is the business of the state to deal. They are problems which the state has neglected for too long.

David Lloyd George, speech made to Parliament, 15 June 1908.

(iii) In the 1880s some poorer couples just about held onto their homes but lived in daily fear of the workhouse. The Poor Law authorities allowed people too old to work a small weekly sum – 'outdoor relief'. But it was not enough to live on. Unless they had children to help support them, there came a time when the home had to be broken up. When, 20 years later, Old Age Pensions began, life was transformed for these aged cottagers. They were relieved of anxiety. They were suddenly rich. At first, when they went to the post office to draw their pension, tears of gratitude would run down their cheeks and they would say, 'God bless that Lord George!' (for they could not believe one so powerful and generous could be plain 'Mr') and, 'God bless you, Miss!'

From Flora Thompson's 'Lark Rise To Candleford', an eyewitness account of life in the 1880s.

ITEM 2 A historian's view (1)

The first three years of Asquith's premiership were a period of success almost unequalled by any other British government. The dragon, in the shape of the House of Lords, was finally slain, or at least had its teeth pulled and perhaps the most important piece of social legislation of the 20th century was placed upon the statute book - the National Insurance Act of 1911. The government took office with no great blueprint of reform, yet the energy of ministers like Churchill and Lloyd George, and the growing influence and skill of civil servants such as Llewellyn-Smith and Beveridge had produced an unparalleled amount of legislation. In part, this was a response to political pressures and both Lloyd George and Churchill felt that the Labour Party had to be seen off by a large dose of social reform. The legislation was also a response to the 'public mood'. The drive for National Efficiency and the growing awareness of unacceptable poverty created a climate in which New Liberalism could flourish. What was acceptable in 1867 was no longer acceptable in 1907. There was a growing faith in the state's capacity to cure problems. No longer could it be left to local government which had shouldered most of the burden of social reform and improvement in the 19th century. The example set by other countries was important. The dynamic new German Empire showed that social reform and economic success could go hand-in-hand. Belgium set up infant welfare centres in 1903. Many national disaster areas remained untouched - the problem of slums, for example, was not tackled. Despite this, social service spending roughly doubled between 1906 and 1914.

Adapted from Pearce & Stewart 1992.

ITEM 3 A historian's view (2)

Between 1880 and 1906, attitudes began to soften towards the 'deserving' poor. This approach culminated in the 1905 Unemployed Workmen's Act which gave local authorities powers to set up labour exchanges and to create work for the unemployed at the ratepayers' expense. The main aim behind the flood of legislation carried out by the Liberal government between 1906 and 1914 was to continue this process by attacking those causes of poverty which Booth and Rowntree had helped isolate and publicise - family poverty, old age, sickness, death of the breadwinner, low wages and unemployment. There was no overall plan and no sharp break with previous practice, yet the cumulative effect was to mark an end to the old approach and a beginning of the new. The amount of legislation is unusual and needs explanation. Credit should be given to two ministers - Lloyd George and Churchill - who pushed the most important legislation through Parliament. Public opinion was changing - but only slowly (many people remained hostile to state control over the individual). On the other hand, there was political pressure from socialists who demanded more state action in defence of the poor. Also, decision makers were aware of the welfare legislation that had been passed in Germany. There was widespread discussion of 'national degeneration' prompted by the eugenics movement (people who believed the British race could be improved by selective breeding) and the low level of health among military volunteers at the time of the Boer War. The desire to rescue and elevate the poor came not only from those conscious of the injustice and waste of individual poverty, but also from people who were anxious to raise and strengthen the British 'race'.

Adapted from Royle 1997.

ITEM 4 Liberal reforms and Lloyd George

David Lloyd George was born in Manchester in 1863, but his family moved to North Wales the following year and he was brought up there in a lower middle-class, non-conformist household. He did not go to university, but trained as a solicitor before being elected as a Liberal MP for Caernarvon Boroughs at a by-election in 1890. In Parliament, he joined the radical wing of the party and first rose to prominence as an outspoken opponent of the Boer War. It was as a social reformer in the period 1906-14 that Lloyd George made his greatest contribution to modern Britain. He linked the Old Liberalism of the farms and the chapels to the New Liberalism of welfare, labour and social reform. The reforms which he and Winston Churchill introduced set the agenda for the remainder of the 20th century. Two of his aims were, first, to frustrate the challenge of the rising Labour Party and, second, to find a Liberal free-trade alternative to the Unionists' tariff reform. Where Unionists said the foreigner should pay, the Liberals said the rich would pay - but without imposing unfair taxes which would hit the poor as well. A man of the Welsh countryside, he became a liberator of the masses of darkest urban Britain. The People's Budget was important not just because it triggered a conflict with the Lords, but because it introduced a new policy which lasted until the 1980s of financing social programmes from the direct taxation of individuals and companies. The National Insurance Act established the principle that benefits should be paid, as of right, to all contributors. This meant a new and dynamic view of the state - though one linked with private and voluntary agencies such as insurance companies and trade unions. All social reformers since 1911 have stood on Lloyd George's shoulders.

David Lloyd George

Adapted from Morgan 1997.

Questions

1. How radical were the Liberal reforms? Use Items 1-4 and your own knowledge in your answer.
2. a) What do Items 1(i) and 1(iii) tell us about reactions to the introduction of old age pensions?
   b) What evidence is there in Item 1(ii) to suggest that the Liberal government was influenced by New Liberalism?
3. a) On what points do Items 2 and 3 agree and on what do they differ?
   b) Why did the Liberal government pass so many reforms in the period 1906-14? Use Items 2 and 3 and your own knowledge.
4. Look at Item 4.
   a) Give arguments for and against the view that Asquith and not Lloyd George should be credited with the Liberal reforms of 1908-14.
   b) To what extent do you agree with the view that it was the threat from the left not New Liberalism which explains the Liberal government's reforms.

3 The constitutional crisis

Key questions

1. What led to the constitutional crisis of 1909-11?

2. How did the constitutional crisis affect the Unionist alliance?

3. Did the crisis result in a triumph for the Liberals?

3.1 What led to the constitutional crisis of 1909-11?

The People's Budget

The catalyst for the constitutional crisis that dominated politics in 1910-11 was Lloyd George's Budget of 1909 - the so-called 'People's Budget' (the main details are outlined in Box 6.13). As noted above, this Budget was controversial because it marked a clear departure in terms of approach to taxation. Taxes were deliberately raised in order to pay for state-run schemes and there was, for the first time, an element of redistribution of wealth:

'[The Budget] changed the whole basis of British public finance from the Victorian pattern to the system that has lasted throughout the 20th century. It shifted the chief source of revenue from indirect to direct taxation; it established the principle that taxation ought to be related to capacity to pay and it inaugurated a limited redistribution of income for the benefit of the poor through social welfare schemes.' (Pugh 1988, p.47)

Since the Budget was particularly targeted against those on high incomes (especially landowners and people with unearned income), it was strongly opposed by the Conservative Party.

Lloyd George's motives

There has been some debate about Lloyd George's motives for introducing such a controversial Budget.

BOX 6.13 | **The People's Budget of 1909**

Summary Box

- Super tax - six pence per pound on incomes of £5000 and over.
- Income tax increased by two pence in the pound on unearned incomes and on incomes over £3000 per annum.
- Increase in death duties.
- Tax on motor vehicles according to horsepower.
- Three pence on a gallon of petrol.
- New land taxes, particularly a 20% tax on land sold at a higher value than when it was purchased.
- Increased duties on liquor licences.
- Duties on spirits raised by a third, those on tobacco by a quarter.

Some historians have suggested that Lloyd George consciously set out to provoke the House of Lords in the hope that a constitutional crisis would break out. Most historians, however, do not accept such a view. They argue that Asquith and Lloyd George did not want the reform programme to be sidetracked and that the aim was to revive the Liberal Party's fortunes:

'It is sometimes argued that the Budget was deliberately framed to incite the Lords. This seems unlikely for two reasons. The first is that both Asquith and Lloyd George gave priority to their reform programme and wanted to maintain its impetus. A constitutional crisis would guarantee its complete halt. In any case it is probable that Asquith had tried to sidestep confrontation in the first place by including in the Budget several measures such as land taxes, hoping that the Lords would abide by convention and not reject anything in a money Bill. Second, Lloyd George was well aware of the need to revive the support of the rank and file who were somewhat disillusioned by the limited measures so far produced. He also had the next election in mind and had to find a quick way of conveying a policy which would get reform moving and appeal to most of the Liberal constituency. Thus the aim of the government was probably to speed up its social legislation by finding a way out of political entanglement.' (Lee 1994, p.230)

The idea that the Budget was designed to revive the political fortunes of the Liberal Party is supported by Lloyd George himself:

'Referring to his Budget plans in a letter to his brother in May 1908, Lloyd George wrote: "It is time we did something that appealed straight to the people - it will, I think, stop the electoral rot, and that is most necessary".' (Blewett 1972, p.68)

Sidestepping the Lords

Most historians agree that a confrontation between the Liberal government and the House of Lords had been brewing for some time before 1909. Reform of the Lords had been one of the demands of Gladstone's 'Newcastle Programme' as long ago as 1891 (see Unit 2, page 62) and it remained in the background from that point onwards. There is some evidence that Campbell-Bannerman was considering challenging the Lords just before he died. According to Lee, however:

'The leadership did not consider it appropriate to escalate early confrontations over, for example, the Education Bill into a full-scale constitutional crisis which would involve a further general election and a complete halt to all other government business.' (Lee 1994, p.230)

Amongst the Bills rejected by the House of Lords between 1906 and 1909 were a group of Land Bills (rejected in 1907) and a Licensing Bill (rejected in

1908). While it was constitutionally acceptable for the Lords to reject such Bills because they were not explicitly finance Bills, it was not conventional for the Lords to reject finance Bills. The composition of the 1909 Budget was, therefore, designed to sidestep the Lords. By dressing up measures previously rejected by the Lords as financial matters, the government hoped to introduce reforms which otherwise would have been blocked.

The constitutional crisis

When the Lords rejected Lloyd George's Budget Bill in November 1909, this was the first time that the House of Lords had rejected a finance Bill for 200 years. The rejection of the Budget was the start of a constitutional crisis:

'It raised a simple but important question. Who governed Britain? Was it the elected majority in the House of Commons or was it that sector of society who saw themselves as - and, indeed, had traditionally been - the "governing class"?' (Green 1996, p.24)

Lee (1994) argues that the Liberal government had three good reasons for rising to the challenge set by the Lords:

1. It was a fundamental constitutional right that the democratically elected Commons should be able to control taxation.
2. The government had a huge majority in the Commons and, therefore, a mandate to complete its legislative programme.
3. By protecting the political and financial interests of the Conservative Party, the Lords were acting in a blatantly partisan manner ie it was supporting the interests of the Conservative Party rather than acting in the national interest.

The course of the constitutional crisis is summarised in Box 6.14.

3.2 How did the constitutional crisis affect the Unionist alliance?

Ewen Green's interpretation

In an article which examines why the People's Budget became the catalyst for a major constitutional crisis, Ewen Green argues that:

'The "backwoodsmen" who descended on London to trample the Budget were venting anger and frustration that had been building up for years - the House of Lords did not reject the Budget reluctantly, but did so with relish.' (Green 1999, p.26)

Green provides five reasons why the People's Budget was the final straw for Unionist peers. These are outlined in Box 6.15 (i) on page 210. He also argues that a large number of peers were so opposed to the People's Budget that they would have voted against it regardless of the stance of the Unionist alliance's leadership. As it happened, however, the Unionist alliance's leadership did support the rejection of the Budget. Green gives four reasons why it adopted this stance. These are outlined in Box 6.15 (ii) on page 210.

Impact of the crisis on the Unionist alliance

There is a consensus amongst historians that, in the short term at least, the Unionist alliance was damaged by the constitutional crisis - not least because, following the introduction of the Parliament Bill, the party split into three groups:

- the 'diehards' insisted on resisting the Bill in the Lords to the bitter end
- the 'hedgers' supported abstention (not voting)
- the 'rats' agreed to vote with the government.

Differences of opinion between these three groups was open and hostile and, according to Ewen

---

BOX 6.14 The constitutional crisis of 1909-11

The defeat of the Budget forced Asquith to dissolve Parliament. The Liberals were returned in the January 1910 general election in roughly equal numbers to the Unionists. Labour and the Irish Nationalists kept Asquith in power. The Budget, now that it had received popular backing, soon became law. King Edward VII then insisted that, before Asquith would be able to move against the Lords, a second election must be held. Following the King's death in May 1910, a constitutional conference was held in an attempt to break the deadlock. The conference failed and Asquith promptly asked for a dissolution and also for a promise that the new King would create enough new Liberal peers to outvote existing peers, if and when the need for this arose. The result of the second general election of 1910 closely followed the first. The government introduced its Parliament Bill. The Unionist opposition objected, but gave way after being informed at the last moment of the King's promise to create enough new Liberal peers to outvote the Conservatives. This caused an internal party dispute which cost Balfour the Conservative leadership. In August 1911, the Parliament Bill became law. Under its terms, the Lords lost their power to reject finance Bills and, in future, they would only be able to delay other forms of legislation. If a Bill passed the Commons in three successive sessions, it would automatically pass into law. So, the Lords could postpone but not permanently veto any Bill, however controversial. In addition, the life of Parliaments was reduced from seven to five years.

Adapted from Searle 1992 and Watts 1995.

Interpretation

BOX 6.15 | The People's Budget and the peers

Interpretation

(i) Why did Unionist peers oppose the Budget?
Green argues that the five reasons why the People's Budget was the final straw for Unionist peers were as follows:

1. Agricultural depression in the late 19th century had resulted in a fall of rents and land prices. This hit some peers hard.
2. Beginning in the 1880s, legislation had been designed to control, tax or eliminate the privileges enjoyed by landowners.
3. Electoral reform made it difficult for landowners to influence voters.
4. Local government reform shifted power from the aristocracy to elected representatives.
5. The 'long game' (the tactic adopted by Salisbury and Balfour of defending aristocratic interests by conceding some reforms but rallying to block important reforms) was frustrating because it meant that some unwelcome measures were passed.

(ii) Why did the Unionist leadership oppose the Budget?
Green gives four reasons why the Unionist alliance's leadership supported the rejection of the 1909 Budget. These were as follows:

1. It was a good chance to force a general election. Recent by-election successes suggested that the Unionist alliance had a good chance of regaining power.
2. Many members of the Unionist alliance were strongly opposed to the Budget on the grounds that its provisions were 'socialist'.
3. Many members of the Unionist alliance realised that the provisions in the Budget undermined the appeal of tariff reform since the Budget raised the cash to finance social reform while retaining free trade (central to the case for tariff reform was the argument that the money raised by tariffs could be used to pay for social reform).
4. It was important to make a stand at this early stage because, once the Budget was implemented, the idea that social reform should be financed by taxing the wealthy would gain momentum. In other words, a precedent would be set.

Adapted from Green 1999.

Green, long-lasting:
'To the diehards and their supporters, those peers that abstained , the "hedgers", and those who actually voted for the government, the "rats", became objects of derision or open hostility. This bad feeling, often personal but also based on deep political differences, was reciprocated and continued to plague the Conservative Party until the outbreak of the Great War. Having entered the fray in 1909 with enthusiasm and high hopes, the Conservative Party emerged defeated and in disarray.' (Green 1996, p.25)

Balfour and the crisis
Many historians have been critical of Balfour's leadership during the constitutional crisis. Balfour's official position on the Parliament Bill was that peers should allow it to pass rather than forcing the government to create new Liberal peers. This position, however, was unacceptable to the diehards and 114 of them rejected Balfour's line and voted against the Bill (131 peers voted for the Bill). One criticism of Balfour is that he was indecisive:
'His inability to take a strong line during the Parliament Bill episode eroded his support, even in the most sympathetic quarters. Hence Balfour's leadership became the most important casualty of the crisis, for his resignation in the autumn of 1911 was prompted by the all-too-evident criticism and ill-feeling to which he was subjected by his own party after the passage of the Parliament Act.' (Green 1996, p.25)
Other critics suggest that the Parliament Act was one disappointment too many:
'No-one questioned Balfour's intellectual primacy, but three election defeats, his climbdown on tariff reform [he moved from being neutral in the run-up to the 1906 election to adopting the policy after the election] and now the Parliament Bill, heightened criticism of his leadership. Leo Maxse of the right wing *National Review*, for long a critic of Balfour, coined the abbreviation BMG in his September 1911 edition - Balfour Must Go...he appears by the action of 1911 to have had enough of division and criticism and when in October 1911 the "Halsbury Club" of diehard "Ditchers" was formed, Balfour decided to resign.' (Pearce & Stewart 1992, p.381)
In the leadership contest which followed Balfour's resignation, the two main contenders - Austen Chamberlain (the son of Joseph) and Walter Long - stood aside and allowed the underdog, Andrew Bonar Law, to become leader.

The effect of Balfour's resignation
Historians are divided about whether Unionist fortunes revived after Balfour's resignation. On the one hand, Dutton (1992) and Green (1995) argue that the Conservative Party (the Liberal Unionists formally merged with the Conservative Party in 1912) remained divided and in crisis throughout the period 1910-14:
'From the first months of 1910 to the outbreak of the Great War, the Conservative Party found it difficult to establish a consensus on any major issue; the party's disagreements led to the resignation of one Leader and the threatened resignation of his successor. Between 1906 and 1910 there had been general agreement that the full tariff programme was a plausible solution to the party's various problems, but between 1910 and 1914, the Conservatives

found problems and no solutions. The years immediately before the Great War saw a continuance and, in some ways, a deepening of the crisis of Conservatism.' (Green 1995, p.270)

On the other hand, Ramsden (1978) and Goodlad (1998) argue that, under Bonar Law's leadership, the Conservative Party revived to such an extent that, by the time was broke out, it was in good shape. This, it is argued, was largely the result of the leadership provided by Bonar Law:

'[Bonar Law] lacked experience at Cabinet level and, as a middle-class businessman with few social graces, he was an outsider to the party's traditional establishment. Down to 1914, Law's position was never fully secure against the factional criticism of those who thought they could do better. Nonetheless, his dry purposeful manner and his readiness to take on the Liberals with brutal directness did wonders for party morale...That the Conservatives were able to survive in the new world which they found in 1918 was due in part to the leadership of Bonar Law in the immediate pre-war years...The Conservatives entered the conflict of 1914-18 in good heart, ready to exploit the political opportunities it offered. (Goodlad 1998, pp.10, 13)

3.3 Did the crisis result in a triumph for the Liberals?

Historians' verdicts

Most historians agree that the constitutional crisis resulted in a victory for the Liberal government. The government had stood up to the Lords and forced it to make major concessions. This is generally seen as a major achievement (see Box 6.16).

Although most historians agree that reform of the Lords was an impressive Liberal achievement, some suggest that the reform was not a complete success, especially in the short term. Lee (1994) and Watts

---

BOX 6.16 The outcome of the constitutional crisis

(i) 'The outcome of the Lords' crisis was ultimately victory for the Liberals, particularly for Asquith who, in the later stages at least, displayed superb parliamentary mastery and control.' (Adelman 1981, p.4)

(ii) 'In the 1880s and 1890s the Liberals had lacked the unity and the political will to confront the constitutional issues raised by the Lords' assaults on Liberal legislation. That the Liberals proved able to do so in 1909-11 speaks volumes for the transformation of the party's outlook, fortunes and morale.' (Green 1999, p.25)

(iii) 'The Act was a substantial Liberal achievement and it resolved a problem which had beset past progressive administrations. As such, it was much to the credit of ministers.' (Watts 1995, p.146)

Interpretations

(1995), for example, point out that the Lords made a great deal of use of their new delaying powers in the period 1911-14 and, as a result, were able to prevent the Liberals bringing in substantial reforms during that period. The outbreak of the First World War postponed the implementation of key reforms still further. Byrne (1995) takes a more negative line, arguing that:

'The outcome of the constitutional crisis was scarcely revolutionary. Its most immediate effect...was on the Irish Question. It did not result in a flood of legislation needing to be forced through the Lords, indeed the main reforming zeal of the Liberals had exhausted itself by 1911...The crisis cost the Liberals their overall majority and exposed them to the demands of the Irish Nationalists. The reputations of their leaders, particularly Asquith and Lloyd George were enhanced, but the necessity for dealing immediately with the question of Irish Home Rule ruled out any chance there might have been of further measures of domestic reform.' (Byrne 1995, p.473)

MAIN POINTS - Part 3

- **The catalyst for the constitutional crisis that dominated politics in 1910-11 was Lloyd George's 1909 'People's Budget'. Most historians now accept that Lloyd George did not deliberately set out to provoke the Lords into rejecting this Budget. The Budget was, however, designed to sidestep the Lords.**
- **When the Lords rejected the Budget, an election was held. The Liberals regained power and the Budget became law. In May, Edward VII died. Constitutional talks were held but broke down. A second election was held in December. The threat of the creation of new peers was enough to ensure the Parliament Bill was then passed.**
- **There were five main reasons why Unionist peers opposed the People's Budget - (1) value of their land had decreased (2) their privileges had been curtailed**

- **(3) electoral reform prevented them controlling the electorate (4) local government reform reduced their influence and (5) the 'long game' was frustrating.**
- **There were four main reasons why the Unionist leadership opposed the People's Budget - (1) to force a general election (2) on ideological grounds (as it was 'socialist') (3) it undermined the appeal of tariff reform and (4) it set a precedent.**
- **Historians agree that the Unionist alliance was damaged by the crisis in the short term. They are divided, however, over whether Conservative fortunes revived in 1911-14, after Bonar Law became leader.**
- **Most historians agree that reform of the Lords was a major success for the Liberal government, although some argue that it was not a complete success.**

Activity 6.5 The constitutional crisis

ITEM 1 The government's attack on the Lords

(i) Let them realise what they are doing. They are forcing a revolution, and they will get it. The Lords may decree [decide on] a revolution, but the people will direct it. If they begin, issues will be raised that they little dream of. Questions will be asked which are now whispered in humble voices and answers will be demanded then with authority. The questions will be asked whether 500 men, ordinary men chosen accidentally from among the unemployed, should override the judgement - the deliberate judgement - of millions of people who are engaged in the industry which makes the wealth of the country. That is one question. Another will be: Who ordained that a few should have the land of Britain as a perquisite [a right]? Who made 10,000 people owners of the soil and the rest of us trespassers in the land of our birth? Who is it who is responsible for the scheme of things whereby one man is engaged through life in grinding labour to win a bare and precarious subsistence for himself and when, at the end of his days, he claims at the hands of the community he served a poor pension of eightpence a day, he can only get it through a revolution, and another man who does not toil receives every hour of the day, every hour of the night, whilst he slumbers, more than his poor neighbour receives in a whole year of toil?

Part of a speech made by David Lloyd George in Newcastle on 10 October 1909.

(ii) This poster was produced for the government during the constitutional crisis.

ITEM 2 The Budget Protest League

This poster was produced by the Budget Protest League, a pressure group set up by the Unionist MP Walter Long in June 1909 (Lloyd George delivered his Budget speech in April 1909. The Lords finally rejected it by 350 votes to 75 on 30 November 1909). Walter Long was a challenger for the leadership of the Unionist alliance when Balfour resigned in 1911.

(iii) The truth is that all this talk about the duty or right of the House of Lords to refer measures to the people is, in the light of our practical and actual experience, the hollowest outcry of political cant [hypocrisy]. We never hear of it, as I pointed out, when a Tory government is in power. ...It is simply a thin rhetorical veneer by which it is sought to gloss over the partisan and, in this case the unconstitutional, action of the purely partisan Chamber. The sum and substance of the matter is that the House of Lords rejected the Finance Bill last Tuesday, not because they love the people, but because they hate the Budget...The real question which emerges from the political struggles in this country for the last 30 years is not whether you will have a single or double chamber system of government, but whether, when the Tory Party is in power, the House of Commons shall be omnipotent [all-powerful] and whether, when the Liberal Party is in power, the House of Lords shall be omnipotent.

Part of a speech made by Herbert Asquith in the Commons on 2 December 1909.

ITEM 3 The view of a diehard

It seems to me that upon a question of principle, if I believed a thing to be wrong, I ought to do my best to prevent it. The temptation given to us is that we must allow the Bill to pass and then, forsooth, agitate until we get the country to take our view. Thus we are told that we shall be satisfied that we have saved this House from degradation [destruction]. Have we? Is it saving this House from degradation when that which it is admitted to be so degrading to it is yielded to as a threat? I myself will certainly not yield to the threat. Let the government take responsibility for introducing 400 or 500 peers - I care not how many - in the circumstances that my noble friend has pointed out and then let him shield himself by saying 'And you forced me to do it'. I have never heard such an extraordinary argument in my life. It is as if a highwayman came and said 'Give me your watch or I cut your throat' and if you did not give him your watch that you are the author of your own throat being cut...Nothing in the world will induce me not to vote against a Bill which I believe to be wrong and immoral and a scandalous example of legislation.

Part of a speech made by the Earl of Halsbury in the House of Lords on 9 August 1911.

ITEM 4 A historian's view

With hindsight, it appears that the Liberals had a carefully formulated strategy. This was not the case. To some extent, the government muddled its way through the crisis, reacting to developments rather than anticipating them. At first, for example, the Cabinet was divided over how the Lords should be reformed. Asquith eventually imposed his view that the Lords' power of veto should be converted to that of delay (Campbell-Bannerman's preferred option). The government was also thrown by the death of Edward VII. It must, however, be credited with a major achievement. It had taken on the most entrenched institution in the land and, for the first time since the 17th century, had forced it to agree to the reduction of its own authority. In this respect, the success for the Liberals in 1911 was even greater than that of the Whigs in 1832. Also, by reducing the Lords' power of veto to the power of delay, the Liberals were able to press ahead with their legislative programme, the flagship of which was the National Insurance Act of 1911. There is, however, another perspective. The Parliament Act stopped short of what the Liberals really wanted. The preamble of the Act referred to more radical reform in the future - the substitution of a democratic body for the current hereditary body. But, that was never taken up. The Liberals, therefore, lost a unique opportunity to follow up while the issue was warm. The House of Lords also had the final say. Between 1911 and 1914, it used its delaying power against a range of Liberal measures. Reasoning that the government had legitimised its power by redefining it, the Lords saw no reason why they should not use it. As a result, they dampened what could have been another reforming phase.

Adapted from Lee 1994.

Questions

1. a) Describe the context in which each of Items 1-3 was produced.
   b) What do these items tell us about the nature of debate during the constitutional crisis?
   c) Why did the People's Budget lead to a constitutional crisis?
2. a) What does Item 2 tell us about Unionist attitudes?
   b) What arguments do you think Unionists would have made in support of this view of the People's Budget?
   c) How did the government counter these arguments? Use Item 1 in your answer.
3. a) Describe the Earl of Halsbury's attitude towards the Parliament Bill in Item 3.
   b) What arguments might a 'hedger' or a 'rat' have used against the Earl of Halsbury?
4. Was the outcome of the constitutional crisis a triumph for the Liberals? Use Item 4 in your answer.

4 The Liberal government and Ireland

Key questions

1. What was the background to the crisis over Ireland in 1912-14?
2. Why did a crisis develop over Ireland in the period 1912-14?
3. Who was to blame for the crisis?

4.1 What was the background to the crisis over Ireland in 1912-14?

The first Home Rule Bill, 1886

Gladstone's 'conversion' to the cause of Irish Home Rule (self-government) in 1885 split the Liberal Party and raised expectations and fears. It raised the expectations of Irish Nationalists who accepted that the terms of the first Home Rule Bill were, in the words of their Leader, Charles Stewart Parnell (see also Unit 1, Section 3.2), 'a final settlement of our national question'. At the same time, it raised the fears of Unionists - in Britain and Ireland - because they were opposed to any measure which weakened the Act of Union of 1801 (which made Ireland a part of the UK). The Conservative politician Randolf Churchill felt so strongly about the matter that he wrote to Gladstone in December 1885 (before Gladstone had publicly declared his support for Home Rule) telling him that, if Gladstone did come out in favour of it, he would not hesitate to 'agitate Ulster even to resistance beyond constitutional limits' (quoted in Shannon 1999, p.399). Two months later he wrote in a letter:

'I decided some time ago that if the GOM [Grand Old Man - ie Gladstone] went for Home Rule, the Orange card would be the one to play. Please God may it turn out to be the ace of trumps and not the two.'

In 1886, Churchill travelled to Ulster to rally opposition to the Bill. His inflammatory slogan 'Ulster will fight and Ulster will be right' caught the mood already prevailing in the Unionist community there:

'Already in that year [1886], symptoms were appearing of what was to become a raging fever between 1912 and 1914 - already there was drilling [organising along military lines], already there were proposals for a solemn oath of resistance and for the purchase of arms to make that resistance effective.' (Lyons 1971, p.186)

As a measure of the political temperature, later in the year riots broke out in Belfast leaving 32 people dead. The first Home Rule Bill, however, was defeated in the Commons, forcing Gladstone's resignation and a general election.

The second Home Rule Bill, 1893

Parliamentary arithmetic had played an important part in raising the issue of Home Rule in 1885 and it played an equally important part in ensuring that Home Rule remained off the agenda in the period 1886-92. In the 1886 general election, the Conservative-Liberal Unionist alliance won 393 seats while the Gladstonian Liberals won just 192 seats (Craig 1989). This ensured that Home Rule remained in the background until after the election of 1892.

In the election of 1892, the Gladstonian Liberals gained 80 seats, giving them a total of 272 seats. The Conservatives and Liberal Unionists won 313 seats while the Irish Nationalists won 81 seats (despite

being split into pro-Parnell and anti-Parnell factions). Once again, therefore, the Irish Nationalists held the balance of power and they backed Gladstone who had promised to introduce a second Home Rule Bill.

This Bill completed its passage through the Commons on 2 September 1893. Less than a week later, however, it was defeated overwhelmingly by the Lords (419 votes to 41). Although some members of the House of Lords argued that they had voted against the Bill because a minority of MPs representing mainland Britain had supported it in the Commons (304 voted against and 266 for, if the 81 Irish Nationalist MPs are subtracted), the House of Lords had an in-built Unionist majority and there was no chance of it supporting a Home Rule Bill.

In reality, therefore, it was not really necessary to 'play the Orange card' either in 1886 or in 1893. On both occasions, there was sufficient opposition in

BOX 6.17 Ulster

This map shows the nine counties of Ulster and the borders of Ireland's other counties and provinces.

Ulster was not, as Unionists liked to claim, a 'Protestant province'. In the years before the First World War, Ulster returned 33 MPs - 16 Unionists and 17 Nationalists and Liberals. Also, Unionist support was not concentrated in a particular area - the Unionists' stronghold in the east was separated from that in the west by the Nationalist seats of Mid-, North and East Tyrone. Southern Ulster was mainly Nationalist, as was the North West. West Belfast was also strongly Nationalist.

Adapted from Boyce 1992.

Parliament to ensure that the Bills were blocked. Nevertheless, the very fact that one of the two major parties was prepared to support Home Rule was enough to lead to a significant hardening of attitudes among Irish Unionists and to the emergence of a well organised opposition to Home Rule:

'Following the 1886 general election, the Unionists worked hard to consolidate their forces in Ulster and justify their stance. Unionist clubs were formed throughout the province, links were established with Unionists in the south and with the Conservative Party on the mainland and a propaganda campaign was carried out in Great Britain on behalf of the Ulster Unionist cause. An Ulster Defence Association was also formed - a portent of what was to come. The defeat of the second Home Rule Bill in 1893, however, lifted the immediate danger to Ulster.' (Adelman 1996, p.113)

Following the defeat of the second Home Rule Bill, there was a decade of calm as the Conservative government attempted to 'kill Home Rule by kindness'.

Ulster and the growth of Unionism

In Ireland, support for Unionism was not confined to Ulster. In the 1890s, there were as many as 250,000 Unionists in the South of Ireland:

'[Unionists in the South] were primarily landed and Anglican, and provided considerable financial and organisational direction to Unionists in all parts of Ireland...Unionists claimed in the 1880s and 1890s to be a movement which embraced the entire island and southern Unionists, though numerically slight, were important in lending credibility to this claim.' (Connolly 1998, p.566)

Nevertheless, it was in Ulster (see Box 6.17 on page 214) that the majority of Unionists lived and, in the early 20th century, it was in Ulster that Unionism developed into a major obstacle to Home Rule.

The origins of the separate identity which developed in Ulster lay in the earlier history of Ireland. Three main factors came to define this identity - religion, economics and political alignment.

1. Religious polarisation

According to the census of 1861, in Ireland as a whole 78% of the population was Catholic, with the Protestant population divided between Anglicans (11.9%) and Presbyterians (8.9%). By 1911, the percentage of Catholics had risen to 81%. In Ulster, however, Protestants remained in the majority during

| BOX 6.18 | The Census of 1911 |

(i) Religious affiliation of the population of Ireland in 1911

	Protestant	Catholic	Total
Ulster	891,000	691,000	1,582,000
Three southern provinces	250,000	2,550,000	2,800,000
Whole of Ireland	1,141,000	3,241,000	4,382,000

(ii) Religious affiliation in the counties of Ulster in 1911

	Protestant	Catholic
Antrim	79.0%	20.5%
Down	68.4%	31.6%
Armagh	54.7%	45.3%
Londonderry	54.2%	45.8%
Tyrone	44.6%	55.4%
Fermanagh	43.8%	56.2%
Monaghan	25.3%	74.7%
Donegal	21.1%	78.9%
Cavan	18.5%	81.5%

Adapted from Brendon 1996.

this period (see Box 6.18), with Presbyterians outnumbering Anglicans. Until the mid-1880s, there were marked political and economic differences between the two Protestant groups. The Home Rule movement, however, forced the groups together:

'Neither the social distinctions nor the political differences between these two main Protestant groups should be pressed too far. Both were to sink quickly into insignificance the moment the supposed threat from Roman Catholicism took visible shape with the development of a dynamic Home Rule movement in the 1880s. Thereafter, the tendency of most northern Protestants was to close ranks against the common enemy; since Catholics reacted in the same way, the sectarianism [division arising out of religious beliefs] which has bedevilled politics in the province from that day to this became inevitable.' (Lyons 1971, p.23)

Fears of Catholicism were popularly expressed in the phrase 'Home Rule means Rome Rule'.

2. Political polarisation

Growing demands for Home Rule led to political as well as religious polarisation. In the general elections held between 1885 and 1910, the Liberal vote in Ireland was squeezed and Liberal candidates lost out to Conservative Unionists and Nationalists. Apart from the two Dublin University seats, Conservative support in Ireland was confined to the nine counties of Ulster. As a result, Unionism came to be increasingly associated with Ulster.

The revival of the Orange Order

Founded in 1795, the Orange Order was an organisation set up to defend Protestant interests against Catholics and to celebrate the memory of William of Orange (the Protestant who defeated

James II, the Catholic King of England, at the Battle of the Boyne in 1690). After the Act of Union, the group lay dormant until the Land War of 1879-81 (see Unit 1, page 25) sparked a revival:

'Faced with the challenge of the Land League, the landlords of southern Ulster joined the Order in the early 1880s: of these new landlord recruits, the most significant was Edward Saunderson, who used the Order to promote a broadly-based Unionist movement in 1885-86. This [encouraged] the massive growth of Orangeism in late Victorian Ulster.' (Connolly 1998, p.415)

The revival of Orangeism had important political consequences:

'Orangeism, in its new incarnation, had both a social and a psychological value for its devotees. On the one hand, it provided a rallying point for Protestant Unionists regardless of denominational, social or economic differences. And, on the other hand, with its parades, its banners and pounding drums, it injected into Ulster life...an element of political hysteria.' (Lyons 1971, p.25)

The development of a Unionist Party

It was in 1885 that the first moves were made towards the setting up of a formal Unionist Party. The fact that an organisation had begun to be built before the first Home Rule Bill was introduced is important since it provided a focus for opposition to the Bill:

'By March 1886, when Gladstone introduced the Home Rule Bill, a coherent Unionist organisation was in place both inside and outside the House of Commons. The strength of this organisation lay in the fact that it was not merely an immediate or improvised response to Gladstone's challenge.' (Connolly 1998, p.566)

3. Economic polarisation

Divisions between Ulster and the rest of Ireland not only resulted from religious and political factors. There were also economic differences. As a whole, by the 1890s, Ireland remained an agrarian economy. The exception to this general rule was Ulster.

'Ulster was the only segment of Ireland where - following on from the linen trades of earlier centuries - a truly industrial economy developed in the first half of the 19th century, centred on the Belfast region and based on linen factories, shipbuilding and engineering. Ulster thus became not only the most progressive and prosperous province in Ireland, but, owing to its dependence on British markets and raw materials, an area which looked outwards to Great Britain rather than southwards to the rest of Ireland.' (Adelman 1996, p.112)

As a result, most historians agree, Ulster's industrial wellbeing depended on the maintenance of links with Britain. In other words, Ulster Unionists had a vested economic interest in preserving the Union while other parts of Ireland did not.

4.2 Why did a crisis develop over Ireland in the period 1912-14?

The Irish Question 1906-10

When the Liberals won power in 1906, the size of their overall majority (128 seats) and a deliberate decision by the Liberal leadership to tread with caution on Ireland (the party adopted a 'step by step' approach to the Irish Question in 1905) ensured that the Irish Question remained low down the political agenda.

In 1910, however, the position changed. The elections of that year, which were fought on the House of Lords issue (see Part 3 above), resulted in the Irish Nationalists once again holding the balance of power (see Box 6.19):

'The Liberals were only able to reduce the powers of the Lords with the help of the Irish Nationalists and the Irish, in return for their help, [forced the government to agree] that Home Rule would again be brought out of cold storage...The constitutional crisis, almost from the start, became over-shadowed by the Irish issue. In early 1910, for example, there were a number of ministers, among them Grey, the Foreign Secretary, who did not want to reduce the powers of the Lords but preferred to alter the composition of the Upper House...But, the Irish reckoned that even a "reformed" Lords would probably be hostile to Home Rule and held out for removing the Lords' veto.' (Searle 1992, p.88)

The passing of the Parliament Act removed a major obstacle in the way of Home Rule. It meant that, at most, the Lords could only delay a Home Rule Bill

---

BOX 6.19 The elements of 1910

Source Box

1. January 1910

Party	Seats
Conservative & Unionist	272
Liberal	274
Labour	40
Irish Nationalist	82
Others	2

2. December 1910

Party	Seats
Conservative & Unionist	271
Liberal	272
Labour	42
Irish Nationalist	84
Others	1

Adapted from Craig 1989.

for two years, after which time it would become law.

The third Home Rule Bill, 1912

It should be noted that, although the Irish Nationalists held the balance of power from 1910, that alone does not explain why the Liberal government introduced a Home Rule Bill in 1912. Patricia Jalland (1980) argues that many Liberals genuinely desired Home Rule and had a long-standing commitment to it. There was, in other words, no question of the Irish Nationalists forcing the Liberals into introducing a Home Rule Bill. Rather, it was the parliamentary arithmetic after 1910 which ensured that Home Rule became a priority.

The third Home Rule Bill (see Box 6.20) was brought before the House of Commons in April 1912. Despite fierce opposition from the Conservatives and from Unionists, the Bill had completed its passage through the Commons by January 1913. A fortnight later, it was (predictably) rejected by the Lords. Due to the Parliament Act of 1911, however, the Lords only had the power to delay, not to defeat the Bill. The Bill would still become law in 1914.

The development of a crisis

The introduction of the third Home Rule Bill in 1912 sparked a major political crisis. The key factor in this crisis was the determination of the Ulster Unionists, fully backed by the Conservative Party, not to accept

BOX 6.20 The third Home Rule Bill, 1912

Interpretation

The third Home Rule Bill was fundamentally the same as that of 1893 (which stated that the Westminster Parliament was supreme and specifically removed decisions on foreign affairs, trade, customs and excise, and military affairs from the Irish government). There was to be an Irish Parliament with two chambers - a small, nominated Senate and an elected House of Commons. The powers of the Parliament were to be even more limited than those proposed in 1893 since, in addition to the powers listed in the 1893 Bill, the Westminster Parliament was to have greater financial control over Ireland. Also Ireland would be represented at Westminster by 42 MPs (not 80 MPs, as was proposed in 1893). The main point about the new Bill, however, was that, once again, Ulster was to be included. This was due not just to the pull of the past. Self-deception and complacency played a part. There was little real discussion of the Ulster problem among Liberals - despite the fact that Ulster Unionists had insisted for a year before the Bill was introduced that they would resist Home Rule. Many Liberals had convinced themselves that Unionist opposition was 'artificial'.
Adapted from Adelman 1996.

Home Rule. The delay between the rejection of the Bill by the Lords and its passage into law as a result of the Parliament Act provided Unionists with time to mobilise support against the Bill. The setting up of illegal volunteer forces, first by Protestants in Ulster and then by Nationalists in response, created a climate in which civil war seemed a distinct possibility. Despite efforts to reach a compromise, the Liberal government failed to find any consensus. It was only when the First World War broke out in August 1914 that tension eased. The Home Rule Bill became law on 18 September, but the government immediately suspended it - for 12 months or until the war ended.

Resistance in Ulster

Preparations in Ireland to resist a third Home Rule Bill began in earnest as soon as the Parliament Act became law. This resistance was coordinated by two men - Edward Carson, the Leader of the Irish Unionist Parliamentary Party and James Craig, Leader of the Ulster Unionist Council (see Box 6.21 on page 218). In September 1911, nearly a year before the Home Rule Bill was put before Parliament, Craig organised a mass meeting of Unionists from Orange Lodges and Unionist groups all over Ulster. Around 50,000 people attended the meeting and heard the main speaker, Carson, condemning the forthcoming Bill and urging Unionists to resist it.

For a year, the Unionists attempted to put pressure on the government by organising mass meetings. This phase culminated in 'Covenant Day' on 28 September 1912. On this day, a public holiday, people were asked to sign a covenant drawn up by Edward Carson. This covenant committed the person signing it to oppose Home Rule 'using all means which may be found necessary'. Around 250,000 people signed, some of them signing in their own blood.

The setting up of paramilitary organisations

In January 1913, the second phase began with the setting up of the Ulster Volunteer Force (UVF) - a paramilitary force whose senior officers had served in the British army. Although, at first, this organisation had few weapons, it soon began to arm. By June 1913, the UVF had around 50,000 members and by March 1914, around 100,000 members.

In response to the setting up of the UVF, Nationalists in the South of Ireland set up the Irish Volunteers - a paramilitary organisation whose aim was to defend Home Rule. At first, members of the Irish Republican Brotherhood (IRB - a republican movement which grew out of Fenianism, see Unit 1, page 7) dominated the Volunteers' leadership, but, in June 1914, John Redmond, Leader of the Nationalist Party, gained control of it.

The position of the Conservative Party

By 1912, the Conservative Party's opposition to

BOX 6.21   Edward Carson and James Craig

(i) Edward Carson (1854-1935)

Edward Carson was born in Dublin into a liberal professional family. He made his name as a successful barrister and was first elected as Unionist MP for Trinity College, Dublin in 1892. In 1910, he was elected Leader of the Irish Unionist Parliamentary Party. He believed in order and discipline and firm government and thought that the administration of such things by the British government through Dublin Castle was in the best interests of his country. In 1911, appalled by the Conservative leadership's attitude of resignation towards the Parliament Bill and knowing that it would be followed by a Home Rule Bill, he wrote from London to James Craig: 'What I am very anxious about is to satisfy myself that the people over there [ie in Ulster] really mean to resist. I am not for a mere game of bluff and, unless men are prepared to make great sacrifices which they clearly understand, the talk of resistance is no good.' Craig convinced him that there was a real will to resist and, during the crisis of 1912-14, Carson contributed his charismatic personality, inspired oratory and skilful parliamentary leadership to the anti-Home Rule campaign. At first, he hoped to block Home Rule for all Ireland, but, by 1913, he had moved to a position where he was prepared to accept Home Rule for Ireland so long as Ulster was permanently excluded from it. Ideally, he wanted the nine counties of Ulster to be excluded, but his final negotiating stance was that six counties should be excluded.
Adapted from Kee 1972 and Connolly 1998.

(ii) James Craig

Craig was the son of a self-made whisky millionaire who became an MP in 1906 and then Leader of the Ulster Unionist Council (a body set up in 1904-05 to unite Unionism). Affection for his home background in Ulster and for the British Empire which he had fought for in the Boer War provided the simple emotional inspiration for this solid upright man. Once, as Craig saw it, the testing time had come for Ulster itself, he devoted all his energies and considerable organising ability to what he saw as Ulster's cause and filled the role of Carson's principal lieutenant. He mediated between Carson and the local Ulster leadership and was responsible for the detailed planning of the local Ulster Unionist activity. It was Craig who arranged the first big Ulster demonstration at his own home of Craigavon in September 1911.
Adapted from Kee 1972 and Connolly 1998.

Biography Box

Home Rule was well established. Just as Randolph Churchill had used the slogan 'Ulster will fight and Ulster will be right' in 1886, so too the Conservative leader, Andrew Bonar Law made it clear that, in his view, armed resistance to Home Rule was justifiable. In July 1912, he attended a mass meeting held at Blenheim Palace and shared the platform with Carson. In his speech he said:

'We shall not be guided by the considerations or bound by the restraints which would influence us in an ordinary constitutional struggle...If an attempt were made to deprive these men of their birthright...they would be justified in resisting such an attempt by all means in their power, including force...I can imagine no length of resistance to which Ulster can go in which I would not be prepared to support them.'

There were a number of reasons why the Conservatives threw themselves so enthusiastically into opposition to Home Rule. First, they had been out of office since 1906 and believed that opposition to Home Rule would increase their popularity. Second, they argued that, because the Liberals lost seats in the first election of 1910 and did not gain any in the second election, they did not have a mandate to introduce Home Rule. Third, they argued that Home Rule was only introduced because the Irish Nationalists were able to bargain with the Liberals.

And fourth, beneath these arguments lay deeper Conservative resentments over the reduction of the powers of the Lords and what they saw as an attack on the British Empire and on the rights of property:

'For many Conservatives in Britain, Ulster was an appropriate area for exerting political energy. An assault on property and Empire had been conspiratorially planned by a minority interest [ie the Liberals], and this legitimised separatist threats on the part of Unionist Ireland.' (Foster 1988, p.466)

The government position

The Parliament Act ensured that there would be a long delay between the Home Rule Bill being passed by the Commons and it reaching the statute book. The third Home Rule Bill, like the first two, did not include any special provisions for Ulster. Rather, the whole island was treated as a single entity. Between 1912 and 1914, there was growing pressure from the Ulster Unionists for separate status. The position of Nationalists, on the other hand, remained firm - as far as they were concerned, there could be no partition. During this period, the government's policy was one of 'wait and see'. Behind the scenes, members of the government tried to find a compromise which would suit both sides. In March 1914, Asquith was able to persuade Redmond to accept a proposal that any Irish county should have

BOX 6.22   The Liberal government and the Irish crisis

The Cabinet began to consider at an early stage the exclusion of Ulster from a Home Rule settlement, but the restraining factor in pursuing this line was that it would undermine the position of Redmond and his Irish Nationalists in Ireland. As the crisis proceeded, the view that Ulster must be offered some separate deal gained ground and influential ministers such as Lloyd George and, above all, Churchill shared it. On the other hand, the violence and, as many Liberals saw it, unconstitutional character of Unionist opposition to Home Rule, increased Liberal determination to see it through. On several occasions, the Liberal government almost broke up under the strain of the Irish crisis as its members hunted desperately for a compromise. The fact was that Irish Home Rule did not command a great deal of support in mainland Britain. That (as well as his dislike of constitutional innovations) explains Asquith's refusal to hold a referendum on the matter. Besides, within the Liberal Party, there was sympathy for the plight of Ulster Protestants fighting for their 'civil and religious liberties'. To use armed force against these 'Loyalists' was politically hazardous. Yet to defy the wishes of Redmond and the Nationalists, who naturally insisted that Ireland be treated as a whole, would probably mean ejection from office since the government depended heavily on Irish Nationalist votes. The Cabinet twisted and squirmed trying to find a compromise and even the King intervened - inviting all the parties to a constitutional conference in July 1914. Before negotiations at this conference could bear any fruit, however, the First World War broke out.
Adapted from Feuchtwanger 1985 and Searle 1992.

the right to opt out of Home Rule for a period of six years. This compromise, however, was rejected by Carson who said in the Commons:

'We do not want sentence of death with a stay of execution for six years.'

The Liberal government's dilemma is outlined in Box 6.22 above.

The Curragh 'mutiny'

Following Carson's rejection of compromise, the War Office ordered the commanding officer in Ireland, General Sir Arthur Paget, to tighten up security (on the grounds that the UVF might take military action). Paget visited London to outline his plans and, while there, asked what he was to do if he found that officers were unwilling to obey orders to take action against the UVF (many of the officers stationed in Ireland either had their home in Ulster or were sympathetic to the Unionist cause). The War Office replied that, in the event of action being taken against the UVF, officers living in Ulster would be allowed to 'disappear' but any others who refused to obey orders would be dismissed.

Paget returned to Ireland and immediately informed officers that those who did not live in Ulster would either have to obey orders to take action against the UVF (when such orders were issued) or face dismissal. In response, 58 officers stationed in the military camp at Curragh informed Paget that they would prefer dismissal. Although, strictly speaking, this was not a mutiny because the officers had not actually refused to obey orders, the effect was that of a mutiny. It was clear that the British army could not be relied upon to take military action against the UVF. This greatly weakened the government's negotiating power and ensured that any plans to use the army to clamp down on paramilitary activity in Ulster were shelved. This changed the balance of power in Ireland and, in effect, ensured that there would have to be partition or no Home Rule.

Gun-running

Despite the ban on importing arms, both paramilitary organisations had slowly been gaining weapons. On the night of 24-25 April 1914, however, the UVF managed to complete successfully a major gun-running operation. More than 20,000 rifles and several million rounds of ammunition were shipped in from Germany and collected at three Ulster ports:

'The police and military had been physically prevented from interfering and the arms were successfully distributed throughout Ulster bringing the total number of rifles available there to more than 40,000.' (Kee 1980, p.149)

This blatant flouting of the law infuriated Nationalists and further weakened the government.

Significantly, when weapons were shipped in to Ireland by the Irish Volunteers in July 1914, the police, supported by c.100 British troops, attempted to seize them. The Volunteers succeeded in preventing this, but later in the day the troops (who had been continually harassed on their way back to their barracks) opened fire on a crowd of civilians, killing three and injuring over 30 people. The contrast between this incident and the UVF gun-running provoked deep resentment amongst Nationalists.

The position by the summer of 1914

By the summer of 1914, the balance of power had changed. The UVF was well armed and the Unionists were in a position of strength in Ulster. In 1912, the government (and the Nationalists) had written off the threats of Ulster Unionists as bluff, but, by the summer of 1914, Unionist demands were being treated very seriously and there was a consensus in the government and amongst moderate Nationalists that Ulster would have to be treated as a special case.

On the other hand, while it had been Carson's aim in 1911 to kill Home Rule off completely, by 1914 he had long accepted the reality that this was not possible. He had reduced his demands to the minimum (that six of the nine counties of Ulster should be permanently excluded from Home Rule). Since he and his supporters would go no further, they were in danger of being pushed into a position where the use of force was their only option.

4.3 Who was to blame for the crisis?

The historical debate

Historians are divided about the crisis which developed over Home Rule in the period 1912-14. Some (for example, Foster 1988 and Adelman 1996) are highly critical of the British government in general and of the Prime Minister, Herbert Asquith in particular. Foster, for example, argues:

'For the Liberals, the Ulster dimension remained in the background until a curiously late stage. This reflected a general lack of realism, or, perhaps, of interest...The intended strategy was apparently to pass the Home Rule Bill and then see what was needed to reconcile Ulster. As a tactic, this left the government vulnerable; and it gave up the initiative to those ready to seize it.' (Foster 1988, p.463)

Adelman, on the other hand, asserts that:

'[Asquith] more or less controlled Irish policy after 1911 and his prevarication and refusal to take hard decisions...meant that there was no real attempt to face up to the realities of the Ulster situation at the outset when a compromise solution was perhaps possible.' (Adelman 1996, pp.118-19)

Other historians (for example, Jenkins 1964 and Watts 1995) are more sympathetic towards the government's policy of 'wait and see', arguing that this was the best way to respond to the crisis. Jenkins, for example, argues:

'Asquith's relative inactivity on Ireland during the sessions of 1912 and 1913 had more to commend it than is commonly allowed. Additional action beyond the trundling of the Bill around parliamentary circuits might easily have made matters worse. Furthermore, for a government which appeared to be beset on all sides...a certain massive calmness on the part of its head was by no means a negligible asset...He remained calm, detached and mildly optimistic.' (Jenkins 1964, p.282)

Watts' agrees that 'wait and see' was the best policy:

'[Asquith] waited for the Bill to become law to see how events then unfolded. He felt that public sympathy would not be with the side which fired the first shots. Any state trial of Carson for sedition or even treason would almost certainly have aggravated the situation. In the circumstances, it was understandable to "wait and see".' (Watts 1995, p.155)

MAIN POINTS - Part 4

- Three main factors came to define the separate identity which developed in Ulster - religion, economics and political alignment.
- Although there was no need to 'play the Orange card' when the first two Home Rule Bills were introduced, the fact that they were introduced led to a hardening of attitudes in Ulster.
- Preparations in Ireland to resist a third Home Rule Bill were coordinated by Edward Carson and James Craig and began in earnest in 1911. The Ulster

- Unionists were strongly supported by the Conservatives. In January 1913, the UVF was set up.
- The Curragh mutiny and Unionist gun-running success ensured that the Unionists were in a strong position to resist Home Rule by the summer of 1914. The outbreak of the First World War pulled Ireland back from the brink of civil war.
- Some historians are critical of the government while others argue that the 'wait and see' policy was the best that could be adopted in the circumstances.

Activity 6.6 Ulster Unionism, 1912-14

ITEM 1 Carson's view

How will Ulster be better under the Bill?...What single advantage will Ulster get under the Bill?...She will be degraded from her position in this House and she will be put in a perpetual minority in the House of Dublin and the great and expanding industries in the North of Ireland will be at the mercy and governed by whom?...Some three or four hundred thousand small farmers with the labourers attached in the South and the West of Ireland with whom they have nothing whatsoever in common, either in ideals or objects, or race or religion, or anything that makes up a homogenous [uniform] nation...In Belfast at all events, and in some of the larger towns around it, you are dealing with men who have to engage in great businesses, and you have given us in this Bill the rottenest finance that has ever been proposed in this House...There is nothing in this Bill that...can improve the material condition of Ulster.

Part of a speech made by Edward Carson in the House of Commons, 1 January 1913.

ITEM 2 The Ulster covenant

This photo shows Edward Carson signing the Ulster covenant at a meeting in Belfast on 19 September 1912. It was then signed by nearly 250,000 of his male followers. A similar covenant was signed by nearly as many women.

The text of the Ulster covenant

Being convinced in our consciences that Home Rule would be disastrous to the material well being of Ulster as well as the whole of Ireland, subversive of our civil and religious freedom, destructive of our citizenship and perilous to the unity of the Empire, we, whose names are underwritten, men of Ulster, loyal subjects of his gracious majesty King George V, humbly, relying on God whom our fathers in days of stress and trial confidently trusted, do hereby pledge ourselves in solemn covenant throughout this our time of threatened calamity to stand by one another in defending for ourselves and for our children our cherished position of equal citizenship in the United Kingdom and in using all means which may be found necessary to defeat the present conspiracy to set up a Home Rule Parliament in Ireland. And, in the event of such a Parliament being forced on us, we further solemnly mutually pledge ourselves to refuse to recognise its authority. In sure confidence that God will defend the right we hereto subscribe our names. And further we individually declare that we have not already signed this covenant. God save the King.

ITEM 3 A historian's view

In the summer of 1912, the Unionists in general and Carson in particular devoted themselves to raising the tension in Ulster to a new high pitch. What gave the tribal ritual of the signing of the covenant its real menace was the fact, insufficiently appreciated either by the government or by the Nationalists, that the Ulstermen were beginning to drill and to organise in support of their threats. Carson raised the idea of partition in January 1913 when he demanded that the nine counties of Ulster be excluded from Home Rule. Redmond continued to dismiss any compromise for the rest of 1913 and he continued to argue that the Ulster Unionists were bluffing. 'I must express the strong opinion', wrote Redmond to Asquith in November 1913, 'that the magnitude of the peril of the Ulster situation is considerably exaggerated in this country.' We know now that even by the end of 1913 the government had become seriously worried that what Redmond was dismissing as Ulster bluff might turn out to be Ulster rebellion. Evidence had been reaching the authorities that arms and ammunition were being brought secretly and in increasing quantities into the North of Ireland. But, Asquith was unable to make any headway towards a compromise which suited all parties and so the situation drifted on to towards the explosive year of 1914 with no peaceful solution whatever in sight.

Adapted from Lyons 1971.

ITEM 4 The UVF

This photograph shows Edward Carson presenting 'colours' to members of the UVF in 1912.

Questions

1. a) What do Items 1-4 tell us about the nature of Ulster Unionism in the period 1912-14?
   b) What is the evidence that it posed a genuine threat to the government?
2. a) Using Items 1, 2 and 4, describe the tactics used by Edward Carson in his campaign to oppose Home Rule.
   b) 'Carson was a key figure in the crisis of 1912-14'. Explain this statement.
3. a) Using Item 3, describe the state of the Home Rule crisis at the end of 1913.
   b) How well did the British government handle the crisis? Explain your answer.

5 Political leadership - Asquith and Lloyd George

Key questions

1. What led to the rise to power of Asquith and Lloyd George?

2. How did the leadership styles of Asquith and Lloyd George differ?

5.1 What led to the rise to power of Asquith and Lloyd George?

The problem of hindsight

In December 1916, Herbert Asquith resigned as Prime Minister and was replaced by David Lloyd George. Whether Asquith's downfall was the outcome of a plot hatched by Lloyd George and the Conservatives is the subject of debate. Some historians claim that it was, while others blame Asquith for miscalculating and backtracking on his agreements (see Adelman 1981, pp.20-21). Whichever viewpoint is correct, one thing is clear. The rift between Lloyd George and Asquith became deep, bitter and very personal. After the war, the Liberal Party remained divided and Asquithian Liberals stood in elections against Lloyd George Liberals. This has even led some historians to argue that the split between the two men was a major cause of the decline of the Liberal Party which took place after 1918 (see Part 6 below).

It is important to be aware, however, that, in 1914, the split between Asquith and Lloyd George was two years in the future. While there is good evidence to show that the two men played very different leadership roles in the years 1908-14, it should not necessarily be assumed that they were on a collision course. Although the two men had very different characters, approaches and leadership styles, they were part of a team which worked closely together, often with a high degree of harmony. It is important not to view the two men simply as rivals constantly plotting against each other.

Asquith's rise to power

Herbert Henry Asquith was born in Yorkshire in 1852. After attending a minor public school in London and winning a scholarship to Oxford, he trained as a barrister before being elected to Parliament in 1886. He served in Gladstone's final administration (1892-94) as Home Secretary and continued in that position under Rosebery, who replaced Gladstone, in 1894-95. Historians have made much of his early promotion to the Cabinet and a great deal also of his marriage to Margot Tennant, the wealthy daughter of an industrialist from Glasgow, in 1894. Feuchtwanger, for example,

comments as follows:

'Asquith went straight into the Cabinet as Home Secretary. It was a remarkable achievement for a man barely 40 years of age and not born to the purple: he came from Yorkshire non-conformist stock, but it was a background that he had already cast well behind him. His brilliant second marriage to Margot Tennant completed his acclimatisation to the metropolitan world of high politics and society.' (Feuchtwanger 1985, p.213)

Similarly, Clarke says:

'Born in Yorkshire, known by his first name (Herbert) in his youth, Asquith was a self-made barrister with a well-oiled mind...As Home Secretary he had been the youngest, brightest member of Gladstone's last Cabinet and had got married, with the Grand Old Man [ie Gladstone] as the chief guest, to a highly articulate heiress, Margot Tennant (his first wife having died leaving a young family). With his second wife, his second name (Henry) was thought more fitting and Margot's egregious [remarkable] influence was to be apparent in more than the stylish parties she gave.' (Clarke 1996, p.31)

Liberal Imperialist

Following the retirement of Gladstone, the Liberal Party soon split into competing factions. In 1896, Gladstone's successor, Lord Rosebery resigned and, at the end of 1898, his successor William Harcourt followed suit. At this point, historians agree, there were two main contenders for the leadership position - Asquith and Henry Campbell-Bannerman. Pearce and Stewart argue that Asquith refused to take on the job because he could not afford to do so:

'Asquith decided that he could not afford the luxury of the position. He was dependent on his earnings at the bar, being a relatively poor man. Sir Henry was rich and at 62 was unanimously elected as Leader on 6 February 1899. The Liberals had acquired a chief totally lacking in charisma, defective in debating talent and generally unknown.' (Pearce & Stewart 1992, p.191)

Feuchtwanger (1985, p.234) agrees with this analysis, but points out that Asquith 'could afford to wait' as he was only 46.

By 1899, Asquith had become a leading member of the Liberal Imperialists or 'Limps' as they became known by their opponents. The Liberal Imperialists aimed to refresh the Liberal Party's appeal by pushing Irish Home Rule (which had dominated Gladstone's third and fourth administrations) down the political agenda and focusing instead on two strands - the development of the British Empire abroad and social reform at home.

When the Boer War broke out, the Liberal

Imperialists strongly supported it whilst the radicals equally strongly opposed it. It was as an anti-Boer War campaigner that David Lloyd George first came to national notice.

The campaign against Tariff Reform

While Asquith had been a contender for the leadership of the Liberal Party at the end of 1898, Clarke argues that it was his campaign against Joseph Chamberlain's tariff reform movement which ensured that he became Campbell-Bannerman's 'heir apparent' (Campbell-Bannerman is often referred to as 'C-B'):

> 'The real leadership in the free trade campaign came from H.H. Asquith, marking him out as the heir apparent to "C-B"...Asquith emerged as his own man; and he successfully mended his fences within the party by championing free trade.' (Clarke 1996, p.31)

Following the Liberal success in the 1906 general election, Asquith was appointed as Chancellor by Campbell-Bannerman. Two years later, following the resignation of Campbell-Bannerman through ill health, he became Prime Minister. His position in 1908 is outlined in Box 6.23.

BOX 6.23 Asquith in 1908

Interpretation

Asquith was not the man to supply new initiatives, but his arrival marked a dramatic change in the tone and approach of the Liberal administration. He had made his reputation as a skilful campaigner for free trade who had, at every opportunity, demolished the case in favour of tariff reform put by Joseph Chamberlain. As Chancellor of the Exchequer, it was he who had made the first provision for old age pensions. He had an exceptional capacity for administration and doing business, and when it came to defending his actions in the House of Commons, he was at his most effective. He inherited and remodelled a talented, if not always harmonious, Cabinet and led it with considerable skill for much of the time. He was willing to back his ministers when they needed his support and could put forward their case clearly and with conviction.
Adapted from Watts 1995.

Lloyd George's rise to power

David Lloyd George's career began in Wales and it was as a campaigner on issues dear to the Welsh that he established his reputation. There is some debate, however, about his background and early life. Lloyd George himself liked to give the impression that he was from a poor background in rural Wales:

> 'To dramatise his achievements, Lloyd George

often implied that he had been brought up in dire poverty. He famously told a newspaper in 1898 that "we scarcely ate fresh meat, and I remember our greatest luxury was half an egg for each child on Sunday morning".' (Packer 1998, p.3)

But, as Packer points out, the reality was rather different. When Lloyd George was born in 1863, his father was the headteacher of a school in Manchester. He was, therefore, actually born in England into a middle-class family. Although the family moved back to Wales shortly after his birth and although his father died in 1864, the family was not condemned to poverty because his mother's family (the Lloyds) owned a prosperous small business and his father left his mother Betsy a reasonable sum of money:

> 'In no sense can this be described...as a working-class or even an impoverished background, though the Lloyd family's circumstances were briefly straitened in the early 1880s when [David and his brother] were training as solicitors and Richard Lloyd [David's uncle] had retired. The capital inherited by Betsy George ensured that her two sons could embark on professional careers.' (Packer 1998, p.4)

Lloyd George did not have the advantages of a member of the aristocracy, therefore, but nor did he have to struggle as hard as members of the working class.

Welsh radical

Although Lloyd George had not lived in poverty himself, he was certainly highly aware of what it meant to live in poverty and, from the outset of his political career, he presented himself as a politician who listened to and understood the poor and disadvantaged. Unlike Asquith, he did not attend university, but trained as a solicitor and, by his mid-20s, had built up a successful practice. There is ample evidence of his early political ambition:

> 'In his diary (4 September 1887), he itemised the steps which might lead to his being accepted as a Liberal parliamentary candidate. First, he would establish his reputation as a public speaker. Secondly, he would strive to make his name with influential people by his speeches and articles in the local press. Thirdly, he would attend to his solicitor's practice and get all cases well advertised.' (Morgan 1974, p.29)

In 1890, these tactics paid off when he was adopted as the Liberal candidate and won the by-election in Caernarvon.

National politician

For the first nine years of his parliamentary career, Lloyd George focused on Welsh issues in Parliament. In 1899, however, he rose to national prominence when he launched an outspoken attack on the Boer War. By so doing, he identified himself as being on the radical wing of the Liberal Party and as opposed to the Liberal Imperialists. At first, Lloyd George's views were decidedly unpopular (on two occasions, he was physically attacked). But, following the general election of 1900, attitudes both within the Liberal Party and within the country as a whole began to change and, by the time that peace came, the Liberal leadership had adopted Lloyd George's stance. Morgan claims:

'The South African war was a crucial phase in the making of Lloyd George as a political leader. The most obvious feature of this was the wider range of issues that he was drawn into, in imperial and international affairs...Lloyd George's links with the radical press were much strengthened...Lloyd George also reinforced his position as a leader of non-conformity...On a wider front, his anti-war stand strengthened his links with the trade unions and with labour. There can be discerned at this time the origins of that close relationship with organised labour which was to play so crucial a part in his later career.' (Morgan 1974, pp.47-51)

Lloyd George's successful campaign over the Boer War was followed in 1902-04 by a campaign against the 1902 Education Act which further enhanced his career (see Box 6.24 and page 189 earlier in this unit).

Lloyd George enters government

Although, according to Packer (1998), Lloyd George had ambitions to be appointed Home Secretary, Campbell-Bannerman offered him the relatively minor Cabinet post of President of the Board of Trade. Pugh comments:

'The new Prime Minister was under no illusions about Lloyd George's view of him; and his elevation to Cabinet, though not unexpected, was by no means automatic. "I suppose we ought to include him", Campbell-Bannerman grudgingly conceded. His appointment had the virtue of flattering Wales, while also maintaining the balance within the Cabinet which was tipping heavily towards the Liberal Imperialists.' (Pugh 1988, pp.30-31)

While the post of President of the Board of Trade might have been more minor than the post Lloyd George hoped for, he took maximum advantage of the opportunities it offered. Morgan (1974) argues that he showed the following qualities:

- he proved himself to be a skilful administrator
- he piloted a considerable number of Bills through Parliament
- he proved himself capable of charming the Commons and managing to steer legislation through the Lords
- he charmed groups of industrialists who came to lobby him
- he refused to be bullied by senior civil servants
- he successfully dealt with labour crises - most notably he managed to prevent a national rail strike going ahead in 1907.

BOX 6.24   Lloyd George and the 1902 Education Act

Interpretation

Some English non-conformists responded to the 1902 Education Act by refusing to pay rates. But, Lloyd George suggested a far more coordinated policy to Welsh Liberals at a conference held in Cardiff in 1903. He proposed that they should concentrate on winning Liberal majorities on all Welsh county councils in the 1904 elections. Then they should refuse any rate aid to Anglican schools - on the grounds that they were in poor repair. This might just be legal. It was a remarkable tribute to the ingenuity of the scheme and to Lloyd George's prestige in Wales that his plan was adopted by all but a handful of Welsh Liberals. They duly went on to win control of all county councils and to implement his idea. This made Lloyd George the most prominent non-conformist politician in Britain. In 1904, he found himself invited to stay with both Rosebery and Campbell-Bannerman and he was consulted by the Liberal front bench over tactics on all issues affecting non-conformists. The defence of free trade reunited the Liberals and established the Liberal Imperialist Asquith as Campbell-Bannerman's heir apparent. But, Lloyd George had established himself as an indispensable lieutenant. He had also gained popularity with some of the younger Liberals who favoured new ideas about social reform. They admired his stance over the Boer War and, increasingly, came to see him as a possible ally in office. *Adapted from Packer 1998.*

Packer concludes that:

'[Time at the Board of Trade] benefited Lloyd George because it helped to erase his previous reputation as a "wild man" and replace it with the image of a sober, respectable statesman. Moreover, it proved to be a distinct advantage to be at a relatively obscure department in 1906-08 because the government's record was so poor on many of its major pieces of legislation. Lloyd George at least escaped any responsibility for such disasters as the 1906 Education Bill, the 1907 Irish Councils Bill and the 1908 Licensing Bill, none of which became law either because they collapsed under their own unpopularity or were blocked by the Tory-dominated House of Lords.' (Packer 1998, p.20)

Lloyd George becomes Chancellor

Morgan (1974) argues that Lloyd George's success at the Board of Trade made it 'inevitable' that he would be appointed Chancellor by Asquith. Pugh (1988) suggests that there were two other contenders - John Morley (but he was too old) and Reginald McKenna (but he was too conservative). He argues that:

'The appointment proved to be the most important single decision of Asquith's career. As Chancellor himself he had prepared certain radical financial innovations and major social reforms; this work must be carried on, but with flair and style if the full political advantages were to be realised...Lloyd George would provide these qualities and make an excellent foil to the Prime Minister's own gravitas [authority]. Together they were a formidable partnership.' (Pugh 1988, p.37)

5.2 How did the leadership styles of Asquith and Lloyd George differ?

Leadership styles

Norton (1987) argues that different Prime Ministers seek or end up in office for different reasons and these different reasons then have a bearing on how they behave in office. He identifies four main categories of Prime Minister.

1. Innovators

Innovators seek power in order to achieve some future goal (they are, in other words, ideologically motivated). They are prepared to risk unpopularity in order to achieve that goal. The goal is not necessarily formulated and agreed by their party. It bears the personal imprint of the innovator.

2. Reformers

Reformers also seek power in order to achieve some future goal (they are also ideologically motivated). But, this goal has been previously formulated and agreed by their party. The goal does not necessarily bear their personal imprint.

3. Egoists

Egoists seek power simply in order to exercise and retain power. They are, in other words, motivated by self-regard, not by ideology. Since their main aim is to retain power for themselves, they are principally concerned with the present and not with some future goal.

4. Balancers

Balancers seek power to ensure that peace and stability are maintained - both within their party and within society as a whole.

While these categories help to explain the different roles played by different Prime Ministers (and other senior ministers), it is important also to consider the political skills required by senior ministers and the effectiveness with which different ministers select and apply such skills. Norton (1987 and 1998) identifies a number of skills which senior ministers may need, depending on political circumstances:

1. At a general level, senior ministers need to develop the skill of 'impression management'. They need to give the appearance that they are suited to the role of senior minister.

2. They should have and sustain a 'feel for the office' - an intuitive grasp of when to use and when not to use the specific skills that they need in order to achieve their purpose in office.

3. They need to know when to lead and when to react. To do this, successful senior ministers know when to command, when to persuade, when to manipulate and when to 'hide' (to keep a distance from a crisis).

Asquith's leadership qualities

Most historians agree that Asquith was not a great innovator. He is generally portrayed as a moderate who preferred a policy of 'wait and see' to a more dynamic, confrontational approach:

'Asquith was no more than Campbell-Bannerman a creative politician capable of setting visionary goals. He was an executant [performer] of great competence; what he lacked in comparison with Campbell-Bannerman was the generosity of instinct that reassured radicals, but he made up for it by bringing superior ability to the support of the causes his formidable intellect had chosen to adopt.' (Feuchtwanger 1985, p.283)

During the period 1908-14, the Liberal government faced four main problems:

- the constitutional crisis over the People's Budget
- the crisis in Ireland over Home Rule
- the increasingly militant campaign conducted by the suffragettes (see Unit 3, Part 2)
- the rapid growth of industrial strife (see Unit 4, Part 3).

While Asquith was prepared to take the Lords on in the constitutional crisis, Adelman suggests that his approach in the face of the other three difficulties can be termed 'cautious intervention' - see Box 6.25 on page 226. It should be noted, however, that it was Asquith as Chancellor who introduced old age pensions (although Lloyd George gained the credit for doing so) and Asquith who appointed Lloyd George - and who then supported his controversial reforms in Cabinet and in Parliament.

Criticisms of Asquith's leadership qualities

Some historians are less positive about Asquith's leadership qualities. With regard to Ireland, for example, Pearce and Stewart argue:

'With Ulster rapidly arming itself under Carson and his Ulster Volunteers being matched by the nationalist equivalent, the Irish Volunteers, there was a need for strong leadership and decisive action. Asquith, Liberal Prime Minister, provided neither. He did not prevent either side from arming itself, he did not pursue the policy of Ulster's inclusion or exclusion beyond an unsatisfactory compromise... and he did not negotiate fully with Redmond.' (Pearce & Stewart 1992, p.128)

Similarly, although prepared to be positive about

BOX 6.25 | Asquith's leadership qualities

Interpretation

The outcome of the Lords crisis was ultimately a victory for the Liberals, particularly for Asquith who, in the later stages at least, displayed superb parliamentary mastery and control. It is true that, in his attitude towards the suffragette campaign, the Prime Minister showed the other side of his political character - timidity and condescension. Yet, in terms of maintaining party unity and pushing through the Liberals' programme after 1910, a case can be made for Asquith's reluctance to give priority to the franchise issue. However misguided the government's motives and however illiberal their methods, the militant suffragette campaign was contained without any disastrous effects on the Liberal Party. A similar point can be made about the industrial unrest. Whatever the causes, the government's response was one of cautious intervention, aimed at bringing about negotiations between the two sides, compromise and speedy settlement. The Liberals' greatest failure by 1914 was over Ireland. But even here, owing to the luck of the outbreak of the First World War, the government was able to stop the slide to anarchy, at least temporarily.
Adapted from Adelman 1981.

Asquith's leadership overall, Adelman does argue that, as far as the government's policy towards industrial relations was concerned:

'Lloyd George was the main instrument of [the policy of cautious intervention], partly because of Asquith's ineptness of dealing with trade unionists compared with the Welshman's negotiating skill and sympathy with the working men.' (Adelman 1981, p.5)

Whilst, therefore, Asquith does have his supporters (notably his biographer Roy Jenkins - see Jenkins 1964 - who argues that his cautious approach was just what was needed), he also has his critics (especially suffragettes and many feminist historians). The problem is that, for any leader, the judgements made about whether they were 'good' leaders or not depend on the criteria being used. For example, Pearce and Stewart in the passage quoted above suggest that 'strong leadership' was needed to settle the Irish problem. But, this may tell us more about the political beliefs of Pearce and Stewart than about the strengths or weaknesses of Asquith's leadership. It could be argued, for example, that Asquith's style of leadership saved Ireland from civil war (as Jenkins does in Section 4.3 above) rather than intensified the conflict.

Lloyd George's leadership qualities

Martin Pugh points out that:

'In view of Lloyd George's long parliamentary career - from 1890 to the Second World War - it is hardly surprising that wildly differing opinions were expressed about him.' (Pugh 1998, p.38)

Whether historians are hostile or sympathetic, however, all are agreed that Lloyd George was a flamboyant leader. In other words, he had striking leadership qualities. They also agree that he displayed these qualities in particular in his first three years as Chancellor when he steered the People's Budget through Parliament, led the campaign against the House of Lords, and devised and introduced key welfare reforms, notably the National Insurance scheme.

As noted above, historians acknowledge that Asquith had laid the groundwork for the reforms introduced by Lloyd George and accept that, since he was Prime Minister, Asquith remained in charge. But, at the same time, there is a consensus that Lloyd George provided the energetic leadership necessary to ensure that the government emerged victorious from its battles with those opposed to the reforms that the government introduced.

Lloyd George and the constitutional crisis

This energetic leadership was particularly apparent during the constitutional crisis of 1909-11. As noted in Part 3 above, most historians now agree that Lloyd George did not set out to produce a Budget which the Lords would reject. Nevertheless, Pugh argues that, once the Conservatives began to talk about rejecting it, Lloyd George deliberately provoked them in the hope of engineering a crisis which would prove beneficial to the Liberals and damaging to the Conservatives:

'At a meeting at the Limehouse in London's East End on 30 July 1909, he deliberately stoked up the controversy by training his guns on wealthy landowners who, he said, were refusing to do their duty by contributing a fair share to the costs of national defence and social welfare...Such language had not been heard from a leading politician since 1885 when Joseph Chamberlain had attacked those "who toil not, neither do they spin"...By raising the stakes [Lloyd George] would ensure that the Liberal Party would be wedded to radicalism and the Tories drawn into the trap.' (Pugh 1988, pp.48-49)

This passage makes a number of points about Lloyd George's leadership style at this time. It suggests:

- he was prepared to 'lead from the front' by setting the agenda
- he was motivated by - or at least wanted to give the impression he was motivated by - political principle
- he was concerned about party advantage
- his aim was to ensure that the government gained and retained popular support
- he was a populist (he wanted to project himself as 'champion of the people')
- he was a clever tactician (he laid a trap for the Conservatives).

Lloyd George, the constitutional crisis and Labour

Pugh goes on to argue that Lloyd George's campaign was not just an attempt to damage the Conservative Party, but also to steal ground from the Labour Party:

'A key part of Lloyd George's triumph lay in outflanking Labour. This did not, in fact, involve preaching socialism or a class war, except in a very limited sense. In attacking parasitic landowners, Lloyd George sought to make common cause between all who created wealth, both entrepreneurs and working men.' (Pugh 1988, p.50)

According to Pugh, therefore, Lloyd George's pose as 'champion of the people' was a clever attempt to outwit the electoral threat to the Liberals on both the right and the left. Underlying this analysis is the assumption that Lloyd George was both a clever politician and a moderniser - a leader who had vision and who realised that, with the birth of the Labour Party, the political ground was shifting.

Lloyd George the opportunist

While the passages cited above suggest that Lloyd George aimed to secure the future of the Liberal Party, many historians have argued that, far from being a committed party man, Lloyd George was an opportunist who was not really committed to his party. This interpretation comes in part from later events (especially his willingness to remain in a coalition government after 1918), but there is some evidence to support the viewpoint in the period before the First World War. In particular, in 1910 during the constitutional crisis, Lloyd George is known to have secretly proposed to leading Conservatives and Liberals the setting up of a coalition government which would tackle the twin problems of social reform and military rearmament. Morgan comments on this scheme as follows:

'But, the idea of a coalition in 1910...never had a chance of succeeding. Quite simply, the roots of the party went too deep, as Lloyd George failed to understand. Asquith in the Liberal camp, Austen Chamberlain in the Unionist, the rank and file on each side, sensed correctly that the "non-contentious" issues outlined by Lloyd George were basic to the politics of the day and could not be spirited away by secret formulae in smoke-filled rooms.' (Morgan 1974, p.72)

This passage also raises a number of points about Lloyd George's leadership style. It suggests that Lloyd George:

- was prepared to propose bold and radical ideas
- did not have such strong party ties as earlier suggested
- was something of an élitist when it came to decision making (despite his pose as 'champion of the people')
- was, on occasion, rather naive or over-ambitious about what could be achieved

- really was or viewed himself as something of an outsider - as somebody who did not quite fit into the Liberal Party.

More cynically, it might be argued that Lloyd George was making a bid for greater power for himself or that he was hoping to engineer a reputation as a leader who put nation above party.

Lloyd George and ideology

It was noted in Section 2.1 above that there is a debate about whether Lloyd George was or became a 'New Liberal'. This debate has some bearing on how he is to be seen as a leader. If it is accepted that he did become a New Liberal, then this would suggest that he had genuine ideological goals and his actions were motivated by a desire to put these ideas into practice. If, on the other hand, it is argued that he was an opportunist who took up what appeared to be New Liberal causes only because it seemed politically advantageous to do so, this would suggest that his leadership should be interpreted differently.

Lloyd George and Asquith

In his biography of Lloyd George, Morgan is at pains to suggest that during the period 1908-14, the political relationship between Lloyd George and Asquith was symbiotic (in other words, each needed and gained benefits from the other). He points out, on the one hand, for example that Asquith backed Lloyd George as he steered through the National Insurance Act even though it was unpopular with many workers (because they would be forced to pay a contribution):

'Even though the Insurance Act at first lost the Liberals votes at by-elections in 1912-13, Asquith backed up his Chancellor throughout.' (Morgan 1974, p.77)

Without the backing of the Prime Minister, he suggests, Lloyd George would have found it much harder to implement his plans. On the other hand, Lloyd George had qualities which, Morgan argues, were greatly valued by and greatly beneficial to Asquith:

'[In 1913, Lloyd George] was still indispensable to Asquith since he was still the main voice of popular radicalism in the government. He was still the vital link with organised labour, with a rare skill in labour negotiations such as in settling the railway strike of August 1911. He was also active in trying to break the deadlock over Ireland.' (Morgan 1974, p.79)

According to this analysis, therefore, Asquith and Lloyd George worked effectively as a team. Each had support from different wings of the party and each had a very different personality. While these differences had the potential to provoke clashes (as happened later), in the period 1908-14 they were a source of strength.

MAIN POINTS - Part 5

- It is important not to interpret the relations between Asquith and Lloyd George 1908-14 in light of their future split. Although the two men had very different characters, approaches and leadership styles, they were part of a team which worked closely together, often with a high degree of harmony.
- Historians have made much of Asquith's early promotion to the Cabinet and a great deal also of his marriage to Margot Tennant, the wealthy daughter of an industrialist. Asquith was a leading Liberal Imperialist before gaining wide support for his attacks on Joseph Chamberlain's campaign for Tariff Reform.
- Although Lloyd George exaggerated the poverty of his childhood, he did not come from a privileged background. A small town solicitor before being elected to Parliament in 1890, he came to national prominence over the Boer War and enhanced his reputation after campaigning against the 1902

Education Act.
- Lloyd George was more successful at the Board of Trade in 1906-08 than many of his more senior colleagues. His success there, as well as his radical stance, ensured his promotion as Chancellor in 1908.
- Most historians agree that Asquith was not a great innovator. He is generally portrayed as a moderate who preferred a policy of 'wait and see' to a more dynamic, confrontational approach. His quiet approach to leadership has brought criticisms from historians who prefer 'strong' leadership.
- Historians agree that Lloyd George was a flamboyant leader who had energy and vision. Whether he is seen as an unprincipled opportunist or as a clever politician who genuinely aimed to safeguard the position of the Liberal Party and to improve the lives of the poor depends on how his actions are interpreted.

Activity 6.7 Asquith and Lloyd George

ITEM 1 The view of Pearce and Stewart

Herbert Henry Asquith

(i) Asquith was 56 when he replaced Campbell-Bannerman. He was to prove an outstanding peacetime Prime Minister. He possessed a refined and disciplined mind which in Churchill's words 'opened and closed like the well-oiled breech of a gun'. He despatched government business with speed and efficiency, leaving ample time for his numerous other pursuits amongst which literature, alcohol and young ladies figured prominently. With regards to alcohol, he was a superb debater in the Commons until dinner time. Yet, on one evening in 1911, he was slumped on the front bench too drunk to speak. With regards to women, the suffragette Ethel Smythe said in 1914 'I think it is disgraceful that millions of women shall be trampled underfoot because of the convictions of one man who notoriously cannot be left alone in a room with a young girl after dinner'. His failings apart, Asquith was an outstanding political leader, holding together a strong team and uniquely avoiding any resignations for six years.

David Lloyd George

(ii) It is said that David Lloyd George described himself as a genius at the age of 13. As in most cases, his intuition was correct. His was not the conventional mind like that of Gladstone or Asquith, schooled in classical scholarship. Rather, he was the local boy made good. He had a flair for popular oratory, a lightning and often cruel wit, but he also possessed charm in abundance. Lloyd George's dislike of conventional work habits at the Treasury drove some of his senior civil servants to distraction. Not for him the orderly submission of memos. He preferred an informal chat. He fizzed with energy and ideas, but lacked the seriousness of Asquith. His cheerful irreverence is captured in a remark made in 1911 when he said 'Good Heavens, if one mayn't tell lies at election times, when may one tell them?' Perhaps there was a dangerous lack of morality. His Cabinet colleague John Burns said in 1911 'Lloyd George's conscience is as good as new for he has never used it'.

Adapted from Pearce & Stewart 1992.

ITEM 2 Leadership qualities

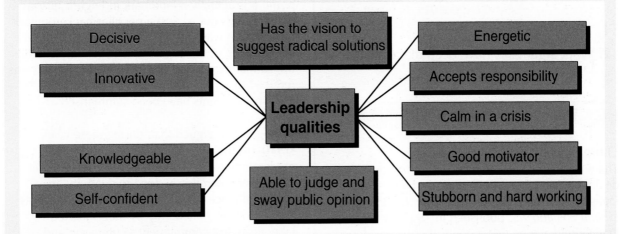

Decisive

Innovative

Knowledgeable

Self-confident

Has the vision to suggest radical solutions

Leadership qualities

Able to judge and sway public opinion

Energetic

Accepts responsibility

Calm in a crisis

Good motivator

Stubborn and hard working

ITEM 3 A cartoon from 1909

"SUPPORTERS" RAMPANT.

This cartoon shows Winston Churchill (left) and David Lloyd George standing on the shoulders of a tottering Asquith. Churchill, as President of the Board of Trade, was closely associated with Lloyd George in the period 1908-11 and the two men were responsible for the key social reforms introduced in this period. The cartoon was published in *Punch* magazine on 29 December 1909.

Questions

1. a) Using Items 1-3 and your own knowledge, describe the leadership roles played by Asquith and Lloyd George in the period 1908-14.
   b) Which of Norton's four leadership categories (see page 225 above) would each man best fit into?
   c) Who was a more effective leader, Asquith or Lloyd George?

2. a) Using Item 2, describe what makes 'good' leadership?
   b) Which of the words in Item 2 best describe the leadership qualities of (i) Asquith and (ii) Lloyd George? Explain why these words fit.
   c) Using Items 1 and 2 explain how people with different personalities can be effective leaders.

3. a) What point is being made by the cartoon in Item 3?
   b) How accurate is the cartoon in describing the relationship between Asquith and Lloyd George in the period 1908-14? Explain your answer.

6 The decline of the Liberal Party

Key questions

1. What was Dangerfield's theory?

2. What arguments have been made against Dangerfield's theory?

6.1 What was Dangerfield's theory?

Dangerfield and Liberal decline

The terms of the current historical debate over the decline of the Liberal Party were set by George Dangerfield whose book *The Strange Death of Liberal England* was published in 1935. In this book, Dangerfield argued that a political crisis developed in the years 1910-14 which was so severe that the Liberal Party never recovered from it. This crisis, he claimed, amounted to an assault on Liberal England by hostile forces on both the left and the right. The crisis had four main elements:

- the struggle over the House of Lords following its rejection of the People's Budget (covered in detail in Part 3 above)
- the growth of syndicalism and industrial strife in the period 1910-14 (which is covered in detail in Unit 4, Part 3)
- the battle for and against Home Rule in Ireland after the passing of the Parliament Act (which is covered in detail in Part 4 above)
- the militant suffragette campaign in support of votes for women (which is covered in detail in Unit 3, Part 3).

Dangerfield is very clear about when this crisis began:

'The year 1910 is not just a convenient starting point. It is actually a landmark in English history, which stands out against a peculiar background of flame. For it was in 1910 that fires long smouldering in the English spirit suddenly flared up, so that by the end of 1913 Liberal England was reduced to ashes.' (Dangerfield 1966, pp.13-14)

His main arguments have been summarised as follows:

'[Dangerfield] argued that, during these years [1910-14] the old Liberal values of toleration, moderation and reason, bruised and battered in 1906, were mercilessly done to death by an unholy alliance of peers, suffragettes, syndicalists and Unionists, linked only by their hatred of Liberalism and commitment to unreason and extremism.' (Adelman 1981, p.4)

The main question that has concerned historians since the publication of Dangerfield's book is whether, as he suggests, the Liberal Party was in decline when war broke out in 1914 or whether it was developments during or after the war which better explain the Liberal Party's rapid decline.

The decline of the Liberal Party

The Liberal Party's decline certainly was rapid (see Box 6.26). Before the outbreak of the First World War, the party was not only the party of government, it was regularly able to win over 40% of the vote and significant numbers of seats in general elections (399 in 1906, 274 in January 1910 and 272 in December 1910). During the war, the party split. The official party machinery remained in the hands of Asquith and his supporters while Lloyd George and his supporters stayed in the government coalition. In

---

BOX 6.26 | **The Liberal decline**

(i) Number of MPs elected in general elections 1900-24

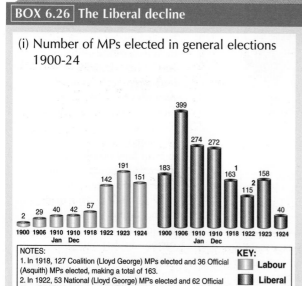

NOTES:
1. In 1918, 127 Coalition (Lloyd George) MPs elected and 36 Official (Asquith) MPs elected, making a total of 163.
2. In 1922, 53 National (Lloyd George) MPs elected and 62 Official (Asquith) MPs elected, making a total of 115.

KEY:
Labour
Liberal

(ii) Percentage of votes in general elections 1900-24

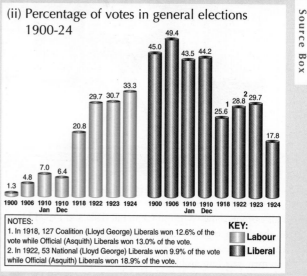

NOTES:
1. In 1918, 127 Coalition (Lloyd George) Liberals won 12.6% of the vote while Official (Asquith) Liberals won 13.0% of the vote.
2. In 1922, 53 National (Lloyd George) Liberals won 9.9% of the vote while Official (Asquith) Liberals won 18.9% of the vote.

KEY:
Labour
Liberal

Adapted from Craig 1989.

Source Box

the general election of 1918, 136 coalition (Lloyd George) Liberals were elected whilst just 27 official (Asquith) Liberals were elected. The split between the two factions remained and, in the 1922 general election, official (Asquith) Liberals fought against National (Lloyd George) Liberals. The official Liberals won 19% of the vote and 64 seats. The National Liberals won 10% of the vote and 51 seats. The Liberal Party reunited in time for the 1923 general election and won 158 seats with 30% of the vote. But, this was the last election in which the Liberal Party won over 100 seats. In the general election held the following year, the party won just 40 seats and, from that point on, it remained very much a third party.

The decline in the Liberal Party after the First World War was in marked contrast to the rise of the Labour Party (see Unit 5, Part 3). While the Labour Party had not won more than 50 seats in any general election held before the war, its rise in support after the war was rapid (see Box 6.26). In January 1924, it was able to form a minority government and, following the general election of October 1924, the party became established as one of the two main parties.

6.2 What arguments have been made against Dangerfield's theory?

Criticisms of the Dangerfield theory

It is common in historical debate to begin by demolishing previous theories before constructing a new one. Since the Dangerfield thesis was the earliest theory to make a mark, it has since come under attack in a number of ways. It should be noted, however, that the conclusions drawn by any one critic have subsequently been disputed by others. One problem is that the evidence is inconclusive:

'A major problem is that two of the main indices by which to gauge a political party's bill of health are not available. Firstly, no general election was held between 1910 and 1918 and, secondly, there were no opinion polls around at the time.' (Lemieux 1995, p.12)

There have been seven main criticisms of Dangerfield's theory.

1. Dangerfield underestimated the impact of New Liberalism

Dangerfield argued that, by 1914, the Liberal Party had become stale:

'[Dangerfield] suggests that by 1914 the Liberal Party had largely run out of steam. It was devoid of fresh ideas and was unequal to new forces at work in society.' (Lemieux 1995, p.12)

According to Clarke (1971) and other writers (such as Byrne 1995 and Fisher 1999), however, this was

by no means the case. Rather, the adoption of New Liberal ideas, especially in the period after Asquith became Prime Minister, ensured that the Liberal Party was transformed into a social democratic party with a broad electoral appeal. In particular, the adoption of New Liberal policies ensured that a large section of the working class remained loyal to the Liberal Party and continued to be prepared to vote for it right up to the outbreak of the war:

'As late as 1912, a Liberal candidate could hold his own in an industrial constituency and as late as February 1913, a Liberal candidate could actually gain ground. What this might have portended for a hypothetical general election in 1915 is an open question.' (Clarke 1971, p.359)

According to this model, therefore, 'class' politics did emerge in the early 20th century but working-class voters continued to identify with an established major party (the Liberal Party) because it proved itself able to adapt to appeal to them rather than leaving it for an untried minor party (the Labour Party). If this model is accurate, then there was nothing inevitable about the rapid decline of the Liberal Party in 1914. On the contrary, the Liberal Party was in a healthy state on the eve of the First World War.

As evidence that the Liberal Party had not run out of steam and that New Liberalism was still making a mark, Byrne refers to Lloyd George's land campaign:

'In 1912, [Lloyd George] began to revive the idea of land reform. The intention was to offer a comprehensive package of reforms, including a guaranteed minimum wage for agricultural workers...Lloyd George intended the land campaign to be the centrepiece of the Liberal revival which would carry them through the next general election, due by the end of 1915 at the latest...The land campaign was specifically intended to damage the Unionists electorally. It aimed to shore up Liberal support in the rural constituencies as well as playing on the sympathies of the urban working class. It was also intended to exacerbate [increase] divisions amongst Unionists who found it difficult to respond with land reform initiatives of their own without risking the alienation of at least some of their supporters.' (Byrne 1995, p.480)

2. Dangerfield missed the target

Dangerfield argued that the target at which opposition groups aimed their attacks in the period 1910-14 was Liberalism. He claims that Liberalism was under attack in these years and that it was the failure of Liberalism to adapt to new conditions which explains the Liberal Party's decline. Some critics (such as Adelman 1981, Searle 1992 and Lemieux 1995), however, argue that Dangerfield missed the target with such an analysis. It is true that the government faced a number of tricky problems in the period 1910-14, they say, but the opposition to the government was directed at the government of the day not at the Liberal Party or at Liberalism. This view is summarised in Box 6.27.

BOX 6.27 | Arguments against the idea that Liberalism was under attack

Interpretation

In terms of historical analysis, without underestimating the seriousness of the problems that faced the Liberal government during the years 1910-14, it is as well to see them in less dramatic and more realistic terms, as problems not essentially different in kind from those that have faced nearly all peacetime governments in this country from Gladstone onwards. In other words, if the Tories had been in power, the government would have faced many of the same sort of problems. So, since the problems faced by the Liberal government were those that would have been faced by the party in government, whichever party that was, and since the problems were handled without the government suffering any major disasters (indeed, the Liberal government of 1908-14 could point to a number of successes), it would be wrong to say that Liberalism was in crisis in 1914.
Adapted from Adelman 1981.

---

3. Dangerfield underestimated the government's achievements

If, as some historians argue (see Section 3.2 above) the constitutional crisis of 1910-11 inflicted damage on the Conservative Party for the whole of the period 1911-14 and really was a triumph for the Liberal Party, then this suggests that Dangerfield's thesis is flawed. Far from being a political battle which weakened Liberalism, the constitutional crisis could be seen as a battle which strengthened it by ensuring that, in the short term, the Liberals' main rival - the Conservative Party - was in disarray and that, in the longer term, a Liberal government with a strong majority would be able to implement its programme of reforms without them being vetoed by the Conservative Lords.

One reason, however, why Dangerfield did not see the struggle over the House of Lords as a Liberal triumph is that the resolution of the struggle ensured that the issue of Irish Home Rule then dominated the political scene. After all, it was the struggle over the House of Lords which led to the elections in 1910 - elections which had resulted in the Irish Nationalists holding the balance of power. Dangerfield's view was that, because the crisis over the Lords was replaced by the crisis over Ireland and because the years 1912-14 were also disturbed by a wave of militant industrial action and militant suffragette protest, the impression grew that Britain was

ungovernable under a Liberal government.

Some contemporary historians, however, deny that the Liberal government's handling of the Irish Question was a failure:

'The belief of an earlier generation of historians that the government's floundering over Ireland between 1911 and 1914 constitutes evidence of the "failure of Liberalism" no longer seems very plausible.' (Searle 1992, p.91)

Second, some contemporary historians (see also Unit 4, Part 3) deny that syndicalism made a serious contribution to the wave of strikes:

'Although syndicalism probably helped to fan the flames, it is more likely that the majority of trade union activity was conducted on traditional lines.' (Lee 1994, p.236)

And third, some contemporary historians argue that the suffragette campaign (see Unit 3, Part 3) alienated the voting public (or left it indifferent) and was handled competently by the government:

'However misguided the government's motives may have been and however illiberal their methods, the militant suffragette campaign was contained during this period without, as far one can tell, having any disastrous effects on the Liberal Party itself or its electoral support.' (Adelman 1981, pp.4-5)

4. Dangerfield underestimated the problems faced by other parties

If, as Dangerfield argues, Liberalism was in crisis by 1914, it might be expected that there is evidence showing rival political parties poised to take advantage of this crisis. Some historians (such as Green 1996 and 1999, and Dutton 1992), however, argue that Conservatism was going through a crisis in the period 1910-14 (see Section 3.2 above). Others (such as Tanner 1990 and Lemieux 1995) suggest that the Labour Party was making little progress in the period 1910-14:

'The Liberals were a powerful force in 1914. Labour often supported both "radical" and "traditional" Liberal policies. It had exposed small weaknesses in the Liberals' appeal, but had few alternatives which seemed credible to the electorate. It was not on the verge of replacing the Liberal Party. On the contrary, it remained a junior ally (albeit one with greater ambitions).' (Tanner 1990, p.26)

This is debated in more detail in Unit 5, Section 3.1.

If there is no evidence of a Conservative revival or a Labour breakthrough by 1914, the idea that the Liberal Party was in crisis appears exaggerated. Lemieux's case in support of the view that the Labour Party was in a weak position in 1914 is outlined in Box 6.28 on page 233.

5. Dangerfield got the date wrong

Dangerfield argued that the turning point for the Liberal Party came in 1910 - four years before the First World War broke out. In 1966, however, Trevor Wilson wrote a book which claimed that it was the

Interpretation

BOX 6.28 Liberals and Labour, 1910-14

Overall between 1910 and 1914, the Liberals lost 15 by-elections and suffered setbacks in many regions at a local government level - for example, losing control of Bradford in 1912. But, it was the Unionists and not the Labour Party who made the advances. In contrast to the period 1906-10 which saw three by-election victories for Labour at the expense of the Liberals, Labour actually lost two by-elections between 1910 and 1914 at Chesterfield and Hanley. The main impact of Labour intervention in constituencies where the electoral pact had broken down was to deliver the seat to the Conservatives. Given recent by-elections where emerging new parties have often done well - such as the SDP in the mid-1980s - it seems all the more unusual that Labour did not achieve some electoral success - unless the answer is that the party was still too weak to win without Liberal backing. It is worth noting that, of the 35 three-cornered contests in the general elections of 1910, Labour failed to win any and came second in all but six. Similarly at local authority level, the Labour Party achieved no real breakthrough and the principal winners in three-cornered contests were the Conservatives.
Adapted from Lemieux 1995.

the arrival of universal manhood suffrage in the Representation of the People Act. The former raised the popularity of the Labour Party, the latter delivered it enough votes to accomplish an electoral breakthrough.' (Lee 1994, p.241)

6. Dangerfield failed to take into account socio-economic factors

Some historians (such as Pelling 1968, Martin 1985 and Laybourn 1997) have argued that analyses like that of Dangerfield have failed to take into account long-term socio-economic trends in their analysis of the decline of the Liberal Party. They disagree with historians who claim that the Labour Party made little progress in the period 1910-14. On the contrary, they argue that growth in trade union membership, the growing number of unions affiliated to the Labour Party (especially the decision of the Miners' Federation to affiliate to the Labour Party in 1909) and a growth in class consciousness were signs that it was making great progress. What the Labour Party lacked was access to its bedrock of support (since many potential Labour voters were disenfranchised). At the heart of the arguments made by historians who support this approach is the idea that there was a trend towards organised labour which began in the 1880s and reached its peak in the inter-war period. This trend helps to explain why the Labour Party grew in support during this period and the Liberal Party declined.

7. Dangerfield underestimated the impact of post-war developments

Some historians (such as Taylor 1965 and Adelman 1981) point out that developments after the war were of significance in explaining why the Liberal Party declined so rapidly. They argue that six factors made a particular impact. First, the fact that the Liberal Party remained split after the war ended was damaging. Second, there is evidence of greater class consciousness (in part, in response to the Russian Revolution of 1917) which favoured the Labour Party. Third, the new voting system was important because the electorate trebled and many of the new voters had no previous ties with a political party. Fourth, the Labour Party improved its organisation and produced a new constitution and a new (socialist) programme which was distinctive and appealing to many new voters (see Unit 8, pages 275-76). Fifth, the Liberal Party's local organisation began to crumble after the war. And sixth, after the war, the Labour Party refused to cooperate with the Liberals at elections. According to Adelman, the strategy of the Labour leader, Ramsay MacDonald, was, as far as possible, to destroy the Liberal Party:

'The key to Labour advance lay, [MacDonald] believed, in the destruction of the Liberal Party as a rival party of the left. Labour must, therefore, retain the lead it had established over the Liberals in the election of 1918 and...push them permanently into

war, rather than the years which preceded it, which was the turning point in Liberal fortunes (Wilson 1966). Wilson argued that the split in the parliamentary Liberal Party which occurred in 1916 was of particular importance (when Lloyd George took over from Asquith as Prime Minister, Asquith and his supporters joined the opposition and refused to support the government coalition, leaving the Parliamentary Liberal Party divided into two groups - official (Asquith) Liberals and coalition (Lloyd George) Liberals). He argued that the persistence of the split meant that the Liberals emerged from the war demoralised and divided. This encouraged voters to look for an alternative (see Unit 8, pages 272-74 for further information on the split).

Lee (1994) denies that the split between Lloyd George and Asquith was of itself enough to spark the long-term decline of the Liberal Party, but he, too, agrees that the impact of the war best explains the rapid decline that took place as soon as the war was over:

'The Liberal decline was not caused primarily by the division between Asquith and Lloyd George; parties have recovered from far worse splits. A far more fundamental dynamic was needed. Between 1914 and 1918 two things happened. One was a social transformation, brought about by the levelling effect of four years of war. The other was third place in the political stakes. Politics would then revolve around a Conservative/Labour struggle...To the consternation and bewilderment of the Liberals it was this policy of "non-cooperation" that was applied skilfully and ruthlessly after 1918. By 1924, it had succeeded triumphantly. It was these six years then that form the key period in the decline of the Liberal Party.' (Adelman 1981, p.64)

MAIN POINTS - Part 6

- Dangerfield argued that the decline of the Liberal Party resulted from a political crisis which developed in 1910-14. This crisis had four main elements - (1) the struggle over the House of Lords (2) the growth of syndicalism (3) the battle over Home Rule in Ireland and (4) the militant suffragette campaign.
- The decline of the Liberal Party was rapid after the war. It never became the party of government again. It only ever won more than 100 seats in one post-war

election (in 1923).
- There have been seven main criticisms of the Dangerfield thesis - (1) it underestimated the appeal of New Liberalism (2) it hit the wrong target (3) it underestimated Liberal achievements (4) it underestimated the problems faced by other parties (5) it got the date wrong (6) it failed to take into account socio-economic factors and (7) it underestimated the impact of post-war developments.

Activity 6.8 The decline of the Liberal Party

ITEM 1 Forced fellowship

This cartoon was produced in October 1909. It shows a middle-class man (representing the Liberal Party) being confronted by a worker (representing the Labour Party).

ITEM 2 Taylor's view

There was still an unmistakable upper class after the First World War. One per cent of the population owned two-thirds of the national wealth. Three-quarters of the population owned less than £100. The political governing class was largely drawn from a few hereditary families. Most were educated at Eton. Nearly all went to Oxford or Cambridge. The war brought some changes. The rich, though still rich, became less idle. They earned their living. The old split between landowners and capitalists almost disappeared - which explains, in part, the decline of the Liberal Party. The Conservatives caught up with the modern world and their leaders added wider experience to their traditional toughness. Broadly speaking, in the 1920s, the Conservatives could count on more cars with which to drive voters to the polls at general elections. Labour could count on more canvassers. In both cases, local organisation was not created for a general election. It already existed. The Liberals failed to transform themselves in this way. They were confused by the feuds between their leaders which began in 1916. Their central fund was usually short of money. But their greatest handicap was that they ceased to make a distinctive contribution in local affairs. Liberalism became a national cause increasingly cut off from its local roots.

Adapted from Taylor 1965.

ITEM 3 Wilson's view

The Liberal Party can be compared to an individual who, after a period of robust health and great exertion, experienced symptoms of illness (Ireland, labour unrest, the suffragettes). Before a thorough diagnosis could be made, he was involved in an encounter with a rampant omnibus - a bus which had gone out of control - namely, the First World War. This mounted the pavement and ran him over. After lingering painfully, he expired. Since then there has been controversy over what killed him. One school argues that, even without the bus, he would have died - the symptoms mentioned above were indeed signs of a terminal illness which would shortly have ended his life. Another school suggests that the encounter with the bus would not have been fatal if the victim had not already been ill. Neither of these views is accepted here. All that is known is that one minute the victim was up and walking and at the next he was flat on his back, never to rise again. And, in the interval, he had been run over by a bus. The bus was responsible for his death.

Adapted from Wilson 1966.

ITEM 4 Adelman's view

There is evidence that the electoral system which existed before 1918 was far less democratic than previously supposed. Not just women, but large groups of men were excluded and, owing to outdated registration and residential qualifications, many men did not vote. It has been estimated that 40-45% of men in pre-war England did not vote for one reason or another. As a result, the industrial working class did not form the majority of the electorate and the Liberal Party's political power was based not on a mass electorate but on the support of the middle classes and an élite of workers. This explains the enormous importance of the Representation of the People Act 1918 which Matthew, McKibbin and Kay (1976) claim 'was of first importance in Labour's replacing the Liberal Party as the principal party of progress'. The Act trebled the electorate, for the first time making the industrial working class a majority in the electorate. It seems probable that it is from these new voters that Labour drew its electoral strength in the post-war world. It was, therefore, the inability of the Liberals to win over the new working-class voters that helps to explain their lack of electoral success. The Liberals failed to do this for a number of reasons. First, the new voters had no existing predisposition to vote Liberal. Second, the split within the Liberal leadership was important. And third, socio-economic trends need to be taken into account - especially the growth in working-class consciousness indicated by the rapid growth of trade union membership from 4 million in 1914 to 8 million in 1919. Mass trade union power helped the Labour Party while the Liberal Party lacked any class basis or class appeal. This was reflected in the leadership. Asquith was always remote from working-class experience while Lloyd George, by leading a Conservative-dominated coalition, lost the confidence of the British labour movement.

Adapted from Adelman 1981.

Questions

1. a) What point is being made by the cartoon in Item 1?
   b) Is it an accurate portrayal of the position of the two parties before the First World War? Explain your answer.
2. Why did the Liberal Party go into decline after the First World War? Use Items 2-4 in your answer.
3. Look at Items 3 and 4.

a) According to each item, what sparked the decline of the Liberal Party?
b) Give arguments for and against the view expressed in each item.
c) In what ways do the analyses in the two items differ from that proposed by George Dangerfield?

References

- **Adelman (1981)** Adelman, P., *The Decline of the Liberal Party 1910-31*, Longman, 1981.

- **Adelman (1996)** Adelman, P., *Great Britain and the Irish Question 1800-1922*, Hodder & Stoughton, 1996.

- **Blake (1985)** Blake, R., *The Conservative Party from Peel to Thatcher*, Fontana, 1985.

- **Blewett (1972)** Blewett, N., *The Peers, the Parties and the People: the General Elections of 1910*, Macmillan, 1972.

- **Boyce (1992)** Boyce, D.G., *Ireland 1828-1923*, Historical Association Studies, Blackwell, 1992.

- **Brendon (1996)** Brendon, V., *The Edwardian Age*, Hodder and Stoughton, 1996.

- **Brown (1985)** Brown, K.D. (ed.), *The First Labour Party: 1906-14*, Croom Helm, 1985.

- **Butler & Butler (1994)** Butler, D. & Butler, G., *British Political Facts 1900-1994*, Macmillan, 1994.

- **Byrne (1995)** Byrne, M., 'Liberals and Unionists 1902-14' in *Scott-Baumann (1995)*.

- **Clarke (1971)** Clarke, P.F., *Lancashire and the New Liberalism*, Cambridge University Press, 1971.

- **Clarke (1996)** Clarke, P.F., *Hope and Glory: Britain 1900-90*, Allen Lane/Penguin Press, 1996.

- **Connolly (1998)** Connolly, S.J., *The Oxford Companion to Irish History*, Oxford University Press, 1998.

- **Cook (1998)** Cook, C., *A Short History of the Liberal Party: 1900-97* (5th edn), Macmillan, 1998.

- **Cooke & Vincent (1974)** Cooke, A.B. & Vincent, J., *The Governing Passion: Cabinet Government and Party Politics in Britain 1885-86*, Harvester, 1974.

- **Cootes (1966)** Cootes, R.J., *The Making of the Welfare State*, Longman, 1966.

- **Craig (1975)** Craig, F.W.S., *British General Election Manifestos 1900-1974*, Macmillan, 1975.

- **Craig (1989)** Craig, F.W.S., *British Electoral Facts 1832-1987*, Gower Publishing Ltd, 1989.

- **Dangerfield (1966)** Dangerfield, G., *The Strange Death of Liberal England*, McKibbon & Kee, 1966 (first published in 1935).

- **Douglas (1971)** Douglas, R., *History of the Liberal Party 1895-1970*, Sidgwick & Jackson, 1971.

- **Dutton (1992)** Dutton, D., *'His Majesty's Loyal Opposition': the Unionist Party in Opposition 1905-15*, Liverpool University Press, 1992.

- **Dutton (1994)** Dutton, D., 'Joseph Chamberlain and the Liberal Unionist Party', *History Review*, Issue 18, March 1994.

- **Feuchtwanger (1985)** Feuchtwanger, E.J., *Democracy and Empire: Britain 1865-1914*, Arnold, 1985.

- **Fisher (1999)** Fisher, T., 'The strange death of Liberal England', *Modern History Review*, Vol.11.2, November 1999.

- **Foster (1988)** Foster, R.F., *Modern Ireland 1600-1972*, Penguin, 1988.

- **Gardiner & Wenborn (1995)** Gardiner, J. & Wenborn, N., *The Companion to British History*, Collins and Brown, 1995.

- **Goodlad (1996)** Goodlad, G.D., 'Lord Salisbury and late Victorian Conservatism', *Modern History Review*, Vol.7.3, February 1996.

- **Goodlad (1998)** Goodlad, G., 'The "crisis" of Edwardian Conservatism', *Modern History Review*, Vol.9.4, April 1998.

- **Green (1995)** Green, E., *The Crisis of Conservatism: the Politics, Economics, and Ideology of the British Conservative Party 1880-1914*, Routledge, 1995.

- **Green (1996)** Green, E., 'Neutering Mr Balfour's poodle', *Modern History Review*, Vol.7.4, April 1996.

- **Green (1999)** Green, E.H.H., 'The People's Budget of 1909: a catalyst for constitutional crisis, *Modern History Review*, Vol.10.3, February 1999.

- **Hay (1983)** Hay, J.R., *The Origins of the Liberal Welfare Reforms 1906-14* (2nd edn), Macmillan, 1983.

- **Hill & Wright (1981)** Hill, C.P. & Wright, J.C., *British History 1815-1914*, Oxford University Press, 1981.

- **Jalland (1980)** Jalland, P., *The Liberals and Ireland. The Ulster Question in British Politics to 1914*, Harvester Press, 1980.

- **Jenkins (1964)** Jenkins, R., *Asquith*, Collins, 1964.

- **Jenkins (1988)** Jenkins, T.A., *Gladstone: Whiggery and the Liberal Party 1874-86*,

- **Kee (1972)** Kee, R., *The Green Flag*, Weidenfeld and Nicolson, 1972.

- **Kee (1980)** Kee, R., *Ireland: a History*, Abacus, 1980.

- **Landes (1969)** Landes, D.S., *The Unbound Prometheus: Technological Change and Industrial Development in Western Europe from 1750 to the Present*, Cambridge University Press, 1969.

- **Laybourn (1997)** Laybourn, K., *The Rise of British Socialism*, Sutton, 1997.

- **Lee (1994)** Lee, S.J., *British Political History 1815-1914*, Routledge, 1994.

- **Lemieux (1995)** Lemieux, S., 'The Liberal Party 1910-14: still a going concern?', *Modern History Review*, Vol.7.1, September 1995.

- **Lyons (1971)** Lyons, F.S.L., *Ireland since the Famine*, Fontana, 1971.

- **Martin (1985)** Martin, D., 1985, 'Ideology and composition' in *Brown (1985)*.

- **Matthew, McKibbin & Kay (1976)** Matthew, H.C.G., McKibbin, R.I. & Kay, J.A., 'The franchise factor in the rise of the Labour Party', *English Historical Review*, Vol.26.1, 1976.

- **McCord (1991)** McCord, N., *British History 1815-1906*, Oxford University Press, 1991.

- **Morgan (1973)** Morgan, K.O. (ed.), *Lloyd George: Family Letters 1885-1936*, University of Wales Press, 1973.

- **Morgan (1974)** Morgan, K.O., *Lloyd George*, Weidenfeld and Nicolson, 1974.

- **Morgan (1997)** Morgan, K.O., 'Lloyd George and the modern world: a rogue elephant among political animals', *Modern History Review*, Vol.9.2, November 1997.

- **Murphy (2000)** Murphy, D., 'The Liberal welfare reforms, 1906-14', *Modern History Review*, Vol.11.4, April 2000.

- **Murray (1999)** Murray, P., *Poverty and Welfare 1830-1914*, Hodder and Stoughton, 1999.

- **Norton (1987)** Norton, P., 'Prime ministerial power: a framework for analysis', *Teaching Politics*, Vol.16.3, September 1987.

- **Norton (1998)** Norton, P., 'Leaders or led? Senior ministers in British government', *Talking Politics*, Vol.10.2, Winter 1997/8.

- **Packer (1998)** Packer, I., *Lloyd George*, Macmillan, 1998.

- **Pearce & Stewart (1992)** Pearce, M. & Stewart, G., *British Political History 1867-1990: Democracy and Decline*, Routledge, 1992.

- **Pelling (1968)** Pelling, H., *Popular Politics and Society in Late Victorian Britain*, Macmillan, 1968.

- **Potter (2000)** Potter, S., 'How new was New Liberalism? New Liberals for old?, *Modern History Review*, Vol.11.3, February 2000.

- **Pugh (1988)** Pugh, M., *Lloyd George*, Longman, 1988.

- **Pugh (1993)** Pugh, M., *The Making of Modern British Politics 1867-1939* (2nd edn), Blackwell, 1993.

- **Pugh (1998)** Pugh, M., 'David Lloyd George', *History Review*, No.32, December 1998.

- **Ramsden (1978)** Ramsden, J., *The Age of Balfour and Baldwin 1902-40*, Longman, 1978.

- **Royle (1997)** Royle, E., *Modern Britain: a Social History 1750-1997*, Arnold, 1997.

- **Scott-Baumann (1995)** Scott-Baumann, M. (ed.), *Years of Expansion: Britain 1815-1914*, Hodder and Stoughton, 1995.

- **Searle (1992)** Searle, G.R., *The Liberal Party: Triumph and Disintegration, 1886-1929*, Macmillan, 1992.

- **Shannon (1999)** Shannon, R., *Gladstone: Heroic Minister 1865-1898*, Allen Lane, 1999.

- **Tanner (1990)** Tanner, D., '"New Liberalism" 1906-14: government reform', *Modern History Review*, Vol.2.2, November 1990.

- **Taylor (1965)** Taylor, A.J.P., *English History 1914-1945*, Penguin, 1965.

- **Watts (1994)** Watts, D., *Tories, Conservatives and Unionists 1815-1914*, Hodder and Stoughton, 1994.

- **Watts (1995)** Watts, D., *Whigs, Radicals and Liberals 1815-1914*, Hodder and Stoughton, 1995.

- **Wilson (1966)** Wilson, T., *The Downfall of the Liberal Party*, Collins, 1966.

- **Winstanley (1990)** Winstanley, M., *Gladstone and the Liberal Party*, Routledge, 1990.

UNIT 7 Britain and the world 1865 -1914

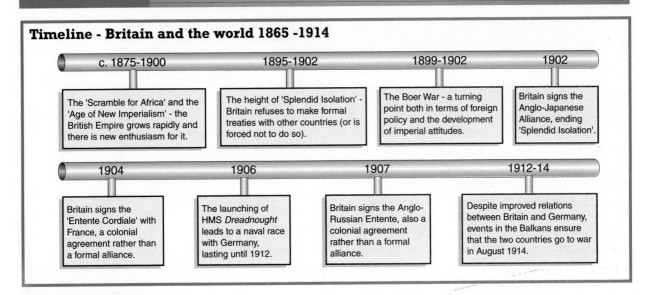

Timeline - Britain and the world 1865 -1914

c. 1875-1900
The 'Scramble for Africa' and the 'Age of New Imperialism' - the British Empire grows rapidly and there is new enthusiasm for it.

1895-1902
The height of 'Splendid Isolation' - Britain refuses to make formal treaties with other countries (or is forced not to do so).

1899-1902
The Boer War - a turning point both in terms of foreign policy and the development of imperial attitudes.

1902
Britain signs the Anglo-Japanese Alliance, ending 'Splendid Isolation'.

1904
Britain signs the 'Entente Cordiale' with France, a colonial agreement rather than a formal alliance.

1906
The launching of HMS *Dreadnought* leads to a naval race with Germany, lasting until 1912.

1907
Britain signs the Anglo-Russian Entente, also a colonial agreement rather than a formal alliance.

1912-14
Despite improved relations between Britain and Germany, events in the Balkans ensure that the two countries go to war in August 1914.

Introduction

In 1865, Britain was not just the world's leading industrial power, it was also the world's leading imperial power. The British Empire was already vast and it was growing. Indeed, between 1865 and 1900, the growth of the British Empire accelerated rapidly. The 'Scramble for Africa' added nearly 5 million square miles to the Empire during this period, for example. But, the British Empire was not the only empire to grow rapidly in the period 1865-1900. Other 'Great Powers' (notably Russia, France and Germany) competed with Britain and each other, ensuring that their empires expanded and their power and prestige grew. At the end of the 19th century, Britain was still ahead of its rivals economically and imperially, but there were signs that they were catching up.

It is often argued that the new phase of empire building which took off after 1865 brought a new attitude towards empire in Britain. For the first time, the mass of people and not just the political class appear to have become genuinely enthusiastic about being part of an empire and genuinely concerned about events in the faraway places which 'belonged' to Britain. The first part of this unit examines imperial attitudes in Britain and considers whether there really was widespread support for the Empire amongst all social classes and whether attitudes towards empire changed over time.

Throughout the period 1895-1914, British foreign policy was based on twin pillars - namely, protection of the Empire and the maintenance of a balance of power in Europe. The standard view is that there was a crucial change in policy in the period 1902-07. Before 1902, the government refused to make alliances or agreements with other states, but between 1902 and 1907, it made agreements with Japan, France and Russia. These agreements, it is often suggested, played an important part in the sequence of events which resulted in Britain's involvement in the First World War. The second part of this unit examines the accuracy of this interpretation of events.

UNIT SUMMARY

Part 1 focuses on the British Empire in the period 1865-1914. It looks at the various reasons which have been given for the growth of the Empire after 1865 and examines how popular the Empire was with the British people.

Part 2 analyses British foreign policy in the period 1895-1914. It considers whether there was a 'revolution' in diplomacy in the period 1902-07 and why Britain went to war in August 1914.

1 The British Empire

Key questions

1. Why did Britain become an imperial power?

2. How did 'New Imperialism' affect attitudes towards the British Empire?

1.1 Why did Britain become an imperial power?

The rise of the British Empire

In 1865, Britain controlled an empire that contained territory in every continent in the world except Antarctica (see Box 7.1). Yet, in 1865, the British Empire had not reached its greatest extent. During the period c.1865-1914 - which is often described as the 'Age of New Imperialism' - the British Empire grew rapidly as Britain gained control of vast new areas, especially in Africa and Asia.

While the roots of the British Empire stretched back to the 17th century (when British colonies first began to be set up overseas) and beyond, historians generally agree that it was in the period 1750-1850 that the main structure of the British Empire was built:

'The foundations were laid in the century 1750-1850, during which Britain acquired India, Australia, Canada, New Zealand, Cape Colony [in South Africa], Gibraltar, Hong Kong, British Guiana [in South America], British Honduras [in Central America], sundry islands and various colonies on the African coast.' (Gardiner & Wenborn 1995, p.103)

How was the British Empire organised?

Most historians would agree with McDonough's view that 'definition is extremely important in the study of empire' and that, in particular, it it is necessary to define the nature of power within an empire. McDonough argues that:

'[The British Empire was] a system of political control which was imposed by a strong (metropolitan) power, based in London, on a number of subordinate (peripheral) societies. These were controlled directly by agents of the British government, and, sometimes, indirectly by locally elected governments, and their foreign policy was dictated by the British government... The nature of the power relationship between the British government and the people within the Empire differed from place to place.' (McDonough 1994, p.2)

In the late 19th century, the British Empire consisted of three main strands:

1. Colonies with dominion status

Between 1840 and 1872, Canada, Australia, New Zealand and Cape Colony in South Africa were granted dominion status. This gave them a large degree of self-government, though Britain retained control over their defence and foreign policy.

2. Dependent colonies

These colonies were ruled directly by Britain. India was the largest and most important of a vast number of dependencies which spanned the continents.

3. The 'informal' British Empire

The 'informal Empire' is what Marshall describes as:

'British domination of large parts of the world, such as Latin America or China, beyond the boundaries of the "formal" Empire that she actually ruled' (Marshall 1990, p.44)

Imperialism

The many empires which have existed throughout history have all differed in terms of their political, economic and military structures. They all, however, have had one thing in common. The relationship between the 'imperial' state (the state which has acquired the empire) and the 'dependent' states (the territory which makes up the empire) is uneven. The imperial state is dominant while the dependent states are, to a greater or lesser extent, subservient. The word 'imperialism' is often used to define this relationship:

'Imperialism has become an umbrella word to describe the relationship between a dominant and subservient

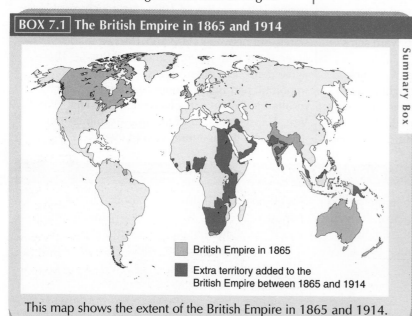

BOX 7.1 The British Empire in 1865 and 1914

- British Empire in 1865
- Extra territory added to the British Empire between 1865 and 1914

This map shows the extent of the British Empire in 1865 and 1914.

society.' (Eldridge 1984, p.9)

Imperialism, however, is a notoriously difficult word to define. McDonough suggests an alternative definition:

'Imperialism really explains the process of establishing rule and the nature of that rule within an empire.' (McDonough 1994, p.2)

When the word 'imperialism' came into usage in Britain in the mid-19th century, it was used both as a term of abuse by those attacking the expansion of empire and as a term denoting patriotic pride in empire. These different uses of the word became important in the debates over empire in the last decades of the 19th century when, historians generally agree, the British Empire entered a new phase (often described as the 'Age of New Imperialism').

Formal and informal empire

Whilst imperialism can be 'formal' (leading to territorial possession), as noted above, it can also be 'informal' (leading to economic dominance). It was Gallagher and Robinson who first stated the case for the existence of this 'informal empire'. While earlier historians had concentrated on areas directly under British rule, Gallagher and Robinson believed that the dominant/subservient relationship of imperialism could equally be exercised through informal means:

'The most common political technique of British expansion in the mid-Victorian period was the treaty of free trade and expansion made with or imposed upon a weaker state.' (Gallagher & Robinson 1953, pp.10-11).

Often, behind the signing of trade agreements and the opening of treaty ports lay the threat of force - 'gunboat diplomacy, the pressure exerted by British consuls [local officials] and naval commanders upon local rulers' (Kennedy 1984, p.24).

Explanations of imperialism in Britain

In attempting to explain why Britain became an imperial power, historians have focused on four main theories. These are outlined below.

The debate over the reasons why Britain acquired an empire is important not just in its own right, but because it helps to shed light on the sort of attitudes which developed towards the British Empire. The different emphases suggested by the different theories outlined below suggest that people had different motives for supporting (or not supporting) the acquisition of an empire. These motives helped to determine the way in which attitudes towards the British Empire developed.

1. Economic imperialism

FOR

One theory is that economic circumstances led to the acquisition of empire. In simple terms, the argument is that growth of the British Empire was closely tied to the changing trading patterns and increase in wealth produced by the Industrial Revolution. This theory was first aired in 1902 by the

New Liberal writer J.A. Hobson (see Unit 6, Section 2.1 for a definition of 'New Liberal'). In his book *Imperialism: a Study*, he put forward the 'surplus capital' theory of expansion of empire. This has been summarised as follows:

'When domestic industry produced more capital than could be profitably reinvested in the domestic economy...financiers sought overseas outlets for their money. Such surplus capital derived from [an unequal distribution] of wealth which left too much money in too few hands. Having invested in unsettled parts of the world, financiers pressed for British intervention to protect their investments.' (Smith 1998, p.74)

Hobson's theory was taken up by the Russian Marxist, Lenin, who published *Imperialism: the Highest Stage of Capitalism* in 1916. In this book, Lenin argued that the search for overseas investments was a final stage of capitalism which inevitably resulted in the 'imperialistic' war of 1914-18:

'Lenin argued in 1916 that the growth of industrial monopoly and finance capitalism in Western states created an enormous "superabundance of capital". If it could not go abroad this capital would stagnate and capitalism would crack.' (Fieldhouse 1982, p.386)

More recent work in support of economic imperialism

AGAINST

The arguments of Hobson and Lenin were later criticised because there was clear evidence to show that only a small amount of British investment was made in the colonies acquired at the end of the 19th century. Nevertheless, the link between economics and imperialism has remained of great interest to historians. The two main strands of thought are outlined in Box 7.2 on page 240.

2. Social imperialism

A second theory is that domestic social concerns led to the acquisition of empire. In other words, imperialist adventures gave the masses a cause behind which they could unite and distracted them from their everyday concerns:

'Most of those who advocated imperialism certainly did see it as a means of uniting their societies behind a great cause and sometimes as a means of heading off working-class discontent.' (Marshall 1990, p.43)

Disraeli and Lord Salisbury in particular have been credited with spotting the vote-winning potential of imperialism and its trappings. Certainly, they had some success in wrapping the Conservative Party in the Union Jack and making it the party of patriotism. Between 1874 and 1906, the Conservatives were in power for 24 out of the 33 years.

A number of authors have linked the growth in empire at the end of the 19th century with the broadening of the electorate and growth in

BOX 7.2 Arguments in support of economic imperialism

Interpretation

(i) Industrialists and manufacturers were the driving force

Between 1875 and 1914, in particular, there was a close link between the rapid growth of empire and the increasing needs that a single global economy had for raw materials and new markets. Without the increasingly dense web of economic transactions, communications and movements of goods, money and people, there was no particular reason why European states should have taken more than the most fleeting interest in the affairs of, say, the Congo basin or engaged in diplomatic disputes about some Pacific atoll.
Adapted from Hobsbawm 1994.

(ii) The City of London was the driving force

The idea that the financial interests of the City of London were the driving force behind the growth of the British Empire has been proposed by Cain and Hopkins (1993). They argue that the importance of the manufacturers and industrialists of the Midlands and the North of England has been exaggerated. Instead, they hammer home the cardinal importance of what they call the 'financial and service sector' (a sector which included merchant banking, shipping services and insurance). This sector was centred on the City of London and the South-East of England. It was, they argue, the focal point of both British domestic economic strength and British imperial power. According to Cain and Hopkins, the 'gentlemanly capitalists' of the City worked closely with those in government and the civil service. They were united by 'like-mindedness' and a 'common world view'. This allowed them to understand the link between the economic and political dimensions of international policy.
Adapted from Dunnett 1999.

democracy (see Unit 2). Hobsbawm, for example, suggests that:

'[The new, wider electorate was offered] glory rather than costly reforms - what was more glorious than conquests of exotic territories and dusky races, especially as these were usually cheaply won?' (Hobsbawm 1994, p.70)

Bolt suggests that a sense of racial superiority was encouraged by 'racial stereotypes' found 'in literary sources, including books for children, in minstrel shows, cartoons, illustrations and advertisements' (Bolt 1984, p.132).

Criticism of this theory

Some historians have questioned the extent to which members of the working class, including working-class political and trade union leaders, were actually influenced by imperialist attitudes (see Section 1.2 below). In addition, Muriel Chamberlain has suggested that:

'[Some politicians supported] the imperial idea, not because they thought it was a distraction from the social question but because they believed it offered a potential solution to that question.' (Chamberlain 1984, p.153)

She cites the example of Joseph Chamberlain. Chamberlain believed that the British Empire (by means of a system of imperial preference - see Unit 6, Section 1.2) could provide the economic salvation for Britain in the increasingly competitive world of the early 20th century.

3. Cultural imperialism

The third theory is that it was a belief in the superiority of British values and culture that led to the acquisition of empire. The argument is that the growth of the British Empire was the result of a desire to 'civilise' the 'uncivilised' parts of the world. Marshall describes this process of 'cultural imperialism' as follows:

'Powerful states are often said to have imposed their values on weaker ones. [This] might be achieved through Christian missions or through educating indigenous élites to accept a view of the world in which the superiority of Europe and North America is explicit. For all their nominal independence, the leaders of non-European countries and even their peoples could thus be manipulated from afar.' (Marshall 1990, p.44)

Underlying this transfer of values was the belief that the British Empire was bringing the blessings of Christianity and civilisation to inferior peoples who lacked them. There was little or no appreciation of the culture and history of the African and Asian societies that became part of the British Empire. Rather, Victorians devised a scale of civilisation, with the British and Americans at the top and the African and Asian communities much lower down. As Hyam (1976) points out, Darwin's doctrine of the survival of the fittest lent pseudo-scientific authority to the idea that there was a racial hierarchy.

The importance of education

A major role in spreading British values was taken by missionaries, especially in missionary schools. These were particularly important because they produced an élite in the colonies which was educated to have Western values. Hobsbawm argues that:

'The most powerful cultural legacy of imperialism was an education in Western ways for minorities of various kinds, the favoured few who became teachers, bureaucrats, clergymen or office workers.' (Hobsbawm 1994, p.79)

The spread of the English language was also a tool for use in spreading the ideas of the imperial power:

'Colonial authorities saw the use of English as the vehicle of an authoritative, essentially superior culture. A common language was widely believed to make government easier, to promote a sense of unity and to reflect shared values. As John Barrow, who had served at the Cape of Good Hope, wrote in 1819: "Let but all official documents be written in the English language and the next generation will become Englishmen".' (Porter 1996, p.188)
The reaction within the colonies towards cultural imperialism is explored in Box 7.3.

BOX 7.3 Reactions within the colonies

Interpretation

The cultures of the countries which were colonised did not simply cease to exist. Sometimes change was resisted and sometimes British ideas were adapted to fit with local values and needs. Indeed, to the annoyance of many missionaries, what indigenous peoples adopted was not so much the faith imported from the West as those elements in it which made most sense to them in terms of their own system of beliefs and institutions. There was, however, a distinct change towards the end of the 19th century. Before c.1865, it is possible to see the encounter between British and other cultures in terms of a dialogue. But, by the time of the New Imperialism in the late 19th century, the balance had changed. From the 1870s on, African cultures found themselves increasingly unable to resist British penetration.
Adapted from Hobsbawm 1994 and McCaskie 1999.

---

4. Strategic imperialism
The fourth theory is that the acquisition of empire can be explained in terms of a nation's strategic interests. In Britain's case, emphasis was always placed on the maintenance of naval supremacy - something which Britain enjoyed throughout the 19th century. This naval supremacy was used, in particular, to keep open the routes to India which was regarded as 'the jewel in the imperial crown':
'The largest single element of British army spending was devoted to the Indian army. The first task of the Royal Navy was to protect the trade routes to India. The anti-Russian tone of British foreign policy, the purchase of shares in the Suez Canal, and the "open door" policy with China were all linked in one way or another with India.' (McDonough 1994, p.51)
A string of naval bases and garrisons for troops was acquired across the world and, until the 1870s, Britain seemed secure in its position as the world's leading nation.

The strategic argument is used particularly in the context of the New Imperialism which developed after 1865, a period when Britain's power was beginning to be challenged by others, including the USA, Germany and Russia. Adding to the British Empire could be seen as part of the developing 'Big Power' struggle:
'Until the 1870s, British industrial and naval supremacy was enhanced effortlessly by the absence of serious challenge from other nations. Thereafter, the rise of industrialising foreign competitors with colonial ambitions altered the international context.' (Burroughs 1999, p.320)
The 'Scramble for Africa', for example, has been seen as a process of grabbing lands to keep out rivals (see below for a brief outline). But, the strategic argument has often been most used by historians who oppose economic explanations of imperialism:
'Of all the supposedly non-economic explanations of imperialism, international rivalry and the defence of what were deemed to be essential strategic interests are the ones most commonly cited.' (Marshall 1990, p.44)

The use of force
Related to strategic concerns is the use of military/naval force in the extension of empire:
'Empires are gained by force and need to be maintained by force, and it was ever so with the British Empire.'(Killingray 1999, p.343)
Wars were fought for economic, political, strategic and many other reasons. It has been estimated that there were 75 small colonial wars, suppressions of rebellions and the launching of 'punitive' and 'pacification' expeditions in the Victorian period (see Dunnett 1999, p.14). Sometimes these wars and the subsequent expansion of territory originated from the actions of 'the man on the spot' rather than from official government policy. The action of General Gordon in the Sudan was one famous example (see Box 7.4 on page 241). Roger Long has found a range of examples of such individual decisions:
'It was the man on the spot who was a factor in imperial expansion as much as, or sometimes more than, imperial policy which was often opposed to further territory as a matter of policy or on the grounds of expense.' (Long 1995, p.1)
Gallagher and Robinson (1981) have also emphasised the role of the 'local crisis' in leading to the expansion of the British Empire. This has helped to move the focus away from the centre to the colonies themselves.

The 'Scramble for Africa'
Between c.1880 and 1900, the continent of Africa was taken over and divided up between a small number of European states (see Box 7.5). As a result of the so-called 'Scramble for Africa', Britain took control of nearly 5 million square miles in Africa, France took control of 3.5 million and Germany, Belgium and Italy shared 2.5 million (figures from McDonough 1994, p.28).

BOX 7.4 Gordon in the Sudan

Rather than waste funds and men fighting a desert war in the Sudan, the Cabinet agreed in January 1884 to evacuate all forces. Supervision of the withdrawal was given to General Charles Gordon. Confident in his own charisma, Gordon, like Gladstone, answered to God for his decisions. He spoke hardly any Arabic, but believed he had the hearts of the Sudanese, especially after an enthusiastic reception on arrival in Khartoum in February 1884. He also believed that there was little threat from the followers of the Mahdi (the holy man who had launched the rebellion against Egyptian occupation of the Sudan). He, therefore, jettisoned his orders to evacuate the Sudan and instead prepared to defend Khartoum. In other words, Gordon single-handedly reversed the government's policy. From Khartoum, he made a number of emotional but powerful appeals in which he called upon his countrymen to shoulder the burden of civilisation and save Sudan from the forces of darkness. His pleas captured the public imagination and the government reluctantly sent an army to the Sudan. But Gordon's position became increasingly precarious. By May, evacuation from Khartoum was impossible as he was hemmed in by the rebels. The following February, Gordon and his men were killed before the relieving army could reach them.

Adapted from James 1994.

There is much historical debate about why the partition of Africa took place:

'The argument that Britain's reasons for becoming involved in the Partition of Africa were a mixture of power politics and economic necessity appears impossible to deny...The issue that remains unresolved, and a matter of major controversy, is the balance between political and economic motives.' (McDonough 1994, p.44)

Even the starting point of the Scramble for Africa is difficult to define clearly. Historians have noted a variety of events in the 1870s and early 1880s which pointed to a new interest in Africa. Hyam summarises these as follows:

'In 1876, King Leopold of the Belgians began his Congo enterprise...France made forward moves in Senegal in 1879. In 1881 France occupied Tunisia and, in 1882, Britain occupied Egypt.' (Hyam 1976, pp.271-72)

From the mid-1880s the partition of Africa gained momentum. Britain and France had long-standing interests in Africa, but new powers also became involved. Belgium was one such power. Another was Germany. Beginning in 1884, German troops took control of several parts of Africa (see Box 7.5). Italy was also a newcomer, taking control of Eritrea in 1885 and Somaliland in 1889.

Britain's role in Africa expanded widely. Before the Scramble, Britain's influence had been mainly in the North (Egypt) and the South (Cape Colony). By 1900, however:

'Britain had acquired huge territorial possessions. A string of British colonies had been established in East and Central Africa as well as in West Africa.' (Marshall 1996a, p.72)

Overall, by 1914 only two areas of Africa - Abyssinia and Liberia - remained outside the European colonial system.

BOX 7.5 The Scramble for Africa

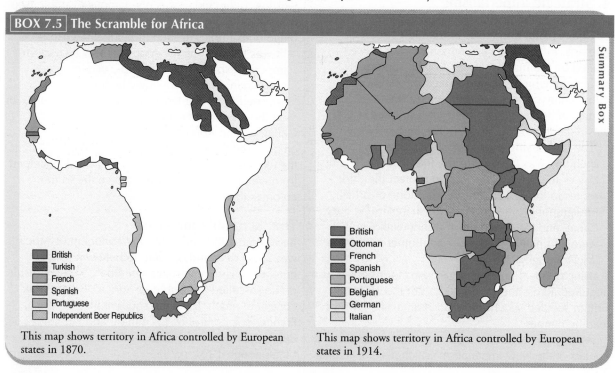

British
Turkish
French
Spanish
Portuguese
Independent Boer Republics

British
Ottoman
French
Spanish
Portuguese
Belgian
German
Italian

This map shows territory in Africa controlled by European states in 1870.

This map shows territory in Africa controlled by European states in 1914.

MAIN POINTS - Section 1.1

- In 1865, Britain controlled an empire that contained territory in every continent in the world except Antarctica. Yet, in 1865, the British Empire had not reached its greatest extent. Between c.1865-1914 (the 'Age of New Imperialism'), the British Empire grew rapidly, especially in Africa and Asia.
- In the late 19th century, the British Empire consisted of three main strands - (1) colonies with dominion status (2) dependent colonies and (3) the 'informal' British Empire.
- 'Imperialism' is a difficult word to define. It has been described as 'an umbrella word to describe the

relationship between a dominant and subservient society' and as 'the process of establishing rule and the nature of that rule within an empire'.
- In attempting to explain why Britain became an imperial power, historians have focused on four main theories - (1) economic imperialism (2) social imperialism (3) cultural imperialism and (4) strategic imperialism.
- Between c.1880 and 1900, the continent of Africa was taken over and divided up between a small number of European states. As a result of the so-called 'Scramble for Africa', Britain took control of nearly 5 million square miles in Africa.

Activity 7.1 Why did Britain acquire an empire?

ITEM 1 Contemporary views

(i) I was in the East End of London yesterday and attended a meeting of the unemployed. I listened to the wild speeches which were just a cry of 'bread!, bread!'. On my way home I pondered over the scene and became more convinced of the importance of the Empire. In order to save the 40 million inhabitants of Britain from a bloody civil war, we colonial statesmen must gain new lands to settle the surplus population and to provide new markets for the goods produced by factories and mines. The Empire, as I have always said, is a bread and butter question. If you want to avoid civil war, you must become imperialists.

Part of a speech made by Cecil Rhodes. Rhodes went to South Africa aged 17 and made his fortune in diamonds. He was Prime Minister of Cape Colony 1890-96 . In the early 1890s, Rhodes' company, the British South African Company, took control of the areas which became known as Northern Rhodesia (now Zambia), Southern Rhodesia (now Zimbabwe) and Nyasaland (now Malawi), adding these areas to the British Empire.

ITEM 2 Ghana after the British occupation in 1896

A British cartoonist's impression of the town of Kumasi in Ghana before and after the British occupation in 1896.

(ii) It is said that our Empire is already large enough and does not need extension. That would be true enough if the world was elastic, but it is not. At present we are 'pegging out claims for the future'. We have to remember that it is part of our heritage to take care that the world (as far as it can be) is moulded by us and that it shall receive an English-speaking complexion and not that of other nations. We have to look forward to the future of our race. We should fail in our duty if we decline to take our share of the partition of the world.

Adapted from a speech made by Lord Rosebery in 1893. Lord Rosebery was a leading Liberal who served as Foreign Secretary in 1886 and 1892-93. In 1894, he took over from Gladstone as Prime Minister.

(iii) When an Englishman wants a thing he never tells himself he wants it. Instead, he waits until the idea comes into his head that it is his moral and religious duty to conquer those who have the thing he wants. Believing that he is a great champion of freedom, he conquers half the world and calls it colonisation. When he wants a market for goods from Manchester, he sends a missionary to teach the natives the Gospel. The natives kill the missionary. The Englishman then flies to arms in defence of Christianity, fights for it, conquers for it and takes the new market as if it were a reward from heaven.

Adapted from 'The Man of Destiny' by George Bernard Shaw, published in 1898.

ITEM 3 The Diamond Jubilee of 1897

This photo shows excited crowds lining the streets to watch the Great Procession during Queen Victoria's Diamond Jubilee celebrations. Representatives from all over the Empire came to London to join the procession.

Questions

1. a) Using Items 1-3 and your own knowledge, explain why Britain acquired an empire.
   b) What do these items tell us about British people's attitudes towards the British Empire at the end of the 19th century?
2. a) Pick out phrases in the passages in Item 1 which provide evidence in support of the four theories used to explain the growth of the British Empire described in Section 1.1 above.
   b) What do these passages tell us about the motives behind the building of the British Empire?
   c) How typical would you expect the attitudes expressed in Item 1 to be?
3. a) Use Items 2 and 3 as evidence to support one or more of the four theories used to explain the growth of the British Empire described in Section 1.1 above.
   b) What do these items tell us about the nature of British imperialism?

1.2 How did 'New Imperialism' affect attitudes towards the British Empire?

What was 'New Imperialism'?

'New Imperialism' is a phrase used to denote a change in attitudes to empire in the last quarter of the 19th century. This appears to have occurred not only in Britain but widely across the Western world. States like Britain, France and Russia, which already had large empires, were joined by newcomers like Germany, Italy, Belgium and the USA, in a scramble for territories in Africa and Asia. In Britain, imperial issues were no longer only the concern of the political classes, but appeared to interest the mass of people as well:

'After 1870, the Empire became a major issue of debate in political circles. An increased interest in the Empire among the working class and within popular forms of entertainment and literature was also apparent. The process began in the 1870s with a major debate over the future of the Empire between Disraeli and Gladstone. By the 1890s, Joseph Chamberlain, "the uncrowned king of the imperialists", had come forward with plans for the expansion of Empire. The climax of all this imperial excitement was reached in the Anglo-Boer War (1899-1902).' (McDonough 1994, p.72)

The reasons that historians have put forward for the heightened imperial activity of the late 19th century develop from the debate on the causes of imperialism examined in Section 1.1 above.

The development of an imperial ideology

As well as exploring the reasons for the New Imperialism, historians have attempted to explain how and why the Empire became the object of so much public interest and, at times, such patriotic enthusiasm in the period 1865-1914:

'During the late 19th century, the Empire became very popular within British society. Britain's imperial expansion, often against European competition, provoked a wide-ranging preoccupation with the Empire, which was fed by the growth in popular forms of entertainment and literature, particularly Music Halls, cheap newspapers and books. From it developed an imperial ideology.' (Surridge 1996, p.7)

According to Smith, this imperial ideology had three main elements - support for the monarchy, an idealistic view of war and the British army, and a belief that the British were racially superior:

'The new-found reverence for empire coalesced around monarchism, militarism and notions of racial superiority, or Social Darwinism...The monarchy became increasingly associated with imperial imagery. This reached a remarkable climax when representatives throughout the Empire came to London in 1897 to celebrate Victoria's Diamond Jubilee. The second half of the 19th century also witnessed a growth in popularity of the armed forces, with military figures such as General Gordon, killed at Khartoum in 1885, raised to the status of national heroes. The depiction of such figures as representatives of a master people fuelled notions of racial supremacy.' (Smith 1998, p.79) Such an ideology allowed military exploits to be seen as an expression of Britain's power in the world and as a necessary part of its civilising mission:

'Nations that had now reached what Cecil Rhodes believed to be the highest state of civilisation were taking control of those who lagged behind or were considered unfit to manage their own affairs.' (James 1992, p.47)

The main ways in which imperial ideology was spread were as follows.

1. The popular press

It has been noted above that the rapid expansion of empire in the late 19th century came at a time when the electorate had been significantly widened. It also came at the time of the so-called 'revolution of the popular press'. MacKenzie notes that:

'New printing techniques made newspapers, magazines and books cheaper and more commonly available...Imperial ideas of all sorts were propagated [spread] through them. High literacy rates also made them highly accessible.' (MacKenzie 1999, pp.288-89)

MacKenzie suggests that the literacy rate in England rose from between 66-75% of the population in the 1840s to c.80% in 1870. Then, between 1870-1900, the rate rose from 80% to 97% (partly as a consequence of the 1870 Education Act - see Unit 1, pages 10 and 13). Greater literacy ensured that there was a mass market for the popular press and, since many newspaper owners were staunch imperialists, many newspapers focused on imperial issues:

'In Britain, the imperialists made alliances with the owners of the new cheap mass-circulation press which had the power to sway lower-middle and working-class opinion...It was soon found that the masses could be whipped into a belligerent [war-like] frenzy whenever it appeared that their country was being flouted...Lord Harmsworth, owner of the Daily Mail (founded in 1896) once remarked that his readers enjoyed a "good hate". There were plenty of opportunities for this pleasure as the 1880s and 1890s unfolded and imperial rivalries intensified.' (James 1994, p.203)

The type of reports that appeared in the popular press are outlined in Box 7.6. Nash (1999, p.43) argues that this type of reporting was evidence of a 'new style of tabloid journalism which was responsible for the formation of opinion as much as for providing news'.

2. Schools

Young people of all classes were encouraged to take pride in the Empire at school - whether attending public school or state school.

Public schools

The major public schools to which members of the

BOX 7.6 The popular press

Interpretation

In the popular press, generals like Gordon and Kitchener were depicted as heroes with almost superhuman power while ordinary soldiers were popularised by Rudyard Kipling's poems (which often appeared in the Times). Sometimes, the horrors of war were passed over by the popular press as unfortunate but necessary. For example, nearly 11,000 Sudanese troops were killed by artillery, machine-gun fire and rifle fire during the battle of Omdurman in 1898. Such blood-letting was unparalleled in a colonial war of this period, but it had been necessary, argued the Daily Mail's war correspondent, G.W. Stevens, to 'secure the downfall of the worst tyranny in the world' and to provide the Sudan with immunity from rape, torture and every extreme of misery. On other occasions, thrilling front-line reports appeared, colouring the public views of empire. During the Sudanese War mentioned above, for example, photographs and sketches showed various battle scenes, British and Egyptian medical orderlies treating wounded Sudanese soldiers and, by way of contrast to this humanity, skeletons of tribesmen massacred at the orders of the Sudanese rebel leader. Further confirmation that Britain was fighting for civilisation came with the illustration in June 1896 of Muslim chiefs in northern Nigeria swearing on the Quran to renounce slavery.
Adapted from Surridge 1996, James 1992 and James 1994.

---

upper class sent their boys were reformed in the 1840s, with greater emphasis being placed on developing 'character' and manly virtues, especially by participation in organised sport. Feuchtwanger claims that:

'By the 1880s, the public-school ethos of the later 19th century had burst into full flower and was having an impact upon all sections of the upper classes...The schools were training not merely a national but an imperial governing class and their playing fields were preparing boys for the work of imperial expansion and administration.' (Feuchtwanger 1985, pp.136-37)

James points out that such an education encouraged a belief in hierarchy since the young boys were controlled by prefects chosen from the older boys who fitted in:

'The public schoolboy...also learned how to control himself and control others through the prefectorial system, a perfect preparation for ruling and chastising [disciplining] the Empire's "lesser breeds".' (James 1994, p.206)

State schools

Teaching the values of the Empire was not confined to the public schools. Such teaching also played an important role in the new elementary school system which grew up after the 1870 Education Act was passed:

'Imperial lessons were taught in the schoolroom. In 1896 the *Practical Teacher* [a journal] advocated regular lessons in elementary schools on the British Empire in which pupils would learn about the supremacy of the Royal Navy, the names of the colonies and trade routes.' (James 1992, p.50)

In addition, school textbooks stressed patriotic themes.

'*The School History of England*, written by Kipling and Fletcher, suggested that "the aim of every boy is to love his country more and more, to praise her sovereign dominion in every part of the globe, to support Britain's brave soldiers in battle and thank God England made him such a happy child".' (McDonough 1994, p.84)

James notes that, in some families, indoctrination into imperial values began before school:

'Even the nursery was not closed to imperialism. An ABC for Baby Patriots produced in 1899 included:

C is colonies
Rightly we boast
That of all great nations
Great Britain has the most.

While the infant mouthed this, its elder brothers and sisters battled with the brightly-painted lead soldiers which became so popular after 1890.' (James 1994, p.210)

3. Children's magazines and books

Growing literacy amongst the young (and technological advances in the printing industry) ensured that children - especially boys - were the targets of a large range of magazines and novels produced in the 1890s and early 1900s. Many of the stories produced during this period were set in distant parts of the British Empire and were designed both to excite the imagination and to reinforce a sense of patriotism and duty:

'Throughout the 1890s, schoolboys were bombarded by popular magazines written specially for them and steeped in the ideas of the New Imperialism. They interwove thrilling adventure yarns with patriotism and reminders of imperial duty.' (James 1994, p.207)

Stories like this appeared in magazines such as *Boys' Own Paper*, *Chums*, *Pluck* and *Union Jack*. In addition, there was a big market in novels written to appeal to the young. Perhaps the most famous writer of such novels was G.A. Henty, who had served as a war correspondent in Africa in the early 1870s. He published an average of three novels a year with titles like:

● *On the Irrawady* (a story about the British fighting in Burma in 1824)
● *By Sheer Pluck: a Tale of the Ashanti* (the Ashanti were a tribe in west Africa)
● *The Dash for Khartoum*
● *With Kitchener to the Sudan*.

MacKenzie notes that the books published by Henty and similar authors were often used as prizes at school prize-giving ceremonies and often bought and distributed by Sunday Schools. He points out that:

'These publications heightened a sense of national identity, of the common purpose of empire.' (MacKenzie 1999, p.289)

The same could be said of the work of Rudyard Kipling - see Box 7.7.

BOX 7.7 | Rudyard Kipling (1865-1936)

Kipling was the son of Methodists, born late in 1865 in Bombay, India, where his father taught at the government's art school. After going away to school in England, he returned to his parents in Lahore where, in 1882, he began work as a newspaper reporter on the *Civil and Military Gazette*. Then, in 1889, he left India for England. Already well known for his verse and short stories, he rapidly became the most celebrated British writer dealing in imperial, military and patriotic themes. His books, such as *Plain Tales from the Hills*, *The Jungle Book* and *Kim*, were widely popular, as was his poetry. They helped to win for him the Nobel Prize for Literature in 1907 and did much to shape attitudes of a conservative British public towards empire and its purposes in the years before the First World War. There is wide agreement that Kipling's writing promoted a powerful brand of imperial patriotism. England's greatness, he believed, lay in its achievements overseas and its true qualities and character could only be understood by those who knew the Empire. In the Empire were to be found the examples of progress achieved by the power, energy, respect for the law, discipline, and expertise which were so lacking at home. Empire was not only the expression of, but also the nursery of, the capacity to govern.
Adapted from Porter 1996.

Biography Box

---

4. Youth movements

It was during the 1880s that youth organisations with military-style structures and patriotic, imperialistic values were first set up. The Boys Brigade was first set up in Glasgow in 1883:

'By 1896, there were over 700 companies in Britain and many soon appeared in the Dominions and colonies. The Anglican Church Lads' Brigade followed in 1891, the Non-conformist Boys Life Brigade in 1899 and there were Jewish and Catholic equivalents. Many other organisations (such as the Boys' Empire League, the Boys' Naval Brigade and the Boys' Rifle Brigade) stressed imperial patriotism with rather less attention to the religious dimension.' (MacKenzie 1999, p.282)

The Boy Scout Movement

These organisations were followed, in 1908, by the setting up of the Boy Scout Movement. This organisation was set up by Robert Baden-Powell, an army officer who had gained fame in the Boer War for his part in the Siege of Mafeking (he had organised the defence of the British forces being besieged, ensuring that they held out long enough to be relieved). Baden-Powell set up the Boy Scout movement with the empire very much in mind:

'Baden-Powell originally conceived scouting as a means to preserve the British Empire against the fate of the Roman Empire. He said that "the main cause of the downfall of Rome was the decline of good citizenship among its subjects, due to want of energetic patriotism, to the growth of luxury and idleness". Britain's enemies abroad were "daily growing stronger and stronger". British boys must not be disgraced "by being wishy-washy slackers without any go or patriotism in them".' (Hyam 1976, p.133)

Baden-Powell translated his experiences in Africa into a movement that, within two years, had over 100,000 members:

'The scouting movement's philosophy was simple patriotism and its activities, largely undertaken outdoors, were derived from Baden-Powell's textbook on fieldcraft and survival which was based on his experiences fighting the Ndebele in Rhodesia. Appropriately, scouts wore a khaki uniform, complete with broad-brimmed bush hat and bandanna.' (James 1994, p.330)

The Boy Scout Movement's sister organisation, the Girl Guides, was set up in 1909. It had similar values, though women were to play a different role from men as this extract from a leaflet suggests:

'Girls! Imagine that a battle has taken place in and around your town or village...What are you going to do? Are you going to sit down and wring your hands and cry, or are you going to be plucky and go and do something to help your fathers and brothers?' (quoted in James 1994, p.331)

5. The Music Hall

One of the most popular forms of entertainment in the late Victorian and Edwardian period was the shows put on by Music Halls (see Box 7.8). These shows were designed to appeal to a predominantly working-class audience and many had a strongly imperialistic and patriotic theme (the term 'jingoism', meaning 'extreme patriotism' came from a Music Hall song):

'It seems there was a concerted effort by pro-Conservative imperialists to push jingoism at the working classes in the Music Halls, especially after 1900 when a spate of imperialist shows began to appear. The emphasis on the racial superiority of

BOX 7.8 Music Halls

Music Halls were the truly distinctive theatrical form of the later 19th century. They developed from traditional entertainment in pubs and 'song and supper' saloons, mainly in working-class areas. By the 1870s, licensing laws were creating a divide between drinking venues and those providing entertainment. The result was an explosion in theatre building. Music Halls sprang up in almost every town and similar entertainments were provided in all of them. There were patriotic songs featuring uniformed performers and much waving of the Union flag. The 'tableau vivant' was another popular form - performers recreated well-known patriotic and imperial scenes as a frozen dumb-show. Such tableaux were sufficiently respectable to appear in church halls as well as theatres. Sometimes they followed a well-known painting or took up a key moment in the Indian Mutiny of 1857-58 (an uprising against British rule which was only put down after a great deal of violence) or re-enacted General Gordon's death. Celebrated singers performed patriotic songs in the Music Halls, gaining considerable fame and fortune as a result. Lesser known imitators carried this material to remoter theatres, while the songs gained further publicity via sheet music for home performance, and concert parties at seaside resorts and in municipal parks. The most famous song was G.W. Hunt's 'By Jingo', source of the word 'jingoism' and first performed in 1878. The song contained the verse: 'We don't want to fight. But, by jingo, if we do. We've got the ships, we've got the men. We've got the money too'.

Adapted from MacKenzie 1999.

the English was a feature of many Music Hall songs such as "It's the English-speaking race against the world".' (McDonough 1994, p.84)

6. Other forms of popular culture

In addition to direct forms of indoctrination into the imperial ideology, British people living in the late 19th century were subjected to many indirect forms of indoctrination. In the late 19th century, as today, towns were full of billboards advertising products and services. These adverts often used imperial images. An advert for Zam-Buk antiseptic cream from c.1880, for example, contains, on the left, a picture of the goddess Britannia standing in front of the Union Jack with the British lion at her feet. On the right, a warrior rubs the cream onto his arm (he is dressed as an ancient Greek hero). Above him, a slogan reads 'The Empire's greatest healer and skin cure'. Similarly, an advert for Paterson's Camp Coffee from the same period shows a group of

British soldiers camping in some remote part of the empire. In the foreground the officers sip Paterson's Camp Coffee which is being served to them by a black servant. Such images were typical.

Another way in which imperial ideology was spread and reinforced was via exhibitions. The Great Exhibition of 1851 began a trend which gained momentum in the 1880s. As well as exhibitions in London, major exhibitions were held in Glasgow, Wolverhampton, Bradford, Edinburgh, Liverpool and Newcastle:

'From the 1880s the exhibitions became explicitly imperial and continued to be so until the Glasgow Empire Exhibition of 1938...The exhibitions featured the products, trade, technology and cultures of mother country and colonies.' (MacKenzie 1999, p.283)

In addition to the major exhibitions, smaller exhibitions were held:

'Missionaries and other societies put on smaller-scale exhibitions in many localities, illustrating their work but also displaying the artefacts and lifestyles of peoples in the Empire.' (MacKenzie 1999, p.284)

How popular was imperial ideology?

There is a consensus that the imperial ideology described above was generally accepted and supported among the middle and upper classes:

'Support was particularly strong in upper-class public school élite groups such as the landed aristocracy, the officer class in the army and navy, colonial administrators, and among middle-class businessmen. There was also support among rising middle-class groups such as shopkeepers and white collar workers, and among many members of the skilled sections of the working class.' (McDonough 1994, p.81)

There is, however, a debate about the extent to which the mass of the working class supported imperial ideology. Certainly, there is an abundance of evidence to show that popular culture in the late 19th century was dominated by images and references to the Empire, but it is hard to be sure whether such images and references were approved of and accepted.

The working class and imperial ideology

The idea that the mass of the working class were enthusiastic imperialists goes back to 1902 when J.A. Hobson published *Imperialism: a Study* (see also page 239 above):

'Hobson was a Liberal and had been a war reporter during the Boer War. He put forward the view that the imperial crusade by the Conservative Party had won over the working classes in the late-Victorian age and he also believed that the working classes had been manipulated into supporting the idea of imperial expansion by "small groups of businessmen and politicians"...This view of small upper-class

élites deliberately seeking to fill the "empty heads" of an uncritical working class with propaganda was based on contemporary observations of working-class public demonstrations of support for the Empire and British military victories abroad.' (McDonough 1994, p.82)

Mafficking

Some of the most enthusiastic of such working-class demonstrations came during the Boer War of 1899-1902. When news of the relief of Mafeking reached Britain in May 1900, for example, there were huge demonstrations throughout the country:

'An explosion of mass patriotism came to a hysterical climax in May 1900 when news came through that the town of Mafeking had been relieved. Everywhere the announcement prompted spontaneous...celebrations, a nationwide street party which produced, hangovers apart, the word "mafficking".' (James 1994, p.212)

People who 'maffick' celebrate wildly and hysterically. Marshall records that:

'In London "staid citizens...were to be seen parading the streets, shouting patriotic songs with the full force of their lungs, dancing, jumping, screaming in a delirium of unrestrained joy".' (Marshall 1996a, p.53)

But, James notes that these celebrations owed as much to relief and uncertainty as to delight:

'Those who "mafficked" were celebrating something more than the rescue of a comparatively insignificant garrison. The high jinks that May were a mass release of tensions and a momentary dispersal of fears that had been deepened by the war. During the winter of 1899-1900, the army had suffered a series of unexpected and humiliating reverses, and the British people discovered that they were no longer invincible. Furthermore they were friendless, for all the Great Powers were hostile...A nation which had been so full of self-confidence 40 to 50 years earlier was now tormented by apprehension.' (James 1994, p.212)

The revisionist view

Despite the mass demonstration of delight at the news of the relief of Mafeking and other public demonstrations of public support for imperial ideology (such as the great interest shown in Queen Victoria's Diamond Jubilee), some historians ('revisionists') have argued against the view that the mass of the working class were fervent imperialists. Price (1972), for example, argues that many members of the working class volunteered to fight in the Boer War in an effort to escape poverty rather than because they deeply supported the cause. Similarly, Pelling (1968) argues that, just because Music Hall songs were jingoistic, it does not mean that the audience fully supported the views expressed. He describes the outpouring of public emotion in May 1900 as an exception, claiming that it was unusual for members of the working class to participate in displays of public patriotism like this. Furthermore, McDonough notes that revisionist historians deny that the result of the 1900 general election (which was known as the 'Khaki Election' because it was held in the middle of the Boer War) was evidence of public support for the Empire:

'The Boer War was certainly the key issue in the election. Yet, the Conservatives polled only 400,000 more votes (out of a total of 4.5 million) than the Liberal Party, which was divided over support for the war. Jingoistic candidates from the Conservative and Liberal parties were rejected in many working-class constituencies. It seems that, among the urban working classes in 1900, opposition to Irish Home Rule remained a stronger reason than imperialism for voting Conservative.' (McDonough 1994, p.83)

MacKenzie (who is not a revisionist historian) sums up the arguments of the revisionists in Box 7.9.

BOX 7.9 The revisionist view

Some historians have continued to deny that imperial ideas and enthusiasms penetrated deeply into the consciousness of the British public. They point out, for example, that many pro-Empire groups which were set up in the late 19th century - such as the Imperial Federation of the 1880s - were short-lived and unsuccessful. They also point out that voters were influenced by hard-headed domestic concerns rather than imperial matters. When Joseph Chamberlain launched his tariff reform campaign, for example, (see Unit 6, pages 190-91), the lack of support for his idea of imperial preference showed that colonial matters were of less concern than dearer food. There is other evidence against the view that the mass of the working class were fervent imperialists. Emigration patterns in the years before 1914 show that the USA was a more attractive destination than parts of the British Empire, for example. Also, men were seldom eager to join the army except when driven to it by unemployment and economic distress.
Adapted from MacKenzie 1999.

Arguments against the revisionists

Hobsbawm agrees with the revisionists that:

'[While] imperialism was extremely popular among the new middle and white collar strata, there is much less evidence of any spontaneous enthusiasm of the workers for colonial conquests or any great interest in the colonies.' (Hobsbawm 1994, p.70)

Nevertheless, he believes that imperialism was popular. He claims that:

'[It gave people] a sense of superiority which united Western whites, rich, middle class and poor.' (Hobsbawm 1994, p.71)

Other work has taken up this point. MacKenzie (1984 and 1999), for example, suggests that this 'sense of superiority' was very deliberately cultivated. He believes that imperialists deliberately set out to influence public opinion - for example, by their use of propaganda in school textbooks, popular literature and Music Hall songs. He argues that:

'Imperial culture almost certainly represented a powerful interaction among the classes, illustrated in the eagerness of the suppliers of entertainment and popular literature, commercial advertisers and the founders of youth organisations to attach themselves to it. The public, largely uninterested in specific imperial principles and policies, were none the less fascinated by the Empire's existence, its racial connotations and the superior self-image which it offered in respect of the rest of the world.' (MacKenzie 1999, p.291)

McDonough argues that oral evidence from working-class people who lived through the period supports this view:

'Large numbers of young people grew up accepting many of the ideas they encountered in popular literature. The fascination with royalty, the armed forces and racial superiority in the Music Hall songs of the day influenced those who were exposed to it. Many of those interviewed remembered being swept along at times by the patriotic fervour that surrounded them.' (McDonough 1994, p.85)

Anti-imperialism

Although there was what MacKenzie (1999, p.291) describes as 'an area of convergence' between the two main political parties (ie the Conservative and Liberal parties) when it came to the Empire, Nash points out that the Liberal Party was suspicious of military adventures for their own sake:

'Liberalism had traditionally entertained an innate distrust, even hatred, of military adventures and their consequences. The fear of the over-eager and over-ambitious "man on the spot" who led Britain into colonial disaster was a commonplace of Liberal rhetoric.' (Nash 1999, p.43)

It was this distrust that lay behind Gladstone's attacks on Disraeli in 1876 and which led to the Midlothian campaigns (see Unit 1, Section 3.1). It should be noted, however, that Gladstone was not opposed to the acquisition of empire or to military action in principle. Indeed, as Prime Minister in 1882, he agreed to the military occupation of Egypt.

It was not until the Boer War that anti-imperialism gained a significant political voice. Before 1899, there were anti-imperialists in the Liberal Party and, particularly, in the labour movement. Keir Hardie (see Unit 5), for example, consistently opposed the jingoism of the 1890s:

'Like other socialists, Keir Hardie was distressed by

Music Hall jingoism, which he believed was deliberately fomented by the bosses in the hope that working men, intoxicated by belligerent patriotism, might forget such knife-and-fork issues as wages and unemployment.' (James 1994, p.323) The Boer War, however, was a turning point not least because it split the Liberal Party between those who supported the war (the Liberal Imperialists) and those who opposed it (the 'Pro-Boers'):

'Criticism of the South African War ranged from mild misgivings to outright opposition with individuals holding a number of overlapping views. The most obviously visible opposition to Britain's stance and its conduct of war were those individuals labelled by domestic opinion, rather too easily, as "Pro-Boers". These included people like David Lloyd George [see Unit 6, Section 5.1] and Emily Hobhouse whose positions varied between championing the rights of Boer republics to criticising Britain's methods of waging war.' (Nash 1999, p.43)

MAIN POINTS - Section 1.2

- 'New imperialism' is a phrase used to denote a change in attitudes to empire in the last quarter of the 19th century. In Britain, imperial issues were no longer only the concern of the political classes, but appeared to interest the mass of people as well.
- From the new interest in empire, there developed an imperial ideology which had three main elements - support for the monarchy, an idealistic view of war and the British army, and a belief that the British were racially superior.
- Imperial ideology was spread by (1) the popular press (2) schools (3) children's magazines and books (4) youth movements (5) the Music Hall (6) other forms of popular culture such as adverts and exhibitions.
- There is a consensus that imperial ideology was generally accepted and supported among the middle and upper classes. While, however, revisionists argue that imperial ideology was never really accepted by the working class, other historians argue that it did influence British people of all classes.
- It was not until the Boer War that anti-imperialism gained a significant political voice. Before 1899, there were anti-imperialists in the Liberal Party and in the labour movement. The Boer War, however, was a turning point not least because it split the Liberal Party between the Liberal Imperialists and the 'Pro-Boers'.

Activity 7.2 New Imperialism and imperial attitudes

ITEM 1 Imperial ideology and militarism

In the late 19th century, imperial ideology encouraged the view that warfare was beneficial because it would cleanse and temper the nation. The popular perception of the army changed as enthusiasm for empire increased. Instead of being seen as brutal and badly behaved, the army came to be respected as the vanguard of British civilisation. From the 1850s, soldiers were, almost for the first time, seen as objects of compassion rather than disgust. In the Indian Mutiny of 1857-58, the soldier became a Christian hero avenging the crimes of the infidel mutineers. Later, the writer Rudyard Kipling enormously popularised the private soldier. In his writing, he pointed out that, while soldiers had a positive image abroad, many were still discriminated against at home - they were often refused entry into pubs, for example. Those who benefited most from the change in attitude were the generals. They became heroes and could cause governments immense problems. Such was the fame of Sir Garnet Wolseley that he became 'the very model of a modern Major-General' in a popular opera written by Gilbert and Sullivan and the term 'All Sir Garnet' came to mean a job well done. The press hero-worshipped these men, suggesting they had almost superhuman powers. If any emergency arose or a delicate colonial matter needed sorting out, the press and public appealed to them. This made it difficult for politicians who had to deal with these idols of the public.

Adapted from Surridge 1996.

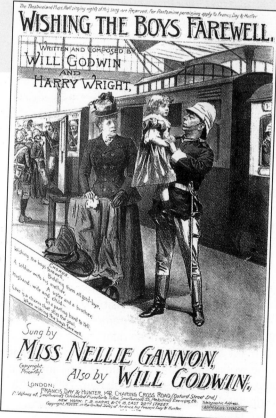

This poster, advertising a Music Hall show, was produced in the early 1880s.

ITEM 2 Imperial enthusiasts and imperial attitudes

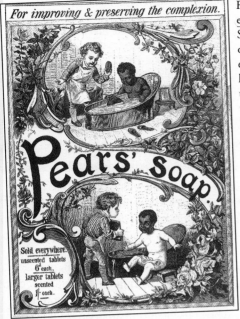

For improving & preserving the complexion.

Pears' Soap.

Sold everywhere.
unscented tablets
6ᵈ each.
larger tablets
scented
1/- each.

This advert was produced in the 1880s.

From Disraeli's time onwards, the Conservative Party remained the party of empire. But, it is necessary to distinguish between, on the one hand, Salisbury, Disraeli and the main body of the Conservative Party and, on the other, the 'High Imperialists' (who believed in the unlimited acquisition of empire or restructuring the Empire on radically new lines to produce some kind of union of the white 'British'). The High Imperialists never captured the Conservative Party, let alone British public opinion as a whole, though they remained a very vocal pressure group. The closest that High Imperialists came to determining policy was in the period 1895-1903 when Joseph Chamberlain sat in the Cabinet as Colonial Secretary (see Unit 6, page 190). It was an essential part of Chamberlain's plan that the British public must be won over to the cause of empire. He saw himself as an educator about empire. Others also took a hand in spreading imperial values with the result that British culture became saturated with imperial themes, images and motifs. For the most part, this relentless exposure of the British public to material about the Empire was not an orchestrated propaganda campaign. Writers and publishers presumably took their own commercial decisions when giving popular songs or children's stories an imperial setting. Advertisers were concerned with selling their goods, not spreading imperial ideology. Expectations that people would buy goods which had been advertised in this way, however, shows that people were generally expected to be well disposed towards the Empire. Nevertheless, some deliberate attempts were made to harness this popular enthusiasm for empire. Rudyard Kipling, for example, had an imperial vision he wanted to be accepted. Similarly, those who founded youth movements had imperial values they wished to instil in the young. Many teachers in the public schools were highly committed to imperialism. In state schools, attempts were made to include 'sound' imperial material into the curriculum and Empire Day was celebrated annually.

Adapted from Marshall 1996a.

ITEM 3 The Boer War

From the start of the Boer War, Lloyd George had to battle hard against the jingoism whipped up by Chamberlain and the Salisbury government and their largely middle- and upper-class supporters. Most of the Liberal Party in the Commons reacted strongly against Lloyd George's attacks. The Liberal Imperialists supported the war on the grounds of 'National Efficiency' (see also Unit 6, Section 2.1). Most of the rest of the party supported the Leader, Campbell-Bannerman, who gave reluctant support to the government. In provincial cities and in the National Liberal Federation (NLF), anti-war sentiment was more widespread and the trade unions supported peace. But, in 1899-1900, outright opposition was dangerous. Lloyd George's solicitor's practice in London suffered severely. His eldest son had to leave school because of bullying. Even in Wales, pro-war sentiment was widespread, especially after the relief of Mafeking. Lloyd George had to escape angry mobs in Caernarvon and to endure the insults of 'jingo' critics. After a speech in Bangor in April 1900, he was struck on the head by a heavy stick. In December 1901, a violent mob broke up a meeting he was addressing and he had to escape disguised as a policeman. In this crisis, the support he received from his uncle, brother and wife (all 'Pro-Boers') was important. In the Khaki Election of 1900, Lloyd George held on to his seat with an increased

This photo shows crowds on the streets of London following the news that the siege of Mafeking had been lifted.

majority and, after the election, there came a dramatic transformation. First of all in the NLF and then in the Parliamentary Liberal Party, the anti-war mood gripped the Liberal conscience. People like Lloyd George became acceptable and respected. People were becoming sickened by the brutality that marked the later stages of the war. As thousands died in Kitchener's concentration camps, the war no longer seemed so glorious. Eventually, Campbell-Bannerman denounced the government's 'methods of barbarism'. When peace came in 1902, the Liberal Imperialists were in a small minority.

Adapted from Morgan 1974.

2 From 'Splendid Isolation' to the First World War

Key questions

1. Why did Britain retreat from 'Splendid Isolation'?

2. Why did Britain go to war in 1914?

2.1 Why did Britain retreat from 'Splendid Isolation'?

What was 'Splendid Isolation'?

In 1895, most historians agree, Britain was the most powerful state in the world. Britain controlled the largest empire in the world (see Part 1 above). The British economy was producing more in most sectors than that produced by its rivals. No other country had a navy to match that of Britain. As Martel points out, these three components - the Empire, the economy and the navy - were the keys to Britain's power:

'Britain's industry provided the appetite for empire, the desire for the resources and markets that her possessions in Africa and Asia, in North America, the Caribbean and Australasia provided; industrial prosperity and technological proficiency enabled the British to construct a large, modern navy; mastery of the seas enabled them to defend their Empire against all opponents. This simplistic picture may be misleading, but the idea that British power was fundamentally industrial, and that British interests were essentially imperial, was entertained by most observers of Victorian Britain.' (Martel 1996, p.46)

Foreign policy

The Empire, the economy and the navy were also the keys to British foreign policy. In broad terms, British foreign policy in the late 19th century rested on twin pillars - protection of the Empire and maintenance of a balance of power in Europe:

'For most of the 19th century, British defence planning was aimed primarily at France and Russia. Both posed threats to British colonial possessions overseas, France in Africa and Russia in the Far East. And, during the course of the century, Britain had gone to war with

both, with France from the end of the 18th century until 1815 and with Russia in the period 1854-55 [the Crimean war]. British interests were also best served by the maintenance of a balance of power in Europe and in the prevention of the continent being dominated by any one state.' (Ray 1998, p.46)

Ray argues that, in the last quarter of the 19th century, this 'balance of power in Europe' was secured by Germany whose unification had been secured in 1871 after Prussia had been victorious in three successful wars - in 1864 (against Denmark), in 1866 (against Austria) and in 1871 (against France). The unification of Germany, he argues, was of concern to France and Russia (both of which had borders with Germany). A united Germany helped to reduce the threat that these countries posed to Britain:

'The rise of Germany into the ranks of the first-class powers helped to counterbalance [the threat from Russia and France] and allowed Britain to keep its distance from events on the continent while remaining in "Splendid Isolation".' (Ray 1998. p.46)

Splendid Isolation - a definition

The traditional view is that, under Lord Salisbury (who was Prime Minister in the years 1885, 1886-92 and 1895-1902 and served also as Foreign Secretary until 1900), Britain pursued a policy of 'Splendid Isolation'. This term has been defined as follows:

'The term "Splendid Isolation" refers to a period in British diplomacy when the British government preferred a policy of isolation to an alliance or close diplomatic ties with other powers. This is usually considered to have lasted from 1895 to 1902.' (Lee 1994, p.254)

Pearce (1996) points out that the term 'Splendid Isolation' was coined in 1896:

'The phrase "Splendid Isolation" was first used by a member of the Canadian Parliament who approved of Britain's refusal to become entangled in European alliances, and it was popularised in the British press.' (Pearce 1996, p.72)

Historians then picked up on the phrase and used it to describe the approach to foreign policy adopted in the period 1895-1902.

In the last quarter of the 19th century, European countries started making formal alliances which, eventually, divided the continent into two main rival blocs:

- Germany, Austria-Hungary and Italy (the Triple Alliance)
- France and Russia (the Franco-Russian Alliance).

Throughout the 1880s and 1890s, despite overtures from various states, Britain refused to make a formal alliance with any other state, preferring to stay, instead, in isolation. This policy continued until 1902 when, for the first time, Britain made a formal alliance - with Japan. Pearce (1996) argues, however, that using the term 'Splendid Isolation' to describe this policy is misleading. His arguments are summarised in Box 7.10.

BOX 7.10 'Splendid Isolation' - a misleading term

Interpretation

Salisbury never used the term 'Splendid Isolation' and he certainly did not approve of it. He knew that isolation - unless, that is, every other power was isolated as well - carried too many dangers. To his mind, isolation was foolish not splendid. He saw the need to intervene extensively in European affairs in order to protect British interests. On the other hand, he also judged that membership of a long-term formal alliance was equally unwise since it might drag Britain into unwelcome and troublesome conflicts. Britain had land frontiers with all the major European powers - not in Europe but in the Empire. It would be difficult to overcome colonial conflicts if Britain were tied to any binding alliance which limited freedom of action. Besides, alliances were of limited value since future governments could break agreements which had been made earlier. In short, Salisbury wanted neither isolation nor alliances. Instead, he wanted cooperation with other states without being committed to them. It was, in his opinion, only from this position that Britain could pursue the flexible policies which national interests demanded. Salisbury, therefore, decided to walk a tightrope, balancing carefully between the two pitfalls of isolation and alliance. Given that this is the case, the use of the term 'Splendid Isolation' is misleading.
Adapted from Pearce 1996.

Enforced isolation?

Lee argues that Britain's isolation in the period 1895-1902 was enforced - 'the result of actual events not of deliberate policy' - and that politicians used the term 'Splendid Isolation' to give the impression that Britain was fully in control when, in reality, it was not. Lee argues that:

'For over a decade, successive British governments were confronted by a series of crises, involving almost every major power and indicating Britain's universal unpopularity'. (Lee 1994, p.258)

The main 'crises' were as follows.

1. The crisis in Turkey 1895-97

Turkey was of great strategic importance to Britain since it controlled the Straits of the Bosphorous - the route between the Mediterranean and the Black Sea. By supporting an independent Turkey, Britain ensured that the Russians had no easy access to the Mediterranean. British support for Turkey, however, came under strain in 1895 when the Turkish government used what the British public regarded as excessive force against Armenians living in Turkey:

'Salisbury, therefore, had to appease the public by pursuing an anti-Turkish policy and doing what he could to prevent further Armenian suffering, and yet at the same time he had also to try to safeguard British interests in the area. In particular, he had to dissuade the Russians from cashing in on the chaos and seizing the straits and Constantinople [Turkey's capital, now know as Istanbul].' (Pearce 1996, p.77)

Although, Pearce argues, Salisbury wanted to send a fleet to the Straits, his Cabinet overruled him. This had the knock-on effect of raising alarm that Russia would attempt to destabilise British rule in India:

'Fears of Russian encroachments on India intensified, especially when it became clear, after 1895, that Britain would be unable to retaliate by passing through the Straits to bombard Russia's flank.' (Pearce 1996, p.79)

The crisis in Turkey, therefore, destabilised relations between Britain and Russia.

2. Britain and the USA

When, in July 1895, a border dispute broke out between Venezuela and British Guiana (a British colony), the Venezuelans appealed to the USA to intervene. The American President responded by arguing that since, according to the so-called 'Monroe Doctrine', the dispute occurred within the USA's legitimate sphere of influence, the USA should arbitrate between the two sides. This was a clear challenge to Britain since that would mean a third party settling a dispute involving a British colony. Salisbury's reaction was as follows:

'Salisbury took the matter calmly, insisting that it would fizzle out and that it was largely created for home consumption [ie to please the American public].' (Pearce & Stewart 1992, p.169)

When, after waiting for four months to respond, Salisbury wrote refusing to accept the USA's right to intervene, President Cleveland replied with a strong note of protest and there seemed the possibility of war breaking out. The Cabinet then insisted that Salisbury should back down and allow American arbitration - which he duly did. Feuchtwanger

(1985, p.226) argues that Salisbury was overruled by his Cabinet, but Pearce argues that:

'The Prime Minister took the realistic decision that there was no point risking war with the USA, especially when there were problems in plenty elsewhere, and arbitration was accepted.' (Pearce 1996, p.80)

This incident was followed by British neutrality during the war between the USA and Spain (which resulted in the USA gaining control of Puerto Rico and Cuba in 1898) and British acceptance in 1901 that the USA alone would control the Panama Canal (even though an agreement had been made in 1850 that the USA and Britain would control it jointly). The result was as follows:

'[This all] added up to British realisation of USA predominance in the New World. Britain would no longer challenge [the USA's] claims and most British warships were now withdrawn from their station in the West Indies.' (Pearce & Stewart 1992, p.170)

Conflict with the USA, therefore, resulted in an important strategic realignment.

3. The Fashoda incident, 1898

Pearce argues that the Turkish crisis described above resulted in an important change of British strategy. Rather than focusing on the Straits of the Bosphorus, Salisbury decided that Egypt was the key to tackling the Russians:

'With the tacit abandonment of the Straits, it now seemed sensible to concentrate on building up the British presence in Egypt. From here, British forces would be able to tackle the Russians, if they proceeded through the Straits. But, the new position assigned to Egypt made the neighbouring Sudan more vital than ever before for Britain.' (Pearce 1996, p.78)

As a result of this change in strategic focus, and (according to Pearce & Stewart 1992) as a result of appeals for help from Italian troops who had been attacked by Dervish (ie Sudanese) troops, British forces were sent to reconquer the Sudan under General Kitchener. Kitchener advanced slowly and successfully south, fighting the decisive Battle of Omdurman in September 1898.

That same month, Kitchener discovered that a French force under Captain Marchand, which had been travelling north from the Congo had reached Fashoda, a position on the Nile just south of the British forces. The result was the 'Fashoda Incident' - see Box 7.11. The Fashoda Incident damaged relations between Britain and France.

4. Britain, Russia and the Far East

Throughout the 1890s, Britain was concerned about the threat of Russian expansion. Byrne argues:

'In the Far East, Britain had two objectives: the security of its trade with China and the maintenance of peace without which trade could not flourish. Both these objectives seemed to be most compromised by

---

BOX 7.11 The Fashoda Incident, 1898

Interpretation

The French government believed, after almost 20 years of fruitless diplomatic efforts to persuade the British to leave Egypt, that they must find some way to prod them into serious negotiations. The strategy they decided upon was to send a military expedition through the Congo into the Sudan. Here, they could, by occupying a position at the headwaters of the Nile, threaten the British position in Egypt. When the force arrived at Fashoda in September 1898, the French claimed the area by the right of prior conquest. But, they were challenged by Kitchener's superior British force. It was unclear who owned the area legally. The key issue was which side would stand its ground and which withdraw. The British government immediately made clear its determination to go to war rather than permit the French to remain in the Sudan. The French were not prepared for war with the British in Africa, partly because Russia, France's ally, was heavily involved in Manchuria (part of China) and could not help. Marchand withdrew and, after six months of prolonged argument, France conceded the Nile to Britain.

Adapted from Martel 1996.

---

the activities of the Russians. Britain suspected Russian ambitions in Persia, Afghanistan and China, whilst the extension of rail networks in Russia itself (largely funded by French money) seemed to offer a threat even to India.' (Byrne 1995, pp.405-06)

When, in 1894-95, Japan invaded Chinese territory, Russia, France and Germany set up a coalition which forced Japan to hand its newly acquired territory back to China. Britain was not involved, leading Byrne to comment that:

'[This] was indicative of the extent to which Britain could be marginalised whenever the other powers acted in concert.' (Byrne 1995, p.406)

In the second half of the 1890s, tension continued to mount over China as Germany took control of territory in 1897 and Russia took control of Port Arthur in 1898. Pearce notes that:

'There was talk of war in the British press, but Salisbury calmed the situation, even concluding an agreement with the Russians to build a railway in northern China. Nevertheless, the situation remained dangerously fluid and in 1900 the "Boxer rebellion" - in which Chinese nationalists attacked Europeans - broke out...The Russians used it as an excuse to send an army into Manchuria to extend their control over the region.' (Pearce 1996, p.79)

Although the European powers eventually agreed on spheres of influence in which they could trade without interference, the instability remained a major concern to the British government.

5. Britain and South Africa

South Africa in the 1890s was divided into four states - two British (Cape Colony and Natal) and two Boer (Transvaal and the Orange Free State). The Boers, or Afrikaners, were descendants of the Dutch colonists who had settled in South Africa in the 17th and 18th centuries.

Jameson's Raid, 1896

In 1886, gold was discovered in Transvaal and, as a result, there was an influx of non-Boers into the state. Transvaal's President, Paul Kruger, treated these newcomers (known as 'uitlanders'), many of whom were British, as second-class citizens:

'[Kruger] subjected the uitlanders to heavy rates of taxation and various restrictions, including virtual exclusion from political rights.' (Byrne 1995, p.402)

In 1895, Cecil Rhodes, Prime Minister of Cape Colony, planned an uprising of uitlanders in the Transvaal, in the hope of overthrowing Kruger's government:

'[Rhodes'] motives were a strange compound of financial interests, resentment at exploitative Boer taxes and fanatical patriotism. Rhodes believed in a vast British African Empire which would stretch from Cairo [in Egypt] to Cape Town [in South Africa].' (Pearce & Stewart 1992, p.172)

The attempt was a complete failure (it became known as 'Jameson's Raid' since a Dr Jameson led a group of armed police from Cape Colony into the Transvaal in the hope of sparking a general uprising there). Rhodes was forced to resign and the British government claimed that it had no prior knowledge of Rhodes' intentions. The incident, however, was followed by the notorious 'Kruger telegram'. This was a telegram sent by the German Kaiser (Emperor) to Paul Kruger, congratulating him on his defeat of the uprising (Germany had colonial interests in the nearby province of German South West Africa which it had occupied in 1884 and Kruger had shipped in German arms on a large scale). The telegram was seen as an attack on Britain and a challenge to British dominance in the region:

'For public opinion at home, the humiliation of the raid's failure was almost eclipsed by anger over the Kaiser's congratulatory telegram to Kruger, and there was general agreement that Germany must not be allowed to undermine Britain's position in southern Africa.' (Feuchtwanger 1985, p.229)

The Boer War, 1899-1902

It was suggested in Section 1.2 above that the Boer War was a turning point for Britain. Most historians agree with Byrne that:

'It was an ugly war in which many Boer women and children perished from disease in British camps and Britain's international reputation was tarnished.' (Byrne 1995, p.403)

During the Boer War, there was talk among some of Britain's European rivals of the setting up of a coalition force (a 'Continental League') to oppose British forces in South Africa. This never materialised, but it was a warning to the British government. Also, although Britain's European rivals did not actually take action against Britain, they were united in their condemnation of British action in South Africa. This encouraged a sense of isolation and concern that the Empire was threatened on all sides. This created a climate in which long-established assumptions began to be questioned. Indeed, most historians agree that the Boer War profoundly altered British thinking on foreign affairs. The standard view is as follows:

'The impact of the Boer War on British diplomacy was dramatic. The war was a traumatic shock for British society and institutions. Britain's military forces performed relatively poorly against a minor adversary. Statesmen began to think about what might happen if Britain became involved in a conflict with a major power.' (Watts 1998, pp.18-19)

Box 7.12 considers ways in which British foreign policy altered as a result of the Boer War.

BOX 7.12 The impact of the Boer War

(i) The Boer War was a profound shock for the British. It revealed a number of weaknesses. As Kipling wrote, it provided 'no end of a lesson'. It damaged British confidence and led to the growth of anti-imperialist feeling. In addition, it profoundly altered British foreign affairs. The war helped to sour Anglo-German relations. During the war, the Germans were highly critical of British policy. In particular, the treatment of Boer prisoners of war was denounced as 'brutal and inhuman'. Germany observed strict neutrality in the war and it was only France and Russia who talked of intervention. But, the war strengthened the position of those who considered that isolation was harmful to British interests.
Adapted from Pearce 1996.

(ii) The Boer War showed that Britain's isolation posed little danger to the Empire. The so-called 'Continental League' amounted to nothing. In fact, no action of any kind was taken against the British. As a result, Britain was able to fight the war in South Africa without having to worry about the consequences in the Far East, Central Asia and the Mediterranean. Indeed, the Empire was never in serious danger after 1900; Fashoda proved to be the last crisis in which Britain contemplated the possibility of a war with a European power arising from its imperial interests. So, the change in approach to diplomacy which took place after 1900 was sparked not by any immediate fear of a threat to the Empire, but by concern for the European balance of power.
Adapted from Martel 1996.

Interpretation

A revolution in diplomacy?

Many historians have argued that there was a distinct change in approach to foreign policy after Salisbury resigned as Foreign Secretary in 1900. Pearce and Stewart (1992, p.175), for example, talk of a 'diplomatic revolution'. This argument is based on three main developments.

1. The Anglo-Japanese Alliance, 1902

In 1902, Britain made a formal alliance with Japan. According to Byrne, the terms of the treaty were 'straightforward':

'If either power was at war with a third party, the other would maintain strict neutrality; if either power was at war with two other powers, the other would come to their aid; both powers asserted their special interests in the [Far East] and Britain recognised Japan's claims in Korea.' (Byrne 1995, p.406)

A number of reasons have been suggested to explain why Britain agreed to make this alliance. These can be summarised as follows:

- Lord Salisbury had resigned as Foreign Secretary and Lord Lansdowne (his successor) had a different approach (see Wilkinson 2000)
- Japan was a rising power which had previously played off one Western power against another and so Britain would gain an advantage over its rivals
- Japan already had connections with Britain (including naval training)
- Salisbury's veto of an alliance with Germany meant that alliance with Japan was a second best option
- the growth of rival Europeans' naval power meant that Britain alone could not deploy sufficient ships in the Far East to protect its trade
- like Japan, Britain was concerned about the threat of Russian expansion in the Far East
- Britain was worried that Japan would make an alliance with Russia.

In 1905, the Anglo-Japanese alliance was extended:

'By the terms of the Treaty of August 1905, the alliance could be invoked if either party was attacked by a single state. In return for British recognition of Japanese claims in Korea, Japan guaranteed military assistance in the defence of India in the event of a war breaking out between Britain and Russia.' (Ray 1998, p.19)

2. The Entente Cordiale of 1904

In April 1904, Britain and France signed an agreement which became known as the 'Entente Cordiale'. This was not a formal alliance. Rather, it was a colonial agreement:

'Several minor, but irritant, colonial disputes were settled: Siam (modern Thailand) was accepted by both sides as a buffer state between French Indochina and British Burma; Britain abandoned claims to Madagascar; the New Hebrides were put under joint administration; and mutually acceptable fishing rights off Newfoundland were agreed. More importantly, the French finally agreed to accept British control in Egypt, while Britain recognised French predominance in Morocco.' (Pearce 1996, p.88)

A number of reasons have been suggested to explain why Britain decided to make this agreement. These can be summarised as follows:

- Britain was alarmed at the growth of the German navy and wanted to strengthen its position against Germany
- a group of senior civil servants were convinced that Britain's best interests would be served by growing closer to France rather than Germany
- Britain was aware that France was more likely to make concessions now that Britain had an alliance with Japan (since France was allied to Russia, a Japanese-Russian clash could escalate into a war involving France and Britain, something which France wanted to avoid)
- the agreement would prevent the war between Russia and Japan (which had broken out in February 1904) escalating
- the agreement would stabilise Britain's commercial interests
- the British government was aware of the weakness of its position in the Mediterranean and was conscious of the dangers of over-commitment.

3. The Anglo-Russian Entente, 1907

In August 1907, Britain and Russia signed an agreement known as the Anglo-Russian Entente. Like the Entente Cordiale, this was not a formal alliance, but a colonial agreement:

'The agreement which was signed on 31 August 1907 resolved all the outstanding differences between Britain and Russia. Tibet was recognised as a neutral buffer state and Russia renounced contact with Afghanistan. Persia [Iran] was the crux of the agreement: Russia was to have a sphere of influence in the North while Britain had a comparable arrangement in the South, with a neutral zone in between where both countries had equal rights of access. The Persians were not consulted about any of this.' (Byrne 1995, p.408)

A number of reasons have been suggested to explain why Britain agreed to make this agreement. These can be summarised as follows:

- Japanese forces defeated Russian forces on land and sea in 1905 and Britain wanted to take advantage of Russia's weakness
- an agreement with Russia would protect India
- an agreement with Russia would increase Britain's security in Europe
- British troops could be released from service in India to make up a force which could be deployed in Europe
- the agreement would be a check on German ambitions.

Since the Entente Cordiale and Anglo-Russian Entente entwined Britain, France and Russia, the arrangement is sometimes referred to as the 'Triple Entente'.

What brought about the new approach?

Although, as suggested above, most historians agree that the Boer War was a turning point, they also accept that the Boer War was not the only reason why Britain shifted from its position of isolation. The following factors have been identified as factors which help to explain the change in approach.

1. Relative economic decline

By the end of the 19th century, it was clear that Britain's economic advantage over other powers was slipping away. Relative economic decline meant that Britain found it harder to maintain its military superiority - see Box 7.13.

BOX 7.13 Britain's relative economic decline

Interpretation

Britain's relative decline in terms of steel production was particularly important since this had a bearing on the production of military arms and equipment. Back in 1870, Britain had led the world with 0.7 million tons of steel produced in that year, with Germany some way behind on 0.3 million. By 1900, both Germany and the United States had overtaken Britain, at 6.7 and 10 million tons respectively compared with Britain's 5 million. The gap widened rapidly. By 1910, the figures for Germany and the United States were 13.8 and 26 million, while for Britain only 5.9 million. In addition, in 1900 Austria, France and Russia were all increasing their steel production at a faster pace than Britain. Although such developments took some time to affect contemporary perceptions of power, politicians were aware of the relative decline and aware, therefore, that Britain's position of strength was being eroded.

Adapted from Lee 1994.

---

2. Britain was overstretched

It was noted above that, in the 1890s, the British began to scale down their commitments in the Americas. By the beginning of the 20th century, politicians realised that Britain was overstretched - it simply did not have the resources to maintain such a huge empire, especially given that other powers were growing more powerful:

'In 1899 Sir Henry Brackenbury, a War Office official, commented on the tenuous nature of British control: "We are attempting to maintain the largest empire the world has ever seen with the armaments and reserves that would be insufficient for a third-class power". This dangerous situation had been recognised by Lord Salisbury over a

decade earlier...At the turn of the century, it became clear that British interests would continue to be better served by cooperation with other powers.' (Watts 1998, p.18)

3. Developments in Germany

Ray describes the deterioration of relations between Britain and Germany at the beginning of the 20th century. Germany, he argues, was keen to establish a close relationship with Britain, but, on a number of occasions, was rebuffed. For example:

'During the Spanish-American war of [1898], Germany had sought to limit the extent of the American victory by raising a united European front against the United States in support of Spain. This failed largely because Great Britain refused to take part in any such diplomatic initiative.' (Ray 1998, p.46)

Similarly, Ray notes, Britain upset Germany when a crisis arose in Venezuela in 1902. In order to force the Venezuelan government to pay debts it owed, British, German and Italian ships set up a blockade. When the German ships fired on Venezuelan ships, the American President intervened, asserting the Monroe Doctrine (see also page 253). Germany did not accept the validity of the Monroe Doctrine and was prepared to fight, but the British ships were immediately removed, forcing the Germans to back down. As a result:

'All attempts to forge a closer relationship with Britain were abandoned in favour of concentrating on a naval building programme designed to give [Germany] more diplomatic room for manoeuvre.' (Ray 1998, p.47)

This naval building programme, Ray argues, was perceived as a threat by the British and it encouraged the British government to take measures to neutralise the threat by forming closer ties with other powers.

4. A change in personnel

Wilkinson argues that the resignation of Lord Salisbury as Foreign Secretary and his replacement by Lord Lansdowne in 1900 meant an important change in emphasis. While Salisbury was firmly opposed to making any agreement which would tie Britain to another power (and, therefore, allow the possibility that Britain would be dragged into conflict by a third party), Lansdowne took a different view:

'Unlike Salisbury, who maintained that ultimately the Royal Navy would protect the Empire and that formal alliances were unnecessary, Lansdowne believed that the prerequisites [conditions] demanded by Salisbury's policy of non-commitment no longer applied. Not only was Britain widely hated, but her navy was now challenged by Germany. Because the fleet was needed at home, diplomacy had to plug the gaps.' (Wilkinson 2000, p.11)

5. A new mood in Britain

Ray argues that the Germans' decision to embark on

a programme of naval expansion produced a new mood in Britain. While, in the 1880s and 1890s, a host of 'invasion stories' had appeared in the press, claiming that the Empire was under threat from France and Russia, in the early years of the 20th century, these invasion stories started to identify Germany as the likely enemy:

'The extent to which these stories gripped the imagination of even sensible people may be gauged by the reaction of Frederick Harrison [a philosopher] who wrote a letter outlining his concerns to the *Times* during this period. There was in existence, he warned, a German army "trained for sudden transmarine descent on a coast" while Britain's only defence lay in keeping its navy at a high level of readiness at all times.' (Ray 1998, p.48)

Such fears helped to create a climate in which closer ties with Germany's opponents would be acceptable.

Was the Anglo-Japanese alliance really a turning point?

Not all historians agree that there was a distinct change in approach to foreign policy after Salisbury resigned as Foreign Secretary in 1900. Pearce, for example, argues that such an interpretation is 'faulty in several respects' and concludes that:

'It may thus be unconvincingly melodramatic to talk of any "revolution" in British foreign policy in 1902-07. There was too much continuity with previous policy for this.' (Pearce 1996, p.90)

Pearce's arguments are explored in Activity 7.3 below.

MAIN POINTS - Section 2.1

- British foreign policy in the late 19th century rested on twin pillars - protection of the Empire and maintenance of a balance of power in Europe. The latter was secured by Germany whose unification in 1871 was of concern to France and Russia (both of which had borders with Germany). A united Germany helped to reduce the threat that these countries posed to Britain.
- The traditional view is that, between 1895 and 1902, Britain pursued a policy of 'Splendid Isolation'- the British government refused to make alliances or have close diplomatic ties with other states. Some authors argue Britain was never really isolated. Rather, the government's policy was 'cooperation without commitment'.
- Some authors argue that Britain's foreign policy in the period 1895-1902 was shaped by a series of crises which included - (1) confrontation with Russia

as a result of developments in Turkey 1895-97 (2) disputes with the USA over Venezuela and the Panama Canal (3) confrontation with France in the Sudan in 1898 (4) tensions with European states in China and (5) tension and then war in South Africa.
- Many historians have argued that there was a major change in approach to foreign policy after Salisbury resigned as Foreign Secretary in 1900. This argument is based on three main developments - (1) the Anglo-Japanese Alliance of 1902 (2) the Entente Cordiale of 1904 and (3) the Anglo-Russian Entente of 1907. Some historians deny there was a major change.
- In addition to the Boer War, historians identify the following factors to explain the change in approach - (1) relative economic decline (2) the difficulty of coping with such a huge empire (3) developments in Germany (4) changes in personnel (5) a new mood in Britain.

Activity 7.3 Splendid Isolation

ITEM 1 The term 'Splendid Isolation'

Britain's refusal to join alliances did not mean total isolation from European affairs. It was never practical or desirable for Britain to adopt a truly isolationist role. The concept of 'Splendid Isolation', if it has any useful meaning at all, should be taken as referring to the fact that Britain felt that it could afford to stand apart from the power blocs emerging in Europe, retaining freedom of action at a time when the other Great Powers were significantly reducing their own. In this sense 'isolation' meant no more than the traditional policy of 'non-entanglement', a policy adopted by the British government throughout the period 1815-70. Nor should the term 'splendid' be taken to imply an increase in power in the strategic sense. Rather, it was splendid only in the sense that, by remaining detached, Britain claimed to have a moral superiority over other nations. There were two main reasons why Britain moved away from complete detachment. First, the burden of the Empire (which had grown rapidly at the end of the 19th century) placed Britain under enormous strain - and this strain was made even more acute by the erosion of naval superiority. And second, the realisation grew in the period 1895-1902 that Splendid Isolation was in danger of turning into genuine isolation, possibly leading Britain into the role of an outcast nation. The distinctive feature of British foreign policy in the 1890s was not so much that Britain was more isolated as such, but rather that it became alienated from so many other powers at the same time.

Adapted from Byrne 1995.

ITEM 2 Two cartoons

DISENGAGED.

Miss Britannia (meditatively). "I THINK UNCLE SAM WOULD BE A GOOD PARTNER; AND SO WOULD LITTLE JAP! I WONDER IF MY 'COUSIN-GERMAN,' WILLIAM, WILL ASK ME TOO!"

PASSIVE ASSISTANCE.

French Tar. "YOUR PAL AND MINE LOOK LIKE HAVING A ROW! DON'T SEE WHY WE SHOULD CHIP IN, DO YOU?"
British Tar. "LOR' BLESS YOU, NO! PASS THE 'CORDIALE'!"

This cartoon was published in *Punch* magazine on 5 June 1898. It shows Miss Britannia (ie Britain), fed up with being 'isolated', considering possible marriage partners (ie partners for a future alliance). She wonders whether to choose, Uncle Sam (the USA), 'Little Jap' (Japan) or 'Cousin-German' (Germany whose Kaiser was related to the British royal family). The absence of Russia and France should be noted. It suggests that Miss Britannia was not contemplating marriage with them at this time. By portraying Britain as a woman, the cartoonist suggests that Britain was not in a position to make proposals of alliance to other countries. Rather, Britain was waiting for other countries to make the initiatve.

This cartoon was published in *Punch* magazine on 5 August 1903. It shows two sailors (representing France on the left and Britain on the right) in the foreground and their two bickering friends in the background (representing Japan on the left and Russia on the right). By representing France and Britain as sailors, the cartoonist reminds the viewer that both are naval powers. The French sailor is drinking from a bottle marked 'Entente Cordiale' (a play on the word 'cordiale' which means both friendly and a soft drink), even though the agreement had not then been finally sealed. The two sailors agree that they should not intervene in the dispute between their friends.

ITEM 3 A revolution in diplomacy?

Salisbury had not pursued Splendid Isolation at all. He had been at pains to become involved in European affairs - had sought association with the European powers while refusing to commit himself to any particular ally. He wished to keep a free and flexible hand to avoid being dragged into war by restless partners. Was this policy really so different from that pursued in 1902-07? The Japanese alliance really committed Britain to very little - Britain merely promised to help Japan if it was attacked by a coalition of powers - a remote possibility. Similarly, the Ententes were not designed to commit Britain to any action - they were the settlement of past disputes, not a guarantee for the future. Unlike most full-scale alliances, they singled out no particular enemy and involved no joint military or naval plans. As a result, they gave Britain the freedom of diplomatic manoeuvre Salisbury had always desired since the less Anglo-French and Anglo-Russian tension existed, the less Britain needed a European ally. Popular misconceptions on this issue have arisen firstly by misunderstanding Salisbury's policies and, secondly, by misinterpreting the Ententes as essentially anti-German. It is true that in 1902-07 fear of Germany was growing and this was a factor influencing the agreements made. But, this did not mean that the agreements were directed against Germany. Rather, worries about German ambitions remained in the background for the British. Nor did the French view the Entente Cordiale as relevant to Germany. French security against Germany at this time lay with the Franco-Russian alliance. Similarly, the Anglo-Russian Entente had little relevance to Germany - Britain's overwhelming concern was with India, not with the Kaiser. It is, therefore, too strong to talk of a 'revolution' in diplomacy. There was too much continuity with previous policy for this. The Ententes were not alliances and they preserved Britain's 'semi-detached' position in Europe.

Adapted from Pearce 1996.

Questions

1. a) Using Items 1-3 describe what the term 'Splendid Isolation' means.
   b) How useful is the term?
   c) To what extent did British foreign policy change in the period 1895-1907?
2. a) Describe the context in which the two cartoons in Item 2 were drawn.
   b) What does each cartoon tell us about British foreign policy at the time?

   c) How did Britain's foreign policy position change in the period between the two cartoons?
3. a) Go through Section 2.1 and find pieces of evidence which could be used to support the interpretation in Item 3.
   b) What arguments could be made against the interpretation in Item 3?
   c) Do you believe there was a revolution in diplomacy in the period 1902-07? Explain your answer.

2.2 Why did Britain go to war in 1914?

The problem of causation

In an article written in 1997, Robert Pearce argues that it is important for historians to consider the question of why the First World War broke out in 1914, but 'difficult, if not impossible' to answer the question satisfactorily. One reason for this is that historians use 'causal labels' (words or phrases which are supposed to aid understanding of why things happen). These labels mean different things to different people:

'Everyone is familiar with the concept of "short-term" and "long-term" causes, but not everyone has the same timespan in mind - and whatever happened to "medium-term"? Historians also write regularly of "objective" and "subjective" causes; of "preconditions" and "precipitants"; of "sufficient" or "necessary" factors, as well as of "occasioning" factors or triggers. In addition, there are still "root", "basic", "fundamental" and "peripheral" causes. And if there are "important" causes of an event, does this mean that there are "unimportant" ones as well?' (Pearce 1997, p.12)

Pearce points out that different historians trace the origins of the First World War back to different points:

'Some books begin in 1911, with the Agadir crisis. Others go back to the first Moroccan crisis of 1905. Or should we look to the naval race and Tirpitz's first naval Bill of 1898 or at the dismissal of Bismarck [German Chancellor] in 1890? All are possible dates. Or is the real beginning the unification of Germany in 1871? (Pearce 1997, p.12)

Pearce then goes on to identify a number of other problems. These can be summarised as follows:

- the problem of hindsight - it is easy to exaggerate the importance of an event because, later, it was shown to be significant
- each of the events which can be said to have contributed to the outbreak of war in 1914 had its own complex causes which require explanation
- a large number of states was involved, each of

which had its own domestic problems and its own reasons for becoming involved
- historians no longer believe that the war can simply be explained by reference to important people (such as ministers and diplomats) - a wider perspective is taken
- since historians disagree, they add to the confusion.

This section focuses on why Britain went to war in 1914. It provides, therefore, only a partial explanation of why war broke out at that time. The focus is on events which took place between 1907 and 1914 since Section 2.1 above covered many of the key developments which took place between 1895 and 1907. It begins, however, with a development which affected Britain's policy towards Germany throughout the period 1898-1914 - Germany's decision to build a navy which would be able to compete with the Royal Navy.

The naval race

It was noted in Section 2.1 above that Germany's relations with Britain deteriorated in the early 1900s. In part, this was due to the German government's decision to adopt what Ray describes as the 'risk-fleet theory':

'The aim of this was to build a fleet based in the North Sea of sufficient size to pose a serious threat to Britain if it found itself at war with a third party. When the Royal Navy left home waters to do battle with such an enemy in defence of the Empire, it risked not only exposing the British Isles to invasion from the continent but also, the theory suggested, loss of its overall naval superiority.' (Ray 1998, p.47)

The construction of the German fleet began in 1898. Over the next 14 years, a new naval base was set up in Heligoland (an island in the North Sea, just off the coast of Germany), the Kiel Canal was widened (allowing ships to move from the Baltic Sea to the North Sea) and new ships began to be built. The aim was to build three new battleships a year. Joll argues:

'The consequence of the German naval programme was not only the realignment of British foreign policy. It also led indirectly to a radical change in British strategic thinking...The War

Office [considered] for the first time in decades the problems of sending an expeditionary [ie a land] force to the continent of Europe.' (Joll 1992, pp.75-76)

Watts accepts that British policy makers and the British military were concerned by Germany's naval programme, but he argues that:

'The "German menace" was more "invented" for political reasons than real. Naval rivalry diverted attention from the vulnerability of the Empire and justified the diplomatic agreements that France and Russia had made with Britain. By 1912, Britain was winning the naval arms race convincingly.' (Watts 1998, p.20)

Dreadnoughts

In 1889, Britain had adopted the 'two power standard' - the policy that the British navy should be at least as big as the next two biggest navies combined. This policy had been directed at the French and Russian navies (in 1898, the German navy was the seventh largest in the world). Britain's response to Germany's naval programme, however, was to begin one of its own. In 1906, HMS *Dreadnought* was unveiled. This led to a new phase in the naval race which continued up to 1912 - see Box 7.14.

Britain's relations with Germany in 1907

At first sight, Britain's decision to make the two agreements which led to the formation of the Triple Entente (ie the Entente Cordiale of 1904 and the Anglo-Russian Entente of 1907) might appear to be directed against Germany. After all, by making these agreements, Britain moved closer to two of Germany's main European rivals and, when war finally broke out in 1914, Britain fought on the side of France and Russia. It is tempting, therefore, to see the agreements of 1904 and 1907 as the seeds of the later conflict. Indeed, this is the way in which some historians have interpreted events (Howard 1974, for example). Such a view has been challenged, however. Reynolds argues that:

'By the time the historian reaches 1907 it is tempting to see the road to 1914 already stretching out ahead - the Triple Entente with France and Russia clearing the way for war with Germany. Yet that is a misconception based on the simplifications of hindsight.' (Reynolds 1991, p.77)

Pearce agrees with such an analysis, claiming that:

'Certainly, the British did not view the Entente Cordiale as much more than the settlement of past disputes. Worry about German ambitions existed in the background, but British diplomats wanted a freer hand in European affairs not a commitment to back up the French in their long-running enmity with Germany...Similarly, the Entente of 1907 had little relevance to Germany: Britain's overwhelming concern was with India not with the Kaiser.' (Pearce 1996, p.90)

BOX 7.14 The naval race 1906-12

Interpretation

HMS *Dreadnought* was a new type of battleship with greater speed and larger guns than other battleships. When it was launched, it seemed that the British had a decisive lead in the naval race. In fact, this was not the case. Dreadnoughts so outclassed other battleships that, in a sense, all other vessels were obsolete, including Britain's and so its existing lead was unimportant. Germany responded with its own version of the new battleship, beginning a new, more menacing and more expensive phase in the naval race. The British Cabinet became divided between those who wanted to outbuild Germany and those who wished to cut the soaring defence budget and to reach some sort of agreement with Germany. But public opinion was strongly in favour of outbuilding Germany. In 1909, the Cabinet responded to the slogan 'we want eight [dreadnoughts] and we won't wait' by ordering eight dreadnoughts to be built. Within a few years, Britain was spending more on its navy than Germany, France and Russia combined. The two-power standard was abandoned in 1909 since the combined navies of the USA and Germany were larger than Britain's, but comfort lay in the fact that these two countries were unlikely to combine. British security was ensured by a 60% margin of superiority over the German navy and by a new concentration of the British navy's ships in home waters. By 1912, however, the naval race was over. Germany concentrated instead on increasing the size of its army. Naval rivalry, therefore, was not a direct cause of the First World War. But, it did harm Anglo-German relations and it prepared the public for war.
Adapted from Pearce 1996.

In fact, relations between Britain and Germany in the period 1907-14 were complex. Most historians agree that there was nothing inevitable about the outbreak of war in 1914 and most agree that the outbreak of war should not be explained simply in terms which suggest that relations between Britain and Germany declined slowly until they eventually reached breaking point. Martel, for example, argues that, while the British government was concerned about Germany's growing naval power and its expansionist tendencies throughout the period 1895-1914, the principles behind British foreign policy remained consistent, regardless of which party was in power:

'Changes in government seldom meant dramatic changes in policy, and the party in power could usually be quite certain that the nation as a whole would support its policies. This coherence was largely the result of the widespread acceptance within the British ruling class of certain basic assumptions that were to guide British relations with Europe...The principles of the balance of power, of a strong navy, and of avoiding commitments that would draw Britain into a European war were generally supported by both political parties and most politicians.' (Martel 1996, p.49)

There were, however, a number of occasions when Britain clashed with Germany in the period after Britain made its agreements with France and Russia. Indeed, the first occasion came in 1905, just a few months after Britain had signed the Entente Cordiale.

The first Moroccan crisis, 1905

In March 1905, Kaiser Wilhelm (who was on a cruise) was persuaded to land at Tangier in Morocco. He then made a speech in which he declared that he was visiting a free and independent state and that the German government was prepared to act to preserve that independence. He also demanded that an international conference be held to sort out Morocco's status. This was a deliberately provocative action since the Entente Cordiale laid down that France should have control of Morocco:

'The point of the first Moroccan crisis was not Morocco, but the nature of the relationship between Germany and France. If the French were forced to give in to German demands...it would make it plain that Germany was so much more powerful in Europe that France could expand her empire overseas only with Germany's consent...The Moroccan crisis was tremendously important because it seemed likely to determine whether or not France was still capable of pursuing an independent foreign policy.' (Martel 1996, p.62)

Most historians accept, therefore, that the Germans' motive for this action was to force the British and French apart:

'Germany hoped to expose what was assumed by her government to be Britain's lack of genuine commitment to France.' (Byrne 1995, p.410)

At the international conference held in January 1906, however, Britain's Foreign Secretary, Edward Grey, strongly supported France:

'[Grey] was solidly behind France - and orchestrated support from Russia, Spain and Italy - when an international conference met at Algeciras in January 1906...The result was that Germany was isolated and outvoted while France's interests were substantially endorsed. Furthermore, Britain and France emerged from the crisis as much closer collaborators than before.' (Pearce 1996, p.102)

Consequences

The main consequence of the first Moroccan crisis was closer relations between Britain and France. Although Britain continued to refuse to make a formal alliance with France and, although it refused

to make a commitment to support France militarily if Germany invaded it, movements were made in this direction:

'In attempting to bolster the French during the German-inspired Moroccan crisis, Grey hit upon a new concept in British diplomacy. He authorised "conversations" between the British and French military general staffs aimed at considering the means by which British forces could assist France on land in the event of war. This was all hypothetical of course, but it pointed to a consideration that had, in a sense, always been evident if never fully accepted - that Britain could not allow France to be dominated by a greater power in Europe.' (Byrne 1995, p.411)

A further consequence of the Moroccan crisis was a change in the direction of German diplomacy. It was significant that Italy voted against Germany at the Algeciras conference since Italy was a member of the Triple Alliance. The only country to support Germany was Austria-Hungary. As a result, German support for Austria-Hungary became a priority:

'The Moroccan crisis and the conference of Algeciras had shown the Germans that their alliance with Austria was all that stood between them and complete diplomatic isolation...The maintenance of Austria-Hungary as a Great Power became a major foreign policy goal for Germany.' (Joll 1992, p.56)

The Bosnian crisis 1908-09

Germany's support for Austria-Hungary became of particular importance in 1908-09 when Austro-Hungarian troops took control of Bosnia and Herzegovina (see Box 7.15 on page 263). Until then, this area had been under Turkish control. The crisis arose because Russia made a deal with Austria-Hungary which, it claimed, the Austro-Hungarians failed to honour. Commenting on the occupation of Bosnia, Henig says:

'This action had been discussed with the Russian Foreign Minister, Isvolsky, who had given his agreement in exchange for Austria-Hungary using her good offices to secure for Russia greater influence at Constantinople and the right to free passage for Russian ships through the Straits [of the Bosphorus] in times of peace and war. However, other powers, especially Britain, were strongly opposed to this second proposition and thus, while Austria-Hungary increased her territories, Russia got nothing.' (Henig 1993, p.19)

The result was a rapid escalation of tension between Austria-Hungary and Russia and talk of war between the two empires. In January 1909, the German Chief of Staff intervened, making a public declaration to his Austrian counterpart that 'the moment Russia mobilises, Germany will also mobilise'. This was enough to force the Russians to back down. The significance of this event has been described as follows:

'Much of this was bluff: neither the Austrians nor the Russians were militarily or economically in a position to go to war, but the effect was to show both the nature and the limitations of the alliance system because, while the effect of Germany's commitment to Austria was made clear, the Russians had found only lukewarm support in Paris and London for their ambitions at Constantinople.' (Joll 1992, p.57)

According to Martel, Britain and France's failure to provide solid support for Russia was seen in Germany as evidence of weakness and led directly to the second Moroccan crisis of 1911 (see below):

'The Germans regarded the Bosnian crisis as convincing proof that neither the alliance with France nor the entente with Britain would provide the Russians with any meaningful assistance in the Balkans. Perhaps the Ententes would prove equally useless to France in North Africa where another crisis began to emerge in Morocco.' (Martel 1996, p.71)

The second Moroccan crisis, 1911

Like the first Moroccan crisis, the second began as a dispute between France and Germany. In April 1911, the French government sent troops to Morocco in response to an outbreak of disorder in the town of Fez:

'The crisis began when internal unrest in Morocco led the French to take military action and thus technically breach the agreement of 1906.' (Pearce & Stewart 1992, p.287)

The German government's response to this was to demand compensation from France and to send a battleship to Morocco. This ship arrived in the Moroccan port of Agadir in July 1911:

'Why had the Germans intervened? The Foreign Office decided that the aim was, as in 1905, to destroy the Entente; but, it is much more likely that the Germans simply wanted a foreign policy success.' (Pearce 1996, p.105)

The British response

Whatever the motives, the German government's action sparked an angry response from the British government. In a speech made in late July 1911, David Lloyd George (the Chancellor of the Exchequer) said:

'If a situation were to be forced upon us in which peace could only be preserved by the surrender of the great...position Britain has won by centuries of heroism...then I say emphatically that peace at that

BOX 7.15 | The Balkans 1908-13

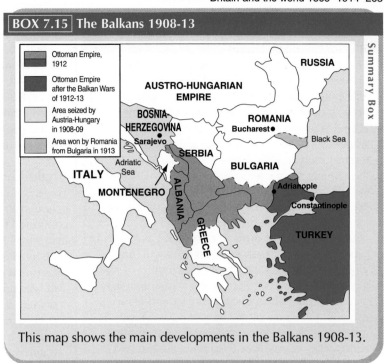

This map shows the main developments in the Balkans 1908-13.

price would be a humiliation intolerable for a great country like ours to endure.'

According to Pearce & Stewart:

'[The speech] was meant as a warning to both France and Germany, but it was interpreted in Germany as another humiliating threat. Throughout August and September, war seemed possible.' (Pearce & Stewart 1992, p.287)

In November, however, the Germans accepted the French offer of some territory in the Congo and the crisis blew over. Martel argues that the reason why the British became involved in this crisis was not because the government was concerned with which country controlled Morocco or the Congo. Rather:

'What worried them was that German power in Europe could be used to control French behaviour overseas; if this proved to be the result of the crisis, then France would be reduced to subordinate status and the balance of power in Europe would have shifted clearly in Germany's favour. In other words, Britain had no immediate fear of Germany's imperialism, but she did regard the balance of power as essential to her security and she was increasingly concerned that this was being endangered by Germany.' (Martel 1996, p.72)

What this crisis reveals about Anglo-German relations is explored in Box 7.16.

Consequences

Historians argue that a number of important consequences resulted from the second Moroccan crisis. These can be summarised as follows:

- an anti-German government was elected in France
- Britain and France signed a Naval Agreement in 1912 - the British fleet would defend the

BOX 7.16 The second Moroccan crisis and Anglo-German relations

The second Moroccan crisis reveals in full the peculiar state of Anglo-German relations. There was talk of war on both sides but there was nothing concrete to fight about. The Germans hoped for a spectacular diplomatic victory and wanted some territorial rewards to show the German public. If the Entente was weakened in the process, so much the better for Germany's foreign position. The British were involved because they believed the Entente was under attack and it was essential to back the French who might give way to German pressure. If Germany triumphed over France, the European equilibrium would be shattered and Britain's security threatened. What is striking is the assumption that a colonial quarrel between Germany and France involved the European balance of power. It was a measure of British insecurity that the government overreacted from fear of German intentions and French weakness. It did not need French prodding to convince the Foreign Office that what could be seen as a piece of German blackmail was a threat to the European status quo. There was something totally unreal about the whole quarrel yet both sides considered war. The Moroccan problem was solved, but the suspicions that underlay the Foreign Office reading of the German action could not be removed. Nor could the conditions in Berlin which provoked the original decision to send a warship to Morocco. As the Germans had neither a fixed plan nor a clear course of action in mind, their diplomacy was erratic and unpredictable and the Foreign Office tended to respond not in terms of the actual challenge, but in accordance with its reading of Germany's ultimate intentions.

Adapted from Steiner 1977.

Channel and France's Atlantic borders while the French fleet would move into the Mediterranean
● there was an upsurge of anti-British feeling in Germany and of anti-German feeling in Britain
● Germany's leaders felt that their ambitions had been held back and they felt increasingly vulnerable
● there was a greater willingness in Europe to believe that a major war was inevitable at some point.

Despite the upsurge of popular hostility in Britain and Germany, there was an attempt to improve relations between the two countries when, in 1912, Lord Haldane, the British Secretary of State for War, visited Germany. His visit, however, failed to produce any concrete agreement:

'The Germans wanted British neutrality in the event of a Franco-German or Russo-German war and, in return, they offered to scale down their naval construction programme. But, all Haldane promised was that Britain would not pursue an aggressive policy towards Germany. He could not accept an unqualified neutrality that would compromise Britain's freedom of action and, in effect, amount to her abdication from European affairs.' (Pearce 1996, p.106)

Anglo-German relations 1912-14

There is a consensus among historians that relations between Britain and Germany improved in 1912 and continued to improve until the summer of 1914. Indeed, as late as May 1914, senior civil servants such as Harold Nicolson were optimistic about relations with Germany:

'It was not the prospect of European war that occupied the British government in 1914, but the crisis over Ireland. Europe seemed calmer than it had for a long time. Even the fierce Germanophobe [German hater], Nicolson, was writing in May 1914: "since I have been at the Foreign Office I have not seen such calm waters". The next month, four British battleships visited Kiel on a goodwill mission.' (Pearce & Stewart 1992, p.288)

Reynolds (1991) argues that this was due to four main factors:
● the end of the naval race
● improved trading relations between Britain and Germany
● diplomatic initiatives
● the extension of the Russian railway system and revival of Russia militarily - see Box 7.17 on page 265.

Signs of improved relations

In the period 1912-14, there were three main signs of improved relations between Britain and Germany. First, the two governments drew up a treaty which settled a long-running dispute over the division of territory in Africa which was part of the decaying Portuguese Empire. In 1898, Britain had made a secret agreement with Germany which divided up the Portuguese empire, but in 1899 Britain had renewed its alliance with Portugal (Portugal was Britain's oldest ally). In 1912-13, however, negotiations between the British and German government resulted in agreement over a new division of territory:

'The actual territorial exchanges were concluded in May 1913. The British granted the Germans a much larger share of Angola than in the earlier arrangement and were given only slight compensation for this alteration in Mozambique.' (Steiner 1977, p.106)

Although the treaty was not published before war broke out in 1914, the fact that negotiations resulted in agreement suggests a climate of cooperation.

Interpretation

BOX 7.17 Russia - a common cause for concern

Developments in Russia were of particular concern to the German army. Ever since the signing of the Franco-Russian alliance in 1894, the strategy of the German army had been based on the need to fight a war on two fronts. This resulted in General Schlieffen's famous plan of 1905. By this plan, France was to be defeated by a rapid strike, allowing the German armies then to concentrate against Russia. The Schlieffen Plan assumed that the German army would be able to defeat France before the Russians had mobilised. The extension of the Russian railway system made this task harder because it promised to halve to 15 days the time required for mobilisation. At the same time, the increase in the term of French military service in 1913 from one to three years made the French army a far harder nut to crack quickly. As a result, the Schlieffen Plan now looked dangerously flawed. The Russian military revival was also of concern to the British. The 1907 Anglo-Russian agreement had not held in Persia where the growth of nationalist unrest had given the Russians the excuse to take complete control of the northern zone. The Indian border with Tibet also became an issue again. British concern about Russia encouraged British diplomats to improve relations with Germany.
Adapted from Reynolds 1991 and Joll 1992.

Second, in June 1914, Britain and Germany reached an agreement over the construction of the Baghdad railway. Under the terms of this agreement, Britain secured its interests in the Gulf area while Germany secured the finance to complete the railway. Referring to the agreement over the Portuguese Empire as well as that over the Baghdad railway, Joll argues:
'The colonial negotiations confirmed that there was no direct territorial rivalry between the two countries, but they also revealed that neither side was prepared to give up its pretensions to world power in a broader sense.' (Joll 1992, p.185)
And third, during the two Balkan Wars which broke out in 1912 and 1913, Britain and Germany cooperated to ensure that the conflict did not escalate. Britain put pressure on Russia not to become involved, whilst Germany put pressure on Austria-Hungary.

Why did Britain go to war?
The events which triggered the war (often described as the 'July crisis') are outlined in Box 7.18. Whereas the German government had been prepared to restrain Austria-Hungary in 1912-13, it refused do so in July 1914. As a result, the crisis escalated rapidly and soon involved Russia and France. Britain's attempts to prevent the crisis from escalating were simply ignored by the German government. Most historians agree that there was little Britain could do in July to prevent war breaking out. But that did not mean that, once the other Great Powers had become involved, Britain had to go to war:
'The Entente Cordiale did not necessitate British support for France, and neither did the military or naval talks held after the Moroccan crises. It is true that Britain, and several other Powers, had guaranteed Belgian neutrality by the Treaty of London of 1839 and that, in their invasion of France, German troops were bound to violate that neutrality. But, would such a violation necessitate British intervention?' (Pearce 1996, p.111)
Historians are divided about why the Liberal Cabinet eventually came to the conclusion that German violation of the Treaty of London did indeed necessitate British intervention.

The British Cabinet and war
It was not until 27 July that the British Foreign Secretary, Edward Grey, raised the possibility of Britain joining a war if Germany invaded France. On that occasion, five members of the Cabinet said that such action would lead to their resignation, much to Grey's disappointment:
'The Foreign Secretary's offers of mediation had been turned down flat by Germany, and he was

BOX 7.18 The outbreak of war in 1914

Summary Box

28 June - the assassination of Archduke Franz Ferdinand, heir to the Austrian throne, begins a chain reaction of events (since the Austrians blame Serbia, an ally of Russia, for the assassination).

5 July - the Kaiser gives the Austro-Hungarian government a 'blank cheque' to respond to the assassination as it sees fit.

23 July - Austria-Hungary gives Serbia an ultimatum.

25 July - Serbia's reply fails to meet all the Austrian demands.

28 July - Austria-Hungary declares war on Serbia.

30 July - Russia mobilises its troops.

31 July - France, Austria-Hungary and Germany mobilise their troops.

1 August - Germany declares war on Russia.

2 August - Germany occupies Luxembourg and sends an ultimatum to Belgium demanding the free passage of troops.

3 August - Germany declares war on France and the Belgians appeal to Britain for support.

4 August - Germany invades Belgium and France and Britain declares war on Germany.

becoming convinced that German militarists were deliberately inflaming the crisis. He, therefore, believed that Britain could have to fight...but without Cabinet agreement he was powerless.' (Pearce 1996, p.110)

Between 27 July and 2 August, Britain's position remained unclear. Since his hands were tied, Grey refused to promise the French support while he tried to put pressure on the Germans by making it clear that Britain's entry into the war had not been ruled out. The crucial change came at a Cabinet meeting held on 2 August. At that meeting, Grey threatened to resign unless the Cabinet backed him. All but two members did so.

What persuaded the Cabinet to support Grey?

Some historians argue that Grey was able to convince the Cabinet that Britain really was under an obligation to go to war against Germany if the Germans violated the Treaty of London. According to this view:

'The defence of a small and helpless state had an irresistible appeal.' (Lee 1994, 267)

Other historians, however, argue that the Belgian issue was a useful justification for rather than the real cause of the Cabinet's decision that Britain should enter the war. These historians argue that the domestic political situation was important. At the meeting of the Cabinet on 2 August a letter was read out from the Conservative Leader, Bonar Law, and former Foreign Secretary, Lord Lansdowne, expressing their support for war. This letter, it is suggested, was a bid by the Conservatives to win power from the Liberals. When Edward Grey threatened to resign if the Cabinet did not support going to war if Germany invaded France, party political considerations were enough to ensure that the vast majority of the Cabinet supported Grey's position:

If, as appeared likely, Asquith resigned along with Grey, the result would have to be either a coalition government or a new Conservative government; neither would prevent the slide to war and the latter might even accelerate it. All but two Liberal Cabinet ministers came to the conclusion that unity had to prevail if the Liberals were to remain in power, and the Belgian issue made their conversion more palatable.' (Lee 1994, p.268)

Other factors

One further factor that needs to be taken into account is public opinion. As the July crisis intensified, public opinion swung in favour of war (although, as Kennedy 1980 points out, some sections of the British public remained hostile to war right up to its outbreak). Public demonstrations in favour of war culminated in a demonstration in London on 3 August:

'Demonstrations were taking place in Trafalgar Square, and crowds - deluded by the belief that a war would be all over by Christmas - assembled outside Buckingham Palace shouting 'We want war!' A police guard had to be mounted to protect the German embassy. Powerful pro-war and anti-German feelings which had been smouldering for many years, now surfaced, removing the last vestiges of doubt from the Liberal Cabinet.' (Pearce 1996, p.111)

Other factors that may have contributed to the decision to enter the war include:

- the government's need for distraction from domestic problems (such as the crisis in Ireland, industrial strife and the suffragette's militant campaign)
- concern that the war would result in a massive growth in German (or Russian) power and that Britain's position of pre-eminence would be eroded.

MAIN POINTS - Section 2.2

- **The origins of the First World War are very complex. One author argues it is 'difficult, if not impossible' to explain the outbreak of war satisfactorily.**
- **The Germans' decision to build a navy which would compete with the Royal Navy led to a naval race. This soured relations with Germany and prepared the British public for war. The naval race was over by 1912, however, and so was not a direct cause of the First World War.**
- **Neither the Entente Cordiale nor the Anglo-Russian Entente was directed at Germany. Rather, Britain's foreign policy was shaped by what the government felt would best preserve the balance of power in Europe.**
- **The two Moroccan crises (of 1905 and 1911) pushed Britain and France closer together whilst Britain's**

failure to intervene in the Bosnian crisis of 1908-09 was interpreted as a sign of weakness.
- **Between 1912 and July 1914, relations between Britain and Germany improved. The two countries made agreements over the Portuguese Empire and the Baghdad railway and both intervened in the Balkan Wars of 1912-13 to ensure that Austria-Hungary and Russia did not become involved.**
- **There was little Britain could do in July 1914 to prevent a major war breaking out, but Britain's decision to join is the subject of debate. Some historians argue that the Treaty of London was the deciding factor. Others argue that Britain would have joined the war regardless of the German violation of Belgium.**

Activity 7.4 Why did Britain enter the war in August 1914?

Long-term and short-term causes

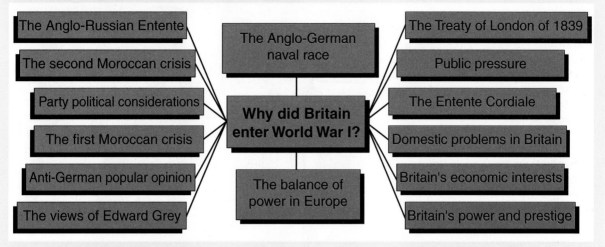

| The Anglo-Russian Entente |
| The second Moroccan crisis |
| Party political considerations |
| The first Moroccan crisis |
| Anti-German popular opinion |
| The views of Edward Grey |

| The Anglo-German naval race |
| **Why did Britain enter World War I?** |
| The balance of power in Europe |

| The Treaty of London of 1839 |
| Public pressure |
| The Entente Cordiale |
| Domestic problems in Britain |
| Britain's economic interests |
| Britain's power and prestige |

This diagram shows some of the the long-term and short-term causes of Britain's entry into the First World War.

The role played by Edward Grey

However the events of July and August 1914 are viewed, the personal influence of Edward Grey was considerable. Grey has been criticised on the grounds that his policy towards Germany was inconclusive and he sent the wrong messages, inadvertently encouraging the German government to increase the pressure. He then suddenly cried halt, but it was too late. According to this view, therefore, Grey's policies were over-ambitious because he believed that Britain could maintain the balance between France, Russia and Germany. On the other hand, it could be argued that nothing that Grey did - or did not do - made any difference to the German invasion of Belgium. Recent historical interpretation has stressed Germany's desire to go to war in 1914 as the way out of a major dilemma. It was considered by the German military and government that German security was being endangered by a rapid increase in the military power of the Franco-Russian alliance. Both countries were catching up quickly and the Russian rearmament programme would be complete by 1917. At a meeting between the Kaiser and his generals on 8 December 1912, Von Moltke, the Chief of Staff, said that war was inevitable and, he added, 'the sooner, the better'. Germany, after all, had the means to inflict a swift and crushing defeat on France (ie the Schlieffen Plan). In the crisis which developed after the assassination of Archduke Ferdinand, therefore, the German Chancellor was content to ignore peace offers made by Grey because it was better for Germany for war to break out immediately rather than in one or two years' time. Grey, therefore, was dealing with a government which had already taken up the view that war was the way out of, not into, a hole.

Edward Grey

Adapted from Lee 1994.

ITEM 3 Britain and Belgium

(i) Belgian independence was a long-standing British commitment which went back to the Treaty of London of 1839. That Belgium was a small power facing a mighty enemy was convenient both for rallying public opinion and for staking a claim to the moral high ground. But, it was not, in itself, decisive. Britain turned a blind eye to the plight of small powers faced by aggression when it suited it to do so. Equally, the Germans had long planned to attack France through Belgium if war came and so Britain's reaction was unimportant. Although the Germans hoped that the British would remain neutral, they never counted on it in their planning. Since they also assumed the war would be short, they attached little importance to the British threat - the British army being, in the Kaiser's words, 'contemptible' in terms of its size.

Adapted from Byrne 1995.

(ii) The rallying point for those members of the Cabinet wishing to avoid war was that, while Britain might have a moral obligation to and a strategic interest in France, the British government was not bound by treaty to come to France's aid. Belgium was different. But, the language of the 1839 treaty was unusual on one point. It gave the signatories the right, but not the duty, of intervention in the case of the violation of Belgian territory. In 1914, as the possibility of German violation loomed, the non-interventionists in the Cabinet clung to this point. Britain, they said, had no obligation to defend Belgium, especially if Belgium itself did not fight. If

NO THOROUGHFARE

BRAVO, BELGIUM!

This cartoon was published in Punch magazine on 12 August 1914 - eight days after Belgium had been invaded by Germany. It shows a Belgian peasant boy trying to protect his land against an aggressive, heavily armed German. The cartoon reflects and promotes the idea that the German invasion of Belgium was an unjustifiable act of violence.

the Belgian army simply lined the roads while the German army passed, British troops need not be committed. Before 2 August, nobody knew what Belgium would do. When news of the threatened German invasion of Belgium became known on 2 August, a wave of indignation rolled over the nation. This wave swept up the mass of Britons who, although reluctant to fight for France, sprang to the side of neutral Belgium.

Adapted from Massie 1992.

(iii) The invasion of Belgium was important. Yet, most historians believed that Britain would have entered the war anyway, sooner or later. This view is based on the notion that there were three main reasons for British participation. First, there was Anglo-German rivalry, which is often seen as the root cause of Britain's entry. Second, public opinion (fed by the glorious image of war) provides an important explanation. A journalist recalled that Asquith did not carry England into war. On the contrary, England carried Asquith. Asquith's government did not share public enthusiasm for war, but it could not afford to ignore it. And third, perceptions of national interest led to Britain's declaration of war. If Britain stayed out, its prestige would suffer and so might more material interests. Besides, whichever side won, the balance of power in Europe would be destroyed, to Britain's disadvantage.

Adapted from Pearce 1996.

ITEM 4 The Cabinet meetings of 2 August

Sunday 2 August was the decisive day in two respects. Having forbidden Churchill (who, from 1911, was First Lord of the Admiralty) to proceed with full mobilisation of the navy on the previous day, the Cabinet now agreed to protect the French northern coastline and French shipping if the German fleet came down the Channel. It was also at this Sunday lunchtime meeting that the pledge of Conservative support was made known. After this, Grey openly stated that he would resign if France was not supported and Asquith said that he would 'stand by Grey in any event'. Talk of a coalition government frightened some and offered others the excuse for standing together as a united Cabinet. Four waverers later explained to friends that they felt it was better to go to war united than to hand over 'policy and control to the Tories'. The moderates' general position appears to be that, if intervention was increasingly difficult to avoid, it would be better to stay in office to carry out a war policy by Liberal methods. At the second Cabinet meeting that day, it was resolved that a 'substantial violation' of Belgian neutrality would 'compel us to take action'. What the Belgian factor did was to give Cabinet waverers and their backbench supporters a recognisably Liberal justification for entry into the conflict, to reduce the number of resignations to two and to undercut the agitation of opponents to war outside the Cabinet. That does not mean that Belgium was the decisive element. In actual fact, it appears that, by 2 August, the majority of the Cabinet felt committed to joining the war even if Belgium supported the Germans (though the King of Belgium's appeal to Britain for help avoided such an embarrassment). Belgium was crucial in keeping the Liberal Party united, but much less so in causing British intervention.

Adapted from Kennedy 1980.

Questions

1. Look at Item 1.
   a) Arrange the causes of Britain's entry into the First World War into short-term and long-term causes.
   b) Make a list of the causes with the most important at the top and least important at the bottom. Explain why you have made this choice.
   c) Why did Britain go to war in August 1914?
2. a) Using Items 2 and 4, describe the role played by Edward Grey in the build-up to the First World War.
   b) To what extent was Grey responsible for Britain's

entry into the war?
3. a) Judging from Items 3 and 4, how important is the 1839 Treaty of London in explaining Britain's entry into the First World War?
   b) Why do you think that the Cabinet came to the conclusion on 2 August 1914 that Britain should enter the war?
   c) Give arguments for and against the view that there was a serious possibility of Britain remaining neutral in 1914.

References

- **Bolt (1984)** Bolt, C., 'Race and the Victorians' in *Eldridge (1984)*.
- **Burroughs (1999)** Burroughs, P., 'Defence and imperial disunity' in *Porter (1999)*.
- **Byrne (1995)** Byrne, M., 'Foreign policy: 1870-1914' in *Scott-Baumann (1995)*.
- **Cain & Hopkins (1993)** Cain, P.J. & Hopkins, A.J., *British Imperialism, Innovation and Expansion 1688-1914*, Longman, 1993.
- **Chamberlain (1984)** Chamberlain, M.E., 'Imperialism and social reform' in *Eldridge (1984)*.
- **Dunnett (1999)** Dunnett, R.E. (ed.), *Gentlemanly Capitalism and British Imperialism*, Longman, 1999.
- **Eldridge (1984)** Eldridge, C.C. (ed.), *British Imperialism in the 19th Century*, Macmillan, 1984.
- **Feuchtwanger (1985)** Feuchtwanger, E.J., *Democracy and Empire: Britain 1865-1914*, Arnold, 1985.
- **Fieldhouse (1982)** Fieldhouse, D.K., *The Colonial Empires*, Macmillan, 1982.
- **Gallagher & Robinson (1953)** Gallagher, J. & Robinson, R., 'The imperialism of free trade', *Economic History Review* (2nd Series), Vol.6.1, August 1953.
- **Gallagher & Robinson (1981)** Gallagher, J. & Robinson, R., *Africa and the Victorians: the Official Mind of Imperialism*, Macmillan, 1981.
- **Gardiner & Wenborn (1995)** Gardiner, J. & Wenborn, N., *The Companion to British History*, Collins and Brown, 1995.
- **Henig (1993)** Henig, R., *The Origins of the First World War* (2nd edn), Routledge, 1993.
- **Hobsbawm (1994)** Hobsbawm, E., *The Age of Empire 1875-1914*, Abacus, 1994.
- **Howard (1974)** Howard, M., *The Continental Commitment: the Dilemma of British Defence Policy in the Era of Two World Wars*, Penguin, 1974.
- **Hyam (1976)** Hyam, R., *Britain's Imperial Century, 1815-1914*, Batsford, 1976.
- **James (1992)** James, L., 'The White Man's Burden? Imperial wars in the 1890's', *History Today*, August 1992.
- **James (1994)** James, L., *The Rise and Fall of the British Empire*, Little, Brown and Company, 1994.
- **Joll (1992)** Joll, J., *The Origins of the First World War* (2nd edn), Longman, 1992.
- **Kennedy (1980)** Kennedy, P., *The Rise of the Anglo-German Antagonism 1860-1914*, Allen and Unwin, 1980.

- **Kennedy (1984)** Kennedy, P., 'Continuity and discontinuity in British imperialism 1815-1914' in *Eldridge (1984)*.

- **Killingray (1999)** Killingray, D., 'Imperial defence' in *Winks (1999)*.

- **Lee (1994)** Lee, S.J., *British Political History 1815-1914*, Routledge, 1994.

- **Long (1995)** Long R.D. (ed.), *The Man on the Spot*, Greenwood Press, 1995.

- **McCaskie (1999)** McCaskie, T.C., 'Cultural encounters: Britain and Africa in the 19th Century' in *Porter (1999)*.

- **McDonough (1994)** McDonough, F., *The British Empire 1815-1914*, Hodder and Stoughton, 1994.

- **MacKenzie (1984)** MacKenzie, J.M., *Propaganda and Empire 1880-1960*, Manchester University Press, 1984.

- **MacKenzie (1999)** MacKenzie, J.M., 'Empire and metropolitan cultures' in *Porter (1999)*.

- **Marshall (1990)** Marshall, P., 'Imperialism: uses of the term', *History Sixth*, No.6, March 1990.

- **Marshall (1996)** Marshall, P. (ed.), *Cambridge Illustrated History of the British Empire*, Cambridge University Press, 1996.

- **Marshall (1996a)** Marshall, P., '1870-1918: the Empire under threat' in *Marshall (1996)*.

- **Massie (1992)** Massie, R.K., *Dreadnought: Britain, Germany and the Coming of the Great War*, Jonathan Cape, 1992.

- **Martel (1996)** Martel, G., *The Origins of the First World War* (2nd edn), Longman, 1996.

- **Morgan (1974)** Morgan, K.O., *Lloyd George*, Weidenfeld and Nicolson, 1974.

- **Nash (1999)** Nash, D., 'The Boer War and its humanitarian critics', *History Today*, Vol.49.6, June 1999.

- **Pearce & Stewart (1992)** Pearce, M. & Stewart, G., British Political History 1867-1990: *Democracy and Decline*, Routledge, 1992.

- **Pearce (1996)** Pearce, R., *Britain and the European Powers 1865-1914*, Hodder and Stoughton, 1996.

- **Pelling (1968)** Pelling, H., *Popular Politics and Society in Late Victorian Britain*, Macmillan, 1968.

- **Porter (1996)** Porter, A., 'Empires in the Mind' in *Marshall (1996)*.

- **Porter (1999)** Porter, A. (ed.), *The Oxford History of the British Empire: the 19th Century*, Oxford University Press, 1999.

- **Price (1972)** Price, R., *An Imperial War and the Working Class*, Routledge, 1972.

- **Ray (1998)** Ray, C., 'Britain and the origins of the First World War', *History Review*, No.30, March 1998.

- **Reynolds (1991)** Reynolds, D., *Britannia Overruled: British Policy and World Power in the 20th Century*, Longman, 1991.

- **Scott-Baumann (1995)** Scott-Baumann, M., *Years of Expansion: Britain 1815-1914*, Hodder and Stoughton, 1995.

- **Smith (1998)** Smith, S.C., *British Imperialism 1750-1970*, Cambridge University Press, 1998.

- **Steiner (1977)** Steiner, Z.S., *Britain and the Origins of the First World War*, Macmillan, 1977.

- **Surridge (1996)** Surridge, K., 'Guardians of the Empire', *Modern History Review*, Vol.7.4, April 1996.

- **Watts (1998)** Watts, C., 'Britain and the origins of the Great War: why Britain went to war', *Modern History Review*, Vol.10.2, November 1998.

- **Wilkinson (2000)** Wilkinson, R., 'Lord Lansdowne and British foreign policy 1900-17', *History Today*, March 2000.

- **Winks (1999)** Winks, R.W. (ed.), *The Oxford History of the British Empire: Historiography*, Oxford University Press, 1999.

UNIT 8 — The impact of the First World War

Timeline - The impact of the First World War

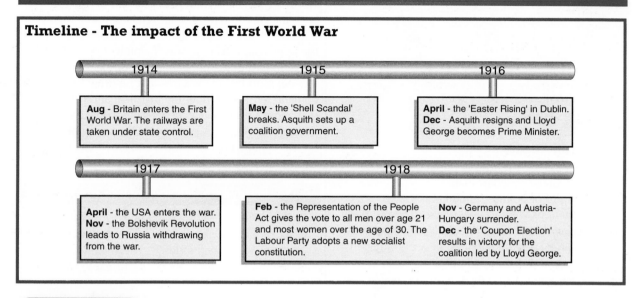

1914

Aug - Britain enters the First World War. The railways are taken under state control.

1915

May - the 'Shell Scandal' breaks. Asquith sets up a coalition government.

1916

April - the 'Easter Rising' in Dublin.
Dec - Asquith resigns and Lloyd George becomes Prime Minister.

1917

April - the USA enters the war.
Nov - the Bolshevik Revolution leads to Russia withdrawing from the war.

1918

Feb - the Representation of the People Act gives the vote to all men over age 21 and most women over the age of 30. The Labour Party adopts a new socialist constitution.

Nov - Germany and Austria-Hungary surrender.
Dec - the 'Coupon Election' results in victory for the coalition led by Lloyd George.

Introduction

Some historians have described Britain's experience in the First World War as its first taste of 'total war' - war in which entire societies are mobilised against one another, with the home front becoming just as important as the fighting front. So, while, it has been estimated, around 6 million British people had direct experience of trench warfare during the First World War, almost the whole of the remaining population became involved in the war effort in some way. This meant change and upheaval in the short term at least. Indeed, most historians agree that the First World War placed unprecedented strains on Britain's political, economic and social structures. There is, however, a debate about the nature and extent of change produced by the war. This debate centres on whether the war is seen as the cause of fundamental change or whether, alternatively, it is seen as a catalyst which accelerated existing political, social and economic trends. Some historians see the First World War as a turning point, arguing that participation in the war fundamentally changed Britain and its relations with the outside world. The war, it is argued, was responsible for the decline of the Liberal Party and the rise of Labour. The war disrupted Britain's economy, ensuring that it went into long-term decline. The war produced a more equal and more democratic society. The war won the vote for women. Other historians, however, argue that all these changes would have taken place eventually even if Britain had not participated in the war. The war may have speeded up change, but it did not shape the direction in which change was heading. This unit examines the two sides of this debate.

UNIT SUMMARY

Part 1 examines the political impact of the war. It considers how the war affected the main political parties and the significance of the Coupon Election of 1918.

Part 2 looks at the ways in which the war affected economic thinking, how the war was financed and the economic consequences of participating in the war.

Part 3 focuses on the way in which the war affected British society. How has the social impact of the war been explained? How did the war affect the class structure and people's attitudes? How did it affect the role and status of women?

1 The political impact of the First World War

Key questions

1. How did the war affect each of the main parties?
2. What was the significance of the 'Coupon Election' of 1918?

1.1 How did the war affect each of the main parties?

The overall impact

In his analysis of the domestic impact of the First World War, Blake observes that:

'In the world of politics, remarkable transformations were to take place...The old party divisions were to blur and fade. New alignments were to arise, new allegiances, new enmities. In this strange and unmapped political territory, every step was fraught with difficulty and peril. The old landmarks had vanished, the familiar scene had disappeared. In its place was a new and unknown landscape, full of false traps for the imprudent and snares for the unwary.' (Blake 1955, p.255)

The process of political change which took place during the First World War had two distinct strands. On the one hand, there was the impact of the war on the fortunes of political parties - an impact which was initially masked by the wave of patriotism and all-party support for the Liberal government's declaration of war in August 1914. On the other hand, there were broader changes in relation to the nature and distribution of political power and political relationships. The increasingly interventionist role played by the state during the war and the new role played by women, for example, both affected the nature and distribution of political power and political relationships. Part 1 deals with the impact of the war on political parties. The broader political changes are examined in Part 2 and Part 3.

A. The Liberal Party

The historian Malcolm Smith (1990 p.59) argues that 'the most obvious political casualty of the test presented by the Great War was the Liberal Party'. Whether or not the decline of the Liberal Party had begun before war broke out is a matter of debate. This debate is discussed in detail in Unit 6, Part 6.

In terms of developments during the war itself, historians have focused on the split within the parliamentary party which occurred following Herbert Asquith's resignation in December 1916 and his replacement as Prime Minister by David Lloyd George.

The crisis of May 1915

Until May 1915, Asquith attempted to conduct the war through the existing structures of party government. The only new appointment to the Cabinet was that of Lord Kitchener as Secretary of State for War. But, despite his reputation as a highly effective imperial campaigner in the Sudan and during the Boer War, Kitchener was 'painfully unprepared for the problems of trench warfare' (Simpson 1986, p.86). Indeed, most historians agree that he struggled to come to terms with both the logistical and political demands of his post. Kitchener's inadequacies destabilised Asquith's position. In the spring of 1915, criticism in the press mounted and Lloyd George clashed with Kitchener (see Box 8.1).

BOX 8.1 Lloyd George and 'total war'

By the spring of 1915, nearly one-third of the employed male labour force had enlisted or joined a war-related industry. This meant that the economy could not work as usual. There were two main options - limit the size of the army or adapt to the new conditions. On 22 February 1915, Lloyd George circulated a memorandum to his Cabinet colleagues. In it, he suggested that, for victory to be ensured, both the army and munitions production would have to expand massively. Munitions were the key, he argued. He wanted to reorganise factories so that all the engineering works in the country were turned to the production of war material. If this could be done, he said, Britain would then be able to equip not only its own huge army but also the armies of Britain's allies. In effect, Lloyd George was arguing for a total commitment to victory from all of society, under the direction of the government. This was his message throughout the war and he believed that he was the man to put the plan into practice. In the spring of 1915, however, he clashed with Kitchener. Kitchener wanted to concentrate production of munitions on existing War Office contracts. Lloyd George, on the other hand, wanted a revolutionary increase in production and that could only be done by developing new sources of supply. The battle dragged on through April and May, becoming increasingly personal and fraught. *Adapted from Packer 1998.*

Then, on 14 May 1915, the so-called 'Shell Scandal' broke when an article was published in the *Times* claiming that British troops were unable to make headway because they were being left short of shells to fire at the enemy. Colonel Repington, the newspaper's war correspondent, wrote:

'We had not sufficient high explosives to lower the enemy's parapets to the ground...The want of an unlimited supply of high explosives was a fatal bar to our success.' (*Times*, 14 May 1915)

The next day, news came of the resignation of Admiral Sir John Fisher, the First Sea Lord, who had fallen out with Winston Churchill, the First Lord of the Admiralty, over the Gallipoli campaign:

'The "shell scandal" and Fisher's resignation precipitated a political crisis which, within a few days, led to an establishment of a coalition government, and thus the demise of England's "last Liberal government".' (Adelman 1981, p.13)

The Asquith coalition

As a result of the formation of the coalition government, Bonar Law became Colonial Secretary, Balfour (a senior Conservative) replaced Churchill at the Admiralty and Lloyd George took over as head of the new Ministry of Munitions. Packer argues that the formation of the coalition opened the way to the split of December 1916:

'There is no need to see in this a deeply laid plot. But a coalition...opened up a new political situation. It was unlikely Lloyd George would ever have succeeded Asquith as Liberal Leader. He was popular in the party at large but he had too many personal enemies in the Cabinet...But, war changed all this. Once the government was a coalition, it was no longer necessary to be Liberal Leader to become Prime Minister.' (Packer 1998, p.47)

During the period May 1915 to December 1916, Lloyd George used his new position as Munitions Minister to promote himself as an alternative War Leader. His position was strengthened in July 1916 when, following the death of Kitchener on a mission to Russia, he took over as Minister for War. During this period, he focused on two issues - the need for conscription (compulsory military service) and the creation of a smaller War Cabinet (which, he claimed, would be more efficient and effective).

Conscription

Lloyd George's campaign to introduce conscription intensified existing tensions within the Liberal Party. Indeed, Bourne argues that:

'The issue which began the unravelling of [Asquith's] authority was that of conscription...Conscription was inherently contentious [controversial], especially for the Liberals, 30 of whom voted against the establishment of a National Register of Manpower in the first parliamentary division [vote] on 5 July 1915.' (Bourne 1989, p.121)

Asquith's response to Lloyd George's demand for conscription was to suggest a compromise - the 'Derby Scheme' of October 1915 - which would allow the adult male population to be classified by age, marital status and occupation as the first step on the road to conscription. Marwick describes this as:

'[A] shot-gun wedding between the fair maid of Liberal idealism and the ogre of Tory militarism.'

(Marwick 1991, p.80)

But Asquith's attempt to reconcile his party's historical commitment to individual freedom with the demands of total war ended in failure. By December 1915, recruitment had fallen to 55,000 per month (450,000 had joined up in September 1914). Despite Asquith's continued reluctance, conscription was introduced in January 1916. To add to Asquith's discomfort, John Simon, the Home Secretary, resigned over the issue.

A small War Cabinet

Lloyd George's call for a small War Cabinet intensified after he succeeded Kitchener at the War Office. It was this issue which triggered the end of the Asquith coalition and his own promotion to the position of Prime Minister. The political intrigue and double-dealing which occurred in the first week of December 1916 are explored in Box 8.2.

BOX 8.2 The end of the Asquith coalition

Interpretation

On 1 December, Lloyd George suggested the formation of a small War Cabinet with himself as Chair and Bonar Law and Edward Carson (the Ulster Unionist - see Unit 6, Section 4.2) as members. Asquith would remain Prime Minister but not take part in the War Cabinet. Lloyd George had already taken the precaution of securing Bonar Law's approval for this suggestion in advance. Asquith was, at first, hostile. But, on 3 December, he agreed to the plan once Conservative resignations had been threatened. But the *Times* published an article on 4 December which discussed the proposal in terms which put Asquith in a bad light. This caused him to change his mind. He would not 'be relegated to a position of an irresponsible spectator of the war'. Asquith's rejection of the plan led to the resignation of, first, Lloyd George, second, Conservative ministers and, finally, Asquith (on 5 December). A conference of Party Leaders attended by Asquith, Bonar Law, Lloyd George, Henderson (Labour Leader) and Balfour (a senior Conservative) took place at Buckingham Palace on 6 December. The position of Prime Minister was offered to Bonar Law who said that he would accept only if Asquith agreed to serve under him. Asquith refused to do this. It then emerged that Conservative ministers were prepared to serve under Lloyd George. On 7 December George V reluctantly invited him to be Prime Minister. With perhaps equal misgivings, Lloyd George accepted. The other Liberal ministers resigned with Asquith. Lloyd George secured the support of the Conservatives, Labour and about 100 Liberal MPs. The other Liberal MPs remained loyal to Asquith. The split within the Liberal Party, therefore, was clearly drawn.

Adapted from Simpson 1986.

The significance of the split

Lee argues that the new Lloyd George coalition shaped the direction of British politics:

'When Lloyd George established himself in power in 1916, he proved that the war could be run by effective leadership without a party base. Hence, the coalition government, combined with the personal appeal and effectiveness of Lloyd George, cancelled out the advantages which the war seemed to hold to the Liberals in 1914.' (Lee 1996, p.30)

Bourne describes Lloyd George's rise to the premiership as a 'watershed in British politics':

'The formation of the Lloyd George coalition was not just a personal defeat for Asquith. It was also a defeat for the Liberal Party which was split between the supporters of Lloyd George and Asquith.' (Bourne 1989, p.127)

While Lloyd George had often been accused of being the 'villain' in the process, Pugh (1988) argues that Lloyd George did not plot to overthrow Asquith. He argues that Asquith's inflexibility and his refusal to cooperate with Bonar Law were the key factors. The subsequent development of the Lloyd George coalition and the Coupon Election of 1918 are discussed in Section 1.2 below.

B. The Conservative Party

In considering the impact of the war on Conservative fortunes, it is important to distinguish between the impact in the short term and that in the long term. In the short term, some historians regard the outbreak of war as a setback in a process of steady recovery since the three election defeats in 1906 and 1910. In view of the range of problems facing the Liberal government in the period 1911-14 (see Unit 6), a Conservative victory in a general election held in 1915 was a possibility. In this light, the war and Lloyd George's emergence as a 'presidential' Prime Minister can be said to have set back the party's re-emergence for another decade, ensuring that the period 1906-22 became the longest period without a Conservative government in modern British history.

On the other hand, the period between 1915 and the outbreak of the Second World War could be described as a period of Conservative ascendancy. Conservative ministers served in coalition governments between 1915 and 1922 and between 1931 and 1935. In addition, the Conservatives governed by themselves between 1922 and 1924, from 1924 to 1929 and from 1935 to 1939. In a sense, the Conservatives were only out of power, therefore, during the nine months when the first minority Labour government served in 1924 and during the two years when the second minority Labour government served in 1929 to 1931. This suggests that, while the war can be described as a setback in the short term, the underlying changes and trends produced by the conflict had the long-term effect of benefiting the party.

Why did the Conservatives gain in the long term?

A number of reasons have been suggested for the revival of Conservative fortunes after the war. First, it has been argued that, in general terms, the Conservatives' political philosophy was better able to respond to the key issues which emerged during the conflict:

'On almost every issue that came up, Conservative tradition and ideology was better suited than Liberal to meet the needs of the hour. Conscription, "defence of the realm", Ireland, indeed all the necessities of a prolonged war, tended to create doubts and divisions in the Liberals. After all, they were the party of liberty, and liberty is the first casualty of war. They were the party of moral conscience - and that is another casualty of war...It was the Conservatives who, before the war, had been anti-German, who had pressed for conscription, for greater armaments, for a tougher foreign policy.' (Blake 1985, pp.195-96)

Second, while the Conservatives remained united, the Liberals divided:

'The suspension of general elections allowed the Liberals to disintegrate into factions rather than regroup as an opposition to a possible Conservative government in 1915.' (Lee 1996, p.31)

Third, the wartime coalition gave the Conservatives vital ministerial experience. And fourth, Adelman points out that, in November 1916, Bonar Law was having difficulty retaining the support of his backbenchers:

'On 8 November, on a minor issue relating to the sale of confiscated enemy property in Nigeria, Sir Edward Carson led 64 Conservatives into the opposition lobby - only 71 voted with their Leader! This was a clear attack on Bonar Law for sustaining Asquith's war policy.' (Adelman 1981, p.18)

By helping to engineer Asquith's downfall, Bonar Law restored his credibility with his party and he ensured that the new government, though led by a Liberal, was dominated by Conservatives. This ensured that the Conservatives could claim credit for victory when it finally came.

C. The Labour Party

Just as there is a debate about the impact of the war on the fortunes of the Liberal Party, so too there is a debate about the impact of the war on the fortunes of the Labour Party. Some historians argue that Labour's strength was growing before war broke out and that the party was on course to replace the Liberal Party as one of the two main parties. Others, however, argue that Labour remained very much a third party at the time war broke out and that it was the war which provided a turning point in the party's fortunes. This debate is examined in detail in Unit 5, Section 3.1.

It should be noted that, while the war did not

harm (and probably enhanced) Labour's prospects in the long term, it initially served to emphasise divisions within the party. When war broke out, Ramsay MacDonald resigned as Chairman of the Parliamentary Labour Party and was joined in opposition to the war by Philip Snowden and a small group of largely Independent Labour Party (ILP) MPs. The majority of party members, however, supported the war and MacDonald and his supporters became a target of abuse from many trade unions and from the popular press. Bourne notes that:

'[MacDonald] spent the remainder of the war as the target for much vitriolic [fierce] abuse, not least from the country's trade unionists, but his courage in the face of this helped later to establish a reputation for integrity of purpose and nobility of character which brought him to national leadership within a decade.' (Bourne 1989, p.107)

MacDonald was replaced as Chairman of the Parliamentary Labour Party by Arthur Henderson. Henderson made no attempt to expel those Labour members who were against the war. The reasons why the split within the party in 1914 did not harm its prospects are examined in Box 8.3.

The 1918 constitution

Adelman argues that Arthur Henderson's resignation from government in August 1917 allowed him to concentrate on the reorganisation of the Labour Party:

'Under the inspiration of Henderson, the Labour Party began to develop a detailed programme for a "just peace", a programme in which Henderson worked closely with [Ramsay] MacDonald and Sidney Webb, and received the tacit [silent] support of the TUC.' (Adelman 1986, p.49)

One of the outcomes of this work was a new constitution for the Labour Party in 1918. According to Pelling:

'[Henderson's] object was to weld the socialist and trade union elements firmly together and to provide for the admission to full membership of people who were not trade unionists - middle-class people for instance, and also women, who were shortly to get the vote.' (Pelling 1991, p.43)

The terms of the new constitution

The main terms of the new draft constitution were:
- local Labour parties were opened to individual membership (until 1918, party membership only came via membership of an affiliated group)
- the composition of the National Executive Committee (NEC) was changed (the number of members went up to 20 - 11 from unions and socialist societies, five from local parties, four women and a Treasurer)
- the NEC was to be elected by the annual conference
- affiliated trade unions were to pay increased fees

BOX 8.3 The Labour Party and World War I

The Labour Party managed to avoid the lasting split which occurred in parallel socialist groups in France and Germany for the following reasons. First, those who opposed the war, for the most part did not campaign against it. Instead, they campaigned for measures to prevent future wars and almost all the party could agree with the safeguards they suggested. Second, patriots and critics alike were united in demanding that the economic welfare of the working class should be defended and protected even during the national emergency. They were able to cooperate amicably on bodies like the Emergency Workers' National Committee which was created to press for adequate government protection for soldiers' families, the restraint of food prices, rent control and so on. Third, even those who supported the war effort were often critical of the way in which the government conducted it. Though the Parliamentary Labour Party was represented in government in May 1915, and in the Cabinet after Lloyd George came to power in December 1916, it was never wholly at ease in the coalition. In August 1917, Henderson resigned from the Cabinet when Labour leaders were refused permission to attend an international socialist conference to discuss peace conditions. By the time Henderson resigned, he and his colleagues were keen to encourage party unity to take advantage of Labour's rising electoral prospects. There was a big growth of party membership in the war and the Representation of the People Act of February 1918 (see Box 8.8 on page 288) trebled the electorate. A majority of new voters were working class and, therefore, within Labour's reach. The split within the Liberal Party added further encouragement.
Adapted from Phillips 1992.

- a commitment to socialism was made in Clause IV.

These terms were accepted at the annual party conference held in February 1918 with just one significant change - the number on the NEC from unions and socialist societies was raised to 13.

Clause IV

A great deal of historical debate has focused on the adoption of Clause IV, the clause in the constitution which committed the Labour Party to a socialist programme. Clause IV read as follows:

'The Labour Party's object is...to secure for the workers by hand or by brain the full fruits of their industry and the most equitable distribution thereof that may be possible upon the basis of common ownership of the means of production, distribution and exchange, and the best obtainable

system of popular administration and control of each industry or service.' (Labour Party 1993)
The clause was controversial because it committed the Labour Party to 'common ownership' - the nationalisation (state ownership) of industry and services. If this programme was put in practice, it could mean an end to the free-market economy and, possibly, the abolition of private ownership. It should be noted, however, that what, in practical terms, was proposed is vague.

The debate over Clause IV

Adelman argues that Clause IV had two main aims. First, it was a response to the Russian Revolution of November 1917. It was designed as an alternative to the type of socialism being experimented with in Bolshevik Russia. And second, it was designed to provide a practical alternative to Liberalism:

'The adoption of the new constitution gave Labour both a modernised organisation and a definite socialist ideology (through the famous Clause IV) with which to oppose the Liberal Party, now divided and weakened. In this way, Labour could capture the new mass electorate created by the Reform Act of 1918.' (Adelman 1986, p.51)

McKibbin (1974), however, argues that Clause IV was out of line with the rest of the constitution and should not be interpreted as a serious commitment to socialism. Rather it was - to use Laybourn's phrase (1997, p.71) - 'a sop to the professional middle class who had found socialism through the wartime experience'. Laybourn himself finds McKibbin's arguments unconvincing. He argues that:

'It was the vagueness of Clause Four which permitted it to act as a unifying force within the Labour Party. The various Labour and socialist organisations which [affiliated] to the Labour Party exhibited widely different views about socialism and war...[Clause IV] was detailed enough to distinguish Labour men from the Liberal Party but sufficiently vague to avoid serious conflict over the variety of socialist programmes on offer.' (Laybourn 1997, p.72).

Sidney Webb's programme

In June 1918, a second party conference was held at which a policy document written by Sidney Webb, one of the authors of the constitution, was adopted. This document laid out a programme which had four main elements:

- a 'National Minimum' - a policy of full employment with a minimum wage and minimum standard of working conditions
- democratic control of industry (though the details were left vague)
- financial reform - heavy taxes on big incomes to fund social services
- surplus wealth to be used for the common good.

Pelling argues that the adoption of Webb's policy document was extremely important:

'[This] was of great importance because it formed the basis of Labour Party policy for over 30 years - in fact, until the general election of 1950.' (Pelling 1991, p.44)

1.2 What was the significance of the 'Coupon Election' of 1918?

Non-party government

The coalition formed by Lloyd George in December 1916 has been described by some historians as a turning point in modern British politics because it led to a four year post-war experiment in non-party government. These historians believe that there was a genuine attempt to 'break the mould' of politics by governing as a 'Centre Alliance'. Others, however, have been more cynical in their interpretation of the motives behind the continuing cooperation between Lloyd George's Liberal supporters and the Conservatives at the end of the war and in the so-called 'Coupon Election' of December 1918. They suggest that talk of a 'Centre Alliance' only served to mask the more limited aim of neutralising the growing threat posed by Labour. What really occurred in December 1918, they argue, was a decisive victory for the Conservatives, the full extent of which was disguised by Lloyd George's continuation as Prime Minister.

Bourne points out that Lloyd George's reliance on the Conservatives (or Unionists, as they were often called at the time) was heavy from the start:

'Apart from Lloyd George himself, the only Liberal to obtain a key post was Addison, rewarded with the Ministry of Munitions. All the other important ministries...were held by Unionists. Lloyd George was the Prime Minister, but he led no political party...His continuance in office depended on the goodwill of his Unionist colleagues and the votes of their supporters...Lloyd George's position was, therefore, one of limited independence and room for manoeuvre. The consequences of this dominated the politics of the next two years - and beyond.' (Bourne 1989, p.127)

The Maurice debate

From December 1916, Lloyd George organised the war effort through a small War Cabinet made up of himself, the Labour Leader, Arthur Henderson, and the Conservatives Bonar Law, Lord Curzon and Lord Milner. Most historians accept that this arrangement increased the efficiency and effectiveness of decision making. But, in May 1918, Lloyd George was criticised in the press by the recently retired Director of Military Operations, General Sir Frederick D. Maurice, for misleading the House of Commons about the number of troops in France. Maurice claimed that there were more there in January 1918 than 12 months previously, even though Lloyd George had promised troops would be held in

Britain where they would not be lost in useless offensives. Asquith seized on Maurice's allegations and called for a select committee to investigate the matter. In a vote which followed, 98 Liberal MPs supported the call for an inquiry into the Prime Minister's conduct. Pearce and Stewart argue that:

'The fiction of Liberal unity had been maintained despite the Lloyd George-Asquith personality struggle. There had, in effect, been no real opposition to government. The Maurice debate on 9 May 1918 ended this. Ninety-eight Liberals voted against the Prime Minister and with Asquith. Two separate organisations now emerged, first at Westminster with their own whips, and later in the constituencies. The Maurice debate had established battle lines.' (Pearce & Stewart 1992, p.218)

Simpson (1986, p.89) points out that the Maurice debate revealed just how dependent Lloyd George was on his Conservative supporters.

The Progressive Centre Alliance

It was in the immediate aftermath of the Maurice debate - and the growing threat of Communist revolution in Europe - that Lloyd George and the Conservatives discussed the possibility of cooperating after the war in a 'Progressive Centre Alliance' (Smith 1990, p.86). By October 1918, these discussions had formed the basis of the 'coupon' arrangement (the term 'coupon' was a reference to ration coupons and was coined by Asquith in an attempt to discredit the arrangement). Under this arrangement, Lloyd George and Bonar Law approved Conservative and Liberal candidates to fight the forthcoming general election. Candidates who gained this approval became, in effect, coalition candidates (the candidates were selected on the basis of their voting record since December 1916). The 'coupon' was, in fact, a letter signed by Lloyd George and Bonar Law confirming that the individual was a genuine coalition candidate. Those 'couponed' in this way would not be opposed by a Conservative or Lloyd George Liberal. While 150 Liberals were 'couponed', the number of Conservatives was over 300. The motives behind this arrangement are considered in Box 8.4.

The Coupon Election

The result of the Coupon Election was a triumph for the coalition (see Activity 8.1, Item 1). In one sense, the coalition's victory did appear to have significantly redrawn Britain's political map:

'Coalition Liberals in 1918 proved to be especially strong in areas where Labour might have hoped to make real inroads - in the industrial areas of the North and North-East - as well as winning over traditional Liberal strongholds in agricultural seats in Wales, Scotland and East Anglia. Lloyd George may have burned his political bridges - the Asquithean Liberals had been effectively smashed

BOX 8.4 | Motivations behind the coupon arrangement

Interpretation

(i) The Conservatives agreed to the arrangement partly out of political calculation, partly out of genuine admiration for Lloyd George's leadership qualities and partly out of a belief that Lloyd George was the only man who could unite the forces of the right against the threat from Bolshevism.
Adapted from Simpson 1986.

(ii) As socialist revolution spread across Europe in the last months of the war, many Conservatives thought that the post-war world would be hostile to Conservatism. They realised that the 1918 election would be the first to be held under universal male suffrage and that the Labour Party's position was strong. By remaining with Lloyd George, they might be able to tempt Liberal votes to the coalition. If Asquith's Liberals could be crushed, a combination of the right and centre in British politics stood a good chance of seeing off socialism. Lloyd George was interested in such an approach. His work with Conservatives during the war had dented his ingrained distaste of them. Also, his attempt to undercut Labour's appeal, especially the promise to build 'homes fit for heroes to live in', needed framing in an anti-socialist context - something the Conservatives could provide better than the party to which he belonged but had no immediate prospect of leading.
Adapted from Smith 1990.

- but he also appeared to have redrawn the political map of Britain at a stroke, leaving himself in control.' (Smith 1990, p.87)

The long-term significance of the Coupon Election

Despite the coalition's apparent success, however, historians have seriously questioned its longer-term significance as an experiment in genuine alliance politics:

'Lloyd George was unable to turn the alliance of convenience of 1918 into a reliable political base. It was, after all, an alliance of opposites, united only in the belief that it was necessary to keep Labour out...By polling day, the coalitionists were campaigning almost entirely on the need to "squeeze Germany until the pips squeaked". Electorally, this may have been successful, for it was an issue on which Labour could easily be made to look very vulnerable, given their attitude towards the war as a whole. But, it also meant that the Conservatives could be allowed to dominate the new Parliament to an extent that threatened the whole idea of a Progressive Centre Alliance.'

(Smith 1990, pp.87-88)

In February-March 1920, there was an attempt to fuse the two elements into a single party and 95 Conservative backbenchers petitioned Lloyd George and Bonar Law, urging them to put the alliance onto a permanent footing. But, the attempt failed and the support for a permanent alliance never re-emerged:

'The alliance with Lloyd George came near to crystallising into permanency. In 1920, there was a serious movement towards "fusion", as it was called, between the National (ie coalition) Liberals and the Conservatives. It came to a head in March. Bonar Law was not enthusiastic, but he would not have blocked it. Lloyd George would have been the beneficiary. It would have given him a real base, a party machine and party funds...But, he ran into opposition from some of the coalition Liberal members of the Cabinet and he did not push the matter very hard. It was a fateful decision, or lack of decision. The chance did not recur.' (Blake 1985, pp.197-98)

The coalition finally collapsed in October 1922 when the Conservatives withdrew their support for Lloyd George. In light of this outcome, Morgan (1979, p.42) has concluded that if the Coupon Election 'embodied anything, it was a mandate for peace, reconstruction and reform' rather than any fundamental party political realignment.

MAIN POINTS - Part 1

- The resignation of Fisher and the Shell Scandal in May 1915 led to the formation of a coalition government. Political intrigue then led to Lloyd George replacing Asquith as Prime Minister in December 1916. Not all historians agree that Lloyd George was the 'villain'.
- In the short term, the outbreak of war prevented a likely Conservative general election victory. In the long term, however, it prepared the way for Conservative domination of the inter-war period.
- While the war did not harm (and probably enhanced) Labour's prospects in the long term, it initially served to emphasise divisions within the party. In 1918, Labour adopted a new constitution which included a controversial commitment to common ownership.

- Some historians argue that the Lloyd George coalition was significant because it led to a four year post-war experiment in non-party government. Others suggest that the main aim was to neutralise the growing threat posed by Labour. The Coupon Election, they claim, was really a decisive victory for the Conservatives, but this was disguised by Lloyd George's continuation as Prime Minister.
- The 'Coupon Election' is named after the letters ('coupons') signed by Lloyd George and Bonar Law which confirmed that an individual was a genuine coalition candidate. Those candidates with the coupon were not opposed by any other coalition candidates.

Activity 8.1 The Coupon Election

ITEM 1 General election results 1910-22

	Conservative & Liberal Unionists	Lloyd George Liberals	Official Liberals	Labour Party	Irish Nationalists	Sinn Fein	Others
1910 (Dec) **%**	46.6	44.2 [1]		6.4	2.5	-	0.3
SEATS	271	272		42	84	-	1
1918 %	47.1 [2]		13.0	20.8	2.2	4.6	12.3
SEATS	473		36	57	7	73	61 [3]
1922 %	38.5	9.9	18.9	29.7	0.4	-	2.6
SEATS	344	53	62	142	3	-	11

BALLOT BOX

NOTES:
1. In December 1910, the Liberal Party was not split and fought the election as a single unit.
2. In the Coupon Election of 1918, coalition candidates were, in the main, from the Conservative and Liberal Parties.
3. The high number of 'others' includes 50 Conservatives who were elected even though they didn't have the 'coupon'.

Adapted from Craig 1989.

ITEM 2 A new voter votes

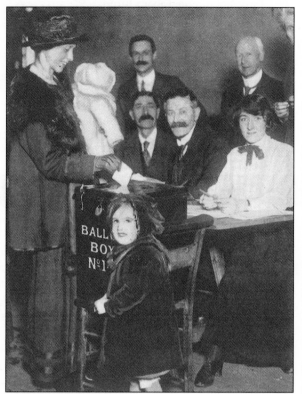

Voting took place on Saturday, 14 December 1918. It was the first time that voting took place in all constituencies at the same time. The result was announced two weeks later after the soldiers' votes had been gathered. In fact, only 2.7 million out of 3.9 million troops received ballot papers. Of these, only one-third voted. The turnout was only 59% of voters, the lowest at a general election in the whole of the 20th century. But, because of the extension of the franchise to all men over 21 and most women over 30 (one of whom is voting in the photo above), the total vote cast was double that of the last general election in 1910.

Adapted from Pearce 1992.

ITEM 3 The Coupon Election (1)

Before the election, in November 1918, Lloyd George offered to make Asquith Lord Chancellor (with the power to appoint two Cabinet ministers and six junior ministers). But, Asquith refused this generous offer. There was now no hope of reuniting the Liberal Party. Lloyd George was, therefore, left with the support of around 150 Liberal MPs and the Conservatives (Labour refused to remain in the coalition). The Conservatives were willing to support Lloyd George because they had not won a general election since 1902 and had, quite simply, lost confidence in themselves. The Coupon Election has gone down in history as a disreputable and jingoistic affair. Overall, however, the campaign was more low-key and sober than is generally realised. The *Times* called the election 'the most orderly campaign of our time'. Lloyd George dominated the campaign. A Liberal colleague wrote to Lloyd George: 'Somebody said to me the other day that the only speeches in the papers were your speeches, that the only thing the country listened to was what you said'. Some historians claim that the election was essentially a referendum in support of Lloyd George. In fact, had this been the case, he would have lost since more votes were cast against the coalition than for it. But, the British electoral system ensured that the coalition won an overwhelming majority of seats. The coupon was remarkably effective - 88% of those endorsed (and, therefore, unopposed by other coalition groups) were elected. Labour won almost a quarter of the votes but only 9% of seats. The two wings of the Liberal Party won similar numbers of votes but massively different numbers of seats. The practical result was a large overall majority for the coalition - made larger by the fact that Sinn Fein MPs refused to take their seats. Asquith lost his seat (he regained a seat at a by-election in February 1920) and so did three leading Labour figures - Arthur Henderson, Ramsay MacDonald and Philip Snowden. What was most noteworthy about the election result was the swing to the right.

Adapted from Pearce 1992 and Adelman 1981

ITEM 4 The Coupon Election (2)

If the Liberals had been united and had had the prestige of Lloyd George on their side, they would very possibly still have lost the 1918 general election, but they would probably have emerged as an opposition of a respectable size, in no danger of being taken over by the Labour Party. But, if Lloyd George and the Conservatives were on the same side, there was very little hope for any Liberal candidate who did not have the support of the 'coupon' - the letter signed by Lloyd George and Bonar Law which stated that a candidate was a good and loyal servant of the coalition. If Lloyd George's influence was going to be thrown against his old party, the coupon was the only way that a Liberal remnant could be preserved. The course of the election campaign ran steadily downhill. During the campaign Lloyd George never fully committed himself to the policy of hanging the Kaiser and making Germany pay (a policy supported by most coalition candidates), but he never made his reservations clear. The ordinary voter was pleased to hear that Germany was going to have to pay for the war, though this was because most voters believed Germany should be punished. Less attention was paid to the idea that the social benefits promised by the slogan 'a land fit for heroes' would have to be paid for by extra taxation. Lloyd George did not use his position and prestige to warn the electorate that things might not be so easy. A general election is a great opportunity for political education and a party which is likely to win a big majority has a particular responsibility to avoid being swept along by uninformed popular feeling. The results of the election are even more devastating to the opposition than the figures suggest. Not a single Liberal ex-minister was re-elected and the most talented Labour leaders were also defeated.

Adapted from Lloyd 1993

Questions

1. a) Using Items 1-4 and your own knowledge, describe the impact of the First World War on Britain's political parties.
   b) Give arguments for and against the view that the war resulted in fundamental changes.
2. a) Using Items 1 and 2, explain how the general election in 1918 differed from previous general elections.
   b) How did the different circumstances in 1918 affect (i) the Liberal Party (ii) the Conservative Party and (iii) the Labour Party?
3. a) What do Items 3 and 4 tell us about (i) the nature of the Coupon Election and (ii) the position of Lloyd George in 1918?
   b) Assess the conduct of Lloyd George in the period between the end of the war and the Coupon Election.
   c) In terms of the development of party politics, how significant was the Coupon Election?

2 The economic impact of the First World War

Key questions

1. What was the impact of the war on established economic thinking?

2. How was the war financed?

3. What were the wider economic consequences of the war?

2.1 What was the impact of the war on established economic thinking?

The economic problem

According to Dewey, the economic problem which developed when war broke out was as follows:

'From the economic point of view, the essential problem was to move the necessary personnel and military supplies into the Armed Forces as quickly and efficiently as possible. This, however, would cause shortages in the supply of civilian goods and services. This, in turn, would cause inflation.' (Dewey 1997, p.23)

Dewey argues that the government took little action to deal with this problem in the early months of the war. The result was rapidly rising inflation and shortages. Before long, the demands on the economy were so severe that the government could no longer rely on the free market. Instead, it became necessary for the state to intervene:

'The First World War made unprecedented demands on the economy...The laws of supply and demand, while by no means in suspense, could be relied upon neither to mobilise the nation's resources nor to secure the equitable distribution of goods and services. A system of controls slowly evolved whereby the state directed more and more of the nation's economic activities.' (Peden 1985, p.36)

Obstacles to state intervention

When war broke out, it was generally accepted that the government should leave people alone, as far as possible, to get on with their own lives as they saw fit. Government employed a small fraction of the number of people it employs today and government expenditure was a small proportion of the national income. The idea that the state should take over the running of industries or services was dismissed out of hand by all but a small number of socialists. Reasons for this included:

- the tradition of economic thought that had been dominated since the early 19th century by a belief in a laissez-faire approach (see Unit 1, page 3)
- the fact that private enterprise dominated the market-based economy
- an emphasis on the rights of the individual - rights which were deeply embodied in common law and defended by an independent judiciary
- the abandonment of protectionism in 1846 and the subsequent commitment by all governments to free-trade principles.

Although, as Peden points out, the war did eventually result in a marked - and essential - extension in the economic role played by the state, this was a slow process. At first, the government hoped to be able to carry on as normal:

'"War", declared Trotsky, "is the locomotive of history". In August 1914, the British government set the signals at red [ie "stop"]. Its aim was "business as usual"...English politics were about bread and butter issues. The state was almost invisible by continental standards...The idea of an omnipotent [all-powerful] state - even a beneficent [kind] one - found no favour.' (Bourne 1989, p.191)

Developments before 1914

Some historians have made a link between New Liberal ideas which emerged before 1914 (see Unit 6, Section 2.1) and the development of government economic policy during the First World War. Bourne, for example, points out that there is good evidence to show that government intervention increased significantly under the pre-war Liberal government.

He points out that:

- the introduction of a national insurance scheme and old age pensions (see Unit 6, Section 2.2) increased the role of the state
- the number of state employees more than doubled in the period 1900-14
- the government intervened in industrial disputes on several occasions.

But, he argues:

'This "New Liberalism" was a response to the social problems and aspirations generated by a mature urban and industrial economy and a prudent adjustment to the political reality of the "rise of labour". It involved no ideological conversion to social engineering, economic planning and the benefits of a powerful state either on the part of government or on the part of the masses who benefited from the fruits of reform. British wartime experience followed the same course. The advance of state control between 1914 and 1918 was cautious, pragmatic, limited and, above all, temporary.' (Bourne 1989, p.192)

Because government was reluctant to intervene, the interventionist measures that were taken tended to be piecemeal reactions to specific problems:

'The extension of government control was only a pragmatic response to the unforeseen stresses on the economy.' (Milward 1984, p.20)

Munitions

It was noted in Box 8.1 on page 272 above that the rapid mobilisation of volunteers in the first nine months of the war was a major cause of concern for the government. The difficulty of supplying these troops with armaments culminated, in May 1915, in the 'Shell Scandal' and Asquith's decision to set up a Ministry of Munitions. The main problem before May 1915 was as follows:

'The War Office was distributing contracts to some 2,500-3,000 companies in Britain and seeking suppliers in North America. But, both in Britain and overseas, shortages of labour (partly due to recruiting), delays in machinery deliveries and trade union restrictions were seriously impeding production. Bottlenecks in production appeared as soon as the war began. Government factories such as the Royal Arsenals could not meet the demand, and neither could private manufacturers. Deficiencies in the War Office system of tendering made things worse; when war broke out, the Army Contracts Department consisted of only 51 officials and clerks.' (Dewey 1997, p.26)

The Ministry of Munitions

The Ministry of Munitions was set up in May 1915, under David Lloyd George, to increase the production of armaments. The Munitions of War Act, passed in July 1915 gave it comprehensive powers - see Box 8.5.

BOX 8.5 | The Munitions of War Act, July 1915

Summary Box

The Munitions of War Act granted the Ministry of Munitions the following powers:

1. Labour
Since 19.5% of male engineering workers had joined the armed forces by June 1915, further loss of personnel was blocked by the introduction of 'exemption badges'. At the same time, trade unions had to accept the principle of 'dilution' - semi-skilled and unskilled workers (men or women) would be allowed to do jobs previously only done by skilled workers. In addition, strike action was prohibited, restrictive practices were abandoned and compulsory arbitration introduced.

2. Profits
Existing munitions factories were identified as 'controlled establishments'. In controlled establishments, profits were limited to their pre-war level plus an excess of one-fifth. In September 1915, 715 munitions factories were identified as controlled establishments. By the end of the war in November 1918, this figure had grown to 20,000.

3. Workplaces
In addition to controlled establishments, 250 new National Shell Factories were built from public funds. This meant that the state became a major employer for the first time.

4. Supply
The Ministry of Munitions directed the purchase, supply and distribution of raw materials and machine goods to the controlled establishments and National Shell Factories.

5. Capital
In order to pay for the expansion of munitions production, £2,000 million of public funds was made available.

Adapted from Milward 1984 and May 1992.

The Ministry of Munitions' impact

The Ministry of Munitions did not just impose state control on the controlled establishments and National Shell Factories. It also increased state control in two further ways. First, the Ministry provides a good example of the so-called 'command spiral' - the idea that increased government intervention in one area of the economy leads to increased intervention in another area or areas. In the case of the Ministry of Munitions, the control of the price of munitions in controlled establishments led to the control of sub-contractors' prices. In effect, therefore, the state ended up exercising control over many more than the 20,000 munitions factories it controlled directly. And second, the standards and practices imposed by the Ministry were increasingly imitated throughout the economy as a whole:

- controlled establishments and National Shell factories set standards of employees' health and welfare which were increasingly adopted by other non-controlled workplaces
- the latest machinery and methods were introduced - for example the use of electricity increased significantly and new Arc furnaces began to replace Bessemer Converters in the steel industry
- mass production techniques of standardisation, simplification and the use of machine tools set examples of best practice
- specialisation and research and development were encouraged, leading to a Department of Scientific and Industrial Research in 1916 (which produced more powerful and efficient weapons)
- modern systems of financial control in the controlled establishments provided models for private companies.

Despite this, however, the long-term significance should not be exaggerated:

'The Ministry of Munitions was...the most obvious of the "extraordinary" demands made by the war, a simply temporary phenomenon, the ideological significance of which was dismantled along with the rest of the state machinery as soon as the demand for weaponry had evaporated.' (Smith 1990, p.60)

Transport

Apart from the production of munitions, transport was the other sector of the economy most immediately and directly affected by the outbreak of war. First the railways and then shipping were brought under government control.

The railways

The use of the rail network to transport troops was central to military thinking in the build-up to war and it is no surprise, therefore, that government intervention was so rapid:

'On 4 August 1914, the railways passed into the control of the government, to be run as a unified system by the Railway Executive Committee, of which the official Chairman was the President of the Board of Trade. The individual railway companies were guaranteed the same level of profits as they had enjoyed in 1913; receipts were pooled and the government, instead of making separate payments for troop movements, from time to time put into the pool the amount by which it fell short of the earnings of 1913.' (Marwick 1991, pp.197-98)

As Bourne points out, the advantages of state control and the rationalisation of train services were 'too great to ignore'. Before the war, there had been 130 companies and many services were duplicated. As a result of the wartime experience:

'There could be no return to wasteful pre-war practices. Nationalisation was resisted, but the Railway Act of 1921 restricted the control and management of the national network to four companies.' (Bourne 1989, p.194)

Shipping

In August 1914, Britain was a world leader in shipping:

'Before the First World War, Britain dominated world shipbuilding, accounting for 58.7% of the world tonnage launched in 1909-13. British registered ships also dominated the world fleet. In 1914, they accounted for 18.9 million (41%) of the world total of 45.5 million tons.' (Dewey 1997, p.92)

There was, therefore, little immediate concern about a shipping shortage when war broke out and the extension of government controls was, initially, minimal. When Lloyd George took over as Prime Minister in December 1916, however, he set up a Ministry of Shipping under John Maclay. In the spring of 1917 a crisis developed as U-boat attacks accounted for the sinking of 3.7 million tons of British shipping:

'By April 1917, one in four ships leaving the British Isles never came home.' (May 1992, p.319)

The government responded to this crisis by adopting the convoy system (battleships travelled with convoys of merchant ships to protect them) and by taking control of the shipping industry:

'Maclay [Minister of Shipping] eased the imports crisis by requisitioning ships for vital imports, coordinating the activities of the docks and the railways and increasing the rate of construction of new merchant ships.' (Packer 1998, p.57)

By the end of the war, most merchant ships had been requisitioned for military use. By then, too, the construction programme was in full swing, though this masked the underlying damage that the war had done to the British shipbuilding industry:

'[Britain's] dominance, already being slowly diminished before 1914, was substantially eroded after 1918. Between 1920 and 1929, Britain accounted for only 44.7% of world output. By 1930, the British fleet, though slightly larger than in 1914, at 20.3 million tons represented only some 30% of the total world fleet of 68 million tons.' (Dewey 1997, p.92)

The reasons for this decline, Dewey argues, were:

- the oversupply of ships at the end of the war meant that there were too many ships to carry the available produce and, as a result, freight rates dropped dramatically
- world trade recovered slowly, with the result that there was less demand for transport
- British shipbuilders were hit by the loss of naval orders
- British shipbuilders were less competitive than shipbuilders abroad
- British ship designs were old-fashioned.

Food production

From the 1870s, Britain had become increasingly reliant on cheap imported food. By 1914, 40% of meat, 80% of grain and fruit, and all sugar was imported. While there was some disruption to supplies before mid-1916, it was only then that serious shortages began to bite. In response, the government took two measures to increase food production:

- the 1917 Cultivation Production Act empowered local Agricultural Committees to force farmers to transform pasture land to arable use
- the 1917 Corn Production Act introduced a minimum wage for agricultural labourers and provided farmers with a guaranteed price for grain.

With respect to food supply, Peden notes:

'Distribution was at first left to the free market.' (Peden 1985, p.38)

The first significant moves towards government control of food distribution were made by the new Lloyd George administration in December 1916 when a Ministry of Food was set up under Lord Davenport. Davenport, a former grocery retailer, resisted demands for food rationing and was replaced in May 1917 by Lord Rhondda. A bread subsidy was introduced in September 1917 (ensuring that the price of bread fell) and, in the autumn, new Food Control Committees began to set up voluntary rationing schemes. National rationing was gradually introduced in 1918 and, eventually, sugar, meat, butter, jam and margarine were rationed. Pope argues that:

'[Rationing] kept prices under control and eliminated shortages, queues and the popular discontent which accompanied them.' (Pope 1991, p.33)

Some historians, however, are critical of the steps taken by the government - see Box 8.6. Rationing continued after the war - for meat until November 1919, for butter until early 1920 and for sugar until November 1920. Following the end of the war, however, government attempts to control farming were relaxed:

'Government showed little interest in the long-term needs of agriculture. Post-war farming returned to the doldrums.' (Bourne 1989, p.195)

Coal

Like shipping - which ensured Britain was supplied with imported goods - coal-mining was essential because coal fuelled Britain's industries and kept the nation warm in winter:

'The industries which were completely indispensable to the nation's survival in time of war were shipping and coal-mining.' (Marwick 1991, p.163)

In 1915, following a serious miners' strike, the government introduced price controls and export

BOX 8.6 Government control and food

Interpretation

Food production was encouraged by giving farmers guaranteed prices, by providing more labour in the form of soldiers, prisoners of war and the Women's Land Army, and by County Committees threatening to force farmers to plough up their grassland for wheat. But, Lloyd George had to be careful not to offend the farming lobby. Farmers had powerful friends in the Tory Party and could not simply be told to take action. As a result, agriculture was persuaded rather than ordered towards greater cereal production. The main problem, however, was food distribution. Many workers were convinced that farmers and retailers were making huge profits out of food shortages and that there was no shortage of luxury goods for the rich. Lloyd George made a mistake in appointing his friend Lord Davenport as Food Controller. As a retailer, he knew all about food distribution, but insisted it be left in the hands of shopkeepers who could operate voluntary schemes. It was only after Davenport was replaced that there were moves towards price control and rationing. This was the reality behind Lloyd George's administration. Rather than fearless new ministers ruthlessly organising the country, the new government was much the same as Asquith's. It lurched from crisis to crisis, only gradually moving towards greater state intervention. All the time, it was held back by party bickering and sectional interests.
Adapted from Packer 1998.

licensing. Then, in 1917, a Coal Controller (a minister in charge of maintaining the coal supply) was appointed by Lloyd George. While mines remained under private ownership, profits were fixed by the Coal Controller at pre-war levels. Bourne argues that the coal industry was, in effect, nationalised, but claims that this had little benefit:

'This produced no lasting benefits. There were no significant technical innovations. Attempts to improve productivity failed. Output declined towards the end of the war. Labour relations remained bitter and strikes were frequent. The wartime legacy of over-capacity and high wages was an explosive combination which finally ignited in [the General Strike of] 1926.' (Bourne 1989, p.194)

The impact of government intervention

By intervening, albeit reluctantly, in the running of many industries and services, the government created new precedents and opened up new possibilities:

'In the first place the precedents had been set, establishing in fact a new measure of tolerance for state intervention...In the second place, ideas which could in pre-war years be laughed off as utopian fantasies, denounced as contrary to economic law or displayed as evidence of the sinister intention of socialism, had been put to work and seen to work.' (Marwick 1991, p.293-94)

Nevertheless, the significance of these moves towards greater state control should not be exaggerated. Once the war was over, the government attempted to return to the approach of the past:

'The degree of state control eventually achieved during the course of the war was striking and impressive. It encompassed all Britain's basic industries. The British people showed a remarkable readiness to accommodate themselves to the fact of this change. This readiness was not, however, extended to the question of principle. State control was not an idea whose time had come, but an exceptional measure for exceptional circumstances, to be abandoned when the world returned to its senses. The power and responsibilities increased, but the nature of the state was not transformed.' (Bourne 1989, p.193)

2.2 How was the war financed?

The overall cost

It was calculated in 1916 that the war was costing the British government £3.85 million per day, or £1,405 million per year. This compared with an immediate pre-war annual expenditure of £29 million on the army and £51.5 million on the navy. Most of the extra expenditure - 70% - was added to the National Debt. This rose from £625 million in 1914 to £7,980 million by the end of the war:

'The result was to create a large burden of debt service which was to haunt Chancellors of the Exchequer throughout the inter-war period.' (Dewey 1997, pp.30-31)

The remaining 30% of money was raised from taxation. Dewey notes:

'The war upset completely the pattern of public finance. Before it, only about one-eighth of the national income was spent by government (central and local combined). With the outbreak of war, it rose rapidly, to account for more than half the national income in the last three years of the war. Even in 1919, more than half the national income was still being spent by the government.' (Dewey 1997, p.28)

Taxation

Taxes can be raised in two ways - either directly or indirectly. Direct taxation is a tax levied directly on an individual or an organisation. Income tax is one form of direct taxation. Everyone earning more than a minimum amount pays a percentage of their earnings to central government in income tax.

Indirect taxation is a tax levied on goods or services. The tax is indirect since it is only paid by those people who buy the goods or use the services which are subject to it. Excise duties - such as the taxes levied on alcoholic drinks and tobacco - are an example of indirect tax. Indirect taxes tend to hit poor people harder than rich people. This is because only some people pay direct taxes - for example, only people above a certain income pay income tax. On the other hand, everybody who buys an alcoholic drink has to pay the same amount of tax - whether they are a millionaire or a pauper.

The tax burden before the war

Before the First World War, most people did not have to pay any income tax:

'Most wage earners were totally exempt from income tax. Salaries between £160 and £500 a year were charged at a rate of 9d [nine pence] in the pound, those above £500 a year at the rate of 1s 3d [one shilling and three pence].' (Bourne 1989, p.191)

Dewey (1997, p.29) notes that, in 1913-14, indirect taxation accounted for a large proportion of the money raised by government. While £88 million was raised in direct taxation (54% of total revenue), £75.3 million was raised from indirect taxation (46% of total revenue). This mainly came from:

- tobacco (£18.3 million)
- duties on spirits (£19.5 million)
- duties on beer (£13.6 million).

The shift during the war

During the war, the burden of taxation moved towards direct taxation, partly because it was difficult to raise indirect taxes too rapidly (people would simply stop buying the goods if tax was raised too rapidly and the result would be that less tax was collected). Most of the extra tax that was raised during the war came from income tax:

'A high proportion of [revenue] came from direct taxation. Income tax rose steadily. By 1918, it stood at 6s [six shillings] in the pound. This was an eightfold increase since 1914. Many workers were required to pay income tax for the first time. The traditional distinction between the taxed and the untaxed, between the "masses" and the "classes", began to blur. The reliance on direct taxation helped to keep down the cost of living for working-class families.' (Bourne 1989, p.205)

Dewey notes that:

'In the financial year 1918-19, direct taxes accounted for 79.5% of total taxation revenue. By then, a large amount of direct taxation (£284 million) was being contributed by taxation of war profits in the form of the Excess Profits Duty (EPD).' (Dewey 1997, pp.29-30)

The EPD was introduced in 1915. It was a tax on all profits which exceeded pre-war levels. It remained a significant source of government revenue until its repeal in 1921.

BOX 8.7 The disruption of trade

While British industry and shipping concentrated on the war, commercial rivals seized what had been British markets - the USA in Latin America, the Japanese in India and East Asia. Japan's share of the China market, for example, rose from 20% in 1913 to 36% in 1929 while Britain's share fell from 16.5% to 9.5% over the same period. The war also stimulated industrialisation in parts of the British Empire - notably India. The extra production from these newly industrialised regions then contributed to the over-capacity in textiles, shipping and steel which underlay the slump of the 1920s. In addition, Britain's loss of 15% of its assets complicated the balance of payments. At the same time, the war converted the USA from a debtor nation to a creditor nation. As a result of its lending in the war, it became a major new player in international finance. A further casualty of the war was the old 'gold standard' economy in which most major currencies were valued at a fixed price in gold. This had ensured that most international payments were made in sterling via London. But, after the First World War, changes in the world economy ensured that both international confidence in Britain and British wealth had diminished. Britain was forced off the gold standard in 1919, though it did return to it in 1925. But, when it returned to the gold standard (at the old rate) interest rates were high and the rate probably overvalued the pound by 10%. This gave no help to domestic industry as it struggled to compete internationally under unfavourable conditions.
Adapted from Reynolds 1991.

2.3 What were the wider economic consequences of the war?

Disruption of the old system

After the war, the British economy suffered because trade had been disrupted and the pattern of trade had changed. The main developments are outlined in Box 8.7 above.

In addition, Simpson points out that Britain was affected by the instability in Europe which followed the war:

'The British economy was affected more adversely by what the First World War did to the world economy in general than what it did to the British economy in particular. The war brought about the collapse of four empires - the Hapsburg [Austria-Hungary], the German, the Russian and the Ottoman. In all these areas, it took several years

before political stability was restored...Europe never again enjoyed the financial stability it had experienced before the war.' (Simpson 1986, p.108) Instability in Europe was particularly damaging for Britain since it relied on Europe for 30% of its exports and 40% of its imports. It should be noted, however, that, although the war weakened Britain's economy, Britain remained in a stronger position than many of its European rivals:

'Though the pressure of war needs had weakened the economy and checked investment, Britain's economy was not devastated as was the case in so many European countries. In fact, after a temporary lull following the armistice, output and incomes soon regained their pre-war levels and during the years 1919-20, Britain experienced one of the most violent and speculative booms on record.' (Aldcroft 1994, p.39)

MAIN POINTS - Part 2

- In the early months of the war, the movement of personnel and supplies into the Armed Forces caused shortages in the supply of civilian goods and services. This, in turn, caused inflation. Before long, the demands on the economy were so severe that the government could no longer rely on the free market. Instead, it became necessary for the state to intervene.
- Despite a growth in government intervention before the war, there was little support for the idea that the state should take over the running of industries or services. As a result, the advance of state control between 1914 and 1918 was cautious, pragmatic, limited and, above all, temporary.
- The degree of state control eventually achieved during the course of the war was striking and

impressive. It encompassed all Britain's basic industries.This created new precedents and opened up new possibilities. But, once the war was over, the government attempted to return to the approach of the past.
- The war was very expensive. Most of the extra expenditure - 70% - was added to the National Debt. This rose from £625 million in 1914 to £7,980 million by the end of the war. The remaining 30% of money was raised from taxation, mainly from increases in direct taxation.
- After the war, the British economy suffered because trade had been disrupted and the pattern of trade had changed. Instability in Europe was also damaging for Britain, though Britain remained in a stronger position than many of its European rivals.

Activity 8.2 The economic impact of the war

ITEM 1 A historian's view

The war familiarised the nation with the scope and potential of an ever-present, interventionist state. Central government involved itself in all spheres of everyday life, as it had never done so before. It conscripted men and women, rationed food and other necessities, fixed rents and wages, ran factories. The state's enterprises and propaganda filled the newspapers and cinema screens. At the same time, the state announced its intention to bring in vast and generous schemes of social reform. These developments changed the common perception of politics, or at least accelerated changes which, up to then, had not been developed. For working people especially the actual and prospective importance of the state in determining their wellbeing was obvious. Until 1914, it had remained possible for them to look to their own organisations - unions, cooperatives and Friendly Societies - to provide many of their needs. These associations were not destroyed by the war, but they were disrupted, and perhaps weakened. To this extent, the protection which could be afforded by the state assumed a higher value. The change in working-class attitudes should not be exaggerated, however. Typically, it was slow and incomplete. But, some groups of workers had particular reasons for concern with the conduct of government. The war had, on the whole, brought higher earnings and more secure employment. In some cases, as in coal mining and the railways, such gains appeared to result directly from the control of industry by the state. Other trades had seen alterations less welcome to the workforce, such as the recruitment of large numbers of women. The government promised that extraordinary working practices would be reversed, but not everybody believed that it would keep its promise.

Adapted from Phillips 1992.

ITEM 2 The Ministry of Munitions

DELIVERING THE GOODS.

This cartoon was published by *Punch* magazine on 21 April 1915. It shows Lloyd George, the new Minister for Munitions driving a truck full of weapons down the road to total war. The two horses, which are harnessed together, represent labour (the workforce) and capital (the owners). Lloyd George is driving them along in unison.

ITEM 3 Public spending and taxation

(i) Government expenditure as % of UK national income, 1913-19

	Government expenditure (£ million)	Gross National Product (GNP) (£ million)	Government spending as % of GNP (%)
1913	302	2,333	12.9
1914	318	2,362	13.5
1915	690	2,682	25.7
1916	1,690	3,186	53.0
1917	2,331	3,960	58.9
1918	2,839	4,790	29.3
1919	2,744	5,023	54.6

GNP ia a measure of national income.

(ii) Central government war expenditure, 1914-18 in £million

	1914-15	1915-16	1916-17	1917-18	1918-19
Fighting services	361 [a]	755	854	1,052	1,415
Munitions	[b]	247	559	715	562
Debt service	23	30	127	190	270
Overseas loans [c]	52	316	545	488	265
Shipping	-	-	8	195	285
War pensions	-	-	2	24	50
Total expenditure	436	1,377	2,096	2,665	2,848

Notes:
a Sub-totals may not add up to total due to rounding
b Expenditure under 'fighting services' in 1914-15
c To parts of the British Empire and Allies

3 The social impact of the First World War

Key questions

1. How has the social impact of the war been explained?

2. In what ways did the war affect the class structure and people's attitudes?

3. How did the war affect the role and status of women?

3.1 How has the social impact of the war been explained?

Total war

It has been estimated that around 6 million British people had direct experience of trench warfare during the First World War. At the same time, the war affected the remainder of the population in ways that earlier generations had not been affected by previous wars. As a result, the First World War has been described as being the British nation's first experience of 'total war'. By this term, historians mean a war in which society is organised in such a way that all available resources are channelled into the war effort. Because all available resources are channelled into the war effort, total war makes a huge impact on the lives of everybody in society, not just on those directly involved in the fighting. This impact is not just political and economic, it also has social, cultural and even psychological dimensions.

Some of the experiences in the First World War which can be said to have made a social, cultural and psychological impact are as follows:

- the emotional trauma suffered by many men who were forced (due to conscription) to serve in the Armed Forces
- the widespread bereavement arising from the death of friends and relatives
- changes in diet and habits resulting from food rationing
- the experience of living in a society in which government propaganda and government controls were much more extensive than in pre-war society

- the new experience that many upper- and middle-class women gained from taking up paid employment for the first time.

The social, cultural and emotional impact of the war was such that it has led some historians to argue that the period after 1918 witnessed a fundamental realignment of moral and social attitudes.

The 'Military Participation Ratio'

Historians clearly face a difficult, if fascinating, task in attempting to quantify the extent of the social, cultural and emotional changes caused by the war since these are areas which cannot easily be measured. The first historian to attempt such an analysis was Stanislaw Andreski who developed the idea of a 'Military Participation Ratio' (Andreski 1954, p.33). Andreski argued that, following times of war, the government rewards proportionately those sections of society upon whose support it has depended. The greater the contribution made by the middle class in the war, for example, the more likely a post-war government is to pass reforms which address middle-class needs. The more 'total' the war, and, therefore, the greater the involvement of the mass of people at the bottom of society, the more likely there is to be a post-war process of social levelling (ie removal of class inequalities). According to Andreski, it was because the First World War was so large in scale and involved, for the first time, virtually all sections of the population that Britain finally became a democracy (see Box 8.8 on page 288). In other words, the war itself was instrumental in providing the environment in which democracy could emerge.

Criticisms of Andreski's theory

Andreski's theory has been challenged on a number of different grounds. First, it is argued that he placed too much emphasis on military participation, suggesting that this was the key to post-war social levelling. Arguably, the most significant social change resulting from the war was the changed role and status of women (see Section 3.3 below). But, women's direct military participation was, in Andreski's terms, limited. Second, the idea of a 'ratio' implies that social change

BOX 8.8 The Representation of the People Act, 1918

Interpretation

Clearly, Britain was more democratic after the passing of the Representation of the People Act in 1918 than ever before in its history. A substantial majority of the adult population - all men over the age of 21 and most women over the age of 30 - could vote in general elections which had to be held at least every five years. Moreover, they could vote in constituencies of approximately equal size and provision was made to change constituency boundaries periodically to take account of changes in population distribution. It was also possible for a greater variety of people than ever before to stand for Parliament. No longer were there any religious restrictions on candidates and candidates no longer had to be especially wealthy. Every candidate had simply to pay a deposit of £150 which would be returned after the election unless he (or for the first time she) failed to poll one-eighth of the total votes cast. Successful candidates would then receive a salary, as they had done since 1911, ensuring people of all social backgrounds could afford to stand for Parliament.
Adapted from Pearce & Stearn 1994.

can be isolated and measured precisely. But, many of the changes that can be observed in British society after the First World War can be traced back to the pre-war period. Indeed, it could be argued that the war alone was responsible for comparatively few of the social changes that took place in the post-war period. Some historians argue that, rather than initiating changes, the war accelerated and intensified changes which were already underway. And third, Andreski's theory has been accused of being an oversimplification. Other societies - hardly affected by the First World War - showed similar patterns of social development during the post-war period.

Marwick's model

A different approach has been adopted by Arthur Marwick. Marwick identifies four 'dimensions' which, he claims, help us to understand the 'complex inter-relationship between society and its experience of the war'. Referring to these four dimensions, he argues that:

'These, inevitably, overlap; the exact number and the exact phrasing is not important: others might well find better ways of expressing the basic idea - and it is the basic idea - that of what happens in "society at war" - which is crucial in explaining why wars may bring about change.' (Marwick 1988, p.xv)

The four dimensions Marwick identifies are as follows:

- the destructive and disruptive dimension - the idea that destruction in the war creates an

impulse towards rebuilding after it
- the test dimension - the idea that wars place societies under a great deal of pressure (ie they provide a test) and societies have to adapt to avoid defeat
- the participation dimension - the idea that total war requires the involvement of underprivileged groups and their participation in the war changes attitudes towards them, bringing the possibility of social change after the war
- the psychological dimension - the idea that war encourages intensity of emotions (it encourages hatred of the enemy, for example) which stimulate a new cultural response.

It is useful to bear in mind these headings when investigating specific areas of social change associated with the impact of the First World War.

> ### 3.2 In what ways did the war affect the class structure and people's attitudes?

Social levelling

The idea that working-class participation in the First World War led to 'social levelling' (a reduction in inequality between the different social classes) is central to Andreski's Military Participation Ratio. But, more recent works have challenged the idea that the war brought about significant changes in Britain's class structure. Reid, for example, argues that:

'There was more continuity with the pre-war experience than might at first be expected.' (Reid 1988, p.19)

The working class

Marwick claims that:

'The working class in 1914 was large and it was poor. In the early 1920s, it was not quite so large and it was not quite so poor.' (Marwick 1991, p.344)

It has often been argued that the First World War had two major effects on working-class experience:

- differences within the working class became less marked as a result of the dilution of skills and the evolution of a more uniform rate of pay
- greater collective action was stimulated through trade union activity and a growth in political awareness.

The idea that there was a dilution of skills has been challenged by Reid (1988), though he does agree that the working class emerged from the war in a stronger position than it had been in before war broke out.

The 'dilution' of skills

The standard argument is that, because many skilled male workers left their jobs to fight, unskilled workers (who had previously been prevented by the unions from doing skilled jobs) took over these jobs - with the result that the gap between unskilled and skilled workers narrowed. Reid, however, argues that this phenomenon was not as widespread as sometimes claimed. Mainly, he claims, it was confined to the engineering industry and particularly to munitions. Since many of the skilled jobs in munitions were taken over by women, at the end of the war it was easy to identify and eject 'diluted' labour (many women simply lost their jobs). Further, Reid argues, the idea behind 'dilution' was often to release skilled workers to do jobs where their skills could be more effectively used. Many actually increased their skills and responsibility during the war by working as tool-makers, tool-setters, inspectors and overseers, for example.

Reid also questions the idea that a more uniform rate of pay evolved during the war. He argues that, in most important manufacturing industries (such as coal, iron and steel, and shipbuilding), there was virtually no change in the skills profile of the workforce. As a result, wage differentials (the difference in pay between different workers within the same company) did not change substantially. There was, he claims, a 7% improvement in shipbuilding and coal compared to a 14% improvement in engineering (where there was substantially more 'diluted' labour).

A stronger position

Reid does not deny that the war brought significant social changes, however. He argues that the working class emerged from the war in a stronger position for four main reasons - see Box 8.9.

Reid's second and third points about the growing power of the trade unions and the growing willingness of government to consult with workers are particularly significant. During the war, the government sought trade union cooperation over a range of issues relating to the successful mobilisation of the economy. The result was that:

'By 1916, a new conception of trade unionism was becoming current in England in which responsibility and representative leadership was seen to merit a role in the country's political life.' (Middlemass 1979, p.40)

The middle and upper classes

Marwick (1991) argues that, while there was a distinct shift in power from the landed to the business interest, there was little change in the proportion of wealth owned by the upper class:

'In 1910, 1.1% of the population took 30% of the income; in 1929, 1.5% took 23% of the income and two-thirds of the wealth was owned by 2.5% of the population.' (Marwick 1991, p.342)

The main change for the middle class was the large increase in the number of people working:

- in the professions (the result of rising material and welfare standards)
- in the civil service (the result of growing bureaucracy)
- as managers (the result of the growth of large-scale modern industry).

In addition, some middle-class women continued to work in the positions they had obtained during the war. One further important change was the fall in the number of servants after the war. In the post-war period, many middle-class families reduced the number of servants they employed or did not employ any. While these changes suggest that the war made some impact on the class structure, there is little evidence of a fundamental shift.

Changing attitudes

While the war did not fundamentally alter the class structure in Britain, there is evidence that there was a significant shift in terms of attitudes - the area of change which Marwick describes as the 'psychological' dimension. Although it is difficult to

---

BOX 8.9 The working class and the First World War

Interpretation

There were four main ways in which the position of the working class was strengthened as a result of the First World War. First, on a straightforward economic level, workers' positions were strengthened as a result of increasing wage rates. This was, in part, due to the shortage of labour (which encouraged employers to raise wages to attract labour). In part also, it was due to increased earnings resulting from higher levels of output, longer hours of work and less frequent spells of unemployment. One consequence of this was an improvement of civilian health during the war. Second, low unemployment and higher earnings led to a marked increase in trade union power, due to the decreased likelihood of 'blacklegging' and the increased ability of prospective members to pay union dues. Union membership rose from 4.1 million in 1914 to 6.5 million in 1918. Third, there was an increased willingness of governments to consult with workers during the war. In order to prevent disruption and encourage high output, governments became more and more involved in the resolution of industrial disputes. They also consulted with workers over changes in production methods and over guarantees to the unions of a return to pre-war practices. This process of consultation amounted, in effect, to a new kind of bargaining. And fourth, many workers were enfranchised for the first time in 1918, giving them new political power.
Adapted from Reid 1988 (trade union figures from Pelling 1987).

measure precisely the impact of war on attitudes, there is no doubt from eyewitness accounts that many people regarded the war as some sort of turning point:

'We found ourselves in an utterly changed world...We could not, even had we wished, join this new, comparatively sane world on the jagged edges of the one that had broken off five years before - this new one was quite a different place. The war had broken down the barriers and customs and conventions. It had left us curiously free.' (an extract from the autobiography of Margaret Rhondda quoted in Alberti 2000, p.271)

Marwick points out that the war affected people's loyalties and made them question the world in new ways:

'War is an enormous emotional experience during which loyalty to one's own group or those with whom one comes to identify in wartime (one's trade union, the working class, other women, the entire nation) intensifies, as does hostility to other outgroups (principally, of course, the enemy). Considerable force is also given to the notion...that such appalling slaughter must be for something, that change in many spheres, including the cultural, must [result]. The special horrors of war, in any case, call forth new intellectual and artistic responses.' (Marwick 1988, p.xvi)

No return to 'old values'
Bourne, on the other hand, emphasises that there was no return to the 'old values' and argues that conventions which relaxed during the war collapsed completely in the 1920s - see Box 8.10.

The impact of military service
Stevenson suggests that experience in the Armed Services broadened many people's social horizons and broke down class prejudices while the experience of victory ensured that there were only muted demands for change:

'The strong communal loyalties which had often led groups of men to join up with their peers tended to be affected by the common experiences of the war. Some jostling of lifestyles and background was almost inevitable. Young boys straight from public school could, and did, find themselves in charge of platoons of Durham miners or Manchester clerks. Where defeat might have emphasised social divisions or produced widespread bitterness at the great sacrifice, the war had been won. Stirrings of unrest in post-war Britain there undoubtedly were, but victory confirmed rather than destroyed the conservatism of British society.' (Stevenson 1990, p.96)

3.3 How did the war affect the role and status of women?

The debate
The extent to which the role and status of women changed during and after the First World War is at the heart of the debate about the nature and extent of change brought about by the war. Historians have tended to explore women's role and status under three headings:
- women and war work
- attitudes towards women
- the political dimensions of change and continuity.

Some historians have argued that there is a direct link between the economic role that women played during the war and the granting of the vote to most women over the age of 30 in the 1918 Representation of the People Act. It was because women made a contribution to the war effort, they argue, that they won the right to vote after the war. Marwick, for example argues that:

'It is difficult to see how women could have achieved so much in anything like a similar

---

BOX 8.10 Changing attitudes

Chaperons disappeared from polite society. Writing in 1966, Harold Macmillan observed: 'It is difficult to recall that 50 years ago a young lady of good position could not walk in the street alone without damage to her reputation'. Some increase in sexual permissiveness was probably inevitable. War exposed the fragility of human happiness. Those who did not love today might not be able to love tomorrow. Sex became a celebration of life in the midst of death. The new attitude was reflected in the rise in illegitimate births and the greater availability of contraception. Manners changed as well as morals. Smoking increased in popularity. Men - and women - not only smoked more, but also more publicly. Swearing became more socially acceptable. The greater financial independence and self-respect of women was reflected in fashion. Hemlines shortened. Hairstyles became more practical - and more mannish. Some women even wore trousers. They were able to enter pubs without being thought 'loose'. During and after the war, there was a longing for the sensuous. The Music Hall - vulgar and boisterous - widened its appeal across all classes. Theatres were full. Plays were romantic and sentimental. Night clubs appeared on the social scene. Good food in good restaurants was always available for those who could pay. The war gave birth to the 'Roaring Twenties'.

Adapted from Bourne 1989.

Interpretation

timespan without the unique circumstances arising from the war.' (Marwick 1991, p.333)

Other historians argue that such an interpretation underplays the importance of the suffragette campaigns before 1914 (see Unit 3, Part 3). Pugh, for example, places great emphasis on continuities and claims that the nature of the pre-war suffrage movement determined the shape of legislation in 1918:

'It is significant that, where women who undertook male tasks during the war have left a record of their feelings, they seem to have taken it for granted that they were stepping in on a purely temporary basis and they vacated their jobs at the end of the war without protest. This is not surprising in view of the relatively conservative, middle-class nature of the pre-1914 women's movement which had confined itself to the narrow question of the franchise and neglected the wider social objectives that the vote might help them to attain. In this light, the grant of the franchise in 1918 to women over 30 years who were either local government electors themselves or the wives of local government electors is [understandable]. Members of Parliament were determined to keep women in a minority among voters, and to enfranchise only those who, as relatively mature, family women, seemed likely to [make up] a stable, loyal section of the community.' (Pugh 1982, p.188)

Women and war work

It has already been noted that the upheavals produced by the outbreak of war resulted in labour shortages in some sectors and that women stepped in to fill the shortages:

'From the outset, women of all social classes were absorbed into the war effort and played a crucial part on the Home Front. Many upper-class and middle-class women experienced their first taste of paid work during the war, entering occupations which would have been deemed unsuitable during peacetime.' (Bartley 1998, p.94)

The extent of women's involvement in war work is described in Box 8.11.

What was new about the pattern of employment?

Although there was an overall rise in the number of women employed during the war, Lewenhak (1980) points out that female employment was an established feature of many pre-war industries, including munitions. What gave the impression of change was the temporary change in the background of the women employed. In particular, many middle-class women took on jobs that had previously been done by working-class women. Lewenhak suggests that both the increase in, and the changing character of, female employment during the war has been exaggerated by some historians' readiness to rely too much on the evidence of contemporary propaganda. This was generated both by the government (which hoped to give the impression that it was solving a national crisis) and by feminists (who hoped to use the image of wartime involvement as a lever for further expansion of employment opportunities after the war). It could be argued that the overall rise in the number of women employed during the war (1.4 million) was not particularly large. Besides, many women lost their jobs after the war was over. In fact, the overall percentage of women in work fell from 35% in 1911 to 34% in 1921. Pope notes that:

'Employers, partly through preference and partly for fear of upsetting male workers and disrupting production through industrial disputes, were often reluctant to employ women. Farmers went to great lengths to retain male workers. Many would-be female volunteers could not find work in agriculture. In spite of the formation of the Women's Land Army, there were only 23,000 more women working on the land in 1918 than there had been in 1914.' (Pope 1991, p.23)

Reid concludes that:

'The net impact of the war was a temporary increase in female unskilled munitions workers

---

BOX 8.11 Women and war work

By November 1918, 947,000 women were employed in munitions work. This was unpleasant and sometimes dangerous. More than 300 lost their lives as a result of TNT poisoning and explosions. Women also served with the military forces. There were 40,850 in Queen Mary's Auxiliary Army Corps by the end of the war. Some 17,000 women were employed with the British Expeditionary Force in August 1918. Many of these were nurses, but they also included cooks, waitresses, mechanics, drivers, clerks, telephonists and shorthand typists. In all, the number of women in paid employment rose during the course of the war from 5.96 million in 1914 to 7.31 million by 1918. Some changes were particularly striking. The number employed in metalworking rose from 170,000 to 594,000, in transport from 18,200 to 117,200, in commerce from 505,200 to 934,500. In national and local government, the number of female employees rose from 262,000 to 460,200, including 15,000 on the headquarters staff of the Ministry of Munitions alone. At the same time as the number of women working in munitions and factories was going up, the number of women working in 'traditional' areas of female employment (such as domestic service and the clothing trade) declined.

Adapted from Bourne 1989.

Interpretation

and a permanent shift in the bulk of women's employment from domestic service to white-collar and service-sector employment. Since, in the cases of new wartime manufacturing employment, women workers knew that they were temporary and frequently felt that they were there for patriotic reasons, they were often prepared to tolerate lower wages.' (Reid 1988, p.18)

Changing attitudes towards women?

During the build-up to the 1918 Representation of the People Act, government propaganda suggested that the sacrifices made by women during the war had earned them the right to vote:

'When women were enfranchised in 1918, billboards announced that "The Nation Thanks the Women". A grateful nation, overwhelmed by the sacrifices of the munitions workers in particular, granted them suffrage as recompense for their efforts. It was also supposed that women were enfranchised because the war had changed masculine perceptions about women's role in society.' (Bartley 1998, pp.93-94)

Most historians agree, however, that, in reality, many men continued to oppose the idea that women should come out of the private sphere (the family) and into the workplace (see Box 8.12). One reason for these negative attitudes was that men were concerned that the employment of women would push down wages:

'There was a great fear that the concept of the family wage (where a man was paid sufficient to keep a wife and children) was being eroded and that low-paid and unskilled women workers would peg wages below acceptable levels.' (Bartley 1998, p.99)

It was not just attitudes towards women in work that did not shift in any fundamental way. Most historians agree that attitudes towards women's political rights did not change a great deal:

'There is little evidence that war service caused a change in attitudes towards women's political rights...The restrictions on women's voting rights...suggest little alteration in the treatment of women as second-class citizens.' (Pope 1991, p.129)

The political dimension

According to the traditional view, an important factor in the granting of the vote to women in 1918 was the stance taken by the suffrage groups during the war. By acting responsibly and supporting the war effort, it is argued, the suffrage groups demonstrated that women were mature and responsible enough to gain the vote. One flaw in this argument is the fact that not all suffrage groups did support the war effort and the main suffrage groups that did so suffered splits over their patriotic stance.

The WSPU

Within the WSPU, both Emmeline and Christabel

BOX 8.12 Male attitudes towards women after the war

Interpretation

Attitudes towards women workers remained, in many instances, negative. To skilled men, women were a threat in both the long and the short term. While the war lasted, by taking on 'men's work' women ensured that increasing numbers of males were vulnerable to military conscription. In the longer term, men were concerned because their traditional protection of skilled jobs had been undermined. Though women's experience varied widely, with some women doing skilled jobs with the full cooperation of male colleagues, many were restricted to unskilled posts and some were the victims of hostility and even sabotage. Trade union views reflected the contrasting attitudes of different sections of the male workforce. Some, including the Electrical Trade Union and the National Union of Railways, recruited women for the first time. Others, including craft societies such as the Amalgamated Society of Engineers refused to admit women as members. Some employers were also reluctant to employ women - partly because they feared upsetting male workers. In evidence to a parliamentary committee, employers criticised women for bad timekeeping (in the chemical industries), for doing inferior work and as incapable of supervising others (china and earthenware). The attention given by press and politicians to women's employment is further evidence of a fundamentally unchanged attitude. There was a patronising wonder at what women achieved. Also, the resentment at the high earnings and criticism of the independent and sometimes boisterous behaviour of some young female munitions workers is further evidence that attitudes had not changed.
Adapted from Pope 1991.

Pankhurst adopted a highly patriotic stance, calling on their members to suspend militant action and to support the British war effort. The WSPU then worked in collaboration with the government (particularly after 1915 with Lloyd George's Ministry of Munitions), publicising and coordinating female recruitment into the workforce. In July 1915, the government gave the WSPU a grant of £2,000 to finance the so-called 'Great Procession of Women' - a march through London designed to heighten awareness of the need for women to actively support the war effort. But, not all WSPU members supported the leadership's stance:

'As a consequence, two different groups split from the WSPU to form their own suffrage organisations: the Suffragettes of the Women's Social and Political

Union (SWSPU) in October 1915 and the Independent Women's Social and Political Union (IWSPU) in March 1916.' (Bartley 1998, p.90) In addition, the East London Federation of Suffragettes (ELFS) - the organisation led by Sylvia Pankhurst which had been expelled from the WSPU in January 1914 (see Unit 3, page 91) - was highly critical of the WSPU's leadership. During the war, Sylvia Pankhurst and the ELFS campaigned against the war and, as well as providing relief for many working-class people in London, demanded the implementation of a socialist programme. As a result, Bartley argues:

'It is difficult to believe that the government wished to reward the ELFS for their emphatically negative reaction to the war.' (Bartley 1998, p.91)

The NUWSS

The NUWSS was also divided between those who supported the war (including Millicent Fawcett, the President) and those who opposed it. In the spring of 1915 a major split occurred in the group over Millicent Fawcett's refusal to allow NUWSS delegates to attend a peace conference for women at the Hague. The pacifist members of the group (including most of the national officers) split away and formed the Women's International League for Peace and Freedom:

'Catherine Marshall, Helena Swanwick and Isabella Ford, for example, supported the pacifists while other leading members like Eleanor Rathbone, Lady Frances Balfour and Millicent Fawcett maintained that women had to prove themselves by patriotic war work...Supporters of the war stressed the right to serve as a basis for citizenship, extending the female sphere into patriotic duty. Feminist pacifists claimed that women were essentially opposed to militarism.' (Rowbotham 1997, p.67)

Unlike the WSPU, the NUWSS continued to press for female suffrage during the war, as well as providing relief work. When the issue of electoral reform was raised in the summer of 1916, the NUWSS immediately began to lobby for the inclusion of female suffrage.

Developments in Parliament

According to Bartley (1998) there were five main reasons why the wartime government came to the conclusion that women should be granted the vote:

- there was a need for franchise reform in general (existing rules meant that voters had to be resident for a year - making large numbers of serving soldiers ineligible to vote)
- the balance in Parliament had swung towards female suffrage, especially when Lloyd George became Prime Minister in December 1916 (unlike Asquith - see Unit 3, page 97 - Lloyd

George and a number of other members of the coalition Cabinet were broadly sympathetic to female suffrage)
- women's contribution to the war effort allowed hostile MPs (especially Asquith) to back down without losing face
- the setting up of a coalition government meant there was less division within parties, allowed an all-party agreement to be made and removed fears that one particular party would benefit from the measure
- there was an international trend towards women's suffrage and this put pressure on the government to act.

The issue is raised

The issue of female suffrage remained in the background until August 1916 when the question of a new voting register was raised:

'All agreed on the need for a new register. The addresses shown on the existing register no longer applied to 80% of male electors and there was no provision for those doing war service. The NUWSS, while insisting that it did not wish to dissipate the government's energies by a controversial argument stated that it would not stand by and allow voting rights to be extended to hundreds of thousands of serving men while nothing was done for serving women. For the first time, Asquith agreed...Once again "Votes for Women" became the subject of open debate and this time it had clear support from the public, politicians and the press.' (McDonald 1989, p.73)

The Speaker's Conference

In August 1916, Asquith set up an all-party parliamentary committee chaired by the Speaker of the House of Commons to examine the issue of electoral reform (the so-called 'Speaker's Conference'). In January 1917, this committee recommended that all men over the age of 21 and women who were over the age of 35 and on the local government electoral register (or whose husbands were on the electoral register) should be given the vote. Bartley notes:

'The Speaker's Conference...took place behind closed doors, no evidence was gathered and no lobbying accepted...Fortunately for women, there were many supporters of women's suffrage within the Speakers' Conference.' (Bartley 1998, p.97)

The Labour Party and the suffrage societies opposed the limited concession recommended by the Speaker's Conference, but agreed to support a Bill if the age limit for women was lowered to 30. This concession was granted and, on 19 June 1917, the clause granting the vote to women over 30 was finally passed by a majority of 385 to 55. The remaining parliamentary hurdles were crossed and the Bill became law in February 1918.

MAIN POINTS - Part 3

- The First World War was Britain's first experience of 'total war'. As a result, it made a huge impact on the lives of everybody in society, not just on those directly involved in the fighting. This impact was not just political and economic, it also had social, cultural and even psychological dimensions.
- Whilst Andreski argues that the impact of the war can be measured by a Military Participation Ratio, Marwick identifies four key dimensions - (1) the destructive and disruptive dimension (2) the test dimension (3) the participation dimension and (4) the psychological dimension.
- While some historians have argued that the war resulted in significant social levelling, others claim that such changes have been exaggerated. Even if the class structure did not change in a fundamental way, however, there is evidence that there was a

significant shift in terms of attitudes.
- Some historians have argued that there is a direct link between the economic role that women played during the war and the granting of the vote to women over age 30 in the 1918 Representation of the People Act. Other historians argue that such an interpretation underplays the importance of the suffragette campaigns before 1914.
- Although attitudes towards women did not really change during the war, the government eventually accepted women's suffrage because (1) there was a need for franchise reform in general (2) Parliament and Cabinet became sympathetic (3) hostile MPs could back down without losing face (4) coalition government allowed party division to relax, and (5) there was an international trend towards women's suffrage.

Activity 8.3 Women and the First World War

ITEM 1 Munitions workers

Women worked as coal-heavers, railway porters, land-girls, carpenters, mechanics, postwomen, policewomen and munitions workers (the photo, left, shows women working in a munitions factory in 1918). An enormous range of semi-skilled and labouring jobs was taken up by women who, previously, would not have been allowed or considered themselves able to do such work. By the end of the war, women had demonstrated that they were not weak, frail, unintelligent creatures. They had helped to win the war and, at the same time, overturned society's views about men's and women's roles.

Adapted from Atkinson 1996.

ITEM 2 A historian's view (1)

In some ways, the war actually obstructed votes for women. First, the war seemed to confirm the Antis' physical force argument - the idea that men and women had separate roles because women are, on average, physically weaker than men. Although many women serving in the Armed Forces were extremely brave, they did not experience the horrors of the front line. The separation of role was also reinforced by geography with many men across the Channel while most women stayed at home. Second, the war weakened the suffragist movement. It pushed all peacetime problems down the political agenda. The WSPU ended their militant campaign and almost all suffragists diverted their energies into war work of some sort or another. Still, the war did help feminism in some ways. It soon became obvious that modern warfare had become so technical that physical strength was less important for success than qualities where women were not necessarily inferior - skill, organisation and courage. The gun and the bomb completely undermined the Antis physical force argument. Besides, modern warfare involves mobilising entire societies against one another, creating a home front as important as the fighting front. If the war was to be won, national unity was essential and this indirectly helped to win votes for women. The challenge of the war was so great that any distraction from squabbles over women's suffrage could not be risked. When the idea of extending the vote to all servicemen was raised, the suffragists at once pointed out that women too were contributing to the war effort. The fact that the government was now made up of an all-party coalition made it easier for MPs to accept suffragist demands. In addition, the overriding need to defeat Germany gave both Antis and suffragettes an excuse for climbing down from the impossible positions they had adopted before the war and accepting a compromise position.

Adapted from Harrison 1993.

ITEM 3 A historian's view (2)

By the late summer of 1914, the varying pressures applied by the NUWSS, the Liberal Women's Suffrage Union and by the new militant groups (such as Sylvia Pankhurst's ELFS) were all pushing the Liberal government towards some commitment on women's suffrage in the near future. Pessimistic accounts which focus on the increasing isolation and continuing organisational decline of the WSPU in the period 1913-14 are inadequate because they ignore the significant political advances other sections of the suffrage movement had secured for their cause. The Liberal government found itself squeezed between the Labour Party's firm commitment to a wide extension of the franchise which included women and the possibility of a limited Conservative measure which would strengthen the propertied vote. At the same time, support for women's suffrage was growing in the Liberal Party and the Cabinet. Further, campaigning by the NUWSS and ELFS had confirmed that the cause had significant support among the working class. It seems reasonable to argue, therefore, that British suffragists would have expected to gain the vote by 1918 if a Liberal government had been returned in the general election due later in 1914 or 1915. It is even possible that there might have been a limited measure of women's suffrage under a Conservative government. All this must significantly modify those interpretations which stress the outbreak of war as the decisive factor in the eventual winning of the women's vote. It might even be that the war postponed such a victory. What is clear is the importance of the suffragists' own efforts in securing the strong position of their cause at the outbreak of war. Women's war work may have converted some former opponents or provided others with a face-saving excuse to alter their positions. But, even before this, the political alliances built by the suffragists ensured that women would have to be included in any future reform Bill.

Adapted from Holton 1986.

ITEM 4 Nancy Astor -- the first female MP to sit in the House of Commons

Nancy Astor

The first woman to be elected to Parliament was Countess Markievicz who won a seat in the 1918 election. She was, however, a member of Sinn Fein and, since Sinn Fein did not accept the legitimacy of the British Parliament, she refused to take up her seat. The first woman actually to take her seat in the House of Commons was the Conservative, Nancy Astor, who won a by-election in her husband's old constituency in Plymouth after he was elevated to the Lords in 1919. Arthur Balfour, the former Conservative Leader, and David Lloyd George, the Prime Minister, acted as her sponsors and the press fully reported a story which, for once, was not about militancy, marriage, the war or scandal. In 1921, a second woman MP was elected in a by-election. Suddenly, MPs found that all legislation had a woman's angle. Conscious of having to win women's votes, they sought their advice on every issue. Some MPs thought that, once women had won the vote, they would support a women's political party, but this did not happen. The structure of the parties remained unchanged. The women's organisations were themselves unsure how to act. In the NUWSS, many members felt that they should use the power of the vote to bring about general changes in education, health and social services. The purists, however, argued that they should act solely with regard to women's own position. These were not essential differences, but rather symptoms of the new environment.

Adapted from McDonald 1989.

Questions

1. a) Judging from Items 1-4, what impact did the war make on the role and status of women?
   b) Give arguments for and against the view that the war marked a major turning point for women.
2. a) 'War work won women the vote'. Using Item 1 and your own knowledge, give arguments for and against this view.
   b) Do you agree that women's war work 'overturned society's views about men's and women's roles'.

3. a) Upon what do Items 2 and 3 (i) agree and (ii) disagree?
   b) How important was the war in securing the vote for women over the age of 30.
4. a) Explain why Nancy Astor's by-election victory in 1919 (Item 4) was an important development.
   b) 'Many of the fears of those opposed to women's suffrage were unfounded'. Explain this statement using Item 4.

Explain your answer.

References

- **Adelman (1981)** Adelman, P., *The Decline of the Liberal Party 1910-31*, Longman, 1981.

- **Adelman (1986)** Adelman, P., *The Rise of the Labour Party* (2nd edn), Longman, 1986.

- **Alberti (2000)** Alberti, J., 'The movement in Britain, 1918-1928' in *Purvis & Holton (2000)*.

- **Aldcroft (1994)** Aldcroft, D.H., 'The locust years? Britain's inter-war economy' in *Catterall (1994)*.

- **Andreski (1954)** Andreski, S., *Military Organisation and Society*, Routledge and Kegan Paul, 1954.

- **Atkinson (1996)** Atkinson, D., *The Suffragettes in Pictures*, Sutton Publishing, 1996.

- **Bartley (1998)** Bartley, P., *Votes for Women 1860-1928*, Hodder and Stoughton, 1998.

- **Blake (1955)** Blake, R., *The Unknown Prime Minister: the Life and Times of Andrew Bonar Law 1858-1923*, Eyre and Spottiswoode, 1955.

- **Blake (1985)** Blake, R., *The Conservative Party from Peel to Thatcher*, Fontana Press, 1985.

- **Bourne (1989)** Bourne, J.M., *Britain and the Great War 1914-18*, Edward Arnold, 1989.

- **Catterall (1994)** Catterall, P., *Britain 1918-51*, Heinemann, 1994.

- **Craig (1989)** Craig, F.W.S., *British Electoral Facts 1832-1987*, Gower Publishing Ltd, 1989.

- **Dewey (1997)** Dewey, P., *War and Progress: Britain 1914-45*, Longman, 1997.

- **Harrison (1993)** Harrison, B., 'The First World War and feminism in Britain', *History Review*, No.16, September 1993.

- **Holton (1986)** Holton, S.S., *Feminism and Democracy: Women's Suffrage and Reform Politics in Britain 1900-18*, Cambridge University Press, 1986.

- **Labour (1993)** Labour Party, *Labour Party Rule Book 1993-4*, Labour Party, 1993.

- **Laybourn (1997)** Laybourn, K., *The Rise of British Socialism*, Sutton, 1997.

- **Lee (1996)** Lee, S.J., *Aspects of British Political History 1914-95*, Routledge, 1996.

- **Lewenhak (1980)** Lewenhak, S., Women and Work, Fontana 1980.

- **Lloyd (1993)** Lloyd, T.O., *Empire, Welfare State, Europe: English History 1906-1992* (4th edn), Oxford University Press, 1993.

- **McDonald (1989)** McDonald, I., *Vindication! A Postcard History of the Women's Movement*, Deirdre McDonald Books, 1989.

- **McKibbin (1974)** McKibbin, R., *The Evolution of the Labour Party: 1910-1924*, Oxford University Press, 1974.

- **Marwick (1988)** Marwick, A. (ed.), *Total War and Social Change*, Macmillan, 1988.

- **Marwick (1991)** Marwick, A., *The Deluge: British Society and the First World War* (2nd edn), Macmillan, 1991.

- **May (1992)** May, T., *An Economic and Social History of Britain 1760-1970*, Longman, 1992.

- **Middlemass (1979)** Middlemass, K., *Politics in an Industrial Society*, Deutsch, 1979.

- **Milward (1984)** Milward, A.S., *The Economic Effects of the Two World Wars on Britain*, Macmillan, 1984.

- **Morgan (1979)** Morgan, K.O., *Consensus and Disunity: the Lloyd George Coalition 1918-22*, Oxford University Press, 1979.

- **Packer (1998)** Packer, I., *Lloyd George*, Macmillan, 1998.

- **Pearce (1992)** Pearce, R., *Britain: Domestic Politics 1918-39*, Hodder and Stoughton, 1992.

- **Pearce & Stearn (1994)** Pearce, R. & Stearn, R., *Government and Reform 1815-1918*, Hodder and Stoughton, 1994.

- **Pearce & Stewart (1992)** Pearce, M. & Stewart, G., *British Political History 1867-1990: Democracy and Decline*, Routledge, 1992.

- **Peden (1985)** Peden, G.C., *British Economic and Social Policy - Lloyd George to Margaret Thatcher*, Philip Alan, 1985.

- **Pelling (1987)** Pelling, H., *A History of British Trade Unionism*, Pelican, 1987 (first published in 1963).

- **Pelling (1991)** Pelling, H., *A Short History of the Labour Party* (9th edn), Macmillan, 1991.

- **Phillips (1992)** Phillips, G., *Rise of the Labour Party*, Routledge, 1992.

- **Pope (1991)** Pope, R., *War and Society in Britain*, 1899-1948, Longman, 1991.

- **Pugh (1982)** Pugh, M., *The Making of Modern British Politics, 1867-1939*, Blackwell, 1982.

- **Pugh (1988)** Pugh, M., *Lloyd George*, Longman, 1988.

- **Purvis & Holton (2000)** Purvis, J. & Holton, S.S. (eds), *Votes for Women*, Routledge, 2000.

- **Reid (1988)** Reid, A., 'World War I and the working class in Britain' in *Marwick (1988)*.

- **Reynolds (1991)** Reynolds, D., *Britannia Overruled: British Policy and World Power in the 20th Century*, Longman, 1991.

- **Rowbotham (1997)** Rowbotham, S., *A Century of Women: the History of Women in Britain and the United States*, Viking, 1997.

- **Simpson (1986)** Simpson, W.O., *Changing Horizons: Britain 1914-80*, Stanley Thornes, 1986.

- **Smith (1990)** Smith, M., *British Politics, Society and the State since the Late 19th Century*, Macmillan, 1990.

- **Stevenson (1990)** Stevenson, J., *British Society 1914-45*, Penguin, 1990.

Index